Who's Who
IN THE MIDDLE AGES

Who's Who
IN THE MIDDLE
AGES

Richard K. Emmerson
Editor

Sandra Clayton-Emmerson
Associate Editor

Volume II

J–Z

Routledge
Taylor & Francis Group

LONDON AND NEW YORK

First published in one volume as *Key Figures in Medieval Europe* in 2006
by Routledge
270 Madison Avenue, New York, NY 10016

Simultaneously published in Great Britain
by Routledge
2 Park Square, Milton Park, Abingdon, Oxon, OX14 4RN

This edition first published as *Who's Who in the Middle Ages*
in 2006
by Routledge

Routledge is an imprint of the Taylor & Francis Group, an informa business

© 2006 Taylor and Francis Group, LLC

Typeset in Sabon by Taylor & Francis Books
Printed and bound in Great Britain by TJ International Ltd, Padstow, Cornwall

British Library Cataloguing in Publication Data
A catalogue record for this book is available from the British Library

Library of Congress Cataloging in Publication Data
A catalog record for this book has been requested

ISBN10: 0-415-42205-1 (Set)
ISBN10: 0-415-42055-5 (Volume I)
ISBN10: 0-415-42056-3 (Volume II)

ISBN13: 978-0-415-42205-5 (Set)
ISBN13: 978-0-415-42055-6 (Volume I)
ISBN13: 978-0-415-42056-3 (Volume II)

Contents

J

JACOB VAN MAERLANT(ca. 1230–ca. 1290) A Flemish poet, Maerlant came from Bruxambacht, or, the "Freedom of Bruges" (*het Brugse Vrije*). His oeuvre, which shows strong didactic tendencies, clearly indicates that he was well educated, even though his exact place in society is unclear. He probably received minor orders and held several positions as a clerk (*clerc*). In the late 1350s, Maerlant moved northward to the island of Voorne (in the estuary of the River Maas in the southern part of the county of Holland), taking his name from the village Maerlant (near Brielle) on that island. He became sexton (*coster, custos*) of the local church of St. Peter (if *Coster* is not his family name), a profession that agreed perfectly with his activities as an author. During his stay in Maerlant he was possibly a tutor to young Floris V (d. 1296), count of Holland. Around 1270 he returned to Flanders, to Damme, near Bruges, earning his livelihood as a civil servant (in toll regulations) and continuing his writing. Tradition (unproved) has it that he was buried after his death ca. 1290 "under the bells" of the church of Our Lady in Damme.

Some of Maerlant's works are only known from references in his other works, such as the *Sompniarijs* (a book on dream interpretation), the *Lapidarijs* (a book on the mineral qualities of stones), and a *vita* (life) of St. Clare of Assisi. Maerlant's authorship of some works is still a matter of dispute, but his oeuvre amounted to at least 225,000 lines in coupled rhyme.

The oldest surviving work is *Alexanders Geesten* [Deeds of Alexander (ca. 1260, 14,277 verses)]. Maerlant wrote this history of Alexander the Great on a commission from Aleide van Avesnes, to whom he gives the pseudonym *Gheile* in an acrostichon (series of first letters in lines of a poem which spell words). The text is a translation and adaptation of the *Alexandreïs* of Walter of Châtillon, which Maerlant took from a manuscript with glosses. But the poet used a broad range of additional sources, including the *Historia Scholastica* (Scholastic History) of Petrus Comestor, Lucanus's *De Bello Civile* (Civil War), Ovid's *Metamorphoses*, Virgil's *Aeneid*, the *Disciplina Clericalis* (Clerical Discipline) of Pedro Alfonso, the *Secreta Secretorum* (Secret of Secrets), and Honorius of Autun's *Imago Mundi* (Image of the World).

For Albrecht of Voorne, Maerlant wrote *Merlijn* in 1261. The text encompasses two separate tales: the *Historie van den Grale* (History of the Grail, 1607 verses) and *Boek van Merline* (Book of Merlin, 8485 verses), which were adaptations of Robert de Boron's *Joseph d'Arimathie* (Joseph of Arimathia) and *Roman de Merlin* (Tale of Merlin). The

Torec (ca. 1262) is Maerlant's second Arthurian romance. This text (about 3,800 verses) has only been handed down to us in an abridged form, included in the vast *Lancelot Compilation* of The Hague.

Maerlant's *Historie van Troyen* (ca. 1264, 40,880 verses) renders the history of the Trojan War, from its preparatory stages to its aftermath. Among the sources he used were the *Roman de Troie* of Benoît of St. Maure, the *Achilleid* of Statius, the *Aeneid* of Virgil, Ovid's *Metamorphoses* and his own *Alexanders Geesten*. In addition, he incorporated the complete *Trojeroman* of Segher Diengotgaf into his text. The patron behind this work is not yet known, but it is likely the *Historie van Troyen* was intended for a noble audience.

The "Mirror of Princes," the *Heimelijkheid der Heimelijkheden* (ca. 1266, 2,158 verses), was possibly written for the young count of Holland, Floris V, and is a translation of the *Secreta Secretorum* of Pseudo-Aristoteles. (Maerlant's authorship of this text is sometimes disputed.) *Der naturen bloeme* [Flower of Nature (ca. 1266, 16,670 verses)], the first bestiary in the vernacular, assimilated Aristotle's books on biology. Maerlant derived his text from his immediate source, the *Liber de Natura Rerum* (Book of Natural Things) by Thomas of Cantimpré. The bestiary was commissioned by the nobleman Nicolaas of Cats (d. 1283).

In 1271 Maerlant finished his *Scolastica*, an abridged adaptation of Petrus Comestor's *Historia Scolastica*. To this book, of some 27,000 verses, he added an adaptation of Flavius Josephus' *De Bello Iudaïco* (On the Jewish War). Maerlant considered the total text of almost 35,000 verses as a single work. Probably commissioned by a noble patron, it was intended to serve an audience of noble laymen (*illiterati*). Even though it was not a translation of the Bible, the *Scolastica* marked the beginning of the popularization of the Bible in the Dutch language.

In the early seventies Maerlant wrote *Sente Franciscus Leven* (10,545 verses). This fairly literal translation of the *Legenda Maior* of St. Bonaventure is perhaps the first *vita* of Saint Francis in the vernacular. Maerlant wrote it at the request of the *fratres minores* (Order of the Lesser Brothers) in Utrecht. During his career as a poet, Maerlant composed several shorter stanzaic poems. These lyrical texts with a didactic aim show a fervent devotion to the Virgin Mary and a strong critical attitude towards society.

Maerlant's *magnum opus* is undoubtedly his *Spiegel Historiael*. He worked from 1283 until 1288 on this world chronicle, dedicated to Count Floris V of Holland. The major source by this text is Vincent of Beauvais's *Speculum Historiale* but Maerlant consulted and absorbed many more sources, among them the Vulgate, the *Secreta Secretorum*, *De Hormesta Mundi* of Orosius, *De Origine et Rebus Gestis Getarum* of Jordanes, two works by Martin of Braga (the *Liber de Moribus* and the *Formulae vitae honestae*), Paulus Diaconus's *Historia Miscella*, the *Historia Regum Brittanniae* by Geoffrey of Monmouth, as well as the Crusade chronicles by Albert of Aken and (probably) William of Tyre. As it has come down to us, the *Spiegel Historiael* (ca. 91,000 verses), is not solely from the hand of Maerlant. He had planned a work in four parts (which he called *partieën*), and he wrote the first, the third, and three "books" of the fourth part. He had postponed work on the second part, containing the years 54–367 C.E., and never was able to complete it. Apart from the lacuna of the second part and the remaining "books" of part four, Maerlant wrote a history from the Creation to the year 1113. The *Spiegel Historiael* was completed by two of his younger contemporaries, Philip Utenbroeke and Lodewijc van Velthem. The latter added a fifth part, bringing the history to the year 1316.

The extent and diversity of his oeuvre, and his exceptionally erudite and critical style, marks Jacob van Maerlant as a leading author of his time whose stature extended beyond his Dutch homeland.

See also **Benoît de Sainte-Maure; Pedro Alfonso, or Petrus Alfonsi; Peter Comester**

Further Readng

Berendrecht, Petra. *Proeven van bekwaamheid. Jacob van Maerlant en de omgang met zijn Latijnse bronnen.* Amsterdam: Prometheus, 1996.

Claassens, Geert H. M. "Maerlant on Muhammad and Islam." In *Medieval Christian Perceptions of Islam. A Book of Essays,* ed. John V. Tolan. New York & London: Garland, 1996, pp. 211–242 and 361–393.

de Pauw, Napoleon, and Edward Gaillard, ed. *Die Istory van Troyen.* 4 vols. Ghent: Siffer, 1889–1892.

de Vries, Matthijs, and Eelco Verwijs, ed. *Jacob van Maerlant's Spiegel Historiael, met de fragmenten der later toegevoegde gedeelten, bewerkt door Philip Utenbroeke and Lodewijc van Velthem.* 3 vols. Leyden: Brill, 1863–1879.

Franck, Johannes, ed. *Alexanders Geesten, van Jacob van Maerlant,* Groningen: Wolters, 1882.

Franck, Johannes, and Jakob Verdam, ed. *Jacob van Maerlants Strophische Gedichten.* Leyden: Sijthoff, 1898.

Gysseling, Maurits, ed. *Corpus van Middelnederlandse teksten. Reeks II: Literaire handschriften,* Vol. 3, *Rijmbijbel/tekst,* Leyden: Nijhoff, 1983.

Maximilianus, O. F. M., ed. *Sinte Franciscus Leven van Jacob van Maerlant.* 2 vols. Zwolle: Tjeenk-Willink, 1954.

Sodmann, Timothy, ed. *Jacob van Maerlant, Historie van den Grale und Boek van Merline.* Cologne/Vienna: Böhlau, 1980.

te Winkel, Jan. *Maerlant's werken beschouwd als spiegel van de 13de eeuw.* Ghent 1892; rpt. Utrecht: HES, 1979.

van Oostrom, Frits P. *Maerlants werteld.* Amsterdam: Prometheus, 1996.

Verdenius, Andries A., ed. *Jacob van Maerlant's Heimelijkheid der Heimelijkheden.* Amsterdam: Kruyt, 1917.

Verwijs, Eelco, ed. *Jacob van Maerlant's Naturen Bloem.* 2 vols. Groningen: Wolters, 1872–1878.

GEERT H. M. CLAASSENS

JACOBUS DA VORAGINE (c. 1228–1298)

Jacobus da Voragine (Jacopo da Varazze) was a Dominican writer, administrator, and archbishop; his name suggests that he or his forbears came from Varazze, a town near Genoa. He entered the Order of Preachers—i.e., the Dominican order—as a youth, in 1244. After completing his education, he is reputed to have distinguished himself both as a public preacher and as a teacher of preachers in training, and also to have been prior (local head) of the Dominican community in Genoa. From 1267 on, his career is more clearly documented. His fellow Dominicans repeatedly elected him prior of the entire province of Lombardy, a post he held from 1267 to 1277 and again from 1281 to 1286. Both the order and the papacy entrusted him with sensitive diplomatic missions. From 1292 until his death, he was archbishop of Genoa, and he had such an exemplary reputation in this office that he was eventually beatified (in 1816).

Among the literary works Joacobus wrote or compiled, the earliest and most famous is a *Legenda sanctorum aurea (Golden Legend).* After the *Legenda,* Jacobus composed four large sets of Latin sermons, which evidently circulated as models for other preachers to use: *Sermones de sanctis,* on major saints and festivals of the church year; *Sermones de tempore,* on the Sunday gospels for the year; *Sermones quadragesimales,* on the weekday gospels for Lent; and *Mariade,* or *Laudes deiparae virginis,* sermons in praise of the Virgin Mary. Jacobus's sermons survive in numerous manuscripts and early printed editions and thus must have enjoyed a wide and long-lasting popularity. His last major work, *Chronicle of Genoa,* which he wrote as archbishop, is noteworthy for the local history and hagi-ography it preserves and for some auto-biographical passages that shed light on his own life.

Further Reading

Kaeppeli, Thomas. *Scriptores Ordini Praedicatorum medii aevi*, Vol. 2. Rome: Ad S. Sabinae, 1975, pp. 348–369.

Monleone, Giovanni. *Iacopo da Varagine e la sua Cronaca di Genova dale origini al MCCXCVII*, 3 vols. Rome: Tipografia del Senato, 1941.

Sermones aurei..., 2 vols. Ed. Rudolph Clutius. Augsburg and Cracow: Apud Christophorum Bartl, 1760. (Latin edition: includes all four sermons).

SHERRY REAMES

JACOPO DA MILANO (13th century) The Franciscan lector Jacopo da Milano (Jacob of Milan, James of Milan, Jacobus Mediolanensis, Giacomo da Milano) was the author of the original version of a spiritual clas-sic in Latin, *Stimulus amoris* (*Prick of Love*). Much has been surmised but little is known for certain about Jacopo. From the date of the earliest evidence for the *Stimulus amoris*, and from the acquaintance it shows with the writ-ings of Saint Bonaventure, Jacopo must have composed it in the second half of the thirteenth century. Jacopo has been plausibly but not conclusively identified with a Brother James of Milan recorded as a lector at the Franciscan convent at Domodossola in 1305. Some scholars have thought him identical or possibly identical with a mid-thirteenth-century Milanese theologian who was known until 1979—incorrectly—as Giacomo Capelli or de Capellis; but this person is no longer credibly a Jacopo. Jacopo could well have been the renowned Franciscan, formerly a lector in Milan, who sometime after 1296 read and ap-proved Arnaldo of Foligno's *Memorial* on the mystic and visionary Angela of Foligno. One modern scholar has as-cribed to Jacopo a meditation on the hymn *Salve Regina*, transmitted in some of his manuscripts and at times attrib-uted to Bernard of Clairvaux (among others), but this idea has not found widespread acceptance.

Recent investigation has revealed *Stimulus amoris* in its Jacopean form to be an unstable "open text" whose very title is uncertain. As now edited, it con-sists of a prologue and twenty-three brief chapters; the first nine chapters guide the reader toward divine rapture, and the rest deal with other aspects of the con-templative life. The writing style is often intense and rhetorically effective; it com-bines direct address, exclamation, and figures of repetition with an intention-ally simple vocabulary. Chapter 14, an especially vivid meditation on Christ's passion, is thought by some to have fur-nished the theological basis for the im-agery in the window of the Glorification of Saint Francis in the upper church of Francis's basilica at Assisi. However, the ideas in question were common in later thirteenth-century Franciscan contexts, and the dating of both the window and the earliest version or versions of the text is uncertain.

Jacopo's *Stimulus* circulated with Bonaventure's works, was soon mis-takenly attributed to Bonaventure, and was expanded twice in the fourteenth century by persons unknown. Modern scholars differentiate these texts by call-ing the original *Stimulus (amoris) minor* and the expansions (treated as a single version) *Stimulus (amoris) maior*. The *maior* was more widely read: there are more than 130 manuscripts of it, as opposed to some ninety manuscripts of the *minor*. A recent suggestion that the *maior* was actually the original seems unpersuasive. Starting in the later fourteenth century, this very different larger version was translated into other European languages, including English. A fourteenth-century translation (now lost) of *Stimulus minor* into Tuscan dialect is thought to underlie its first printing in Italian (Venice, 1521).

See also **Angela da Foligno, Saint; Bonaventure, Saint**

Further Reading

Edition

Fathers of the College of Saint Bonaventure, eds. *Stimulus amoris fr. Iacobi Mediolanensis— Canticum pauperis fr. Ioannis Peckam.* Bibliotheca Franciscans Ascetica Medii Aevi, 4. Quaracchi: Collegium S. Bonaventurae, 1905, pp. vi–xvii, 1–132. (Reprint, 1949).

Critical Studies

Alberzoni, Maria Pia.' "L'*approbatio*': Curia Romana, ordine minoritico e *Liber.*" In *Angèle de Foligno: Le dossier*, ed. Giulia Barone and Jacques Dalarun. Collection de l'École Française de Rome, 255. Rome: École Française de Rome, 1999, pp. 293–318. (See especially pp. 311–114.)

Canal, Jose M., "El *Stimulus amoris* de Santiago de Milán y la *Meditatio in Salve regina.*" *Franciscan Studies*, 26, 1966, pp. 174–188.

Cremaschi, Chiara Giovanna, trans. "Introduzione" and *Stimulus* (Giacomo da Milano, *Il pungolo dell'amore*). In *I mistici: Scritti dei mistici francescani*. Assisi: Editrici Francescane, 1995–, Vol. 1, pp. 795–881.

Eisermann, Falk. "*Diversae et plurimae materiae in diversis capitulis*: Der 'Stimulus amoris' als literarisches Dokument der normativen Zentrierung." *Frühmittelalterliche Studien*, 31, 1997, pp. 214–232.

——. *Stimulus amoris: Inhalt, lateinische Überlieferung, deutsche Übersetzungen, Rezeption.* Münchener Texte und Untersuchungen zur Deutschen Literatur des Mittelalters, 118. Tübingen: Max Niemeyer Verlag, 2001.

Mostaccio, S. "Giacomo da Milano." In *Dizionario biografico degli Italiani*, Vol. 54. Rome: Istituto della Enciclopedia Italiana, 2000, pp. 221–223.

Piana, Celestino. "Il 'fr. Iacobus de Mediolano lector' autore dello pseudo-Bonaventuriano *Stimulus amoris* ed un convento del suo insegnamento." *Antonianum*, 61, 1986, pp. 329–339.

Poulenc, Jerôme. "Saint François dans le 'vitrail des anges' de l'église supérieure de la basilique d'Assise." *Archivum Franciscanum Historicum*, 76, 1983, pp. 701–713.

Wessley, Stephen E., "James of Milan and the Guglielmites: Franciscan Spirituality and Popular Heresy in Late Thirteenth-Century Milan." *Collectanea Franciscana*, 54, 1984, pp. 5–20.

JOHN B. DILLON

JACOPO DE CESSOLIS (fl. 1275–1322) Jacopo Jacobus was born in the small town of Cessole, near Asti, in Piedmont. He entered the Dominican order, probably at the convent of Santa Maddalena near Asti. From 1317 to 1322, he lived in Genoa, where he became vicar of the Inquisition attached to the convent of San Domenico. At the request of fellow Dominicans and several laypeople, he wrote his only extant work, *De moribus hominum ed de officiis nobilum super ludo scaccorum* (*On the Customs of Men and Their Noble Actions with Regard to the Game of Chess*), known simply as *Ludus scaccorum*.

Ludus scaccorum is a moralized explanation of chess based on the medieval estates, whereby each chess piece represents a different social class. It consists of twenty-four chapters divided into four sections (*tractatus*). The first section consists of three chapters that narrate when, how, and by whom chess was invented. The narrative, in the form of a medieval *exemplum*, recounts how a Greek philosopher named Xerxes or Perses invented the game to show his cruel king Evilmerodach "the maners and conditicions of a kynge of the nobles and of the comun people and of theyr offices and how they shold be touchid and drawen. And how he shold amende hymself & become vertuous." Xerxes explains that he invented the game to keep the king from "ydlenesse," which can induce men to sin, and to satisfy man's desire for "noueltees & tydynges," which in turn sharpen the mind. The *exemplum* ends with Evilmerodach's eventual conversion, thus setting a precedent for using chess to teach people how to behave.

The second section is divided into five chapters describing, respectively, the five different chess pieces in the first row: (1) king, (2) queen, (3) alphinus (judge), (4) knight, and (5) rook (legate). Each piece is described in terms of its clothing, its symbols of power, the moral significance of those symbols, and—most important—the way a represented by the piece must behave in society. Jacopo narrates several *exempla* to illustrate the kind of behavior he has in mind for each person.

The third section deals with the pawns and is divided into eight chapters, each taking up a particular group of commoners (one pawn representing one group): (1) laborers (farmers), (2) smiths, (3) notaries, (4) merchants, (5) physicians, (6) innkeepers, (7) city watchmen and guards, and (8) ribalds and town couriers. Each pawn is described in terms of the tools of its trade, its relationship to the chess piece behind it, and how the person represented should behave. For each group of commoners, Jacopo narrates one or more *exempla*, illustrating either appropriate or inappropriate behavior of that group.

The fourth section is also divided into eight chapters. The first chapter describes the chessboard as an allegorical representation of Babylon, where the game was presumably invented. The next six chapters deal with the actual moves of each chess piece on the chessboard. These moves reflect the rules of chess that were then in effect in Lombardy and are allegorized to illustrate a moral. For example, when a pawn becomes a queen, the fact that many great rulers had humble origins is illustrated. In the eighth chapter in this section—the final chapter—Jacopo reiterates the history of the origins of chess, reminding his readers that chess is a social allegory of the various classes of

medieval society working together for the common good.

As Kaeppeli (1960) noted, the convent of San Domenico in Genoa produced a considerable amount of popular religious literature. It is not surprising, therefore, that *Ludus scaccorum* spread rapidly throughout western and eastern Europe; there were even a Scottish translation and a Czech translation. When *Ludus scaccorum* was translated from Latin into a vernacular, or from one vernacular into another, the content was sometimes modified to reflect a country's particular ways of representing its own social classes (Buuren 1997).

The diffusion and popularity of *Ludus scaccorum* during the fourteenth and fifteenrh centuries are reflected in the numerous manuscripts and early printed editions of the work. It was the second book to be printed in the English language: William Caxton printed an English translation of Jehan de Vignay's French translation (c. 1350) of *Ludus scaccorum* in 1474. Despite the popularity of *Ludus scaccorum* in the late Middle Ages and the early Renaissance, there are no critical editions in print of the Latin original, nor are there any modern translarions in either English or Italian. There are, however, modern critical editions of Jean Ferron's French translation of 1347 (the best of the medieval French translations), and of the Middle Scots translation of c. 1515.

Further Reading

Editions

Burt, Marie Anita. "Jacobus de Cessolis: *Libellus de moribus hominum et officiis nobilium ac popularium super ludo scachorum.*" Dissertation, University of Texas, Austin, 1957.

Jacobus de Cessolis. *Libellus de ludo scachorum*, ed. Ernst Köpke. Mittheilungen aus den Handschriften der Ritter-Akademie zu Brandenburg a. H., 2. Brandenburg a. d. Havel: G. Matthes, 1879.

Das Schachbuch des Jacobus de Cessolis: Codex Palatinus Latinus 961, 2 vols. Belser Faksimile Editionen aus der Biblioteca

Apostolica Vaticana, 74. Zürich: Belser Verlag, 1988.

Vetter, Ferdinand, ed. *Das Schachzabelbuch Kunrats von Ammenhausen, Mönchs, und Leutpriesters zu Stein am Rhein, nebst den Schachbüchern des Jakob von Cessole und des Jakob Mannel*. Frauenfeld: Huber, 1892.

Translations

Caxton, William. *The Game and Play of Chesse (1474)*, intro. N. F. Blake. London: Scolar, 1976.

Caxton's Game and Playe of the Cheese, 1474: A Verbatim Reprint of the First Edition with an Introduction by William E. A. Axon. London: Elliot Stock, 1883.

The Game of the Cheese by William Caxton: Reproduction in Facsimile with Remarks by Vincent Figgins. London: John Russell Smith, 1860.

Volgarizzamento del libro de' costumi e degli offizii de' nobili sopra il giuoco degli scacchi di frate Jacopo da Cessole: Tratto nuovamente da un codice Magliabechiano, ed. Pietro Marocco. Milan: Dalla Tipografia del Dott. Giulio Ferrario, 1829.

Critical Studies

Buuren, Catherine van, ed. *The Buke of the Chess: Edited from the Asloan Manuscript (NLS MS 16500)*. Edinburgh: Scottish Text Society, 1997.

Collet, Alain, ed. *Le Jeu des Eschaz Moralisé: Traduction de Jean Ferron (1347)*. Paris: Honoré Champion, 1999.

Di Lorenzo, Robert D. "The Collection Form and the Art of Memory in the *Libellus super Ludo Scaccorum* of Jacobus de Cessolis." *Mediaeval Studies*, 35, 1973, pp. 205–221.

Kaeppeli, Thomas, O.P. "Pour la biographie de Jacques de Cessole." *Archivum Fratrum Praedicatorum*, 30, 1960, pp. 149–162.

Mann, Jill. *Chaucer and Medieval Estates Satire*. Cambridge: Cambridge University Press, 1973. Murray, Harold James R. *A History of Chess*. Oxford: Clarendon, 1913, pp. 537–549. (Reprints, 1961, 1987.)

STEVEN GROSSVOGEL

JACOPONE DA TODI (c. 1230 or 1236–1306)

The Franciscan friar and mystic Jacopone da Todi (Jacobus de Benedictis, Jacopus de Tuderto, Jacopo de' Benedetti, Giacopone de' Benedetti) is considered by some to be Italy's greatest poet before Dante. The principal type of verse that Jacopone used is the *lauda*, a nonliturgical song of praise in vernacular ballad form, although some works in Latin are also attributed to him.

Details about Jacopone's life before his religious conversion are sketchy, but it is generally accepted that he was born (as his name implies) in Todi, Umbria, to a family of the lesser nobility. He received an education typical of his time and social class (he may have studied at the University of Bologna) and then is believed to have practiced the profession of notary in Todi and, in his mid-thirties, to have married Vanna di Bernardino di Guidone, of the counts of Collemedio (or Coldimezzo). According to early *vitae* (lives) of Jacopone, Vanna's accidental death at a party devastated him, provoked a profound psychological crisis, and led to his religious conversion in 1268. The precipitating factor in this rapid chain of events appears to have been his discovery that Vanna, like many others during this tumultuous period of Italian history, had practiced self-mortification as a form of religious penance—in her case, by wearing a hairshirt under her beautiful and costly outer garb. To the consternation of his family and the disbelief of his fellow citizens, Jacopo divested himself of all his worldly goods and habits and became a *bezocone*, or mendicant Franciscan tertiary (*Laude*, ed. Mancini, 1974, 151). For the next ten years, he traveled the highways of Umbria, singing God's praise and preaching salvation, not in the Latin of the church but in the language of the people, as was the custom of the Franciscans. In 1278, on his second request, he was finally admitted to the order of Friars Minor (i.e., the Franciscan order; Casolini 1966, 620). He thus became Fra Jacopone—a name that can be translated as Big Jim or Big Jake.

In the years following the death of Saint Francis (1226), the Franciscans split into two opposing camps. The Spirituals believed in the strict interpretation of Francis's rule, which called for complete poverty; the Community, sometimes referred to as the Conventuals, supported a more relaxed interpretation that permitted ownership of property and other material comforts. Jacopone sided with the more extreme Spirituals and, as a consequence, found himself locked in the bitter and sometimes dangerous struggle between the two factions. When Boniface VIII became pope, Jacopone allied himself with the Colonna family, Boniface's enemies. Jacopone's open and virulent opposition to the powerful new pope earned him excommunication and five years of solitary confinement.

While he was in prison, Jacopone wrote many *laude*. In one of them—*Que farai, fra Iacovone?* ("What will you do, Brother Jacopone?" number 55 in Ageno's edition, 53 in Mancini's)—he comments with mordant irony on the dire conditions of his imprisonment. We know from two *laude*—*O papa Bonifazio/io porto el tuo prefazio* ("O Pope Boniface, I bring your sentence," number 56 in Ageno and 55 in Mancini) and *Lo pastor per mio peccato/posto m'à for de l'ovile* ("Because of my sin the shepherd has cast me out of the sheepfold," number 57 in Ageno and 67 in Mancini)—that Jacopone twice begged the pope for absolution. Although the pope granted absolution to many in the jubilee year of 1300, Jacopone was not among them. In 1303, however, Jacopone received personal liberty and release from religious censure from Boniface's more compassionate successor as pope, Benedict XI.

The elderly Jacopone then retired to the convent of San Lorenzo in Collazzone, where he died on Christmas eve, 1306. In 1433, his remains were discovered in the convent of Santa Maria di Montecristo, and in 1596 his tomb in the crypt of the Franciscan church of San Fortunato in Todi was dedicated. Although he has not been beatified or canonized by the church,

Jacopone is inscribed in the Franciscan martyrology and is popularly referred to and venerated as "blessed" or "saint."

Jacopone wrote approximately 100 *laude* in the Umbrian vernacular that express the mystic's innermost sentiments about the state of his soul and seek to instruct others who are seeking greater closeness to God. Unlike many *laude* composed by others at this time (which was the form's most fertile period), Jacopone's hymns were written not for the general lay public but for his own personal use, and possibly for his Franciscan brothers. Jacopone's *laude* treat a wide range of subjects and present a variety of tones and moods. His important themes include the following (for each example, the number in Ageno is followed by the number in Mancini): praise of God (e.g., *La bontade enfinita*, "The infinite goodness," 79, 21), Christ (*Ad l'amor ch'è venuto*, "To the Love that came," 65, 86), and the Virgin Mary (*O Vergen più che femina*, "O Virgin more than woman," 2, 32); Saint Francis and the Franciscan ideal of poverty (*Povertade enamorata*, "Beloved poverty," 59, 47); the condemnation of all types of secular temptation (*Guarda che non caggi, amico*, "Be careful not to fall, my friend," 6, 20); detailed descriptions of disease, death, and dying (*Quando t'alegri*, "When you are glad," 25, 61); soul-searching self-criticism (*Que farai, fra Iacovone?* "What will you do, Brother Jacopone?" 55, 53); extreme self-abnegation (*O Signor, per cortesia,/mandame la malsanìa*, "O Lord, please infect me with disease," 48, 81); biting political satire (*Que farai, Pier da Morrone?* "What will you do, Pier da Morrone?" 54, 74); laments on the state of the church (*Piange la Ecclesia*, "The church weeps," 53, 35); descriptions of the mystical stare of ecstasy, akin to madness, that the poet entered during his spiritual meditation (*Senno me pare e cortesia*, "It seems to be wise and courteous," 84, 87); and the passionate praise of divine love (*O iubilo del core*, "O heartfelt joy," 76, 9;

and *Sopr'onne lengua amore*, "Ineffable love," 91, 92). Misogyny is patently evident in some of his *laude* (e.g., *O femene, guardate*, "Women, beware," 8, 45), revealing Jacopone to be a man of his time. However, there is also evidence that he gave some thought to the difficult living conditions of many women in the late thirteenth century (e.g., *O vita penosa*, "O sorrowful life," 24, 58). One simple yet supremely elegant *lauda*—*Donna del paradiso* ("Lady of Paradise," 93, 70)—is important because it represents the pinnacle of Jacopone's poetic art and also because it constitutes a crucial step in the evolution of Italian religious theater: it has four speakers, and many scholars consider it the first religious drama in Italy.

Although critics are not in complete agreement regarding Jacopone's authorship of a number of works in Latin, the following have variously been attributed to him: the famous sequence *Stabat mater dolorosa*, now a part of the Roman Catholic liturgy; pithy moral sayings known as the *Detti*; and *Trattato* (*Treatise*), whose subject is mystical union with God.

See also **Boniface VIII, Pope; Celestine V, Pope**

Further Reading

Editions

Contini, Gianfranco, ed. *Poeti del Duecento*, 2 vols. Milan and Naples: Ricciardi, 1960, Vol. 2, pp. 61–166.

Jacopone da Todi. *Le laude, ristampa integrale della prima edizione (1490)*, ed. Giovanni Papini. Florence: Libreria Editrice Fiorentina, 1923.

——. *Le laude secondo la stampa riorentina del 1490*, ed. Giovanni Ferri. Bari: Laterza, 1930.

——. *Laudi, Trattato, e Detti*, ed. Franca Ageno. Florence: Le Monnier, 1953.

——. *Le laude*, ed. Luigi Fallacara. Florence: Liberia Editrice Fiorentina, 1955.

——. *Laude*, ed. Franco Mancini. Bari: Laterza, 1974.

Menestò, Enrico, ed. *Le vite antiche di Iacopone da Todi*. Florence: La Nuova Italia, 1977.

——, ed. *Le prose latine attribuite a Jacopone da Todi*. Bologna: Pàtron, 1979.

Ugolini, Francesco A., ed. *Laude di Jacopone da Todi tratte da due manoscritti umbri*. Turin: Istituto Editrice Gheroni, 1947.

Translations

Jacopone da Todi. *The Lauds*, trans. Serge Hughes and Elizabeth Hughes. New York: Paulist, 1982.

Underhill, Evelyn. *Jacopone da Todi: Poet and Mystic 1228–1306: A Spiritual Biography*. London: Dent; and New York: Dutton, 1919. (Reprint, Freeport, N.Y.: Books for Libraries, 1972.)

Studies

Ageno, Franca. "Modi stilistici delle laudi di Iacopone da Todi." *La Rassegna d'Italia*, 5, 1946, pp. 20–29.

——. "Motivi francescani nelle laudi di Iacopone da Todi." *Lettere Italiane*, 2, 1960, pp. 180–184.

Apollonio, Mario. *Jacopone da Todi e la poetica delle confraternite religiose nella cultura preumanistica*. Milan: Vita e Pensiero, 1946.

Bettarini, Rosanna. *Jacopone e il Laudario Urbinate*. Florence: Sansoni, 1969.

Casolini, Fausta. "Iacopone da Todi." *Biblioteca Sanctorum*, 7, 1966, pp. 617–628.

Convegni del Centro di studi sulla spiritualità medievale: Jacopone e il suo tempo (13–15 ottobre 1957). Todi: Accademia Tudertina, 1959.

D'Ascoli, Emidio. *Il misticismo nei canti spirituali di fra Iacopone da Todi*. Recanati: n.p., 1925.

Dick, Bradley B. "Jacopone da Todi and the Poetics of Franciscan Spirituality." Ph.D. dissertation, New York University, 1993.

Furia, Paola. "Sulla lingua delle 'laude' di Iacopone da Todi." *Cultura e Scuola*, 28(110), 1989, pp. 44–49.

Katainen, V. Louise. "Jacopone da Todi, Poet and Mystic: A Review of the History of the Criticism." *Mystics Quarterly*, 22, 1996, pp. 46–57.

Lograsso, A. H. "Jacopone da Todi." In *New Catholic Encyclopedia*. New York: McGraw Hill, 1967.

McGinn, Bernard. *The Flowering of Mysticism: Men and Women in the New Mysticism (1200–1350)*. The Presence of God: A History of Western Mysticism, 3. New York: Crossroad, 1998.

Menestò, Enrico, ed. *Atti del convegno storico iacoponico in occasione del 750 anniversario della nascita di Iacopone da Todi: Todi, 29–30 novembre 1980*. Florence: La Nuova Italia, 1981.

Neri, Ferdinando. "La pazzia e la poesia di Jacopone da Todi." In *Saggi di Letteratura Italiana, Francese, Inglese*. Naples: n.p., 1936.

Parodi, Ernesto Giacomo. "Il Giullare di Dio." *Il Marzocco*, 19(26), 1915. (Reprinted in *Poeti antichi e moderni: Studi critici*. Florence: Sansoni, 1923, pp. 129–141.)

Peck, George T. *The Fool of God: Jacopone da Todi*. Tuscaloosa: University of Alabama Press, 1980.

Petrocchi, Giorgio. *Scrittori religiosi del Duecento*. Florence: Sansoni, 1974.

Russo, Luigi. "Jacopone da Todi misticopoeta." In *Studi sul Due e Trecento*. Rome: Edizioni Italiane, 1946, pp. 31–57.

Sapegno, Natalino. *Frate Jacopone*. Turin: Baretti, 1926.

Toschi, Paolo. *Il valore attuale ed eterno della poesia di Jacopone*. Todi: Res Tudertinae, 1964. Triplo, Gary. "Mysticism and the Elements of the Spiritual Life in Jacopone da Todi." Ph.D. dissertation, Rutgers University, 1994.

Ungaretti, Giuseppe. "Sulla vita di Iacopone da Todi e la poesia di Iacopone da Todi." In *Invenzione della poesia moderna: Lezioni brasiliane di letteratura*, ed. Paola Montefoschi. Naples: Edizioni Scientifiche Italiane, 1984, pp. 41–68.

V. Louise Katainen

JACQUES DE VITRY (ca. 1160/70–1240)

The son of a wealthy bourgeois family in Vitry-en-Perthios near Reims, Jacques studied in Paris at a time when Peter the Chanter, one of the most celebrated preachers of his day, was master of the cathedral school. In 1211, he entered the monastery of Augustinian regular canons dedicated to St. Nicolas in Oignies, not far from Cambrai. Over the next five years, he was close to the lay religious group known as the béguines, whose leader was Marie d'Oignies. During this same period, he became a preacher of crusades, first against the Albigensians in 1213 and then against the infidels in the Holy Land in 1214. His preaching won him the see of Acre on the coast of Palestine. Jacques arrived in Palestine in 1216 and accompanied the armies of the Fifth Crusade at Damietta, 1218–21. Weary of constant strife, Jacques left Acre in 1225 and served Pope Gregory IX in Italy and in the Low Countries over the next three years. In 1228, Gregory appointed him cardinal bishop of Tusculum, and he remained in Rome until his death. Jacques was buried at the monastery in Oignies, where he had begun his ecclesiastical vocation.

Jacques's most significant contribution to the history of the church comprised his collections of sermons intended to serve as models for preachers. One collection, *Sermones dominicales* (*de tempore*), gives three sermons for each of the Sundays of the ecclesiastical calendar; *Sermones de sanctis* gives 115 sermons for saints' days and special feasts; *Sermones communes et feriales* gives twenty-seven sermons for daily use; *Sermones vulgares* (or *ad status*) gives seventy-four sermons addressing social classes and religious groups. The first small collection of such model sermons was compiled only the generation before by Alain de Lille, and Jacques went far beyond them with his collections, particularly in their homiletic illustrations, or exempla, which provide a wealth of amusing and instructive anecdotes.

Jacques also composed a biography of Marie d'Oignies (1213) that helped gain papal approval for the béguine movement and has since become a valuable historical source for the early days of that controversial movement. Several of his letters date from his sojourn in Palestine (up to 1221), and his *Historia Hierosolymitana abbreviata* in three books recounts not only the history of Jerusalem during the

Crusades but also, and perhaps more importantly, the new and often controversial religious movements of the day, such as the béguines, the Humiliati, and even the Franciscans (at least in their more colorful manifestations), as they relate to the renewal of the church and to the success of its mission.

Although Jacques's religious vocation took the more traditional form of an Augustinian canon, both his sympathies for the spiritual revival of his day and his talents as an extraordinary preacher place him firmly in the mainstream of the life of the church in the 13th century.

See also **Alain de Lille; Marie d'Oignies**

Further Reading

Jacques de Vitry. *The Historia occidentalis of Jacques de Vitry,* ed. John F. Hinnebusch. Fribourg: University Press, 1972.

——. *Lettres de Jacques de Vitry, 1160/70–1240, évêque de Saint-Jean d'Acre,* ed. R.B.C. Huygens. Leiden: Brill, 1960.

——. *Sermones vulgares.* In *Analecta nouissima spicilegii Solesmensis, altera continuatio,* ed. Jean Baptiste Pitra. 2 vols. Paris: Typis Tusculanis, 1885–88, Vol. 2.

Funk, Philipp. *Jakob von Vitry: Leben und Werke.* Leipzig: Teubner, 1909.

MARK ZIER

JAIME (JAUME) I OF ARAGÓN-CATALONIA

(1208–1276) Jaime (Jaume) I "the Conqueror," count-king of the realms (*regnes*) of Aragón-Catalonia, was the leading figure of the Reconquest in eastern Spain, founder of his realms' greatness in the western Mediterranean, and an innovative contributor to Europe's administrative, educational, legal, and literary evolution. The only son of Pedro II (Pere I of Catalonia), "the Catholic," he was born in a townsman's home at Montpellier, the principality inherited by his half-Byzantine mother, Marie. His father, hero of the battle of Las Navas (1212), which opened Almohad Islam

to Jaime's later conquests, died at Muret (1213) at battle in the Albigensian crusade in Occitania. Simon de Montfort, leader of the Albigensian crusade, kidnapped Jaime and held him at Carcassonne. Jaime was rescued by Pope Innocent III, who then placed his realms under Templar protection. The orphan Jaime—his mother had died at Rome—was brought up from his sixth to his ninth years at the Templar headquarters castle of Monzón in Aragón. By the time he was almost ten, he had begun his personal rule (1217), and had captained armies in a league for order—the beginning of his intermittent domestic wars with refractory nobles (particularly in 1227 and 1273–1275).

In 1225 Jaime led an abortive crusade against Peñíscola in Islamic Valencia. Four years later he mounted a successful amphibious invasion of Mallorca, adding Minorca in 1232 and Ibiza in 1235 as tributaries. Organizing his Balearic conquests as a separate kingdom of Mallorca, Jaime embarked on a nearly fifteen-year campaign to conquer Almohad Valencia piecemeal (1232–1245). Only three major cities fell to siege (Burriana, Valencia, Biar), with consequent expulsion of Muslims, and Játiva succumbed to a combination of siege, feint, and negotiated arrangements from 1239 to 1248 and on to 1252. One set-piece battle was fought in 1237 at Puig; and Valencia surrendered in 1238. Flanking naval power supplied Jaime's war and fended off Tunisian help. Alfonso X of Castile was conquering northward out of Murcia, and the two kings narrowly averted war over southernmost Valencia by the treaty of Almizra in 1244.

Historians have followed Jaime's own account in ending this crusade (actually a series of papal crusades) in 1245, followed by Mudéjar revolts in the 1250s, 1260s, and 1270s. It now seems clear that he patched up a truce with Al-Azraq, the last leader in the field, to take advantage of his last opportunity to recover Provence. He rushed north, personally led a raid to kidnap the heiress of Provence at Marseilles, was foiled by a counterraid by Charles of Anjou, protested noisily to the pope, and withdrew. Hailed as a hero of Christendom for his conquest of Valencia at this lowest point of Europe's crusading movement, in 1246 Jaime rashly announced a crusade to help Latin Byzantium. However, Al-Azraq plunged Valencia into a decade of countercrusade (1247–1258), put down piecemeal again by Jaime in a new papal crusade. Jaime continually organized his Valencian realm as his original invasion progressed, down to his last years of life. Some of his massive land distribution is recorded in his detailed *Repartiment*. His Mudéjar treaties set up semi-autonomous Muslim enclaves throughout Valencia, on a scale unmatched elsewhere in Spain, forming a colonialist society with a thin grid of Christians dominating until the following century. He brought in more Muslims, and also attracted Jewish settlers from Occitania and North Africa, as part of a planned program. He set up Valencia as a separate kingdom with its own law code, money, parliament, and administration.

Meanwhile, Jaime signed away all but his coastal rights in Occitania to Louis IX of France in the treaty of Corbeil (1258). His peninsular politics, notably with Alfonso X of Castile, are only beginning to be explored in depth. Both kings were ambitious to absorb Navarre; they confronted one another as champions, respectively, of the Guelph and Ghibelline movements in the Mediterranean, especially after Jaime married his heir, Pedro, to the Hohenstaufen heiress, Constance of Sicily. In 1265–1266 Jaime helped Alfonso recover the Murcian kingdom from Mudéjar rebellion, an adventure counted as Jaime's third conquest of an Islamic power. From that time on, the confrontational character of their mutual policies turned to friendship.

Jaime also negotiated with the Mongols, who wanted allies against Islam, in 1267. In 1269 he finally mounted his long-awaited crusade to the Holy Land, but abandoned his fleet due to storms (his own excuse) or to reluctance to leave his mistress (the charge by his enemies). After a brief estrangement from his heir, Pedro, and a bitter baronial revolt led by Jaime's bastard son Ferran Sanxis, the conqueror had a moment of triumph again on the world stage. Pope Gregory X summoned him to the Second Ecumenical Council of Lyons in 1274, particularly for his expertise in crusading; Jaime devoted twenty chapters of his autobiography to recounting his reception and activities there. In 1276 the worst of Valencia's Mudéjar revolts erupted, a sustained effort with North African and Granadan help, to recover the land. Jaime fell ill while fighting at Alcira (20 July 1276) and died at Valencia (27 July).

He abdicated on his deathbed, to take the vows and habit of a Cistercian monk, a not uncommon deathbed piety then. The Mudéjar war required his burial at Valencia; only in May 1278 could his successor inter him properly at Poblet monastery near Tarragona. When mobs sacked his tomb during the nineteenth-century Carlist wars, his body was removed to Tarragona cathedral, and only recently has been returned to Poblet. At his death the troubadour Matieu de Carsin hailed him as exalter of the cross "beyond all kings here or overseas," another Arthur of Camelot. His younger contemporary Ramón Muntaner records that people called him "the Good King"; another chronicler records his title as "James the Fortunate," founder of two thousand churches. A myth grew that he had co-founded the Mercedarian ransomer order. A later movement to canonize him did not receive ecclesiastical encouragement.

Jaime had his dark side, however. He could be cruel in warfare after the manner of the times. He cut out the tongue of the bishop of Girona in 1246, for which he suffered papal thunders and public penance. And he was notoriously a womanizer. His guardians had married him in

1221 to an older woman, Leónor, the sister of Fernando III of Castile, for reasons of state. When he was able to consummate the union, Jaime produced his son and first heir, Alfonso (who died in 1260). Rome annulled the marriage in 1229, and in 1235 he married the true love of his life, Violante, the daughter of King Bela IV of Hungary, by whom he had two sons and two daughters. She died in 1251, and in 1255 Jaime married Teresa Gil de Vidaure, by whom he had two sons. Historians often count Teresa as a mistress, but Pope Gregory X regarded the marriage as firm in his thunders against Jaime's efforts to divorce her (1274) after he had relegated her to a nunnery in Valencia. Jaime also had seven formal or contract mistresses and at least five illegitimate children. This led some moderns to dub him "the Henry VIII of Spain."

Jaime promulgated the first Romanized law code of general application, *the furs of Valencia* (1261), as well as the *fueros of Aragón* (1247), the Lérida *Costums* (1258), and the *Costums de la mar* (ca. 1240). Besides founding the papal University of Valencia (1245), he reorganized the statutes of the University of Montpellier to make it the first effective royal university in Europe. He fully supported the mendicant movement and its Arabic/Hebrew language schools, including the Dominicans' 1263 Disputation of Barcelona with the Jews. By his prodigal use of Játiva paper he elaborated the first substantial archives in Europe after the papacy's, leaving a remarkable record of life and administration in his registers. He promoted commerce in many ways, particularly by his trade monopoly at Alexandria, his tributary control of Ḥafṣid Tunis, the North Africa–Valencia–Mallorca–Occitania trade, and his monetary policy. He presided over a literary court (Bernat Desclot and the troubadour Cerverí de Girona stand out) and contributed his *Llibre dels feyts*, the only autobiography by a medieval king except for his great-great-grandson's imitation, to

European letters. Done by collaborators at Játiva in 1244 (the first three hundred chapters) and at Barcelona in 1274, it is a lively personal account of himself as a military Roland or Cid. Desclot describes him as taller than most, with athletic frame and reddish-blond hair, a man cordial to everyone and adventurously bold. His skeletal remains confirm the physical details, and a portrait in Alfonso X's *Cantigas de Santa María* shows him at around sixty, majestic, with his short beard gone white.

See also **Alfonso X, El Sabio, King of Castile and León; Louis IX**

Further Reading

Belenguer Cebrià, E. *Jaume I a través de la història.* 2 vols. Valencia, 1984.

Burns, R. I. *Society and Documentation in Crusader Valencia.* Princeton, N.J., 1985.

——, ed. *The Worlds of Alfonso the Learned and James the Conqueror: Intellect and Force in the Middle Ages.* Princeton, N.J., 1985.

Jaime I y su época: X Congrés d'història de la Corona d'Aragó. 5 vols. in 2. Zaragoza, 1979–82.

Tourtoulon, C. de. *Études sur la maison de Barcelone: Jacme Ier le Conquérant, roi d'Aragón.* 2 vols. Montpellier, 1863–67. Rev. in trans, by Teodoro L'orente. *Don Jaime I el Conquistador.* 2 vols. Valencia, 1874.

ROBERT I. BURNS, S. J.

JAIME II (1267–1327) Second son of Pedro III (r. 1276–1285) and Constanza de Hohenstaufen, Jaime II was an amalgam of the stubborn courage of his grandfather Jaime I (1213–1276) and a keen and crafty mind that provided a clear ruling template for his grandson Pedro IV (1336–1387). With his father's acquisition of Sicily in 1283, Jaime as a teenager became a pivotal figure in central Mediterranean affairs, serving as king of Sicily from 1285 to 1291. In this post, he developed a ruling style which combined unbridled force with patient diplomacy. Holding at bay his family's archenemy, Charles of Anjou, by the development of a strong fleet, Jaime established such an efficient Sicilian government that, according to one chronicler, the island population "grew prosperous in a very short time."

With the death of his brother, the ineffectual Alfonso III (1285–1291), Jaime quickly realized that far greater power was open to him on the Iberian mainland than as Sicilian ruler. Shamefully deserting his island vassals, the new Aragónese sovereign began transforming old enemies into new friends. Making peace with Charles of Anjou and sealing the new relationship by marrying his old foe's daughter in 1295, Jaime then rapidly mended fences with Pope Boniface VIII (papacy 1294–1303), becoming the standard bearer and protector of the papacy in exchange for conquest rights to Sardinia and Corsica. The changed reality of this *realpolitik* was especially dramatic in regard to Sicily, which chose Jaime's younger brother, Fadrique, as its sovereign and then supported their new lord in a war of survival with his sibling (1296–1298) that guaranteed at least temporarily Sicilian independence.

The combination of specifically applied force and wide-ranging diplomatic activity marked all of Jaime's subsequent forays into foreign affairs. Maintaining generally peaceful relations with Castile, he used the death of his cousin, Sancho IV of Castile (1284–1296) to block the accession of the young heir, Fernando IV (1296–1312), in favor of another contender for the Castilian crown, hoping to gain the pivotal district of Murcia in the process. Though this conspiracy proved unsuccessful, Jaime persistently pressed his claim to Murcia. By 1304, the Castilians relented partially and granted Jaime the right to conquer Almería and its surroundings. Since the region was still under Muslim control, an Aragónese attack of the city brought overwhelm-

ing response from the Granada emir, Muḥammad III (1302–1309) and this effectively ended Aragónese military operations in Andalusia until the era of the Catholic kings.

Despite these aftershocks of the great Reconquest, events soon convinced Jaime that much greater geopolitical prizes awaited him in the Mediterranean than on the Iberian Peninsula. When the Sicilian war ended in 1302, mercenary forces (*almogávares*) who had served Fadrique were out of a job. Accepting an offer for employment from the Byzantine emperor Michael IX (1295–1320), the company was soon thrown out of work again by a premature peace with the Ottoman Turks and then went into business for itself by ravaging much of the central Mediterranean and establishing a loose colonial structure, the Duchy of Athens, which remained in Catalan hands until 1388. Indirectly thrust into Mediterranean affairs by this "Catalan Vengeance," Jaime bided time until 1322 when he attempted to make good his claim to Sardinia with extensive military operations that, however, never brought the island under his control and ultimately consumed the very Barcelona dynasty itself when in 1410 the last heir to the dynasty died putting down yet another Sardinian uprising. Despite this lingering Sardinian debacle, Jaime's reign had ushered in a new economic era in the Mediterranean that made the Catalans, with bases in Athens, Sardinia, the North African litoral, and the Balearics, a strong rival to Pisa and Genoa for market dominance.

Jaime also played a significant role in domestic affairs. Trained in Sicilian politics, which gave much greater power to the sovereign, Jaime brought to eastern Spain not a revolution, but a steady manipulation of legal and constitutional norms. Under his tutelage, royal government became steadily more efficient and productive. Quickly realizing the disparate nature of his realms, the king soon moved to set up structures that firmly tied the ruling center to its many peripheries. His most far-reaching action in this regard was the Privilege of Union (1319), which affirmed "whoever was the king of Aragón would also be the king of Valencia and the count of Barcelona." To further this unity, Jaime completely reformed royal government, dividing it into such departments as the chancellery and the treasury, and staffing these with university educated specialists such as the chancellor, treasurer, and master of accounts. From this pool of curial talent, he chose advisers who, along with trusted nobles and clergy, constituted the royal council.

The wholesale administrative changes that accompanied Jaime's accession enraged his conservative realms of Aragón and Valencia, which had spent the last three decades in stamping out royal "innovations" and in legally subordinating the crown to baronial control. Rather than using military means to confront this insurgency (occasionally bound together as the *Unión*), the king, in August 1301, used the very laws forced on his ancestors to charge his rebellious barons with treason and did so before the unionist functionary, the *Justicia de Aragón.* Despite this temporary triumph, Jaime knew he could not fully defeat the barons and admitted as much in the *Declaration of the General Privilege* (1325), in which he formally accepted many of the legal restrictions the *Unión* had previously imposed on the crown.

Jaime II died on 2 November 1327. He married four times: to Isabel of Castile (1291), Blanche of Anjou (1295), Maria de Lusignan (1317), and Elisenda de Montcada (1322). The most fecund of these unions was the second, which produced ten children, including the princes Jaime, Alfonso (the eventual successor), and Juan (late archbishop of Tarragona). To later historians, Jaime was known as "the Just" or "the Justiciar" because he would allow no one but himself to

"render verdicts for disputes." Despite these judicial sobriquets, his greatest accomplishment was the transformation of the Crown of Aragón from a solely Iberian to a strong Mediterranean power.

See also **Pedro III, King of Aragón; Sancho IV, King of Castile**

Further Reading

Abulafia D., *A Mediterranean Emporium: The Catalan Kingdom of Majorca.* Cambridge, 1994.

Archivo de la Corona de Aragón, Cancillería real, Regs. 90–350; Pergaminos, Carp. 128–214.

Kagay D. J. "Rebellion on Trial: The Aragónese *Union* and Its Uneasy Connection to Royal Law, 1265–1301," *Journal of Legal History* 18, no. 3(1997): 30–43.

Martínez Ferrando, J. E. "Jaime II," in *Els Descendants de Pere el Gran.* Barcelona, 1980.

Salavert, V. *Cerdena y la expansion mediterránea de la Corona de Aragón, 1297–1314.* Madrid, 1956.

DONALD J. KAGAY

JAN VAN BOENDALE (ca. 1280–1351)

A Brabantine poet and a native of Tervuren, a small town between Leuven and Brussels, Jan van Boendale spent most of his working life as secretary to the aldermen of the city of Antwerp. In this position he dealt with all levels of society, an experience that affected his writing. His oeuvre consists of some seven works, although some of those texts cannot definitively be attributed to him. Boendale wrote several versions of some of his works, mainly updates of his historiography texts, which were then dedicated to other patrons.

His first work, the *Brabantsche yeesten* (Brabantine Deeds), is a chronicle in coupled rhyme, dealing with the history of the Brabantine ducal house in the period from ca. 600 to ca. 1350. This chronicle is divided in five parts ("books"), of which the first four describe the history of Brabant before Boendale's own lifetime, and the fifth is devoted to the three dukes contemporaneous with him: Jan I (d. 1294), Jan II (d. 1312), and Jan III (d. 1355). This voluminous work of some 16,000 lines was not written in one effort; the first version dates from ca. 1316, the fifth from 1347, and a sixth version may have been written around 1351, each one providing an updated version of the history of the duchy. This does not imply that Boendale was completely original in his chronicle. Large parts of his text were copied from the *Spiegel historiael* (Mirror of History) by Jacob van Maerlant—whom Boendale elsewhere called "the father of all Dutch poets"—and the anonymous *Chronica de origine ducum Brabantiae* (Chronicle of the Origins of the Duchy of Brabant); only when writing about his own lifetime is Boendale original.

After completing a second version of the *Brabantsche yeesten* in 1318 he used the text in 1322 as the source for a very short rhyme-chronicle, the so-called *Korte kroniek van Brabant* (374 lines). He later wrote a second version of this text too, in the years 1332–1333.

But between 1325–1330, he composed an extensive didactic poem of more than 20,000 lines, called *Der leken spiegel* (The Layman's Mirror). In using this title, Boendale explicitly addresses an audience of non-readers (*illiterati*), offering them an encyclopedic text, dealing with cosmology, the nature of human body and soul, the history of the Old and New Testaments, church history, devotional practice, etc. The poem is structured according to the *Heilsgeschichte* (divine plan) and divided into four books. Books one and two deal with God's Creation, the structure of the universe, and the course of history; book three is concerned with the present, and book four with the future. *Der leken spiegel* contains the oldest poetical treatise in Dutch: in book three, chapter fifteen, Boendale presents, under the title *Hoe dichters dichten sullen ende wat si hantieren sullen* (How writers

should write and what they should pay attention to), his views on literature. This is not a treatise on technical aspects of poetry, but a declaration by a self-conscious author concerning the cultural responsibilities inherent in authorship. Here, Boendale presents his ideas on, among other topics, the prerequisites of true authorship, the value of literary tradition, and the relationship between genre and fictionality.

Between 1330–1334 Boendale wrote his *Jans teesteye* (Jans testimony), a dialogue in some 4100 lines of coupled rhyme. In this polemic-didactic dialogue the participants are "Jan," Boendale's *alter ego*, and "Wouter," probably a fictitious person, playing the role of the pupil. The topic of discussion is *grosso modo*, the quality of life in their time. Jan takes a positive, but not uncritical position; Wouter's position is negative: he is the "praiser of times past" (*laudator temporis acti*).

Shortly after 1340 Boendale wrote *Van den derden Eduwaert*, describing in 2,018 lines the role of the English king Edward III (d. 1377) in continental European politics. The poem was not only a tribute to this king, whom Boendale probably had met in person; it was first and foremost a panegyric to Duke Jan III of Brabant, an ally of the English king at the outbreak of the Hundred Year's War in 1337.

Boendale's authorship of two poems is disputed. The first is the very short *Hoemen ene stat regeren sal* (18 lines, before ca. 1350), a poem advising officials on "how to rule a town." The poem is known in several versions, some written on the tie-beams of city halls, including those in Brussels and Emmerich. The oldest known version is incorporated in a manuscript of *Der leken spiegel* (Brussels, Koninklijke Bibliotheek, manuscript no. 15.658, fol. 122r).

The second disputed poem is called the *Boec van der wraken* [The book of punishment (5,870 lines, ca. 1346)]. Reacting to the conflict between Pope

Clemens VI and the German emperor Louis of Bavaria, in which he chose the imperial side, Boendale has written a pamphlet-like poem around the theme of God's punishment for human sinfulness, with strong eschatological overtones. A second, updated version was written in 1351.

Typical of Boendale's historiographic works is his orientation on Brabantine history, apparent in the recurrent *origo*-motive (the tracing back of the origin of the ducal house to the Trojans) and the *reditus*-motive (the dukes of Brabant as the true inheritors of Charlemagne). Boendale's didactic perspective revolves around the theme of the *ghemeyn oirbaer* ("the common good"), which is the basis for his social criticism. Boendale criticizes clergy, aristocracy, and commoners alike, but evidently tends to identify himself with his urban environment. This somewhat intermediate position shows itself clearly in the dedications of his poems. Though often explicitly intended for a broad audience of laymen, many of the manuscripts contain dedications to members of the aristocracy, including Willem van Bornecolve, alderman of Antwerp, Rogier van Leefdale, viscount of Brussels, and Duke Jan III of Brabant.

Jan van Boendale is an example of what is called the Antwerp School, a designation for the explosive literary output of Antwerp in the first half of the fourteenth century. When cities began to emerge as centers of literary activity in the late thirteenth century, Antwerp was the third most culturally important town of Brabant (after Brussels and Leuven). In Antwerp this increased literary activity resulted in a rather homogeneous group of texts, which included, besides Boendale's works, the *Sidrac*, the *Melibeus*, and the *Dietsche doctrinale*. The *Sidrac* is an extensive encyclopedic and didactic dialogue in prose, translated from French in 1318. The *Melibeus* (1342) is a translation of the *Liber consolationis et consilii* (Book of Consolation and Counsel) by Albertanus of Brescia (d. after 1246). In 3,771 lines, a moralizing dialogue between allegorical characters is presented.

The *Dietsche doctrinale* (German Doctrine 1345) is another translation of a misogynistic didactic text by Albertanus of Brescia, *De amore et dilectione Dei et proximi et aliorum rerum et de forma vitae* (On God's love...). This work of some 6,650 lines, divided in three "books," deals with love and friendship, virtues and vices, and closes with an interesting section on the nature of God. It thus presents a compendium of laymen's ethics. The thematic similarities between the *Melibeus*, the *Dietsche doctrinale*, and Boendale's oeuvre—that history is a framework for laymen's ethics as well as the central concept of the "common good"—has sometimes led to the attribution of these two texts to Jan van Boendale.

See also **Jacob van Maerlant**

Further Reading

Avonds, Piet. "*Ghemeyn Oirbaer*. Volkssoevereiniteit en politieke ethiek in Brabant in de veertiende eeuw." In Reynaert, Joris et al. *Wat is wijsheid? Lekenethiek in de Middelnederlandse letterkunde*. Amsterdam: Prometheus, 1994, pp, 164–180 and 405–411.

Gerritsen, Willem P., et al. "A fourteenth-century vernacular poetics: Jan van Boendale's 'How Writers Should Write'." In Erik Kooper, ed. *Medieval Dutch Literature in its European Context*. Cambridge, Cambridge University Press, 1994, pp. 245–260.

De Vries, Matthijs, ed. *Der leken spieghel, leerdicht van den jare 1330, door Jan Boendale, gezegd Jan de Clerc, schepenklerk te Antwerpen*. 3 vols. Leyden, Du Mortier, 1844–1848.

Heymans, Jo, ed. *Van den derden Eduwaert*. Nijmegen, Alfa, 1983.

Heymans, Jo. "Geschiedenis in *Der Leken Spiegel*." In Geert R. W. Dibbets and Paul W. M. Wackers, ed. *Wat duikers van is dit! Opstellen voor W.M.H. Hummelen*. Wijhe: Quarto, 1989, pp. 25–40.

Jonckbloet, Willem J. A., ed. *Die Dietsche Doctrinale, leerdicht van den jare 1345, toegekendaanJanDeckers.*TheHague,1842.

Kinable, Dirk, *Facetten van Boendale. Literair-historische verkenningen van Jans teesteye en de Lekenspiegel.* Leyden: Dimensie, 1998.

Lucas, H.S. "Edward III and the poet chronicler John Boendale." *Speculum* 12 (1937): 367–369.

Reynaert, Joris. "Ethiek en 'filosofie' voor leken: de *Dietsche doctrinale.*" In Joris Reynaert, et al. *Wat is wijsheid? Lekenethiek in de Middelnederlandse letterkunde.* Amsterdam: Prometheus, 1994, pp. 199–214 and 415–419.

Snellaert, Ferdinand A., ed. *Nederlandsche gedichten uit de veertiende eeuw van Jan Boendale, Hein van Aken en anderen naar het Oxfordsch handschrift.* Brussels, Hayez, 1869 [*Jans teesteye; Boec van der Wraken; Melibeus*].

Van Anrooij, Wim, ed. "Hoemen ene stat regeren sal. Een vroege stadstekst uit de Zuidelijke Nederlanden." *Spiegel der Letteren* 34 (1992): 139–157.

Van Anrooij, Wim. "Recht en rechtvaardigheid binnen de Antwerpse School." In Reynaert, Joris et al. *Wat is wijsheid? Lekenethiek in de Middelnederlandse letterkunde.* Amsterdam: Prometheus, 1994, pp. 149–163 and 399–405.

Van Eerden, Peter C. "*Eschatology in the Boec van der wraken.*" In Werner Verbeke, Daniel Verhelst, and Andries Welkenhuysen, ed. *The Use and Abuse of Eschatology in the Middle Ages.* Leuven: Leuven University Press, 1988, pp. 425–440.

Van Tol, J. F. J., ed. *Het boek van Sidrac in de Nederlanden.* Amsterdam: H. J. Paris, 1936.

Willems, Jan Frans, ed. *De Brabantsche yeesten of rymkronyk van Braband.* 2 vols. Brussels: Hayez, 1839, 1843 and J. H. Bormans, *De Brabantsche yeesten, of rijmkronijk van Braband,* vol. 3. Brussel, Hayez, 1869 [with the *Korte kronike van Brabant*].

GEERT H. M. CLAASSENS

JAN VAN RUUSBROEC (1293–1381)

Jan van Ruusbroec, a Brabantine mystic, was born in 1293 in the village of Ruisbroek southeast of Brussels. When he was eleven, he went to live in the city with a relative, John (Jan) Hinckaert (d. 1350/1358), who was a canon of the collegiate church of St. Gudula. The boy attended the school attached to the church, and after the required studies, he was ordained a priest in 1317 and became a chaplain there. In Brussels he began to compose his first treatises on mystical life, among which were some of his most important writings: *Die geestelike brulocht* (The Spiritual Espousals) and *Vanden blinkenden steen* (The Sparkling Stone).

The *Spiritual Espousals* is the most famous and most translated of his works. It describes the entire path to a mystic life from a humble beginning to complete development and indicates the risks and possible deviations at each stage. According to Ruusbroec, the essence of mystical life is the direct and passive experience of God. To describe the different stages, he uses three terms in the *Espousals* which recur in all his treatises: *dat werkende leven* (the active life), *dat inninghe leven* (the interior life), *and dat schouwende leven* (the contemplative life). Each is a way to live one's relation with God. In the active life, love manifests itself in the exercise of virtue; in the interior life, a new dimension of love is discovered: to adhere intimately to the Beloved; finally, in the contemplative life, the loving person is elevated above him- or herself and introduced into the most intimate life of God, the love of the Father, Son and Spirit in one divine being. Ruusbroec strongly emphasizes the point that, at each level, the higher life does not neglect, let alone reject, the lower life. A person who has discovered the interior life should not despise the active life. And, one who has been introduced into the contemplative life should not disdain God nor active service to his neighbor. Just as the interior life does not replace the need for an active life, but inspires and purifies it, the contemplative life enhances and elevates both.

Whereas the *Espousals* is famous for its all-encompassing view, Ruusbroec's small treatise, *The Sparkling Stone*, is a masterpiece of conciseness. It briefly describes the three lives of the *Espousals* and then concentrates on the highest of the three, the contemplative life.

In 1343 Ruusbroec, together with John Hinckaert and Frank of Coudenberg (d. 1386), another Canon of St. Gudula, left Brussels to live a contemplative life in Groenendaal (Green Valley), a site in the Wood of Soignes about ten kilometers south of Brussels. To cope with the juridical problems, resulting from their living together as a religious community without belonging to an established order or following a recognized rule, the group, which had meanwhile increased, became a provostry of canons regular of St. Augustine. Ruusbroec was the first prior of the newly founded monastery.

In Groenendaal he continued his work as a writer. There, he finished his largest work, *Van den geesteliken tabernakel* (The Spiritual Tabernacle). As the number of the manuscripts still preserved indicates, this treatise must have been very popular in its time. For the modern reader, access is difficult because the *Tabernacle* is a continuous allegory on some passages from the biblical books, Exodus and Leviticus, which describe the construction of the tabernacle and give ritual prescriptions during Israel's stay in the desert. The link between material image and spiritual reality may seem somewhat farfetched today, but the way in which Ruusbroec masters the complex whole of image and reality is astonishing.

In Groenendaal Ruusbroec not only wrote books, but also met people who came to him with their questions about a life of prayer. Among the most famous was Geert Grote (1340–1384), the founder of the religious movement, the Modern Devotion. Very rarely, Ruusbroec left Groenendaal to visit those who were not allowed to leave their monasteries. At an advanced age, he traveled on foot to a monastery of Carthusians to help them with some difficulties concerning his description of the highest stages of mystical life. This visit gave rise to one of his last works, *Boecsken der verclaringhe* (Little Book of Enlightenment). By means of another tripartition, *enecheit met middel* (unity with intermediary), *sonder middel* (without intermediary), and *sonder differencie* (without difference), he tries to explain to his friends that—though the distinction between Creator and creature is eternal—there is a moment in mystical life when nothing of the opposition between the beloved "you" and the loving "I" is left.

In 1381 Ruusbroec died in Groenendaal at the age of eighty-eight, but his works have survived him. During his lifetime, some were translated from the Brabantine Middle Dutch into High German for the *Gottesfreunde* (Friends of God) in Strasbourg and Basle, and into Latin. About the middle of the sixteenth century his *Opera Omnia* (entire works) were translated into Latin by a Carthusian in Cologne, Laurentius Surius (1523–1578). This was the basis for many later translations into modern languages, including German and Spanish. Ruusbroec's influence is evident in the first generations of the Modern Devotion: the canons regular of the Windesheim Chapter, Gerlach Peters (d. 1411), Hendrik Mande (d. 1431), and Thomas à Kempis (1379/1380–1471). Another member of the Modern Devotion, Hendrik Herp (d. 1477), was so deeply influenced by Ruusbroec that he earned the name of "Herold of Ruusbroec." Through him, Ruusbroec's influence reached France through Benedict of Canneld (1562–1610) and John of Saint Samson (1571–1636). Born in England, Benedict passed much of his life in France, where he became a Capuchin. There, he introduced Ruusbroec to mystical circles, for example, to one Madame Acarie (1566–1618). John, blind from his early youth, joined the Carmelites and became one of the most outstanding mystical writers of his order.

See also **Thomas à Kempis**

Further Reading

Dupré, Louis. *The Common Life: The Origins of Trinitarian Mysticism and its Development by Jan van Ruusbroec.* New York: Crossroad, 1984.

Mommaers, Paul and Norbert de Paepe, ed. *Jan van Ruusbroec: the sources, content and sequels of his mysticism.* Mediaevalia Lovaniensia ser. 1. Studia 12. Leuven: Leuven University Press, 1984.

Underhill, Evelyn. *Ruysbroeck.* London: Bell, 1915.

van Ruusbroec, Jan. *Werken.* Naar het stand-aardhandschrift van Groenendaal uitge-geven door het Ruusbroec-genootschap te Antwerpen. 4 vols. Mechelen/Amsterdam: Kompas, 1932–1934; 2nd ed. Tielt: Lannoo, 1944–1948.

——. *Opera Omnia.* Studiën en tekstuitgaven van Ons Geestelijk Erf, XX. Leiden: Brill; Tielt: Lannoo; Turn-hour: Brepols, 1981ff. [Middle Dutch text, English and Latin trans.; Dutch and Latin introd.; 10 vols. planned, 4 published].

——. *The Spiritual Espousals and Other Works,* Trans. James A. Wiseman. New York/Mahwah/Toronto: Paulist, 1985.

Wiseman, James A. *"Minne in Die gheestelike brulocht* of Jan van Ruusbroec." S.T.D. Thesis. Catholic University of America, 1979.

GUIDO O. E. J. DE BAERE

JAUFRE RUDEL (fl. 1120–48) The troubadour Jaufre Rudel, lord of Blaye in the Gironde, sang of earthly love infused by a mystical quest expressed also through his participation in the Second Crusade. Of his six surviving songs of certain authenticity, Jaufre's most successful *canso* is directed to his love from afar, or *amor de loing,* which gives this lyric its leitmotif and keyword. In this song and in *Qan lo rius,* he voices his yearning for a distant love, diversely interpreted by critics as a woman, the Virgin Mary, God, or the Holy Land. Recent scholarship underlines instead the deliberate ambiguity in jaufre's fusion of linguistic registers and love objects drawn from both profane and sacred traditions. The legend of his love for the Countess of Tripoli dates from the pseudobiographical *vida* and earlier. It has been echoed in every century since the 13th by authors as varied as Petrarch, Stendhal, Rostand, Browning, Heine, Carducci, Pound, and Döblin.

See also **Petrarca, Francesco**

Further Reading

Jaufre Rudel. *The Songs of Jaufre Rudel,* ed. Rupert T. Pickens. Toronto: Pontifical Institute of Mediaeval Studies, 1978.

——. *The Poetry of Cercamon and Jaufre Rudel,* ed. and trans. George Wolf and Roy Rosenstein. New York: Garland, 1983.

——. *Il canzoniere di Jaufre Rudel,* ed. Giorgio Chiarini. Rome: Japadre, 1985.

Rosenstein, Roy. "New Perspectives on Distant Love: Jaufre Rudel, Uc Bru, and Sarrazina." *Modern Philology* 87 (1990): 225–38.

ROY S. ROSENSTEIN

JEAN DE GARLANDE (Johannes de Garlandia; ca. 1195–ca. 1272) Born in England, Jean first studied at Oxford shortly after 1200 and went to Paris in 1217 or 1218, first to complete his studies and then to teach. At Paris, he lived in the Clos de Garlande, from which he derives his name. At the close of the Albigensian Crusade, the papal legate Romain Frangipani commissioned him to teach at the newly formed University of Toulouse (April 2, 1229), together with the Dominican master Roland of Cremona. Jean remained at Toulouse for only a few years. He may have returned to England during the 1230s but in any case was again teaching in Paris by 1241.

Jean's interests ranged primarily over the field of literary studies: etymology, rhetoric, grammar, and poetics. One of his earliest and best-known works, the *Parisiana poetria* (ca. 1220; revised a decade later), was a treatise on the art of poetry in the tradition of Matthieu de Vendôme and Geoffroi de Vinsauf. In this work, he stresses the place of both verse and prose composition in the arts curriculum. From this same period comes his *Dictionarius*, perhaps the first word book to be so entitled. Jean also wrote a brief verse commentary to Ovid's *Metamorphoses*, the *Integumenta Ovidii*, giving interpretations sometimes moral, sometimes scientific or historical, to the fables. Like many of his works, the *Integumenta* presupposes a vast general knowledge of the subject and is not intended for the novice.

Jean was also concerned about the moral formation of his students and wrote several works with that aim, among them the *Morale scolarium* (1241), an admonition on the values and habits of the ideal scholar, and the *Stella maris* (ca. 1249), in praise of the Virgin Mary as a paragon of Christian virtue and action. A later work, *De triumphis ecclesiae* (ca. 1252), is a polemic against pagans and heretics, based on his earlier experiences in Toulouse.

Jean had a prominent reputation in the 13th century. But though his promotion of lay piety was in keeping with the contemporary mission of the Dominicans and Franciscans, his resistance to Aristotelian studies and to the new emphasis on logic in the curriculum bespeak a conservatism more in keeping with the schools of the 12th century than with the universities of the 13th.

Jean must not be confused with the musician of the same name.

Further Reading

Jean de Garlande. *Morale scolarium of John of Garland (Johannes de Garlandia), a Professor in the Universities of Paris and Toulouse in the Thirteenth Century,* ed. Louis J. Paetow. Berkeley: University of California Press, 1927.

Wilson, Evelyn Faye. *The Stella maris of John of Garland.* Cambridge: Mediaeval Academy of America, 1946.

MARK ZIER

JEAN DE MEUN (Jehan de Meung; 1235/40–1305) Born at Meung-sur-Loire, Jean Chopinel (or Clopinel) obtained the Master of Arts, most likely in Paris. He dwelt for much of his adult life in the capital, where from at least 1292 to his death he was housed in the Hôtel de la Tourelle in the Faubourg Saint-Jacques. Jean's works exhibit a rich classical and scholastic culture. Among the works he translated into French are Vegetius, *De re militari*, dedicated to Jean de Brienne, count of Eu; Boethius, *De consolatione Philosophiae*, dedicated to Philip the Fair; and the correspondence of Abélard and Héloïse. He also claims two additional translations, which are not extant, versions of Giraldus Cambrensis, *De mirabilibus Hiberniae*, and of Aelred of Rievaulx, *De spirituali amicitia*. More likely than not, Jean was also the author of the satirical *Testament maistre Jehan de Meun* and *Codicile maistre Jehan de Meun*.

But Jean is best remembered as the second author of the *Roman de la Rose*, an allegorical narrative begun by Guillaume de Lorris. This masterwork has survived in over 250 manuscripts. It also had twenty-one printed editions from 1481 to 1538. The *Rose* was translated partially or *in toto* during the medieval period once into Dutch, twice into Italian, and three times into English—the first English fragment is attributed to Chaucer. Jean de Meun influenced Dante, Boccaccio, Machaut, and Froissart; he played a crucial role in the formation of both Chaucer and Gower. Jean's section of the *Rose* became the subject of the first great literary quarrel, at the beginning of the 15th century. Jean de Meun was the first recognized *auctor* and *auctoritas* in French literary history, and his book the first true French classic, glossed, explicated, quoted, indexed, anthologized, and fought over—treated as if it were a masterpiece from antiquity.

Guillaume de Lorris wrote his *Roman de la Rose*, 4,028 lines left unfinished, in the early 1220s. In the decade 1264–74 Jean de Meun brought Guillaume's text to a conclusion. Jean's *Rose*, some 17,722 lines, does not merely complete the earlier poem: he grafts a totally original sequel onto it.

The God of Love comes with his army to succor Guillaume's forlorn Lover. First, False Seeming and Constrained Abstinence slay Foul Mouth, permitting the Lover to speak with Fair Welcome. A pitched battle occurs between the attackers and the defenders of the castle, ending in a truce. Finally, Venus leads a victorious assault, flinging her torch into the sanctuary: the castle bursts into flames, and the Lover wins the Rose.

The action and the allegory no longer play a primary role, as they did for Guillaume de Lorris. They serve as supports, and pretexts, for discourse: exhortations from Reason and Friend to the Lover, False Seeming's confession of his true nature to the God of Love before he is admitted into the army, the Old Woman's exhortation to Fair Welcome, Nature's confession to her priest, Genius, and Genius's exhortation to the army before the final battle.

The God of Love refers to Jean's book as a *miroër aus amoreus* (1. 10,621). It is, in one sense, a *speculum* or anatomy, a medieval encyclopedia, treating all knowledge, including ethics, economics, cosmology, astronomy, optics, alchemy, and the university. The knowledge in the *speculum*, however, is granted unity and coherence by means of its inclusion under the category of love, which Jean expounds in all facets, both good (sex and reproduction, friendship, justice, the love of reason, one's neighbor, and God) and bad (lust for money, enslavement to Fortune, clerical celibacy, and the hypocrisy and deceit that exist between false lovers and false friends).

That the *Roman de la Rose* is didactic no one denies, but the precise nature of the message, the world vision that Jean de Meun wishes to instill, is subject to controversy. Most scholars believe that Jean transforms and refutes Guillaume de Lorris's *Rose*, that he derides, undermines, and destroys the ideal of *fin'amors* at every turn. One school of thought argues that Jean counters *fin'amors* with a call to procreation, to free love in the service of cosmic plenitude. Another school proposes that Jean treats all his characters, with the exception of Lady Reason, with irony and that his philosophy conforms to orthodox, Augustinian Christianity. The reason scholarly opinion differs so strikingly, why it is so difficult to pin down the author's personal doctrine, lies in the fact that Jean de Meun has chosen to exploit a unique version of narrative technique, quite different from that of his predecessors. Jean distinguishes himself as author from the dreamer-protagonist of his story, proclaimed to be Guillaume de Lorris, thus creating a first level of irony and distance. Second, the dreamer-protagonist, Fair Welcome, and Genius listen to and approve or disapprove of the lengthy discourses listed above, all of which are also presented with comedy and irony. Speakers have a proclivity to contradict themselves, and to cite texts from antiquity that refute rather than support their position. There is no foolproof method for determining which, if any, of the discourses are to be given greater weight than the others; which, if any, carry Jean's own conviction. Readers must judge each of these delegated voices in turn, analyzing the facts and rhetoric, to come to their own conclusions. The result, perhaps intended by Jean de Meun, is a state of doctrinal indeterminacy, in which the Lover and the audience are offered a sequence of philosophies and worldviews. The Lover, in the end, decides—he opens the sanctuary with joy—but the reader-audience is not obliged to applaud his decision. The indeterminacy remains, part and parcel of Jean's text and of a certain late Gothic mentality of which he is the first outstanding master.

Less controversial are the texture and ambience of Jean's imaginative world, a domain in which he is as great an innovator as in narrative technique. Compared with Guillaume de Lorris, Jean is a master of truculent vulgar speech, material detail, and picaresque naturalism. He shifts the audience's perspective from top to bottom, from rose petals to what they hide. A generation before Dante, three generations before Chaucer, Jean juxtaposes lofty and humble registers of style. Scenes, images, and speech once reserved to the fabliaux or excluded from polite letters altogether are now included in a serious work of art, alongside the sublime.

Jean's demystification of courtly love assumes several forms. His characters underscore the role of money in the erotic life, that so often the opposite sex is an object to be purchased, bartered, or exchanged for money or other commodities. The process of reification, and perhaps of antifeminism, is crowned by Jean de Meun's transformation of the woman-rose into a piece of lifeless architecture, a sanctuary, which the Lover pries open with his pilgrim's staff.

Still more striking is the role the author applies to manipulation and duplicity. Speech serves two purposes: to instruct and to trick. All people can be divided into knaves and fools, masters and slaves, deceivers and deceived. The deceivers create illusion by hiding behind masks; it is not easy for the Lover, Fair Welcome, or anyone else to distinguish appearance from reality, the mask from the flesh, the literal bark from an allegorical kernel. The author tells us that, since the end of the Golden Age, dissimulation, violence, and evil are part of the human condition and that we must learn to cope with them. Throughout the *Rose*, he implicitly urges the Lover and the audience to go beyond appearances and seek the truth, to open our eyes and rip aside the mask of falsehood. Knowledge can then lead to action. Some of Jean's characters remain passive, blind, impotent. Others, including the Lover, attain a measure of freedom, becoming masters not slaves, adults not children.

Jean's is a world of comedy. Several of his characters embody comic archetypes derived from the classics of ancient Rome. They are rigid, mechanical, obsessed with their narrow concerns. Furthermore, the narrative line, such as it is, constitutes the triumph of young love over old constraint. In spite of the blocking figures, Venus's torch burns and the story ends, as comedies must, with the couple packed off to bed. Whatever Jean's doctrine, whether for good or ill, the victory of our animal nature is achieved in a denouement of erotic explosion and the exaltation of life. It is for this reason that many scholars, especially in France, associate Jean de Meun with the awakening of humanism, the rebirth of reverence for antiquity, lust for life, and the revaluation of art that are hallmarks of the 12th- and 13th-century renaissance.

See also **Abélard, Peter; Boccaccio, Giovanni; Chaucer, Geoffrey; Dante Alighieri; Guillaume de Lorris**

Further Reading

Guillaume de Lorris and Jean de Meun. *Le roman de la Rose*, ed. and trans. Armand Strubel. Paris: Livre de Poche, 1992.

——. *Le roman de la Rose*, ed. Félix Lecoy. 3 vols. Paris: Champion, 1965–70.

——. *The Romance of the Rose*, trans. Charles Dahlberg. Princeton: Princeton University Press, 1971.

Arden, Heather M. *The Romance of the Rose*. Boston: Twayne, 1987.

——. *The Roman de la Rose: An Annotated Bibliography*. New York: Garland, 1993.

Badel, Pierre-Yves. *Le roman de la Rose au XIVe siècle: étude de la réception de l'œuvre*. Geneva: Droz, 1980.

Brownlee, Kevin, and Sylvia Huot. *Rethinking the Romance of the Rose: Text, Image,*

Reception. Philadelphia: University of Pennsylvania Press, 1992.

Calin, William. *A Muse for Heroes: Nine Centuries of the Epic in France*. Toronto: University of Toronto Press, 1983, chap. 5.

Fleming, John V. *The Roman de la Rose: A Study in Allegory and Iconography*. Princeton: Princeton University Press, 1969.

Gunn, Alan M. F. *The Mirror of Love: A Reinterpretation of the Romance of the Rose*. Lubbock: Texas Tech Press, 1952.

Payen, Jean-Charles. *La Rose et l'utopie: révolution sexuelle et communisme nostalgique chez Jean de Meung*. Paris: Éditions Sociales, 1976.

WILLIAM C. CALIN

JEANNE D'ARC (ca. 1412–1431) The most heroic of France's saints, Jeanne d'Arc was born to a peasant family in Lorraine. At thirteen, Jeanne began hearing the "voices" (of SS. Michael, Catherine, and Margaret) that inspired her. In February 1429, she persuaded a Valois captain to provide an escort for her dangerous journey to the court of Charles VII. At Chinon, Jeanne convinced the king of her divine mission to defeat the English and to assist at his overdue coronation. After formal inquiry into her orthodoxy and chastity, she was given a commanding role in a relief force for Orléans and led reinforcements into the besieged city on April 29. She inspired counterattacks that compelled the English to abandon the siege on May 8. A month later, her army's decisive victory at Patay ensured Valois control over the Loire Valley and destroyed the myth of English invincibility. The subsequent campaign that brought Charles to Reims for a triumphant coronation on July 17 was the high point of Jeanne's meteoric career.

Now a political force, Jeanne became a recognized leader of the court faction favoring renewed war over negotiations with the Anglo-Burgundians. Failure in war soon destroyed her influence. When, she was defeated and wounded in an ill-considered assault on Paris in September, Charles arranged a truce and disbanded his army. Though her family had been ennobled, Jeanne was politically isolated and left the court in the spring to bolster Compiègne's resistance to a Burgundian siege. She was captured there on May 24, 1430, and, to his eternal discredit, abandoned by Charles. Jeanne's cross-dressing, claims to divine guidance, and success had aroused suspicions of sorcery, but her subsequent trial and execution for heresy were acts intended primarily to discredit the Valois cause. In response to an accusation by

Arrival of Joan of Arc at Chinon. German tapestry (called Azeghio tapestry), 15th c. Photo: Bulloz. © Réunion des Musées Nationaux/Art Resource, New York.

representatives of the University of Paris, her Burgundian captors delivered her for trial at Rouen under the direction of Bishop Pierre Cauchon. Eloquent in testimony and steadfast when threatened with torture, Jeanne submitted only when weakened by illness and faced with execution. Sentenced to a life of imprisonment and penance, she relapsed and was condemned. Courageous to the end, she insisted on her innocence and asked the executioner to hold the cross high so she could see it through the flames. Jeanne remained a controversial figure, and in 1456 Charles VII arranged the annulment of her conviction mainly to clear himself of a suspect association.

Shrouded in myth and exalted by unceasing artistic glorification, Jeanne endures as a figure inspiring even the most skeptical. Her historical importance could be narrowly construed: she was essentially a military figure whose inspirational leadership and ephemeral battlefield success helped restore the prestige of the Valois dynasty, ensuring its survival but not its eventual triumph. Few, however, would restrict themselves to such a reductive assessment. Jeanne's courageous example and her martyrdom assure her an enduring role in modern life, not unlike that played by Roland in the Middle Ages. She has become a symbolic figure emblematic of many and varied hopes. Above all, she is the symbol of 20th-century France at war with both itself and its German invaders. In the late 19th century, the "Maid of Orléans" become a popular heroine who inspired generations of French conservatives in the struggle against the secularism of the Third Republic and reminded all Frenchmen of the need to regain the lost provinces of Alsace and Lorraine seized by Germany in 1870. This popular devotion led to her canonization in the aftermath of the First World War and final confirmation that her greatness transcends if not defies historical analysis.

See also **Charles VII, Christine de Pizan**

Further Reading

Doncoeur, Paul, and Yvonne Lanhers, eds. Documents et recherches relatifs à Jeanne la Pucelle. 5 vols. Vols. 1–4, Melun: Librairie d'Argences, 1921–58; Vol. 5, Paris: De Brouwer, 1961.

Tisset, Pierre, and Yvonne Lanhers, eds. Procès de condamnation de Jeanne d'Arc. 3 vols. Paris: Klincksieck, 1960–71.

Gies, Frances. Joan of Arc: The Legend and the Reality. New York: Harper and Row, 1981.

Margolis, Nadia. Joan of Arc in History, Literature, and Film: A Select, Annotated Bibliography. New York: Garland, 1990.

Vale, Malcolm G.A. Charles VII. Berkeley: University of California Press, 1974.

Warner, Marina. Joan of Arc: The Image of Female Heroism. New York: Knopf, 1981.

PAUL D. SOLON

JEANNE OF NAVARRE (1273–1305) Queen of France. The daughter of Henri III of Champagne and Navarre and Blanche of Artois, granddaughter of Louis VIII, Jeanne inherited her father's lands in 1274. Plans for her to marry the heirs, first of Edward I of England and then the king of Aragon, failed after problems in Spain led Blanche and Jeanne to seek asylum with Philip III. In May 1275, Blanche put Navarre under Philip's protection and affianced Jeanne to one of his sons. Raised at the French court, Jeanne was declared of age on May 17, 1284, and on August 16 married Philip IV the Fair, who on October 6, 1285, succeeded his father as king. Jeanne was closely involved with the administration of Champagne and Navarre, but Philip effectively controlled them.

Jeanne was a popular queen, and Philip was devoted to her. In 1288, he deferred until after her death collection of money owed for the defense of Navarre. In October 1294, he appointed her regent of France if he died before their eldest son came of age. Her name was associated with Philip's in important acts, and she accompanied him on his grand tour of the Midi in 1303–04.

She showed independence in supporting the Franciscan Bernard Délicieux and accepting gifts from citizens of Béziers, whose orthodoxy and loyalty were suspect. She pressed the prosecution of Guichard, bishop of Troyes, accused of cheating her and her mother (and later charged with killing Jeanne by sorcery). A woman of considerable culture, she commissioned Joinville's *Vie de saint Louis*; Ramon Lull and her confessor Durand de Champagne dedicated works to her, and Raymond of Béziers began for her his translation of *Kalila et Dimna*. She was godmother of Enguerran de Marigny's wife, and Enguerran was the officer in charge of Jeanne's pantry before joining Philip's service in 1302.

Jeanne bore Philip four sons and a daughter before dying on April 2, 1305. In her lavish testament, she used 40,000 *livres parisis* and three years' revenues of Champagne, assigned her by Philip, to endow a hospital at Château-Thierry and the Collége de Navarre in Paris. Having rejected burial at Saint-Denis, the royal mausoleum, she was interred at the Franciscan church in Paris.

See also **Llull, Ramón; Philip IV the Fair**

Further Reading

Arbois de Jubainville, Henry d'. *Histoire des ducs et des comtes de Champagne.* 7 vols. Paris: Durand et Lauriel, 1859–69.
Brown, Elizabeth A.R. *The Monarchy of Capetain France and Royal Ceremonial.* London: Variorum, 1991.
Favier, Jean. *Un conseiller de Philippe le Bel: Enguerran de Marigny.* Paris: Presses Universitaires de France, 1963.
Lalou, Elisabeth. "Le gouvernement de la reine Jeanne, 1285–1304." *Cahiers Haut-Marnais* 167 (1986): 16–30.

ELIZABETH A.R. BROWN

JEHAN BODEL (d. 1210) A trouvère from Arras in the second half of the 12th century and one of the most prominent writers of his time. Jehan Bodel's life is only sketchily known—neither the date nor the place of his birth has been established with accuracy.

Jehan Bodel had strong links with the city of Arras and its surroundings. He introduces himself as a minstrel in his *Congés*: he was a member of the Arras minstrel and burgher brotherhood and contributed to the rapid expansion of this society. Stanza 40 of the *Congés* suggests that he was a familiar of the Arras *échevinage*, or town council, to which he was presumably attached. Elated by Foulque de Neuilly's preaching, he was about to follow Baudouin of Flanders, the future conqueror of Constantinople, to the Holy Land, when he began to suffer from the first signs of leprosy. In 1202, he withdrew to a leprosarium in the Arras region, most likely at Grant Val near Beaurains, where he died, according to the death-roll of the brotherhood, between February 2 and June 16, 1210.

Jehan's work has only gradually unveiled its secrets. Long underestimated, it now appears as one of the richest, most original *œuvres* in medieval literature. Because he tackled various genres simultaneously, the chronology of his works is difficult to establish. He is one of the earliest writers of *pastourelles* in *langue d'oïl*; five have been ascribed to him. Such narrative lyrics had already been composed by troubadours, but the Arragese minstrel left his mark upon the genre. Within a conventional framework, he proved original in his skilled composition in a wide range of prosodic structures and in the impression of truthfulness he gives due to subtle characterization and concrete details taken from peasant life.

Slightly different in inspiration were his one fable and eight fabliaux, those merry tales that give full scope to the imagination of an artist aiming at entertaining a noble audience at the expense of the middle class, peasants, women, and churchmen. If not as incisive as Gautier le Leu's, Jehan's fabliaux evince acute observation and a rich experience of the life of Picard peasants and merchants. The genre, free enough to encompass risqué tales and cautionary fables, appealed to this storyteller keen on Gallic mirth: *Jehan Bodiax, un rimoieres de flabiax*, as he called himself.

His versatility led him to widen the scope of his writings. A connoisseur of chansons de geste, he soon realized that the Saxon wars, a landmark in Charlemagne's reign, were a fit subject for a vast epic, and by 1180 he undertook the composition of the *Chanson des Saisnes*, which his disease prevented him from completing. Four drafts of this work are extant, the shortest one known as *A* (4,337 lines) and the longest as *T* (8,019 lines). Analysis shows that later writers tried to bring the unfinished poem to completion after the 12th century. The first 3,307 lines of *A* provide us with a text as close as possible to what Jehan's original work may have been. Here, we can recognize the innovator at once by his art and literary theories as well as his idea of history. In keeping with the Roland tradition of the chanson de geste, he foregrounds Charlemagne but also humanizes the God-chosen emperor, whose character underwent further transformation with the continuators. Nor is Jehan's inspiration purely epic: with the amours of Baudouin, the young Frenchman, romance is woven into the martial narrative, while the comedy peculiar to fabliaux creeps into the episode of Saint-Herbert du Rhin. The poem synthesizes all the components of the author's craftsmanship: a scholarly minstrel, fascinated by history and committed to his times, both an observer of reality and a visionary, but first and foremost a poet capable of breathing life into whatever he portrayed.

Jehan dealt once more with an epic subject in the *Jeu de saint Nicolas*, a semiliturgical drama produced during the *grand siège*, or convention, of the Arras brotherhood, between 1194 and 1202. As in the *Chanson des Saisnes*, the background is the war of Christians and heathens. After an initial victory by the king of Africa's Saracens, the only survivor of the Christian host eventually ensures the triumph of his party, thanks to the protection of the saint; the king and his men convert to Christianity. The *Jeu* is a chanson de geste in miniature. Yet once more, the narrow frame of the genre, the dramatized miracle play, bursts under the poet's creative power. "Throughout the play," Albert Henry writes, "sacred and profane, sublime and comic, marvelous … and realistic elements are to be found side by side." In this powerful and original work, a masterpiece of medieval dramatic literature, is reflected the multifarious personality of an author who showed as much sincerity in praising Auxerre wine as in extolling the crusade.

Disease turned Jehan into one of our great lyric poets. When obliged to withdraw from the society of his contemporaries, he wrote a long supplication to his friends and benefactors in his farewell poems (*Congés*), composed in 1202. Taking up the stanzaic form of Hélinant de Froid-mont's *Vers de la Mort*, he bade a pathetic farewell to the world in forty-five octosyllabic stanzas. The regret of bygone joys, rebellion against and resignation to his misfortune, faith in God, gratitude to those who harbored him "half sound and half rotten"—all the themes of a new genre are to be found here. A work of harrowing sincerity, the *Congés* stand, in the early 13th century, as the first example of "ordeal lyricism" to be found in so many poets from Rutebeuf to Verlaine.

A teller of spicy stories, the author of a chanson de geste, a skillful dramatist, a lyric poet, and a critic (in the prologue to the *Chanson des Saisnes*, he puts forward a classification of the three principal poetic genres), Jehan Bodel tackled most contemporary forms and achieved creativity in each.

Further Reading

Bartsch, Karl, ed. *Altfranzösische Romanzen und Pastourellen*. Leipzig: Vogel, 1870, pp. 287–91. [Based on MS *F* (B.N. fr. 12645).]

Berger, Roger, ed. *La nécrologie de la confrérie des jongleurs et des bourgeois d'Arras (1194–1361): texte et tables.* Arras: Imprimerie Centrale de l'Artois, 1963.

Bodel, Jehan. *La chanson des Saisnes,* ed. Annette Brasseur. 2 vols. Geneva: Droz, 1989.

——. *La chanson des Saxons,* trans. Annette Brasseur. Paris: Champion, 1992.

——. *Le jeu de saint Nicolas de Jehan Bodel,* ed. Albert Henry. Brussels: Palais des Académies, 1980. [Based on MS *V* (B.N. fr. 25566).]

——. *Les fabliaux de Jean Bodel,* ed. Pierre Nardin. Paris: Nizet, 1965. [Based on MS *A* (B.N. fr. 837).]

——. *Les congés d'Arras (Jean Bodel, Baude Fastoul, Adam de la Halle),* ed. Pierre Ruelle. Paris: Presses Universitaires de France, 1965, pp. 83–104. [Based on MS. *A* (Arsenal 3142).]

Brasseur, Annette. *Étude linguistique et littéraire de la "Chanson des Saisnes" de Jehan Bodel.* Geneva: Droz, 1990.

——. "Index des rimes de Jehan Bodel." *Olifant* 15 (1990): 211–336.

Foulon, Charles. *L'œuvre de Jehan Bodel.* Paris: Presses Universitaires de France, 1958.

ANNETTE BRASSEUR

JIMÉNEZ DE RADA, RODRIGO (ca. 1170–1247)

Jiménez was born about 1170 in Puente la Reina in Navarre, to a family of the minor nobility. His father was Jimeno Pérez de Rada, and his mother, Eva de Finojosa. His uncle, Martín, was abbot of the monastery of Santa María ais de la Huerta. Family connections probably led to a stay at the royal court of Navarre before his departure to secure a higher education at the Universities of Bologna and of Paris. The dates of his stay at those institutions are unknown, although it appears that he was in Paris in 1201. He had returned to Navarre and the court of Sancho VII well before 1207. In that year he participated in the negotiation of a peace between Sancho and Alfonso VIII of Castile. His ambition and talent must have recommended Rodrigo instantly to the latter, to whom he became a major adviser and confidant for the rest of his reign.

Their relationship had become so strong by 1208 that Jiménez, not yet an ordained a priest, was nominated by Alfonso to the see of Osma, although he was never consecrated to it. Instead, further royal favor propelled him in that same year into the primatial see of Toledo. In that capacity he toured western Europe in 1211, soliciting aid for a crusade against Muslim Andalusia. In July 1212 he was present in the army of Alfonso VIII when the great victory over Muslim forces from North Africa was won at Las Navas de Tolosa.

During the next few years the debility of the king and realm prevented any immediate exploitation of that victory, but Jiménez was active in consolidating the resultant territorial gains of the kingdom and of his see in La Mancha. He was a major political figure in the brief reign of Enrique I (1214–1217) and again during the minority of Fernando III. When the latter reached his majority, Jiménez became a royal confidant and one of the chief royal advisers as Fernando ruled Castile (1217–1252) and then León (1230–1252) after the reunion of the two realms, In those capacities he assisted the king in the campaigns that saw the definitive conquest of eastern and central Andalusia—Baeza (1225), Úbeda (1233), and Córdoba (1236)—although he did not live to see the conquest of Seville (1248).

Jiménez's tenure as archbishop also saw the territorial and juridical consolidation of the see of Toledo, whose aggrandizement was one of the great passions of his life. The other peninsular archiepiscopates—Braga, Santiago de Compostela, and Tarragona—were forced to recognize the primacy of Toledo. Bishoprics for the newly conquered cities of Baeza and Córdoba in Andalusia were made suffragans of Toledo. However, claims to Zamora and Plasencia, where sees had been created during the earlier re-conquest period, were lost to Santiago de Compostela. Also, despite much acrimony, newly conquered Valencia was assigned by Rome to Tarragona rather than Toledo, and the ancient see of Oviedo in the north continued to be exempt from all metropolitan jurisdiction.

Given the conditions of the age, none of this could be carried through without the cooperation of the papacy, and Jiménez was well known at Rome. He had gone there first in 1211 to secure backing for the campaign of Alfonso VIII against the Almohads in 1212. He returned there to attend the Fourth Lateran Council in 1215. And in 1236 and 1241 he visited the pope. In 1218 he was named papal legate in the peninsula, and from 1224 was entrusted by the papacy with a contemplated creation of a diocese for North Africa in Morocco. Nevertheless, Jiménez had his problems with Rome. Often they flowed from the collection and utilization of ecclesiastical revenues for the reconquest of the south. Jiménez had helped to persuade Rome of their necessity, and was involved in their application to the benefit of the crown. Inevitably he was caught between the necessities of the crown, the reluctance of the Spanish clergy, and the suspicions of Rome.

Some of the moneys from this source certainly contributed, directly or indirectly, to the glorification of the church at Toledo and of its archbishop. Jiménez had hardly been consecrated when he began the construction of a new archiepiscopal palace in Alcalá de Henares (ca. 1209). The present Gothic cathedral at Toledo was begun under his aegis (ca. 1221) to replace the mosque that had served as a cathedral since 1085.

Without question Jiménez was the dominant figure in the Iberian Church during the first half of the thirteenth century, and a major political and court figure as well. Even so, he found time to produce six historical works, and so became the major historian of that period. The most important of these is his *De rebus Hispaniae*, in which he carried on the tradition of the Latin chronicle from Genesis down to the recent conquest of Córdoba. In large measure he continued the work of his older contemporary, Lucas of Túy, and supplied the materials that would underpin the new vernacular history of the *Primera crónica general*, begun in the second half of the century. His *Historia Arabum*, on the other hand, had no known precursor in Christian Iberia, and few in western Europe. Beginning with the biography of Muḥammad, the work deals primarily with the Muslim conquest of Iberia down through the arrival in the peninsula of the North African Murābit (Almoravids). It demonstrates his acquaintance with both the Arabic language and some of the Muslim historians, as well as the breadth of his interests. A *Historia Romanorum* displays his classical interests, and a *Historia Ostrogothorum* and a *Historia Hunnorum, Vandalorum, Suevorum, Alanorum, et Silingorum* demonstrate his debt to the school of Iberian historians of Visigothic times, especially Isidore of Seville.

During the spring of 1247 Jiménez traveled to France to visit Pope Innocent IV at Lyons. On his return journey to Iberia he drowned in the Rhone on 10 June. His body was embalmed and returned to the monastery of Santa María de la Huerta, where it was entombed. His tomb was opened for examination as recently as 1907.

See also **Fernando III, King of Castile**

Further Reading

Ballesteros Gaibros, M. *Don Rodrigo Jiménez de Rada.* Madrid, 1943. (A highly laudatory and semipopular introduction.)

Gorosterratzu, J. *Don Rodrigo Jimémez de Rada: Gran estadista, escritor y prelado.* Pamplona, 1925. (The only modern biography; old-fashioned, but thorough.)

Jimémez de Rada, Rodrigo. *Rodericus Ximenius de Rada. Opera.* Ed. María

Desamparades Cabanes Pecourt. Valencia, 1968. (Reprint of the 1793 complete edition of his work.)

——. *Historia Arabum*. Ed. J. Lozano Sánchez. Anales de la Universidad Hispalense, serie Filosofía y Letras. Vol. 21. Seville, 1974.

——. *Historia de rebus Hispaniae sive Historia gothica*. Ed. J. Hernández Valverde. Corpus Christianorum, Continuatio Medievalia, Vol. 72. Tumhout, 1987.

BERNARD F. REILLY

JOACHIM OF FIORE (c. 1135–30 March 1202) Joachim of Fiore (Flora, Floris) was a biblical exegete and the founder of the order of San Giovanni in Fiore, commonly known as the Florensians. Joachim's attempts to explain the patterns of Christian history gained him a reputation as a prophet in the thirteenth century, as well as a following among the Spiritual faction of the Franciscan order. His reputation as a prophet made his thought very influential in the later Middle Ages, but some people considered him a heretic because of his Trinitarian doctrine and his adoption by the Spirituals.

Joachim was born in Celico, near Cosenza in Calabria. As a young man, he trained to be a notary like his father, and for some years he served in this capacity at the Corte del Giustiziere in Calabria and later at the court of King William II of Sicily in Salerno. Around 1167, a serious illness led Joachim to make a pilgrimage to the Holy Land, where he decided to become a monk. On his return to Calabria, Joachim retired first to the Cistercian monastery of Sambucina and then to the monastery of Corazzo, near Catanzaro. There he professed and was ordained in 1168. Sometime before 1177, he was elected abbot. Joachim found administration arduous; and when negotiations to have Corazzo officially accepted by the Cistercian order led to a two-year residence at the Cistercian monastery of Casamari (1182–1184), he took advantage of the respite to begin two major works of biblical exegesis. These were *Liber de concordia Novi ac Veteris Testamenti* (*Book on the Concordance between the Old and the New Testaments*) and *Expositio in Apocalypsim* (*Exposition of the Apocalypse*). Now convinced that exegesis was his real calling, Joachim turned to the papacy to obtain a release from administration. When Pope Lucius III took up residence in nearby Veroli during 1184, Joachim obtained Lucius's permission to devote himself to writing for a year and a half. He received a renewal of this permission from Pope Urban III in 1186, and another from Pope Clement III in 1188. Clement also seems to have approved Joachim's resignation as abbot of Corazzo, which was now fully incorporated into the Cistercian order.

In the mid-1180s, Joachim became dissatisfied with the Cistercian life. He moved to a hermitage at Petralata, and then to San Giovanni in Fiore, in the Sila mountains. Meanwhile, his reputation as a prophet was growing. In 1191, he was summoned to an interview with Richard I Coeur de Lion (Lion-Heart) at Messina; later that year he was summoned to another, with Emperor Henry VI near Naples. The Cistercian leadership did not approve of Joachim's activities, however. In 1192, the order's chapter general declared that if Joachim and his companion Ranier of Ponza did not return to Corazzo by the feast of John the Baptist in 1193, they would be considered fugitives. Joachim ignored the deadline and instead founded his own order at Fiore. Again he turned to the papacy to legitimize his actions. The rule of Joachim's new order, based on that of the Cistercians but more austere, was approved by Pope Celestine III in 1196. Joachim also received a charter for his monastery and an annual stipend from Emperor Henry VI. The new order spread rapidly, establishing thirty-eight houses in Calabria and twenty-two elsewhere within the first few decades of its existence. But its growth stopped in the mid-thirteenth century, apparently because of competition from the Mendicant orders. It was united with the Cistercian order in 1570.

Joachim died at the Florensian monastery of San Martino di Giove near Canale. In 1240, his body was translated to San Giovanni, where it became the center of a local cult.

Joachim's fame rests on his novel method of scriptural exegesis. He sought understanding of what he called *concordia*—harmony between the Old Testament and the New Testament, manifested in parallel events. Joachim described this as "a similarity of equal proportion between the Old and the New Testaments, equal, I say, as to number, not as to dignity." The idea of *concordia* had no real precedent in earlier Christian exegesis. Typology had been used to argue that certain Old Testament events and figures foreshadowed Christ and that Christ was therefore the fulfillment of Old Testament prophecies, but Joachim's *concordia* presumed a steady parallel between Old Testament and Christian history. Moreover, Joachim treated Christ as one of many parallel figures and events in scriptural *concordia*, whereas previous exegetes had seen Christ as the only figure foreshadowed in the Old Testament. It has been suggested that Joachim's *concordia* derived from a desire, common in the twelfth century, to find meaning and pattern in human history. In this sense, Joachim's exegesis was very much in the spirit of his time.

Joachim believed that three visions had given him the spiritual insight to perceive scriptural *concordia*. His study of *concordia* revealed, in turn, the patterns of history. These were overlapping numerical sequences of events, arranged mainly in twos, threes, and sevens. The two most important were the synchronous *diffinitio alpha* and *diffinitio omega*. *Diffinitio alpha* divided history into three *status* or states, corresponding to the persons of the Trinity and symbolizing the spiritual progress of humanity. *Diffinitio omega* was arranged in two stages corresponding to the Old Testament on the

one hand, and the New Testament, the Christian era, and a final period of special spiritual understanding on the other. This final period would be the completion of the Christian era. The first *status* of *diffinitio alpha* was marked by an order of married people and the second by an order of clerics; the third would be characterized by an order of monks. This third *status* would be a time of joyous contemplation and understanding of the scriptures, in which the church would become truly spiritual. Joachim thought that the second *status* was gradually giving way to the third in his own rime. On the basis of the pattern of twos that he saw throughout the Old and New Testaments, he predicted that the church would be led into the new *status* by two new orders of spiritual men: one an order of hermits, the other of preachers. These orders would not end the Roman church but would, rather, lead its transition to a higher quality of spiritual life. There would be a period of peace before the last great persecution preceding the last judgment.

Joachim subdivided the stages of historical *diffinitiones* into lesser overlapping patterns, also numerically based. For example, the first *status* featured twelve patriarchs who founded twelve tribes, the second had twelve apostles who founded twelve churches, and the third had twelve great religious who founded twelve monasteries. Although each set of twelve dominated its own *status*, it also had roots in the previous *status*, thus producing the overlap. By far the most important of these lesser sequences was a pattern of sevens arranging the Old and New Testament stages of history. There was some precedent for this among previous exegetes, who had often divided history into seven periods. But whereas traditional commentators such as Augustine envisioned the seventh period as a time of peace beyond the end of history, Joachim placed his seventh age before the last judgment. He considered this seventh age to be concomitant with the third *status*. Joachim was also original in imposing a pattern of concordant double sevens subdividing the seven ages: one a sequence of seven seals that appeared during the second and third ages, the other a sequence of seven openings of the seals that occurred in the sixth age. Joachim believed that he was living at the end of the sixth age and near the end of the fifth seal-opening, so he speculated a good deal on the identity of contemporaries who might figure in the transition to the next age. This established an important precedent for his followers.

Joachim's Trinitarian concerns led him to question Peter Lombard's commonly accepted description of the unity of the Trinity, *vera et propria*, suggesting instead *collectiva et similitudi-naria*. This formulation was condemned as tritheistic at the Fourth Lateran Council in 1215. The council's failure to comment on the rest of Joachim's doctrines created uncertainty about his orthodoxy, and this uncertainty was never really resolved. While many were drawn to Joachim's vision of a coming spiritual age, others remained suspicious of his doctrine. In the mid-thirteenth century and the early fourteenth, Joachim's reputation suffered further blows. His predictions regarding the two orders of spiritual men who would herald the new *status* attracted the interest of the newly founded Dominicans and Franciscans. Soon radical Franciscans had woven their own apocalyptic notions around Joachim's thought. Gerard of Borgo San Donnino's *Eternal Evangel* was condemned as heretical in 1255. The doctrines of the Spiritual Franciscans met a similar fate in the 1310s. Both were deeply rooted in Joachim's teachings, and their censure increased doubts about his orthodoxy.

Joachim's double reputation as a prophet and a heretic continued into modern times. Thomas Aquinas, Duns Scotus, and the sixteenth-century historian Cesare Baronius all considered him heterodox; Dante, Boccaccio, and the usually skeptical Bollandist Daniel Papebroch considered him a prophet. Early Protestant writers were similarly divided. During the Enlightenment, attacks on the notion of prophecy drastically diminished Joachim's influence, but in the nineteenth and twentieth centuries it could still be found in figures as diverse as Auguste Comte and Carl Jung.

See also **Dante Alighieri; Henry VI; Richard I**

Further Reading

Editions

Joachim of Fiore. *Liber de concordia Novi ac Veteris Testamenti*, ed. E. Randolph Daniel. Transactions of the American Philosophical Society, 73(8). Philadelphia, Pa.: American Philosophical Society, 1983.

———. *Enchiridion super Apocalypsim*, ed. Edward Kilian Burger. Studies and Tests, 78. Toronto: Pontifical Institute of Mediaeval Studies, 1986.

Studies

Bloomfield, Morton. "Recent Scholarship on Joachim of Flora and His Influence." In *Prophecy and Millenarianism: Essays in Honour of Marjorie Reeves*, ed. Ann Williams. Essex: Longman, 1980, pp. 23–52.

Daniel, E. Randolph. "The Double Procession of the Holy Spirit in Joachim of Fiore's Understanding of History." *Speculum*, 55, 1980, pp. 469–483.

Emmerson, Richard K., and Bernard McGinn, eds. *The Apocalypse in the Middle Ages*. Ithaca, N.Y.: Cornell University Press, 1992.

Lee, Harold, Marjorie Reeves, and Giulio Silano. *Western Mediterranean Prophecy: The School of Joachim of Fiore and the Fourteenth-Century Breviloquium*. Studies and Texts, 88. Toronto: Pontifical Institute of Mediaeval Studies, 1989.

McGinn, Bernard. *The Calabrian Abbot: Joachim of Fiore in the History of Western Thought*. New York: Macmillan, 1985.

Potestà, Gian Luca, ed. *Il profetismo gioachimita tra Quattrocento e Cinquecento: Atti del III Congresso Internazionale di Studi Gioachimiti, S. Giovanni in Fiore, 17–21 settembre 1989*. Genoa: Marietti, 1991.

Reeves, Marjorie. *The Influence of Prophecy in the Later Middle Ages: A Study in Joachimism.* Oxford: Clarendon, 1969.

——. *Joachim of Fiore and the Prophetic Future.* London: SPCK, 1976.

——. "The Originality and Influence of Joachim of Fiore." *Traditio*, 36, 1980, pp. 269–316. Reeves, Marjorie, and Beatrice Hirsch-Reich. *The Figurae of Joachim of Fiore.* Oxford-Warburg Studies. Oxford: Clarendon, 1972.

West, Delno C., ed. *Joachim of Fiore in Christian Thought: Essays on the Influence of the Calabrian Abbot,* 2 vols. New York: Burt Franklin, 1974.

West, Delno C., and Sandra Zimdars-Swartz. *Joachim of Fiore: A Study in Spiritual Perception and History.* Bloomington: Indiana University Press, 1983.

THOMAS TURLEY

JOANNA I OF NAPLES (1326–1382, r. 1343–1382)

Joanna (Joan, Joanne, Giovanna) was queen regnant of Naples. She was the elder daughter of Robert the Wise, king of Naples, and was married four times: to Andrew of Hungary (in 1340), Louis of Taranto (1347), James of Majorca (1362), and Otto of Brunswick (1375). She had no surviving issue.

In 1345, Andrew was assassinated. His death provoked an invasion by his brother, Louis the Great of Hungary, who accused Joanna of complicity in Andrew's murder and claimed the throne for himself (as the grandson of Charles Martel, firstborn son of Charles I of Anjou). Louis entered Naples in 1348. Few Italians opposed him, and some, including Cola di Rienzo, were actively supportive. (Cola, however, fell before the Hungarian triumph, his defeat having been partly engineered by Joanna's supporters.) Joanna, seeking allies, married one cousin, Louis of Taranto, secretly and without papal sanction (she and Louis were related closely enough to require a dispensation in order to marry); and appointed another cousin, Charles of Durazzo (d. 1348), guardian of her son, though Charles played an equivocal role in the invasion. As the Hungarians approached, Joanna and Louis fled to their overlord, Pope Clement VI, at Avignon. To recover his support after their marriage and the murder of Andrew and to obtain money with which to renew the fight against Hungary, Joanna sold Avignon to Clement for 80,000 florins, considerably less than its worth. Meanwhile, the black death broke out, and the Hungarians, much reduced in number, returned home, taking as hostage Joanna's son (who died in Hungary) but leaving Joanna and Louis of Taranto in possession of the Regno. The Hungarians returned later, but never successfully. By 1352, Louis of Taranto, with help from the papacy, was recognized in Naples and had also established his rights against his wife's claims to sovereignty. Organized by the grand seneschal, Niccolò Acciaiuoli, the Regno experienced a brief period of recovery before war was renewed. The war was undertaken again partly in an unsuccessful attempt to reunite Sicily (which had been under Aragonese rule since 1285) with the Regno, and pardy because of renewed rebellion by the Durazzo branch of the Angevins, who resented the dominance of Louis of Taranto.

Louis died in 1362. Joanna's third husband, James of Majorca, was given no authority in government. James—who had recently escaped from fourteen years' imprisonment in an iron cage by his uncle, Peter IV of Aragon—was half mad and periodically violent. He soon returned to Spain, and from 1362 to 1375 Joanna ruled alone. Despite minor rebellions initiated by her sister Maria, who was the widow of Charles of Durazzo, and by Maria's sons, the realm achieved a measure of peace. In 1368—1370, Urban V briefly returned to Italy from Avignon, with Joanna's protection.

In 1378, Urban VI, formerly archbishop of Bari and Joanna's subject, became pope and quickly indicated his intention to revive and support the Hungarian claim to Naples. Accordingly, when a rival pope,

Clement VII, was elected, Joanna took Clement's part; and her next husband, Otto of Brunswick, proved entirely willing to persecute Urban's followers. Urban reacted by excommunicating Joanna and conceding her throne to Louis of Hungary. Charles III of Durazzo (nephew of Maria and the late elder Charles) encouraged Louis, so, although Charles III was her nearest relative, Joanna excluded him from the succession. Instead, with Clement VII's approval, she bequeathed all her rights to Louis of Anjou, eldest brother of Charles V of France (in January 1380). In 1381, Urban, despairing of the Hungarians, crowned Charles III of Durazzo king of Naples. In the ensuing civil war, Charles was successful: in August Otto was taken prisoner and Joanna surrendered. She died in prison, probably stifled to death on Charles's orders, in July 1382, while her adopted heir, Louis of Anjou, was coming over the Alps to her rescue.

Joanna's lament "I regret only one thing, that the Almighty did not make me a man" has some justification. Urban VI's main complaint against her was apparently that he disliked queens regnant. She had some devotees, notably Giovanni Boccaccio, but she was more usually scorned as immoral and incompetent. Still, she did her best work when she ruled alone: although her reign was a disaster, the problems were not all of her making.

See also **Boccaccio, Giovanni; Charles V the Wise**

Further Reading

Editions

Caracciolo, Tristan. *Vita Joannae primae Neapolis regina*, ed. Giuseppe Paladino. Rerum Italicarum Scriptores, 22. Bologna: Zanichelli, 1933, pp. 1–18.

Dominicus de Gravina. *Cronicon de rebus in Apulia gestis, 1333–1350*, ed. Albano Sorbelli. Rerum Italicarum Scriptores, 12. Città di Castello: Tipi dell'Editore S. Lapi, 1903.

Villani, Mattreo. *Cronica*, 5 vols., ed. Ignazio Moutier. Florence: Magheri, 1926.

Studies

De Feo, Italo. *Giovanna d'Angiò, regina di Napoli*. Naples: F. Fiorentino, 1968.

Léonard, Émile G. *Histoire de Jeanne Ire, reine de Naples, comtesse de Provence (1343–1382)*, 3 vols. Paris: Picard, 1932–1936.

——. *Les Angevins de Naples*. Paris: Presses Universitaires de France, 1954.

Louis the Great, King of Hungary and Poland, ed. S. B. Vardy, Geza Grosschmid, and Leslie. S. Domonkos. New York: Columbia University Press, 1986.

CAROLA M. SMALL

JOÃO I, KING OF PORTUGAL (1357?–1433)

João, the illegitimate son of Pedro I and Teresa Lourenço, was born probably in Lisbon on 14 August 1357 and died there on 14 August 1433. In 1363, when he was still a child, he became the master of the Order of Avis.

In normal circumstances, he would never have acceded to the throne, but the situation created in the latter years of Fernando I's reign (1367–1383) opened a crisis of succession. By his marriage to Leonor Teles in 1372, Fernando had a daughter, Beatriz (1372–ca. 1409), who married Juan I of Castile in 1383. Under Fernando, Portugal had three wars with Castile, and this marriage was intended to settle the conflict between the two countries. The marriage contract laid down that Portugal would be ruled by the first heir born to Beatriz, and until the child reached fourteen, Queen Leonor would govern the country as regent. This marriage gave Juan I the possibility of one day sitting on the Portuguese throne. However, Queen Leonor, in collusion with her lover, João Fernandes Andeiro, kept an oligarchic rule that excluded the merchants from the privy council. These, fearing the regency by the queen, persuaded João to kill Andeiro in order to force an accommodation with her. But, following the death of Andeiro and the rising of the people against her, the queen appealed to Juan I, who invaded Portugal.

João immediately organized the defense of Lisbon, relying on the military support of Nuno' Alvares Pereira (Nun' Alvares), a knight who proved to be a supreme strategist. The peasants, artisans, and merchants rallied to Dom João's cause, and the younger sons of noble families with no land of their own joined his forces. While João held Lisbon against the Castilian army, Nun' Alvares fought in the south and eventually neared Almada, close to Lisbon, wreaking havoc upon the Castilians. On 3 September 1384, Juan I, fearing the plague that had smitten his camp, lifted the siege of the city, which had lasted four months, and withdrew to Castile. *Cortes* (parliament) were convened at Coimbra to solve the problem of succession. And while João besieged the castles loyal to Beatriz, Nun' Alvares harassed the Castilian loyalists.

João and Nun' Alvares arrived in Coimbra on 3 March 1385. At the *cartes*, the lawyer João Afonso das Regras argued João's case, showing that the other pretenders, the sons of Pedro I and Inês de Castro, were illegitimate in view of the irregular relationship between their parents. As for Juan I, his invasion of Portugal had disqualified him, because it was a breach of the treaty. Having disposed of the argument of rights by birth, João das Regras claimed that since João was the one who had taken up arms to defend the realm from the Castilian invader, he deserved to be king. By acclamation he became João I on 6 April 1385.

Yet the war with Castile was not over. Following Fernando's previous policy of getting military support from England, João I gained some assistance from the duke of Lancaster. An English contingent fought alongside the Portuguese in the battle of Aljubarrota (14 August 1385), which was a decisive victory for the Portuguese. Portugal's ties with England were strengthened by the Treaty of Windsor (9 May 1386), a military alliance between the two countries. This was followed by the marriage of João I to Philippa of Lancaster (1359–1415), daughter of John of Gaunt, duke of Lancaster, on 2 February 1387. From this marriage were born Duarte (1391), Pedro (1392), Henrique (1394, known as Prince Henry the Navigator), João (1400), and Fernando (1402). In 1415, four years after the peace treaty with Castile had been signed, João I, encouraged by his minister of the treasury, complied with the wishes of his sons and led an expedition to Ceuta in Morocco, taking the city. This initiated the period of Portuguese expansion in which all the princes were deeply involved. Between 1418 and 1427, Prince Henrique promoted the discovery of the islands of Madeira and the Azores.

João I was a popular king who listened to his subjects and tried to satisfy their demands. The dynastic crisis of 1383–1385 gave Portugal its independence and enabled the productive classes—traders, merchants, and artisans—to take a leading role in the development of the country. By relieving the people of Lisbon and Oporto from the payment of tithes and seigniorial rights, João I paved the way for a new age. He was a cultivated man and wrote a remarkable treatise on hunting (*Livro da montaria*) that reflects his views on court life and a pre-Renaissance awareness of the value of the human body.

Further Reading

Bernardino, T. *A revolução portuguesa de 1383–1385*. Lisbon, 1984.
Eannes de Zurara, G. *Crónica da tomada de Ceuta por el rei dom João I*. Lisbon, 1915.
Lopes, F. *Crónica de dom Pedro*. Rome, 1966.
——. *Crónica del rei dom Johan I*. 2 vols. Lisbon, 1968–73.
——. *Crónica de dom Fernando*. Lisbon, 1975.
Peres, D. *Dom João I*. Oporto, 1983.
Suárez Fernández, L. *Historia del reinado de Juan I de Castilla*. 2 vols. Madrid, 1977.

LUIS REBELO

JOHANN VON WÜRZBURG (fl. ca. 1300)

As in most cases of medieval German literature, hardly anything is known about the author, except for some self-references in his courtly romance, *Wilhelm von Österreich*. He mentions that he was born in Würzburg and worked as a scribe, perhaps for the counts of Hohenberg and Haigerloch, especially Count Albrecht von Haigerloch (d. 1298). He also expresses his thanks to a citizen of Esslingen, Dieprecht, for helping him with his work. *Wilhelm von Österreich* was completed in May of 1314 and was dedicated to the Dukes Leopold and Frederick of Austria. It appears to have been rather popular, since it has come down to us in a large number of manuscripts (in Gießen, Gotha, The Hague, Heidelberg, etc.). In total, there are ten complete manuscripts and ten fragments extant.

Wilhelm von Österreich is a biographical romance combining chivalrous with amorous adventutes providing a mythical-historical background for the ruling House of Hapsburg. Duke Leopold of Austria and the heathen king Agrant of Zyzia make a pilgrimage to the holy site of John of Ephesus to pray for an heir. They meet by chance and make their sacrifices together. Leopold's wife delivers a son, Wilhelm, and Agrant's wife has a daughter, Aglye. The goddess Venus awakens love in both children through dreams and instigates Wilhelm to leave home on a search for Aglye. After exotic travels he meets Aglye, and the children fall in love. Her father, Agrant, separates them, however, because he wants to marry his daughter to a heathen prince. The lovers exchange an extensive correspondence that documents the high level of literacy that members of the higher aristocracy could acquire in the later Middle Ages. Aglye is twice promised as wife to heathen princes, but Wilhelm kills them both in battles and jousts. Only after he has liberated Queen Crispin of Belgalgan's kingdom of monsters are the lovers able to meet again. Soon afterwards a massive battle involves the heathen and Christian forces, which concludes with the Christians' victory

and the heathens' baptism. Finally, King Agrant agrees with the marriage of Aglye and Wilhelm, to whom a son is born called Friedrich. Wilhelm dies thereafter when he is ambushed by an envious brother-in-law. Aglye's heart breaks when she hears the news and dies as well.

Wilhelm experiences a large number of allegorical adventures throughout his quest for his beloved. These, and other aspects, are often commented on by the narrator, who fully enjoyed the use of the so-called *geblümter Stil* (flowery style). Johann von Würzburg refers to Gottfried von Straßburg, Wolfram von Eschenbach, and Rudolf von Ems as his literary models. He also knows Albrecht's *Jüngeren Titurel* and other thirteenth century romances.

Wilhelm von Österreich displays a surprising openness toward the heathen culture, although the paradigm of Christianity as the only true religion is not abandoned in favor of global tolerance. Johann von Würzburg enjoyed considerable success with his work, which glorifies the House of Austria and combines the exotic world of the Orient with the world of Arthurian romance. The text was copied far into the fifteenth century and discussed by other writers such as Püterich of Reichertshausen and Ulrich Fuetrer. Anton Sorg printed a prose version in 1481 and 1491 in Augsburg, which was also reprinted, probably in Wittenberg in 1530–1540. Wilhelm and Aglye, the main characters in the romance, are portrayed in the fifteenth-century frescoes on Castle Runkelstein as ideal lovers, next to Tristan and Isolde, and Wilhelm of Orleans and Amelie.

See also **Gottfried von Straßburg;**
Wolfram von Eschenbach

Further Reading

Brackert, Helmut: "*Da stuont daz minne wol gezam,*" *Zeitschrift fur deutsche Philologie, Sonderheft,* 93 (1974): 1–18.

Juergens, Albrecht: *'Wilhelm von Österreich'. Johanns von Würzburg 'Historia Poetica von 1314 und Aufgabenstellung einer narrativen Fürstenlehre.* Frankfurt am Main: Lang, 1990.

Johanns von Würzburg *"Wilhelm von Österreich.* "*Aus der Gothaer Hs.,* ed. Ernst Regel. Berlin: Weidmann, 1906; rpt. Zurich: Weidmann, 1970.

Mayser, Eugen. *Studien zur Dichtung Johanns von Würzburg.* Berlin: Ebering, 1931.

Ridder, Klaus. *Mittelhochdeutsche Minne- und Aventiure-romane: Fiktion, Geschichte und literarische Tradition im späthöfischen Roman: Reinfried von Braunschweig, Wilhelm von Österreich, Friedrich von Schwaben.* Berlin: de Gruyter, 1998.

Straub, Veronika: *Entstehung und Entwicklung des frühneuhochdeut schen Prosaromans. Studien zur Prosaauflösung 'Wilhelm von Österreich'.* Amsterdam: Rodopi, 1974.

Wentzlaff-Eggebert, Friedrich-Wilhelm: *Kreuzzugsdichtung des Mittelalters.* Berlin: Walter de Gruyter, I960, pp. 290–293.

ALBRECHT CLASSEN

JOHANNES VON TEPL (ca. 1350–early 15th c.)

Born in German and Czech-speaking Bohemia, Tepl (also known as Johannes von Saaz or Johannes Henslini de Sitbor) has been identified as the author of the *Ackermann aus Böhmen* (The Bohemian Plowman) by means of the acrostic IOHANNES, and by the signature de Tepla ("of Tepl") in a letter accompanying the work sent to friend Peter Rothirsch of Prague. Appointments as rector of the Latin school and notary of the cities of Saaz and later Prague-Neustadt show Tepl to have been literate in both Czech and Latin as well as German. Besides the *Ackermann aus Böhmen*, only a few German and Latin verses, plus parts of a Latin votive office (1404), have been identified as Tepl's work. It is unclear whether the *Czech Tkadlecek* (ca. 1407), a text similar to the *Ackermann* in which a weaver laments the loss of his unfaithful sweetheart, might also have been composed by him. *The Ackermann* is preserved whole or in part in sixteen manuscript editions, mostly of upper German provenance, as well as in seventeen early printed editions. The Pfister edition of 1460 is one of the two earliest printed books in German.

The work, an audacious debate with death, is framed as a legal proceeding in which a grief-stricken widower, a "plowman of the pen" (i.e., a scribe) brings a complaint against the justice and justification of death in God's world order. The plowman bewails the loss of his virtuous young wife, Margaretha, and rails at Death's cruelty and unfairness. In sixteen rounds of spirited debate, the plowman condemns Death while defending life, love, and man, God's finest creation. Death, in his turn, denies any dignity of man and any right to life, vaunting, instead, his own power and arbitrariness. Only in chapter 33 is the argument silenced when God is called on to deliver a verdict in the case. Because the plaintiff has fought well, God awards him honor, but gives the victory to Death by affirming the status quo. The work ends with an impassioned prayer for the soul of Margaretha.

The emotional verisimilitude of the argumentation and the correspondence of biographical data in the text to certain facts of Tepl's life have raised the question whether the work might not have been precipitated by an actual bereavement of the author, perhaps his first wife, the mother of his two oldest children. Records show Tepl to have been survived by a widow, Clara (possibly a second wife), and five children. The autobiographical thesis seems to be at odds, however, with the tone of the author's letter to Rothirsch, which emphasizes the stylistic devices and rhetorical strategies deployed in the work.

More significant than the unresolved autobiographical issue is the controversy over whether the arguments and style place the work further within the realm of late medieval or of early humanist thought. Although thematically and formally the

Ackermann remains largely indebted to earlier medieval traditions, stylistically its language echos that of Johann von Neumarkt's chancellery German, which shows the strong influence of the Latin rhetorical forms of Italian humanists.

Further Reading

Hahn, Gerhard. *Der Ackermann aus Böhmen des Johannes von Tepl.* Erträge der Forschung 215. Darmstadt: Wissenschaftliche Buchgesellschaft, 1984.

Hruby, Antonín. *Der Ackermann und seine Vorlage.* Munich: Beck, 1971.

Hübner, Arthur. "Deutsches Mittelalter und italienische Renaissance im *Ackermann aus Böhmen.*" *Zeitschrift für Deutschkunde* 51 (1937): 225–239.

Jafre, Samuel. "Des Witwers Verlangen nach Rat: Ironie und Struktureinheit im *Ackermann aus Böhmen.*" *Daphnis* 7 (1978): 1–53.

Johannes von Saaz. *Der Ackermann aus Böhmen*, ed. Günther Jungbluth. 2 vols. Heidelberg: Winter, 1969–1983.

Johannes von Tepl. *Death and the Plowman; or, The Bohemian Plowman*, trans. Ernst N. Kirrmann from the Modern German version of Alois Bernt. Chapel Hill: University of North Carolina Press, 1958.

Schwarz, Ernst, ed. *Der Ackermann aus Böhmen des Johannes von Tepl und seine Zeit.* Wege der Forschung 143. Darmstadt: Wissenschaftliche Buchgesellschaft, 1968.

ANNE WINSTON-ALLEN

JOHN (1167–1216; r. 1199–1216) Born on December 24, 1167, he was the youngest of the four sons of Henry II and Eleanor of Aquitaine to reach manhood. His father intended him to be the ruler of an autonomous kingdom of Ireland (and from 1185 he bore the title Lord of Ireland), but with the deaths of his elder brothers he aspired to wider ambitions. After the death of the childless Richard (1199) he became king of England, duke of Normandy, duke of Aquitaine, and count of Anjou, and he prevailed against the claims of his nephew Arthur of Brittany, son of his brother Geoffrey.

It was a difficult inheritance. The financial burdens of Richard's reign had been extraordinarily heavy, for his crusade and ransom, and for the defense of the continental dominions against persistent attacks and subversion by Philip II (Philip Augustus) of France. The revenues of England, vital for survival, were devalued by inflation. The balance of advantage in resources and influence had tipped decisively in favor of the French crown. Normandy was war-weary, weakened, and demoralized; when Philip renewed his attack in 1204, the will to resist suddenly collapsed and John retired to England without putting up a fight.

John never reconciled himself to the loss of Normandy. His efforts to accumulate a war chest were remarkably successful, but achieved by a relentless and ruthless exploitation of royal rights over subjects that exposed the arbitrary nature of many of his royal powers and called their legitimacy into question. His barons, seeking to rebuild family fortunes after the loss of their Norman estates, had to bid expensively for royal favors granted, or withheld, capriciously.

Disaffection was for a time deflected by John's resistance to Pope Innocent III, who set aside a royal nominee for the archbishopric of Canterbury and instead appointed Stephen Langton, whom the king rejected. John's stand was generally supported by the laity, who patiently endured an interdict for six years. John confidently disregarded a sentence of excommunication while his coffers were augmented by the appropriated revenues of the clergy. That the English clergy should be so completely at his mercy was, however, a chilling demonstration of royal power to override established rights, and there was a growing feeling among some of the barons that their own safety and their families' fortunes depended on getting rid of him.

Faced by incipient rebellions and an invasion fleet mustered by Philip of France, John could not ignore the ultimate papal weapon, a sentence of deposition. He accepted the pope's terms for lifting the sanctions and in addition offered his kingdoms of England and Ireland as fiefs of the papacy, in effect putting them under the protection of the Holy See.

John's carefully nurtured grand strategy for the defeat of the French king collapsed when his allies, the count of Flanders and his nephew Emperor Otto IV of Germany, were decisively defeated by Philip at the Battle of Bouvines, May 1214. Open rebellion erupted in England. At a moment when neither side could be sure of winning, an attempt at a negotiated peace produced Magna Carta (June 1215), by which the crown's claims to executive privilege were brought within the bounds of agreed law. As a peace formula it failed, and John had it annulled by the pope. He was winning the civil war when he died (October 1216). Loyalists reissued Magna Carta to rally support for his infant son, Henry III.

While curtailing the possibility of tyranny Magna Carta also recognized the advantages of efficient royal government, which John had done much to foster. He understood administration and did much in a short reign to refine and rationalize it. He created a precedent (in the Thirteenth of 1207) for a proper taxation system. He created the navy that thwarted Philip's projected invasion. He failed, however, at the crucial arts of government in the management of men and what was currently recognized as "good lordship."

John has been portrayed as a monster of depravity. This is a fanciful elaboration of a distorting half-truth. He was no more domineering than his father and brother, and hardly more morally reprehensible, but he lacked their redeeming qualities. He was crafty and vindictive and instead of charismatic leadership could offer only dogged determination. Failing to inspire loyalty, he tried to dominate by menace and—constantly fearing disloyalty—he fed his fears by a corrosive suspicion. He is a classic case of a ruler undone not merely by adverse circumstances but by defects of personality.

See also **Eleanor of Aquitaine; Henry II; Innocent III, Pope; Philip II Augustus**

Further Reading

Hollister, C. Warren. "King John and the Historians." *Journal of British Studies* 1 (1961): 1–29

Holt, J.C. *The Northerners: A Study in the Reign of King John.* London: Oxford University Press, 1961

Holt, J.C. *Magna Carta and Medieval Government.* London: Hambledon, 1985 [collected papers especially valuable are "King John," first published in 1963, and "The End of the Anglo-Norman Realm," from 1975]

Turner, Ralph V. *King John.* New York: Longman, 1994

Warren, W.L. *King John.* 2d ed. London: Eyre Methuen, 1978

Warren, W.L. "Painters King John Forty Years On." *Haskins Society Journal I* (1989): 1–9.
W.L. WARREN

JOHN II THE GOOD (1319–1364)

King of France, 1350–64. The elder son of Philip VI and Jeanne of Burgundy, John became heir to the throne when his father succeeded to it in 1328. In 1332, John married Bonne de Luxembourg, daughter of the king of Bohemia. Before she died of plague in 1349, Bonne bore him nine children, among whom were the future Charles V and Jeanne, who married Charles the Bad of Navarre.

In the early campaigns of the Hundred Years' War, John's first important command was at the abortive siege of Aiguillon in 1345. He was much attached to his mother and to the strong Burgundian faction in French politics, with which she was aligned. When Philip VI finally tried to mollify the dissident northwestern nobility in the 1340s and reduce the role of Burgundians, John remained linked to the latter in opposition to his father.

John's accession to the throne in 1350, soon followed by the summary execution of the constable Raoul de Brienne, revived the old tension between the Valois monarchy and the northwestern nobles. Leadership of the opposition passed to the Évreux branch of the royal family, headed by Charles of Navarre, who engineered the murder of the new constable, Charles of Spain, in 1354. After two provisional settlements with his dangerous son-in-law, John finally lost patience and arrested Charles in April 1356, executing several of his Norman allies and plunging northwestern France into civil war.

John also attracted criticism for his style of government, which gave great responsibility to the heads of administrative bodies, who tended to be men of modest social origins. Their continuity in office contrasted with that of the royal council, which frequently changed in composition as John had to appoint representatives of political factions rather than trusted men of his own choosing. Reformers on this council resented their lack of control over the administrative bodies. Bourgeois reformers, led by Parisians, harbored personal and political resentments against these royal officials. Noble reformers had an agenda based on class and geography as well as governmental philosophy, while clergy were found in both camps.

These opposition groups both played a role in the Estates General of 1355, but their failure to generate needed revenues provoked the king into policies that alienated both groups during 1356. In September, with an army consisting of his own noble supporters, John II met defeat and capture at the hands of an Anglo-Gascon army at Poitiers. For the next four years, he was a prisoner in England, trying to negotiate a treaty that would secure his release, while his son Charles struggled to preserve some authority for the monarchy in Paris.

As the bourgeois reformers showed increasing hostility to the nobles, and as the nobles became disillusioned with their erratic leader Charles the Bad, the crown managed to recruit important dissident nobles and rebuilt its power around a new coalition. This realignment occurred during the last six years of John's reign, but historians differ as to whether he or his son deserves credit for the royal recovery. Released for a large ransom under the terms of the Treaty of Brétigny in 1360, John had to contend with the violence of thousands of unemployed soldiers. After considering a crusade to lure them away, he secured from the Estates in December 1363 an important new tax, the *fouage*, to finance an army to restore order. Continuing unresolved problems with England were complicated when the king's son Louis, a hostage for his father's ransom, broke parole and fled. John returned to captivity in England and died there in the spring of 1364.

See also **Charles II the Bad; Charles V the Wise**

Further Reading

Bordonove, Georges. *Jean le Bon et son temps.* Paris: Ramsay, 1980.

Cazelles, Raymond. "Jean II le Bon: quel homme? quel roi?" *Revue historique* 509 (1974): 5–26.

———. *Société politique, noblesse et couronne sous Jean le Bon et Charles V.* Geneva: Droz, 1982.

Deviosse, Jean. *Jean le Bon.* Paris: Fayard, 1985.

Henneman, John Bell. *Royal Taxation in Fourteenth Century France: The Captivity and Ransom of John II, 1356–70.* Philadelphia: American Philosophical Society, 1976.

JOHN BELL HENNEMAN, JR.

JOHN OF SALISBURY (ca. 1115–1180) John was born in Old Sarum, England, and entered a clerical career as a young man, studying in the schools of Paris from 1136 until the mid-1140s. There, he heard lectures by Peter Abélard, Robert of Melun, William of

Conches, Thierry of Chartres, Gilbert of Poitiers, and other masters of the day. He then traveled to Rome, where he entered the service of the pope. In 1148, he attended the synod at Reims where Gilbert of Poitiers was tried for heresy, a trial that John recounts in his *Historia pontificalis*. In 1153–54, he returned to England, where he served as secretary to Theobald, archbishop of Canterbury, and to his successor, Thomas Becket. John was part of one of the most striking public conflicts of royal and ecclesiastical power in the 12th century, that between Becket and King Henry II Plantagenêt of England. Becket's exile to France took John of Salisbury there as well. John was present in Christ Church cathedral, Canterbury, when Becket was attacked, but he fled the scene before the actual murder. In 1176, John was consecrated bishop of Chartres and died there in 1180. He knew well the worlds of episcopal patronage, education in the schools of Paris, the papal and royal courts, and the web of personal and professional friendships woven by the exchange of letters. Each of these circles influenced his life and writings.

The *Metalogicon*, a spirited defense of the Trivium, with emphasis upon the discipline of logic, is a valuable resource for understanding the world of the 12th-century schools and lists the masters with whom John studied. His *Policraticus* combines political theory, a handbook for government, criticism of court life, and a program of education for courtiers. In the *Historia pontificalis*, John offers a history focused on the papal court from the Synod of Reims (1148) through the year 1152. Among his other writings are a *vita* of Anselm of Bec and a brief *vita* of Becket, probably meant to serve as preface to a collection of the murdered archbishop's letters. Some 325 of John's letters survive.

See also **Abélard, Peter; Becket, Thomas; Gilbert of Poitiers; Henry II**

Further Reading

John of Salisbury. *Memoirs of the Papal Court*, ed. and trans. Marjorie Chibnall. London: Nelson, 1956.

——. *The Metalogicon of John of Salisbury: A Twelfth-Century Defense of the Verbal and Logical Arts of the Trivium*, trans. D.D. McGarry. Berkeley: University of California Press, 1955.

——. *The Letters of John of Salisbury*, 1: *The Early Letters (1153–1161)*, ed. W.J. Millor and H.E. Butler, rev. Christopher N.L. Brooke. London: Nelson, 1955.

——. *The Letters of John of Salisbury*, 2: *The Later Letters (1163–1180)*, ed. W.J. Millor and Christopher N.L. Brooke. Oxford: Oxford University Press, 1979.

Smalley, Beryl. *The Beckett Conflict and the Schools: A Study of Intellectuals in Politics*. Oxford: Blackwell, 1973, pp. 87–108.

Webb, C.C.J. *John of Salisbury*. London: Methuen, 1932.

Wilkes, Michael, ed. *The World of John of Salisbury*. Oxford: Blackwell, 1984.

GROVER A. ZINN

JOHN OF SEVILLE (fl. 1133–1135) John of Seville was an astrologer and translator of scientific works from Arabic into Latin. His full name appears to have been Iohannes His-palensis et Lunensis (or Limiensis). Attempts to identify him with Avendauth, the collaborator of Dominigo Gundisalvo, John David of Toledo, and other Johns are not convincing. He is known only through his translations, which include Abū Ma'shar's *Greater Introduction to Astrology* (1133), Al-Farghānī's *Rudiments of Astronomy* (1135), 'Urnar ibn al-Farrukhān's *Universal Book* (on astrology), Al-Qabīsī's *Introduction to Astrology*, Thābit ibn Qurra's *On Talismans (De imaginibus)* and astrological works by Māshā'allāh and Sahl ibn Bishr. These were the most important texts on astrology in the Arabic world, and established Latin astrology on a firm scientific footing. To them, John added his own *Epitome of Astrology* or *Liber* *quadripartitus* (1135), which covered all the main aspects of astrology and, having four books, was clearly meant to be analogous to, and perhaps to replace, the best-known text on astrology from classical antiquity, Ptolemy's *Quadripartitum.*

John appears to have ventured also into the field of medicine, for he is credited with a translation of the medical portion of Pseudo-Aristotle's *Secret of Secrets, On the Regimen of Health,* and Qusta ibn Lāqā's *On the Difference between the Spirit and the Soul.* These medical texts are the only works that put their author into a historical context, since the first is dedicated to a queen of Spain with the initial T.—often identified with Tharasia, daughter of Alfonso VI of Castile and León, who married Henry of Burgundy, count of Portugal (1057–1114), and the second is dedicated to Raymond, archbishop of Toledo (1125–1152), and thereby is the earliest text to have some connection with the cathedral.

John's astrological translations are pedantically literal, suggesting that Arabic may have been his first language. The medical translations are more fluent, and the excerpt from the *Secret of Secrets* is preceded by a preface in which the translator justifies departing from the literal sense of the original. Both the astrological and the medical texts remained popular throughout the Middle Ages and several of the astrological texts, including the *Epitome,* were printed in the Renaissance.

Further Reading

Lemay, R. *Abū Mashar and Latin Aristotelianism in the Twelfth Century.* Beirut, 1962.
Thorndike, L. "John of Seville." *Speculum* 34 (1959): 20–38.

CHARLES BURNETT

JOHN, DUKE OF BERRY (1340–1416) The son of John II the Good of France and Bonne de Luxembourg, John was born in the castle of Vincennes on

Jean de Cambrai (fl. 1397–1438). John, Duke of Berry, life-size statue. © Erich Lessing/Art Resource, New York.

November 30, 1340. His father named him count of Poitou in 1356, but when this territory was ceded to England by the treaty of 1360 John became duke of Berry and Auvergne. During the years 1360–64, he was one of the hostages sent to England after the release of his father from captivity.

In 1369, John was charged with guarding the western frontier to keep the English contained within Poitou, and his brother Charles V reassigned him this county as an incentive to recover it from the English. His ineptitude at military strategy soon became clear. In 1374, Charles V's attitude toward John changed, perhaps because of a distaste for his private life. In October, when arranging for the succession, Charles V ordered that John not be one of his son's guardians if the dauphin, the future Charles VI, should succeed to the throne as a minor. Despite some rapprochement between the brothers in 1375 and 1376, John never regained Charles's full confidence. With the accession of Charles VI in 1380, however,

John was officially accorded a place in the government and began to act as mediator between his two surviving brothers, the dukes of Anjou and Burgundy.

In November 1380, John was named royal lieutenant-general in Languedoc, where his officers and his policies soon made him unpopular. He rarely visited the Midi personally, and his lack of direct involvement produced near-anarchy in the province. When the king resolved to go to the south in person in 1389, John resigned his lieutenancy. The details of John's political behavior, especially in the years following the assassination of his nephew Louis of Orléans in 1407, show him to have been unethical, unreliable, and selfish. Despite this evidence, contemporaries viewed him as gregarious, eloquent, and philanthropic. He did show both consistency and determination in his ecclesiastical policy, being the French prince most committed to ending the papal Schism.

After April 1404, as the king's sole surviving paternal uncle, John enjoyed a prestigious position and important role at court, serving as mediator between the Burgundian and Armagnac parties, particularly after the murder of the duke of Orléans. He was married twice: in 1360 to Jeanne d'Armagnac and, after her death, in 1389 to Jeanne de Boulogne. He died in Paris on June 15, 1416, leaving no male heirs.

One of the greatest patrons in the history of art, John was an inveterate collector—of books, dogs, castles, tapestries, jewels, and *objets d'art*, whether antique or contemporary. If he overtaxed his people, as has been claimed, it was to transform his immense wealth into works of art. Probably the best-known work commissioned by him is the unfinished *Très Riches Heures* (Chantilly, Musée Condé), illuminated by the limbourg brothers and Jean Colombe. The famous calendar illuminations in this manuscript picture some of the duke's seventeen castles: Lusignan, Dourdan, Hôtel de Nesle, Clain, Étampes,

Saumur, the Louvre, and Vincennes. Another favorite castle, Mehun-sur-Yèvre, dominates the Temptation of Christ scene. Other works illuminated by the brothers include the *Très Belles Heures de Notre Dame* (B.N. lat. 3093) and the *Belles Heures* (New York, The Cloisters). They also contributed a miniature of the duke setting off on a journey in the *Petites Heures* (B.N. lat. 18014) and some scenes in *grisaille* for a *Bible historiale* (B.N. fr. 166). Another famous book of hours associated with the duke is the *Grandes Heures* (B.N. lat. 919), commissioned in 1407 and completed in 1409. Unfortunately, its original sixteen large miniatures, possibly by Jacquemart de Hesdin, who had illuminated the *Heures de Bruxelles* (before 1402) for the duke, have been lost. The list of artists contributing small miniatures reads like a who's who of the day, including the Boucicaut and Bedford Masters, as well as the Pseudo-Jacquemart. Other artists in the duke's employ were his master architect Gui de Dammartin, André Beauneveu, and Jean de Cambrai, who sculpted the duke's tomb.

John's extensive library included thirty-eight chivalric romances, forty-one histories, as well as works by Aristotle, Nicole Oresme, and Marco Polo. His secular books were outnumbered by religious works, especially prayer books: fourteen Bibles, sixteen psalters, eighteen breviaries, six missals, and fifteen books of hours. Of the over 300 illuminated manuscripts in the duke's library, some one hundred are extant today. Most of the other objects in his collections are known to us only through the extensive registers he caused to be kept after 1401.

See also **Charles VI; John II the Good; Limbourg Brothers**

Further Reading

Guiffrey, J. *Inventaires de Jean, duc de Berry (1401–1416)*. 2 vols. Paris, 1894–96.

Lacour, René. *Le gouvernement de l'apanage de Jean, duc de Berry 1360–1416*. Paris: Picard, 1934.

Lehoux, Francoise. *Jean de France, duc de Berri: sa vie, son action politique*. 4 vols. Paris: Picard, 1966–68.

Longnon, Jean, and Raymond Cazelles. *The Très Riches Heures of Jean, Duke of Berry*. New York: Braziller, 1969.

Meiss, Millard. *French Painting the Time of Jean de Berry: The Late Fourteenth Century and the Patronage of the Duke*. 2nd ed. 2 vols. London: Phaidon, 1969.

——, and Elizabeth H. Beatson. *The Belles Heures of Jean, Duke of Berry*. New York: Braziller, 1974.

Thomas, Marcel. *The Grandes Heures of Jean, Duke of Berry*. New York: Braziller, 1971.

RICHARD C. FAMIGLIETTI
WILLIAM W. KIBLER

JOINVILLE, JEAN DE (1225–1317) Joinville's *Vie de saint Louis*, a French prose memoir by a powerful aristocrat, is one of our most valuable accounts of noble society in the 13th century. Joinville's father was seneschal of Champagne, an office he inherited. In 1248, he decided to take part in the Seventh Crusade and thus met St. Louis, becoming a close friend. The two endured captivity together, then Joinville served as royal steward at Acre (1250–54) before returning to France. Joinville began his memoirs of the king in 1272, just after Louis's death, but undertook the second part (composed 1298–1309) when Jeanne of Navarre, wife of Philip IV, requested it.

Joinville's narrative has many virtues. As an important noble, he advised the king during the crusade; as a warrior, he fought in it. Although a close friend, Joinville, unlike other biographers of Louis, respected but was not overawed by the king and sometimes disapproved of his actions, particularly when Louis's saintliness conflicted with what Joinville perceived to be his duties as king, aristocrat, and layman. Louis's decision to go on crusade in 1270 was one such occasion, but there were others. Joinville felt free at the time to speak his mind and records a number of salty interchanges between himself and his ruler. He was also candid about his own prejudices; he defended aristocratic privileges and was contemptuous of bourgeois upstarts. His observations are vivid, and his frankness makes the *Vie* delightful reading.

Joinville's work was overshadowed in his own day by Guillaume de Nangis's biography of Louis; of the three extant manuscripts, only one is medieval, a copy of the presentation manuscript of 1309.

See also **Louis IX**

Further Reading

Joinville, Jean de. *La vie de saint Louis*, ed. Noel L. Corbett. Sherbrooke: Naaman, 1977.

—— and Villehardouin. *Chronicles of the Crusades*, trans. Margaret R.B. Shaw. Harmondsworth: Penguin, 1963.

Billson, Marcus K. "Joinville's *Histoire de Saint-Louis*: Hagiography, History and Memoir." *American Benedictine Review* 31 (1980): 418–42.

Perret, Michèle. "'À la fin de sa vie ne fuz-je mie': Joinville's *Vie de Saint-Louis*." *Revue des sciences humaines* 183 (1981): 16–37.

LEAH SHOPKOW

JUAN MANUEL (1282–1348) Son of Alfonso X's younger brother, Manuel, and grandson of Fernando III; born in Escalona (Toledo) in 1282. From a very young age, he participated both in war (particularly in the advances on Murcia, which lasted from 1284 to 1339) and in politics, though not without differences with his council.

Along with his hectic political life during the reigns of Fernando IV (1295–1312) and Alfonso XI (1312–1350), which was largely motivated, as he himself says, by questions of *onra* [honor/reputation] and *facienda* [property/wealth], Juan Manuel displayed an encyclopedic knowledge that was indicative of his desire to emulate his uncle, Alfonso X, whom he admired from an exclusively cultural (and not political) perspective. He was also a devout man, influenced by the Dominican tradition, which he followed throughout the various didactic works of his career. After retiring from active political life, Juan Manuel died in 1348; he is buried in the monastery at Peñafiel, which he founded.

In the general prologue to his works, the author expresses the philological/critical anxiety that his texts might be poorly copied, declaring that the authentic, original books, against which any potentially confusing transcripts can be compared, are in the convent at Peñafiel. Although this is essentially nothing more than a repetition of what Nicolás de Lira had already said, this disclaimer serves as a mark of authenticity for Juan Manuel's work. With this notice, the author participates in the medieval concept of an ethics of language opposing the lie, and is thus able to forestall any willful error on his part. For those inevitable involuntary errors, he resorts to the *topos* of modesty—already in use since antiquity—attributing such lapses to his lack of intelligence. Juan Manuel manipulates the vernacular language in a fresh, renewed manner, and with a wider vocabulary and a more purified syntax than Alfonso X. He is partial to concision and clarity, qualities he praises in his uncle's writing, although he does experiment with a more hermetic, obtuse style. The discovery of a skillful use of dialogue is frequently attributed to Juan Manuel, who arguably anticipates certain subtleties of the Renaissance.

A list of Juan Manuel's works appears both in the *Prólogo general* and in the prologue to *El conde Lucanor,* although there are discrepancies between the two prologues with regard to the order and number of works listed. Without the lost Peñafiel codex, what remains of the author's writings is found in various fourteenth-century manuscripts, among them Manuscript 6376 in the Biblioteca Nacional in Madrid. This manuscript lacks the *Crónic abreviada,* which in turn was found by Sánchez Alonso (in MS. F. 81 [now 1356]), also in the Biblioteca Nacional. Both have served as the basis for the edition of Juan Manuel's *Obras completas.*

Of the preserved texts one must first cite the *Libro del cavallero et del escudero.* Written before 1330, the work is one of many encyclopedic treatises of the time. Similar to Ramón Llull's *Llibre de l'ordre de cavalleria,* to which Juan Manuel seems to allude, the plot consists of the encounter between a young squire on his way to the court, and a former knight—now a hermit—who answers the young man's numerous questions. The hermit upholds knighthood as the most honorable estate in this world and indoctrinates the squire through a brief discourse on chivalry; later, the former knight gives the young man, now a novice *caballero,* a treatise on theology, another on astrology, and several expositions on the animal, vegetable, and mineral kingdoms; finally he tells the young man about the sea and the land, ending with an exaltation of creation as "manifestación de la gloria de Dios" (manifestation of God's glory).

Libro de los estados, finished in 1330, consists of two books distributed in three parts: the first book's hundred chapters, which address different religions and the estates of the lay population; the first fifty chapters of the second book, concerning the different laws (among which only the Christian law is true) as well as the mysteries of Christ and the estates of the secular clergy; and the fifty-first chapter of the second book, dedicated to religious orders and their regulations, especially the orders of preaching friars and of lesser friars. The structure is that of a work within a work, all written using dialogue as a technique supported by the main characters: the pagan king Morobán, the *infante* Johas and his tutor/teacher Turín, and a Christian preacher named Julio. The basic framework is similar to that of *Barlaam y Josafat.* Turín, committed to avoid having to address the concept of mortality, ends his phase of the prince's education by explaining the meaning of death in front of a fortuitously discovered cadaver. Chapter 22 introduces the Castilian preacher Julio, "omne muy letrado et muy entendido" [a very educated and intelligent man] in matters of Christian doctrine. Julio claims to be tutor to Prince Juan, son of the *infante* Don Manuel, and from that moment on he will carry the burden of Prince Johas's education. The work teaches that, in order to be saved, he who did not keep the law of nature should follow Christian law, which fulfilled Old Testament designs. This law is contained in the Holy Scriptures and is preached by the church, whose accepted hierarchy, divided into "legos" [the lay population] and "eclesiásticos" [the clergy], is described in detail.

Crónic abreviada, written during the tutelage of Alfonso XI (around 1320), was thought lost until Sánchez Alonso found it in 1941. It is a summary of Alfonso X's *Estoria de España,* and though Juan Manuel claims to follow his uncle's work step by step, it is actually much more than just a faithful copy.

Libro de la caza, thought by some to be written late in the author's life, is a treatise on the art of falconry, addressing the care, training, and medication of falcons and hawks. Juan Manuel relates not only his knowledge of the hunt, but also his own personal experience, to which he alludes in the text.

Libro infinido, or *Castigos y consejos a su hijo don Fernando* (1337), is inscribed within the tradition of the education of princes, although it also contains a strong dose of personal and autobiographical content. It refers frequently to *Libro de los estados.*

Libro de las armas, or *Libro de las tres razones,* written after 1335, addresses three issues: the meaning of the coat of arms given to Juan Manuel's father; the reason a person may knight others without having been knighted himself; and the content of Juan Manuel's conversation with King Sancho at his deathbed (1295). The author explains the symbolism of the coat of arms (especially the angelic *ala* [wing]) that appeared in his grandfather's prophetic vision while his father, Don Manuel, was in the womb. He relates various anecdotes told both to his father and to himself, among them the legend of Doña Sancha de Aragón, similar to the legend of Saint Alexis. He concludes that both his uncle, Alfonso X, and his father had wanted him to knight others during their lifetime. Finally, the author describes Ring Sancho's deathbed speech, in which he tells Juan Manuel of the anguish caused by his parents' misfortune, and entrusts the young man to the king's wife María and their son Fernando. This work, which has been praised by Américo Castro as "la primera página, íntima y palpitante de una confesión escrita en castellano" [the first intimate, true life confession written in the Spanish language], has recently been analyzed from a literary perspective.

Tratado de la Asunción de la Virgen María was likely the last work to leave Juan Manuel's pen. A brief theological treatise on the Christian miracle of the Virgin's Assumption, the work gives several reasons why "omne del mundo no deve dubdar que sancta María no sea en cielo" [men in this world should not doubt that Saint Mary is in heaven].

Finally, *Libro del conde Lucanor,* (or *Libro de los Enxiemplos del conde Lucanor et de Patronio*), finished in 1335, has come down to the modern reader in a rather contaminated state. The preservation of five manuscripts, all from the fifteenth century, attest to its wide diffusion. The work is divided into five parts, of which the first is the most extensive, consisting of fifty-one known *exempla*. In the second part the style changes, and in its prologue the author praises the use of subtlety as a way of making the merit of his work known. Books 2, 3, and 4 are essentially one book of proverbs, and the fifth and final book is a general reflection on Christian doctrine. It is difficult to separate the didactic from the narrative; the work's rhetoric manages to overcome the dichotomy of the two elements.

The sources—especially of the *exiemplos*—can be found in stories of Oriental origin that, like the *Disciplina clericalis*, were well known in the Western world through their Latin versions. It is important to remember that in Alfonso X's day *Calila e Dinna* and *Sendebar* had already been translated into Castilian. Other works also circulated in medieval translations, including Aesop's fables, *Barlaan e Josafat, Sintipas,* the *Gesta romanorum,* the *Legenda aurea,* which was used by preachers who collected exempla, and contemporary works such as chronicles and bestiaries.

Some of the exempla may come from oral sources later recorded in some textual form selected by the author. Others are indications of Juan Manuel's own originality as a creator, as well as his artistic manner of reelaborating extant texts.

The purpose of the majority of Juan Manuel's writings is to teach through pleasure (*docere delectando*); in several occasions, the author expresses his goal of morally attending to his readers, orienting their conduct—including the increase of *onras* and *faciendas*—according to their estate. Consequently, and especially in *El conde Lucanor,* the author filled his exiemplos with the most useful and entertaining stories he knew, hoping that his readers would benefit from the work's *palabras falagueras et apuestas* (delightful and elegant words), while at the same time taking in the *cosas aprovechosas* (useful things) mixed in.

Starting in the thirteenth century, the exemplum played a didactic role, offering models of behavior for its readers. With Juan Manuel, however, the exemplum becomes something much more: it is an explicitly structural, well-determined genre chosen consciously by the author. Furthermore, it allows Juan Manuel to establish a perfect accord between the duelling narrative and didactic elements, a desire already implicit in the prologue's affirmations.

See also Llull, Ramón

Further Reading

Caldera, E. "Retórica narrativa e didáttica nel "Conde Lucanor," *Miscellanea di studi ispanici,* 14 (1966–67), 5–120.

Catalán, D. "Don Juan Manuel ante el modelo alfonsí. El testimonio de la *Crónica abreviada*" In *Juan Manuel Studies.* Ed. I. Macpherson. London, 1977, 17–51.

Don Juan Manuel. VII Centenario. Murcia, 1982.

Giménez Soler, A. *Don Juan Manuel. Biografia y estudio critico.* Zaragoza, 1932.

Juan Manuel, *Obras Compietas.* Ed., prologue, and notes by J. M. Blecua. Vols. 1–2. Madrid, 1983.

Rico, F., "Crítica del texto y modelos de cultura en el *Prólogo General* de Don Juan Manuel." In *Studia in honorem prof. M. de Riquer.* Vol. 1. Barcelona, 1990, 409–423.

JESÚS MONTOYA MARTÍNEZ

JUDITH, EMPRESS (ca. 800–843) Adulated as a Rachel, vilified as a Jezebel, Empress Judith (r. 819–840) has likely suffered more than any other Carolingian from a polarized historiography. Primarily known as the second wife of Emperor Louis the Pious (r. 814–840) and mother of King Charles the Bald (r. 840–877), she assumed a commanding role in the volatile world of ninth-century Frankish politics, earning the respect of many, and the enmity of many more.

Presented at the February, 819, Aachen assembly by her parents (Welf, count of Alemannia, and the Saxon noblewoman Heilwig), a beautiful Judith caught the recently-widowed emperor's eye; they were married immediately. Judith gave birth in 821 to a daughter, Gisela, but did not pose a real threat to her three stepsons until producing a rival male heir, Charles, on June 13, 823. From that day forth she strove to procure a stable future for her son (and herself) by arranging advantageous marriage alliances, installing relatives in key imperial offices, and using her proximity to her husband on behalf of several influential courtiers. She achieved her greatest successes in Louis's territorial grants to Charles in 829 (Alemannia), 832 (Aquitaine), and 837 (Neustria), followed by the actual crowning of Charles as "king" in August, 838. Among such auspicious occasions, however, lay a series of rebellions in 830 and 833–834, each led by Louis's eldest son, Lothar, in an attempt to assert his own imperial authority. He and his followers focused much of their hostility on Judith, accusing her in 830 of adultery and sorcery (charges later cleared by her oath of innocence at Aachen on February 2, 831), and banishing her to Poitiers. They exiled her again in the later revolt to a convent in Tortona, Lombardy. Lothar's overconfidence and the ephemeral help of his brothers (Louis and Pepin) assured his failure in both instances, however, leaving Judith and Charles several years to consolidate their position (and according to some accounts, to wreak revenge) before Louis died on June 20, 840.

Civil war ensued, despite Louis's revised division of the empire in 839 between Lothar and Charles. In the end, it was the help of Louis the Bavarian (who had married Judith's sister, Emma, in 827) that made possible Charles's and Judith's victory over Lothar at Fontenoy on June 25, 841. Afterward, Charles further shored up his powerbase, benefiting particularly from his mother's activities in Aquitaine from her base in Bourges. On December 13, 842, Judith witnessed the strategic marriage of her son to Ermentrude (niece of Adalard, count of Tours). Charles soon enhanced this declaration of independence by dispossessing his mother of her lands and placing her in "retirement" at Tours, probably in February, 843. She died there two months later, on April 19, 843, comforted, perhaps, that her consistent efforts on behalf of her son had changed the course of Carolingian history.

Acclaimed by several contemporary writers for both her beauty and erudition, Judith also fostered Carolingian learning. She arranged for Walahfrid Strabo to tutor Charles from 829 to 838, and commissioned the second book of Freculf of Lisieux's important *Chronicle*. Hrabanus Maurus's dedication of a commentary on the biblical books of Judith and Esther, as well as a figure poem to Judith also testifies to her literary patronage, and has supported the contention that she may have personally supervised the creation and expansion of Louis the Pious's court library.

See also **Lothair I; Rabanus Maurus; Walafrid Strabo**

Further Reading

Bischoff, Bernhard. "Benedictine Monasteries and the Survival of Classical Literature." In *Manuscripts and Libraries in the Age of Charlemagne*, trans. Michael Gorman. Cambridge, England: Cambridge University Press, 1994, pp. 134–160.

Boshof, Egon. *Ludwig der Fromme*. Darmstadt: Primus, 1996.

Cabaniss, Allen. "Judith Augusta and Her Time." *Studies in English* 10 (1969): 67–109.

Konecny, Silvia. *Die Frauen des karolingischen Königshauses*. Vienna: VWGÖ, 1976.

McKitterick, Rosamond. *The Frankish Kingdoms under the Carolingians, 751–987*. London: Longman, 1983.

Nelson, Janet L. *Charles the Bald*. London: Longman, 1992.

Ward, Elizabeth. "Caesar's Wife: The Career of the Empress Judith, 819–829." In *Charlemagne's Heir: New Perspectives on the Reign of Louis the Pious (814–840)*, eds. Peter Godman and Roger Collins. Oxford: Clarendon, 1990, pp. 205–227.

STEVEN A. STOFFERAHN

JULIAN OF NORWICH (1342/43–after 1416) Mystical writer and the first known woman author in English literature. Her book of *Showings*, or *Revelations of Divine Love*, ranks with the best medieval English prose and is a primary text in the literature of mysticism. It is extant in a short version, probably written first, and in an extended form, completed 20 years later.

Biographical information about Julian is sparse. It is limited to tacts in her own text, mention in a few wills, and a passage in the *Book of Margery Kempe*. Julian's birthplace is unknown. The dialect in the oldest extant copy of her book shows northern features, leading to the conjecture that she may have come from Yorkshire. Sometime between 1413 and 1416 Margery Kempe visited Julian and received counsel from her. As late as 1416 Julian was living in Norwich in Norfolk as an anchoress, enclosed in a cell attached to the Church of St. Julian. She may have received the name Julian upon her entrance into the anchorhold.

On 8 May (or possibly 13 May) 1373, at the age of 30 and a half, she fell seriously ill, most likely while still at home. She then recalled having prayed in her youth for a bodily sickness, to prepare her for death, and for the wounds of true contrition, natural compassion, and resolute longing for God. Surrounded by her mother and friends, and attended by a priest, she believed, with them, that she was about to die. Suddenly, however, while she was looking at a crucifix, her health returned. Then followed a series of fifteen visions, mostly of the crucified Christ. These were interrupted by attacks from the Devil, and then confirmed in a sixteenth and final showing. This experience gives the content to the short version of her book, in which she explains that the visions were threefold in character—visual, intellectual, and spiritual or intuitive. The long version of the text is enriched with 20 years of theological reflection, pastoral counseling, and spiritual growth. Her teachings are oriented to the instruction of other believers, her "even-Christians."

The shorter version of Julian's book is extant in one manuscript copy—the 15th-century Amherst Manuscript (BL Add. 37790). The longer text is complete in three manuscripts: the Paris Manuscript (BN Fonds angl. 40), copied around 1650; and two Sloane manuscripts (Sloane 1—BL Sloane 2499, early 17th century; Sloane 2—BL Sloane 3705, an 18th-century modernization of Sloane 1). Excerpts from the longer version exist in Westminster Treasury 4 (W), written in the early 16th century; and in a 17th-century manuscript from Upholland Northern Institute (formerly St. Joseph's College). The Upholland manuscript was written by English Benedictine nuns, living at Cambrai, after the Dissolution of the monasteries. The earliest printed edition (1670) is by Serenus Cressy, an English Benedictine, chaplain for the Paris house of the nuns.

T.S. Eliot, in the *Four Quartets*, familiarized the literary world with Julian's key phrase, "All shall be well," and with some of her mystical symbolism. Thomas Merton cited her as "one of the greatest English theologians" (1967). An observance at Norwich (1973) commemorated the sixth centenary of her showings. Since then Julian has become the focus of extensive study by literary scholars and theologians and has a growing following as a spiritual guide.

Textual critics disagree on the choice of a preferred copy text for a Julian edition. Colledge and Walsh (1978) opted for Paris, favoring its more conventionally correct rhetorical structures. Marion Glasscoe selected Sloane 1 for a student edition (2d ed. 1986). Glasscoe notes the pitfalls of following, in disputed readings, either Sloane 1 or Paris, or creating an eclectic text; nonetheless, she finds special qualities to recommend reliance on Sloane 1, which, she says, often reflects "a greater sense of theology as a live issue at the heart of human creativity" (1989: 119) thereby coming closer to Julian's central concern.

Theological approaches diverge widely. A plethora of devotional books have been based on a surface reading of the *Revelations*, stressing Julian's optimism and oversimplifying her doctrine of love. Her terms "substance" and "sensuality" are often misunderstood. A misreading, sometimes abetted by inaccurate translations, assumes that by "substance" Julian means the human soul and by "sensuality" the body or the five senses. Substance designates, rather, "the truth of our being, body and soul: the way we are meant to be, as whole persons" (Pelphrey, 1982: 90): "Where the blessed soul of Christ is, there is the substance of all souls that will be saved by Christ.... Our soul is made to be God's dwelling place, and the dwelling place of the soul is God.... It is a high understanding inwardly to see and to know that God our creator dwells in our soul; and a higher understanding it is inwardly to see and to know that our soul which is created dwells in God's substance, of which substance, through God, we are what we are" (Long Text, ch. 54).

Usually "sensuality" refers to that human existence which becomes God's in the Incarnation: it is the "place" of the city of God, the glory of the Trinity abiding in collective humanity. Human beings are called to be helpers or partners in the unfolding of what humanity is meant to become—a city fit for God to reign and find rest in. These difficult concepts are carefully explored by Pelphrey, who succinctly summarizes Julian's teaching about divine love: "The reflection of divine love into humanity is...seen to take place in three ways: in the creation of humanity (our capacity for God); in the maturing or 'increasing' of humanity (to which she also refers as our 'remaking' in Christ); and in the perfecting or fulfilling of human beings through the indwelling Christ" (1982: 90).

Julian presents this theology principally through the parable of the Lord and the Servant: "This story conveys Julian's insights about the first Adam, the cosmic Christ, the Trinity, and the unity of all who are to be saved. The one great reality in the parable is the person of Christ, in whom are mysterious compenetrations of other realities—the Adam of Genesis; the total Adam (all humanity); Christ as the second Adam (and in one sense the first Adam, since to his eternal image all things were made); and Christ, meaning all humanity to be saved. The basic parable weaves into other metaphors: for example, the sinful Adam fell in misery to the earth, but likewise the divine Adam falls on the earth—into human nature in Mary's womb—and makes the garden of the earth spring forth with food and drink for which the Father thirsts and longs, in his unending love for the treasure which was hidden in the earth" (Bradley, 1984: 209). The Trinity is revealed in Christ. God is active as "maker, preserver, and lover," an insight Julian experienced when she saw creation in the likeness of a hazelnut. Since God is the ground of the soul, the desire for God is natural, and sin (all chat is not good) is unnatural. Prayer unites the soul to God, the foundation from which the prayer arises. In the depths or core of the believer, the being of God intersects with the being of the creature and is the root of a "godly will" that always inclines toward the good. Nonetheless, humanity continues to sin, for evil was permitted to arise contrary to goodness, which will triumph in the end in the form of a good greater than what would otherwise have been. How "all things shall be well," as Christ promised Julian, will remain hidden until a great deed is accomplished on the Last Day (Long Text, ch. 32).

Literary and linguistic critics contribute to the explication of this mystical core, Reynolds explores the key images of Christ as courteous and "homely," in its medieval sense. Courtesy signifies that Christ possesses without limit the largesse and fidelity attributed to the medieval knight. Courtesy fuses with "homeliness," the familiar manner used at home, among equals, and implies nearness, so that "we are clothed and enclosed in the goodness of God" (Long Text, ch. 6). In his familiar aspect Christ is mother, an image rooted in scripture and in biblical exegesis but developed with originality by Julian. As the archetypal mother Christ bears his children not to pain and dying but to joy and endless living. His Passion is a birthing, which entailed the sharpest throes that ever were, and was undertaken to satisfy his love. The maternal image further signifies that humanity dwells in Christ, as in a mother's womb, and is also fed, nurtured, chastised, and tenderly cared for, as a child. The sensual nature of humanity (that which is born into time) is in the second person, Jesus Christ, and is knit—as in fabric making—to its ground in God. This motherhood metaphor has attracted the attention of feminist criticism, adding to Julian's popularity today. The overall lesson of the revelations is love in three meanings: uncreated love, or God; created love—the human soul in God; and a love that is bestowed as virtue, enabling believers to love God, themselves, and all creation, especially their "even-Christians."

See also **Kempe, Margery**

Further Reading

Primary Sources

Colledge, Edmund, and James Walsh, eds. *A Book of Showings to the Anchoress Julian of Norwich.* 2 vols. Toronto: Pontifical Institute, 1978

Colledge, Edmund, and James Walsh, trans. *Showings.* New York: Paulist Press, 1978

del Mastro, M.L., trans. *Revelation of Divine Love in Sixteen Showings.* Liguori, Mo.: Triumph Books, 1994

Glasscoe, Marion, ed. *A Revelation of Love.* 2d ed. Exeter: University of Exeter, 1986.

Secondary Sources

New *CBEL* 1:522–24

Manual 9:3082–84, 3438–44

Bradley, Ritamary. "Julian of Norwich: Writer and Mystic." In *An Introduction to the Medieval Mystics of Europe,* ed. Paul E. Szarmach. Albany: SUNY Press, 1984, pp. 195–216

Bradley, Ritamary. *Julian's Way: A Practical Commentary on Julian of Norwich.* London: HarperCollins, 1992

Glasscoe, Marion. "Visions and Revisions: A Further Look at the Manuscripts of Julian of Norwich." *SB* 42 (1989): 103–20

Lagorio, Valerie Marie, and Ritamary Bradley. "Julian of Norwich." In *The 14th-Century English Mystics: A Comprehensive Annotated Bibliography.* New York: Garland, 1981, pp. 105–26

Llewelyn, Robert, ed. *Julian: Woman of Our Day.* Mystic: Twenty-Third Publications, 1987

Molinari, Paolo. *Julian of Norwich: The Teaching of a 14th Century English Mystic.* London: Longmans, Green, 1958

Nuth, Joan. *Wisdom's Daughter.* New York: Crossroad, 1991

Pelphrey, Brant. *Love Was His Meaning: The Theology and Mysticism of Julian of Norwich.* Salzburg: Institut fur Anglistik und Amerikanistik, 1982

Reynolds, Anna Maria. "'Courtesy' and 'Homeliness' in the Revelations of Julian of Norwich." *14th-Century English Mystics Newsletter (Mystics Quarterly)* 5/2 (1979): 12–20

von Nolcken, Christina. "Julian of Norwich." In *Middle English Prose: A Critical Guide to Major Genres and Authors,* ed. A.S.G. Edwards. New Brunswick: Rutgers University Press, 1984, pp. 97–108.

RITAMARY BRADLEY

JULIAN OF TOLEDO (b. ca. 640) Born around 640, Julian was of partly Jewish descent. Knowledge of his career comes primarily from the brief "Eulogy" of him written by Bishop Felix of Toledo (693–ca. 700). He was a pupil of Bishop Eugenius 11 (647–657), and subsequently became a member of the clergy of the church in Toledo while following a rigorous ascetic regime. Following the death of Bishop Quiricus (667–680) he was chosen by King

Wamba to take over the see. The choice may have been influenced by Julian's eulogistic *Historia Wambae,* an account of the opening events of that king's reign. However, before the end of 680 Julian had been caught up in, or even had initiated, the chain of events leading to Wamba's enforced abdication and retirement to a monastery. With the new king, Ervig (680–687), to whom he had previously dedicated a now lost work on divine judgment, Julian seems to have cooperated closely. In 686 he dedicated to the king his most significant surviving book, *On the Proof of the Sixth Age,* a polemical reply to Jewish denials of Christ's messiahship. This work redefined the chronological framework of human history within an apocalyptic context, and was to be highly influential in Spain and western Europe throughout the Middle Ages. He died in Gao.

Other extant writings by Julian include the *Anti-keimenon* and *the Prognosticum futuri saeculi.* In these, as in lost collections referred to in the "Eulogy," Julian is revealed as an assiduous reader of the works of Augustine. Like Ildefonsus, Julian is credited by Felix with the composition of verse and also of a substantial body of liturgy. The latter cannot be disentangled from the vast corpus of Mozarafaic liturgical texts.

During his episcopate Julianus presided over four Councils of Toledo: the twelfth (680–681), thirteenth (683), fourteenth (684), and fifteenth (688). The first of these formalized the primacy of Toledo over all the other churches of the Visigothic kingdom. Julian himself contributed to this by his emphasis on the role of the anointing of the king in the "royal city" as a precondition for a new ruler's legitimacy.

Further Reading

Collins, R. "Julian of Toledo and the Royal Succession in Late Seventh-Century Spain." In *Early Medieval King-ship.* Eds. P. Sawyer and I. Wood. Leeds, 1977. 30–49.

Hillgarth, J. N. "St. Julian of Toledo in the Middle Ages." *Journal of the Warburg and Courtauld Institutes* 21 (1958), 7–26.
Murphy, F. X. "Julian of Toledo and the Fall of the Visigothic Kingdom in Spain." *Speculum* 27 (1952), 1–21.

ROGER COLLINS

JUSTINIAN I (c. 482 or 483–565, r. 527–565) Justinian I (Flavius Sabbatius) was the sovereign of the eastern Roman, or Byzantine, empire during an age of vast transition and was a figure of both glory and paradox. Born a peasant, he appreciated the awesome Roman heritage as few others could appreciate it; but in seeking to be its steward and restorer, he also opened the way to its transformation. His reign—one of the longest in the Byzantine empire—saw achievements that were substantial and enduring but brought ruin and disaster as their price. In his very quest to restore the territorial and doctrinal unity of the Roman world, Justinian guaranteed its further fragmentation.

Justinian was of Thracian-Illyrian stock and was born in a Latin-speaking district of the Macedonian Balkans. His uncle, Justin, having achieved success as a member of the new imperial guards in Constantinople, sent for the boy and several other nephews in order to give them an education, and opportunities, in the capital. Adopting a new name in tribute to his uncle, Justinian learned Greek, took a liking to intellectual pursuits such as theology, and learned the workings of the military and the court. In 518, by a quirk of fortune, Justin seized the throne, and Justinian quickly emerged as his right-hand man, becoming heir-designate in 525 and full successor two years later.

By that time, Justinian had met and married Theodora, the remarkable woman who was to be his invaluable partner in rule. He had also identified administrators and commanders on whom he could rely and had formulated the main lines of his policies. During the first four years of his reign, he was trapped in an unwanted war with his powerful eastern neighbor, Persia; and just as he was winning peace and freedom there, the devastating Nika riots of January 532 nearly swept him off the throne. He recovered quickly, however, thanks partly to the advice of Theodora and to the soldiers of the young general Belisarius, and was then in a stronger position that allowed him to initiate an array of projects. These included a codification of the Roman legal tradition as *Corpus juris civilis*, schemes to end the religious and political dissent of the Monophysites and other heterodox movements, and a large-scale building program that was to culminate in the triumphant cathedral of Hagia Sophia in the capital.

Justinian's chief project, though, was his program of reconquest, aimed at recovering the western provinces that had been detached by various Germanic tribes during the previous century. He was inspired in this by his duty to rescue the orthodox provincials in those districts from their Arian Christian rulers, and he was also prodded by dispossessed landowners who sought the restitution of their property; more broadly, he was motivated by his broad perception that the barbarian "successor states" in the west were only a temporary aberration, and by a sense that he was responsible for restoring the Roman empire to its former scope, encompassing the entire Mediterranean.

Exploiting diplomatic opportunities, Justinian dispatched the brilliant Belisarius to North Africa, where the destruction of the Vandal kingdom was effected with lightning speed (533–534). Meanwhile, given the deterioration of relations with the Ostrogoths in Italy during the last years of their king, Theoderic, and the dynastic crisis attending the succession of Theodoric's daughter Amalasuntha, Justinian was next able to address the conquest of the Ostrogoth kingdom. While another general was sent to seize the Ostrogoths' holdings in the Balkans, Belisarius landed in Sicily in the summer of 535, beginning the long episode of the Gothic wars in Italy.

Uneasy about Belisarius's popularity and military prowess, Justinian vacillated in his support for his general and was then furious when Belisarius dared to entertain an offer from the Goths to take the imperial title in the west. When the settlement of 540 with the Goths broke down and a counter-offensive by Totila began undoing Belisarius's work, Justinian sent Belisarius back to Italy, though grudgingly and without adequate support or resources. Only when Belisarius asked to be recalled and the outlook in Italy seemed hopeless did Justinian commission Narses to organize a new army and complete the conquest of Italy.

When Justinian's commitment to the reconquest was most intense and the reconquest itself was in full tide and was proving more prolonged than he had intended, the rapacious Persian king reopened war with the empire on a wide range of fronts. This drained the emperor's manpower and resources, which were further reduced by a plague that ravaged the Mediterranean world in 542–543. Justinian, increasingly pressed, was forced to impose oppressive taxes and to skimp on expenditures wherever he could. His economies and his withdrawals of troops particularly weakened the Balkan regions, which were exposed to raids by various peoples, notably the Huns, who menaced Constantinople several times. This weakening allowed even more disastrous penetrations of the Balkans by Avars and Slavs in the decades following Justinian's death.

Throughout his reign, Justinian strove to achieve religious unity in the face of intractable dissent and regional resistance. His continually shirting responses included persecution, conciliation, schemes for compromise, and the bullying of Pope Vigilius to win the accord of Rome. Justinian's increasing obsession with religious coercion poisoned his last years, during which the ruinous effects of his overstrained finances darkened his reputation and made his death in November 565 a relief to his subjects.

Among Justinian's achievements, for good or ill, must be reckoned his lasting impact on Italy. Although his wars of reconquest left the peninsula devastated and exhausted, he nevertheless set the pattern for its restored government through his Pragmatic Sanction of 554; and the extraordinarily comprehensive powers that he granted to Belisarius and Narses laid the foundation for the governmental agency of the exarchate, through which the Byzantine empire was to rule its Italian holdings in the face of invasions by the Lombards. The exarchs' capital, Ravenna, provided a model for imperial style and imagery for centuries and had an important influence on Charlemagne. This model was conveyed most notably through the wondrous mosaic decorations carried out under Justinian, which include the famous portraits of him and Theodora in San Vitale. As the sponsor of the great *Corpus juris civilis*—whose rediscovery in Italy in the eleventh century was influential in reviving Roman law and legal studies in later medieval Italy and the west in general—Justinian himself became a symbol of the traditions of Roman sovereignty. Dante was to celebrate Justinian as a paradigm of imperial majesty in Canto 6 of *Paradiso*.

See also **Theodora**

Further Reading

Barker, John W. Justinian and the Later Roman Empire. Madison: University of Wisconsin Press, 1966. (General account setting the reign in the context of the fourth-seventh centuries.)

Browning, Robert. Justinian and Theodora, rev. ed. London: Thames and Hudson, 1987. (Vivid and insightful.)

Bury, J. B. A History of the Later Roman Empire from the Death of Theodosius I to the Death of Justinian I (A.D. 395–565), Vol. 2. London: Macmillan, 1923. (Reprint, New York: Dover, 1958. Fullest modern scholarly study in English.)

Downey, Glanville W. Constantinople in the Age of Justinian. Norman: University of Oklahoma Press, 1960. (Lively evocation of the era.)

Holmes, W. G. The Age of Justinian and Theodora: A History of the Sixth Century, 2 vols. London: G. Bell and Sons, 1905–1907. (2nd ed., 1912. Extended and detailed but somewhat uninspired and dated.)

Procopius of Caesarea. History of the Wars, Secret History, and Buildings. Loeb Classical Library Series, 7 vols. London and Cambridge, Mass.: Heinemann and Harvard University Press, 1914–1940. (With reprints. Full English translation of the complete works of the most important contemporary historian of Justinian.)

Ure, Percy N. Justinian and His Age. Harmondsworth and Baltimore, Md.: Penguin, 1951. (Stimulating and perceptive study.)

JOHN W. BARKER

K

KEMPE, MARGERY (ca. 1373–after 1438) Controversial mystic and author of the first extant autobiography in English. *The Book of Margery Kempe* is both a mystical treatise consisting of the author's visions and conversations with Christ and a narrative of her life, including her conversion, pilgrimages, and arguments with church authorities. Kempe, who was illiterate, dictated her autobiography to two different scribes. The original manuscript has been lost, but a 15th-century copy was discovered in 1934.

Born in the East Anglian town of King's Lynn ca. 1373, Margery was the daughter of John Brunham, mayor of the town. At the age of twenty she married John Kempe. After the difficult birth of their first child Kempe suffered a breakdown. This experience, followed by business failures in brewing and milling, led eventually to her mystical conversion. Her first ordeal as a mystic was to convince her husband to be celibate, but only after twenty years of marriage and fourteen children did he agree, on the condition that she pay off all his debts. With the consent of her husband and the church Kempe was finally free to pursue her vocation as a mystic.

The "way to high perfection," however, was fraught with difficulties. Kempe encountered hostility from people who doubted her holiness and questioned her orthodoxy. She traveled around England seeking support and verification of her visions from many holy people, including the anchoress Julian of Norwich. Nevertheless, she continued to arouse suspicion and persecution for her behavior, including her bold speech and her "boisterous weeping." She was arrested as a Lollard, threatened with burning at the stake by her English detractors, and deserted by her fellow pilgrims on her travels abroad. Kempe's weeping in particular inspired her contemporaries to revile her and modern readers to label her "hysterical."

Kempe's travels took her to the Holy Land, Italy, Santiago de Compostela, and finally, near the end of her life, to Danzig, Prussia. The *Book* ends with her return to King's Lynn, where she still inspires both hostility and marvel as a woman in her sixties.

The Book of Margery Kempe departs from the medieval saint's life and mystical treatise. Unlike the saint's life, which is biographical, Kempe's book is autobiographical. As author and narrator of her own life Kempe develops some hagiographic conventions, such as the themes of her suffering, patience, and charity, while ignoring others. Her book is also unusual as a mystical treatise. Kempe's visions and revelations are grounded in everyday, autobiographical details, including her struggles for acceptance, her fears for her own safety, and her travels.

Kempe's work is divided into two sections, or books. The first book ends with the death of her scribe. Kempe spent four years trying to convince the second scribe to recopy and finish her book. He hesitated because of her notoriety and the illegibility of the first scribe's writing but finally agreed. The 15th-century manuscript that survives may be a copy of the original dictated by Kempe to the second scribe. This copy belonged to Mount Grace, a Carthusian monastery in Yorkshire, but was later lost. William Butler-Bowdon discovered it in 1934 in his family library, and Hope Emily Allen identified it as *The Book of Margery Kempe.* (It is now BL Add. 61823.) Until 1934 only brief extracts of Kempe's book had been known; these extracts, printed by Wynkyn de Worde (ca. 1501) and Henry Pepwell (1521), misleadingly omit Kempe's autobiographical passages, and one incorrectly labels her a "devout anchoress."

As a mystical treatise Kempe's *Book* is often compared with the work of her contemporary Julian of Norwich. Kempe's mysticism, like Julian's, belongs to the tradition called affective piety, characterized by personal devotion to Christ's humanity, particularly in the Nativity and Passion. The emotions, or affections, play a crucial role in this devotion. By identifying with the suffering humanity of Christ the mystic is transported through her emotions to spiritual love.

Kempe's life and mysticism, however, differ considerably from Julian's. Her boisterous weeping, her insistent identification with Christ, her self-preoccupation, and her refusal to live the more orthodox life of a nun or recluse distinguish her from Julian of Norwich. Critics in her own time as well as today fault her for the excessive emotionalism and literalness of her visions. Yet Kempe's mysticism was not unique. She found models for it in the lives and mystical works of other female mystics, such as Marie d'Oignies, Birgitta (Bridget) of Sweden, and Elizabeth of Hungary, and in the writings of the English mystic Richard Rolle.

The core of the controversy about Margery Kempe is her version of imitating Christ. Although the practice of imitating Christ's suffering was common in medieval spirituality, Kempe is preoccupied with this suffering. Her meditations on the Passion elicit this suffering and her roaring draws attention to it, disrupting sermons and disturbing the people around her. In addition Kempe's use of erotic language to describe mystical union—words like ravishment, dalliance, and even homeliness—is boldly literal. She translates the mystical concept of marriage to Christ into an alarmingly worldly one, as Christ instructs Kempe to take him to bed with her as her husband (ch. 36). Although Rolle before her had used sensual imagery to describe mystical union, Kempe's usage startles with its emphasis on the literal rather than the figurative or symbolic.

Kempe's book poses problems for literary analysis as well. Her narrative is not strictly chronological, and with its digressions and repetitions it seems unconstructed. How much Kempe's scribes contributed to the shape of the narrative is a further problem facing literary analysis. Finally Kempe s illiteracy makes the question of influence an interesting one. She exhibits some knowledge of both Latin and vernacular religious texts in spite of her inability to read or write.

Like her book Margery Kempe is an interesting and problematic subject. As a woman charting her own "way to high perfection" she challenged the religious, social, and gender expectations of her time. Her book offers valuable insight into the struggles of an extraordinary medieval woman who refused to conform to those expectations in her pursuit of a "singular grace."

See also **Julian of Norwich; Rolle, Richard, of Hampole**

Further Reading

Primary Sources

Butler-Bowdon, William, ed. and trans. *The Book of Margery Kempe,* New York: Devin-Adair, 1944.

Meech, Sanford Brown, and Hope Emily Allen, eds. *The Book of Margery Kempe.* EETS o.s. 212. London: Oxford University Press, 1940.

Windeatt, B.A., trans. *The Book of Margery Kempe.* New York: Penguin, 1985.

Secondary Sources

New *CBEL* 1:524.

Manual 9:3084–86, 3444–45.

Atkinson, Clarissa W. *Mystic and Pilgrim: The Book and the World of Margery Kempe.* Ithaca: Cornell University Press, 1983.

Beckwith, Sarah. "A Very Material Mysticism: The Medieval Mysticism of Margery Kempe." In *Medieval Literature: Criticism, Ideology & History,* ed. David Aers. New York: St. Martin, 1986, pp. 34–57.

Fries, Maureen. "Margery Kempe." In *An Introduction to the Medieval Mystics of Europe,* ed. Paul E. Szarmach. Albany: SUNY Press, 1984, pp. 217–35.

Goodman, Anthony E. "The Piety of John Brunham's Daughter, of Lynn." In *Medieval Women,* ed. Derek Baker. Oxford: Blackwell, 1978, pp. 347–58.

Hirsh, John C. "Margery Kempe." In *Middle English Prose: A Critical Guide to Major Authors and Genres,* ed. A.S.G. Edwards. New Brunswick: Rutgers University Press, 1984, pp. 109–19.

Lochrie, Karma. *Margery Kempe and Translations of the Flesh.* Philadelphia: University of Pennsylvania Press, 1991.

McEntire, Sandra J., ed. *Margery Kempe: A Book of Essays.* New York: Garland, 1992.

KARMA LOCHRIE

KOERBECKE, JOHANN (ca. 1420–1491)

A contemporary of Stefan Lochner and Konrad Witz, this painter contributed to the transition from the international Gothic style to a more realistic one, inspired by Netherlandish art. Koerbecke was probably born circa 1420 in Coesfeld (Northrhine Westphalia).

He is first recorded in Münster in 1443, when he purchased a house. He led an important workshop there until his death on June 13, 1491.

Koerbecke's sole documented work is the Marienfeld Altarpiece, for which he received payment in 1456. Installed on the high altar of the Marienfeld monastery church in 1457, it originally consisted of a carved shrine and painted wings with scenes from the life of the Virgin and the Passion. In the seventeenth century, the wings were sawn into sixteen panels, now located in several collections (Avignon, Musée Calvet; Berlin, Gemäldegalerie; Chicago, Art Institute; Cracow, National Museum; Madrid, Thyssen Collection; Moscow, Pushkin Museum; Münster, Westfälisches Land esmuseum; Nuremberg, Germanisches Nationalmuseum; Washington, National Gallery). They reveal knowledge of works by important painters of the preceding generation in Westphalia and Cologne. Koerbecke's Crucifixion is inspired by Conrad von Soest's paintings of that subject, his Presentation is an interpretation of Stephan Lochner's 1447 version (Darmstadt, Hessisches Landesmuseum), and his Resurrection is based on Master Francke's 1424 *Englandfahrer Altarpiece* (Hamburg, Kunsthalle). Koerbecke's volumetric figures and detailed, naturalistic treatment of interiors and landscapes derive from Netherlandish art.

Other attributed works are the wings of the Langenhorst Altarpiece with eight scenes from the Passion (Münster, Westfälisches Landesmuseum), ca. 1445, and three panels from an altarpiece with scenes from the life of Saint John the Baptist: the baptism of Christ and Christ with Saint John (Münster, Westfälisches Landesmuseum), and the beheading of the Baptist (The Hague, Meermanno-Westreenianum Museum), ca. 1470. A wing with Saints John the Baptist and George, and a fragment with Saint Christopher, survive from the Freckenhorst Altarpiece of ca. 1470–1480 (Munster, Westfalisches Landesmuseum).

See also Francke, Master; Lochner, Stefan

Further Reading

Kirchhoff, Karl-Heinz. "Maler und Malerfamilien in Münster." *Westfalen* 4 (1977): 98–110.

Luckhardt, Jochen. *Der Hochaltar der Zister zienserklosterkirche Marienfeld.* Münster: Westfälisches Landesmuseum für Kunst und Kulturgeschichte, 1987.

Pieper, Paul, *Die deutschen, niederländischen und italienischen Tafelbilder bis um 1530.* Bestandskataloge des Westfälischen Landesmuseum für Kunst und Kulturgeschichte. Münster: Aschendorff, 1986, pp. 140–200.

Sommer, Johannes. *Johann Koerbecke: Der Meister des Marienfelder Altars von 1457.* Dissertation, Universtität Bonn, 1937. Münster: Westfälische Vereinsdruckerei, 1937.

SUSANNE REECE

KONRAD VON WÜRZBURG (ca. 1230–1287)

Included among the "twelve old masters" revered by Meistersingers, Konrad produced one of the largest and most varied oeuvres in all of Middle High German literature. Initially neglected by modern scholars as an epigone and mannerist, critics are now examining Konrad's work in its own context. Konrad embodies a turn in German literature, he was neither noble (Song 32, line 189: *waere ich edel*, if I were noble) nor a part of the court. Konrad plied his trade in the cities and wrote for the wealthy bourgeoisie and the urban nobility. Archives, official documents, and Konrad's works themselves provide us with an extraordinary amount of information about his life and patronage. Born in Würzburg, Konrad began as a wandering poet, spent time in Strasbourg and eventually settled in Basle. Konrad wrote two lays. *Got gewaltec waz du schickest* (Powerful God, what you send) is a religious lay in praise of the Virgin and the Trinity. *Vênus diu feine diust entslâfen* (Elegant Venus has fallen asleep) is a secular lay treating courtly love. Unfortunately, the melodies to both of these have been lost. Konrad's shorter love lyric consists primarily of nine summer songs and eleven winter songs characterized by floral metaphors and the *jârlanc* introduction (nos. 5, 6, 10, 13, 17, 21, 23, 27). Konrad also produced three dawn songs (nos. 14, 15, 30), as well as exempla (nos. 18, 24, 25), maxims, and religious poetry. In Konrad's short lyric, one finds all the qualities of literary mannerism. For example, in song 26, every single word is part of a rhyming pair: *Gar bar lît wît walt, kalt snê wê tuot: gluot sî bî mir.* The excessive, albeit impressive rhyme schemes, especially in songs 26, 27, 28 and 30, ultimately obscure the meaning and emotion of the poetry and Konrad's use of traditional imagery often undermines the originality of his stylistic innovations. Konrad's allegory, *Die Klage der Kunst* (Art's Complaint), appeals for patronage and support of "true art" (*rehte kunst*). His hymn in praise of the Virgin Mary, *Die goldene Schmiede* (The Golden Smith), draws on and synthesizes an extraordinary range of medieval images and symbols. This work may have been commissioned by the Strasbourg Bishop Konrad von Lichtenberg. Other religious-oriented works include Konrad's verse legends. *Silvester* (1260) was commissioned by Liutold von Roeteln, the legend of Alexius (1265), by Johannes von Bermeswil and Heinrich Iselin, and Konrad composed the story of Pantaleon (1258) for Johannes von Arguel. The patronage of Konrad's earliest narrative work, *Das Turnier von Nantes* (The Tournament of Nantes, 1257–1258) is unknown, but critics suspect that it was written for someone affiliated with the Lower Rhine region. The tournament takes place at the Arthurian capital of Nantes and pits the German princes under the leadership of Richard of England against the French princes, under the leadership of the king of France. This poem was probably intended to win the support of the lower German princes for the recently crowned king of the Romans, Richard, earl of Cornwall (May 17, 1257). Konrad's fragment, *Schwannritter* (Swan Knight), also seems to have been written during this period. The tale is related to the French *Chevalier au Cygne* (1200) and the Lohengrin story found at the end of Wolfram von Eschenbach's *Parzival* (1210). Undoubtedly, Konrad's *Mären* (lyric novellas) are the most impressive and well-known works in his oeuvre. *Das Herzemaere* relates the popular tale of the jealous lord who feeds his wife the heart of her beloved knight. Konrad's introduction to this story recalls the work of Gottfried von Straßburg. This reference serves to underscore Gottfried's conspicuous influence on Konrad's style. In *Der Welt Lohn* (Worldly Reward), Konrad describes Wirnt von Grafenberg's (the poet of the courtly verse novel *Wigalois*) encounter with *Frau Welt* (Lady World). Although no certain source has been identified for this tale, it belongs to the *contemptus mundi* (contempt of the world) tradition. After gazing upon the infested backside of *Frau Welt*, Wirnt rejects the world, takes up the cross, and achieves martyrdom in the Holy Land. The dark comedy *Heinrich von Kempten* (also called *Otte mit dem Bart*, Otto with the Beard, 1261), illustrates the benefits of loyalty. Composed for the dean of Strasbourg Cathedral, Berthold von Tiersberg, the story plays on the traditions of the ill-tempered Emperor Otte (probably Emperor Otto II), Critics dispute the authorship of other Maren attributed to Konrad (*Die halbe Birne*, Half of the Pear, *Der Mvnch ah Liebesbote*, The Monk as Go-between, etc.).

Konrad composed three romances. *Engelhard*, set in the time of Charlemagne, tells a tale of fidelity (*triuwe*) in friendship. Engelhard and Dietrich resemble one another almost exactly and develop a close friendship at court in Denmark. Dietrich leaves the court to assume his position as the duke of Brabant but returns to Denmark to help Engelhard win the hand of Engeltrud, the daughter of the king of Denmark. Later, Dietrich is stricken with leprosy. Reminiscent of Hartmann von Aue's tale, *Der Arme Heinrich*, the poem culminates after Dietrich reveals that the blood of Engelhard's children is the only remedy for his illness. In *Partonopier und Meliur* (1277), Konrad draws on the extremely popular French romance *Partonopeus de Blois* (1200). While out hunting, Partonopier chances on a boat that takes him to the invisible island castle of the heiress of the Byzantine imperial throne, an enchantress named Meliur. At the castle, invisible hands tend to the youth. Partonopier lies with the invisible Meliur each night. Meliur plans to marry him when he comes of age under the condition that he does not look upon her before the appointed time. After a year has passed, Partonopier, plagued by doubts, chances to look upon Meliur and she rejects him. A year later, the pair is reconciled. Partonopier wins Meliur's hand through knightly prowess and becomes the Byzantine emperor. The romance comprises a mix of several different traditions, including: fairy tales, antique epics, *matèrie de Bretange* (tales of Bretange), and the *chansons de geste* (songs of heroic deeds). Similar motifs appear in *Die Königen von Brennenden See* (The Queen of the Burning Lake, 1220–1240), Egenolf von Staufenberg's courtly tale, *Ritter Peter* (1310), and in Thüring von Ringoltingen's verse tale *Melusine* (1456).

Konrad's last and greatest endeavor, *Trojanerkrieg* (The Trojan War, 1281) surpasses, with its 40,424 verses, Herbert von Fritzlar's Middle High German rendition of the fall of Troy, *Liet von Troye* (1190–1217) in both length and quality. Benoît de Sainte-Maure's *Estoire de Troie* is the main source for both German works. Konrad's narrative includes the birth of Paris and Achilles, relates the tale of Jason and Medea, the kidnapping of Helen and the preparation for war. Konrad's tale breaks off in the middle of the siege of Troy. The poem, concluded by a lesser, anonymous poet, was well received. The exact nature of the relationship of Konrad's *Trojanerkrieg* to the *Göttweiger Trojanerkrieg* (1270–1300) has not yet been determined. However, at the very least, Konrad's *Schwannritter* seems to have influenced the anonymous poet of *Götttweiger Trojanerkrieg*, erroneously attributed to Wolfram von Eschenbach. Konrad died in Basle either on August 31 or between October 8–22, 1287. He and his wife, Bertcha, had two daughters Gerina and Agnese. He was buried in Basle. Konrad von Würzburg was highly esteemed by contemporaries and successors. He is depicted dictating his work in the Codex Manesse. Hugo von Timberg praises Konrad in *Der Renner* (II. 1202–1220), and Frauenlob (Heinrich von Meißen) mourns him with the lament that art itself had died with the passing of Konrad: *ach kunst ist tôt!* (313, 15–21).

See also **Frauenlob; Gottfried von Straßburg; Hartmann von Aue**

Further Reading

Brandt, Rüdiger. *Konrad von Würzburg.* Darmstadt: Wissenschaftliche Buchgesellschaft, 1989.

Kokott, Hartmut. *Konrad von Würzburg: Ein Autor zwischen Auftrag und Autonomie.* Stuttgart: Hirzel, 1989.

Konrad von Würzburg. *Der Trojanische Krieg,* ed. Adelbert von Keller. Amsterdam: Rodopi, 1965.

——. *Die goldene Schmiede,* ed. Edward Schröder. Göttingen: Vandenhoeck & Ruprecht, 1969.

——. *Die Legenden: Silvester, Alexius, Pantaleon,* ed. Paul Gereke. Halle: Niemeyer, 1925–1927.

——. *Engelhard,* ed. Paul Gereke. Tübingen: Niemeyer, 1982.

——. *Kleinere Dichtungen,* ed. Edward Schröder. 3 vols. Berlin: Weidmann, 1959–

1963 [*Der Welt Lohn, Das Herzmaere, Heinrich von Kempten, Der Schwanritter. Das Turnier von Nantes, Die Klage der Kunst,* songs].

——. *Partonopier und Meliur,* eds. Karl Bartsch and Franz Pfeiffer. Berlin: de Gruyter, 1871; rpt. 1970.

——. *Trojanerkrieg: Staatsbibliothek Preussischer Kulturbesitz, Ms. germ. fol. 1.* Munich: Lengenfelder, 1989 [color microfiche].

Musica practica. *Minnesänger und Meistersinger Lieder um Konrad von Würzburg.* Freiburg: Christophorus, 1988 [audio recording].

STEPHEN M. CAREY

KORMÁKR QGMUMDARSON (ca. 930–970)

KORMÁKR QGMUMDARSON (ca. 930–970) Kormákr Qgmumdarson was an Icelandic poet, the chief character of *Kormáks saga.* The name (Irish *Cormac*) suggests Celtic family connections. According to Haukr Valdísarson's *Íslendingadrápa,* Kormákr was of high birth (*kynstórr*). The saga belongs to the category of *skáldasögur,* and is particularly remarkable for the large number of verses (*lausavísur*) it contains scattered throughout. Sixty-four of the eighty-five verses are spoken by the hero. Of the remaining ones, fifteen are attributed to his chief rival, Bersi. A few verses are faked, corrupt, or of doubtful origin (in particular 6, 24, 61, 73, and 79). The prose story of the saga, the biography of the poet, is unusually short and constitutes little more than a connecting framework around the many verses. There are linguistic indications that it was composed at the beginning of the 13th century, the earliest period of saga writing.

Its all-dominating theme is the hero's unhappy love story, a love that is never consummated. Right from the start, it contains bizarre elements. A glimpse of a young girl's beautiful ankles is enough to make the poet fall in love and causes a flow of poetic inspiration. He realizes that love for the young Steingerðr is to be his fate for the rest of his life. But although his feelings are reciprocated, and, after incidents in which blood is shed, her father's resistance is overcome, the planned marriage falls through. Paradoxically enough, the direct cause of the failure is Kormákr himself: when the time comes, he does not turn up at the wedding that has already been prepared. According to the saga, the real reason is the harmful spell put upon him by a woman whose sons the poet had killed. Against her will, Steingerðr is married to the scarred warrior Bersi. With the arrogance that always characterizes him, Kormákr insists on his first right to the girl and challenges Bersi to single combat, but after a slight wound has to admit defeat. Scornful verses, challenges, and single combats follow. Steingerðr leaves Bersi and later marries again, this time a peaceful man whom Kormákr deeply despises and mocks.

Off on his Viking journeys, the poet dreams of his beloved and sings the praises of her beauty. What seems to be a promising meeting between the two occurs when Kormákr visits his country, but a night spent with Steingerðr ends in a frustrating anticlimax: the physical role of a lover seems to have been something denied to Kormákr.

One thing is certain: no Icelandic skald can compete with Kormákr as the master of love poetry, which is not, however, his only genre. *Skáldatal* informs us that Kormákr had sung the praises of both Earl Sigurðr in Hlaðir and Haraldr gráfeldr ("grey-cloak") Eiríksson. Only a part of the former's poem has survived; there are seven half-strophes from *Sigurðardrápa*, cited in *Skáldskaparmál* in Snorri's *Edda*, and one complete strophe in *Heimskringla*. An original artistic device of the poet is his way of replacing the *drápa's* refrain (*stef*) by varying mythological allusions that do not seem to have any connection with the content of the rest of the poem. In Snorri's *Háttatal,* this variety of *dróttkvætt* is called *hjástælt.*

A much-discussed theory would have us believe that *Kormáks saga* is an entirely literary product, with prose and poetry as equally authentic literary components. The author, it is suggested, was a 13th-century writer who had been influenced by continental European troubadour poetry and the medieval love poetry of which Tristan is the hero (Bjarni Einarsson 1976). This theory has been contested on both linguistic and literary-historical grounds (Einar Ól. Sveinsson 1966–69, Andersson 1969, Hallberg 1975).

Further Reading

Editions

Einar Ól. Sveinsson, ed. *Vatnsdœla saga.* Íslenzk fornrit, 8. Reykjavik: Hið íslenzka fornritafélag, 1939.

Literature

Wood, Cecil. "Kormak's Stanzas Called the *Sigurðardrápa.*" *Neophilologus* 43 (1959), 305–19.

Hallberg, Peter. *The Icelandic Saga.* Trans. Paul Schach. Lincoln: University of Nebraska Press,' 1962.

Einar Ól. Sveinsson. "Kormákr the Poet and His Verses." *Saga-Book of the Viking Society* 17 (1966–69), 18–60.

Andersson, Theodore M. "Skalds and Troubadours." *Mediaeval Scandinavia* 2 (1969), 7–41.

Frank, Roberta. "Onomastic Play in Kormákr's Verse: The Name Steingerðr." *Mediaeval Scandinavia* 3 (1970), 7–34.

Bjarni Einarsson. "The Lovesick Skald: A Reply to Theodore M. Andersson (*Mediaeval Scandinavia* 1969)." *Mediaeval Scandinavia* 4 (1971) 21–41.

Hallberg, Peter. Old *Icelandic Poetry: Eddic Lay and Skaldic Verse.* Trans. Paul Schach and Sonja Lindgrenson. Lincoln: University of Nebraska Press, 1975.

Turville-Petre, E. O. G. *Scaldic Poetry.* Oxford: Clarendon, 1976.

Bjarni Einarsson. To *skjaldesagaer. En analyse af Kormáks saga og Hallfreðar saga.* Bergen, Oslo, and Tromsø: Universitetsforlaget, 1976.

See, Klaus von. "Skaldenstrophe und Sagaprosa. Ein Beitrag zum Problem der mündlichen Überlieferung in der altnordischen Literatur." *Mediaeval Scandinavia* 10 (1977), 58–82.

Frank, Roberta. *Old Norse Court Poetry: The Dróttkvætt Stanza*. Islandica, 42. Ithaca and London: Cornell University Press, 1978.

See, Klaus von. "Mündliche Prosa und Skaldendichtung. Mit einem Exkurs über Skaldensagas und Trobadorbiographien." *Mediaeval Scandinavia* 11 (1978–79), 82–91.

Schottmann, Hans. "Der Bau der Kormáks saga." *Skandinavistik* 12 (1982) 22–36.

Lie, Hallvard. *Om sagakunst og skaldskap. Utvalgte avhandlinger.* Øvre Ervik: Alvheim & Eide, 1982.

Clover, Carol J., and John lindow, eds. *Old Norse–Icelandic Literature: A Critical Guide*. Islandica, 45. Ithaca and London: Cornell University Press, 1985.

FOLKE STRÖM

KÜRENBERC, DER VON (fl. late 12th c.) Der von Kürenberc is the earliest named German lyric poet. His poems are preserved only in the famous Heidelberg University library *Minnesang* manuscript "C," where he is grouped among the barons. He is possibly a member of the Kürenberg family who had a castle near Linz, Austria, during the mid-twelfth century. He is part of what is known as the Danube or indigenous school, showing very little French influence.

Fifteen stanzas have been preserved. The basic metrical unit is the four-beat half-line; the long lines formed of two such halves are combined in rhyming couplets. There are two stanza patterns: the predominant one of four long lines, which is the basis of the so-called Nibelung stanza, or *Nibelungenstrophe*, and that where a rhymeless line is inserted as the odd fifth half-line. Several are so-called "Women's stanzas," or *Frauenstrophen*, written from the woman's point of view. In one poem, a lady stands at night on battlements, listening to a knight singing from among the crowd, in *kürenberges wîse* (*Minnesangs Frühling [MF]*, no. 8,1). In another poem, the lady is compared with a falcon: women and falcons are easily tamed, if one entices them rightly, they will seek the man (*MF* 10, 17).

Kürenberc makes dramatic and effective use of the *Wechsel*, or lyrical dialogue, alternating speeches of identical length. Frequently the speeches do not make contact; the man and woman talk past each other. In a *Wechsel*, he parodies the figure of the lover who so idealizes the lady that he stands beside her bed and does not dare wake her up, much less think of enjoying her favors (MF8, 9–15). He has a dramatic sense of situations; his lyrics often tell little stories. His best known song has the falcon as its subject, *Ich zôch mir einen valken*, for which many widely differing interpretations have been proposed (MF 8, 33). A person rears a falcon for more than a year, trains and adorns it with gold wire and silken jesses. The falcon flies away "into other lands." Later, the person sees the falcon, still with the gold and the silk, and says: *Got sende si zesamene, die geliep wellen gerne sîn* (God bring those together who wish to be lovers!). The poem might be the literal story of the loss of a falcon or the falcon might be a symbol for a messenger of love, or for the yearning of lovers, or for an unfaithful lover. If the woman is speaking, the poem may be identified as *Frauenstrophen*, if a man, as a *Botenlied*. If it is first the man and then the lady, it is a *Wechsel*.

Der von Kürenberc introduces several elements that appear in later *minnesang*: the message and messenger taken from medieval Latin epistle form; the need for secrecy and fear of spies, *merkære* (slanderers) and *lügenære* (liars); the submissive role of the man.

Further Reading

Agler-Beck, Gayle. *Der von Kürenberg: Edition, Notes, and Commentary*. German Language and Literature Monographs 4. Amsterdam: John Benjamins, 1978.

Heffner, R.-M.S, and Kathe Peterson. *A Word-Index to Des Minnesangs Frühling.*

Madison: University of Wisconsin Press, 1942.

Koschorreck, Walter, and Wilfried Werner, eds. *Codex Manesse. Die Große Heidelberger Liederhandschrift. Faksimile-Ausgage des Cod. Pal. Germ. 848 der Universitdts-Bibliothek Heidelberg.* Kassel: Ganymed, 1981 [facsimile].

Moser, Hugo, and Helmut Tervooren. *Des Minnesangs Frühling unter Benutzung der Ausgdben von Karl Lachmann und Moriz Haupt, Friedrich Vogt und Carl von Kraus.* Stuttgart: Hirzel, 1982.

Rakel, Hans-Herbert S. *Der deutsche Minnesang. Eine Einfrührung mit Texten und Materialien.* Munich: Beck, 1986.

Sayce, Olive. *Poets of the Minnesang. Introduction, Notes and Glossary.* Oxford: University Press, 1967.

Schweikle, Günther. *Die mittelhochdeutsche Minnelyrik,* vol. 1. *Die frühe Minnelyrik. Texte und Übertragungen, Einführung und Kommentar.* Darmstadt: Wissenschaftliche Buchgesellschaft, 1977.

——. *Minnesang.* Stuttgart: Metzler, 1989.

Tervooren, Helmut. *Bibliographie zum Minnesang und zuden Dichtern aus "Des Minnesangs Frühling."* Berlin: Schmidt, 1969, pp. 55–58.

Wapnewski, Peter. "Des Kürenberger's Falkenlied." *Euphorion* 53 (1959): 1–19.

STEPHANIE CAIN VAN D'ELDEN

L

LA VIGNE, ANDRÉ DE (ca. 1457–ca. 1515) Late-medieval poet and playwright. Born between 1457 and 1470 in the port city of La Rochelle, La Vigne was in the service of Marie d'Orléans from ca. 1488 until her death in 1493, when he became secretary to the duke of Savoy. In 1494, in an effort to attract a more powerful protector, he presented a work to King Charles VIII, the *Ressource de la Crestienté*. This poem is a dream allegory in which the king, in the personage of Magesté Royalle, is shown as the protector of Dame Crestienté, who is in peril. Impressed with La Vigne's talents, Charles appointed him historiographer of his military expedition into Italy to conquer the kingdom of Naples (1494–95). The resulting chronicle, the *Voyage de Naples*, is an eyewitness record of the events of the Italian campaign. Like the *Ressource*, it is written in alternating verse and prose.

In May 1496, La Vigne was invited to the town of Seurre in Burgundy, where he was commissioned to write a play on the life of St. Martin, patron of the town. Within five weeks, he had completed not only the *Mystère de saint Martin*, comprising more than 10,000 lines of verse, but also a comic morality play, the *Aveugle et le boiteux*, and a farce, the *Meunier de qui le diable emporte l'âme en enfer*. The mystery play was written to edify the people with scenes from the holy and devout life of their patron saint. To this end, there are sermons, miracles, and conversions, as well as scenes set in Heaven and Hell. The play is also a rich tapestry of daily life, showing people of all sorts and conditions engaged in their daily tasks. La Vigne portrays this milieu from a variety of stylistic perspectives. He sympathetically treats family difficulties and explores the psychology of suffering; he satirizes the abuses of the powerful, the faults of the clergy, and the venality of the merchant class; he depicts the bombast of braggart soldiers and the antics of drunken messengers. All these strands are woven together in a seamless dramatic action in which the playwright deftly alternates affective and comic scenes for maximum effect.

Toward the end of the century, La Vigne collected a number of his early works in the *Vergier d'honneur*. In 1504, he brought suit against Michel Le Noir, a Parisian printer, to stop an unauthorized edition of this work; the Parlement de Paris issued the injunction. Before the death of Charles VIII in 1498, La Vigne had been appointed secretary to the queen, Anne of Brittany. He remained in this capacity until her death in 1514. His later works included epitaphs for his patrons and other panegyric poems. He wrote two other plays, the *Sotise à huit personnages*, attacking the abuses of his day, and the *Moralité du nouveau monde* against the abolition of the Pragmatic Sanction, as well as political poems. In the *Louenge des roys de France*, for example, he supported Louis XII in his quarrel with the pope. Francis I in the year of his accession (1515) named La Vigne his historiographer and charged him with writing the history of his reign. Since only a few pages of the chronicle were completed, La Vigne is thought to have died shortly after.

Further Reading

La Vigne, André de. *Le mystère de saint Martin, 1496*, ed. André Duplat. Geneva: Droz, 1979.
——. *Le voyage de Naples*, ed. Anna Slerca. Milan: Pubblicazioni della Università Cattolica del Sacro Cuore, 1981.
Brown, Cynthia Jane. *The Shaping of History and Poetry in Late Medieval France*: *Propaganda and Artistic Expression in the Works of the Rhétoriqueurs*. Birmingham: Summa, 1985.
Duplat, André. "La *Moralité de l'aveugle et du boiteux* d'Andrieu de la Vigne: étude littéraire et édition." *Travaux de linguistique et de littérature* 21 (1983): 41–79.

ANDRÉ DUPLAT

LANDINI, FRANCESCO (c. 1325–2 September 1397)

Francesco Landini was a composer, organist, singer, instrument maker, and poet of the second generation of the Italian *Trecento*. He may have been born in Fiesole or Florence and was the son of the painter Jacopo Del Casentino (d. 1349), a cofounder of the Florentine guild of painters. Landini lost his sight after having smallpox as a child; as a result, he turned to music with a passion. He mastered several instruments, including the organ; worked as an organ builder, organ tuner, and instrument maker; and played, sang, and wrote poetry. As a scholar, he is recorded as following the teachings of William of Ockham, and

he was knowledgeable in many areas of astrology, philosophy, and ethics. Landini was very active in religious and political events. His musical works indicate that he spent some time in northern Italy before 1370, probably in Venice. He was organist at the monastery of Santa Trinita in 1361; and from 1365 until his death he was *capellanus* at the church of San Lorenzo. His acquaintances included the Florentine chancellor of state and humanist Coluccio Salutati and the composer Andreas de Florentia. In 1379 and 1387, Landini was involved in building organs at the church of Santa Annunziata and at the cathedral of Florence. Giovanni da Prato, in *Il paradiso degli Alberti* (1389), a narrative poetic account of Florence, portrays Landini as an active musician and humanist, taking part in extensive philosophical and political conversations as well as singing and playing the organ. Landini died in Florence, in the church of San Lorenzo; his tombstone was discovered in Prato in the nineteenth century. A picture of Landini can be seen on folio 121v of the Squarcialupi Codex (I-Fl 87). His fame continued well into the fifteenth century. The French musicologist Fetis rediscovered Landini's music in 1827.

Not only was Landini a very prolific composer, but the survival of his musical works attests to his popularity and importance. His extant works represent almost a quarter of the entire known repertoire of secular *Trecento* music. One hundred fifty-four works can be definitely attributed to Landini: ninety *ballate* for two voices, forty-two *ballate* for three voices, eight *ballate* that survive in two-part and three-part versions, one French *virelai*, nine madrigals for two or three voices, one three-voice canonic madrigal, and one *caccia*. Works of doubtful authenticity include two or three *ballate* for two voices, and four motets with fragmentary single voices. More than 145 works by Landini are contained in the Squarcialupi Codex.

Landini's musical style is multifaceted; he wrote works ranging from simple dances to complex isorhythmic and canonic pieces. His compositional technique is often described as a synthesis of French and Italian musical influences. The melodic inventiveness of Landini's music is readily apparent. A special musical cadence—which musicologists call the Landini cadence—appears frequently in his music; it is recognizable at the end of phrases as a leaping upward by an interval of a third. Landini's music points toward the polyphonic imitation in fifteenth-century early Renaissance music.

Further Reading

Editions

The Works of Francesco Landini, ed. Leonard Ellinwood. Cambridge, Mass.: Medieval Academy of America, 1939. (2nd ed., 1945; reprint, New York: Kraus Reprint, 1970.)

The Works of Francesco Landini, ed. Leo Schrade. Polyphonic Music of the Fourteenth Century, 4. Monaco: Éditions de l'Oiseau-Lyre, 1958.

Studies

Ellinwood, Leonard. "Francesco Landini and His Music." *Musical Quarterly*, 22, 1936, pp. 190ff. Fischer, Kurt von. "On the Technique, Origin, and Evolution of Italian Trecento Music." *Musical Quarterly*, 47, 1963, pp. 41ff.

"Landini, Francesco." In *New Grove Dictionary of Music and Musicians*, Vol. 10, pp. 428–434.

BRADFORD LEE EDEN

LANFRANC OF BEC (ca. 1010–1089) Born into a good family in Pavia, Lanfranc was educated in that city and more generally in northern Italy. He left Italy for France while still a young man and made his reputation as an itinerant teacher in the area around Avranches. In 1042, he entered the new monastery at Bec (founded 1041); he was abbot of Saint-Étienne, Caen, in 1063; in 1070, he was made archbishop of Canterbury. He had a dual reputation, first as a teacher and scholar and later as a brilliant administrator and leader.

His scholarship falls into two periods, before and after his entry into Bec. The earlier works, no longer extant, are on the Trivium; after 1042, he devoted himself to theology, writing commentaries on the Psalms and Pauline epistles that circulated widely. About 1063, he wrote a treatise *De sacramento corporis et sanguinis Christi*, against the opinions of Berengar of Tours's *De eucharistia*, and to which Berengar replied in *De sacra coena*. Berengar's ideas caused widespread antagonism and were finally condemned by Pope Gregory VII in 1079. The issue centers on the changes taking place in the bread and wine of the eucharist in order for them to become the body and blood of Christ. Both Berengar and Lanfranc believed in the Real Presence, but they differed on the necessity and type of any change in the elements, Berengar insisting that no material alteration was needed and Lanfranc arguing for outward identity concealing inner grace. The question was compounded by difficulties of language: no clearer statement of the central issue was to be possible until the introduction of Aristotelian notions of substance and accident in the 13th century.

Lanfranc's leadership of the school at Bec made it into one of the most famous of its day, and pupils included Anselm of Bec, Ivo of Chartres, and Guitmund of Aversa (later Pope Alexander II). He was a valued counselor to Duke William of Normandy (the Conqueror) despite having declared William's marriage invalid.

Lanfranc was a great holder of synods (in 1075, 1076, 1078, 1081), which he used to promulgate canon law, and he was the first to create separate courts of ecclesiastical jurisdiction. His legal turn of mind (he seems to have practiced or at least studied civil law in Pavia) was coupled with a traditionalist viewpoint, so that his outlook reminds us of Carolingian attitudes and practices rather than any innovation. The collection of canon law, the so-called *Collectio Lanfranci*, which Lanfranc brought to Canterbury from Bec, has an old-fashioned cast, in contrast to the *Collection in Seventy-Four Titles* (*Diversorum patrum sententiae*) or Ivo of Chartres's *Panormia* and other legal works, the new breed of legal collections that it seems Lanfranc preferred to ignore.

As archbishop of Canterbury, Lanfranc replaced many Saxon bishops with Normans, to the displeasure of some in the English church, but in doing so he increased ties with the Continent and with Gregory VII's reforms, with which, at least in the area of the moral reform of the church, he was largely in sympathy. Lanfranc rebuilt the church at Canterbury and established its library. He reestablished many of the old monastic privileges and lands.

See also **Anselm of Bec; Gregory VII, Pope; William I**

Further Reading

Lanfranc of Bec. *Opera. PL* 150. 1–782.
——. *The Letters of Lanfranc, Archbishop of Canterbury*, ed. Helen Clover and Margaret T. Gibson. Oxford: Clarendon, 1979.
Gibson, Margaret T. *Lanfranc of Bec.* Oxford: Clarendon, 1978.
Huygens, R.B.C. "Bérenger de Tours, Lanfranc et Bernold de Constance." *Sacris Euridiri* 16 (1965): 355–403.
Southern, Richard W., ed. *Essays in Medieval History.* London: Macmillan, 1948.

         Lesley J. Smith

LANGMANN, ADELHEID (ca. 1312–1375)

Born to a politically and socially powerful family in Nuremberg around 1312, at the age of thirteen, Adelheid Langmann was betrothed to Gottfried Teufel, who died shortly afterward. Following what she describes as a lengthy spiritual struggle, around 1330, Adelheid entered the Franconian Dominican cloister of Engelthal. Regarded as a particularly prosperous and renowned cloister, Engelthal housed the daughters of many of the prominent burghers of the area. Among them was Christina Ebner, whose widespread praise included bishops and kings. Adelheid was cloistered at Engelthal in 1350 when King Charles IV (later Emperor Charles) visited the monastery for spiritual advice. She was educated in Latin and learned to read and write in her vernacular German dialect. Shortly after Christina wrote her spiritual autobiography, Adelheid recorded her visions and revelations along with a lengthy prayer dedicated to the Trinity. Her *Revelations*, extant in three manuscript variations, were written in a Bavarian dialect and chronicle her spiritual life from 1330 to 1344. While the content is essentially autohagiographical, representing the religious experiences of its author, there are stylistic similarities and thematic parallels with the mystical lives narrated in the convent chronicles of Helfta, Toss, Unterlinden, Diessenhoven, and Adlehausen. Influenced by biblical sources, especially the Song of Songs, Adelheid's ecstatic mysticism reflects the bride mysticism of the Middle Ages. Her texts, as well as several other manuscripts written by Dominican cloistered women in Southern Germany, were rediscovered and edited by nineteenth-century scholars interested in the linguistic history of German.

See also **Charles IV; Ebner, Margaretha**

Further Reading

Die Offenbarungen der Adelheid Langmann: Klosterfrau zu Engelthal, ed. Phillip Strauch. Strasbourg: Trübner, 1878.
Hale, Rosemary Drage. "*Imitatio Mariae*: Motherhood Motifs in Devotional Memoirs." *Mystics Quarterly* 16 (1990): 193–214.
Hindsley, Leonard P. *The Mystics of Engelthal: Writings from a Medieval Monastery.* New York: St. Martin's Press, 1998.

        Rosemary Drage Hale

LAUFENBERG, HEINRICH (ca. 1390–1460) Laufenberg, a cleric active in Freiburg im Breisgau and Zofingen, composed the bulk of his verses between 1413 and 1445. In the latter year he entered a cloister in Strasbourg that had been founded by Rulman Merswin (d. 1382), the lay mystic and guiding spirit for the so-called Friends of God. Laufenberg is best known as the author of some 120 sacred songs written in the German vernacular, among them Christmas and New Year's verses. His Christmas song *Jn einem krippfly lag ein kind* (In a little crib lay a child) is representative in its straightforward narration, plain diction, and heartfelt religious devotion. Especially pronounced is Laufenberg's veneration of the Virgin Mary; few medieval poets command his breadth of Mariological symbols and tropes. The culmination of his Mariology is the *Buck der Figuren* (1441), a massive versified catalogue and interpretative commentary on more than 100 prefigurations of the Virgin in the Old Testament. Another lengthy work from his pen is the *Regimen sanitatis* (1429), a combination cosmology and medical reference tool of more than 6,000 German verses based on many source texts, Avicenna among them. The *Regimen*, besides treating health concerns, pregnancy, and child-care, examines the solar system, the elements, and natural phenomena—including pestilence. Very popular, Laufenberg's *Regimen* was an early printed book. Rounding out his longer works is a 1437 translation, in 15,000 verses, of a fourteenth-century discourse on salvation, *Speculum humanae salvationis*.

The prolific author, who had regular ecclesiastical duties as pastor, curate, and dean, evinces broad learning, theological sophistication, and mastery of a wide range of vernacular and Latin literary forms. At home in verse and prose, Laufenberg translated Latin church hymns and sequences and composed "mixed" poetry, that is, songs in alternating Latin and German verses. Musical composer and self-aware author in one person (Laufenberg liked to sign and date his compositions), he influenced hymn writing in the Reformation and beyond. As Martin Luther was to do, Heinrich Laufenberg penned many pointed *contrafactura*, appropriating secular texts and melodies for the Christian sphere. His most famous example—and his most famous song—is *Ich wölt, daz ich doheime wer* (I wished I were at home). The "home" of which the singer speaks is heaven; he longs for a home far from earth where he can gaze eternally upon God. In like vein, Laufenberg wrote Christian dawn songs and adapted secular love songs for worship of the Virgin Mary. She appears typically in his verse as the *mülnerin* (the miller's wife/female operator of a mill), a figure who threshes, grinds, and bakes the biblical "corn of wheat" (John 12:24) that is Jesus Christ. Evident everywhere in Laufenberg's work is the desire to increase piety in his broad audience, be these nuns, religious societies, or laymen. That his texts were read silently by individual readers for meditation and private devotion is very probable.

Scholarly research on Heinrich Laufenberg has labored under the loss of unique versions of most of his creations, the result of destruction of manuscripts in Strasbourg during the Franco-Prussian War in 1870. A critical edition of his works has not yet appeared and would necessarily contain presumed transcriptions.

Further Reading

Schiendorfer, Max. "Der Wächter und die Müllerin 'verkert,' 'geistlich.' Fußnoten zur Liedkontrafaktur bei Heinrich Laufenberg." In *Contemplata aliis tradere, Studien zum Verhältnis von Literatur und Spiritualität. Festschrift für Alois Haas zum 60. Geburtstag*, eds. Claudia Brinker, et al. Bern: Lang, 1995, pp. 273–316.

Wachinger, Burghart. "Notizen zu den Liedern Heinrich Laufenbergs." In *Medium aevum deutsch, Beiträge zur deutschen Literatur des hohen und späten Mittelalters. Festschrift für Kurt Ruh zum 65. Geburtstag*, eds. Dietrich Huschenbett, et al. Tübingen; Niemeyer, 1979, pp. 349–385.

WILLIAM C. McDONALD

LA3AMON OR LAYAMON (fl. ca. 1200–25?) Author of the *Brut*, a major poem of the early ME period that contains, among other items of interest, the first account in English of the Arthurian legend. La3amon identifies himself in the opening lines of his poem as a priest residing in Ernle3e (Areley Kings, Worcestershire). Having resolved to write a history of England, he says, he consulted as source material Bede's *Ecclesiastical History*, a Latin book written by Sts. Albin and Augustine, and Wace's *Roman de Brut*. In fact La3amon appears to have made little use of Bede's history (tentatively identified by scholars as the OE translation of Bede) or the untitled Latin text (identified still more tentatively as a book containing selections by Albin and Augustine of Canterbury, the Latin text of Bede, or a mere fiction invented by the poet to display his erudition). Thus, with some significant modifications and additions, La3amon's poem is essentially an English paraphrase of Wace's *Brut* rendered into alliterative long lines, some 16,000 in number. Because of an allusion in the opening lines of the poem to Eleanor, "who was Henry's queen," it is generally accepted that the *Brut* was written some time after the death of Henry II in 1189 and possibly even after the death of Eleanor herself in 1204; but scholarly opinion relating to the precise date of composition ranges from the late 12th century to the second half of the 13th.

The *Brut* survives in two manuscripts dating from 1250–1350. Although both are thought to derive from a common archetype, BL Cotton Caligula A.ix is commonly held to be closer to its exemplar—and hence to La3amon's original text—than is BL Cotton Otho C.xiii. The latter is considered an inferior text because its scribe apparently attempted to modernize his original by eliminating many of the rhetorical embellishments intended to give it what has been called an "antique colouring" (Stanley). These embellishments include lengthy repetitions of detail and incident and archaisms of the type that survive in and characterize the Caligula text—that is, the many coinages and poetic compounds with a distinctly Anglo-Saxon ring about them and the marked preference for words of Anglo-Saxon origin (many of which have been replaced in the Otho text by French loanwords).

In subject matter and method La3amon imitates Wace so as to be able to afford his readers a history of the Britons from the time of Brutus, great-grandson of Aeneas, to the ascendancy of the Saxons over the Britons during the reign of Cadwalader in the 7th century. Lazamon's additions to and modifications of his Anglo-Norman source have much to tell us, however, about his purpose in adapting Wace's poem into English: as scholars have been quick to notice, Lazamon's numerous accounts of feasts, sea voyages, and battles, many of which have no counterparts in Wace's poem, evoke the ethos of OE poetic accounts of such events and seem to have been intended to do so. Similarly Wace's interest in love, courtesy, and the ideals of chivalry is not one that La3amon shares: indeed, in his adaptation of many of the events described in Wace's poem, we find La3amon attempting to recreate the ethos of the heroic, as opposed to the chivalric, world. His Arthur, for example, is not a Norman king presiding over a chivalric court as in Wace, but a Saxon chieftain as disposed to committing acts of brutality and violence as to rewarding his faithful retainers, after a battle, with rings, garments, and horses. As in the meadhalls of OE poetry, there are *scops* in Arthur's court and *dream* (joy) when a victory is being celebrated; by the same token here and elsewhere in the poem there prevails, as in OE verse, an overwhelming sense of the role played by Fate in the human lives, but especially in the lives of those destined to enter the field of battle.

Further evidence of La3amon's familiarity with and desire to imitate the verse of OE poets can be discerned in his use of formulas, not simply as tags and line fillers but also to advance his narrative in a manner in keeping with the formulaic practices of OE poetry. Not surprisingly, perhaps, the *Brut* is most noticeably formulaic in passages tliat have no counterpart in Wace and in which La3amon seems to have been particularly eager to recreate the ethos of the past, such as his accounts of feasts, sea voyages, and battles. Equally indicative of La3amon's admiration for the verse of the OE poets is his use of certain rhetorical tropes and patterns found in their poetry. With an unmistakable sense of what he is about La3amon employs, with varying degrees of frequency, the kenning, the descriptive epithet, the simile, litotes, variation, chiasmus, and more complex structural repetitions, such as the envelope pattern, repetition parallels, and balance parallels.

La3amon's unmistakable nostalgia for the pre-Conquest period is reflected not only in the poem's style and content but also in its verse form. He patterns his verse, like his language and themes, after that of the OE poets. La3amon's basic metrical unit is the alliterative long line consisting of two two-stress hemistichs linked by alliteration, rhyme, or both. His use of rhyme as well as alliteration, of a longer line (to accommodate the hypotactic constructions of ME), and of some metrical patterns that do not conform to the metrical patterns of OE verse suggest that La3amon was working within a much more flexible prosody than that governing the composition of OE poetry; however, his verse should not be relegated, as some of his critics have suggested, to the ranks of "popular" poetry. Rather it is an evolutionary form of the "classical" alliterative verse of the English Middle Ages.

See also **Geoffrey of Monmouth; Wace**

Further Reading

Primary Sources

Brook, G.L., and R.F. Leslie, eds. *La3amon: Brut*. 2 vols. EETS o.s. 250, 277. London: Oxford University Press, 1963–78.

Bzdyl, Donald G., trans. *Layamon's Brut: A History of the Britons*. Binghamton: MRTS, 1989.

Secondary Sources

New *CBEL* 1:460–63

Le Saux, Françoise H.M. *La3amon's Brut: The Poem and Its Sources*. Cambridge: Brewer, 1989.

Le Saux, Françoise H.M. *The Text and Tradition of La3amon's Brut*. Cambridge: Brewer, 1994.

Reiss, Edmund, et al. *Arthurian Legend and Literature: An Annotated Bibliography*. Vol. 1. New York: Garland, 1984, pp. 79–80.

Stanley, E.G. "Layamon's Antiquarian Sentiments." *MÆ* 38 (1969): 23–37.

JAMES NOBLE

LEO III, EMPEROR (c. 680–741, r. 717–741) Leo III (Conon) was a Byzantine—i.e., eastern Roman—emperor. In older works he was mistakenly called "the Isaurian," but research has now established that he was from Germanicea (modern Marash or Maraš in southeastern Turkey). His native tongue was Syriac or Arabic, and as regards religion he was most likely a Jacobite (Syrian Monophysite).

Conon probably changed his original name to the more "Roman" Leo and became religiously orthodox when he joined the Byzantine army. As a young man he became a protégé of Emperor Justinian II during Justinian's second reign (705–711), and he continued to rise during the short reigns of emperors Philippicus (711–713) and Anastasius II (713–715). When Theodosius III (715–717) deposed the latter, Leo marched on Constantinople to avenge Anastasius. With a large Arab land and naval force also approaching Constantinople, Theodosius voluntarily handed Leo the throne.

Leo's greatest achievement was to thwart the Arab siege of Constantinople in 717–718. Although the Arabs continued to be a threat, they never again endangered the existence of the empire. Also important was his promulgation of the *Ecloga*, the first Byzantine legal collection since the *Corpus iuris civilis* of Justinian I.

Leo's espousal of Iconoclasm, which condemned religious art, in 726 caused a revolt in those portions of Italy still under imperial control (Sicily had already shown signs of resistance early in Leo's reign). Tax increases imposed by Leo may also have been a factor in this revolt. Pope Gregory II—who lacked sufficient resources to withstand the Lombards and thus was still dependent on the Byzantines' military power—urged the Italians to exercise moderation, even though Leo (probably at about this time) removed parts of Illyricum from papal jurisdiction. Pope Gregory III, who was less conciliatory, also continued a limited cooperation with the empire; but by this time the popes were allies of the empire rather than its subjects. Leo may have caused some immigration to Italy from the empire's heartland, though this mainly occurred during the reign of his son. Refugees, many of them monks, augmented the existing Italo-Greek population—especially monastic communities—in Rome and central and southern Italy. Iconoclasm seems to have been little enforced in Byzantine Italy.

Further Reading

Editions and Translations

Gouilland, Jean. "Aux origines de l'iconoclasme: Le témoinage de Grègoire II." *Travaux et Mémoires*, 3, 1968, pp. 243–367. (Greek text and French translation of two letters of Pope Gtegory II to Leo III protesting Leo's Iconoclastic policies.)

Le liber pontificalis, ed. Louis Duchesne. Bibliothèque des Écoles Françaises d'Athènes et de Rome. Paris, 1955. (Not a new edition, but incorporates the editor's corrections, deletions, and emendations up to his death and thus supersedes earlier printings. The life of Gregory II in *Liber pontificalis* is the most important source for the effects of Leo III's policies in Italy. As of the present writing there was no English translation of Gregory II's biography or of any other from the Iconoclastic period.)

Nicephorus, Saint, Patriarch of Constantinople. *Breviarium historicum* (*Short History*), trans., with commentary, Cyril Mango. Dumbarton Oaks Texts, 10; Corpus Fontium Historiae Byzantinae, 13. Washington, D.C.: Dumbarton Oaks, 1990. (Short chronicle covering some of the same rime as Theophanes. Nicephorus was an Iconophile patriarch of Constantinople, dismissed by Emperor Leo V.)

Santoro, Anthony, trans. *Theophanes' Chronographia: A Chronicle of Eighth-Century Byzantium*. Gorham, Me.: Heathersfield, 1982. (With maps; translates only the notices from 717 to 803, but these years included most of the Iconoclastic epoch.)

Theophanes. *Chronographia*, ed. Charles de Boor. Leipzig: Teubner, 1883–1885. (Reprint, 1963. Principal Greek source for Leo's reign, but badly informed and often confused on Italian affairs.)

———. *Chronographia: The Chronicle of Theophanes Confessor—Byzantine and Near Eastern History, A.D. 284–813*, trans., with introduction and commentary, Cyril Mango and Roger Scott, with Geoffrey Greatrex. Oxford and New York: Oxford University Press, 1997.

Turtledove, Harry, trans. *The Chronicle of Theophanes: An English Translation of Annus Mundi 6095–6305 (A.D. 602–813)*, with Introduction and Notes. Philadelphia: University of Pennsylvania Press, 1982.

Critical Studies

Anastos, Milton V. "The Transfer of Illyricum, Calabria, and Sicily to the Jurisdiction of the Patriarchate of Constantinople in 732–733." In *Silloge Bizantina in Onore di Silvio Giuseppe Mercati*. Rome, 1957, pp. 14–31.

———. "Leo III's Edict against the Images in the Year 726–727 and Italo-Byzantine Relations between 726 and 730." *Byzantinischen Forschungen*, 3, 1968, pp. 281–327.

Barnard, Leslie W. *The Graeco-Roman and Oriental Background of the Iconoclastic*

Controversy. Byzantina Neerlandica, 5. Leiden: Brill, 1974.

Gero, Stephen. *Byzantine Iconoclasm during the Reign of Leo III, with Particular Attention to the Oriental Sources.* Corpus Scriptorum Christianorum Orientorum, 384, Subsidia, 52. Louvain: Corpussco, 1977. (Source for Leo's early years, though occasionally mistaken on western matters.)

Hodgkin, Thomas. *Italy and Her Invaders,* Vol. 6, *The Lombard Kingdom.* Oxford: Oxford University Press, 1916. (Classic account.)

Noble, Thomas F. X. *The Republic of Saint Peter: The Birth of the Papal State, 680–825.* Philadelphia: University of Pennsylvania Press, 1984. (Full bibliography through the early 1980s.)

Richards, Jeffrey. *The Popes and the Papacy in the Early Middle Ages, 476–752.* London: Routledge and Kegan Paul, 1979.

MARTIN ARBAGI

LEO IX, POPE (1002–1054)

Pope Leo IX was born as Bruno of Egisheim in 1002 into a noble Alsatian family. His early studies were at the regional center in Lorraine of Toul, where, in 1017, he became a canon at the cathedral. Related to the German ruler Conrad II, he served prominently in the royal army in Lombardy in 1026. Conrad appointed him the bishop of Toul in 1027. Inspired by the monastic reform efforts of the tenth and eleventh centuries, Bruno sought to bring the fruits of these movements to such monasteries in his diocese as St. Aper, St. Dié, Moyenmourier, and Remiremont. Reform of the diocesan clergy also was the order of a number of the synods he held. His efforts to reinvigorate his diocese as the bishop of Toul would prepare him for extending these activities to the whole Western Church when he became pope.

The emperor Henry III, his cousin, selected him to be pope in 1048, after the brief reigns of Henry's previous two appointees, and he was crowned at St. Peters with the acclamation of the Roman people. From Lorraine he would summon such like-minded reformers as Humbert, abbot of Moyenmoutiers; Frederick of Liege, the future Pope Stephen IX, and Hugh of Remiremont. Joining the men of the north would be such Italian churchmen as Peter Damian and Hildebrand, the future Pope Gregory VII, to become the nucleus of what became the college of cardinals. Aided by the efforts of these and other reforming churchmen, the new pope sought through the holding of numerous regional synods in Italy, Germany, and the kingdom of the French to curb the problems of simony, nicolaitism (opposition to celibacy), and violence against churchmen and the poor and to deal with numerous other problems facing the church in this period. Pope Leo presided over these gatherings and exhibited the presence of the papacy to a substantial portion of Western Christendom, quite unlike that of his predecessors. He extended papal protection to monasteries in a series of charters and in 1050 issued a canonical collection that drew on earlier rulings to support his papal activities. His aggressive attempt to deal with the problems faced by the church is also apparent in his personally leading an army into southern Italy in 1053, with the approval of Henry III, to oppose the Normans, a major preoccupation in the latter part of his papacy, because they were such a threat to the ecclesiastical and papal political holdings in the region. The Normans defeated the army of the pope in June of that year and held Leo captive. Incensed by this invasion into a region where the Byzantines had claims, Patriarch Michael Cerularius of Constantinople closed the Latin churches in his city. Humbert was dispatched from Rome to lead a papal embassy to try to solve the problem. The result was not the desired rapprochement but a mutual excommunication by Humbert and the patriarch and the beginning, in July of 1054, of the great schism between Rome and Constantinople, between the Western Church and the Eastern Church that continues to the present. Pope Leo, however, was not alive to witness the separation. He died in April of that year in Rome shortly after his release from Norman captivity.

John of Fécamp called Pope Leo "the marvelous pope" (*papa mirabilis*), a title that in many ways he well deserved. His papacy marks an important moment in the history of the church. His achievements provided the foundation for the Gregorian reform and the future papal monarchy. He brought the presence of the bishop of Rome to many parts of Western Christendom, in a manner comparable to the papal global travels in the late twentieth century. At the Council of Rheims, he used the title of universal to emphasize the scope of the power of the vicar of Peter. His very name demonstrates his awareness of the singular importance of his position, so clearly delineated in the Petrine doctrine of Leo the Great. But he also utilized the Donation of Constantine to justify his actions in southern Italy where he aggressively displayed his leadership in a new papal militarism that looked forward to the summons of the First Crusade by Urban II in 1095. This aggressive leadership, however, also led to the great schism of 1054, a separation that has had a profound importance in the history of the church and of Europe as a whole. Few papacies, if any, have marked such a major change in the direction of the church.

See also **Conrad II; Gregory VII, Pope; Henry III; Damian, Peter; Urban II, Pope**

Further Reading

Analecta Bollandiana 25 (1906): 258–297 [Brussels, 1892ff.; continues *Acta Sanctorum*].

Brucker, P. P. *L'Alsace et l'Eglise au temps du pape saint Léon IX (Bruno d'Egisheim) 1002–1054*, 2 vols. Strasbourg: F. X. Le Roux, 1889.

Fliche, A. *La réforme grégorienne*, vol. 1 Louvain: Spicilegium sacrum louvaniense, 1924.

Leo IX, in *Acta Sanctorum*. London: Snowden, 164lff. April 11, pp. 641–673 [lives of saints by calendar].

Migne, Jaques-Paul, ed. *Patrologia Latina*, vol. 143. Paris: Migne, 1882, cols. 457–800.

Nicol, D. M. "Byzantium and the Papacy in the Eleventh Century." *Journal of Ecclesiastical History* 13 (1962): 1–20.

Tellenbach, Gerd. *The Church in Western Europe from the Tenth to the Early Twelfth Century*, trans. T. Reuter. Cambridge, England: Cambridge University Press, 1993.

Daniel F. Callahan

LEODEGUNDIA In addition to Egeria, other Iberian women were involved in literary activities in the early Middle Ages. Some wrote letters of a more or less artistic nature. Some participated, in various ways, in producing texts. Such is the case with Leodegundia of Bobadilla, a Galician nun who wrote a *Codex regularum,* a Visigothic compendium that was widely read for centuries. Her manuscript is one of the oldest versions of this work, which typically contains the teachings and lives of the holy fathers of the church.

The manuscript, which was moved from Oviedo to the Escorial (a.I.13) in the sixteenth century, includes the following colophon: "O vos omnes qui legeritis hunc codicem mementote/clientula et exigua Leodigundia qui hunc scripsi in monasterio Bobatelle regnante Adefonso principe in era 950 quisquis pro alium oraver it semetipsum deum commendat." The manuscript appears to refer to King Alfonso II and presumably was written in 850 rather than 950.

Leodegundia's calligraphy has been highly praised. However, it is logical to assume she did more than copy the manuscript. In addition to the usual teachings and lives of the holy fathers, her version of the *Codex regularum* contains St. Jerome's letters to women friends, St. Augustine's letter to his sister Marceline, St. Leander's letters to his sister Florentina, and the lives of a number of women saints. That the additions have to do with women would seem not to be a coincidence. Neither would the fact that some of the women saints are of Spanish origin, and one, St. Melanie, is believed to have made her living by writing. Rather, this collection appears to be a mirror in which its author and her audience, the nuns of her convent, recognize themselves, a feminine adaptation of a masculine work.

Further Reading

Antolín, G. "Historia y descriptión de un *Codex regularum* del siglo LX (Eiblioteca del Escorial: a.1.13)." *Ciudad de Dios 75* (1908), 23–33, 304–16, 460–71, 637–49.
Benedictines of Bouvert. *Colophons de manuscrits occidentaux des origines au XVIᵉ sie"le*. Fribourg, 1976, 36.
Pérez de Urbel, J. *Los monjes españoles en la Edad Media*. 2 vols. Madrid, 1934.

CRISTINA GONZÁLEZ

LEÓN, MOSÉS DE (1250–1305) Spanish cabalist. *Cabala* means "receiving," referring to that which has been handed down by tradition. By the time of Mosés de León, the term was used to denote the mystic and esoteric teachings and practices of a growing body of mystical literature.

Little is known about his life; he settled in Guadalajara sometime between 1275 and 1280 and relocated to Avila sometime after 1291. Best known for his revelation of the *Zohar* (*The Book of Splendor or Enlightenment*) to fellow cabalists, he also composed twenty cabalistic works, only two of which have been printed: *Ha-Nephesh ha Hakhamah* (*The Wise Soul*) and *Shekel ha-Kodesh*. (*The Holy Shekel, or Weight*). By 1264 he undertook the study of Maimonides' Neoplatonic philosophy, a belief system that rejected a literal interpretation of Torah and sought to spiritualize its teachings.

While in Guadalajara, Mosés de León composed a mystical midrash, which he titled *Midrash ha-Ne'elam* (*Concealed, Esoteric Midrash*). A midrash is an analytical text that seeks to uncover the meaning of biblical passages, words and phrases

and often employs philology, etymology, hermeneutics, homiletics, and imagination. This work represents the earliest stratum of the *Zohar* and contains commentary on parts of the Torah and the Book of Ruth. Between 1280 and 1286, he produced the main body of the *Zohar,* a mystical commentary on the Torah written in Aramaic, which is spoken by Rabbi Shim'on ben Yohai and his disciples as they ruminate over distinct passages of the Torah.

The text upon which the *Zohar* was purportedly based was said to have been sent from Israel to Catalonia, where it fell into the hands of Mosés de León of Guadalajara, who assumed the task of copying and disseminating different portions of it from the original manuscript. After the Mamluk conquest of the city of Acre (Israel) in 1291, Isaac, son of Samuel, was one of the few to escape to Spain. When he arrived in Toledo in 1305, he heard reports about the existence of a newly discovered midrash of Rabbi Shim'on ben Yohai. Ostensibly written in Israel, the manuscript was unfamiliar to Isaac. He sought out Mosés de León, who assured him that he owned the original ancient manuscript upon which the *Zohar* was based and offered to show it to him if he came to his residence in Avila. After their separation, Moses became ill and died in Arévalo on his way home. When Isaac learned of the news, he traveled to Avila, where he was told that the wife of provincial tax-collector Joseph of Avila was living. After Mosés de León's death, Joseph de Avila's wife had made a deal in which she would offer her son's hand in marriage to the daughter of Mosés de León's widow in exchange for the ancient manuscript. During Isaac's visit, Joseph de Avila's wife denied that her late husband had ever possessed such a book, insisting instead that Mosés de León had composed it himself.

Mosés de León attributed the work to Shim'on ben Yohai, a famous teacher of the second century A.D. known for his piety and mysticism. Ben Yohai lived in

Israel, where he reportedly spent twelve years in seclusion in a cave. After his death, his book was either hidden away or secretly transmitted from master to disciple. When Mosés de León began circulating booklets among his friends containing previously unknown teachings and tales, he claimed to be a mere scribe copying from an ancient book of wisdom. In addition, he distributed portions of the book rather than entire copies. No complete manuscript of the work has ever been found. When the *Zohar* was first printed in Italy in the fifteenth century, the editors combined several manuscripts to produce a complete text. Other manuscripts located later were added to an additional volume which was printed later. Today, most standard editions comprise some 1,100 leaves consisting of at least two dozen separate compositions.

The *Zohar* consists of a mystical commentary on the Pentateuch, describing how God—referred to by the cabalists as *Ein Sof* (the infinite, endless)—rules the universe through the Ten *Sefirot* (Ten Spheres). In other cabalistic texts, the sefirot are often organized in the form of a hierarchy of divine emanations from the apex of the Godhead with *Keter* or *Da'at* (the highest aspect of God) being followed by *Hokhmah* and *Binah* (divine wisdom and understanding respectively). Ein Sof is rarely emphasized in the *Zohar*. Instead, the work focuses on the sefirot as the manifestations of Ein Sof, its mystical attributes in which God thinks, feels, and responds to the human realm. The characters include Rabbi Shim'on and his comrades, biblical figures and the sefirot. At times the distinction between the latter two is ambiguous. Throughout the work, the *Zohar* never loses sight of its goal: to create a mystical commentary on the Torah in which God is simultaneously revealed and concealed. To study Torah is to meditate on the name of God. As Daniel C. Matt explains, "*Zohar* is an adventure, a challenge to the normal workings of consciousness. It dares you

to examine your usual ways of making sense, your assumptions about tradition, God, and self. Textual analysis is essential, but you must engage *Zohar* and cultivate a taste for its multiple layers of meaning. It is tempting and safe to reduce the symbols to a familiar scheme: psychological, historical, literary, or religious. But do not forfeit wonder."

The authorship of the text, its method of composition and its use of sources (contemporary or ancient) have remained polemical among scholars. Among the most representative opinions in this controversy are Jellinek, Graetz, Scholem, and Giller. Jellinek concluded that many of the passages in the *Zohar* were derived from ancient sources and that Mosés de León was at least one of the authors of the work. Graetz concurred with Jellinek on the nature of its sources, but believed that the text represented a forgery executed entirely by Mosés de León. Scholem argued that the text was purely a product of the thirteenth century and was based on medieval Jewish Neoplatonism and Gnosticism. For him, the author and the translator were one and the same. More recent scholarship in the tradition of Giller and Liebes tends to view the *Zohar* as the product of a group collaboration among thinkers who grappled with cabalistic doctrine. Mosés de León was a main figure in this group but is not the sole author.

Regarding the overall structure of the *Zohar*, there is some consensus among scholars. The work is divided into distinct sections or strata, each of which has its own literary nature and mystical doctrines which are unique to it. The *Midrash ha-Ne'elam* is the earliest and is followed by the long midrash on the Torah and another group of compositions resembling it; the *Tiqqunei ha-Zohar* (*Embellishments on the Zohar*) and the *Ra'aya Meheimna* (*The Faithful Shepherd*) constitute another stratum. The *Midrash ha-Ne'elam* establishes an organizing fulcrum for the entire work in creating a protagonist

Shim'on bar Yohai who does not appear until later. Until his subsequent appearance in the text, the teachings are conveyed by other rabbis from the second century with no single dominant figure. Further, there is a pattern of development in which certain ideas and themes are developed and reach their culmination over the course of the work's composition.

The *Zohar* was not accepted immediately as an ancient work. Students of Rabbi Solomon ibn Adret of Barcelona treated it with restraint. In 1340, the philosopher and cabalist Joseph ibn Waqqar warned about the preponderance of errors in the book. Slowly, its antiquity became accepted by cabalists, but as late as the mid-fifteenth century was not read or circulated except in small circles. It did not become the Bible of the Cabalah movement until after the Jewish expulsion from Spain in 1492. After 1530, Safed (Israel) gained importance as a meeting place for cabalists. Among them was Mosés Cordovero who wrote two systematic books based on the *Zohar*, along with an extensive commentary. Isaac Luria developed a new system based on Cabalah that relied heavily on portions of the *Zohar*. The trend of mystical-ethical literature emerging from this circle helped popularize the *Zohar*'s teachings as did the messianic fervor that encouraged the dissemination of its enigmas. If early qabbalists had drawn an analogy between spread of Cabalah and the redemption of Israel, in the sixteenth century, studying the *Zohar* became elevated to the level of a divine command, equal in importance to studying the Bible and the Talmud. Today, the *Zohar* retains its distinction as the fundamental text of cabalistic thought.

See also **Ibn Adret, Solomon; Maimonides**

Further Reading

Fine, L. *Essential Papers on Kabbalah*. New York, 1995.

Giller, P. *Reading the Zohar: The Sacred Text of the Kabbalah*. Oxford, 2001.

Holtz, B. (ed.) *Back to the Sources: Reading the Classic Jewish Texts*. New York, 1984.

Liebes, Y. *Studies in the Zohar*. Trans. A. Schwartz, St. Nakache, and P. Peli. Albany, N.Y., 1993.

Matt, D. C. (ed.) *Zoliar: Book of Enlightenment*. New York, 1983. 38.

MATTHEW B. RADEN

LÉONIN (Leoninus; fl. 1154–ca. 1201) Anonymous 4's epithet *optimus organista* ("the best singer/improviser/composer/compiler/notator of organum") assured Léonin a significant place in music history long before any convincing identification of the person was suggested. Since he was responsible for the new polyphonic repertory of the cathedral of Notre-Dame in Paris in the decades after its founding in the 1160s, his place was evidently among the dignitaries of its ecclesiastical hierarchy, but the familiar use of the Latin diminutive of his name, as "Magister Leoninus," in the theoretical treatise of Anonymous 4—the only source for information on his considerable musical achievement—long seemed to belie this. Anonymous 4 credited Léonin with the *Magnus liber organi de gradali et antifonario* some one hundred years after its compilation, a fact that recommends cautious use of his testimony and the need for independent verification. Three major manuscript sources (*W1*, *F*, and *W2*) confirm a repertory of organum that fits Anonymous 4's description of a *Magnus liber organi*, and the melodies of the plainchant that form the basis of that organum match notated plainchant sources used at Notre-Dame. Still, this does not clarify what Léonin's role may have been in making such a book. *Optimus organista* suggests a youthful man in full voice, while the diminutive implies a beloved elder whose practical contributions may have been overshadowed by his administrative usefulness—two very different "portraits" of the individual. It may not have been so much by his initiative as by his approval that modal rhythm became the primary innovation of the Notre-Dame School, and there is no certain evidence that such rhythm was subject to systematic theoretical or notational principles during his lifetime.

Archival evidence only recently brought to light establishes a probable identity for Anonymous 4's Magister Leoninus as Magister Leoninus presbyter, a canon active in the affairs of the cathedral during the late 12th century and a Latin poet whose hexametric Old Testament commentary, *Hystorie sacre gestas ab origine mundi*, was long praised after his death. There is, however, no document, except possibly the treatise of Anonymous 4, to substantiate the involvement of Leoninus presbyter with music at all, a striking omission given the significance of the *Magnus liber organi* and the stature of the poet. Thus, while the search for independent, corroborating evidence continues, the hypothesis that Leonin, known also as Magister Leoninus presbyter, was responsible for the vanguard of virtually a new era in music with the *Magnus liber organi* should remain compelling.

See also **Pérotin**

Further Reading

Reckow, Fritz. *Der Musiktraktat des Anonymus 4*. Wiesbaden: Steiner, 1967.
Wright, Craig. "Leoninus, Poet and Musician," *Journal of the American Musicological Society* 39 (1986): 1–35.

SANDRA PINEGAR

LEOVIGILD (d. 586) The brother of Liuva I (r. 568–72/3), who made him coruler in 569, with responsibility for the south and center of the Iberian Peninsula, Leovigild proved to be perhaps the greatest of the kings of Visigothic Spain. Even those who opposed his religious policies, such as Isidore of Seville and John of Biclaro, admired his military capacity and achievements. At the time of his accession the kingdom was threatened by Frankish aggression from the north and Byzantine aggression in the southeast. Much of the north of the peninsula and various areas in the south, including the city of Córdoba, had broken free of royal control. An independent Suevic kingdom survived in the northwest. Leovigild's initial campaigns were directed against the Byzantine enclave, and he regained Sidonia and Málaga. In 572, he reimposed Visigothic rule on Córdoba. Following the death of his brother Liuva I, Leovigild turned his attention northward, and in a series of campaigns between 573 and 577 made himself master of most of the north of the peninsula, from the Rioja to the frontiers of the Suevic kingdom, whose ruler Miro became tributary to him. In the peaceful years of 578 and 579, the king established the new town of Recco-polis, named after his younger son, and also set up his elder son Hermenegild in Seville as coruler with responsibility for the south. This failed when Hermenegild rebelled, at the instigation of Leovigild's second wife, Goisuintha, widow of the former Visigothic king Athanagild (r. 554–568). Initially Leovigild made no move to curtail his son's independence, and in 581 launched a campaign northward to contain the Basques. There he founded another new town, called Victoriacum (probably Olite in Navarre). Only when an alliance between Hermenegild and the Byzantines developed, symbolized by the former's conversion to Catholicism, did Leovigild act. In 583 he took Mérida and Seville, and in 584 Córdoba, where Hermenegild was captured. After the suppression of the revolt in the south, Leovigild overran the Suevic kingdom in the northwest, where the son of his former ally Miro had recently been overthrown by a usurper. With this achieved, the Basques temporarily pacified, and a Frankish invasion of the province of Narbonensis repelled in 585, Leovigild had achieved a military reunification of the Visigothic kingdom in the peninsula and Septimania. To turn this into a genuine political and cultural unification required the solution of the theological division between Arians and Catholics, which had provided a context for factionalism and local power struggles. This problem Leovigild hoped to tackle by holding a council in Toledo in 580 with the aim of modifying the theological tenets of Arianism, to make this view of the Trinity more acceptable. In the outcome, the polarization of religious and political opinion following the conversion of Hermenegild in 582 made such a compromise unworkable. The only solution was the acceptance by all of the uncompromising doctrinal stand of the Catholics. It is reported in Gregory of Tours's *histories* that Leovigild himself secretly converted prior to his death in 586, but the public resolution of the issue was left to his heir Reccared.

Further Reading

Collins, R. "Mérida and Toledo, 550–585." In Visigothic Spain: New Approaches. Ed. E. James: Oxford, 1980. 189–219.

Stroheker, K. F. "Leowigild. Aus einer Wendezeit westgotischer Geschichte," Die Welt als Geschichte 5 (1939), 446–485.

Thompson, E. A. The Goths in Spain. Oxford, 1969, 57–91.

ROGER COLLINS

LEVI BEN GERSHOM (GERSONIDES)

(1288–1344) Although he was born and lived his entire life in then French Provence, Gersonides was the heir of the Spanish Hebrew-Arabic medieval culture. Deeply influenced by Averroës and Maimonides in philosophy and by Abraham ibn Ezra in biblical exegesis, Gersonides not only excelled in both these areas but also made important contributions to astronomy and mathematics. Besides inventing or improving upon several astronomical observational instruments, he compiled his own astronomical tables, made many of his own observa-

tions, and engaged in a critical analysis of several of Ptolemy's hypotheses. In mathematics he wrote a commentary on parts of Euclid's *Elements* and a treatise on trigonometry.

But it was in philosophy and biblical exegesis that Gersonides was most influential. Continuing the tradition of the Córdoban philosopher Averroës, Gersonides wrote many supercommentaries on Averroës's commentaries on Aristotle, in which he exhibited a critical and independent approach to both his predecessors. But it is *The Wars of the Lord* that is his most important philosophical work. In this long treatise most of the topics of medieval philosophy and science are discussed in detail and with acuity. Some of his more novel or radical conclusions were (1) the individual human intellect is immortal (contrary to Averroës); (2) God does not have knowledge of particular future contingent events (contrary to Maimonides); (3) yet there is divine providence over deserving individuals; (4) the universe was divinely created out of an eternal shapeless body (contrary to Averroës and Maimonides); (5) although it has a beginning, the universe is indestructible (contrary to Aristotle).

Whereas *The Wars of the Lord* elicited considerable criticism from his coreligionists, Gersonides' commentaries upon the Bible were widely studied, even among nonphilosophical Jews; his *Commentary on Job* was particularly popular. This is remarkable because in these commentaries Gersonides pulls no punches: the ideas of *The Wars of the Lord* are repeated or assumed, and there is no effort to mute their impact. He did not obey Averroës's and Maimonides' rule that the teaching of philosophy ought to be reserved for the philosophers alone. In his *Commentary on Job*, for example, he has each character represent a distinct philosophical position on the question of divine providence. These various positions are philosophically analyzed, and eventually one emerges as the true solution to Job's predicament.

Thus, the Book of Job is transformed into a Platonic dialogue.

See also **Averroës, Abu 'L-Walīd Muhammad B. Ahmad B. Rushd; Gregory of Tours; Isidore of Seville, Saint**

Further Reading

Levi ben Gershom. *The Wars of the Lord*. 2 vols. Trans. Seymour Feldman. Phildelphia, 1984–87. Touati, C. *La Pensée philosophique et théologique de Gersonide*. Paris, 1974.

SEYMOUR FELDMAN

LIMBOURG BROTHERS (fl. late 14th–early 15th c.) Three brothers (Paul, Jean, and Herman), nephews of the painter Jean Malouel, came to Paris

Limbourg Brothers. January: The Feast of the Duke of Berry. Illustrated manuscript page from *Les Très Riches Heures de Duc de Berry*, 1416. Ms. 65; fol. 1V. Photo: R.G. Ojeda. © Réunion des Musées Nationaux/Art Resource, New York.

from Nijmegen in the Low Countries as youths to serve as apprentices under a goldsmith but had to leave because of the plague. Imprisoned on their way home in 1399, they were ransomed by Philip the Bold, duke of Burgundy, for whom they illuminated a Bible, now lost, between 1400 and 1404. They may have been in the service of John, duke of Berry, by 1405; for him, they produced their most notable works: miniatures in the *Très Belles Heures de Notre Dame* (B.N. n.a. lat. 3093), a miniature of the duke of Berry embarking on a journey in the *Petites Heures* (B.N. lat. 18014), some scenes in *grisaille* for a *Bible historiale* (B.N. fr. 166), the illuminations of the *Belles Heures* (New York, The Cloisters), and, most notably, miniatures in the *Très Riches Heures* (Chantilly, Musée Condé), which remained unfinished in 1416, when all three brothers and their patron appear to have died in an epidemic.

Their miniatures, particularly in the *Très Riches Heures*, are representative of the height of the International Gothic style in France, combining courtly elegance, sumptuous coloration, and a mixture of fanciful and remarkably naturalistic landscape settings. Although attempts have been made to define the style of each of the brothers, these have not always been successful, and they are generally regarded to have participated collectively on their productions.

See also **John, Duke of Berry; Philip the Bold**

Further Reading

Longnon, Jean, and Raymond Cazelles. *The Très Riches Heures of Jean, Duke of Berry*. New York: Braziller, 1969.

Meiss, Millard. *French Painting in the Time of Jean de Berry: The Limbourgs and Their Contemporaries*. 2 vols. New York: Braziller, 1974.

——, and Elizabeth H. Beatson. *The Belles Heures of Jean, Duke of Berry*. New York: Braziller, 1974.

ROBERT G. CALKINS

LIUDPRAND OF CREMONA (c. 920–972) Liudprand (Liutprand, Liuzo) was bishop of Cremona (961–972) and also a historian and diplomat. He was born in Pavia in northern Italy into a wealthy family who may have been either merchants or urban aristocrats. His father (who died young) and stepfather had served Hugh of Aries, king of Italy, as diplomats. Liudprand himself went to Constantinople, capital of the Byzantine (eastern Roman) empire, in 949 during the reign of Constantine VII (called Porphyrogenitus) on a mission for Hugh's successor, Berengar of Ivrea. Liudprand fell out with Berengar and went into exile at the court of Otto I, duke of Saxony. There, Liudprand met Recemund, bishop of Elvira in Muslim Spain, who suggested that Liudprand write a history of their time. The result was *Antapodosis*. Liudprand rose in Otto's favor, was granted the see of Cremona, and accompanied Otto on an expedition to Italy that resulted in Otto's coronation as emperor in February 962. Liudprand went on at least two missions to Constantinople on behalf of Otto: in 960 (when he seems not to have reached Constantinople); and in 968–969, during the reign of Nicephorus II Phocas, to arrange a marriage with a Byzantine princess for Otto's son, Otto II. The second embassy was a miserable failure, but later Nicephorus's successor, John I Tzimisces, did consent to a match between Otto II and Theophano. Liudprand probably went to Constantinople a fourth time in 972 (though he seems to have been reluctant to do so, possibly because of ill health) to help escort Theophano to the west; and apparently he died at some point during that trip.

Liudprand's principal works are *Antapodosis* (translated into English as *Tit for Tat* or *The Book of Retribution*); *Relatio de legatio Constantinopolitana* (*Report on the Embassy to Constantinople*), i.e., the embassy of 968–969; and *Liber de rebus gestibus Ottonis* (*The Deeds of Otto*), i.e., Otto I. Recent scholarship (Bischoff 1984) has also identified Liudprand as author of a sermon given at Easter c. 960.

Antapodosis is a gossipy history running from 887 to 949. It forms our principal guide to northern and central Italy during that confused period and contains much information on other areas: Germany, Burgundy, southern Italy, and the Byzantine empire—especially Constantinople. *Antapodosis* was written to show that the major figures in Italian politics of the first half of the tenth century whom Liudprand disliked—notably Berengar of Ivrea and his wife, Willa—eventually met bad ends. Though an excellent storyteller, Liudprand obviously does not pretend to be impartial.

Relatio is bitterly anti-Byzantine. It is often cited to show the growing estrangement of the Latin west from Byzantium but in fact demonstrates no such thing. Liudprand's tirades against the "Greeks" are a result of the hostile and demeaning treatment he received at the hands of Emperor Nicephorus. There is no trace of anti-Greek sentiment in *Antapodosis*, which gives a good-natured account of Liudprand's mission of 949. The fascinating narrative and Liudprand's caustic humor compensate for the whining tone of *Relatio*.

The Deeds of Otto is a record not of the great Saxon ruler's entire reign (Liudprand died a year before Otto), but of one incident: the deposition of Pope John XII by Otto in 963.

Despite his admiration for and devotion to Otto and the Saxons, Liudprand is a figure essentially centered on the Mediterranean. He claimed to know Greek and interlarded his work with Greek words (followed by their Latin translations). Although some scholars consider this merely a display of pedantry, most now believe that Liudprand did know the spoken Byzantine tongue of his day (which was closer to modern than to classical Greek), and perhaps some classical or *koiné* Greek as well. Although Liudprand had the requisite education and social background for a diplomat, his effectiveness was vitiated by his explosive temper (amply demonstrated in *Legatio*) and his acerbic disposition (of which *Antapodosis* is a prime example). His urbane, witty, sarcastic, and occasionally ribald style makes him sound curiously modern, especially if one reads him in a good translation.

See also **Otto I; Otto II**

Further Reading

Editions

Bischoff, Bernard. "Einer Osterpredigt Liudprands von Cremona (um 960)." In *Anecdota novissima: Texte des vierten bis sechzehnten Jahrhunderts—Quellen und Untersuchungen zur lateinischen Philologie des Mittelalters*, Vol. 7. Stuttgart, 1984, pp. 93–100. (First publication of the text of an Easter sermon by Liudprand, previously anonymous, c. 960.)

Liudprand of Cremona. *Opera omnia Liudprandi Cremonensis*, ed. Paolo Chiesa. Corpus Christianorum. Continuatio Mediaevalis. Turnholti: Brepois, 1998.

Translatio Sanctae Hymeri, ed. Ferdinand Ughelli. Itala Sacra, 4. Rome: Vitale Mascardi, 1592, cols. 797–798. (Includes a notice of Liudprand's death. Reprinted in Monumenta Germaniae Historica, Scriptorum, 3. Hannover and Leipzig: Hanische Buchhandlung, 1839, pp. 266–267, note 23.)

Translations

Relatio de Legatio Constantinopolitana, ed., trans., intro., and commentary by Brian Scott. Reading Medieval and Renaissance Texts. Bristol: Bristol Classical Press, 1993. (With textual notes.)

The Works of Liudprand of Cremona, trans. and intro. F. A. Wright. Broadway Medieval Library. London: Routledge, 1930. (Classic English translation. Includes *Translatio Hymeri* but not the Easter Sermon. Wright substitutes French for the Greek words in the original, creating much the same effect.)

Critical Studies

Halphen, Louis. "The Kingdom of Burgundy." In *The Cambridge Medieval History*, Vol.

3, *Germany and the Western Empire*. Cambridge: Cambridge University Press, 1922, ch. 6.

Hiestand, Rudolf. *Byzanz und das Regnum italicum im 10. Jahrhundert*. Geist und Werke zu Zeit. Zurich: Fretz and Wasmuth, 1964.

Koder, Johannes, and Thomas Weber. *Liutprand von Cremona in Konstantinopel*. Herausgegeben von der Kommission für Fühchristliche und Östkirchliche Kunst der Österreichischen Akademie der Wissenschaften und vom Institut für Byzantinistik und Neograzistik der Universität Wien, 13. Vienna: Verlag der Österreichischen Akademie der Wissenschaften, 1980. (Two brief monographs: one is on Liudprand's knowledge of Greek, with a glossary of all Greek words in his works; the second essay uses Liudprand as a source for the diet of the period in Byzantium and the west.)

Kreutz, Barbara. *Before the Normans: Southern Italy in the Ninth and Tenth Centuries*. Philadelphia: University of Pennsylvania Press, 1991.

Leyser, Karl. "Ends and Means in Liudprand of Cremona." In *Byzantium and the West, c. 850–c. 1200: Proceedings of the XVIII Spring Symposium of Byzantine Studies, Oxford, 30th March–1st April 1984*, ed. J. D. Howard-Johnston. Amsterdam: Adolf Hakkert, 1988, pp. 119–143. (Survey in English of Liudprand's work that also summarizes scholarship.)

Lintzel, M. *Studien über Liudprand von Cremona*. Historische Studien, 3. 1933. (A standard monograph.)

Previté-Orton, Charles. "Italy in the Tenth Century." In *The Cambridge Medieval History*, Vol. 3, *Germany and the Western Empire*. Cambridge: Cambridge University Press, 1922, ch. 7.

Rentschler, Michael. *Liudprand von Cremona: Eine Studie zum öst-westlichen Kulturgefälle im Mittelalter*. Frankfurter Wissenschaftliche Beiträge, 14. Frankfurt: Vittorio Klosrermann, 1981.

Sutherland, J. N. "The Idea of Revenge in Lombard Society in the Eighth and Tenth Centuries: The Cases of Paul the Deacon and Liudprand of Cremona." *Speculum*, 50, 1975, pp. 391–410 (Revenge is a major theme in *Antapodosis*.)

MARTIN ARBAGI

LLULL, RAMÓN (1232/3–1316)
Catalan lay missionary, philosopher, mystic, poet, and novelist, Ramón Llull was one of the creators of literary Catalan; the first European to write philosophy and theology in a vernacular tongue; the first to write prose novels on contemporary themes; and the founder of a combinatory "art" that was a distant forerunner of computer science. He wrote some 265 works in Catalan, Latin, Arabic (none of these last have been preserved), and perhaps Provençal. In addition we have medieval translations of his works into Spanish, French, and Italian.

Life

Born on the island of Mallorca (modern-day Majorca), which had only recently been reconquered (at the end of 1229), and brought up in a wealthy family in a colonial situation, amid a still considerable Muslim population (perhaps a third of the entire population of the island), Llull's youth was that of a courtier who dabbled in troubadour verse. He married, had two children, and was appointed seneschal to the future Jaume II of Mallorca. Then, in 1263, repeated visions of the Crucifixion made him decide to dedicate his life to the service of Christ, and specifically to carrying out three aims: to try to convert Muslims even if it meant risking his life; to "write a book, the best in the world, against the errors of unbelievers"; and to found monasteries for the teaching of languages to missionaries. Llull bought a Muslim slave in order to learn Arabic and began nine years of study not only of that language, but also of Latin, philosophy, theology, and logic, as well as a certain amount of law, medicine (surely in Montpellier), and astronomy. At the end of this period he wrote a compendium of Al-Ghazālī's logic and the *Llibre de contemplació en Déu* (Book of Contemplation), a vast work combining semi-mystic effusions with the germs of most of his later thought. The changing methodological tactics of the work,

however, were finally resolved on Mount Randa in Mallorca, where, after a week's meditation, "The Lord suddenly illuminated his mind, giving him the form and method for writing the aforementioned book against the errors of the unbelievers." (See below for *Contemporary Life* from which this and other passages are quoted.) This "form and method" was the art, of which he now wrote the first work (*Ars compendiosa inveniendi veritatem*, c. 1274), thereby fulfilling the second of his three aims. The third was soon (1276) to be fulfilled with the founding of the monastery of Miramar on the northwest coast of Mallorca for the teaching of Arabic to thirteen Franciscan missionaries.

From this point on, apart from his feverish literary activity, Llull's life became one of ceaseless travel in an attempt to interest the world in his missionary projects. Using Montpellier as a base (it then formed part of the kingdom of Mallorca), he visited Paris four times, where he lectured at the university and had audiences with the king (Philippe IV the Fair, nephew of his patron, Jaume II of Mallorca); he traveled to Italy some six times (to Genoa, where he was in contact with rich merchants, to Pisa, to Rome, where he had audiences with at least three popes, to Naples, and near the end of his life to Sicily); he went three times to North Africa (Tunis and Bougie [modern-day Bejaïa]), thereby fulfilling the first of his three proseltyzing aims; and once to Cyprus (from where he visited the Turkish port of Ayas, and perhaps Jerusalem). Llull's lack of success was typical for an idealist approaching practical politicians with schemes for the betterment of mankind. As he himself admitted in a work of the same title, he was everywhere treated as a *phantasticus*, or as he put it in earlier works, "Ramon lo Foll." And in a touching passage from the poem *Desconhort* (1295), he complained that people read his art "like a cat passing rapidly over hot coals." But these epithets and complaints must not make us forget that he did manage to have the ear of kings and popes, that he presented them with political tracts that recent research has shown to have been far more realistic than was formerly believed. Nor must we forget that on his last trip to Paris, overcoming at last the incomprehensions attendant on his former attempts to teach his peculiar system there, Llull received (1310–1311) letters of commendation from Philippe IV and the chancellor of the university, as well as a document in which forty masters and bachelors in arts and medicine approved of Llull's lectures in *Ars brevis*. The Council of Vienne (1311–1312) subsequently endorsed his proposal for the founding of schools of Oriental languages.

After Llull's discovery of the methodology of the art, his literary and philosophical production can be divided into three periods.

The Quaternary Phase (ca. 1274–1289). This was so called because the basic components of the art (divine attributes, relative principles, and elements) appear in multiples of four. The first work of the art, *Ars compendiosa inveniendi veritatem*, was rapidly accompanied by a series of satellite works explaining it and showing the other fields to which it could be applied. Among these, the most important was *Llibre del gentil e dels tres savis* (Book of the Gentile and the Three Wise Men), Llull's principal apologetic work. It was also around this same time that Llull wrote a pedagogical tract for his son, *Doctrina pueril*, and a manual of knighthood, the *Llibre de l'orde de cavalleria* (*Book of the Order of Chivalry*), destined to become popular in its French translation, and later translated into English by William Caxton. It was also during this time (1283) that he wrote his first didactic novel, *Blaquerna* (this seems to have been the original form of the name, and not the later *Blanquerna*), which included his most famous mystic work, the *Llibre d'amic e amat* (*Book of the Lover and the Beloved*).

In the same year of 1283, Llull decided to refashion many minor aspects of his system in a new version called *Ars demonstrativa*, around which he wrote a new cycle of explicative and satellite works. It was during this period that he wrote his second didactic novel, *Félix o El libre de meravelles* (Felix, or the Book of Wonders), which includes the political animal fable, *Llibre de les baèsties* (*Book of the Beasts*).

The Ternary Phase (1290–1308). In this phase the principles of the art appear in multiples of three (and the four elements disappear as one of its foundations). Because of "the weakness of human intellect" that Llull encountered on his first trip to Paris, he reduced the number of figures with which his system invariably began from twelve (or sixteen) to four, and he removed all algebraic notation from the actual discourse of the art. This phase begins not with a single work surrounded by satellites, but with twin works: *Ars inventiva veritatis* which, as Llull says, treats *ciència* or knowledge, and *Ars amativa* which treats *amància* or love of God; it ends with the final formulation of his system in *Ars generalis ultima* (1305–1308), and in shorter form in *Ars brevis* (1308). This period is rich in important works, among which one might mention the immense encyclopedia, *Arbre de ciència* (Tree of Science, 1295–1296), as well as his principal work on logic, epistemology, and politics, *Logica nova* (1303), *Liber de ascensu et descensu intellectus* (1305), and *Liber de fine* (also 1305).

The Postart Phase (1308–1315). With the definitive formulation of his system now out of the way, Llull is free to concentrate on specific logical and epistemological topics, many directed toward his campaign against the Parisian "Averröists" while on his last trip there (1309–1311). It was at the end of this stay that he dictated what has come to be known in its English translation as *Contemporary Life*. He also became more and more involved in the art of preaching, writing a vast *Summa sermonum* in Mallorca (1312–1313).

Llull's last works are dated from Tunis, December 1315, after which he disappears from history. He probably died early the following year, either there on the ship returning to his native Mallorca, or on the island itself, where he is buried. The story of his martyrdom (he was stoned to death) is a legend bolstered by pious falsifications in the early seventeenth century, in which an earlier (1307) stoning in Bejaï'a was transposed and made into the cause of his death.

Thought and Influence

The unusual nature of Llull's system and of his thought in general is due to his insistence that any apologetic system that hoped to persuade Muslims and Jews would have to abandon the use of Scripture, which only caused endless discussions over validity and interpretation, and try to prove the articles of the Christian faith, above all those of the Trinity and Incarnation that Muslims and Jews found most difficult to accept. The first consideration forced Llull to forge an abstract system that could stand completely by itself. This was the art, each work of which begins with a series of concepts distributed amid geometric figures, and then proceeds to describe the correct method of combining these concepts. The point was to display the basic structure of reality, which, noted Llull, begins with the attributes of God, goodness, greatness, eternity, and so forth, which are not static but unfold into three correlatives of action. Thus *bonitas* (goodness) unfolds into an agent (*bonificativum*) and a patient (*bonificabile*), and the act joining them (*bonificare*). Their necessary activity *ad intra* produces the Trinity, and their: contingent activity *ad extra* the act of creation. Moreover, this triad of action is then reproduced at every level of creation, so that, for instance, man's intellect

is composed of *intellectivum, intelligibile,* and *intelligere,* and fire of *ignificativum, ignificabile,* and *ignificare.*

This metaphysics of action exerted a strong influence on Nicholas of Cusa, as did the combinatorial art on Giordano Bruno and Gottfried Wilhelm Leibniz. But at the same time, Llull's system was taken over by alchemists, and eventually over one hundred such works were falsely attributed to him. This, plus his self-image as a *phantasticus,* the unusual nature of his system, and the fact that his attempts to prove the articles of the faith made him suspect to the Inquisition, helped propagate the image of a peculiar, countercultural figure.

Llull's influence in the Iberian Peninsula was less hetorodox and countercultural than in the rest of Europe. Aside from the fifteenth-century Llullist schools of Mallorca and Barcelona, there were a certain number of Castilian translations of his works done in the later Middle Ages, although interest in him seems to have been of a dispersed, sporadic nature, at least until the beginning of the sixteenth century. Then we find a Lullist school at Valencia (where some of his works were published), the chief figure of which was the humanist Alonso de Proaza. He in turn was in contact with Cardinal Francisco Jiménez de Cisneros, who in his foundation in 1508 of the University of Alcalá de Henares, instituted a chair of Lullian philosophy and theology. Later in the century, Felipe II was an admirer of Llull, as was his chief architect, Juan de Herrera, who not only wrote a *Tratado del cuerpo cúbico* based on Llull's art, but in 1582 founded a mathematical-philosophical academy in Madrid in whose program the art was to have a prominent place.

Literary Works

Llull's most unusual literary feature is that he dared to modify the conventional genres of contemporary romance tradition to fit his own didactic needs. Llull first attempted the novel, in the *Libre de Evast e Blaquerna* (Book of Evast and Blaquerna, 1283), and *Félix o El libre de meravelles* (Felix, or the Book of Wonders, 1288) he recounted stories morally useful to his readers. He similarly adjusted the narrative wrapping of an early apologetical work, the *Llibre del gentil e dels tres savis* (Book of the Gentile and the Three Wise Men), in which an unbeliever struggles to find the truth and finally embraces the faith.

The plot of *Blaquerna* follows the outline of a hero's biography; the main character is endowed with the mental strength permitting him to overcome the obstacles in the way of his becoming a contemplative hermit. These "obstacles" are the ties that link a man to society: a family, a religious order, a diocese, and the whole of Christianity ruled by the pope. Blaquerna abandons his parents, Evast and Aloma, and convinces his bride, Natana, to become an exemplary nun, whereupon he enters a monastery and becomes a reforming abbot who is then elected bishop. Blaquerna improves the spiritual life of his diocese and as a result is elected pope; from Rome Blaquerna manages to reorganize the world and to change the moral attitudes of people. Finally he renounces the papacy and becomes the perfect hermit, which permits him to write *Llibre d'amic e amat* (*Book of the Lover and the Beloved*), a collection of short mystical proverbs lyrically embellished and artistically constructed.

The *Book of Wonders* follows the spiritual journey of Felix through events that cause him "wonder" because they seem to be contrary to God's will, and that allow various hermits and philosophers to explain the fundamental points of Christian knowledge about God, angels, the heavens, the elements, plants, minerals, animals, man, paradise, and hell. Like *Blaquerna,* this novel offers plenty of morally meaningful exempla, but unlike the earlier work, it betrays considerable pessimism about the capacity of mankind

to better its moral behavior. One chapter of *Félix* has become particularly famous: *Llibre de les baèsties* (*Book of the Beasts*), a Llullian adaptation of the old Iranian *Book of Kalila and Dimna* with some references to the French *Roman de Renard.*

In search of a literary vehicle for his message, Llull attempted autobiography, so *Desconhort* (1295) and *Cant de Ramon* (1300), two splendid lyric poems, explain from a personal point of view the disappointments and failures of his career. In the process Llull himself becomes a new literary character: a poor, old, and despised man who has devoted his life to revealing a treasury of knowledge, an art given to him by God. A short late prose work, *Phantasticus* (1311), offers the most complete picture of this personage, whom, as was noted above, he sometimes called "Ramon lo Foll."

Plant de la Verge and *Llibre de Santa Maria,* both probably written between 1290 and 1293, are two pieces of devotional literature: the former, in verse, is a moving description of Christ's Passion, the latter, in prose, an unusual application of the Llullian art to a prayer to the Virgin Mary. Another treatise with rich literary contents is the *Arbre de filosofia d'amor* (*Tree of Philosophy of Love,* 1289), which encloses a short, touching mystical novel.

In his immense encyclopedia of 1295–1296, the (*Arbre de ciència*) (Tree of Science) Llull included a little *Arbre exemplifical* (Tree of Examples), in which a preacher could find the way to "translate science into exemplary literature." This work is the first of Llull's contributions to homiletics, a trend that later developed both into theoretical treatises—*Rhetorica nova* (1302), *Liber de praedicatione* (1304), *Ars brevis pradicationis* (1313)—and sermon writing. Llull in later years, in fact, put aside romance literary genres and devoted himself to sermon collections; the most important being *Summa sermonum* of 1312–1313, which offers an unusual model for preaching, since

Llull wanted to persuade lay audiences intellectually rather than to touch their hearts with moving anecdotes.

See also **Caxton, William; Nicholas of Cusa; Philip IV the Fair**

Further Reading

Bonner, A., and Badia, L. *Ramon Llull: Vida, pensament i obra literària*. Barcelona, 1988.

Carreras y Artau, T., and J. *Historia de lafilos-ofía espa[ola: Filosofía cristiana de los siglo XIII al XV*. 2 vols. Madrid, 1939–43.

Hillgarth, J. N. *Ramon Lull and Lullism in Fourteenth-Century France*. Oxford, 1971.

Llull, R. *Obres essencials*. 2 vols. Barcelona, 1957–60.

——. *Selected Works of Ramon Llull (1232–1316)*. 2 vols. Ed. A. Bonner. Princeton, N.J., 1985. Catalan version in *Obres selectes de Ramon Llull (1232–1316)*. 2 vols. Majorca, 1989.

ANTHONY BONNER AND LOLA BADÍA

LOCHNER, STEFAN (1400/1410–1451) The most important painter of the early Cologne school of painting, Lochner is the only artist whose name can be associated with individual works. However, the entire attribution of his body of works is based on Albrecht Dürer's 1530 diary entry, in which he mentions the altar-piece in Cologne he saw painted by a "Master Stefan." The work in question is presumed to be the altarpiece representing the patron saints of the city in attendance at the Adoration of the Magi (now in Cologne cathedral), the most significant altarpiece produced in Cologne. All other works associated with Lochner are attributed through stylistic affinity to this piece. As a result of the meager documentation, some scholarship has cast doubt on the identity of the creator of these works. The historical Stefan Lochner, the only Stefan in the Cologne guilds, was active ca. 1435–1451, and is presumed to have been born between 1400 and 1410 in Meersburg, on Lake Constance. Little is known of his life, but he was first documented as a master in Cologne in June, 1442, and died, probably of the plague, in September, 1451. His life was probably short, as he died within a year of his parents. Two works are dated: the 1445 Presentation in the Temple (Lisbon, Gulbenkian Collection), and the 1447 work of the same subject (Darmstadt, Hessisches Landesmuseum).

Lochner's work often shows traces of Flemish realism, causing some to question the nature of his training. His paintings show little stylistic relationship to works from Lochner's homeland near Constance. Also, Lochner introduced numerous innovations to the essentially conservative Cologne school of painting. Lochner's figures inhabited landscapes and architectural settings full of specific details that clearly reflect a familiarity with Flemish works. His work shows figures that have somewhat more volume than previously seen, and these figures exist in space far more effectively than those of his Cologne predecessors.

Several of his works, such as the Nativity (Munich, Alte Pinakothek), the Gulbenkian Presentation in the Temple, and the St. Jerome in his Cell (Raleigh, North Carolina Museum of Art), all bear numerous similarities to the works of Robert Campin and his followers, particularly in the representation of interior spaces. Lochner's largest extant work, and the best known, is the previously noted City Patrons' Altarpiece or *Dombild*. This work seems to reflect both the knowledge of the Ghent Altarpiece, particularly on the exterior Annunciation, and Lochner's characteristic sweetness, grace, and delicacy. The figures in this altarpiece are the first life-size figures painted in Cologne.

Nevertheless, Lochner's paintings maintained links to the past and are noted for a tension between their fully modeled forms and linear patterns. He also often used gold backgrounds and, like earlier Cologne painters, outlined figures in red. Lochner's paintings are also characterized by a distinctly personal quality of calm and sweetness, creating a sense of quiet mysticism. These qualities are created through idealization of features, particularly those of women, and rich, glowing colors, often created with oil glazes. All these qualities are perhaps best seen in his Madonna of the Rosebower (Cologne, Wallraf-Richartz-Museum).

Further Reading

Corley, Brigitte. "A Plausible Provenance for Stefan Lochner?" *Zeitschrift für Kunstgeschichte* 59 (1996): 78–96.
Förstesr, Otto H. *Stefan Lochner: Ein Maler zu Köln*. Frankfurt am Main: Prestel, 1938.
Goldberg, Gisela, and Gisela Scheffler. *Altdeutsche Gemälde, Köln und Nordwes tdeutschland. Alte Pinakotek, München*. 2 vols. Bayerische Staatsgemäldesammlung Gemäldekataloge 14. Munich: Bayerische Staatsgemäldesammlung, 1972, vol. 1, pp. 190–210.
Stefan Lochner, Meister zu Köln: Herkunft, Werke, Wirkung, ed. Frank Günter Zehnder. Cologne: Wallraf-Richartz-Museum, 1993.
Zehnder, Frank Günter. *Katalog der Altkölner Malerei*. Kataloge des "Wallraf-Richartz-Museums 11. Cologne: Stadt Köln, 1990, pp. 212–244.

DANIEL M. LEVINE

LÓPEZ DE AYALA, PERO (1332–1407) Pero López de Ayala was a chronicler, poet, and statesman who lived in a period that spanned the reigns of five Castilian kings. He was born into a wealthy, noble family in the northern province of Alava. Although not a great deal is known of his youth, Ayala's knowledge of Latin and French, plus his interest in the Bible and other religious writings may have come from early ecclesiastical training by his uncle, Cardinal Pedro Gómez Barroso, who raised and educated him. Much of what is known of Ayala's activities is derived from the chronicles he wrote describing the reigns of Pedro I (1350–1369), Enrique II (1369–1379),

Juan I (1379–1390), and Enrique III (1390–1406). Beginning with his first appearance in the *Crónicas des los reyes de Castilla: don Pedro* (Chronicle of the Kings of Castile: Peter I) in 1353 as a page selected to carry the king's banner, Ayala served Pedro in various capacities for over a dozen years. By 1367, however, he had joined Enrique of Trastámara, Pedro's illegitimate half-brother and rival for the throne. Shortly afterward, Ayala was taken prisoner by the English at the battle of Nájera.

During the reign of Enrique II, Ayala received many royal favors, including territorial possessions and political posts. His political activity greatly increased during the reign of Juan I, when he served as royal counselor and as ambassador to France. Although he opposed the plan of Juan I to assume the Portuguese throne and thereby unite the two kingdoms, Ayala participated in the disastrous battle of Aljubarrota, where he was captured by the Portuguese and imprisoned for two years. It is probable that some of his writings were done during this period, especially the *Libro de la caza de las aves* and some poetic works. Ayala's importance and influence continued to grow during the reign of Enrique III. He was a member of the Council of Regents during the king's minority and served as a negotiator in the peace talks with Portugal. In the mid-1390s, Ayala spent several years in semiretirement at his estate in Álava and at the adjacent Hieronymite monastery. It is believed that he wrote his chronicles and *Libro del linaje de Ayala* during this time. In 1399, he was appointed grand chancellor of Castile.

In addition to being an impressive political and military leader who was personally acquainted with popes and kings, Ayala must also be acknowledged as one of the three major literary figures of his century. Juan Ruiz, Juan Manuel, and Pero López de Ayala all in their own way reflect the social, economic, and political milieu in which they lived as well as their own personal reactions to their circumstances. Although a self-consciousness as literary creators is apparent in the work of each of these authors, their primary purpose remains didactic—ranging from the jocular tongue-in-cheek admonitions of Ruiz to the chivalric preoccupations and moralizing of Manuel to the almost ascetic severity of Ayala. As the most important writer of the last half of the fourteenth century, Ayala's prose and poetic works are significant for a number of reasons. Linguistically, they comprise an extensive and reliable source of late-fourteenth- and early fifteenth-century Spanish. His chronicles are of great historical value as they are a major source of information concerning events in Spain from 1350 to 1396. The epoch that Ayala chronicles is a period of crisis and of such peninsular and international conflicts as civil and religious wars in Spain, the Hundred Years' War, the Black Death, and the schism in the Catholic Church. An eyewitness to many of these events, Ayala identifies himself with the purpose and norms of ancient chroniclers, explaining in his preface that the purpose of knowing about events in the past is to serve as a guide for present actions. He further comments that his sole intention is to tell the truth based on what he himself observed and from testimony of trustworthy persons. Nevertheless, the chronicler's impartiality, and at times even his veracity, has been questioned because he reports so many barbarous acts, and because he views Pedro I primarily as a negative example. Ayala's support of the Trastámaran pretender and his later involvement in the royal court further clouds the picture. The two manuscript traditions *abreviada* and *vulgar* suggest a process of revision that served to soften the condemnation of Pedro I after the reconciliation of the two dynastic lines, with the marriage of the grandchildren of the two contenders.

The literary nature of these narratives and the chronicler's acute awareness of literary style must also be taken into account. Among the variety of literary devices used in the chronicles, Ayala includes the skillful arrangement of all the contributing elements to form an organic unity: tense choice, paired words or doublets, alternation, contrast, parallelism, repetition, and portraiture. The author's skill in the use of direct address such as dialogues, one-liners, discourses, letters, and sayings enliven narrative passages and reveal the dramatic nature of the events. The dramatic structure of the death scenes is also evident in other episodes; for example, the farewell scene between Leónor de Guzmán and her son Fadrique, the confrontation with the Queen Mother at Toro, the departure of Pedro I from Burgos, and the papal election that began the schism. Ayala must be recognized as a talented prose stylist as he relates events more varied and fascinating than many fictional sagas, consisting of wars, fratricides, marriages, mistresses, international intrigues, and power struggles at the highest levels of government.

Ayala's long poetic work *Rimado de Palacio*, completed in 1404, is a highly personal and creative expression of the author's moral and philosophical preoccupations. Most of its 2,168 stanzas (totalling more than 8,000 lines) are written in the verse form *cuaderna via*, characterized by four-line stanzas, each fourteen-syllable line divided by a caesura after the seventh syllable and ending in uniform consonantal rhyme. In spite of being the last of the *cuaderna via* poets, Ayala demonstrates poetic innovations that include increased use of the eight-syllable line and the introduction of *arte mayor*, both most apparent in the *Cancionero* portion, stanzas 732–919. At the center of *Cancionero*, the poet again reveals his concern for the Church in a long allegory in which the ship of St. Peter is being torn apart by the destructive storm of the Great Schism.

The *Rimado* consists of a large number of poems of varied content and structure whose composition undoubtedly spans decades and whose impetus springs from the experiences of a long, adventurous life as well as from periods of reading and meditation. To say that it is a didactic-moral work or a long confessional poem is true. Nonetheless, this would slight the literary value and variety of Ayala's forcefully sober verse. Ayala's fine, satirically traced pictures of medieval society have, above all else, attracted readers to *Rimado*. These vigorous scenes of contemporary society and court life are found in the first part of the book, along with other poems that arise from the chancellor's personal experiences and his reflections. The poet's description of personages in the royal courts, the almost caricaturelike presentation of merchants and lawyers, prefigure later satirical works that culminate in the mordant sarcasm and ridicule of Francisco Quevedo, as well as in subsequent vignettes of manners and customs.

The more extensive final part of the work provides a focus on doctrine rather than experience. Ayala demonstrates originality in combining confessional and doctrinal themes and materials based on the Bible and the *Morals* of St. Gregory in order to produce a didactic exposition in verse. Many of the themes of the fifteenth-century rhymmed confessions undoubtedly received some impetus from the meditations on life, death, original sin, and the brief duration of worldly gains portrayed in *Rimado*. In addition to influencing the verse forms, topics, and themes of later poets, Ayala's devout and moving poems dedicated to the Virgin had an impact on religious lyrical poetry of the fifteenth century. Ayala also made an important contribution to Castilian intellectual life through his translations of works of Livy, Gregory, Isidore, and Boethius.

See also **Enrique II, King of Castile; Juan Manuel**

Further Reading

García, M. *Obra y personalidad del Canciller Ayala*. Madrid, 1983.

López de Ayala, P. *Libra Rimado de Palacio*. 2 vols. Ed. J. Joset. Madrid, 1978.

Strong, E. B. "The *Rimado de Palacio*: López de Ayala's Rimed Confession." *Hispanic Review* 37 (1969), 439–51.

Tate, R. B. "López de Ayala, Humanist Historian?" *Hispanic Review* 25 (1957), 157–74.

Wilkins, C. *Pern López de Ayala*. Boston, 1989.

CONSTANCE L. WILKINS

LÓPEZ DE CÓRDOBA, LEONOR (b. 1362)

Born in 1362, Leonor López de Córdoba composed one of the most singular chronicles of the late Middle Ages in Castile. Her *Memorias*, which were dictated to a scribe around the beginning of the fifteenth century, are a personal testimony of a society ravaged by civil war, pestilence, and class upheaval.

Due to the dramatic circumstances of the narrator's life, the *Memorias* present a point of view that is rare in the historiography of this period. Leonor López was the sole survivor of a family destroyed because of its allegiance to Pedro I, the legitimate king of Castile, during the dynastic struggle he waged against his half-brother, Enrique de Trastámara. The social climate of the decades following this civil war was dominated by the usurper's followers, who spread propaganda alluding to the brutality of Pedro "the Cruel," and the low social class of his supporters, as a means of justifying their overthrow of the rightful monarch. In an effort to repudiate such rumors in her *Memorias*, Leonor López described in detail the nobility of her lineage, the bravery of her father in defense of the loyalist cause, and the atrocities that Enrique de Trastámara himself inflicted upon her family. Her work is a historical curiosity, both as a document of a dispossessed class, and as a feat of honor performed verbally by a woman.

Memorias also merits attention for its literary significance as one of the earliest examples of autobiographical expression produced in medieval Spain. In order to

exonerate herself, Leonor López elaborated a self-portrait that exemplified the
conduct deemed appropriate for a noble
lady. Her persuasive manipulation of language is particularly evident in her use of
motifs derived from pious literature to
associate herself with a popular ideal of
Christian virtue.

Despite their limitations as a historical
record and artistic work, the *Memorias* of
Leonor López are notable as a re-creation
of the past that preserves a uniquely feminine interpretation of the values of medieval Castilian society.

See also **Pedro I the Cruel, King of Castile**

Further Reading

Ayerbe-Chaux, R. "Las memorias de Leonor
    López de Córdoba." *Journal of Hispanic
    Philology* 2 (1977–78), 11–33.
Deyennond, A. "Spain's First Women Writers."
    In *Women in Hispanic Literature: Icons
    and Fallen Idols.* Ed. B. Miller, Berkeley,
    Calif., 1983. 26–52.

                                AMANDA CURRY

LÓPEZ DE MENDOZA, IÑIGO (1398–
1458) Born in 1398, Iñigo López de
Mendoza (first marqués de Santillana,
and señor de Hita and Buitrago) was the
son of Diego Hurtado de Mendoza, the
influential admiral of Castile. His uncle
was Pero López de Ayala, poet, statesman, military figure, and the commanding chancellor of Castile during the last
quarter of the fourteenth century. During
the reign of Juan II of Castile, López
de Mendoza was head of the powerful Mendoza clan, which was connected
through marriage to many of the most
influential families of the kingdom.

López de Mendoza is one of the major
cultural and political figures of the fifteenth century. He spent a part of his youth
in Aragón, where he became friends and
shared intellectual pursuits with Enrique
de Villena, one of the great learned men of
his time. López de Mendoza distinguished

himself both militarily and literarily on
the Granadan frontier, at Ágreda in 1429
and again at Jaén in 1438. Although he
fought alongside Juan II and his confidant
Álvaro de Luna, Constable of Castile, at
the battle of Olmedo in 1445 defending
the interests of the monarchy against the
challenges of the Infantes de Aragón,
López de Mendoza quickly became don
Álvaro's sworn enemy. Along with other
powerful nobles, López de Mendoza then
conspired to topple Luna from power
and went on to write admonitory poetry
about the example of Luna's life and execution in 1453.

The Marqués, as López de Mendoza
was referred to simply in his time, surrounded himself in Guadalajara with artists, writers, and thinkers like Nuño de
Guzmán, Pero Díaz de Toledo, and Martín
González de Lucena, and was perhaps the
greatest single cultural and artistic force
of his time. As both intellectual and patron, López de Mendoza was the single
most important figure in the propagation
of humanistic knowledge in Castile during
the first half of the fifteenth century. In addition to having gathered in Guadalajara
the most significant library of humanistic
works in lay hands and patronized the
translation of Homer's *Iliad*, Plato, Ovid,
Cicero, Seneca, Dante, and Boccaccio into
Castilian, López de Mendoza was in his
own right a celebrated poet, literary critic,
and theoretician. Although he collected
Latin manuscripts, he could not read
Latin, but he read several vernaculars flu-
ently and was aware of contemporary developments in European poetry, especially
in France and Italy. His *Carta e prohemio
al Condestable de Portugal*, which draws
heavily on classical and patristic writers as
well as Boccaccio's *De genealogia deorum*,
is considered the first concerted work of
literary theory and criticism in Castilian.
Its novelty lies in its historical descriptions of different genres and the catalogue
of works that it contains, just as it offers
an evaluation of the qualities and defects
of the poets he mentions. In addition, his

Sonetos fechos al itálico modo (1438), which follow the example of Dante and Petrarch, mark the first coherent attempt to cultivate the sonnet form in Castilian. Besides these two works and his patronage, López de Mendoza was a prolific writer responsible for a vast body of work in both prose and verse that deals with moral, religious, political, and sentimental themes, all of which contributed to his vast fame during his lifetime. Among the best known of his lyrical works are his *serranillas,* or pastourelles, that tell of rural love encounters between knights and rustic shepherdesses. His ambitious narrative and allegorical poems, known as *decires* (*Bías contra Fortuna, Doctrinal de Privados, Comedieta de Ponza*), are replete with mythological, biblical, and other learned themes that attest to his humanistic knowledge and intellectual aspirations. The *Comedieta* (1436), a patriotic composition that exalts the Aragónese in their Italian campaign at the naval battle of Ponza, represents the culmination of López de Mendoza's allegorical works. It is built upon a complicated image pattern developed through the use of highly learned language and allusion. *Bías contra Fortuna*, written in 1448 as a consolation to mark the political imprisonment of a cousin by don Álvaro de Luna, marks the climax of the theme of Fortune in his work. In contradistinction to the difficult allegory of the *Comedieta*, Bías, the Greek philosopher who is the spokesperson for Santillana, makes his views on Fortune and the world clearly known. The *Doctrinal* reveals a final vindictive side of López de Mendoza's character, in which he employs Fortune and confession to make Álvaro de Luna, his dead enemy, denounce his own transgressions.

When López de Mendoza died in 1458, the event inspired his contemporaries to write a number of elegies and other literary compositions to mourn his passing.

See also **Boccaccio, Giovanni; Dante Alighieri; Guzmán, Domingo de; Petrarca, Francesco**

Further Reading

Lapesa, R. *La obra literaria del Marqués de Santillana*. Madrid, 1959.
Nader, H. *The Mendoza Family in the Spanish Renaissance, 1350–1550.* Rutgers, N.J., 1979.
Schiff, M. *La bibliothèque du marquis de Santillane*. Paris, 1905.

E. MICHAEL GERLI

LORENZETTI, PIETRO (c. 1280–1348) AND AMBROGIO (c. 1290–1348) The brothers Pietro Lorenzetti and Ambrogio Lorenzetti were Sienese painters; they represent two of the most radical and innovative forces in *Trecento* art. Pietro and Lorenzetti were probably pupils of Duccio, and they both enlarged on the study of narrative and pictorial realism common to Sienese and Florentine art at this time. Their art manifests an interesting admixture of the styles of both schools, combining Sienese sensitivity to color and line with Florentine monumentality.

Relatively few documents regarding the life or artistic activity of either Pietro or Ambrogio have come down to us. Although Lorenzo Ghiberti, in the first written account of Ambrogio, provides a long and enthusiastic discussion of his work (*Commentarii,* c. 1450), he never mentions Pietro in his survey of Sienese artists. Vasari (*Lives,* 1568) did not even realize that the two artists were brothers; he misidentifed one of them as Pietro Laurati. Reconstruction of their careers has understandably proved to be difficult, especially because some of their most celebrated compositions have been lost. Although the brothers worked quite independently of each another, some commissions appear to have been joint undertakings, and the intensity of each brother's exploration of pictorial realism suggests a greater degree of contact and collaboration between the two than we now suppose.

Pietro, traditionally considered the elder brother, has usually been overlooked in comparison with Ambrogio, who has a greater reputation for invention. However, Pietro's own brilliant technical innovation is shown as early as his first documented work, a polyptych painted for the high altar of rhe parish church of Santa Maria in Arezzo (1320). In one portion of the *Arezzo Polyptych*, the frame is treated as if it were contiguous with the architecture of the painted narrative, so that the pilasters and arches framing the *Annunciation* are seen as supporting elements for the front wall of Mary's chamber. The space of this room is seen logically as extending back from the supporting columns and arches on the surface, creating an illusion of a box of space extending beyond the frame. This was an advance in a direct line with the development of one-point perspective a century later, and it was an idea to which Pietro would subsequently return even more daringly. Analysis of Pietro's forms in the *Arezzo Polyptych* reveals a mélange of stylistic sources influencing his art. In the central panel of the *Madonna and Child* especially, the Madonna exhibits a graceful sway and pattern indebted to Duccio; the pronounced twist of her neck recalls Giovanni Pisano's sculptures for the facade of the cathedral in Siena; and her firm support of the child's solidly rounded body echoes Giotto's massive forms.

Important pictorial features are found in Pietro's most extensive surviving work, the frescoes in the left transept of the lower basilica of San Francesco in Assisi. These narrate the *Passion and Resurrection of Christ* and the *Stigmatization of Saint Francis*; and there is an unusual section of trompe l'oeil depictions of chapel furnishings, including an unoccupied pew, a fictive altarpiece, and a niche containing liturgical objects. These frescoes are undocumented, and their dating has provoked controversy, but most scholars place them c. 1320. Many scenes, such as the *Entry into Jerusalem* and the epic *Crucifixion*, continue the Sienese tradition of sensitivity to color and love of profusion, but they are characterized by an unprecedented wealth of observation. The *Last Supper*, for example, deftly juxtaposes three distinct types of light in a confrontation of the mundane and the divine. A remarkably detailed night sky, the first portrayal of its kind, meticulously differentiates the light of the moon, stars, and meteors streaking across the heavens above the structure containing the main scene. This natural light is contrasted with the artificial light of the hearth fire in the kitchen, which casts the first shadows in western art since antiquity. Both of these lights pale in relation to the floodlit interior of the supper chamber, which seems to be illuminated by the supernatural glory of Christ and his disciples. In another astonishing step toward realism, Pietro makes it clear that the narratives are to be understood as a sequence of stories unfolding over time; the moon, high over the pavilion in the *Last Supper*, is shown to be setting behind the Mount of Olives in the adjacent *Arrest of Christ*. Other frescoes in the left transept, such as the *Deposition from the Cross* and the *Entombment*, do away with all anecdotal detail to approach the monumental grandeur and dramatic tension of Giotto's narratives. The *Deposition*, in which Christ's broken body is ingeniously interlaced with the living, forms one of the most sustained images of grief in western art.

Three securely dated works succeeded the Assisi frescoes: the *Carmine Altarpiece* of 1327–1329 (Siena, Pinacoteca; New Haven, Yale Museum; Princeton, Princeton Museum), a polyptych made to celebrate the final approval of the Carmelite order by Pope John XXIII in 1326 for its Sienese church of San Niccolò; the *Uffizi Madonna and Child* (Florence, Uffizi; signed and dated 1340); and the *Birth of the Virgin* (Siena, Museo dell'Opera Metropolitana; commissioned 1335, signed and dated 1342). This last altarpiece, made as part of a cycle of Marian altarpieces celebrating feasts of the Virgin surrounding Duccio's

Maestà in the cathedral of Siena, returns to the integration of frame and painting seen in the *Arezzo Polyptych* of twenty-two years earlier. Here the illusion of continuity is much more thorough. We seem to be peering into a miniature Gothic palace which is structurally supported by the columns and arches of the frame and from which the exterior walls have been removed (as in a dollhouse) to allow us to witness the events within. And although this work is technically a polyptych (the two lateral panels of saints originally flanking the *Birth* are now lost), there is none of compartmentalization traditionally seen in separate panels. The space of one panel is treated as continuous with that of the next; thus, the two panels on the right convey information concerning the same time and place, Mary's birthing chamber. To emphasize this, the figure of the woman bearing a fly whisk continues on either side of the vertical pier of the frame. Also gone is the traditional flattening backdrop of gold leaf signifying a sacred event. Instead, an opulently appointed interior, described in rich patterns from the vault to the floor tiles, defines a remarkably convincing illusion of spatial recession. In the left panel depicting Joachim and the herald, the setting suggests a vast structure beyond the two visible chambers, indicating Pietro's concern to construct a completely plausible world for his figures to inhabit.

Pietro worked, together with Ambrogio and Simone Martini, on a cycle of frescoes illustrating the life of the Virgin for the facade of the hospital of Santa Maria della Scala in Siena. (These frescoes are now lost, but a recorded inscription bore the date 1335.) Pietro also worked alongside Ambrogio on a fresco cycle for the chapter hall of the monastery of San Francesco in Siena, of which a *Crucifixion* and a *Resurrected Christ* survive (possibly 1336). A *Massacre of the Innocents* from a fresco cycle in San Clemente ai Servi in Siena and an altarpiece depicting stories of the *Life of the*

Blessed Humilitas (Florence, Uffizi) are two other works frequently attributed to Pietro.

Lorenzo Ghiberti considered Ambrogio Lorenzetti the greatest Sienese painter of the 1300s, surpassing even Simone Martini in ability and sophistication. A *Madonna and Child* from Vico L'Abate (signed and dated 1319; Florence, Museo Arcivescovile del Cestello) is the earliest of only three dated works by Ambrogio. It shows the originality of the artist's concepts from the beginning of his career. Ambrogio's panel is based on a Byzantine type of the Virgin as the throne of God, and the rigidly frontal, iconic pose of the Madonna adheres closely to the archaic format. The sovereign detachment between mother and God, typically upright in front of the Madonna, has, however, here been replaced by a restless, squirming Christ child seeking his mother's attention. Both figures have the solidity and roundness of Giotto's paintings, and the throne is also presented as a spatially receding three-dimensional structure. This modernization of an ancient type in the latest Giottoesque idiom reveals Ambrogio's special understanding of the Florentines' achievement. In fact, Ambrogio worked periodically in Florence between 1318 and 1332, and he is listed in the registry of the Florentine painters' guild in 1327. The Vico L'Abate panel is a prime example of the astonishing variety and inventiveness that both Pietro and Ambrogio brought to the theme of the Madonna and child. Both artists composed ceaseless variations on this popular devotional subject, but Ambrogio's Madonnas, especially, attained a level of iconographic and aesthetic sophistication that seems to belong more to the Renaissance, or even to the Baroque, than to the *Trecento*. A few of Ambrogio's groupings of the Madonna and child are shown as if responding to the viewer's presence, as in the *Madonna del Latte* (Siena, Palazzo Arcivescovile), in which the suckling child looks out at the viewer with intense curiosity; or the

Rapolano Madonna (Siena, Pinacoteca), which portrays a Christ child so surprised and frightened by the attention coming from our direction that he crushes his pet goldfinch. This psychologizing of the mother's and the child's response to their surroundings reaches a climax in the Sant'Agostino *Maestà* in Siena (possibly 1339), the last surviving fragment of a fresco cycle illustrating episodes of the life of Saint Catherine of Alexandria for an Augustinian chapter house formerly adjacent to the church. The *Maestà* depicts Mary and Christ adored by saints who bear the attributes of their faith; these include some who were brutally martyred: Saint Bartholemew with his flayed skin, Saint Agatha with her breasts, and Saint Catherine with her severed head all kneel and present their tokens of faith to the child. This grisly spectacle strikes terror into the child, who staggers unsteadily backward in an attempt to escape—the most natural response a child could have.

Some of Ambrogio's patrons apparently felt that his daringly human interpretation of the divine breached the limits of decorum. The chapel of Monte Siepi in the rural abbey of San Galgano near Siena was built to honor this Sienese saint and to commemorate a vision of the Madonna that Galgano had on this site. The surviving frescoes are fragmentary; but Ambrogio's original program for the chapel, c. 1336, included a depiction of Galgano's vision, portraying a procession of saints and angels on the side walls converging, along with the visitors inside the chapel, toward the Madonna enthroned as queen of heaven on the wall behind the altar. By portraying saints on the walls flanking the enthroned Madonna, Ambrogio involved the entire space of the chapel, surrounding the viewer with Galgano's vision—a bold experiment that anticipates the carefully coordinated chapel interiors of the seventeenth century. The complex iconographic program for the wall portrayed the Virgin's central role in the mystery of human redemption:

she was shown both as the exalted queen of heaven at the top of the fresco and as the humble *Virgin Annunciate* at the bottom. As the discovery (in 1996) of the *sinopie* underlying the frescoes revealed, Ambrogio originally portrayed the Virgin of the annunciation cowering in utter terror before the angel, while the *Maestà* above showed her enthroned without the child, wearing a crown, and bearing worldly symbols of power—the orb and scepter—in her hands. Both of these unique images were suppressed shortly after completion of the frescoes: the trembling annunciate was painted over by another artist, who replaced her with a typical meekly accepting Madonna; and the empress was transformed into the more usual image of motherhood by placing the Christ child on her lap. Presumably, the patrons had been disturbed by Ambrogio's provocative interpretations and had subsequently commissioned something more conventional.

From 1337 to 1340, under commission from Siena's ruling Council of Nine, Ambrogio worked on the most important surviving cycle of medieval secular decorations, the *Allegory and Effects of Good and Bad Government*, painted on three walls of the Sala della Pace (or Sala dei Nove), one of the ruling council's meeting rooms in the Palazzo Pubblico in Siena. This cycle is almost completely devoid of religious content; its complex philosophical underpinnings—along the lines of antique Aristotelian, Ciceronian, or more strictly medieval tracts—are still disputed. We may take comfort in the fact that even during the *Trecento*, visitors to the *sala* needed the learned interpretation of a guide in order to understand the extremely intricate allegorical message of the cycle. The fresco juxtaposes the elements of just and harmonious rule with the evil elements of tyranny, contrasting the effects of each form of rule on city and country. The mural is filled with visual puns (Harmony, for instance, is shown with a wood plane, smoothing out any unevenness) and references to the antique (the figure of Peace is derived from an antique Roman coin). In his depiction of the prosperous city, Ambrogio created an unparalleled catalog of the myriad activities of town life. Nothing else in medieval art prepares us for the panoramic landscape adjacent to the well-governed city, which is the first landscape since antiquity, and really the first "portrait" of a particular terrain—a glance out the window of this hall reveals the close affinity between the fresco and the Tuscan countryside surrounding Siena.

As noted above, Ambrogio collaborated with Pietro on (lost) frescoes for a hospital in Siena, and on frescoes for a Franciscan chapter house (the latter included a painting of a typhoon, since lost, that Ghiberti praised highly). Ambrogio also painted an altarpiece of the *Presentation at the Temple and Purification of Mary* (1342; Florence, Uffizi) for the same cycle in the cathedral at Siena for which Pietro executed his *Birth of the Virgin*. Like Pietro's work, Ambrogio's *Presentation* is startling for its sophisticated suggestion of space and light. Ambrogio's last signed and dated work is from 1344: an *Annunciation* (Siena, Pinacoteca) painted for the chamber of the tax magistrate in the Palazzo Pubblico in Siena. The moment of incarnation depicted here presents an interpretation of great theological subtlety, and the spatial construction of the panel shows the tile floor converging to a single vanishing point; this is the closest any *Trecento* painting comes to true one-point perspective.

Ambrogio and Pietro both evidently died of the plague in 1348; with their deaths, Siena's period of cultural ascendancy came to an end.

See also **Duccio di Buoninsegna; Martini, Simone**

Further Reading

Borsook, Eve. *Ambrogio Lorenzetti.* Florence: Sadea Sansoni, 1966.

Brandi, Cesare. *Pietro Lorenzetti: Affreschi nella basilica inferiore di Assisi.* Rome: Pirelli, 1957.

——. *Pietro Lorenzetti.* Rome: Edizioni Mediteranee, 1958.

Carli, Enzo. *Pietro Lorenzetti.* Milan: A. Martello, 1956.

——. *I Lorenzetti.* Milan: Fabbri, 1965.

——. *La pittura senese del Trecento.* Milan: Electa, 1981.

Cole, Bruce. *Sienese Painting from Its Origins to the Fifteenth Century.* New York: Harper and Row, 1980.

DeWald, Ernest T. *Pietro Lorenzetti.* Cambridge, Mass.: Harvard University Press, 1930.

Frugoni, Chiara. *Pietro and Ambrogio Lorenzetti,* trans. L. Pelletti. Florence: Scala, 1988. Maginnis, Hayden B. J. "Pietro Lorenzetti: A Chronology." *Art Bulletin,* 66, 1984, pp. 183–211.

——. *Painting in the Age of Giotto: A Historical Reevaluation.* University Park: Pennsylvania State University, 1997.

Norman, Diana. "'Love Justice, You Who Judge the Earth': The Paintings of the Sala dei Nove in the Palazzo Pubblico, Siena." In *Siena, Florence, and Padua: Art, Society, and Religion 1280–1400,* Vol. 2, *Case Studies,* ed. Diana Norman. New Haven, Conn.: Yale University Press, 1995, pp. 145–167.

Offner, Richard. "Reflections on Ambrogio Lorenzetti." *Gazette des Beaux Arts,* 56, 1960, pp. 235–238.

Rowley, George. *Ambrogio Lorenzetti,* 2 vols. Princeton, N.J.: Princeton University Press, 1958. Rubinstein, Nicolai. "Political Ideas in Sienese Art: The Frescoes by Ambrogio Lorenzetti and Taddeo di Bartolo in the Palazzo Pubblico." *Journal of the Warburg and Courtauld Institutes,* 21, 1958, pp. 179–207.

Southard, Edna. *The Frescoes in Siena's Palazzo Pubblico, 1289–1359: Studies in Imagery and Relations to Other Communal Palaces in Tuscany.* New York: Garland, 1979.

——. "Ambrogio Lorenzetti's Frescoes in the Sala della Pace: A Change of Names." *Mitteilungen des Kunsthistorischen Institutes in Florenz,* 24, 1980, pp. 361–365.

Starn, Randolph, and Loren Partridge. "The Republican Regime of the *Sala dei Nove* in Siena, 1338–1340." In *Arts of Power: Three Halls of State in Italy, 1300–1600.* Berkeley: University of California Press, 1992, pp. 11–59.

Volpe, Carlo. *Pietro Lorenzetti.* Milan: Electa, 1989.

GUSTAV MEDICUS

LOTHAIR I (795–855) King of Lotharingia and emperor.

The eldest son of Emperor Louis the Pious (778–840) and Irmengarde, Lothair I is remembered chiefly for his role in dismembering the empire constructed by Charlemagne. In 817, Louis the Pious sought to ensure the empire's unity after his death by promulgating the *Ordinatio imperii*. This divided the Carolingian territories into kingdoms for Lothair I and his brothers, Pepin of Aquitaine (800–838) and Louis the German (804–876), while leaving Italy under their father's nephew, Bernard. Lothair, who was made co-emperor, was granted the largest, central realm, including Aix-la-Chapelle and Rome. After his father's death, he was to exercise supremacy over his brothers and Bernard.

Difficulties emerged in 817 with the revolt of Bernard, who died after being blinded as punishment. Italy was transferred to Lothair. In 823, the birth of another son, Charles the Bald, to Louis the Pious (by his second wife, Judith) forced the emperor to modify his plans for the inheritance by allotting to Charles lands earlier assigned to his half-brothers. Lothair revolted in 830, and again in 833 with the help of his brothers Louis the German and Pepin. While their father emerged victorious and in 834 confined Lothair to Italy, the remaining years of Louis's reign saw continued political unrest.

Upon Louis's death in 840, Lothair I proclaimed again the *Ordinatio imperii* and turned against his surviving brothers, Louis the German and Charles. The power struggle among those rulers led to the Treaty of Verdun (843), dividing the Carolingian territories into separate king-

doms for Louis, Charles, and Lothair. This testified to the end of the ideal of a united empire, though Lothair retained the imperial title.

Lothair was in conflict with one or both brothers most of the rest of his life. Upon his death in 855, his lands were divided among his sons, Louis II (d. 875), Lothair II (d. 869), and Charles of Provence (d. 863). Louis II alone was left the imperial crown, which he had received in 850.

See also Louis the Pious

Further Reading

Ganshof, François L. *The Carolingians and the Frankish Monarchy: Studies in Carolingian History,* trans. Janet Sondheimer. London: Longman, 1971, pp. 289–302.

McKitterick, Rosamond. *The Frankish Kingdoms Under the Carolingians, 751–987.* London: Longman, 1983.

Nelson, Janet L. *Charles the Bald.* London: Longman, 1992.

Riché, Pierre. *The Carolingians: A Family Who Forged Europe,* trans. Michael I. Allen. Philadelphia: University of Pennsylvania Press, 1993.

CELIA CHAZELLE

LOTHAR III (1075–1137) Lothar III

of Supplinburg was born shortly after his father, Count Gebhard of Supplinburg, died in battle against King Henry IV. Historians know little about his youth, his rise to prominence, or exactly why King Henry V named Lothar as successor to the late Magnus Billung, duke of Saxony, on August 25, 1106. Soon after, having grown still more powerful through other inheritances and his own political and military ability, Lothar became the leader of the opposition to Henry V.

With the death of Emperor Henry V in 1125 without a son, German princes reasserted their traditional right to elect a new king. Representative magnates of the four ethnic divisions of Swabia, Bavaria, Saxony, and Franconia were delegated to the election at Mainz under the leadership of the archbishop. Although Duke Frederick II of Swabia, Henry V's nephew and heir, and Margrave Leopold III of Austria found a great deal of support, the archbishop promoted the case of the duke of Saxony, Lothar von Supplinburg. Lothar's party probably gained the support of the main hold-out, the Welf duke of Bavaria, Henry the Black, with a promised marriage alliance between Henry's son, Henry the Proud, and Lothar's only child and heir, Gertrude. Elected on August 30 as king of the Romans, Lothar was crowned in Aachen about two weeks later.

The succession did not go smoothly, however. Between the Staufen Frederick II of Swabia and Lothar a new rivalry developed. The new king needed to assert his control over royal and imperial rights and properties. But royal prerogatives were mixed together with the personal inheritance of Henry V and the Salian dynasty inherited by the Staufen. Because Frederick was reluctant to turn over certain possessions, Lothar outlawed him at Christmas, 1125. Distracted by the defiance of Sobeslav of Bohemia, Lothar could not begin a military campaign against the Staufen until summer 1127, when he began to besiege Nuremburg. There the Staufen party elected Frederick's younger brother Conrad as anti-king in December, 1127. This conflict disturbed the peace of the empire until Conrad's capitulation in 1135. Nineteenth-century historians inflated these disagreements into a grand vendetta between two dynasties, the Welf (or in Italian, Guelph) versus the Staufen (or in Italian, Ghibelline after the castle Waiblingen). While such a view oversimplified the issues involved, the competing interests of these powerful families would recurrently affect imperial affairs for decades.

Meanwhile, Lothar was capably handling the affairs of his kingdom. His exploitation of extinct noble dynasties changed the political landscape. Lothar helped establish the Zähringens in Burgundy as rivals to the Staufen. Lothar's intervention of the succession of the duchy of Lower Lotharingia led to its breakup into the duchies of Brabant and Limburg. In Saxony, his home territory, he enfeoffed the Askaniens with the Nordmark and the Wettins with the Marches of Meissen and Lausitz, dynasties that would, however, later become rivals of the Welfs. Lothar made his will felt beyond his kingdom's borders. He carried out several campaigns against the Slavs, collecting tribute from Poland and granting Pomerania as a fief. And a quick military demonstration against the Danish, where rivalry for the throne had caused disorder, encouraged the various candidates to acknowledge his overlordship almost without bloodshed.

Most importantly, Lothar became entangled in the papal schism between Innocent II and Anacletus II. Since both sides had respectable claims to the papacy, Lothar faced a real dilemma about whom to recognize as legitimate pope. Under the influence of the important Cistercian Abbot Bernard of Clairvaux and Norbert of Xanten (the founder of the Premonstratentian order, whom Lothar had made archbishop of Magdeburg), Lothar decided at a synod at Würzburg in 1130 to give allegiance to Innocent. Greeting the pope in Liège in March, 1131, Lothar acted as a groom and horse-marshal (*Strator- und Marschaldienst*), leading the pope's horse by the bridle and holding his stirrup during dismounting. The memorialization of this act with a fresco in the Vatican, implying that Lothar served as a vassal of the pope, later caused tension between imperial and papal ideologues.

In return for offering to conquer Rome for Innocent, Lothar tried to get back the old rights of investiture of bishops that had been lost for the monarchy in the Concordat of Worms. But Innocent only gave a promise of the imperial election. In late summer 1132, Lothar began an expedition to Italy with a small army.

His attack on Rome brought one success: Innocent crowned Lothar and his wife, Richenza, emperor and empress on June 4, 1133, although in the Lateran Palace, since Anacletus's forces still held the Vatican. Again Lothar tried to reclaim investiture, but only received confirmation that his rights would be the same as his predecessors. In negotiations about the Mathildine lands, he gained more success. Lothar recognized the claims of overlordship by the church, but he gained use of the lands in exchange for an annual payment of 100 pounds silver. Although the emperor immediately enfeoffed his son-in-law Henry the Proud with the lands, the papacy tried to portray him as a vassal of the church.

Within months Lothar returned to Germany, unable to defeat Anacletus's main ally, King Roger II of Sicily. Soon, Innocent was forced to flee Rome. Once the Staufen had reconciled with Lothar, however, the worsening plight of Innocent prompted Lothar to lead a second, much larger, Italian expedition in 1136. In northern Italy Lothar was triumphant; by the beginning of 1137 he invaded the kingdom of Roger of Sicily. But the quarrels between pope and emperor over the disposition of conquests and leadership, as well as the heat of summer, led to the breakup of the campaign before lasting success could be won. On the return northward Lothar sickened, finally dying in Breitenwang near Reutte in Tyrol on December 4, 1137.

Both his contemporaries and later historians have tended to judge Lothar harshly, especially those who resented his rather friendly relations with leaders of the church. Other modern historians reject his image as *Pfaffenkönig* (parson's king): his quarrels with the pope and his wars with local territorial bishops belie that charge. The conflicts after his death that ruined his legacy were largely caused by the change in dynasty, which Lothar had tried to forestall by giving the imperial insignia to Henry the Proud. In many ways Lothar successfully expanded political authority in Saxony, Germany, and the empire.

See also **Henry IV, Emperor; Roger II**

Further Reading

Bernhardi, Wilhelm. *Lothar von Supplinburg (1125–1127).* Jahrbücher der deutschen Geschichte 15. 1879; repr., Berlin: Duncker und Humblot, 1975.

Crone, Marie-Luise. *Untersuchungen zur Reichskirchenpolitik Lothars III. (1125–1137) zwischen reichskirchlicher Tradition und Reformkurie.* Frankfurt am Main: Lang, 1982.

Wadle, Elmar. *Reichsgut und Königsherrschaft unter Lothar III. (1125–1137): Ein Beitrag zur Verfassungsgeschichte des 12. Jahrhunderts.* Berlin: Duncker & Humblot, 1969.

BRIAN A. PAVLAC

LOUIS IX (1214–1270) King of France and saint. The son of Louis VIII, Louis IX came to the throne as a child in 1226. He spent his early years as king under the tutelage of his mother, Blanche of Castile. Many northern barons resented the assignment of the regency to a woman, let alone a foreigner. Others resented the growing authoritarianism of the crown during the preceding fifty years, the reigns of Philip II Augustus and Louis VIII. Many baronial families in the west nursed grievances from the period of the conquest of the Plantagenêt fiefs in the early years of the century. And in the south, local notables remained unreconciled to the French regime established in the wake of the Albigensian Crusade. These resentments periodically broke into rebellion: the late 1220s and early 1230s saw the crown confronting shifting alliances of northern barons (including the count of Brittany, Pierre Mauclerc) in defense of aristocratic interests. In the opening years of the 1240s, nobles and townsmen in the southwest and Languedoc banded together with the support of the Plantagenêt king of England to undo the conquests of the previous half-century. The crown defeated all these movements. The credit for the early successes goes largely to Blanche of Castile, but gradually in the 1230s her son became the effective ruler of the kingdom.

Married in 1234 to Marguerite of Provence, who came to dislike his mother, Louis remained devoted to Blanche and responsive to her political advice. Only in one matter is there evidence of political disagreement between mother and son: Louis's decision in late 1244 to take the crusader's vow. Despite Blanche's objections, Louis fulfilled the vow after almost four years of preparation that included commissioning *enquêteurs*, or special investigators, to identify the perpetrators of injustices in his government. In addition to the goodwill that these investigations produced, the information allowed Louis to improve the machinery of government by retiring or reassigning certain of his administrators. At the same time, he worked hard to encourage national and international support for his venture and to build a port, Aigues-Mortes, in the south of France for the embarkation of his army, estimated at 15,000–25,000 men.

Louis departed for the Seventh Crusade in 1248, leaving his mother as regent; his wife accompanied him on the expedition. After wintering in Cyprus, he began the invasion of Egypt in May 1249. The crusaders captured the coastal city of Damietta, and then, after a considerable respite, they began the invasion of the Egyptian interior late in the year, continuing into the early months of 1250. Daily running up against fiercer opposition, they were decisively defeated in April at Al-Mansura; Louis and the remnants of his army were captured. After difficult negotiations, the king and his men were ransomed, and many, including the king's two surviving brothers, Alphonse of Poitiers and Charles of Anjou, took ship

for Europe. The king and a small group of crusaders, spent the next several years in the Christian states of the Holy Land helping to rebuild fortifications and to formulate effective strategies against the enemy.

The queen-mother died in November 1252. Although he learned of her death in the spring of 1253, it was not until a year later that Louis was persuaded by the steady stream of information that reached him from France that conditions there necessitated his return. Landing at Hyères, not far from Marseille, in July 1254, he began immediately to transform the governance of his realm. Convinced that his failure on crusade was the result of his own sinfulness, and translating this conviction into a decision to live up to his notion of the ideal Christian ruler, he set about restraining the excesses of the Inquisition, reintroducing the *enquêteurs*, reforming the administration of the city of Paris, and, most far-reaching, undertaking a thorough overhaul of royal administrators in the provinces. Louis ceaselessly traversed the realm to hear petitions and do justice personally. Traditional institutions of rule, like Parlement, were improved in their organization and were leavened by his commitment to equity. He worked hard, too, to execute a severely restrictive policy toward the Jews that was in part intended to encourage them to convert.

In the late 1260s, Louis committed himself to another crusade. After considerable preparations, he departed in 1270. His wife remained in France. Following a brief stopover in Sardinia, the army, perhaps 5,000–10,000 strong, launched its attack on Tunis. Before the city could be taken—and in the event it never was—the king died (August 25, 1270). He was succeeded by his son, Philip III. As his bones were being transported to their final rest at Saint-Denis, miracles began to be reported. A few years later, the canonization process began in earnest. In 1297, the former king was raised to the catalogue of saints as St. Louis Confessor.

See also **Blanche of Castile; Joinville, Jean de; Philip II Augustus**

Further Reading

Jordan, William C. *Louis IX and the Challenge of the Crusade: A Study in Rulership.* Princeton: Princeton University Press, 1979.

Richard, Jean. *Saint Louis: Crusader King of France,* trans. by Jean Birrell. Cambridge: Cambridge University Press, 1992.

Sivéry, Gérard. *Saint Louis et son siècle.* Paris: Tallandier, 1983.

WILLIAM CHESTER JORDAN

LOUIS THE PIOUS (April 16, 778–June 20, 840) Louis (*Hludowicus*) and Lothar, a twin who soon died, were born on April 16, 778, in the palace of Chasseneuil near Poitiers to Hildegard, the wife of Charles the Great (Charlemagne). "Pious," not a contemporary epithet, was applied to Louis only at the end of the ninth century. In 781, Charles appointed Louis king of Aquitaine, an office he would grow into and hold for the next thirty-three years. In 794, sixteen-year-old Louis, already the father of two children by concubines, married Irmingard (d. 818), the daughter of Count Ingram. The royal couple produced five children within the decade.

Louis, as Charles's only surviving legitimate son, was crowned co-emperor at Aachen on September 11, 813. The implications of the imperial title Charles received in 800 remained ambiguous during his last years. The increasing involvement of churchmen in the administration of his realm suggests that Charles's concept of empire embraced religious as well as political leadership. A capitulary from this period wonders, "Are we indeed Christians?" One of Louis's great tasks after his father's death in January, 814, was to continue to define a Christian empire. Under Louis, Aachen became a beehive of activity. Charles had issued twenty diplomas during his last thirteen

years; Louis nearly doubled that in his first year as emperor. Louis regarded his empire as a divine gift for whose welfare and improvement he was chiefly responsible. Much of his early legislation focused on monastic and ecclesiastical reform. With the help of Benedict of Aniane, a monk who had joined his inner circle back in Aquitaine and whom he installed at Inden nearby Aachen, Louis crafted a vision of empire in which religion, society, and politics coalesced. Concern for the unity of the Christian people animated the *Ordinatio imperii* of 817, his attempt to establish the imperial succession in a manner that would preserve the integrity of the empire. Lothar (b. 795) became co-emperor with Louis while his other sons, Pippin (b. 797) and Louis the Younger (b. 806), were assigned subordinate roles. In placing the unity of the empire before division among his heirs, Louis proposed a transpersonal vision of empire that emulated the unity of the church. Louis saw himself as emperor of the Christian people, not of various ethnic groups. His reforms and concept of empire owed nothing to papal guidance or initiative. The historic *Pactum Hludowicianum* agreement of 817 for the first time outlined specifically the nature of the papal-imperial relationship, a relationship that Louis dominated. Elsewhere he referred to the pope as his helper (*adiutor*) in caring for God's people.

Louis was equally forceful in the political realm. When his nephew, King Bernard of Italy, challenged his authority in 817 he acted swiftly to quash the rebellion, blinding Bernard and exiling the conspirators. (When Bernard died of his injuries, Louis demonstrated the depth of his commitment to Christian kingship by performing public penance.) To preempt further dynastic challenges, he had his half-brothers Drogo, Hugo, and Theodoric tonsured and placed in monasteries. After the death of Irmingard (October 3, 818), Louis married Judith, daughter of Count Welf and his wife,

Eigilwi, who bore him two children, Gisela (821) and Charles (June 13, 823). The birth of Louis's fourth son later triggered searing conflicts within the family and Carolingian society at large. Other problems also challenged his reign during its second decade. Churchmen such as Bishop Agobard of Lyon began to complain about rampant corruption in Carolingian society, including exploitation of church lands and oppression of the poor by the warrior class. With the expansion of Carolingian hegemony at an end, powerful nobles who little understood the ideals of Louis's empire ransacked the Christian people and churches for material gain. The many groups ranged along the empire's extensive borders required continual attention. In the southeast, the Slovenians proved troublesome, while in the northeast Louis was able to effectively manage the Danish threat, which was defused when the Danish king Harald was baptized and adopted by Louis in 826. In the west, Louis campaigned personally in Brittany where he established nominal authority. In Gascony and the Pyrenees borderlands chronic instability reigned, partly because counts Hugo and Matfrid failed to support Louis's military efforts, a dereliction for which the emperor stripped them of their positions. Count Bernard of Barcelona was much more effective and for his efforts was appointed in 829 as the emperor's chamberlain, an office that brought him into intimate contact with the imperial family. Judith saw Bernard as a protector while Louis regarded him as the second man in the empire. Louis's forceful handling of counts Hugo and Matfrid and the empowerment of Bernard and Judith combined with the fear that any provision made for the young Charles would come at the expense of his half-brothers provoked a palace revolt in 830. Pippin and the younger Louis, aided by Hugo and Matfrid, sought to "free" the emperor from the tyrant Bernard and the Jezebel Judith, but Louis's supporters, sowing discord among his older sons,

restored him to authority in October, 830. Although abortive, the coup claimed a victim when the vision of empire outlined in the 817 *Ordinatio imperii* was annulled. The new *Divisio regnum* of 831 restored traditional Frankish practice when it partitioned the empire into four approximately equal kingdoms on Louis's death. The new status quo, however, was only temporary. Adherents of a unified empire agitated against the *Divisio*, while conflict among the brothers continued and was exacerbated when enterprising nobles took sides. On June 30, 833, Louis met with Lothar near Colmar in Alsace to compose their differences, but instead the emperor found himself on the "Field of Lies" facing a coalition of his older sons, their supporters, Pope Gregory IV, and several leading clergy, who took him and Judith into custody. Judith was sent to a monastery in Italy while Louis was confined to the monastery of Saint-Medard in Soissons. Leading clerics, including Agobard of Lyon and Ebbo of Reims, argued that Louis failed as a king and must abdicate the throne. In a humiliating ceremony, he acknowledged his crimes, removed his imperial regalia, and was condemned to perpetual penance. This mistreatment of a father by his sons, another round of conflict among the older brothers and their supporters, and increasing violence soon swung sympathy and support back to Louis who, from his confinement, was orchestrating his return. Freed from captivity, his weapons, his wife, and his youngest son were restored to him.

Emperor once again, Louis continued to rule energetically, bestowing key appointments on his supporters and punishing those such as Agobard and Ebbo who had betrayed him. He continued successfully to provide for Charles against the resistance of the younger Louis. When Pippin died in 838, Louis ignored the complaints of Pippin's son and granted the kingdom of Aquitaine to Charles. Lothar dedicated himself to his Italian lands and never challenged his father again. Louis rebuilt his own political network by holding frequent assemblies after 835 and by presiding at ceremonial and ritual activities, especially hunting, his favorite pastime. He continued to see to the collection of public revenue and directed successful military campaigns. In 839, an embassy from the Byzantine Empire arrived to congratulate him for his stout defense of Christendom.

On June 20, 840, Louis died on Petersaue, an island in the Rhine near his palace at Ingelehim. His last words reportedly were *Hutz, hutz* (German for "Away, away"), shouted as his mourners imagined to circling evil spirits. He was laid to rest in the monastery of Saint-Arnulf of Metz beside his mother and his sisters, Rotrud and Hilde-gard. Bishop Drogo, his half-brother, chose a late antique sarcophagus for him that depicted the flight of the Israelites across the Red Sea before the pursuing Egyptians. The motif symbolized baptism and triumph. Bitter civil war broke out among his sons, resulting in 843 in the formal division of the empire recorded in the Treaty of Verdun.

See also **Charlemagne; Judith, Empress; Lothair I**

Further Reading

Boshof, Egon. *Ludwig der Fromme*. Darmstadt: Primus, 1996.
De Jong, Mayke. "Power and Humility in Carolingian Society: The Public Penance of Louis the Pious." *Early Medieval Europe* 1 (1992): 29–52.
Godman, Peter, and Roger Collins, eds. *Charlemagne's Heir: New Perspectives on the Reign of Louis the Pious*. Oxford: Clarendon Press, 1992.

JOHN J. CONTRENI

LOUIS XI (1423–1483) The eldest son of Charles VII, Louis XI was raised in isolation from his father, and their subsequent animosity made Louis XI a political force long before he ascended the throne.

Charged with the defense of Languedoc in 1439, he fell under the influence of rebellious nobles and joined the Praguerie. He was soon forgiven, but the continuing animosity between Louis and Charles seems to have increased after the death of Louis's wife, Margaret of Scotland, in 1445 and Louis retired to his apanage of the Dauphiné in 1447. There he began an apprenticeship for the throne by reforming provincial government. A disobedient remarriage to Charlotte of Savoy completed the family breach, and Louis fled the realm in 1456.

Louis began his reign in 1461 by ambitiously seeking to expand his authority both abroad, through the invasion of Catalonia, and at home, with his vengeful dismissal of his father's advisers and foolish rejection of previous allies. He barely survived the subsequent *Guerre du Bien Publique* and the indecisive Battle of Montlhéry in July 1465, but the rest of the reign was marked by a remarkable ability to learn from his mistakes. Henceforth, Louis handled his domestic adversaries by isolating and destroying each in turn and sought international success through diplomacy rather than war.

By judicious gifts and appointments, Louis reconciled himself to his father's advisers, Dunois and Chabannes and such dangerous peers as the duke of Bourbon. He isolated his brother Charles of France by the award of the apanage of Guyenne. Louis supported first the Lancastrians and then the Yorkists to prevent English intervention in France, subsidized Swiss resistance to Burgundy, and supported Angevin ventures in Italy to secure the southwest. The birth of a son in 1470 (the future Charles VIII), the death of his brother Charles in 1472, the destruction of remaining Armagnac strongholds in 1473, the execution of the count of Saint-Pol in 1475—all these combined to secure Louis's domestic authority.

Thereafter, Louis concentrated on Charles the Bold, duke of Burgundy, who, at Péronne in 1468, had humiliated him by extorting a guarantee of the independence of Flanders. Charles's death in 1477 was Louis's greatest stroke of good fortune. The remaining years of the reign were devoted to the acquisition of Burgundian territories. In these same years, Louis's annexation of Anjou and inheritance of Maine and Provence virtually completed the territorial unification of modern France before his death.

Louis's successes came as a fulfillment of his predecessors' policies. Ugly and socially isolated from his peers, Louis's rejection of medieval courtly behavior, dress, and ritual later endeared him to 19th-century romantics but in his own day alienated many whose help he needed. Louis was not some sort of "New Monarch" but rather an idiosyncratic medieval king whose breaches with convention often proved self-defeating and whose greatest successes came through the traditional means of diplomacy and warfare made possible by the military and fiscal reforms of his less colorful father.

See also **Charles VII**

Further Reading

Bittmann, Karl. *Ludwig XI. und Karl der Kuhne: Die Memoiren des Phillipe des Commynes als historische Quelle.* Göttingen: Vandenhoeck und Ruprecht, 1964.

Champion, Pierre. *Louis XI.* New York: Dodd, Mead, 1929.

Kendall, Paul M. *Louis XI: The Universal Spider.* New York: Norton, 1970.

Lewis, Peter S. *Later Medieval France: The Polity.* New York: St. Martin, 1968.

Tyrell, Joseph M. *Louis XI.* Boston: Twayne, 1980.

PAUL D. SOLON

LUITGARD OF AYWIÈRES (Luitgard of Tongres; 1182–1246) Born into a wealthy family, Luitgard entered the monastery of Sainte-Catherine at Saint-Trond at the age of twelve. Twelve years later, she was elected prioress but chose instead to leave for the Cistercian monastery at Aywières. After a long life of exemplary holiness, Luitgard died among her fellow sisters on July 16, 1246. She eventually became the patron saint of Flanders. Several *vitae* of Luitgard exist, the most notable being composed by Thomas de Cantimpré three years after her death. Luitgard's life was filled with an extravagant array of visions and miracles. The visions include highly abstract apparitions of light, concrete personal admonitions by Christ and by angelic messengers, political and ecclesiastical messages (e.g., asking her to fast for seven years because of the Albigensians), and contacts with souls in Purgatory. Among her miracles are such physical phenomena as levitation, profuse sweating and crying, ecstasies, healing with spittle and the laying on of hands, prophecy, and raptures.

Illiterate and unable to speak French, Luitgard nonetheless contributed powerful images to the growing movement of christocentric mysticism: Christ urges her repeatedly to drink directly from his bleeding wound and receives her heart in his own. Luitgard's *vita* offers remarkable insight into the flourishing communities of spiritual women and their mutual influence on each other. Marie d'Oignies, for example, is present at her deathbed and predicts Luitgard's miraculous activities from beyond the grave. A Cistercian nun, Sybille de Gages, composes a poem in her honor; Luitgard's spirit frequently appears to other nuns in visions.

See also **Marie d'Oignies**

Further Reading

Thomas de Cantimpré. *Vita Lutgardis*, ed. Pinius. *Acta Sanctorum* (1867) 3.187–209.

——. *The Life of Lutgard of Aywières*, trans. Margot H. King. Saskatoon: Peregrina, 1987.

Deboutte, A. "S. Lutgarde et sa spiritualité." *Collectanea cisterciensa* 44 (1982): 73–87.

Dinzelbacher, Peter. "Das Christusbild der heiligen Luitgard von Tongeren im Rahmen der Passionsmystik und Bildkunst des 12. und 13. Jahrhunderts." *Ons geestelijk erf* 56 (1982): 217–77.

ULRIKE WIETHAUS

LUNA, ÁLVARO DE (1388–1453) Don Álvaro, as he is commonly referred to, was the illegitimate son of a minor noble of Aragónese origin by the same name. He was born in Castile at Cañete in 1388, and his mother was from that village. When his father died in 1395, Álvaro was taken in by his uncle, Juan Martínez de Luna. In 1408 Álvaro de Luna was sent to court to further his education. There he was known for his elegance and wit, and quickly became the friend, companion, and favorite of Prince Juan, the considerably younger boy who had inherited the throne during infancy and would become Juan II, king of Castile. From their earliest days together, Luna and the king were constant companions and confidantes. Fearing the worst of the association, the young prince's mother, the Queen Regent Catalina de Lancaster, arranged to have Luna removed from court in 1415. Juan was miserable without his friend's company, and Luna was quickly recalled. By 1418, when Catalina had died, Luna and the king's relationship had grown to the point that it inspired both public gossip and private envy among many of the nobles, who sought influence to augment their power at the expense of the crown. (In later years the king would be confronted by the nobles with rumors of their homosexual relationship). Luna, however, remained confident of the king's support and relied heavily on the backing of others who associated the crown's interests with their-own, namely the lower and middle layers of society. Luna brilliantly exploited the concerns and aspirations of the non-noble sectors of society and, at the same time, sought to increase his own influence as well as centralize the power of the monarchy. As a result, he undermined the power of the *cortes* (parliament) and the local municipalities, as he gathered more and more power for the crown and for himself. The king, who remained largely disinterested in affairs of state, became a virtual pawn of the ambitious Luna.

In 1420 Luna, who had been elevated to count and been given large estates, rescued the king from the Infantes de Aragón, who had seized the monarch and taken him to Talavera de la Reina. The Infantes, brothers of Alfonso V of Aragón, were closely allied with the Castilian nobles who sought to curb the power of the monarchy in the kingdom. Both had regal ambitions themselves and looked to protect their family's enormous interests in Castile. Luna was made the constable of Castile in 1423, a step which greatly increased his power and influence by making them official. The move provoked the nobles and the Infantes to multiply their efforts against him, which met with success in 1427, when they and the other nobles forced the king to exile Luna. Neither the king nor the nobles, however, were capable of governing Castile without Luna, whose talents had ensured his indispensability. As a result, he was quickly recalled and fully reinstated. The Castilian victory in the war against Aragón (1429) not only restored but amplified Luna's power and influence.

Luna seemed unstoppable. At one point, the mastery of the military Order of Santiago was conferred upon him after it had been stripped from the Infante Enrique, heir to the throne. With this new power in hand, Luna began to campaign against the Muslim south and led the Castilians to an important victory at the battle of La Higueruela in 1431. The nobles, presided over by the Manrique and Enríquez clans, continued to resist Luna and plot against him at court. Although their efforts led to a second exile in 1438, by 1445 Luna had been restored to favor and had handed the nobles a resounding defeat at the battle of Olmedo. Only King Juan's second wife, Isabel of Portugal, managed to rid the kingdom of Luna. With the collaboration of the nobles, especially the conde de Haro and the marqués de Santillana, she persuaded the king to arrest Luna and condemn him to death. He was taken prisoner at Easter, 1453, and publically beheaded at Valladolid on 22 June of that year.

As he went to his death, Luna, whose bravery was legendary, calmly requested that his executioner not tie his hands with the customary rope but with the silk cord he had brought for that purpose. Luna's spectacular rise and dramatic fall would continue to haunt the Castilian imagination for the next several centuries as an example of the whims of Fortune, inspiring many literary works that commemorated it. He is buried in the cathedral at Toledo. Juan II died the year after Luna's execution, overcome by personal grief and remorse.

Álvaro de Luna's diplomatic and military skills rank him among the most influential Iberian political leaders of the fifteenth century. Committed to a powerful monarchy and centralized authority based on broad popular support, his vision was only betrayed by an indecisive king and his own venality.

See also **Alfonso V, King of Aragón, The Magnanimous**

Further Reading

Round, N. G. *The Greatest Man Uncrowned: A Study of the Fall of Don Alvaro de Luna.* London, 1986.

E. MICHAEL GERLI

LYDGATE, JOHN (ca. 1370–1449) The most prolific versifier of the 15th century. Lydgate was probably born in the village of Lydgate in Suffolk and apparently educated at the Benedictine monastery at Bury St. Edmunds, at which he was professed at the age of fifteen. He later studied at Oxford, probably at Gloucester Hall. He was ordained priest in the Benedictine order in 1397. In 1406 Prince Henry supported his return to study at Oxford. It was possibly while at Oxford that he wrote his translation of Aesop's *Fables.* His subsequent career suggests that he enjoyed Henry V's patronage. In 1423, after Henry's death, Lydgate became prior of Hatfield Broadoak in Essex. But from 1426 to 1429 he was in Paris as part of the entourage of John duke of Bedford, regent of France. By 1433 he had returned to Bury. Most of his later works seem to have been written there. He received a royal annuity in 1439 and died ten years later.

Lydgate's earliest major work was probably his *Troy Book,* a translation of Guido delle Colonne's *Historia destruccionis Troiae* (30,117 lines in couplets), which was begun at the behest of Henry V in 1412 and completed in 1420. Its composition appears to have been interrupted by the writing of *The Life of Our Lady,* ca. 1415–16 (5,932 lines, mostly in rime royal stanzas), written, he says, at Henry's "excitacioun." *The Siege of Thebes,* a history of the Theban legend, apparently based on a French source, was probably composed ca. 1420–21, as a continuation of Chaucer's *Canterbury Tales.* While in France in the late 1420s Lydgate probably wrote his translation of Deguileville's *Pilgrimage of the Life of Man* (24,832 lines in couplets) for Thomas Montacute, earl of Salisbury. Some of his shorter poems, including the *Danse Machabre,* also date from this time.

After his return to England in 1429 Lydgate wrote a number of celebratory verses for Henry VI's coronation. His *Lives of Sts. Edmund and Fremund* (3,508 lines in rime royal) was presented to the king in the 1430s, probably after the king's visit to Bury St. Edmunds in 1433–34. For the king's brother, Humphrey, duke of Gloucester, Lydgate wrote his longest work, *The Fall of Princes* (36,365 lines in rime royal), between ca. 1431 and 1438. It is a rendering of Laurent de Premierfait's French prose translation of Boccaccio's

De casibus virorum illustrium. His last major works seem to have been his *Lives of Sts. Albon and Amphibel* (4,724 lines in rime royal), commissioned in 1439 by John Whethamstede, abbot of St. Albans, and a rime royal translation of the Pseudo-Aristotelian *Secreta secretorum,* left incomplete on his death and finished by Benedict Burgh. Other substantial poems attributed to Lydgate include a lengthy allegory, *Reason and Sensuality* (7,042 lines in couplets), and many shorter poems of doubtful canonicity.

In addition to these long poems there are numerous shorter ones on a variety of subjects. These include a popular dream vision, *The Temple of Glass,* and short verse narratives, such as his *Debate of the Horse Sheep and Goose* and *The Churl and the Bird,* several mummings, and a number of devotional lyrics. But the variety of Lydgate's poetic output resists concise summary: it ranges from his translation of Aesop to a treatise for laundresses and a dietary (instructions on healthy diet and behavior). By the most capacious estimates it runs to about 150,000 lines of verse. His sole prose work, *The Serpent of Division,* is a brief history of Rome.

This range of subject matter is reflected in the range of his patrons, which extended from royalty and nobility through a broad spectrum of English society, both religious and lay, male and female, individual and institutional. He was at the call of those who wished him to entertain, instruct, admonish, and propagandize on their behalf.

Lydgate stands crucially between Chaucer and the later evolution of English poetry. He wrote in the generation immediately after Chaucer's death and acknowledges Chaucer as his "master" in frequent lavish tributes. A number of his works are self-consciously conceived within a tradition of Chaucer's works that is reflected in imitation at conceptual, stylistic, and verbal levels. Thus his *Troy Book* sets itself in relation to the subject matter of *Troilus and Criseyde;*

The Siege of Thebes contains an imitation of the beginning of the General Prologue and extensive verbal borrowings from the *Knight's Tale; The Complaint of the Black Knight* and *The Temple of Glass* imitate Chaucer's dream visions, *The Book of the Duchess* and *The House of Fame,* respectively. Lydgate was to play an important role in the creation and dissemination of the Chaucer tradition, particularly through his own popularizing of Chaucerian style and subjects.

Lydgate's Chaucerian imitation is related to the most distinctive tendency in his art, its rhetorical amplification. His instinct was to elaborate his materials, often on a massive scale. The most striking—or notorious—example of this tendency is the opening sentence of his *Siege of Thebes,* which imitates the opening sentence of Chaucer's General Prologue, Lydgate's sentence extends Chaucer's from eighteen to 65 lines. Indeed much of Lydgate's amplification comes from a natural tendency nurtured by a careful reading of Chaucer, through which poetic hints of his "master" could be vastly expanded. Thus, out of suggestions in Chaucer's language, he created a distinctive aureate diction, a Latin-derived, polysyllabic language that often characterizes his "high style," particularly in his religious verse. At its least successful, in conjunction with elaboration of allusion and syntax, it could lead to the obscurity that has earned him the condemnation of many modern critics.

Lydgate's meter systematizes Chaucer's versification through a regular use of five types of iambic pentameter line. One particularly striking feature of this systematization is the frequent use of the "headless" line (one that lacks an initial stressed syllable). Lydgate's own development of Chaucer's metrics was the "broken-backed" line, in which stressed syllables clash across the caesura.

It was probably through his amplification and systematization of Chaucer's art that Lydgate gained his considerable reputation in the 15th and 16th centuries. Allusions in that period acclaim him as part of a great triumvirate of ME poets, together with Chaucer and Gower. And in simple quantitative terms, in numbers of surviving manuscripts, Lydgate was the most popular of all ME poets. His *Fall of Princes* survives in complete or selected forms in over 80 manuscripts, his *Life of Our Lady* in nearly 50, *The Siege of Thebes* in 30. Among Lydgate's shorter poems both his *Verses on the Kings of England* and his *Dietary* exist in over 50 copies. In addition many of his works were issued by the early printers, Caxton, Pynson, and de Worde, often more than once.

This massive dissemination of Lydgate's works during the later Middle Ages led to his wide-ranging influence on later writers and forms. *The Fall of Princes* shaped literary conceptions of tragedy in the early Renaissance. His mummings are important texts in the evolution of English drama. And the works of (among others) Dunbar, Henryson, Douglas, Hawes, and Skelton, as well as many lesser figures, show the influence of his work in their writings, an influence that extended into the 17th century.

See also **Boccaccio, Giovanni; Chaucer, Geoffrey; Digulleville, Guillaume de; Gower, John; Henry V**

Further Reading

Primary Sources

Bergen, Henry, ed. *Lydgate's Troy Book*. 4 vols. EETS e.s. 97, 103, 106, 126. London: Humphrey Milford, 1906–35.

Bergen, Henry, ed. *Lydgate's Fall of Princes*. 4 vols. EETS e.s. 121–24. London: Humphrey Milford, 1924–27.

Erdmann, Axel, and Eilert Ekwall, eds. *Lydgate's Siege of Thebes*, 2 vols. EETS e.s. 108, 125. London: Kegan Paul, Trench, Trübner, 1911–30.

Furnivall, Frederick J., and Katherine B. Locock, eds. *The Pilgrimage of the Life of Man*. 3 vols. EETS e.s. 77, 83, 92. London: Kegan Paul, Trench, Trübner, 1899–1904.

Lauritis, Joseph A., R.A. Klinefelter, and V.F. Gallagher, eds. *A Critical Edition of John Lydgate's Life of Our Lady*. Pittsburgh: Duquesne University, 1961.

MacCracken, Henry Noble, ed. *The Minor Poems of John Lydgate*. 2 vols. EETS e.s. 107, o.s. 192. London: Kegan Paul, Trench, Trübner, 1911.

Humphrey Milford, 1934.

Norton-Smith, John, ed. *John Lydgate: Poems*. Oxford: Clarendon, 1966.

Reinecke, George F., ed. *Saint Albon and Saint Amphibalus*. NewYork: Garland, 1985.

Steele, Robert, ed. *Lydgate and Burgh's Secrees of Old Philisoffres*. EETS e.s. 66. London: Kegan Paul, Trench, Trübner, 1894.

Secondary Sources

New *CBEL* 1:639–46, 740.

Manual 6:1809–1920, 2071–2175.

Edwards, A.S.G. "Lydgate Scholarship: Progress and Prospects." In *Fifteenth Century Studies: Recent Essays*, ed. Robert F. Yeager. Hamden: Archon, 1984, pp. 29–47.

Pearsall, Derek. *John Lydgate*. London: Routledge & Kegan Paul, 1970.

Schirmer, Walter F. *John Lydgate: A Study in the Culture of the XVth Century*. Trans. Ann E. Keep. Berkeley: University of California Press, 1961.

A.S.G. EDWARDS

M

MACHAUT, GUILLAUME DE (ca. 1300–1377) The greatest French poet and composer of the 14th century. Machaut's narrative *dits* set a style in poetry that would predominate in France and England through the 15th century; his lyrics, many set to music, established and popularized the *formes fixes*; his *Messe de Nostre Dame* is the earliest surviving polyphonic setting of all movements of the Mass Ordinary by one composer; his strong interest in manuscript production made him a prime force in creating an awareness of the artist as a professional figure.

Born near Reims, Machaut probably received a university education in Paris. After his studies, he served from ca. 1323 to the late 1330s as personal secretary and clerk to Jean l'Aveugle of Luxembourg, king of Bohemia. In 1333, Jean procured a canonry at Reims for Machaut, whose name appears regularly in the records of Reims after 1340. With Jean's death in 1346 at the Battle of Crécy, Machaut did not lack for patrons. He composed his *Remede de Fortune* for Jean's daughter, Bonne of Luxembourg, who was also the mother of two of his most important patrons, Charles, duke of Normandy (later Charles V), and John, duke of Berry. Machaut praises Charles in his *Voir dit* (1363–65) and probably composed his last major poem, the verse chronicle *Prise d'Alexandrie* (ca. 1369–71), at his instigation. Machaut dedicated his *Fonteinne amoureuse* to the duke of Berry, and one of the most elaborate manuscripts of Machaut's collected works bears the duke's signature. In the early 1350s, Machaut established an important association with Charles the Bad, king of Navarre, whose family had hereditary connections with Champagne and who had married a daughter of Bonne and King John II. Although he apparently continued to cultivate royal patrons, no major works by Machaut are known after the *Prise*, and public records do not speak of him again until his death in April 1377.

Most of Machaut's poetic and musical production can be dated to the period after he settled at Reims in the late 1330s until ca. 1370. He composed some 420 lyric poems, most in the *formes fixes* of *chant royal* (eight extant), ballade (239), rondeau (seventy-seven), virelai (forty), and *lai* (twenty-three). He also wrote twenty-three motets, nine *complaintes*, eight long and four shorter *dits amoureux*, a poem of comfort and counsel (*Confort d'ami*), the *Prise d'Alexandrie*, as well as a *Prologue* that introduced his late complete-works manuscripts. In total, Machaut produced some 60,000 lines of verse. He set about 140 of his lyrics to music, providing polyphonic settings of forty ballades, twenty-one rondeaux, four *lais*, one virelai, and twenty-three motets and monophonic settings for one ballade, sixteen *lais*, thirty virelais, one *complainte*, one chant *royal*, and two miscellaneous lyrics. The manuscripts also include music for his famous *Messe de Nostre Dame* and a textless three-voice hocket.

Machaut's earliest narrative poem, the *Dit du vergier* (late 1330s; 1,293 lines), is an allegorical dream vision in the tradition of the *Roman de la Rose*. It is a first-person account of an encounter with the God of Love, who together with six youths and six maidens appears to the narrator in a grove. In three lengthy speeches, the god discourses on love and promises to help the narrator in his own amours, if he proves worthy.

The *Jugement du roy de Behaigne* (late 1330s; 2,079 lines) narrates a love debate and its resolution by Jean l'Aveugle. The allusions to this poem and the large number of extant manuscripts (twenty) are evidence that this was the most popular of Machaut's works. The question debated is who suffers more, the knight whose lady has taken a new lover or the lady whose beloved has died. Jean decides in favor of the knight, then entertains both parties at his castle of Durbuy for a week. Elements of verisimilitude and the participation of a historical king bring a new air of realism to the *dit amoureux*.

Remede de Fortune (ca. 1340; 4,300 lines) is arguably the best and most influential French love poem of the 14th century. The Lover/Narrator tells of his long but silent love service to his lady. To pass time, he writes poems in the *formes fixes* about his love and circulates them anonymously, until one day a *lai* comes into his lady's hands. When she asks him who had written it, he is unable to speak and retreats in despondency to the Park of Hesdin, where he delivers a lengthy *complainte* against Love and Fortune. In response, Lady Hope appears and tells him that both Fortune and Love had treated him as well as could be expected. Encouraged by Hope, the Lover finally goes to his Lady's chateau and declares his love. Although they exchange rings, the Lady, prompted by the need for discretion and secrecy in love, later ignores him, and the poem ends on an ambiguous note. *Remede de Fortune* is an important didactic poem, serving as a manual for courtiers and providing a poetic and musical model for each of the *formes fixes*. Among the last and best of a line of French love poems that integrated lyrics with narrative, it also provided a model for the nonmusical narratives of such poets as Froissart, Granson, and especially Chaucer.

The *Dit du lyon* (2,204 lines), with the action set on April 2, 1342, is sometimes thought to be the original of Chaucer's lost *Book of the Lion*. The narrator comes onto an island, where he encounters a friendly lion; the lion leads him through a wasteland into a grove, where they are received by a noble lady and her retainers. Here, the narrator observes the love experience of the lion, who is harassed by the persecution of hostile beasts whenever his lady takes her gaze from him. The narrator intercedes on behalf of the lion before returning to his manor.

In the *Jugement du roy de Navarre* (1349; 4,212 lines), Machaut returns to the love debate of *Behaigne* and this time pronounces, through the person of Charles the Bad, king of Navarre, in favor of the Lady. Much more than a simple love debate, the poem is a complex commentary on the role of a poet and poetry in society. An important prologue evokes the Black Death.

The *Dit de l'alerion* (1350s; 4,814 lines) is a bird allegory that presents extensive analogies between birds of prey and women, between hawking and *fin'amors*. The Narrator/Lover tells of four raptors he has acquired, loved, and lost: a sparrowhawk, an alerion (a type of large eagle), an eagle, and a gerfalcon. Like the *Remede*, it is a didactic treatise on love; unlike that poem, it incorporates exempla drawn from historical and literary sources to make its points.

The *Fonteinne amoureuse* (1360–62; 2,848 lines) is a dream vision in which Machaut offers advice to his patron, Duke John of Berry. One night, the Narrator overhears a Lover bemoaning the fact he must go into exile (in actuality, John went to England in 1360 as a hostage after the Treaty of Brétigny) and be separated from his Lady. The next day in a garden, the Narrator and the Lover fall asleep near a fountain and are visited by Venus, who brings the Lady to comfort her suitor and assure him of her fidelity. The two men awaken and return to the castle; several days later, the Lover crosses the sea, but with joy in his heart.

In his last and lengthiest *dit amoureux*, the *Voir dit* (1363–65; 9,009 lines with intercalated prose letters), Machaut gives a pseudoautobiographical account of an affair with a young admirer, Toute-Belle. A sort of epistolary novel in verse, the work is more likely a fiction than an account of a real affair, though many early scholars sought to see in it a *roman à clef*. It is notable for its verisimilitude and for its apparently parodic depiction of *fin'amors*.

The shorter *dits* include the *Dit de la Marguerite*, the *Dit de la Fleur de Lis et de la Marguerite*, the *Dit de la Harpe*, and the *Dit de la Rose*.

In addition to his *dits amoureux*, Machaut composed two other long poems: *Confort d'ami* (1356–57; 4,004 lines) and *Prise d'Alexandrie* (1369–71; 8,886 lines and three prose letters). The *Confort*, incorporating many exempla, was written to console Charles the Bad, who had been taken prisoner by John II in April 1356. The *Prise* is a verse account of the career of Pierre de Lusignan, king of Cyprus, which culminated with the capture of Alexandria in 1365.

Machaut's musical works fall into three genres: motets, settings of fixed-form lyrics, and Mass. Fifteen of Machaut's motets set French texts, six set Latin texts, and two mix French and Latin. The earliest date we have for a work by Machaut is the Latin motet *Bone pastor Guillerme/ Bone pastor qui/Bone pastor*, written for the occasion of the election of Guillaume de Trie as archbishop of Reims in 1324. Most of the remaining motets, dated before ca. 1350, celebrate *fin'amors*. The invective against Fortune in Machaut's most popular motet, *Qui es promesses/ Ha Fortune/Et non est*, was known to Chaucer. The last three of Machaut's motets appear to relate to political events of the late 1350s. Formally, the motets use isorhythmic designs based on chant tenors and are evenly divided among bipartite designs with diminution and unipartite designs. Three motets are based on secular tenors in virelai or rondeau form, one of which, *Lasse comment oublieray/ Se j'aim mon loyal/Pour quoy me bat mes maris*, sets a 13th-century dance song, the complaint of a *malmariée*.

Machaut is unique among 14th-century composers in his cultivation of the difficult *lai* with music. Although most of the musical *lais* are monophonic, their great length, demanding a half-hour or more in performance, requires an attention to formal balance and development unprecedented in medieval music.

The composition of polyphonic songs based on the *formes fixes* of ballade, rondeau, and virelai, began probably in the 1340s. Several experimental early works give the impression that Machaut was decisive in the development of this new musical style. The mature works, with a highly melismatic text carrying voice accompanied by textless tenor and contratenor, remained standard through most of the 15th century. A small core of works, mostly ballades, circulated widely, reaching Languedoc, Italy, and the empire, especially the popular *De petit po*, *De Fortune me day plaindre*, and *De toutes fleurs*. The learned enumeration of mythological characters in the *Voir dit* double ballade *Quant Theseus/Ne quier veoir* and the clear musical setting-off of the refrain are characteristics imitated in later 14th-century ballades.

Machaut's Mass, formerly thought to have been composed for the coronation of Charles V at Reims on May 19, 1364, is now considered to have been composed for a foundation made by Guillaume and his brother Jean for services to commemorate their deaths. The Mass appears to have been performed regularly at these services at the cathedral of Reims until after 1411.

Machaut stands at the culmination of a movement in French literature marked by a growing interest in the manuscript presentation of an author's works. Several manuscripts, prepared at various stages of Machaut's career, collect his complete works, carefully organized into sections by genre, most usually retaining the same order from manuscript to manuscript, with new works added at the end of each series. In general, it appears that each genre is arranged in chronological order. Such complete-works manuscripts had an influence on later poets, such as Froissart and Christine de Pizan; the transmission of musical works after Machaut, however, was confined largely to mixed anthologies.

The Machaut manuscripts are often elaborately illuminated, and the series of illustrations for a given narrative poem was in many cases doubtless determined by the author. The several artists who illustrated Machaut's manuscripts include figures known for their work on manuscripts of kings John II and Charles V. Unfortunately, the original owners of these volumes, except for a posthumous collection belonging to the duke of Berry, have not been conclusively identified.

See also **Charles II the Bad; Charles V the Wise; Christine de Pizan**

Further Reading

Machaut, Guillaume de. *Œuvres de Guillaume de Machaut*, ed. Ernest Hoepffner. 3 vols. Paris: Didot, 1908–21.

——. *Guillaume de Machaut: poésies lyriques*, ed. Vladimir Chichmaref. 2 vols. Paris: Champion, 1909.

——. *Guillaume de Machaut: Musikalische Werke*, ed. Friedrich Ludwig. 4 vols. Leipzig: Breitkopf and Härtel, 1926–54.

——. *Polyphonic Music of the Fourteenth Century*, ed. Leo Schrade. Monaco: L'Oiseau-Lyre, 1956, Vols. 2–3: *The Works of Guillaume de Machaut*.

——. *Guillaume de Machaut: Le jugement du roy de Behaigne and Remede de Fortune*, ed. and trans. James I. Wimsatt, William W. Kibler, and Rebecca A. Baltzer. Athens: University of Georgia Press, 1988.

——. *The Judgment of the King of Navarre*, ed. and trans. R. Barton Palmer. New York: Garland, 1988.

——. *Le confort d'ami*, ed. and trans. R. Barton Palmer. New York: Garland, 1992.

Avril, François. *Manuscript Painting at the Court of France: The Fourteenth Century*. New York: Braziller, 1978.

Brownlee, Kevin. *Poetic Identity in Guillaume de Machaut*. Madison: University of Wisconsin Press, 1984.

Calin, William. *A Poet at the Fountain: Essays on the Narrative Verse of Guillaume de Machaut*. Lexington: University of Kentucky Press, 1974.

Cerquiglini, Jacqueline. "*Un engin si soutil*": *Guillaume de Machaut et l'écriture au XIVe siècle*. Paris: Champion, 1985.

Earp, Lawrence. *Guillaume de Machaut: A Guide to Research*. Forthcoming.

Guillaume de Machaut: poète et compositeur. Paris: Klincksieck, 1982.

Huot, Silvia. *From Song to Book: The Poetics of Writing in Old French Lyric and Lyrical Narrative Poetry*. Ithaca: Cornell University Press, 1987.

Imbs, Paul. *Le Voir-dit de Guillaume de Machaut: étude littéraire*. Paris: Klincksieck, 1991.

Leech-Wilkinson, Daniel. *Machaut's Mass: An Introduction*. Oxford: Clarendon, 1990.

Machabey, Armand. *Guillaume de Machaut: La vie et l'œuvre musicale*. 2 vols. Paris: Richard-Masse, 1955.

Poirion, Daniel. *Le poète et le prince: l'évolution du lyrisme courtois de Guillaume de Machaut à Charles d'Orléans*. Paris: Presses Universitaires de France, 1965.

WILLIAM W. KIBLER/LAWRENCE EARP

MACROBIUS (fl. 400–425) The identity of Macrobius is disputed. Although not a Roman by birthplace, he lived in Rome and received a good education by the standards of his time. His two major works—written for the education of his son, Eustathius—were *Saturnalia* and *Commentary on the Dream of Scipio.* These had the greatest influence in the Middle Ages and Renaissance, although one or two other writings have also been attributed to Macrobius. Macrobius's thought is based on Platonic philosophy and cosmology; he also was recognized as an authority on the virtues.

The *Saturnalia* has not survived in its entirety. All extant manuscripts derive from a single codex of the late eighth or early ninth century. Today the work is divided into seven books that constitute a symposium or banquet; that is, the *Saturnalia* purports to relate how a gathering of learned men celebrated in seemly fashion the three-day feast of the Saturnalia by discussing learned or entertaining features of Virgil's life, knowledge, and poetry. Virgil is esteemed by almost every celebrant as a master of all knowledge; his *Aeneid* is itself viewed as a kind of sacred poem deserving admiration and understanding. Various topics are chosen for discussion and debate during the gathering. On the first day, the men take up different Roman institutions such as the Saturnalian feast itself, the calendar, and religion; these subjects are followed, in the afternoon, by striking sayings from antiquity and, later, topics such as wine and pleasure (Books 1 and 2). On the second day, they take up philosophical and astronomical topics and legal institutions, then commentary on civilization, and finally the quality of different fruits (Book 3). On the third and last day, there is discussion of Virgil as an artist, and especially as a rhetorician and a consummate imitator of Homer and other Greek and Latin antecedents; this section includes extensive quotations from, and cross-references to, Virgil's three

masterpieces: *the Aeneid, Bucolics,* and *Georgics* (Books 4, 5, and 6). The last book treats scientific and medical matters. The *Saturnalia* therefore illustrates what was of interest to educated, civilized Romans in Macrobius's time.

The *Commentary on the Dream of Scipio* survives complete. Its two books contain extensive commentary on scientific and philosophical topics suggested by Cicero's account of Scipio's dream of his elevation to the heavens after death. The most influential part of the *Commentary* is found at the beginning. Here Macrobius discusses the uses of fables *(narratio fabulosa)* in philosophical discourse and the distinction between true and false dreams. Philosophical fables are allegories in which the myth covers a truth about divinity, science, or morality. Among the allegories are dreams, which Macrobius classifies as true or false prophecies (he categorizes them according to mode). The most important are enigmatic dreams that may be true *(somnium)* or false *(insomnium)*, as in wish-fulfillment dreams or nightmares. The *visum* shows the dreamer what will actually happen, and the *oraculum* has someone tell him or her of future events. However, if what is seen or foretold in the dream is false, it is termed a *visio*. These definitions serve as an introduction to Cicero's text, the fictional account of a dream. The commentary that follows draws its abundant philosophical and scientific information from Platonic cosmology.

The *Saturnalia* and the *Commentary* were widely disseminated during the Middle Ages, although their relative influence varied, if we can judge by the dates and numbers of manuscripts that survive from different periods. Both served as encyclopedic sources in Platonic and Neoplatonic philosophy and cosmogony. The influence of the *Commentary* reached a high point in the twelfth and thirteenth centuries, whereas the *Saturnalia* came into its own in the late medieval period and the Renaissance. This is not to say, however, that both were not widely known and used in all periods. In Italy, Macrobius influenced Boccacio, Petrarch, and probably Dante, among others. Moreover, the discussion in *Saturnalia* concerning Virgil's art fit medieval ideas on literary composition and interpretation, especially in the art of invention and rewriting of antecedent sources. Such rewriting could be original. The way Virgil is said to imitate and allude to his Greek and Latin antecedents might well have influenced Dante's rewriting of his master Virgil in the *Divine Comedy.* The representation of his universe might well have been influenced by cosmogonies like that in Macrobius's *Commentary.*

See also **Boccaccio, Giovanni; Dante Alighieri; Petrarca, Francesco**

Further Reading

Editions and Translations

Macrobius. *Commentary on the Dream of Scipio,* trans. William Harris Stahl. Records of Civilization: Sources and Studies, 48. New York: Columbia University Press, 1952.

——. *Commentarii in somnium Scipionis,* ed. Jacob Willis. Leipzig: Teubner, 1963a.

——. *Saturnalia,* ed. Jacob Willis. Leipzig: Teubner, 1963b.

——. *I saturnali,* ed. and trans. Nino Marinone. Classici Latini. Turin: Unione Tipografico-Edkrice Torinese, 1967.

——. *The Saturnalia,* trans. Percival Vaughan Davies. Records of Civilization: Sources and Studies, 79. New York: Columbia University Press, 1969.

Studies

Barker-Benfield, B. C., and P. K. Marshall. "Macrobius." In *Texts and Transmission: A Survey of the Latin Classics,* ed. L. D. Reynolds. Oxford: Clarendon, 1983, pp. 222–235.

De Paolis, Paolo. "Macrobio 1934–1984." *Lustrum,* 28–29, 1986, pp. 107–254.

——. "Addendum." *Lustrum,* 30, 1988, pp. 7–9.

Dronke, Peter. *Fabula: Explorations into the Uses of Myth in Medieval Platonism.*

Mittellateinische Studien und Texte, 9. Leiden, Cologne: Brill, 1974.

Hüttig, Albrecht. *Macrobius im Mittelaker: Ein Beitrag zur Rezeptionsgeschicbte der Commentarii in Somnium Scipionis.* Freiburger Beiträge zur Mittelaiterlichen Geschichte: Studien und Texte, 2. Frankfurt, Bern, New York, and Paris: Peter Lang, 1990.

Kelly, Douglas. *The Conspiracy of Allusion: Description, Rewriting, and Authorship from Macrobius to Medieval Romance.* Studies in Christian Thought, 20. Leiden: Brill, 1999.

Maronine, Nino. "Macrobio." *Enciclopedia virgiliana,* Vol. 3. Rome: Istituto della Enciclopedia Italians, 1987, pp. 299–304.

Rabuse, Georg. "Macrobio, Ambrosio Teodosio." *Enciclopedia dantesca.* Vol. 3. Rome: Istituto della Enciclopedia Italiana, 1984, pp. 757–759.

DOUGLAS KELLY

MAGNÚS HÁKONARSON (r. 1263–1280)

Magnús Hákonarson son of Hákon Hákonarson, ruled Norway 1263–1280; he became king in 1257, and ruled together with his father until Hákon died in 1263.

Magnús Hákonarson and his closest advisers, the "good men," concentrated on the domestic conditions of Norway. Legislative and organizational work characterized Magnús Hákonarson's reign, and secured him the name *lagabætir* ("law-mender"). During his reign, the State Council was more firmly structured than before. Furthermore, he saw to it that a staff of civil servants was educated at the royal chapel, the Apostolic Church in Bergen. We are able to distinguish a group of diplomats employed in his service during his reign.

The object of his legislation was a comprehensive revision of the old law books. The legal revision was a continuation of the State Laws dating from the time of Magnús Erlingsson (1161–1184) and Hákon Hákonarson (1217–1263). The latter had initiated the revision of the Frostuþing Law. The revision of the law went through two stages. The first one included a revision of the law books for Gulaþing in 1267, and Eiðsifa- and Borgarþing in 1268. The latter consisted of the working out of the National Law in 1274 (which also came to apply to the Faroe Islands), a Town Law in 1276, and two law codes for Iceland, *Járnsíða* in 1271 and *Jónsbók* in 1281. An older court law was expanded and revised, and became the *Hirðskrá* (1273–1277).

The object of this legislative work was to create uniform laws for the entire country. The legislation increased the authority of the king with regard to the administration and execution of the laws, as well as the public regulation of society. At the same time, it entailed important reforms, regulation of the tax system and of the institutions for the poor. There is no actual Christian Law in the National Law. The reason for this exclusion was a major conflict between the monarchy and the Church concerning Christian legislation, dating from the end of the 1260s. Magnús Hákonarson claimed that the king and the Church should administer the Christian legislation in unison. On the basis of this claim, Christian legislative decisions were publicized in a statute dating from the middle of the 1260s. The revision of the Gulaþing Law and the Eiðsifa-and Borgarþing law in 1267 and 1268 included the Christian Law. During the revision of the Frostubing Law, the king was strongly opposed by the new archbishop, Jón rauði ("the red"), who independently started to make a Trondic Christian Law in accordance with purely ecclesiastical principles. The conflict between the king and the archbishop was difficult, but an agreement was reached in Tønsberg in 1277.

Magnús Hákonarson's first task as absolute monarch was to conclude a peace treaty with Scotland. Thus, he abandoned his father's expansive foreign policy. The negotiations with the Scottish king began in 1264, and an agreement was reached two years later, the Treaty of Perth.

Magnús Hákonarson gave up his claim to the contested islands, the Hebrides and the Isle of Man, in return for a one-time compensation of 4,000 pounds sterling and 100 pounds sterling annually in perpetuity; at the same time, Norwegian control over the Orkney Islands and the Shetland Islands was secured. Magnús Hákonarson preserved the contact his father had established with neighboring countries and with Europe. His relations with Sweden and Denmark were peaceful, even though he became involved in the dispute over the throne in Sweden in the 1270s and in inheritance claims in Denmark. He also extended legal rights of all German-speaking merchants in Norway, surpassing the rights of native and other foreign merchants. This was the first step in the development of special privileges for the Germans in Norway, based upon their special role in the economy of the country.

See also **Hákon Hákonarson**

Further Reading

Literature

Koht, Halvdan. "The Scandinavian Kingdoms Until the End of the Thirteenth Century." In *The Cambridge Medieval History 6*. Ed. J. R. Tanner *et al.* Cambridge: Cambridge University Press, 1929, pp. 362–92.

Seip, Jens Arup. *Sættargjerden i Tunsberg og kirkens jurisdiksjon*. Oslo: Det Norske Videnskaps-akademi i Oslo, 1942.

Helle, Knui. "Tendenser i nyere norsk høymiddelalderforskning." *Historisk tidsskrift* (Norway) 40 (1960–61), 337–70.

Helle, Knut. "Trade and Shipping Between Norway and England in the Reign of Håkon Håkonsson(1217–1263)." *Sjøfartshistorisk årbok* (Bergen) (1967), 7–33.

Helle, Knut. "Anglo-Norwegian Relations in the Reign of Håkon Håkonsson 1217–63." *Mediaeval Scandinavia* 1 (1968), 101–14.

Gunnes, Erik. "Kirkeligjurisdiksjon i Norge 1153–1277." *Historisk tidsskrifi* (Norway) 49 (1970), 121–60.

Crawford, Barbara E. "The Earls of Orkney-Caithness and Their Relations with the

Kings of Norway and Scotland: 1150–1470." Diss. St. Andrews University, 1971.

Helle, Knut. *Konge og gode menn i norsk riksstyring ca. 1150–1319.* Bergern Universitetsforlaget, 1972.

Crawford, Barbara E. "Weland of Stiklaw: A Scottish Royal Servant at the Norwegian Court." *Historisk tidsskrift* (Norway) 52 (1973), 329–39.

Helle, Knut. *Norge blir en stat 1130–1319.* 2nd ed. Handbok i Norges historie, 3. Bergen: Universitetsforiaget, 1974.

Lunden, Kåre. *Norge under Sverreætten 1177–1319.* Norges historie, 3. Oslo: Cappelen, 1976.

Bagge, Sverre. "Kirkens jurisdiksjon i kristenrettssaker før 1277." *Historisk tidsskrift* (Norway) 60 (1981), 133–59.

Helle, Knut. "Norway in the High Middle Ages: Recent Views on the Structure of Society." *Scandinavian Journal of History* 6 (1981), 161–89.

Bagge, Sverre. "The Formation of the State and Concepts of Society in 13th Century Norway." In *Continuity and Change: Political Institutions and Literary Monuments in the Middle Ages. A Symposium.* Ed. Elisabeth Vestergaard. Odense: Odense University Press, 1986, pp. 43–61.

Bagge, Sverre. "Borgerkrig og statsutvikling i Norge i middelalderen." *Historisk tidsskrift* (Norway) 65 (1986), 145–97.

Sandvik, Gudmund. "Sættargjerda i Tunsberg og kongens jurisdiksjon." In *Samfunn. Rett. Rettferdighet. Festskrifttil Torstein Eckhoffs 70-årsdag.* Ed. A. Bratholm *et al.* Oslo: Tano, 1986, pp. 563–85.

Bagge, Sverre. *The Political Thought of the King's Mirror.* Mediaeval Scandinavia Supplements, 3. Odense: Odense University Press, 1987.

JÓN VIÐAR SIGURÐSSON

MAIMONIDES (1138–1204) Likened by more than one medieval Jewish writer to the prophet Moses ("From Moses to Moses there was none like Moses"), Moses ben Maimon (correctly, Maimūn) was born in Córdoba not in 1135, as is usually assumed (and so the 850th anniversary was universally celebrated in 1985) but in 1138, where he was educated and began writing his first works.

His father, Maimkn, was a *dayan* (religious judge) of the Jewish community of Córdoba, and a student of the great Joseph ibn Megash, and himself author of some responsa and "Letters of Consolation" meant to strengthen the Jews in the face of the Almohad persecution. It was due to this that the family left Spain around 1160, settling first in Fez, Morocco, and then briefly in Palestine. From there they went to Egypt and settled at Fustat, a suburb of Cairo, where Jews were allowed to live. The twin tragedies of the death of his father and then his brother David devasted the young scholar, who had to support himself and his family by becoming a doctor and court physician to the *wazīr* (prime minister) and his son. Never did he convert, or even appear outwardly to do so, to Islam, as a long-discredited legend maintains.

Within a few years he had become by reputation the most famous physician of the Muslim world. At the same time, his reputation in Jewish learning, established already by his brilliant commentary on the Mishnah, was growing. Questions poured in from all parts of the world. Working almost entirely from memory, and under the most difficult conditions imposed upon him by the demands of his medical practice, he composed in clear and simple Hebrew the *Mishneh Torah*, a work in fourteen volumes that encompasses the whole of Jewish law. This work quickly became the accepted authority for Jewish law, the only such composition ever written by someone who was not a rabbi.

Nevertheless, there were critics. First, he had not cited his sources, and although sources have been found for virtually every statement, lesser scholars had difficulty in accepting some of his rulings. Second, there were disagreements in some cases as to the rulings themselves. Finally, certain religious zealots who lacked training in philosophy objected strenuously to his philosophical notions, contained both in his commentary on the Mishnah and in the legal code. The situation worsened when he wrote his great philosophical work, *Dalālat al-bā'irīn* (*Guide for the Perplexed*). Clearly intended only for those with the necessary preliminary background of rigorous study, the book was translated twice from Judeo-Arabic into Hebrew and thus soon fell into the hands of those without such background. Its clear denial of such fundamental popular beliefs as miracles, creation in time, resurrection, and so forth combined with allegorizing of many biblical and rabbinic statements, gave rise to charges of heresy. The result was a controversy that lasted in Spain and Provence for hundreds of years, and actually led to Jewish-inspired condemnation and burning of the book at Montpellier around 1232.

In spite of the philosophical controversy, Maimonides continued to be revered as a legal authority throughout the Middle Ages in Spain and elsewhere. Even those who disagreed with him, such as Nahmanides and Ibn Adret, cite him constantly and respectfully. Communities, such as Tudela, enacted decrees according to which only his rulings were to be followed; similar decisions were made throughout North Africa and Yemen.

No less important was his impact on Christians in Spain. In Aragón-Catalonia, various kings ordered translations of the *Guide* and even of the *Mishneh Torah*. Philosophers in Spain (and, of course, the scholastics in general) who were influenced by him include Poncio Carbonell (fourteenth century) and, more important, Alfonso de la Torre (fifteenth century). Sancho, son of Jaime I, archbishop of Toledo (1266–1275), and Archbishop Gonzalo García Gudiel (1280–1299) both possessed copies of his work. In the fifteenth century, Pedro Díaz de Toledo, possibly a *converso* (Jewish convert to Christianity), made a Spanish translation of the *Guide*.

Maimonides died in 1204, and tradition maintains that his grave is near Tiberias.

Further Reading

Maimonides. *Guide for the Perplexed*. Trans. P. Díaz de Toledo. Ed. Moshé Lazar. Madison, Wisc., 1989.

Ormsby, E. (ed.) *Moses Maimonides and His Time*. Washington, D.C., 1989.

Roth, N. *Maimonides: Essays and Texts*. Madison, Wisc., 1985 (also with bibliographies, including Spanish).

NORMAN ROTH

MALISPINI, RICORDANO (probably 14th century) Ricordano Malispini was allegedly the thirteenth-century author of a history of Florence from its legendary origins to 1282; a continuation down to 1286 was ascribed to a nephew, Giacotto. Some scholars consider this chronicle an important source for Giovanni Villani and Dante. Documentary evidence has been found for Giacotto's existence, though not for Ricordano's. However, the chronicle itself contains anachronisms, some of which were first noted by Scheffer-Boichorst (1870), and these make a fourteenth-century date very probable. A chief purpose of the chronicle appears to have been to celebrate the exploits of members of the Bonaguisi family, and to link the Bonaguisi with the aristocratic and once-powerful Malispini family. Malispini writes that he derived his information from chronicles he found in the house of his Capocci kinsmen in Rome, and also in the Badia of Florence. The Capocci records seem identifiable with the *Libro fiesolano*, which is a translation and adaptation of the *Liber de origine civitatis*, the first surviving account of the founding of Florence. The Badia records seem identifiable with an anonymous compendium of Giovanni Villani. The only known text of this compendium, discovered by Lami (1890), is manuscript 2.1.252, held in the

Biblioteca Nazionale Centrale in Florence. Malispini also includes information about some families that are not mentioned either in the *Libro fiesolano* or in the compendium of Villani.

The *Libro fiesolano* covers the period from the legendary origins of Florence to its rebuilding after Totila's sack (which is fictitious) and the final capture of Fiesole. The anonymous compendium abridges and paraphrases Villani's chronicle from chapter 30 of the first book (Catiline's conspiracy) until 1336. Malispini copies his account of early Florentine history from the *Libro fiesolano*, rather than from the anonymous compendium, but he includes Charlemagne's supposed participation in the rebuilding of Florence, which is mentioned in the compendium but omitted in *Libro fiesolano*. Malispini then follows the anonymous compendium to 1282, and Giacotto's coda follows it to 1286.

One manuscript, often considered the oldest and most reliable copy of Malispini, has a distinctive relationship to the anonymous compendium. This is manuscript 2.4.27, in the Biblioteca Nazionale Centrale in Florence. It corresponds almost exactly to the anonymous compendium not only for the period from Charlemagne to 1286, but also for 1286–1317. The only novelty in this concluding post-Malispinian portion of the manuscript is its interpolated passages praising the Bonaguisi and other related families. These passages are very similar to others praising the same families in this and other manuscripts of the Malispinian chronicle. The presence of such passages in both the Malispinian and the post-Malispinian portions of this manuscript points to the genealogical purpose and the fourteenth-century date of the Malispinian compilation. A further confirmation of its late date is furnished by Porta (1986, 1994), who discovered links between the texts of the anonymous compendium of Villani and Malispini on the one hand, and a revised version, made after 1333, of Giovanni

Villani's chronicle on the other. If Villani had copied Malispini, diese links would be present in the first version of Villani's chronicle as well.

Such evidence should lay to rest the old theory that Malispini was the thirteenth-century father of Florentine historiography. Malispini was, rather, a late fourteenth-century compiler, whose originality was limited to celebrating the nobility and antiquity of certain Florentine families and to furnishing information about himself and his sources designed to validate such genealogical lore.

Further Reading

Editions

Libro fiesolano, ed. Otio Hartwig. In *Quellen und Forschungen zur ältesten Geschichte der Stadt Florenz*, Vol. 1. Marburg: N. G. Elwert'sche Verlagsbuch, 1875, pp. 37–65.

Malispini, Ricordano. *Storia fiorentina, col seguito di Giacotto Malispini, dalla edificazione di Firenze sino all'anno 1286*, ed. Vincenzio Follini. Florence: G. Ricri, 1816.

Villani, Giovanni. *Nuova cronica*, 3 vols., ed. Giuseppe Porta. Parma: Ugo Guanda Editore, 1990–1991.

Critical Studies

Aquilecchia, Giovanni. "Malispini, Ricordano." In *Encyclopedia dantesca*, Vol. 3. Rome: Istituto della Encyclopedia Italiana, 1971, pp. 791–792.

Barnes, John C. "Un problems in via di chiusura: La 'Cronica' malispiniana." *Studi e Problemi di Critica Testuale*, 27, 1983, pp. 15–32.

Davis, Charles T. *Dante and the Idea of Rome*. Oxford: Clarendon, 1957, pp. 244–263.

——. "The Malispini Question." *Studi Medievali*, Series 3(10), 1970, pp. 215–254. (Reprinted in *Dante's Italy and Other Essays*. Philadelphia: University of Pennsylvania Press, 1984, pp. 94–136.)

De Matteis, Maria C. "Ancora su Malispini, Villani, e Dante: Per un riesame dei rapporti tra cultura storica e profezia Erica nell'Alighieri." *Bullettino dell'Istituto Storico Italiano per il Medio Evo e Archivio*

Muratoriano, 82, 1970, pp. 329–390. (Published 1973.)

——. "Malispini da Villani o Villani da Malispini? Una ipotesi sui rapporti tra Ricordano Malispini, il 'Compendiatore,' e Giovanni Villani." *Bullettino dell'Istituto Storico Italiano per il Media Evo e Archivio Muratoriano,* 84, 1973, pp. 145–221. (Published 1978.)

Lami, Vittorio. "Di un compendio inedito della cronica di Giovanni Villani nelle sue relazioni con la storia fiorentina malispiniana." *Archivio Storico Italiano,* Series 5(5), 1890, pp. 369–416.

Maissen, Thomas. "Actila, Totila, e Cario Magno." *Archivio Storico Italiano,* 152 (fasc. 561), 1994, pp. 586–639.

Morghen, Raffaello. "Note malispiniane." *Bullettino dell'Istituto Storico Italiano per il Media Evo e Archivio Muratoriano,* 40, 1920, pp. 105–126.

——. "Dante, il Villani, e Ricordano Malispini." *Bullettino dell'Istituto Storico Italiano per il Media Evo e Archivio Muratoriano,* 41, 1921, pp. 171–194.

——. "Ancora sulla questione malispiniana." *Bullettino dell'Istituto Storico Italiano per il Media Evo e Archivio Muratoriano,* 46, 1931, pp. 41–92.

Porta, Giuseppe. "Sul testo e la lingua di Giovanni Villani." *Lingua Nostra,* 47, 1986, pp. 37–40.

——. "Le varianti redazionali come strumento di verifica dell'autenticità dei testi: Villani e Malispini." *Convegno della società italiana di filologia romanza, Università di Messina, December 19–22, 1991.* Messina, 1994, pp. 481–529.

Scheffer–Boichorst, Paul. "Die florentinische Geschichte der Malespini, eine Fälschung." *Historische Zeitschrift,* 24, 1870, pp. 274–313. (Reprinted in *Florentiner Studien.* Leipzig: S. Hirzel, 1874, pp. 1–44.)

CHARLES T. DAVIS

MALORY, THOMAS (1414/18–1471)

One of the latest and most effective of the many medieval writers about King Arthur and his knights of the Round Table. In his book traditionally called *Le Morte Darthur (The Death of Arthur)* Malory gathers together the results of centuries of storytelling, mainly by medieval French authors. He synthesizes the narratives into one massive, varied book of the life, acts, and death of Arthur and his company. The wealth of incident, rich implications, and laconic style make his the only version of the huge number of medieval Arthurian tales in European languages that continues to be read directly and simply for pleasure by the modern reader. The main characters—King Arthur himself; Sir Lancelot, his best knight, but also lover of his queen, Guinevere; his sister's son the violent Sir Gawain; his incestuously begotten son and nephew Sir Mordred, who kills him; Merlin the magician—are at the center of a set of tales of wonders, bravery, love, joy, and tragedy. But Malory tells romance as history—the history of England said to be in the 5th century, but actually represented in terms of the feelings, strivings, ideals, betrayals, even the armor and the geography (e.g., Camelot is identified with Winchester) of Malory's own troubled 15th-century England. Malory's achievement is the source of many of the retellings of Arthurian story so common today in the United States and Britain.

Life

Identification of the Sir Thomas Malory who names himself as author of *Le Morte Darthur* has been controversial, but thanks to the work of P.J.C. Field and others it seems once more to be probable that he was the Sir Thomas Malory of Newbold Revel in Warwickshire. He was the son of a country gentleman, inherited his lands in 1433 or 1434, was knighted, and perhaps served as a soldier in France. In 1445 he became a member of parliament—a sign of gentry status, not of democratic election. He also became embroiled in the factional disturbances of the times and was on numerous occasions in the next ten years accused of such violent crimes as ambush, rape, extortion, cattle stealing, theft of money, and prison breaking. He underwent a series of imprisonments and despite his escapes spent much time in jail. Some of the accusations, perhaps some of the violence, may have been politically motivated, for Malory supported various noblemen (including Warwick the "Kingmaker") who contended for power during the Wars of the Roses, following now one king, the Lancastrian Henry VI, and now another, the Yorkist Edward IV.

After a period of freedom Malory spent the years 1468–70 in prison, where he wrote *Le Morte Darthur*. The book is full of violent adventure and concludes in civil war and Arthur's death. But it is also deeply concerned with the high ideals of chivalry, with honor, loyalty, and goodness. It may seem that the book's inherent nobility contrasts strangely with the apparent criminality of the author. But perhaps Malory saw himself in imagination as a modern Sir Lancelot fighting for and asserting his own and his lord's rights against other "false recreant knights," as he might have called them.

Text

Two versions of *Le Morte Darthur* survive, neither originating immediately from Malory's hand. One is the edition printed by Caxton in 1485, reprinted 1498, 1529, 1557, circa 1578, again (somewhat changed) in 1634, then not again till 1816, In the later 19th century began the modern series of editions based on Caxton, including that notoriously illustrated by Aubrey Beardsley (1893–94). But in 1934 a manuscript of *Le Morte Darthur* now in the British Library (Add. 59678) was discovered in Winchester College; it was first edited in 1947 by Eugène Vinaver.

The Winchester manuscript contains a text slightly different from Caxton's, including fuller versions of eight addresses by Malory to the reader, varying in length from a few sentences to the paragraph at the end of the whole book. They come at the end of substantial sections and are known as *explicits* (*explicit*, "it is finished"). From these *explicits* Vinaver deduced that, instead of one book, Malory wrote eight entirely separate romances. Their apparent separateness is enhanced in his edition by such typographical devices as capitals at the end of the sections for which there is no manuscript justification. Vinaver's edition is thus confusingly entitled *The Works of Sir Thomas Malory*. Virtually all scholars and critics now reject this concept of totally separate works but do accept the episodic nature of the work even within the eight main sections and the existence of a number of inevitable inconsistencies both between and within the main sections.

The Winchester manuscript is separated from Malory's own writing by at least one intermediate copy and lacks a few leaves at beginning and end. Although Caxton had the Winchester manuscript in his shop for a period of time, his own edition differs from it significantly. He edited the text by cutting it into 21 books comptising 507 chapters, adding a fine Prologue and chapter headings, reducing some of the *explicits*, shortening (to its advantage) the episode of the Roman War by almost half, and making some other minor verbal changes. By comparing the two versions we can reconstruct Malory's authentic text, which is now most nearly approached by Vinaver's edition.

The language of the Winchester manuscript and Caxton's edition is mainly standard mid-15th-century London English, with occasional northernisms. Being prose, it is easily modernized; the original, though old-fashioned and containing a few unfamiliar words, offers no difficulty apart from idiosyncratic spelling. As a narrative the story is engrossing, but it is not at all like a modern novel, and to read it as such is to court disappointment and misunderstanding.

Summary

Malory plunges straight into his story, telling of the begetting of Arthur by Uther

Pendragon, king of all England, on the beautiful widow (as she has just unwittingly become) of the duke of Cornwall, Uther being magically transformed by Merlin into the duke's likeness so as to enter her bedroom. The laconic matter-of-fact style, concentrating on essentials, contrasts piquantly with the drama of passionate feeling and the magic. This contrast, much developed, is part of Malory's unending fascination. As his great story progresses, he makes less use of magic, though it is always an element of mystery in the background, suggesting a dimension beyond the material world and becoming prominent again near the end, with the return of Excalibur to the lake and the queens who carry off the dying Arthur.

We learn of Arthur's fostering, his acceptance as king by the miracle that he alone can draw a sword from a stone, and the gradual establishment of his power over dissident barons and neighboring kings. Merlin's magic helps. Arthur lusts after King Lot of Orkney's wife, Morgause, mother of Gawain and other heroic knights and, unknown to him, his own half-sister. On her he begets Mordred, who will ultimately be his death. Arthur loves and marries Guinevere, though Merlin warns him that she and Lancelot will love each other. She brings with her the Round Table, which henceforth will denote the elite company of knights in Arthur's court.

This first section thus sets the scene and establishes Arthur's supremacy, though with its account of wars it is a little less typical of Malory's mature style, which concentrates more on individual adventures. Malory is attempting to summarize his complex sources of French prose romance, turning them into a kind of history, and minor inconsistencies inevitably arise. This section also contains the tragic tale of the brothers Balin and Balan; with its concentration on individuals, its fated accidents, nobility of temper, deceit, dissension, and tragedy it is as stark and moving a story as any Icelandic saga.

But there are also stories of mystery, magic, adventure, betrayal, and mishap that end in triumph. Arthur gains the magic sword Excalibur from the Lady of the Lake. The noble concept of the High Order of Knighthood is affirmed, reinforced as it is by the oath, sworn by knights of the Round Table at the annual feast of Pentecost, never to do wrong, always to honor ladies, and so on.

Malory's *explicit* to the first main section refers to himself as a "knight-prisoner" and appears to suggest that he may not be able to continue to write. But the opening words of the second section echo this *explicit* so clearly as to make continuity certain. This next section is based mainly on a 14th-century English alliterative poem, the *Morte Arthure*, which makes Malory's own style more alliterative. It tells how Arthur rejects the obligation to pay tribute to the emperor of Rome and how he wages successful war right into Italy. Here Lancelot makes his first appearance as a brave young warrior.

The third main section moves into the area Malory has made his own for ever—the feats of individual knights wandering in search of adventure in strange forests and castles. The hero of this book is Lancelot himself, Malory's favorite knight, killing wicked knights, rescuing ladies, resisting seduction. He is rumored to be the lover of Queen Guinevere, which he denies, and Malory does not describe their love. It is a relatively short section, delightfully varied and vividly interesting in event, created from a cunning selection of incidents widely spaced in Malory's voluminous source, the French prose *Lancelot*.

Having now established both Arthur with his Round Table and Lancelot, the supreme example of chivalry, Malory turns in his fourth section to the story of another knight, significant to the whole history, exemplary in himself, and an adornment to the Round Table—Sir Gareth of Orkney, brother to Sir Gawain.

The source is unknown. The story is based on the familiar general pattern of the Fair Unknown, who is a young hero, handsome, brave, and clever but unrecognized. He achieves success by defeating foes older and more experienced than he, winning his beloved, and establishing his identity and his place in society. This has been termed a version of the "family drama," common in fairy tale and romance. It also illustrates the Malorian themes of bravery, noble bearing, and courtesy.

There follows the long section, over a third of the whole work, centered on the story of Tristram and Isolde, with so many other knights and adventures intermingled that it is impossible to summarize adequately. The ancient tragedy of Tristram's and Isoldes obsessive mutual infatuation had already been diluted by Malory's French sources, and at the end of Malory's version the lovers retire to adulterous bliss in Lancelot's castle of Joyous Gard. Tristram is here an adventurous knight similar and almost equal to Lancelot. He has a jesting companion, Sir Dinadan, who brings commonsensical skepticism to the craziness of knight-errantry but is a good knight of his hands for all that. King Mark, husband of Isolde, is portrayed as a treacherous villain. Only incidentally, in a later section, is Mark's murder of Tristram noted. This Tristram section, full of adventures, disguises, unexpected meetings, unexplained departures, and arbitrary battles, has all the mystery and excitement of romance. It is the part of Malory's work least like the world of plausible appearances of the novel.

A digression toward the end of the Tristram section tells how Lancelot was tricked into begetting Sir Galahad upon Elaine, daughter of Sir Pelles. This leads naturally to the sixth section, in which Sir Galahad, now a pure virginal young knight, comes to King Arthur's court. Miraculous events initiate the Quest of the Holy Grail. The Grail, according to Malory, is the dish from which Christ ate with the apostles on Easter, brought to England by Joseph of Arimathea and endowed with properties both holy and magical. Hermits exhort the knights in their quest, visions and allegories abound, though Malory greatly abbreviates the religious didacticism of his French source. Only Galahad, Percival, and Bors succeed in seeing the Grail; Galahad and Percival both die, passing beyond human ken, and Bors is the only successful Grail knight to return to Camelot. Lancelot is granted only a partial vision of the Grail. He is flawed by his love of Guinevere, but Malory changes the monastic spirit of the original, so that Lancelot remains in a sense the hero. Despite all the changes many beautiful and magical scenes remain, as in the appearance of the ship with Percival's sister.

The last two sections of *Le Morte Darthur*, the seventh and eighth, may be considered as one, for they tell of the supreme glory of the Round Table and its tragic end in a series of closely connected episodes. Malory's art is here at its greatest. He blends French and English sources, but what he makes, fleshed out with his own invention, is entirely his own and one of the great achievements of English literature. The core of the story is the continuing love between Lancelot and Guinevere, and the determination of some malcontents to trap them, so that King Arthur has to condemn them. Lancelot has to rescue the queen three times, and on one occasion he accidentally kills Sir Gareth, his beloved friend, whom he had himself knighted. This joins Gareth's brother Gawain to Lancelot's enemies, and eventually Arthur is forced by Gawain to declare war on Lancelot.

During Arthur's absence at the war Mordred claims the throne and attempts to marry Guinevere. Ultimately, after Gawain has repented of his vengeful feud against Lancelot and died from wounds, Mordred confronts Arthur in battle. The bastard son and noble father kill each other in the desolation of the corpse-strewn battlefield. Arthur dies slowly by a "water-side." Excalibur is thrown into a lake and a hand mysteriously grasps it. Queens come in a boat to take Arthur to Avalon. It is an unforgettably eerie scene, rich in the ancient potent symbolism of the separation, dissolution, and healing power of death. Guinevere enters a nunnery; after a final interview with her Lancelot withdraws to a hermitage, and they die without meeting again.

No mere summary can convey the power, beauty, and pathos of these two sections. Much of the action is conveyed through brilliant terse dialogue, occasionally with a touch of grim or sarcastic humor. There is a wealth of incident in such episodes as Lancelot's rescues of Guinevere, or in the beautiful account of the Fair Maid of Ascolat (later spelled Astolat), who dies for love of Lancelot, or the moving story of Lancelot's healing of Sir Urry. The best knight in the world weeps in humility as he performs the miraculous cure, yet he is the one who causes the destruction of Arthur's Round Table.

Malory's imaginative world is narrow. It is composed only of Arthur, of good or bad knights, and a few desirable or treacherous ladies who, with two or three exceptions, are hardly more than ciphers. No ordinary concerns of life appear. Simple themes are illustrated by simple actions, performed by characters with few traits and virtually no inner life. Yet Malory's earnest concentration on fundamental issues of loyalty, love, and combat, guided by a complex system of honor, is intensely alive. The encounters, friendly or hostile, the wanderings, the seemingly arbitrary events combined with the sense of destiny, the comradeship and the betrayals, create a profound symbol of life that we can easily relate to. Malory's prose creates a sense of the man as in his essence he would be: no mere "narrator" but writing directly to us in the colloquial yet dignified manner of a brave and courteous country gentleman,

on a subject that deeply matters to him, the history of Arthur, of England, of all of us.

See also **Caxton, William**

Further Reading

Primary Sources

Brewer, Derek Stanley, ed. *The Morte Darthur, Parts Seven and Eight.* London: Arnold, 1968 [modernized text].

Cowen, Janet, ed. *Le Morte D'Arthur.* 2 vols. Harmondsworth: Penguin, 1969 [Caxton's edition in modernized spelling].

Le Morte D'Arthur Printed by William Caxton 1485. London: Scolar, 1485 [facsimile].

Spisak, James W., ed. *Caxton's Malory.* 2 vols. Berkeley: University of California Press, 1983.

Vinaver, Eugène, ed. *The Works of Sir Thomas Malory.* 3d ed. Rev. P.J.C. Field. 3 vols. Oxford: Clarendon, 1990.

The Winchester Malory. EETS s.s. 4. London: Oxford University Press, 1976 [facsimile].

Secondary Sources

New *CBEL* 1:674–78.

Manual 3:757–71, 909–24.

Archibald, Elizabeth, and A.S.G. Edwards, eds. *A Companion to Malory.* Cambridge: Brewer, 1996.

Bennett, J.A.W., ed. *Essays on Malory.* Oxford: Clarendon, 1963.

Benson, Larry D. *Malory's Morte Darthur.* Cambridge: Harvard University Press, 1976.

Brewer, Derek Stanley. *Symbolic Stories: Traditional Narratives of the Family Drama in English Literature.* Cambridge: Brewer, 1980 [on the story of Sir Gareth].

Field, P.J.C. *The Life and Times of Sir Thomas Malory.* Cambridge: Brewer, 1993.

Gaines, Barry. *Sir Thomas Malory: An Anecdotal Bibliography of Editions 1485–1985.* New York: AMS, 1990.

Ihle, Sandra Ness. *Malory's Grail Quest: Invention and Adaptation in Medieval Prose Romance.* Madison: University of Wisconsin Press, 1983.

Kato, Tomomi, ed. *A Concordance to the Works of Sir Thomas Malory.* Tokyo: University of Tokyo Press, 1974.

Kennedy, Beverly. *Knighthood in the Morte Darthur.* Cambridge: Brewer, 1985.

Knight, Stephen. *Arthurian Literature and Society*. London: Macmillan, 1983.

Lambert, Mark. *Malory: Style and Vision in Le Morte Darthur*. New Haven: Yale University Press, 1975.

Life, Page West. *Sir Thomas Malory and the Morte Darthur: A Survey of Scholarship and Annotated Bibliography*. Charlottesville: University Press of Virginia, 1980.

McCarthy, Terence. *An Introduction to Malory*. Cambridge: Brewer, 1993.

Parins, Marylyn Jackson, ed. *Malory: The Critical Heritage*. London: Routledge, 1988.

Riddy, Felicity. *Sir Thomas Malory*. Leiden: Brill, 1987.

Sandved, Arthur O. *Studies in the Language of Caxton's Malory and That of the Winchester Manuscript*. Oslo: Norwegian Universities Press, 1968.

Spisak, James W., ed. *Studies in Malory*. Kalamazoo: Medieval Institute, 1985.

Takamiya, Toshiyuki, and Derek S. Brewer, eds. *Aspects of Malory*. Cambridge: Brewer, 1981. Repr. with updated bibliography, 1986.

Whitaker, Muriel. *Arthur's Kingdom of Adventure: The World of Malory's Morte Darthur*. Cambridge: Brewer, 1984.

DEREK S. BREWER

MANDEVILLE, JEAN DE (d. 1372) Composed at Liège ca. 1357 by an otherwise unidentifiable English knight-voyager, Mandeville's *Voyages d'outre-mer* was the most popular secular book of its day, surviving in over 250 manuscripts and some ninety incunabula, including translations into Latin, English, Danish, Dutch, German, Italian, Spanish, Czech, and Irish. Of the three distinct versions, the earliest was certainly composed in French on the Continent. An "insular" version, done ca. 1390 in England, is a Middle English classic, whose anonymous author is sometimes considered the "father" of English prose. The *Voyages* popularized the newly discovered wonders of the East, including much fabulous material, and gives a lengthy description of the Holy Land. Mandeville compiled the work at third hand from French translations by Jean Le Long of Saint-Omer (d. 1383) of genuine Latin travel accounts from the early 14th century. Le Long's translations of five Latin travel accounts are found together in several manuscripts, of which the best known is the *Livre des merveilles* (B.N. fr. 2810), copied ca. 1400 for the duke of Burgundy. Mandeville also drew liberally from Vincent de Beauvais's *Speculum naturale*, Marco Polo's *Devisement du monde*, Gossuin de Metz's *Image du monde*, and Brunetto Latini.

Though filled with fabulous accounts, the *Voyages* relates in a simple and unselfconscious prose the sum of medieval knowledge of the world. It explains, for example, why the world is round and incorporates many other accurate observations. Through the centuries, it has been alternately praised for its style and richness and damned for absurdities and plagiarism. The author has on occasion been confused with a Liège physician, Jean de Bourgogne, and with the writer and notary Jean d'Outremeuse. Mandeville is also credited with a French prose lapidary found in 15th-century manuscripts and early printed editions.

See also **Brunetto Latini; Polo, Marco; Vincent de Beauvais**

Further Reading

Mandeville, Jean de. *Mandeville's Travels, Texts and Translations*, ed. M. Letts. London: Hakluyt Society, 1953. [Edition of B.N. fr. 4515 and the English "Egerton" translation.]

———. *Mandeville's Travels*, ed. Michael C. Seymour. Oxford: Clarendon, 1967. [Edition of the English "Cotton" translation.]

———. *The Metrical Version of Mandeville's Travels*, ed. Michael C. Seymour. London: Early English Text Society, 1973.

———. *The Travels of Sir John Mandeville*, trans. C.W.R.D. Moseley. Harmondsworth: Penguin, 1983. [Modern English translation.]

De Poerck, Guy. "La tradition manuscrite des *Voyages* de Jean de Mandeville." *Romanica gandensia* 4 (1955): 125–58.

Goosse, A. "Les lapidaires attribués à Mandeville." *Dialectes belgo-romans* 17 (1960): 63–112.

WILLIAM W. KIBLER

MANFRED (1232–26 February 1266) Manfred was the natural son of Emperor Frederick II Hohenstaufen and Bianca Lancia of Monferrato; he closely resembled his father physically and, to a considerable degree, temperamentally. Manfred was an astute politician and courageous soldier; he was the emperor's intellectual soulmate, but his own personality was less dynamic. Manfred's career was confined to Italy. His illegitimate birth limited his political effectiveness, and he ultimately lost his kingdom to the combined forces of the papacy, Charles of Anjou, Tuscan financiers, and Sicilian barons. The defeat of Manfred sent the *Mezzogiorno* (southern Italy) into a centuries-long decline, the effects of which linger to the present.

Manfred may have studied at Paris and Bologna, and he was active in the courtly culture of the kingdom of Sicily. When Frederick died in December 1250, Manfred became the regent of his half brother, Conrad IV (1250–1254), who was in Germany. Manfred was generally popular among the feudal nobles of the kingdom, but he faced persistent opposition from important barons and cities. In December 1251, he tried but failed to reach an accord with Pope Innocent IV (r. 1243–1254). Manfred may have offered to exchange recognition of papal overlordship for the Sicilian crown. In December 1251, Conrad went to the kingdom to establish his own royal authority. He revoked all of Manfred's fiefs except the principality of Taranto and forced the humiliated Manfred to remain at court.

Conrad died in May 1254. Guelf chroniclers insist that Manfred poisoned him, but other sources do not concur. Manfred then faced great difficulties. Conrad had named the church as guardian of his son, Conradin, and appointed the leader of the German barons, Berthold of Hohenburg, as his bailiff. Innocent IV invested Edmund, the second son of King Henry III of England, with the kingdom. Meanwhile, Pietro Ruffo, who controlled Calabria and Sicily, played Manfred against Innocent.

Most of the nobility of the kingdom rallied to Manfred, whom they considered the natural regent of young Conradin. The pope refused to recognize Conradin's rights and demanded possession of the kingdom. Open warfare ensued, and Innocent excommunicated Manfred and his adherents. Manfred was unprepared for war and quickly sued for peace. During the negotiations he killed a papal partisan and fled to Lucera, the imperial Muslim stronghold near Foggia. Manfred seized the treasury of Frederick II and Conrad IV and raised a powerful army. He defeated the papal army near Foggia. Almost all of Apulia had fallen into his hands by the time Innocent died (10 August 1254).

Manfred could not placate Innocent's successor, Pope Alexander IV (r. 1254–1261), but Alexander actually put little effort into the vendetta of the papacy against the Hohenstaufen. Manfred was thus free to put the kingdom in order. By 1257, he had imprisoned Berthold and banished Pietro Ruffo. On the false rumor that Conradin had died, the Sicilian barons proclaimed Manfred king. He was crowned at Palermo on 10 August 1258. Manfred soon became deeply involved in central and northern Italy. He attempted to create a federation of barons, cities, and factions under his leadership by providing military assistance, negotiating treaties and marriages, and courting urban factions. In 1258, he joined in a promising but unsuccessful alliance with the despot of Epirus, Michael II, against the Byzantine emperor, Michael

VIII Palaeologus. In 1262, Manfred arranged a marriage between his daughter Constance and the *infante,* Peter of Aragon; this marriage would later justify Aragon's intervention in the Sicilian Vespers uprising of 1282.

Manfred reached the height of his power when he and the Ghibelline factions of Florence and Siena defeated the Guelfs of Tuscany at Montaperti on 4 September 1260. He subsequently posed as lord of Italy and sent vicars throughout the peninsula, but he did not have the force to sustain his ambitions. When the energetic Urban IV (r. 1261–1264) became pope, he renewed the assault on Manfred. Urban found a champion in Charles of Anjou, count of Provence and brother of Louis IX of France. Louis had previously blocked papal overtures to Charles, but Urban argued that Manfred had unlawfully dispossessed his nephew Conradin, and this reasoning apparently laid the scruples of the saintly king to rest. The pope also persuaded Florentine and Sienese bankers to finance an invasion of the kingdom of Sicily.

Late in 1262, Manfred attempted to make a deal with Urban, but the negotiations collapsed. The pope invested Charles with the kingdom in December 1262. War soon followed. Manfred's allies scored several early victories against papal and Guelf forces and almost captured the city of Rome in 1264. After Urban died, the new pope, Clement IV (r. 1265–1268), quickly confirmed the treaty with Charles, who left Provence for Rome in May 1265. Manfred dispatched a manifesto to Rome, in which he revived Frederick's argument that the Romans—not the pope—had the right to choose the emperor. There is no extant reply. Charles arrived in Rome on 28 June 1265 and took charge of the war against Manfred.

After an unsuccessful attack on Rome in August 1265, Manfred returned to his kingdom to find his domestic enemies ranged against him and his treasury empty. Many of his allies went over to Charles, made peace with the pope, or became neutral. In December 1265, Charles's army from Provence passed through Piedmont and Lombardy without opposition. Charles moved into Campania in January 1266 without a fight. Betrayed and deserted by the Sicilian barons, Manfred died bravely on the plain of Grandella near Benevento on 26 February 1266. He was buried outside Benevento, but the archbishop of Cosenza later had his remains disinterred and removed from the kingdom to an unmarked grave near Garigliano.

Manfred's fall may have been inevitable. The papacy was determined to extinguish the Hohenstaufen dynasty, and Charles of Anjou was a hard and relentless campaigner, whose talents and war chest were equal to his greed and ambition. The fickle Sicilian barons who betrayed Manfred did not prosper as a result. After slaughtering Manfred's adherents, Charles replaced the treasonous barons with his own French supporters. Charles exploited the efficient Sicilian fiscal apparatus to bleed the kingdom white, but he returned none of the good government that had accompanied the Normans' and the Hohenstaufen's exactions. Commerce fell into the hands of Venetian and Genoese merchants and Tuscan bankers, and wealth flowed to the Angevins or migrated from the *Mezzogiorno* altogether. The powerful, well-ordered, and prosperous kingdom of Sicily gave way to bad government and chronic poverty.

Manfred was an active patron of poets and scientists and a scholar in his own right. He sponsored and perhaps engaged in the translation of Greek and Arab treatises on philosophy. He revised and commented on the *De arte venandi cum avibus* of Frederick II, which the emperor had dedicated to him. In the *Commedia,* Dante depicts Manfred at the base of the mount of Purgatory with a band of souls who had repented their sins at the moment of death (*Purgatory,* 3.103–145).

The legend of Manfred's heroic and pious end, which inspired Dante, was turned to nationalist purposes in the nineteenth century during the Risorgimento.

See also **Frederick II**

Further Reading

Edition

Capasso, Bartolommeo, ed. *Historia diplomatica regnt Siciliae inde ab anno 1250 ad annum 1266.* Naples: Typographia Regiae Universitacis, 1874.

Critical Studies

Abulafia, David. *Frederick II: A Medieval Emperor.* London: Allen Lane/Penguin, 1988. (See the final chapter.)

Housley, Norman. *The Italian Crusades: The Papal–Angevin Alliance and the Crusades against Christian Lay Powers, 1254–1343.* Oxford: Clarendon, 1982.

Leone, Gino. *La salvazione dell'anima di Manfredi in Dante ad opera di Dante nel III canto del Purgatorio.* Matera: Montemurro, 1969. (Reprinted as *Un re nel purgatorio: Manfredi di Svevia—Dalla vita terrena all'oltretomba dantesco.* Fasano: Schena, 1994.)

Morghen, Raffaello. *Il tramonto della potenza Sveva in Italia.* Rome: Tunninelli, 1936. (Reprinted as *L'età degli svevi in Italia.* Palermo: Paiumbo, 1974.)

Nardi, Bruno. *Il canto di Manfredi e il Liber de pomo sive De morte Aristotilis.* Turin: Società Editrice Internazionale, 1964.

Pispisa, Enrico. *Il regno di Manfredi: Proposte di interpretazione.* Messina: Sicania, 1991.

JOHN LOMAX

MANRIQUE, JORGE (ca. 1440–1479) The reputation of Jorge Manrique has long rested principally upon his *Coplas por la muerte de su padre*, most familiar to English-speaking readers through Longfellow's translation. His poetic range extends, however, beyond the serious mood of the *Coplas* to a wide variety of compositions found in the late medieval and fifteenth-century *cancioneros*, in which Manrique dem-onstrates a fluent handling of the current verbal and conceptual conventions of the genres and categories involved. These include personal satire and various approaches to conventional amorous themes, among them verses in which a lady's name is conveyed acrostically, and renderings of the traditional motif of love as a siege (*Escala de amor*), a castle (*Castillo de amor*), or membership of a religious order (*Profesion que hizo en la orden de amor*). Critical evaluation of Manrique's verse has concentrated primarily upon the *Coplas*, but the importance of his other writings is now generally recognized.

Jorge Manrique's life was marked by active involvement in the politics of his day and their military extension. His family was prominent in the turbulent events of the reign of Enrique IV; his father Rodrigo (1406–1476), count of Paredes and a master of the Order of Santiago, was involved in the abortive elevation of the puppet-king Alfonso against Enrique (an event alluded to in the *Coplas*). To Jorge fell the role of maintaining this involvement in the next phase of the succession dispute, and, having actively espoused the cause of Fernando and Isabel he was fatally wounded in a minor action.

The military aspect of Manrique's career fundamentally marked his poetry; his work stands comparison with that of any war poet of any period. Imagery drawn from the experience and equipment of medieval warfare abounds even in the amorous poems (it is, indeed, the very foundation of *Escala* and *Castillo*, while isolated images occur in other poems), and permeates the *Coplas*, where death is expressed in terms of an ambush and an arrow, against whose force the strongest fortifications and armies are powerless and ineffective. The tournament panoply of the warrior caste (among other dimensions of its courtly existence such as music and dancing) is richly evoked in the poet's examination of the meaning of life. For Manrique, war is a necessary element in existence: the noble's duty is to fight for his faith against its enemies (just as that of the priest is to pray), and by doing so he merits salvation. His father, Rodrigo, is praised for his effectiveness in this sphere, and his entry to paradise is, as a result, taken for granted in the idealized deathbed scene that closes the poem. But Rodrigo is also commended by the poet for his part in the civil wars in support of the legitimate candidate for the throne, and also for fighting fellow-Christians in the maintenance of his own status and domains. The political aspect of his career is thus an essential element in the poet's eulogy of his father Rodrigo's greatness. In this Jorge Manrique is merely reflecting the importance attached to *estado* (state) and to the behavior appropriate to one's rank, in contemporary thinking; beyond mere physical existence lies a further dimension of *fama*, the existence implied in one's reputation, which survives after death; this itself is, of course, a poor second to eternal life, though an essential prerequisite for it in so far as it indicates a worthy life. In addition to the doctrinal statements made and political points scored in the poem, various conscious statements of literary attitude are explicit, as in the rejection of traditional poetic invocations and classical examples in the *Ubi sunt?*, while others remain implicit. Although the *Coplas* have been widely praised, and is indubitably in many respects a masterpiece, problems have been noted in various aspects of the poem from the earliest commentators to the present. The *Coplas* make use of a wide range of traditional imagery drawn from the Bible and other sources in addition to the author's military experience, with the transience of earthly life and the inevitability of death being conveyed in a densely textured series of metaphors. The skillful updating of the topos of the *Ubi sunt?* by reference to politically prominent persons of recent memory is but one dimension of Manrique's artistry in handling traditional concepts and poetic commonplaces. The eulogy of his father (apparently controversial among early commentators, and ignored by most glossators) draws upon classical archetypes and established medieval concepts of hierarchy and makes effective use of the personification of death.

Despite the prominence traditionally assigned to the *Coplas* in Spanish literary studies, the first truly critical edition (which is likely to become the standard text) was not published until 1991; the many previous editions vary, because of problems in the complex transmission of the text, both in the number of stanzas (forty or forty-two) and in their order. The stanza that begins "Si fuesse en nuestro poder," in particular, has been variously placed as number seven or thirteen; the earlier location is undoubtedly the original. The additional two stanzas found in many early editions (and in Longfellow's translation) are problematic; they do not form a natural part of the poem. Their attribution to Manrique remains questionable; even if ultimately proven to be by his hand, they are best viewed as originally independent stanzas that later became an accretion to the *Coplas*. During the sixteenth century, the *Coplas* were frequently printed, and private manuscript copies further attest their popularity. It is clear that the poem circulated in a wide variety of forms and contexts. Important among these are the early printed editions in which the text is accompanied by a poetic gloss; the *Coplas* soon attracted the attention of glossators, the earliest of whom was Alonso de Cervantes (first printed in 1501).

Further Reading

Editions

Beltrán, V. *Coplas que hizo Jorge Manrique a la muerte de su padre.* Barcelona, 1991.
Serrano de Haro, A. *Jorge Manrique; Obras.* Madrid, 1986.

Studies

Domínguez, F. A. *Love and Remembrance: The Poetry of Jorge Manrique.* Lexington, Ky., 1988.

Serrano de Haro, A. *Personalidad y destino de Jorge Manrique.* 2d ed. Madrid, 1975.

DAVID HOOK

MANṢŪR, AL- (fl. 976–1002) Ibn ʿAbī Āmir, later known as Al-Manṣūr was the last of the great rulers during the caliphate period in al-Andalus. Initially he served as vizir, virtually assuming effective control of the caliphate after the death of Al-Ḥakam II, who appointed his young son Hishām to succeed him in 976. Allegedly acting on Hishām's behalf, Al-Manṣūr eliminated all who wished to compete for power, including his father-in-law Al-Ghālib, securing it all for himself. Al-Manṣūr remained in power from 976 to 1002 and was feared and noted for his decisive action, vigilance, and ruthlessness; it was in 981 that he assumed the sobriquet (*laqab*) Al-Manṣūr, "The Victorious."

The caliph Hishām, who was a virtual captive of Al-Manṣūr, was a weak individual who allowed his weaknesses to be exploited. A brilliant politician, Al-Manṣūr filled the political vacuum created by the death of Hishām's father, Al-Ḥakam II. He ruled with an iron hand, galvanizing the army and leading daring incursions into Christian territory that struck terror into the hearts of the northern populations. His name alone was enough to make them shudder with fear. As a response to the Christians who, sensing disunity among the Muslims in al-Andalus, had begun to make their first incursions into Muslim territories, Al-Manṣūr led some fifty expeditions against the Christians. In 997 he struck at their very heart, taking Santiago de Compostela, the alleged burial place of the apostle James. When he entered Santiago the town was all but deserted, except for a Christian monk whom Al-Manṣūr allowed to go free. Although Al-Manṣūr rode his horse into the cathedral to show his contempt for Christianity, the tomb of the apostle was not disturbed. He destroyed all the surrounding buildings and took the bells of the cathedral back to Córdoba both as booty and as a sign of humiliation. He converted the bells into lamps for the mosque, where they remained until the thirteenth century. Besides warrior and statesman, Al-Manṣūr was a poet and a builder, and he expanded the Great Mosque of Córdoba. A devout religious man, he publicly abjured philosophy and ence by burning the books in Al-akam II's library that dealt with these subjects, and always carried with him a Qu'rān that was copied out in his own hand. Whenever the name of Allah was uttered in his presence, he never failed to repeat it. If tempted to act in an impious way, he was reputed always to have resisted temptation. Nevertheless, he was known to have enjoyed all pleasures—even wine, which he failed to renounce until two years before his death.

In 991, virtually ignoring Hishām, he made his eighteen-year-old son ʿAbd al-Mālik chamberlain, and later designated ʿAbd al- Mālik as his successor. Al-Manṣūr died in 1002 while on an expedition against the Christians. His other son, Al-Muzaffar, succeeded him, but died six years later. Al-Muzaffar was briefly succeeded by his brother, ʿAbd al-Rahmān, known as Sanchuelo, who conspired to grasp the title of caliph for himself. The death of Al-Manṣūr was followed by a crisis of authority and struggles among his family; Hishām II, the grandson of ʿAbd al-Rahmān III, who was incapable of ruling; and several other contenders, including Al-Mahdi, who eventually seized power. Al-Manṣūr's biography, *al-Ma'āthir al-ʿAmiriyyah* was written by Husayn Ibn ʿĀsim at the end of the eleventh century.

Further Reading

Chejne, A. G. *Muslim Spain: Its History and Culture.* Minneapolis, 1974.

E. MICHAEL GERLI

MARCABRU (fl. 1130–49) Little can be said for certain about the origins of the troubadour Marcabru. Relying in part on the lyrics, his two *vidas* are probably right to describe him as an early Gascon singer of low birth. Evidence in the songs ties him to courts in southern France and Spain, where he was evidently a jongleur. In some forty-two surviving lyrics, Marcabru is preoccupied largely with social satire and moral allegory. He vehemently denounces a decline in societal mores. One *vida* also describes him as "maligning women and love." But it is still debated whether Marcabru's many pronouncements on love in society are entirely negative or rather idealize love along the lines of a Christian or courtly model. His voice is raw and bitter, his images original and forceful, his language aphoristic and difficult. He is sometimes read as a precursor of the *trobar clus* school. Aside from his thirty-two *sirventes*, his lyrics include the romance *A la fontana del vergier*, the crusade song *Pax in nomine domini*, and the *pastorela Autrier jost' una sebissa*. Marcabru's thematic and stylistic influence on subsequent troubadour song was massive and pervasive.

Further Reading

Marcabru. *Poésies complètes du troubadour Marcabru*, ed. Jean-Marie-Lucien Dejeanne. Toulouse: Privat, 1909.

Harvey, Ruth E. *The Troubadour Marcabru and Love*. London: Westfield College, 1989.

Pirot, François. "Bibliographie commentée du troubadour Marcabru." *Moyen âge* 73 (1967): 87–126. ["Mise à jour," by Ruth E. Harvey and Simon Gaunt. *Moyen âge* 94 (1988): 425–55.]

Thiolier-Méjean, Suzanne. *Les poésies satiriques et morales des troubadours du XIIe siècle à la fin du XIIIe siècle*. Paris: Nizet, 1978.

ROY S. ROSENSTEIN

MARCEL, ÉTIENNE (1310–1358) A prosperous Parisian draper who, as *prévôt des marchands*, led a rebellion against the monarchy in 1357–58. Born into a less wealthy cadet branch of a large and influential family, Marcel was successful in business, a supplier for the royal household, and a respected figure in Paris by the late 1340s. He was elected *prévôt* in 1354. Connected by kinship or marriage to many Parisians who had gained wealth and sometimes ennoblement in royal service, risking disgrace and destitution for corrupt practices but often regaining royal favor, Marcel was perhaps too cautious or too honest to follow their example, and he increasingly resented these rich royal officers from his own circle.

In December 1355, the Estates General met in Paris, and Marcel became the spokesman for the towns of Languedoil, as the assembly worked out an ambitious plan to raise a large tax to support the army, in exchange for governmental reforms and a return to stable currency. Marcel and the Parisians were then staunch supporters of John II in his campaign against the kings of England and Navarre, who had claims to the French throne and sought to partition the realm. By May 1356, however, the tax plan was failing, and without adequate revenues for his troops John II resumed manipulating the currency and restored to power the officials he had agreed to dismiss. These actions caused Marcel to break with the king, no longer providing him with Parisian troops. When John met defeat and capture at Poitiers in September, he had no bourgeois troops but relied solely on nobles.

In the last months of 1356, Marcel seems to have become a partisan of Charles the Bad, the rebellious king of Navarre. An inflammatory Navarrese partisan, Robert Le Coq, dominated the Estates that met after Poitiers, and the urban representatives, led by Marcel, lent at least tacit support to his demands. In December, Marcel organized his first large Parisian street demonstration against the government. He made frequent use of such intimidating tactics in subsequent months.

The Estates obtained a sweeping ordinance of reform in March 1357, but when they failed repeatedly to deliver the taxes needed to prosecute the war, the government ceased to feel bound by the reforms. Marcel and the Parisian crowd became increasingly intimidating, and in February 1358 they murdered two military commanders in the presence of the dauphin Charles, thereby alienating the nobles who had originally spearheaded the reform movement. Marcel and his followers became increasingly radical in their hostility to nobles and gave some support to the Jacquerie of late May. The dauphin, meanwhile, left Paris in March and began to rally noble support. Marcel failed in his effort to organize a league of towns to oppose them, and Paris became increasingly isolated. At the end of July, one of the citizens murdered Marcel, paving the way for the dauphin's triumphant return to the capital.

See also **Charles II the Bad**

Further Reading

Avout, Jacques d'. *Le meurtre d'Étienne Marcel*. Paris: Gallimard, 1960.
Cazelles, Raymond. *Étienne Marcel: champion de l'unité française*. Paris: Tallandier, 1984.

JOHN BELL HENNEMAN, JR.

MARCHETTO DA PADOVA (early 14th century) Marchetto da Padova (Marchetus de Padua) was the most important and most influential music theorist in Italy during his time. Documents at the cathedral of Padua attest to his presence as a teacher in 1305–1307. Three treatises of his survive: *Lucidarium in arte musice plane* (Cesena and Verona, 1317 or 1318), *Pomerium in arte musice mensurate* (Cesena, later than *Lucidarium* but no later than 1319), and *Brevis compilatio in arte musice mensurate pro rudibus et modernis* (later than *Pomerium)*. An acrostic in the text of the motet *Ave re-*

gina celoruml Mater innocencie identifies Marchetto as its author.

Marchetto made fundamental contributions to the theories of mode, chromaticism, and tuning in *Lucidarium,* and to the theory or mensuration in *Pomerium* and *Brevis compilatio.* The theory of mode involves the classification of plainchant melodies by final (a sort of keynote), range, scale structure, and melodic articulation. This classification is crucial for the correlation of (among other sorts of pieces) recitation tones for the psalms with the antiphons that frame them. Whereas traditional modal theory had stressed final and range as determinants of mode, Marchetto stressed scale structure and articulation; this change of perspective, along with his development of the concept of modal mixture, enabled the classification of melodies that had earlier been dismissed as anomalous. Marchetto's modal doctrine spread through Italy and beyond during the next 200 years and became the foundation of the modal theory of polyphonic music during the Renaissance.

Earlier theories of melody based on hexachords (six-note *ut-re-mi-fa-sol-la* prototypes) and their connection through a process called mutation allowed only for diatonic progressions; though they served plainchant melodies well, these theories failed the chromatic progressions (e.g., progressions directly from c-natural to c-sharp) favored by Italian composers of the early fourteenth century. Marchetto developed a theory to accommodate such progressions and coined the term "permutation" for the hexachord connections they entail; though the term gained a certain currency in music theory of the fourteenth century, it disappeared as fifteenth-century composers abandoned chromatic progressions.

Though he espoused the traditional so-called Pythagorean tuning system, in which all perfect fifths are pure, Marchetto modified the system by describing the slight raising of sharped notes in certain contrapuntal contexts, a process that increases the harmonic piquancy of some combinations of notes and makes them seem to drive toward notes of resolution; this procedure has important implications for the performance of fourteenth-century music. Marchetto's "fifths" of whole tones must surely be taken as rough approximations rather than precise measurements; nonetheless, the concept of fractional division of whole tones represents a crucial step in the abandonment of the arithmetic strictures of the Pythagorean system, in which equal division of the whole tone was conceptually impossible. This step was necessary for the eventual development of equal temperament.

The thirteenth century had seen far-reaching developments in the theory of mensural notation, a theory which Franco of Cologne codified late in the century. Franco based his system on a note value called the breve (corresponding roughly to a measure in modern notation) that was divisible only into thirds at primary and secondary levels; Franco worked out elaborate rules for notating rhythms within these limitations. A handful of theoretical and practical sources from around 1300 documents attempts to expand Franco's system, but the earliest comprehensive treatise to succeed in doing so was Marchetto's *Pomerium*, which describes primary and secondary divisions of the breve into two or three parts and tertiary division into two parts, resulting in divisions of the breve into two, three, four, six, eight, nine, or twelve parts, which can then be combined in various ways, even involving syncopation within and between breve units. *Pomerium* became the foundation of Italian mensural theory of the fourteenth century, and it sheds light as well on the early stage of French mensural notation, a system that coexisted with the Italian and eventually supplanted it.

Further Reading

Editions

Coussemaker, Edmond de, ed. *Scriptorum de musica medii aevi nova series*, Vol. 3. Paris: Durand, 1869. (Reprint, Hildesheim: Olms, 1963. Includes *Brevis compilatio*, 1–12.)

Gallo, F. Alberto, and Kurt von Fischer, eds. *Italian Sacred Music*. Polyphonic Music of the Fourteenth Century, 12. Monaco: Éditions de l'Oiseau-Lyre, 1972. (Includes *Ave regina celoruml Mater innocencie*.)

Gerbert, Martin, ed. *Scriptores ecclesiastici de musica sacra potissimum*, Vol. 3. Saint Blasien, 1784. (Reprint, Hildesheim: Olms, 1963. Includes *Lucidarium*, 64–121; and *Pomerium*, 121–188.)

Herlinger, Jan, ed. *The Lucidarium of Marchetto of Padua: A Critical Edition, Translation, and Commentary*. Chicago, Ill., and London: University of Chicago Press, 1985.

Vecchi, Giuseppe, ed. *Marcheti de Padua Pomerium*, Corpus Scriptorum de Musica, 6. Rome: American Institute of Musicology, 1961.

Critical Studies

Berger, Karol. *Musica Ficta: Theories of Accidental Inflections in Vocal Polyphony from Marchetto da Padova to Gioseffo Zarlino*. Cambridge: Cambridge University Press, 1987.

Gallo, F. Alberto. "Marchetus in Padua und die 'franco-venetische' Musik des frühen Trecento." *Archiv für Musikwissenschaft*, 31, 1974, pp. 42–56. (Includes *Ave regina celoruml Mater innocencie*.)

Herlinger, Jan. "Fractional Divisions of the Whole Tone." *Music Theory Spectrum*, 3, 1981a, pp. 74–83.

——. "Marchetto's Division of the Whole Tone." *Journal of the American Musicologkal Society*, 34, 1981b, pp. 193–216.

——. "What Trecento Music Theory Tells Us." In *Explorations in Music, the Arts, and Ideas: Essays in Honor of Leonard B. Meyer*, ed. Eugene Narmour and Ruth A. Solie. Festschrift Series, 7. Stuyvesant, N.Y.: Pendragon, 1988, pp. 177–197.

——. "Marchetto's Influence: The Manuscript Evidence." In *Music Theory and Its Sources: Antiquity and the Middle Ages*, ed. André Barbera. Notre Dame Conferences in Medieval Studies, 1. Notre Dame, Ind.: University of Notre Dame Press, 1990, pp. 235–258.

Martinez–Göllner, Marie Louise. "Marchettus of Padua and Chromaticism." *L'Ars Nova Italiana del Trecento,* 3, 1970, pp. 187–202.

Pirrotta, Nino. "Marchettus de Padua and the Italian Ars Nova." *Musica Disciplina,* 9, 1955, pp. 57–71.

Rahn, Jay. "Marchetto's Theory of Commixture and Interruptions." *Music Theory Spectrum,* 9, 1987, pp. 117–135.

Ristory, Heinz. *Post-franconische Theorie und Früh–Trecento: Die Petrus de Cruce-Neuerungen und ihre Bedeutung für die italienische Mensuralnotenschrift zu Beginn des 14. Jahrhunderts.* Europäische Hochschufschriften, Series 36; Musicology, 26. Frankfurt and New York: Peter Lang, 1988.

Strunk, Oliver. "Intorno a Marchetto da Padova." *Rassegna Musicale,* 20, 1950, pp. 312–315. (Trans., "On the Date of Marchetto da Padova." In Oliver Strunk. *Essays on Music in the Western World.* New York: Norton, 1974, pp. 39–43.)

Vecchi, Giuseppe. "Su la composizione del *Pomerium* di Marchetto da Padova e la *Brevis compilatio.*" *Quadrivium,* 1, 1956, pp. 153–205. (Includes *Brevis compilatio,* pp. 177–205.)

JAN HERLINGER

MARGARET OF CORTONA, SAINT

(c. 1247–1297) Margaret of Cortona was a penitent and mystic. Her Legenda, the most authoritative account of her life, begins like a tragic romance: Margaret, the beautiful daughter of a peasant farmer in Laviano, ran away at sixteen with a nobleman who promised to marry her but did not. They lived together for nine years and had a son, but then Margaret's lover was killed, and she was shocked into repentance. She left all her possessions and tried to return home, asking forgiveness. When her father and stepmother turned her away, she and her child found refuge in Cortona with two gentlewomen who were associated with the Franciscan community there. A few

years later Margaret was admitted to the Franciscan-sponsored Order of Penitents (which later became the third order). She spent the rest of her life as a humble penitent in Cortona, enduring extreme deprivations to atone for her sins and devoting her time to charity, peacemaking, and intense periods of prayer and meditation. By the time she died, local belief in her sainthood was so strong that miraculous cures were spontaneously reported at her tomb. Despite repeated petitions to the papacy, however, annual celebration of her feast day (22 February) in Cortona was not officially authorized until 1515, and her actual canonization was delayed until 1728.

The early documents about Margaret raise tantalizing questions because they speak with multiple and sometimes clashing voices. Although her *Legenda* is attributed to the Franciscan friar Giunta Bevegnati, who served as one of her confessors and eventually compiled most of the text, in reality it has several layers of authorship: Margaret recounted her visions while Fra Giunta took notes; another priest filled this role during the last seven years of her life, when Fra Giunta was absent from Cortona; other witnesses supplied supplementary information; and the final text was reviewed and further edited by both civil and ecclesiastical officials. Recovering Margaret's authentic voice and experience from such a composite text may be impossible, although feminist scholars have begun to try. What does emerge clearly from the *Legenda* and other early sources is the struggle that went on after her death over the right to display her relics and claim the benefits of her patronage. Recent studies have identified three main parties in this struggle: Franciscan friars; civic leaders of Cortona; and adherents of San Basilio, the church that became Margaret's shrine.

In the *Legenda* itself, the strongest voice is Franciscan. Indeed, the text recounts numerous visions in which Christ expresses special favor toward the

Franciscans, reminds Margaret that he has personally entrusted her to their keeping, and urges her always to obey them. The *Legenda* also holds Margaret up as an example for other Franciscan teftiaries to follow and portrays her, in effect, as a testimonial to the virtues that a lay penitent could acquire under Franciscan guidance: humility, self-discipline, reverence for the clergy and the eucharist, perfect orthodoxy (always a key question about uncloistered women), and even the restoration of virginity. As Schlager (1998) has suggested, these emphases may have been chosen partly to overcome the friars' own resistance to the papal mandates that made them responsible for potentially dangerous female penitents.

Other portions of the *Legenda*—*including* practically all the miracle stories, which were originally omitted from Fra Giunta's account and appended in the last chapter—link Margaret more closely with local needs and aspirations in Cortona. And Margaret's own reported words and actions sometimes support the local agendas too. In the decade before her death, she distanced herself somewhat from the Franciscan friars by moving to a solitary cell near San Basilio, which was then just a small secular church in poor condition, and choosing its priest, *ser* Badia, as her final confessor. She supported this church by obtaining an indulgence for those who helped with its rebuilding, and she founded a charitable confraternity whose first chaplain was *ser* Badia. When she died, it was San Basilio that received her body for burial, although the Franciscans insisted for decades that she had made a permanent commitment to them. Civic leaders asserted the town's own claim to her body, arguing that she had chosen to live in Cortona and had contributed significantly to the general welfare by founding a hospital for the poor, resolving conflicts between rival factions, and negotiating an agreement that persuaded the warlike bishop of Arezzo to cancel an impending attack.

As Bornstein (1993) has shown, using archival sources that survive in Cortona, the contest over Margaret's relics had economic and political ramifications. When the miracles began around her tomb, San Basilio reaped the most obvious benefits. In the next few decades, this church acquired an impressive new sanctuary, suitable for welcoming pilgrims, and a rich endowment based on bequests. Civic leaders invested generously in the expansion and adornment of San Basilio (eventually renamed Santa Margherita) and the promotion of Margaret's cult, and the investment evidently paid off in terms of Cortona's increasing prestige and political independence. The Franciscans were shut out until the end of the fourteenth century, when town leaders invited them to replace the secular clergy who had hitherto administered the new church and Margaret's shrine. But the town itself retained—and still retains—legal ownership of Margaret's body.

An ambitious study by Cannon and Vauchez (1999) enriches and complicates this picture by reminding us that the contest over Margaret's cult was partly about the right to define the religious and symbolic identity of Cortona's patron saint. This issue mattered greatly not only to the Franciscans, but also to the civic authorities of Cortona and certain subgroups within the town, including the local clergy and the next generation of male and female terriaries. The different ways in which these Cortonese groups reconstructed Margaret's identity, in the light of their own corporate traditions and priorities, are barely suggested in the *Legenda* and other written sources. But, as Cannon demonstrates, a great deal can still be learned about them by studying what remains of the paintings and sculpture that were added to the church of Santa Margherita in the fourteenth century to honor this not yet canonized saint. More work will surely be done with the wealth of fascinating detail that Cannon and Vauchez have brought to light.

Further Reading

Benvenuti Papi, Anna. "*In castro poeniten-tiae*": *Santità e società femminile nell'Italia medievale.* Italia Sacra, 45. Rome: Herder, 1990. (Collection of Benvenuti's articles that includes her most detailed and important pieces on Margaret of Cortona.)

——. "Mendicant Friars and Female *Pinzochere* in Tuscany: From Social Marginality to Models of Sanctity." In *Women and Religion in Medieval and Renaissance Italy,* ed. Daniel Bornstein and Roberto Rusconi, trans. Margery J. Schneider. Chicago, Ill.: University of Chicago Press, 1996, pp. 84–103. (Overview suggesting societal patterns; the original title of the edited collection was *Mistiche e devote nell'Italia tardomedievale.)*

Bevegnati, Giunta. *Leggenda delld vita e dei miracoli di Santa Margherita da Cortona,* trans. and ed. Eliodoro Mariani, Vicenza: LIEF, 1978. (With historical notes.)

——. *Legenda de vita et miraculis beatae Margaritae de Cortona,* ed. Fortunato Iozzelli. Bibliotheca Franciscans Ascetica Medii Aevi, 13. Grottaferrata: Ediciones Collegii S. Bonaventurae ad Claras Aquas, 1997. (Published in Rome. Critical edition of the Latin text, with detailed discussions of its structure, genre, sources, and major themes, plus extensive bibliography.)

——. *Life and Miracles of Saint Margaret of Cortona,* trans. Thomas Renna. (Forthcoming from Franciscan Institute.)

Bornstein, Daniel. "The Uses of the Body: The Church and the Cult of Santa Margherita da Cortona." *Church History,* 62, 1993, pp. 163–177.

Cannon, Joanna, and André Vauchez. *Margaret of Cortona and the Lorenzetti: Sienese Art and the Cult of a Holy Woman in Medieval Tuscany.* University Park: Pennsylvania State University Press, 1999. (See especially parts 1 and 5.)

"Margherita da Cortona." In *Bibliotheca sanctorum,* Vol. 8. Rome: Istituto Giovanni XXIII nella Pontificia Università Lateranense, 1961–1971, cols. 759–773.

Schlager, Bernard. "Foundresses of the Franciscan Life: Umiliana Cerchi and Margaret of Cortona." *Viator, 29,* 1998, pp. 141–166.

SHERRY REAMES

MARGRETHE I (1353–October 27, 1412) Queen of Norway, Sweden, and Denmark, Margrethe was the daughter of King Valdemar IV Atterdag ("everday") of Denmark and Queen Helvig. At the age of six, she was betrothed, and at the age of ten married, to King Hákon of Norway, son of King Magnus of Sweden of the Folkungs dynasty. Rebellion in Sweden brought Albrecht of Mecklenburg to the throne, but Hákon kept a firm grip on the western parts of the country. Thus, by marriage, Margrethe acquired the additional titles of queen of Norway and Sweden. The upbringing of the young queen was overseen by the Swedish noblewoman Merethe Ulfsdotter, together with that of Merethe's own daughter, and "both often tasted the same birch." Merethe herself was of notable birth; her father was a Swedish nobleman, and her mother St. Birgitta of Vadstena. The young Queen Margrethe was from the very beginning made familiar with current political themes, and was raised in an environment that doubtless shaped her opinion of the possibilities for women in society.

In 1370, around Christmas, she gave birth to her only child, Óláf (Óláfr), the legitimate heir to the crown of Norway and, more or less, Sweden. In Denmark, the problem of succession was deliberately kept undecided. Margrethe's rebellious brother, Christoffer, had died, and King Valdemar had made vague promises to the son of Margrethe's sister Ingeborg, Albrecht of Mecklenburg (not to be confused with King Albrecht of Sweden, his father's brother). When King Valdemar died on October 24, 1375, the Danish Council was faced with a difficult choice, since the Mecklenburg candidate was heavily supported by the German emperor, Charles IV. Margrethe acted swiftly, as if she were the recognized ruler of the realm. After many negotiations, the Danes elected Olaf king in May 1376. But under the military threat by Albrecht, an agreement was reached in September that opened the way for recognition of Albrecht's rights, without detracting from Olaf's, by submitting the issue to arbitration by a number of German princes. Margrethe thwarted this accord by claiming that all arbitration had to follow Danish rules of succession, of which there were none, since Danish kings were elected freely. The death of Emperor Charles in November 1378 and of Duke Albrecht in February 1379 left Margrethe to skirmish only with Albrecht of Sweden. King Hákon died in the late summer of 1380, only forty years old. The next summer, Olaf was acclaimed with all rights as hereditary king of Norway.

In 1386, diplomacy separated the Holsteinians from the Mecklenburg party, albeit at the cost of concessions regarding tile status of the duchy of Schleswig under the Crown, but, as usual, with an enfeoffment of doubtful character, supplemented with clauses that cried out for interpretation. In Sweden, Albrecht gradually lost control over the main fiefs to the councilors. Details of their contacts with Margrethe are not known. But Olaf's sudden death on August 3, 1387, for the moment upset all possible plans. Then, on August 10, Margrethe established herself as "authorized lady and husband and guardian of all of the realm of Denmark," until a new king could be elected according to her proposal. The following year, she performed a similar "coup d'état" in Norway, and managed to secure similar recognition from a number of Swedish magnates. The resulting war with King Albrecht was decided on February 24, 1389, by her victory at Axevall and Åsle, where Albrecht was captured while the German faction still kept Stockholm. The same year, Margrethe adopted her sister's maternal grandson, Bugislav of Pomerania, now renamed Erik, who would become king of all three kingdoms. Everything seemed settled, when a war of revenge with Mecklenburg broke out. The peace in 1395 secured the release of Albrecht, who put up Stockholm

as a pledge for the release sum. As this sum was not paid, Stockholm finally fell into the hands of Margrethe by 1398. Margrethe had already instituted her famous Union of Kalmar the year before. The resulting document, when compared with the coronation document for Erik, suggests that the outcome was not fully in accord with her ideas of monarchial reign. This may explain why the document was written only as a semivalid paper draft, kept secret in Denmark. The stipulated parchment copies to be sent to all three countries were never made, but the document was later used to curb the government of Erik of Pomerania. The lack of a son and the varying rules of succession in the three kingdoms would eventually prove to be the ultimate obstacle for Erik and thus for the life work of Margrethe. Nevertheless, the union between Denmark and Norway lasted until 1814, and with Sweden until the 1520s, indirectly giving fuel to the wars of the 17th and 18th centuries, and playing a major role in the politics of Scandinavia from the 19th century to the present day.

Further Reading

Literature
Erslev, Kristian. *Danmarks Historie under Dronning Margrethe og hendes nærmeste Efterfølgere 1375–1448. 1. Dronning Margrethe og Kahmarunionens Grundlæsggelse.* Copenhagen: Erslev, 1882.

Lönnroth, Erik. *Sverige och Kalmarunionen 1397–1457.* Gothenburg: Elander, 1934; rpt.: Akademiförlaget, 1969.

Linton, Michael *Drottning Margareta. Fullmäktig fru och rätt husbonde. Studier i kalmarunionens förhistoria.* Studia Historica Gothoburgensia, 12. Gothenburg: Akademiförlaget, 1971.

Christensen, Aksel E. *Kalmarunionen ognordisk politik 1319–1439.* Copenhagen: Gyldendal, 1980 [with extensive references to scholarly literature].

Hørby, Kai. *Danmarks historie. 2.1: Tiden 1340–1648.* Copenhagen: Gyldendal, 1980 [with extensive bibliography in vols. 2.1 and 2.2].

Albrectsen, Esben. *Herredømmet over Sønderjylland 1375–1404. Studier over Hertugdømmets lensforhold og indre opbygning på dronning Margrethes tid.* Copenhagen: Den danske historiske forening, 1981.

Etting, Vivian. *Margrethe den Første.* Copenhagen: Fogtdal, 1986 [lavishly illustrated].

SØREN BALLE

MARGUERITE D'OINGT (ca. 1240–1310)

Marguerite was born to noble parents in the French Beaujolais region. By 1288, she became prioress of the Carthusian monastery of Poletains at Lyon. Although she was never canonized, a popular cult in her honor flourished until the Revolution, and she was revered as blessed. Marguerite is the only medieval Carthusian woman writer known to us. The *Pagina meditationum*, a response in Latin to a visionary experience during Mass, interweaves liturgical sections with reflections on Christ's Passion and the Last Judgment. In a remarkable passage, Marguerite develops the image of Christ as a woman undergoing the suffering of labor. The *Speculum*, written in Franco-Provençal and dedicated to Hugo, prior of Vallebonne, describes three visions and their meaning. In the first, Christ shows her a book with white, black, red, and golden letters symbolizing his suffering. In the second, the book opens and reveals a vision of Paradise and the heavens, whence all goodness emanates. In the third, she is shown the glorified body of Christ and meditates on its meaning for Christian spirituality. Marguerite's final work is the biography of Béatrice of Ornacieux (ca. 1260–1303/09), a stigmatized nun at the charterhouse of Parmenie, whose cult was recognized by Pope Pius IX in 1869. Also written in the vernacular, the biography stresses Beatrice's intense mystical experiences, including frequent apparitions, the gift of tears, severe acts of penance to ward off the Devil, and eucharistic visions and miracles. Marguerite's christocentric mysticism includes not only Carthusian but also Franciscan and Cistercian elements. Some letters by Marguerite also survive.

Further Reading

Marguerite d'Oingt. *Les œuvres de Marguerite d'Oingt*, ed. Antonin Duraffour, Pierre Gardette, and Paulette Durdilly. Paris: Les Belles Lettres, 1965.

——. *The Writings of Margaret of Oingt, Medieval Prioress and Mystic*, trans. Renate Blumenfeld-Kosinski. Newbury-port: Focus Information Group, 1990.

Dinzelbacher, Peter. "Margarete von Oingt und ihre *Pagina meditationum.*" *Analecta cartusiana* 16 (1988): 69–100.

Maisonneuve, Roland. "L'expérience mystique et visionnaire de Marguerite d'Oingt (d. 1310), moniale chartreuse." *Analecta cartusiana* 55 (1981): 81–102.

ULRIKE WIETHAUS

MARGUERITE OF PROVENCE (ca. 1221–1295)

Marguerite was the eldest of four daughters of Count Raymond-Berenguer V of Provence. In 1234, at the age of twelve or thirteen, she became queen of France by her marriage to Louis IX. The wedding and her coronation as queen were celebrated at the cathedral of Sens. Eleven children were eventually born to the couple. The marriage was difficult in a number of respects. From the beginning, Marguerite resented and was resented by her mother-in-law, Blanche of Castile; yet she admired Blanche's influence with Louis. She tried to achieve the same position with her son, the future Philip III, but provoked her husband to intervene and have the young Philip's ill-considered oath to obey her until the age of thirty quashed. Though Marguerite by no means lacked in courage or ability (e.g., she successfully preserved order in Damietta in Egypt in 1250 at a particularly difficult moment in her husband's first crusade), Louis almost always ignored her political advice.

After the king's death in 1270, Marguerite became a more active political figure. She was particularly exigent—to the point of raising troops—in defending her rights in Provence, where her husband's brother, Charles of Anjou, maintained his political authority and control of property after his wife's (her sister's) death, contrary to the intentions of the old count, who had died in 1245. Philip III had his hands full in restraining her. Only his death in 1285 and Charles of Anjou's in the same year resolved the situation. At the behest of the new king, Philip IV, she accepted an assignment of income from Anjou as compensation for recognizing the preeminent rights of Charles of Anjou's heirs in Provence. Her last years were spent in doing pious work, including founding in 1289 the Franciscan nunnery of Lourcines, which eventually became a focal point of the cult of her late husband, Louis. Although she does not seem to have testified for her husband's canonization, Marguerite was active in the propagation of his memory: her confessor, Guillaume de Saint-Pathus, for example, wrote an important and reverential biography of the king. Marguerite died on December 30, 1295, nearly two years before the process of canonization was completed.

See also **Blanche of Castile**

Further Reading

Le mariage de saint Louis à Sens en 1234. Sens: Musées de Sens, 1984.

Sivéry, Gérard. *Marguerite de Provence: une reine au temps des cathédrales.* Paris: Fayard, 1987.

WILLIAM CHESTER JORDAN

MARGUERITE PORETE (d. 1310)

Biographical information about Marguerite Porete comes from inquisitorial documents, which tell us that she was a béguine from Hainaut. Quite possibly, she was a solitary itinerant who expounded her teachings to interested listeners. She wrote the *Mirouer des simples ames anienties* in Old French sometime between 1296 and 1306. Since there is no indication that someone else wrote the text of the *Mirouer* from the author's dictation, we can surmise that the author wrote the treatise herself and that she was well educated.

The text received approvals from three Orthodox Church leaders, one of whom was Godfrey of Fontaines, a scholastic at Paris between 1285 and 1306, who also counseled the author to use caution in her expressions. Approval was not universal, however, and the text was condemned and burned in the author's presence with the orders not to spread her views under threat of being turned over to the secular authorities. Marguerite was arrested at the end of 1308 and remained in prison for a year and a half before being condemned to the flames as a relapsed heretic. Despite the condemnation, the *Mirouer* apparently enjoyed widespread popularity, for in addition to copies made of the text in Old French it was translated into Middle English, Italian, and Latin.

The *Mirouer* is a dialogue among allegorical figures who represent the nature of the relation between the soul and God. The fundamental structure of the discourse is grounded in traditional Neoplatonic philosophy, and courtly language is used to express theological abstractions. The *Mirouer* is a theological treatise that analyzes how love in human beings is related to divine love and how the human soul by means of this relation may experience a lasting union of indistinction with God in this life. The *Mirouer* is also a handbook, or "mirror," that aims to teach the "hearers of the book" about themselves and how to attain union with God.

Further Reading

Marguerite Porete. *Le mirouer des simple ames anienties*, ed. Romana Guamieri and Paul Verdeyen. CCCM 69. Turnhout: Brepols, 1986.

———. *The Mirror of Simple Souls*, trans. Ellen L. Babinsky. New York: Paulist, 1993.

Lerner, Robert E. *The Heresy of the Free Spirit in the Later Middle Ages.* Los Angeles: University of California Press, 1972.

Verdeyen, Paul. "Le procès d'inquisition contre Marguerite Porete et Guiard de Cressonessart (1309–1310)." *Revue d'histoire ecclésiastique* 81 (1986): 47–94.

ELLEN L. BABINSKY

MARIE DE FRANCE (fl. 1160–1210) Recognized today among the major poets of the renaissance of the 12th century, Marie de France was equally admired by her contemporaries at court, according to the testimony of Denis Piramus in his *Vie seint Edmunt le rei*. Three works of the period are signed "Marie" and are usually attributed to the same author: the *Lais*, the *Fables*, and the *Espurgatoire saint Patrice*. In the epilogue to the *Fables*, the author adds to her name *si sui de France* (l. 4). This is probably an indication of continental birth, a fact to be remarked if, as seems likely, she was living in England. A number of identities have been proposed for Marie, none of which can be established with certainty: the natural daughter of Geoffroi Plantagenêt (and half-sister of Henry II), abbess of Shaftsbury (1181–1216); Marie de Meulan or Beaumont, widow of Hugues Talbot and daughter of Waleron de Beaumont; and the abbess of Reading (the abbey where the Harley 978 manuscript may have been copied). Identifying her literary patrons is equally problematic. The *Lais* are dedicated to *vus, nobles reis* (l. 43), who may be either Henry II (1133–1189), the most likely candidate, or his son, Henry the Young King (crowned 1170, d. 1183). The Count William named in the *Fables* has been linked to a number of prominent figures, including William Marshal, William Longsword (the natural son of Henry II), William of Mandeville, William of Warren, William of Gloucester, and Guillaume de Dampierre.

Marie's works can be dated only approximately with reference to possible patrons and literary influences. The works themselves suggest that Marie knew Wace's *Brut* (1155) and the *Roman d'Énéas* (1160), an undetermined Tristan romance, classical (notably Ovid) and Celtic sources, but not the romances of Chrétien de Troyes. The *Lais* are therefore dated between 1160 and 1170, the *Fables* between 1167 and 1189, and the *Espurgatoire* after 1189 and probably between 1209 and 1215, since its Latin source, the *Tractatus de purgatorio sancti Patricii* (in the version of Hugh or Henry of Saltrey), has been placed no earlier than 1208.

Five manuscripts contain one or more of Marie's *lais*; only Harley 978 contains a general prologue, which presents the twelve *lais* that follow as a collection specifically arranged by the author (the same manuscript also contains a complete collection of the *Fables*). Marie appears to be the initiator of a narrative genre that flourished between about 1170 and the late 13th century. About forty narrative *lais* are extant. The lyric *lai*, which flourished from the 12th to the 15th century, seems to be an unrelated form.

The prologues and epilogues that frame each of Marie's tales refer to the *lais* performed by Breton storytellers in commemoration of past adventures truly lived. Celtic and English place-names and personal names corroborate Marie's claimed sources: four *lais* take place in Brittany, three in Wales, two in both places, and one in an undetermined *Bretagne*. Marie did not simply write down orally circulating stories. Her artfully crafted compositions combine the written traditions of Latin and vernacular writings with the legendary materials of Celtic and popular tales. While it may be impossible to untangle historical reference and literary topos in Marie's repeated claim to retell well-known *lais bretons*, her indications suggest a process of transmission that begins with an adventure heard by

Bretons, who then compose a *lai*, sung with harp accompaniment. Marie has heard the music and the adventure, the latter perhaps told as a prelude to the song. She then tells us the adventure in rhymed octosyllables, the form used also in the *Fables* and the *Espurgatoire*, elaborating simultaneously its truth, or *reisun* (cf. the *razos* in the Provençal lyric tradition). The title itself, carefully designated in each case and sometimes translated into several languages, guarantees the authenticity of the process.

The general prologue opens with a traditional exordium on the obligation of writers to share their talents and then cites the authority of Priscian to describe the relationship between ancient and modern writers: do philosopher-poets hide a *surplus* of meaning to be found later in the obscurities of their writing, or do later, more subtle poets add it to their predecessors' works? Scholars have variously interpreted these verses (9–22): we are drawn into the problem of interpretation at the very moment the subject of glossing is introduced by Marie's authorial persona. She then explains the nature of her project: not a translation from the Latin as many have done, but something new, demanding hard labor and sleepless nights, the writing down in rhyme of those adventures commemorated in *lais*. Hoping to receive great joy in return, Marie then offers her collection to an unnamed king. She names herself in the following verses, printed by modern editors as the prologue to *Guigemar* (ll. 3–4) but set off in the manuscript only by a large capital indicating a new section (G1).

The twelve *lais* that follow in Harley 978 are *Guigemar* (886 lines), *Equitan* (314), *Fresne* (518), *Bisclavret* (318), *Lanval* (646), *Deus amanz* (254), *Yonec* (558), *Laüstic* (160), *Milun* (534), *Chaitivel* (240), *Chievrefoil* (118), and *Eliduc* (1184). As indicated by the considerable variations in length, the *lais* offer great diversity, but they also operate as a collection unified by the themes of love and adventure. Indeed, they seem to invite exploration as an open-ended set of theme and variations, in which Marie reveals the complexities and varieties of human experience, without trying to contain them within the confines of any single doctrine of love. Heroes and heroines, all noble, beautiful, and courteous, are individualized not by psychological development but by the situations in which they find themselves. Consider the two short anecdotes that constitute *Laüstic* and *Chievrefoil*. Both involve a love triangle: married couple plus lover. *Chievrefoil* relates an episode in the story of Tristan and Iseut, a secret reunion of the lovers vouchsafed during one of Tristan's returns from exile. Whereas Marc here remains ignorant of the tryst, the husband of *Laüstic* discovers his wife's nocturnal meetings with her lover. Although their affair remains innocent, limited to their mutual gaze across facing windows, the angry husband puts an end to their meetings by trapping and killing the nightingale the lady claims as reason for her nightly visits to the window. When the lady sends to her lover the nightingale's body wrapped in an embroidered cloth, along with a messenger to explain the events, he has a golden box made, adorned with precious stones. The nightingale's body is placed in it, and the reliquary accompanies him wherever he goes—hence the name of the *lai*: *laüstic* is the Breton word for *russignol* in French, *nihtegale* in English (ll. 3–6).

The emblem that thus closes the *lai* figures the end of the lovers' meetings, though it may also suggest the triumph of continued love, however impossible to realize: optimistic and pessimistic readings of the ending are both possible. The emblem of *Chievrefoil* also testifies to the enduring nature of Tristan and Iseut's love: just as the hazelwood dies (so it was thought) if the honeysuckle growing around it was cut away, so the two lovers would die if separated: "*Bele amie, si est de nus: ne vus sanz mei, ne jeo sanz vus*" (ll. 77–78). But while that phrasing is negative, what we see realized in this episode is the reunion of the lovers thanks to the piece of hazelwood that Tristan prepares as a signal to Iseut, so that the queen will know he must be hiding in the woods near the route of her cortege. Whereas the emblem of *Laüstic* ends the lovers' meetings, *Chievrefoil's* emblem initiates Tristan and Iseut's reunion, as it symbolizes their love. And just as the repetition of characters, scenes, and situations in *Laüstic* and *Chievrefoil* creates doubles, echoes, and contrasts in positive and negative variations at all levels of the text, so the tendency to present and explore different combinations of the same materials characterizes the links between the *lais* and invites readers to analyze their interactions. The arrangement of twelve *lais* in a collection considerably increases the potential for meaning, however elusive that meaning remains in the beautiful obscurities of Marie's text, and begins to give her *lais* the weight and proportion we normally associate with romance.

The brevity of most *lais* limits their plot development to a single anecdote or episode, although in the mid-length and longer *lais*, especially *Guigemar* and *Eliduc*, there may be a fuller elaboration as the characters' love develops through a series of episodes. The type of adventure that appears in the *lais* differs somewhat from that of romance: it does not involve a quest, even in the longer *récits*; the hero is more passive and his experience leads to private fulfillment and happiness; no special relationship exists between the hero's destiny and that of his society.

While some *lais* have marvelous and folktale elements that recall their Celtic sources (e.g., *Guigemar, Yonec, Lanval*), others remain realistically placed in the courtly world of the 12th century (*Equitan, Fresne, Milun, Chaitivel*). All explore the intersection of two planes of existence, where otherness may be magically encountered or simply introduced by the new experience of love. Although efforts to thus categorize the *lais* often remain problematic, leading to overlap, omissions, and the like, they do respond to the sense of intertextual play that links the *lais* across echoes and contrasts.

Marie's art is as carefully crafted as the precious reliquary she describes in *Laüstic*. The economy and brevity of her style are enriched by the subtlety of her narrating voice. Her use of free indirect discourse, in particular, allows her to merge her voice with that of her characters, while maintaining the distinctness of both. Marie's literary art, sustained throughout the collection of twelve *lais*, joins her work to that of the philosopher-poets, described in the general prologue as worthy of glossing and interpretation.

The twenty-three extant manuscripts of Marie's *Fables*, two of which are complete with prologue, epilogue, and 102 fables, attest their popularity. Marie claims to translate from the English of King Alfred's adaptation from Latin. No such translation is known, and Marie may have invented a fictitious source. Her fables derive from the Latin *Romulus* in combination with other traditions: some details bring her collection closer to the Greek fables than to the Latin; evidence of oral tradition is also apparent. Hers is the first known example of Old French *Isopets*. Each short narrative (eight–124 lines) leads to an explicit moral lesson. This framework of moral and social values provides an underlying unity for the diversity of the fables. The political stance is basically conservative, reflecting an aristocratic point of view, but also shows concern for justice available to all classes: social hierarchy should be maintained for the sake of harmony; people should accept their place, as well as their responsibilities. Marie's concern for justice in terms of feudal loyalty between lord and vassal is demonstrated in a number of fables; elsewhere appears a more specific regard for mistreatment of the poor, as in Fable 2, *De lupo et agno*, in which the wolf invents a series of false accusations to justify killing the lamb. Marie's moral targets the abuse of rich robber barons, viscounts, and judges who exploit those in their power with trumped-up charges.

Extant in a single manuscript, the *Espurgatoire* combines in its over 2,000 lines a variety of materials, romanesque, hagiographic, and homiletic. In addition to various anecdotes, the principle narrative concerns the proselytizing efforts of St. Patrick, thanks to whom an entrance to Purgatory for the still-living has been established in a churchyard, in order to strengthen belief in the afterlife. After suitable prayers and instructions, many have descended to witness the tortures of the damned and the delights of the saved. Not all have returned from the perilous journey. The greater part of the story follows in detail the preparation and descent of the knight Owein. Through a series of diabolical torments, Owein is saved each time when he invokes the name of Jesus. Upon his return, he is confirmed in his knightly career, now purified and dedicated to saintly pursuits. The *Espurgatoire* offers one of the earliest vernacular examples of the same visionary tradition that inspires Dante's *Commedia*.

See also **Dante Alighieri; Gautier d'Arras; Henry II; Wace**

Further Reading

Marie de France. *Les lais de Marie de France*, ed. Jean Rychner. Paris: Champion, 1969.
——. *Les fables*, ed. and trans. Charles Brucker. Louvain: Peeters, 1990.
——. *The Lais of Marie de France*, trans. Glyn S. Burgess and Keith Busby. Harmondsworth: Penguin, 1986.
——. *Marie de France: Fables*, ed. and trans. Harriet Spiegel. Toronto: University of Toronto Press, 1987.
——. *The Espurgatoire Saint Patriz of Marie de France, with a Text of the Latin Original*, ed. Thomas Atkinson Jenkins. Chicago: Chicago University Press, 1903.
——. *Das Buch vom Espurgatoire s. Patrice der Marie de France und seine Quelle*, ed. Karl Warnke. Halle: Niemeyer, 1938.
——. *The Lais of Marie de France*, trans. Robert W. Hanning and Joan Ferrante. New York: Dutton, 1978.
——. *The "Fables" of Marie de France: An English Translation*, trans. Mary Lou Martin. Birmingham: Summa, 1984.
Burgess, Glyn S. *Marie de France: An Analytic Bibliography*. London: Grant and Cutler, 1977; First Supplement, 1985.
Ménard, Philippe. *Les lais de Marie de France: contes d'amour et d'aventure au moyen âge*. Paris: Presses Universitaires de France, 1979.
Mickel, Emanuel J., Jr. *Marie de France*. New York: Twayne, 1974.
Sienaert, Edgar. *Les lais de Marie de France: du conte merveilleux à la nouvelle psychologique*. Paris: Champion, 1978.

MATILDA T. BRUCKNER

MARIE D'OIGNIES (1177–1213) Mystic and one of the founding mothers of the béguine movement. Testimonies of her life were recorded by Jacques de Vitry (ca. 1215) and Thomas de Cantimpré (ca. 1230/31).

Born in Nijvel (Brabant), Marie was married at the age of fourteen but did not consummate her marriage. Together with her spouse, she practiced the *vita apostolica* and cared for the sick. At the age of thirty, she retired to a cell at the Augustinian monastery of Aiseau-sur-Sambre and gained in stature as a spiritual healer and holy woman. According to her pupil Jacques de Vitry, Marie's spirituality was characterized by eucharistic devotion and christocentrism. She lived a life of strict asceticism, abstained from sleep and food, and frequently experienced visions, ecstasies, and trances. Her death was an example of a saintly *ars moriendi*, surrounded by miracles; most noteworthy perhaps is her feat of three days of incessant chanting and scriptural exegesis performed during ecstasy. Jacques de Vitry stressed Marie's allegiance to the church by structuring her *vita* in two parts: Part 1 records the outline of her life's journey towards holiness and aspects of saintliness; Part 2 describes her interior life according to the seven gifts of the Holy Spirit. As with other texts of this genre, it is difficult to distinguish between Marie d'Oignies as a prototype (exemplum) and her individuality and original contributions to medieval spirituality.

See also Jacques de Vitry

Further Reading

Jacques de Vitry. *The Life of Marie d'Oignies,* trans. Margot H. King. Saskatoon: Peregrina, 1986.

Thomas de Cantimpré. *Supplement to the Life of Marie d'Oignies,* trans. Hugh Feiss. Saskatoon: Peregrina, 1987.

Kowalczewski, J. "Thirteenth Century Asceticism: Marie d'Oignies and Liutgard of Aywières as Active and Passive Ascetics." *Vox benedictina* 3 (1986): 20–50.

——. The Life of "Marie d'Oignies." In *Medieval Women's Visionary Literature,* ed. Elizabeth Petroff. Oxford: Oxford University Press, 1986, pp. 179–84.

ULRIKE WIETHAUS

MARSILIO OF PADUA (c. 1275 or 1280–1342 or 1343) Marsilio of Padua (Marsiglio, Marsilius de Mainardino) was an antipapal political theorist. He was the son of the notary of the University of Padua and studied Aristotelian philosophy there; later, he taught this philosophy at Paris, where he was rector in 1313 and eventually studied theology. His obscure career took many turns: he also was a priest, a physician, and a diplomat. In 1319, he went on an embassy for the Ghibelline leaders Matreo Visconti and Cangrande della Scala. Among Marsilio's associates were the astrologer Peter of Abano; the humanist Albertino Mussato; the Averroist John of Jandun; and, in later years, William of Ockham.

In 1324, in Paris, Marsilio completed his masterwork, *Defensor pads (The Defender of Peace),* which circulated anonymously until his authorship was discovered in 1326. Expecting to be condemned as a heretic for his antipapal opinions, he took refuge at the court of the pope's archenemy Lewis of Bavaria, whom he served for the rest of his life. Lewis was guided by Marsilio's theories when he went to Rome in 1327 and was crowned emperor in the name of the people. Likewise, Lewis claimed that the Roman church should be administered by the emperor, and, accordingly, he appointed Marsilio as his administrator, with the title of imperial vicar for spiritual affairs in Rome. The emperor could not maintain himself for long in Italy, however, and by 1330 he was back in Bavaria. In 1342, Marsilio was still with Lewis, serving as his physician and counselor. At this time Marsilio wrote *Defensor minor,* in which his earlier work was summarized and extended to prove that the emperor had jurisdiction over questions of marriage.

Marsilio's central concern was the political power of the papacy, which he, like Dante, saw as the principal cause of civil strife in Italy. To restore peace, Dante sought to revive the Roman empire; Marsilio was more realistic. He insisted that the state should control the church, but he devised a generalized theory of the state that could fit not only the empire but also national monarchies and even city-states. Thus, his proposals, far from threatening civil governments, offered them control over their several churches. *Defensor pacis* is accordingly divided into two principal parts: the first discourse (*dictio*) argues that political power belongs exclusively to the secular state; the second counters the papacy's claims to independent political status and makes the state the administrator of organized religion.

Marsilio's concept of the state is closely modeled on Aristotle's *Politics.* The state is a natural phenomenon, arising from man's nature as a political animal. Government exists so that all men may lead the "sufficient life," i.e., "live and live well." The form of government is not set by nature, however; instead, a community is formed by the mutual agreement of its members to live together under laws to which they have consented. Thus, for Marsilio, the foundation of all government is the "human legislator," i.e., the people of the community who make the laws. Marsilio is not a democrat; he realizes that not everyone is fit to participate in legislation, and he restricts the *legislator humanus* to the "prevailing part" (*valentior pars*) of the citizens, who are better or more numerous (or both) than the others. The Marsilian "legislator" is usually too numerous to do more than authorize the actual ruler (*the pars principans*), e.g., an elective emperor, a hereditary king, *apodestà*, or a council. In practice, all legislative, judicial, and executive functions are delegated to this ruler, who can, however, be deposed by the human legislator that appointed him. Thus, Marsilio's general theory of the state allows for diverse constitutions—monarchical, aristocratic, and even democratic. The main point, for his purpose, was that the ruler has a monopoly on political power within his state. A competing power independent of the ruler would be contrary to nature.

The second discourse of *Defensor pads* defines the proper place of the clergy, and especially the pope, within this political framework. In general, the job of the clergy is to preach the gospel and administer the sacraments. Clergymen are chosen and supported by the state, which administers all the worldly affairs of the church. In effect, the Franciscan ideal of poverty is extended to the whole clergy. Furthermore, Marsilio regards bishops as priests to whom the ruler has delegated certain executive duties, and the bishop of Rome is superior to the rest only insofar as he has been granted a few broader powers. Marsilio elaborately rebuts the papacy's position that the pope is Peter's successor as vicar of Christ and denounces its claim to "plenitude of power" (*plenitudo potestatis*) as the "singular cause of strife or civil discord." Thus, each state controls the church within it. When questions of faith arise that affect the church as a whole, the emperor can call an international council, consisting of laymen as well as clergy, to settle the matter. Enforcement of the council's decisions, however, is wholly up to the local rulers.

Marsilio completely reversed the dominant view that church and state exercise coordinate jurisdictions ("Gelasian dualism"). For more than three centuries, *Defensor pacis* was the arsenal of antipapalists, especially in the age of conciliarism and the Reformation. Many of its ideas were already current in university circles, but Marsilio gave them coherent, scholarly, and passionate expression. Moreover, his arguments appealed to a broad audience trained in Aristotle's logic and political philosophy; no special knowledge of law or theology was required. He moved beyond scholasticism in his use of history to explain institutional development.

Marsilio's theory of the state was not the main thrust of his work, but many readers have been unduly impressed by this theory because it appears to anticipate such modern doctrines as popular sovereignty and the social contract; they thus overlook the other, deeper medieval roots of these ideas.

See also **Albertino Mussato; Cangrande della Scala; Ockham, William of**

Further Reading

The Cambridge History of Medieval Political Thought, c. 350-c. 1450, ed. J. H. Bams. Cambridge: Cambridge University Press, 1988, p. 680. (Bibliography.)

Marsilius of Padua. *The Defender of Peace,* 2 vols., crans. and intro. Alan Gewirth. Records of Civilization: Sources and Studies, 46. New York: Columbia University Press, 1951–1956.

Rubinstein, N. "Marsilius of Padua and Italian Political Thought of His Time." In *Europe in the Late Middle Ages,* ed. John Hale et al. London: Faber and Faber, 1965 pp. 44–75.

RICHARD KAY

MARTÍ, RAMÓN (b. ca 1210/15) The most erudite and accomplished Arabist and Hebraist of his day, missionary to Muslims and fierce polemicist against Jews, Ramón Martí was born at Subirats near Barcelona (ca. 1210/15). He joined the Dominican mendicants at Barcelona's Santa Caterina priory by 1240, and studied at Saint-Jacques College of the University of Paris alongside Thomas Aquinas under Albert the Great (Albertus Magnus). The order sent him in 1250 to help found a missionary school of Arabic at Tunis. In 1264 King Jaime I commissioned him to censor rabbinic texts at Barcelona (but probably he had no role or presence at the Barcelona Disputations of 1263). Martí perhaps worked at the Murcia Arabicum in 1266; in 1268 he was again at Tunis. In 1269 he successfully visited Louis IX of France to urge a North African crusade; while there he probably commissioned Thomas Aquinas, for the order's master general, to write his masterwork the *Contra gentiles*. Martí spent the 1270s and 1280s at Barcelona, where he held the chair of Hebrew in 1281. His contemporary Marsili titled him "Philosophus in arabico," and "beloved intimate" not only of Jaime I and Louis IX but of "the good king of Tunis." Martí's friend Ramon Llull has an anecdote about his nearly converting that Muslim ruler. King Jaime mentions him as a friend in his own autobiography, noting his trip from Tunis to Montpellier. Arnau de Villanova was one of his students.

Martí's prolific writings are a key to the contemporary anti-Talmudism and growing animosity toward Jews. Until 1260 his main focus had been the conversion of Muslims, beginning with his *Explanatio symboli apostolorum* at Tunis in 1257. He is most probably the author of the *Vocabulista in arabico*, an Arabic word list of some 650 printed pages in Celestino Schiaparelli's edition, a missionarys' dictionary of unrivaled importance today for studying the Arabic of eastern Spain. His Islamic phase ended in 1260 with the now lost *Summa* against the Qu'rān. In 1267 came his *Capistrum iudeorum*, which Aquinas seems to have used for his own *Contra gentiles*. Martí's masterwork was *Pugio fidei contra Mauros et iudeos* (*Dagger of Faith*), finished in 1281, filling over a thousand pages in its printed version, of wide influence over the next three centuries. Recent redating of Aquinas's *Contra gentiles* suggests that the hundreds of parallels between these two works show a strong dependence on Martí. With a wealth of rabbinic materials from and in Hebrew, *Pugio* is the most thorough of all the medieval anti-Judaic polemical works. Martí's writings are currently being studied intensively.

See also **Aquinas, Thomas; Llull, Ramón; Vilanova, Arnau de**

Further Reading

Cohen, J. *The Friars and the Jews.* Ithaca, N.Y., 1982. Chap. 6.

Robles, L. *Escritores dominicos de la corona de Aragón, siglos XIII-XV.* Salamanca, 1972.

ROBERT I. BURNS, S. J.

MARTIANUS CAPELLA (fl. first half of the 5th c) Between 410 and 439, Martianus Capella wrote his *De nuptiis Philologiae et Mercurii*. This non-Christian allegorical treatise, an encyclopedic work on the Seven Liberal Arts, was to have a widespread influence in the Christian schools of the late Middle Ages, as a source for teaching the Trivium and Quadrivium. The *De nuptiis* is in nine books, the first two describing the allegorical marriage and each of the next seven dealing with one of the liberal arts. In time-honored tradition, Martianus drew his material from a variety of earlier sources, chiefly Apulaius, Varro, Pliny, and Euclid. This (to us) derivative method only heightened its status in the Middle Ages.

Martianus had three clear "vogues": the first was among the scholars of the Carolingian renaissance centered on Charles the Bald. Johannes Scottus Eriugena and Remigius of Auxerre wrote commentaries on Martianus, and it is through Remigius's commentary that the *De nuptiis* became so influential. The second group of admirers were 10th-century Italians, like Notker of Saint-Gall, Rather of Verona, and Luitprand of Cremona. Finally, Martianus was one of the cosmographical authors most admired by the 12th-century Chartrians, like Alexander Neckham (who wrote a commentary), John of Salisbury, and Thierry of Chartres.

Of Martianus himself, little is known, except that he was a Roman citizen who spent most of his life at Carthage. One Victorian scholar, D. Samuel, describing the *De nuptiis* as a "mixture of dry traditional school learning and tasteless and extravagant theological ornament, applied to the most incongruous material, with an absolutely bizarre effect," illustrates the extant to which Martianus's work, with its interweaving of fact and fiction, has become foreign to our sensibility, although some earlier Christian writers, such as Cassiodorus and Gregory of Tours, similarly disliked this hybrid style.

See also **Eriugena, Johannes Scottus**

Further Reading

Martianus Capella. *De nuptiis Philologiae et Mercurii*, ed. Adolfus Dick, rev. Jean Preaux. Stuttgart: Teubner, 1983.
——. *The Marriage of Philology and Mercury*, trans. William Harris Stahl and Richard Johnson with E.L. Burge. New York: Columbia University Press, 1977.
Shanzer, Danuta. *A Philosophical and Literary Commentary on Martianus Capella's* De nuptiis Philologiae et Mercurii, *Book 1*. Berkeley: University of California Press, 1986.

LESLEY J. SMITH

MARTINI, SIMONE (c. 1284–1344) The birthplace of the painter Simone Martini is unknown, but he must have been a citizen of Siena, for he is referred to as *de Senis*. We find no mention of Martini (as he will be called here, though he is often called simply Simone) in archival records before 1315. However, the year of his birth may be deduced from Vasari, who saw a memorial inscription in the church of San Francesco in Siena, according to which Martini died at age sixty. Martini's training is undocumented. He may have been a pupil of Duccio and may even have been one of several collaborators working on Duccio's *Maestà*; or, as Vasari wrote, he may have been a pupil of Giotto in Rome. Many scholars see in Martini's work the influence of the French courtly style, to which he may have been exposed during visits to Naples and Rome, where French culture throve at the time. Martini married Giovanna, the sister of the Sienese artist Lippo Memmi, in 1324; he bought the house they lived in from Memmi. The couple had no children. After 1333, there is no mention of

Simone Martini. Saints Clare and Elizabeth of Hungary. Fresco. © Scala/Art Resource, New York.

Martini in Siena. By 1336, at the latest, he was in Avignon, where he remained until his death. Only his brother Donato, also a painter, and his wife traveled with Martini to France. The move may have been prompted by competition in Siena from the Lorenzetti brothers, who had been on the rise since c. 1328, or by an unrealized hope for papal commissions.

Siena, Naples, and Assist (c. 1315–1320)

By consensus, the fresco of the *Maestà* (Palazzo Pubblico, Siena) is Martini's earliest dated work; it was probably completed for the commune in 1315–1316 and repaired in 1321. It shows the Virgin and Child enthroned beneath a canopy supported by some of the saints standing on either side. In the foreground, four saintly protectors of the commune kneel with two angels, who present bowls of flowers to the holy pair. A surrounding border contains images in roundels of God the father, prophets, evangelists, church doctors, and others. This fresco is a unique example of a dialogue between the Virgin and the kneeling saints. The Virgin's statements still remain inscribed on the step below her, but the prayers originally offered by the saints have disappeared from the scrolls that only two of them still hold. The sense of space, defined by the canopy, is noteworthy, as is the textured surface, which creates the impression of a tapestry and includes insertions into the plaster of colored glass and imitation gems, as well as the earliest examples of patterned halos.

The *Saint Louis Altarpiece,* tempera on panel (Naples, Capo-dimonte Museum) is signed. It was probably commissioned by Louis's brother, King Robert of Anjou, and shows angels crowning an enthroned Louis, while the saint himself deposits a second crown on a minuscule figure of Robert, kneeling at the right. It is datable between 1317, when Louis was canonized, and 1319, when his remains were translated to a new tomb in Marseilles in

a ceremony attended by Robert, who returned to Naples with Louis's brain as a relic. Martini probably traveled to Naples to execute the picture. Louis's royal status is emphasized by the fleur-de-lis and other emblems on the frame and the saint's robe. The intricate tooling and use of glass, stones, silver, and gold lend the work opulence. The narrative predella, the earliest of this form to survive, illustrates five events from the life, death, and miracles of Louis. Though the scenes are set in different architectural interiors, the intuitive perspective is synchronized in all five, with orthogonals moving toward the vertical axis of the central scene.

The narrative frescoes in the chapel of Saint Martin of Tours (Assisi, basilica of San Francesco) have been attributed to Martini since the nineteenth century for stylistic reasons. The commission was funded by Gentile di Partino da Montefiore, a Franciscan cardinal from the Marches who died in 1312. The paintings include ten scenes from the legend of Martin and many separate pictures of saints and angels, as well as a portrait of the donor kneeling before Martin. The cycle was probably painted after the donor's death in 1312 but before 1319, when a period of political strife in Assisi would have prevented artistic activity in the basilica. The dedication of an Italian chapel to Martin, a patron saint of France who was born in Hungary, is surprising. Perhaps the donor's education in Paris and a later trip to Hungary on a diplomatic mission inspired his choice. The pictures treat Martin's secular life, reign as bishop, death, and funeral. Their narrative sequence is unusual, moving from the bottom of the wall to the top. Though the space is shallow in all the scenes, whether set in architectural interiors or outdoors, the pictorial drama is clearly articulated through the gestures and glances of the figures—for example, a pauper in the first scene who grasps Martin's cloak. Also impressive are the facial expressions of singers and details of costume such as the colorful peaked hats from Hungary, both seen in *The Knighting of Saint Martin*. Some scholars believe that the frescoes illustrating the life of Saint Francis elsewhere in the basilica influenced Martini's style, both in the Saint Martin cycle and in his later work. Martini may also have been responsible for the three stained-glass windows in the chapel. These windows (of uncertain date) show Saint Martin and other figures. According to Vasari, the *Virgin and Child with Saints* and *Five Saints*, frescoes in the chapel of Santa Elisa-betta in the basilica, were begun by Martini and finished by Lippo Memmi.

Siena, Orvieto, San Gimignano, and Pisa (c. 1320–1335)

The *Grieving Saint John* (Barber Institute, Birmingham), in tempera on wood, is dated 1320 but undocumented before 1932. The saint's emotions are beautifully expressed. This work is small in scale and was probably part of a triptych painted for a private patron.

The frescoed *Equestrian Portrait of Guidoriccio da Fogliano* (Siena, Palazzo Pubblico) is controversial. Documents show that *Simone dipentore* painted at least four pictures of castles in the Palazzo Pubblico in 1330 and 1331; Since *Guidoriccio* shows castles in the background, some scholars assume that it is among the documented pictures. However, the fresco was not mentioned by Ghiberti or Vasari, and it is not signed. Moreover, there are errors in the treatment of military details that lead some to conclude not only that the painting is not by Martini, but that it is later than the fourteenth century. A relatively recent discovery of a fresco containing a castle lower down on the same wall as *Guidoriccio* allows us to attribute that work to Martini in lieu of die disputed picture. But if *Guidoriccio* is by Martini, and the inaccuracies are due to sloppy restorations in later times, the fresco demonstrates the painter's innovativeness. The warrior, identified as

Guidoriccio by his heraldry, rides alone immediately behind the picture plane, a broad landscape stretching far beyond him—an image without precedent in medieval secular palaces.

The *Saint Ansanus Annunciation* (Florence, Uffizi) is signed by both Simone Martini and Lippo Memmi and dated 1333. It is painted in tempera on wood and is an early example of an altarpiece illustrated with a narrative scene. The work shows Saint Ansanus and an unidentified female saint (Margaret?) at either side and prophets in roundels. It was the first of four altarpieces for the cathedral of Siena, dedicated to the four saintly protectors of the city, one of whom was Ansanus. The frame was added in the late nineteenth century. The records of payment shed no light on the respective responsibilities of the two collaborators. Probably Martini painted the Annunciation and Memmi painted the two saints and the prophets. A fifth roundel most likely portrayed God the father. The Annunciation is noteworthy for its Immediacy: Gabriel has just alighted, his cape still flying, while the Virgin recoils in fear. Elegant details include Mary's intarsia throne; the marble floor; and Gabriel's brocaded robe, plaid cape, and rose-tinged wings. As in other Sienese Annunciations, Gabriel bears an olive branch instead of a lily. He also wears a crown of olive leaves. Symbolic of peace, these leaves perhaps allude to the coming of Jesus, the prince of peace. The words of Gabriel's announcement, *Ave Gratia Plena Dominus Tecum* (Luke 1:28), are in relief; they can thus be read metaphorically as the word that becomes flesh in Mary's womb at this instant. The *Altarpiece of the Blessed Agostino Novello* (Siena, Pinaco-teca Nazionale) is a tempera painting in an old-fashioned *pala* format. Though it is unsigned and undated, most scholars believe that Martini was the artist. It was painted for Saint' Agostino in Siena and was first documented in 1638, together with the sarcophagus of the Beatus (now lost) that it decorated. Agostino, a hermit monk who died in 1309 outside Siena, was venerated locally. The central panel of the altarpiece portrays him standing amid four trees, book in hand, an inspirational angel at his ear. The side panels illustrate four posthumous miracles—two drawn from Augustinian texts, two unrecorded. Each contains two episodes, a disaster followed by salvation. Three of the four stories show Agostino saving small children, an emphasis compatible with the protohumanism of the early *Trecento*.

Martini and his workshop painted other polyptychs, typically showing a half-length Virgin and child in the center flanked by panels containing busts of saints. At least two rested on a predella, and all apparently were crowned with gables filled with bust-length figures. The altarpiece painted for Santa Caterina in Pisa (Pisa, Museo Nazionale di San Matteo) and signed by Martini seems to have survived intact. The others, broken up and with many panels missing, apparently were painted as altar-pieces for churches in Orvieto and San Gimignano.

Avignon (c. 1335–1344)

The frescoes originally in the porch of the cathedral of Notre Dame des Doms, Avignon, were probably commissioned by Cardinal Jacopo Stefaneschi (d. 1341). When the badly damaged fragments that survive were transferred to the museum of the Palais des Papes, up to three layers of *sinopie* were revealed. Two works are completely lost: *Andrea Corsini Healing a Blind Man*, a portrayal of a miracle that took place in the porch itself; and *Saint George and the Dragon,* known through a seventeenth-century copy. The extant fragments and *sinopie* portray the earliest known Madonna of Humility and an adult Jesus with an orb flanked by six angels. In the former, the donor kneels before the Virgin, and the child holds a scroll inscribed "I am the light of the world"; in the latter, the unusual orb con-

tains a landscape framed between rippling water and a starry sky. The changes in the skillfully drawn series of *sinopie* suggest that the patron played an active role in the artist's progress.

The *Holy Family* (Liverpool, Walker Art Gallery) is signed and dated 1342. This small picture in tempera is a unique portrayal of Jesus, Mary, and Joseph immediately after the disputation with the doctors in the temple. The codex in the Virgin's lap contains an abbreviated quotation from Luke 2:48—"Son, why hast thou dealt with us thus?"—and the gestures indicate a parental reprimand of the defiant Jesus. This work is an unusual example of the Holy Family as an ordinary family with ordinary problems; as such, it reflects the human values of the time.

The *Virgil Frontispiece* (Milan, Biblioteca Ambrosiana) was painted on vellum for Petrarch between 1338 and 1344. A couplet inscribed on it states that the artist was Simone Martini. This painting was made for Petrarch's volume of classical texts, which included most of Virgil; it originally faced the first work, a fourth-century commentary by Servius on the *Bucolics*. The image seems to be an allegory explained by two other couplets that refer to the "unveiling" of the "secrets" of Virgil by Servius. It depicts Servius pulling back a curtain to reveal a reclining Virgil; nearby are a knight (representing the *Aeneid*), a farmer (*Georgics*), and a shepherd (*Eclogues*).

Two lost portraits by Martini probably also date from the Avignon period. The first, made for Petrarch, depicted Laura; it is known only through two of the poet's sonnets that refer to it. The second was of Cardinal Napoleone Orsini, and to it Martini added verses by Petrarch, which appear to come from the sitter's mouth. It was mentioned in a fifteenth-century text. These were the first-known individual portraits in Italy.

The seven surviving tempera panels of the *Antwerp (Orsini) Polyptych* (Antwerp, Musées Royaux des Beaux-Arts;

Berlin, Staatliche Museen, Preussischer Kulturbesitz; Paris, Musée du Louvre) are dated by most scholars to Martini's years in Avignon. Originally a double-sided work, the polyptych probably folded like a concertina. The panels portray Gabriel, the Virgin Annunciate, and the *Via Crucis* (backed by the Orsini arms), *Crucifixion, Deposition,* and *Entombment*. One narrative panel and a second set of the family arms are lost. The patron, shown in the *Deposition,* was one of the four Orsini brothers, all of whom became cardinals. Most remarkable is the *Via Crucis,* which includes perturbed children; a rare depiction of Simon of Cyrene bearing the cross behind Jesus (Matthew 27:32); and a compassionate Saint John already protecting the Virgin, before Jesus asks him to do so from the cross. The polyptych was signed by Martini.

Saint Ladislas (Altomonte, Santa Maria della Consolazione, Museo), a small devotional panel in tempera known only since 1929, is attributed to Martini on the basis of style. It probably was made at Avignon. The veneration of Ladislas was rare in Italy at this time, and the portrayal of a saint standing in isolation was also unusual.

Other Lost or Destroyed Works

Account books in Siena mention other works done in the city but no longer extant. In addition, Ghiberti cites an altarpiece for the cathedral of Siena, now lost, and frescoes on the facade of the Opera del Duomo and the Ospedale della Scala, both destroyed. Finally, Vasari refers to an untraced panel in Santa Maria Novella in Florence.

See also Duccio di Buoninsegna; Giotto di Bondone; Petrarca, Francesco; Robert of Anjou

Further Reading

Borsook, Eve. *The Mural Painters of Tuscany, from Cimabue to Andrea del Sarto.* London: Phaidon, 1960. (Rev. ed. Oxford: Clarendon, 1980, pp. 19–27.)

Brink, Joel. "Francesco Petrarch and the Problem of Chronology in the Late Paintings of Simone Martini." *Paragone,* 28(331), 1977a, pp. 3–9.

———. "Simone Martini, Francesco Petrarch and the Humanistic Program of the Virgil Frontispiece." *Mediaevalia,* 3, 1977b, pp. 83–117.

Cannon, Joanna. "Simone Martini, the Dominicans, and the Early Sienese Polyptych." *Journal of the Warburg and Courtauld Institutes,* 45, 1982, pp. 69–93.

Carli, Enzo, ed. *Simone Martini: La Maestà.* Milan: Electa, 1996.

Contini, Gianfranco, and Maria Cristina Gozzoli. *L'opera completa di Simone Martini.* Milan: Rizzoli, 1970.

Denny, Don. "Simone Martini's *Holy Family.*" *Journal of the Warburg and Courtauld Institutes,* 30, 1967, pp. 138–149.

Enaud, François. "Les frèsques de Simone Martini en Avignon." In *Les Monuments Historiques de la France.* Paris, 1963, pp. 114–180.

Gardner, Julian. "Saint Louis of Toulouse, Robert of Anjou, and Simone Martini." *Zeitschrift für Kunstgeschichte,* 39, 1976, pp. 12–33.

Garzelli, Annarosa. "Peculiarità di Simone Martini ad Assisi: Gli affreschi della cappella di San Martino." In *Simone Martini: Atti del convegno: Siena, 27, 28, 29 marzo 1985,* ed. Luciano Bellosi. Florence: Centro Di, 1988, pp. 55–65.

Hoch, Adrian S. "A New Document for Simone Martini's Chapel of Saint Martin at Assisi." *Gesta,* 24, 1985, pp. 141–146.

Hueck, Irene. "Die Kapellen der Basilika San Francesco in Assisi: Die Auftraggeber und die Franziskaner." In *Patronage and Public in the Trecento: Proceedings of the Saint Lambrecht Symposium, Abtei Saint Lambrecht, Styria, 16–19 July 1984,* ed. Vincent Moleta. Florence: L. S. Olschki, 1986.

Mallory, Michael, and Gordon Moran. "New Evidence Concerning *Guidoriccio.*" *Burlington Magazine,* 128, 1986, pp. 250–256.

Martindale, Andrew. "The Problem of *Guidoriccio.*" *Burlington Magazine,* 128, 1986, pp. 259–273.

———. *Simone Martini.* Oxford: Phaidon, 1988.

Milanesi, Gaetano. *Documenti per la storia dell' arte senese.* Siena: O. Porri, 1854–1856.

Paccagnini, Giovanni. *Simone Martini*. Milan: A. Martello, 1955.

——. "Martini." In *Encyclopedia of World Art*, Vol. 9. New York: McGraw-Hill, 1964, cols. 502–508.

Stubblebine, James H. *Duccio di Buoninsegna and His School*. Princeton, N.J.: Princeton University Press, 1979.

Vasari, Giorgio. *Vite*, ed. Gaetano Milanesi. Florence: G. C. Sansoni, 1878–1885. (Originally 1550, rev. 1568.)

MARY D. EDWARDS

MASLAMA DE MADRID (d. 1007)

Abū-l-Qāsim Maslama ibn Aḥmad al-Majrīṭī, Andalusian astronomer and mathematician, was born in Majrīṭ (Madrid). He studied in Córdoba and practiced astrology: interested by the Saturn-Jupiter conjunction that took place in 1007, he predicted a series of catastrophes usually associated with the fall of the caliphate and the period of civil wars (*fitna*, 1009–1031). He is the author of the first documented astronomical observation in al-Andalus (the longitude of *Qalb al-Asad*, Regulus, 135° 40' in 977 or 979). He wrote a set of notes on the only trigonometrical tool used in antiquity, Menelaos' theorem (*al-shakl al-qaṭṭā'*), as well as a commentary, with frequent original digressions, on Ptolemy's *Planisphaerium*, which is the first of the studies dedicated by Andalusian astronomers to the astrolabe: its influence is clear in the thirteen-century Latin compilation on the instrument ascribed to Messahalla (Māshā'allāh, fl. Bacra, 762–809) the echoes of which reach the treatises on the astrolabe written by the collaborators of Alfonso X and by Geoffrey Chaucer (ca. 1340–1400). He is the creator of an important school of mathematicians and astronomers, and two of his disciples (Aḥmad ibn al-Ṣaffār and Abū-1-Qāsim Aṣbag ibn al-Samḥ) collaborated with him in his revision of the *Sindhind zīj* (astronomical handbook with tables) of Al-Khwārizmī (fl. 800–847), a work having an Indian pre-Ptolemaic origin, probably known in Al-Andalus since ca. 850. This revision, extant in a Latin translation by Adelard of Bath (fl. 1116–1142), adapted certain tables to the geographical coordinates of Córdoba, changed the Persian calendar used in the original for the Hijra calendar, introduced Hispanic and, possibly, Ptolemaic materials and added a considerable amount of new astrological tables (about one-fifth of the extant set of numerical tables), which improve considerably the techniques used by Al-Khwārizmī himself. He also introduced Ptolemaic astronomy in al-Andalus: he studied the *Almagest* and wrote astrological additions for the Ptolemaic *zīj* of Al-Battānī (d. 929).

Further Reading

Burnett, C. (ed.) *Adelard of Bath: An English Scientist of the Early Twelfth Century*. London, 1987. 87–118.

Mercier, R. *Astronomical Tables in the Twelfth Century*. London, 1988.

Neugebauer, O. *The Astronomical Tables of Al-Khuārizmī*. Trans. with commentary by H. Suter. Copenhagen, 1962.

Samsó, J. *Las Ciencias de los Antiguos en al-Andalus*. Madrid, 1992. 84–98.

Suter, .*Die Astonomischen Tafeln des Muḥammed ibn Mūsa al-Khuārizmī in der Bearbeitung des malama ibn Ahmed al-Madjrīṭī und der latein. Uebersetzung des Athelhard von Bath*. Copenhagen, 1914.

Vernet, J., and M. A. Catalá. "Las obras matematicas de Maslama de Madrid." In *Estudios sobre Historia de la Ciencia Medieval*. Ed. J. Vernet. Barcelona, 1979. 241–71.

JULIO SAMSÓ

MATILDA, EMPRESS (1102–1167)

The daughter of King Henry I of England and his wife, Matilda of Scotland, Matilda became the empress by virtue of her marriage to the Salian emperor, Henry V. Her father accepted the marriage proposal during Whitsuntide of 1109, at which time she was only eight years old. In the spring of 1110 she was sent to Germany under the care of Bishop Burchard of Cambrai, betrothed to Henry V at Utrecht, and crowned at Mainz by Archbishop Frederick of Cologne. Henry V then dismissed all her English attendants, and the child was taken under the guardianship of Archbishop Bruno of Trier to learn the German language and customs. The marriage finally took place in January 1114 at Worms, the new consort now being twelve years old and her husband some thirty years her elder. Henry V had used the years between the betrothal and marriage to spend Matilda's enormous dowry of ten thousand silver marks on a major Roman expedition, during which he extracted the short-lived treaty of Ponte Mammolo from Pope Paschal II in hopes of decisively ending the Investiture Conflict.

Matilda soon played the crucial roles of patron and intercessor at court; she appeared on charters in subsequent years as the sponsor of many royal grants, and acted as petitioner several times on behalf of nobles or prelates who sought reconciliation with the emperor. Her imperial role expanded when she joined her husband on a military campaign in Rome in 1117. The imperial army occupied the city, and Matilda was crowned with her husband on Pentecost in St. Peter's Basilica by the archbishop of Braga. Matilda would choose to retain the imperial dignity even after leaving Germany, at least as a courtesy title. When her husband's presence was required north of the Alps after the coronation, Matilda remained in Italy as imperial regent. She assisted in the administration of imperial territories and presided over courts such as the session at Rocca Capineta near Reggio. She appears to have continued in this capacity during the year 1118, and then rejoined the emperor in Lotharingia in 1119. This royal apprenticeship at such a tender age prepared her well for the tumultuous years ahead. She was with Henry V in Utrecht at his untimely death in 1125,

which left her a childless widow in possession of the imperial insignia at the age of twenty-three.

Her husband's hopes that she would produce an heir for the Salian line were quickly replaced by her father's need for an heir to the Norman dynasty, since Henry I's only son died in 1120. He therefore recalled her to England, and Matilda handed over the imperial insignia to Archbishop Adalbert of Mainz before returning to her Anglo-Norman homeland in 1125. After a sixteen–year absence she began yet another new life, with the only tokens of her imperial childhood in Germany being a treasure of jewels and personal regalia (most of which she would give to religious houses) and the precious relic of the hand of St. James (which she gave to the family abbey at Reading). She was recognized as the legitimate heir of Henry I in England and Normandy, and in 1128 Henry I married her to the unpopular Angevin suitor, Geoffrey Plantagenet. Matilda was the child in her first marriage, but in this second union Geoffrey was the child, being ten years her junior and only fifteen years old. Her second marriage of political expediency was a rocky one, but it did produce the needed heir in 1133 (Henry II Plantagenet). After her father's death in 1135 Matilda spent some twenty years asserting her son's claim to the Anglo-Norman throne against her cousin, Stephen of Blois.

Once Henry II succeeded Stephen in 1154, Matilda lived the remainder of her life in Normandy, and was buried at the abbey of Bec upon her death in 1167. She proved to be a valuable and trusted adviser to her royal son. Although she recommended against the appointment of Thomas à Becker as the archbishop of Canterbury, Matilda was turned to repeatedly by all sides as a mediator (*mediatrix*) in the subsequent dispute between the king and cleric. This remarkable woman's Anglo-Norman-German life was summed up in the epitaph on her tomb: "Great by birth, greater by marriage, greatest by offspring. Here lies the daughter, wife, and mother of Henry." Yet surely the legacy of this indomitable woman reaches beyond the men whose political needs set the boundaries of her life.

See also **Henry I**

Further Reading

Chibnall, Marjorie. *The Empress Matilda: Queen, Consort, Queen Mother and Lady of the English.* Oxford: Basil Blackwell, 1991.

Geldner, Ferdinand. "Kaiserin Mathilde, die deutsche Königswahl von 1125 und das Gegenkönigtum Konrads III." *Zeitschrift für bayerische Landesgeschichte* 40 (1977): 3–22.

Leyser, Karl. "Frederick Barbarossa, Henry II and the hand of St. James." *English Historical Review* 90 (1975): 481–506; rpt. in *Medieval Germany and its Neighbors.* London: Hambledon, 1980, pp. 215–40.

Pain, Nesta. *Matilda: Uncrowned Queen of England.* London: Weidenfeld and Nicolson, 1978.

Rössler, Oskar. *Kaiserin Mathilde, Mutter Heinrichs von Anjou, und das Zeitalter der Anarchie in England.* Berlin: E. Ebering, 1897; rpt. Vaduz: Kraus Reprint, 1965.

Schnith, Karl. "*Domina Anglorum,* Zur Bedeutungsstreite eines hochmittelalterlichen Herrscherinentitels." In *Grundwissenschaften und Geschichte: Festschrift für Peter Acht,* ed. Waldemar Schlogl and Peter Herde. Kallmunz: Lassleben, 1976, pp. 101–111.

JOSEPH P. HUFFMAN

MATTEO DA PERUGIA (d. by 1418) Matteo da Perugia (Matheus de Perusia) was born in the latter fourteenth century and belongs, officially, to the third and last generation of Italian *ars nova* musicians; however, his curious career and his stylistic focus make him almost a French musician.

Except for his presumed Perugian origin, we know nothing of Matteo's early life, although it is apparent that he chose to become a professional musician rather than a priest. At some point, he became a singer at the cathedral of Milan (which was then still unfinished), and in 1402 he was appointed to be its first choirmaster (*magister capellae* or *maestro di cappella*). This appointment is thought to reflect the influence of the colorful man who became Matteo's chief patron, Pietro Filargo di Candia (Petros Philargos). Pietro Filargo was born a Greek; joined the Roman church; studied and then taught theology at the University of Paris; was an adviser to Gian Galeazzo Visconti; was made bishop, successively, of Piacenza (1386), Vicenza (1387), and Novara (1389); became archbishop of Milan in 1402; was made a cardinal in 1405; and became the antipope Alexander V in 1409.

Filargo took up his episcopal residence in nearby Pavia, where he could teach at its university and hold a lavish court. Matteo, loyally, came to this court to serve Filargo, so annoying his own employers in Milan that he felt compelled to give up his cathedral post in 1407 and devote himself fully to Filargo. In 1409, when Filargo was elected as antipope Alexander V by the Council of Pisa, Matteo presumably moved with his master to a new residence in Bologna. It was apparently then that Matteo participated in the preparation of one of the most important musical manuscript collections of the day (now in the Estense Library in Modena). When Alexander V died in 1410 (by poison), Matteo evidently stayed on with his successor, John XXIII, until John was assured of deposition by the Council of Constance. In May 1414, Matteo resumed his post at the cathedral in Milan, officially until October 1416. However, but not until January 1418—by which time Matteo himself seems to have died—was his successor given full status as *maestro di canto.*

There is no evidence that Matteo himself ever visited France, but French cultural influences had been present in northern Italy for decades, thanks partly to the proximity of the absentee papal court at Avignon. Filargo's Francophile tastes, in particular, probably caused Matteo to develop an identification with French rather than Italian musical styles—whether by imposition or voluntary affinity. Matteo's output of compositions must have been extensive, and what survives of it, though small by some standards, is the largest of any of the Italian *ars nova* composers. Aside from some six Latin liturgical pieces (two of them complex polytextual motets), the surviving works are secular. Only two *ballate* are in Italian. The remainder (four *ballades,* seven *virelais,* ten *rondeaux,* and one canon) are all in French, presumably to suit the Francophile tastes of his patrons. Most of Matteo's compositions are for three vocal parts, and in virtually all his work—sacred or secular—he applies the arcane techniques of isorhythmic integration, carrying them to elaborate extremes (disjunct lines, conflicting time signatures, etc.) in the style of the so-called *ars subtilior,* the "mannerist" school of exaggerated effects, which he seem to have embraced wholeheartedly. Indeed, Matteo, along with Antonello da Caserta, was a leader of this imported stylistic movement.

Beyond his own authenticated compositions, there survive a number of substitute contratenor parts written for music by other composers. If these parts are indeed by Matteo, as is generally believed, they show him attempting, through these substitute voices, to update or enhance the work of earlier or contemporaneous masters (such as Machaut, Bartolino da Padova, and Antonello). It has been proposed that Matteo's supposedly "modern" style made him an important shaper of new musical directions for the *Quattrocento*; but there is also an argument against this idea, buttressed by the fact that Matteo's music survives in only a few manuscripts and apparently did not circulate widely. For all his fascination as a bold compositional personality, Matteo seems to have played a less significant role than the more focused and disciplined Johannes Ciconia in the transition from the age of Machaut to the age of Dufay.

See also **Ciconia, Johannes**

Further Reading

Apel, Willi. *French Secular Vocal Music of the Late Fourteenth Century.* Cambridge, Mass.: Mediaeval Academy of America, 1950.

——, ed. *French Secular Compositions of the Fourteenth Century,* 3 vols. Corpus Mensurabilis Musicae, 53. Rome: American Institute of Musicology, 1970–1972.

Besseler, Heinrich. "Hat Matheus de Perusio Epoche gemacht?" *Die Musikforschung,* 8, 1955, 19–23.

Fano, Fabio. "Origini della cappella musicale del Duomo di Milano." *Rivista Musicale Italiana,* 55, 1953, pp. 1ff.

——. *La cappella musicale del Duomo di Milano,* Vol. 1, *Le origini e il primo maestro di cappelia*: *Matteo da Perugia.* Milan: Ricordi, 1956.

Gombosi, Otto. "French Secular Music of the Fourteenth Century." *Musical Quarterly,* 36, 1950, pp. 603–610.

Günther, Ursula. "Das Manuskript Modena, Biblioteca Estense, a M.5.24." *Musica Disciplina,* 24, 1970, pp. 17–67.

Korte, Werner. *Studien zur Geschichte der Musik in Italien im ersten Viertel des 15. Jahrhunderts.* Kassel: Bärenreiter, 1933.

Marrocco, William Thomas, ed. "Italian Secular Music". In *Polyphonic Music of the Fourteenth Century,* Vol. 10. Monaco: Éditions de Oiseau-Lyre, 1977.

Pirrotta, Nino. *Il Codice Estense lat. 568 e la musica francese in Italia al principio del 1400.* Palermo: Reale Accademia di Scienze, Lettere, e Arti, 1946.

Reese, Gustav. *Music in the Middle Ages.* New York: Norton, 1940.

Sartori, Claudio. "Matteo da Perugia e Bertrand Feragut." *Acta,* 28, 1956, pp. 12–27.

JOHN W. BARKER

MATTHEW PARIS (ca. 1199–1259) A monk at St. Albans from 1217 until his death in 1259, Matthew inherited the duties of historian from his predecessor in that capacity, Roger of Wendover, and continued work on Rogers *Chronica majora*, to some extent rewriting but primarily extending and illustrating the text (Cambridge, Corpus Christi College 26 and 16, and BL Royal 14.C.vii, fols. 157–218). He also produced other Latin historical texts generally associated with the Chronicles (*Historia Anglorum*, BL Royal l4.C.vii, fols. 1–156; *Liber additamentorum*, BL Cotton Nero D.i; *Abbreviatio chronicorum*, BL Cotton Claudius D.vi) among others, and four saints' lives in Anglo-Norman.

The great bulk of Matthew's illustrative work in the historical texts may be characterized as *signa*, abbreviated symbols that help readers find their way in the text and signal important events. In addition Matthew included itineraries, maps, illustrated genealogies, and the oldest preserved record of heraldic arms. Narrative illustrations are added to the histories but tend to take a minor part and assume a telegraphic, hurried, yet also vividly dramatic aspect. A few full-page iconic illustrations (the Virgin and Child, the Veronica head of Christ) appended to the Chronicles are the only miniatures that could be considered polished works of art.

It is in his illustrated saints' lives that Matthew fully explores the possibilities of narrative and, in the *Vie de seint Auban* in Dublin, produces his most artistically complex work. The Dublin manuscript has been dated in the 1240s as Matthew's first attempt to illustrate the life of a saint and contains Latin versions of the lives, liturgical offices, and charters in addition to Matthew's Anglo-Norman text. The romance text is illustrated by framed miniatures across the top of the three-column page, and these continue above the Latin texts, after the romance text has ended, to detail the foundation of the monastery through the efforts of King Offa. Matthew worked in an accomplished but late version of the "Style 1200." His illustrations for the Dublin manuscript are done in line with some touches of color, primarily green, but also vermilion, blue, and ocher. Notes at the bottom of the pages in Matthew's hand give evidence that the iconography of the miniatures was carefully planned.

It would seem that similar planning would explain Matthew's involvement in the illustration of two other manuscripts of lives of saints. The *Life of St. Thomas of Canterbury* in Anglo-Norman (BL Loan 88) and the *Estoire de seint Aedward le rei* (CUL Ee.3.59) are executed in a different style from the Dublin manuscript but retain many of the features associated with Matthew, even compositions and the drawing of such details as ships and horses. All three manuscripts show an involvement with contemporary political concerns and were intended for an aristocratic audience: the life of Edward is dedicated to Queen Eleanor, and notes on the flyleaf of the Dublin manuscript detail its loan and that of other manuscripts of the lives of saints to aristocratic ladies.

Although Matthew made important innovations in format and narrative in illustrated lives of the saints that in turn influenced the illustration of Apocalypses and other English manuscripts, in general his work must be characterized as eccentric and isolated. He apparently worked apart from the scriptorium at St. Albans and produced his manuscripts as virtually a one-man effort, even writing his own fair copy. If he did plan the London and Cambridge manuscripts, he probably sent them off to London or Westminster for execution.

Matthew received a special commission as historian from Henry III and harbored many courtly prejudices, yet he lived in a monastery away from court and voiced some remarkably strong antiroyal opinions. Similarly he was a religious man who had little patience with the papacy. The unique form and visual content of his Chronicles, which he surely counted as his greatest achievement, had no successor and, as a recent scholar has lamented, have been little studied.

Further Reading

Primary Sources

Lowe, W.R.L., and E.F. Jacob, eds. *Illustrations to the Life of St. Alban*. Intro. M.R. James. Oxford: Clarendon, 1924.

Paris, Matthew. *Chronica majora*. Ed. Henry R. Luard. 7 vols. Rolls Series. London: Longman, 1872–83.Paris, Matthew. *La estoire de seint Aedward le rei*. Ed. Montague Rhodes James. Oxford: Roxburghe Club, 1920 [facsimile].

Secondary Sources

Backhouse, Janet, and Christopher de Hamel. *The Becket Leaves*. London: British Library, 1988.

Hahn, Cynthia. "Absent No Longer: The Saint and the Sign in Late Medieval Pictorial Hagiography." In *Hagiogmphie und Kunst*, ed. G. Kerscher. Berlin: Dietrich Reimer, 1993, pp. 152–75.

Lewis, Suzanne. *The Art of Matthew Paris in the Chronica majora*. Berkeley: University of California Press, 1987 [extensive bibliography and analysis of Chronicle illustrations].

Morgan, Nigel. *Early Gothic Manuscripts 1190–1285*. 2 vols. A Survey of Manuscripts Illuminated in the British Isles 4, ed. J.J.G. Alexander. London: Harvey Miller, 1982–88.

Vaughan, Richard. *Matthew Paris*. Cambridge: Cambridge University Press, 1958.

CYNTHIA HABN

MAXIMILIAN (1459–1519) Emperor, patron of the arts, "the last knight," Maximilian I Habsburg enjoys a popular modern reputation. As the son of Emperor Frederick III, Maximilian experienced a youth tarnished by the wars and defeats his father suffered. His first important step into politics came in 1473, when his father negotiated with Duke Charles the Rash of Burgundy for the hand of his daughter, Mary. Although Charles's original demand of a royal crown was too high, the negotiations continued over the next few years. Then when Charles died unexpectedly at the Battle of Nancy in 1477, the king of France moved to seize Mary, who was holding out in Ghent. Maximilian sealed their marriage first through procurators in April, and finally concluded it in person when he arrived at the head of a rescuing army in August. Their marriage became a true love match. The emperor enfeoffed his son with the lands of the late duke of Burgundy. Yet Maximilian only truly secured most of the lands in a series of wars with France. His victory at the battle of Guinegate in 1479 guaranteed his possession of the Lowlands and most of Burgundy, some of the richest lands in Europe.

These new lands were not so easy to hold onto, however, since the citizens of the prosperous towns disputed the power of the new dynasty. After Mary died from a riding accident in 1482, many in the Lowlands openly rebelled against Maximilian's authority. Allied with France, town forces managed to wring from Maximilian the supervision of his children, Philip and Margaret. Even worse, the city of Bruges took him prisoner for fourteen weeks in 1488. His rather, in a rare but certainly necessary act of support, actually gathered an army that marched on the city, frightening the town into freeing Maximilian. Returning at the head of his own army, Maximilian conquered Bruges and many other towns, completing their defeat by 1493 in the Treaty of Senlis.

In the midst of these conflicts Frederick had managed to get Maximilian elected king of the Romans in Frankfurt on February 16, 1486, and crowned in Aachen on April 9. For the first time in a century a son had followed as king an imperial father during the father's lifetime. In 1490 Maximilian replaced his incompetent cousin, Sigismund "the Rich in Coins," as duke of Tyrol. He made that province, located between Burgundy and Austria on the way to Italy, and its capital, Innsbruck, the center of his imperial organization. From there to Mecheln in the Netherlands he established the first regular postal route in Europe. The silver of Tyrol helped to finance the reconquest of Austria from Matthias Corvinus, while the growing business with the Fugger banking family helped to underwrite many more imperial schemes. But with interest rates of over 35 percent on loans, Maximilian rarely had enough cash to fund all his plans.

After Mary's death, Maximilian fathered several illegitimate children, but he knew the importance of political marriages. To gain both cash and leverage against France, in 1490 Maximilian arranged his marriage by proxy with the twelve-year-old Anne of Brittany, who had just inherited that important province on her father's death. The next year Charles VIII invaded Brittany, dissolved his (unconsummated) marriage to Maximilian's daughter Margaret, and, without returning Margaret or her dowry of Burgundy, married Anne. Maximilian tried to gather an army to oppose these actions but was hopelessly outnumbered by French forces and hampered by his daughter's hostage status. The Brittany affair gained France a strategic province, earned Maximilian frustration and humiliation, and helped engender a centuries-long rivalry between the Habsburg and Valois dynasties. In 1497 Maximilian found another marriage partner in Bianca Maria Sforza, sister of Ludovico il Moro Sforza, who had usurped control of Milan. She brought a dowry of four hundred thousand gulden (guilders), or about three times what Maximilian could draw annually from the Habsburg Austrian lands. That money quickly disappeared also.

Soon after his father's death in 1493, Maximilian responded to a call for an imperial reform proposed for the Reichstag (imperial council) of Worms in 1495. There the archbishop of Mainz, Berthold von Henneberg, tried to gain a reform suitable to the princes. At the Reichstag, Maximilian agreed to the "eternal terri-torial peace" *(Ewige Landfriede),* once and for all, legally forbidding the many private wars and feuds among nobles that had disturbed the empire. To keep the peace, the Reichstag also created the Imperial Chamber Court (Reichskammergericht) and established a general tax, the "common penny" *(gemeine Pfennig).* Afterward many princes wanted further reform and withheld the general tax to put pressure on Maximilian. After his defeat in a brief war against the Swiss, the princes temporarily were able to further restrict Maximilian's authority, imposing an imperial regime *(Reichsregiment)* at Augsburg in 1500. By 1504, however, he had largely defeated the fractious princes. The possibility of a unified, effective imperial government vanished in these quarrels.

Maximilian's involvement in wars on the empire's fringes brought mixed results. He encouraged new developments in military tactics, like cannon. Or he increasingly abandoned the cavalry charge of armored knights in favor of infantry on foot with sword and pike, his *Landsknechte.* Maximilian regularly participated in the shifting diplomatic alliances, and he managed to maintain a reputation as an able commander. But he lost many wars, often through lack of funds. He fought frequently in Italy, which had become an open battleground since the invasion in 1494 by Charles VII of France. In 1508 Pope Julius II, needing Maximilian's military support in the League of Cambrai against Venice, offered to crown him emperor. Yet Maximilian was unable to fight his way to Rome. So he proclaimed himself "elected emperor of the Romans" on February 4, 1508, in Trient. Thus, with Julius's belated acceptance, he became emperor without a papal coronation.

Maximilian gained lasting importance for both his dynasty and European history because of two important double marriages he arranged. First in 1496 he married his son Philip "the Handsome," and daughter Margaret from his marriage with Mary, to the heirs of Spain, Juana "the Mad" and Juan, the children of Ferdinand of Aragon and Isabella of Castille. Philip and Juana had several children. The elder son, Charles V, eventually inherited both the Spanish and Austrian possessions and had an empire "on which the sun never set." The second double marriage was arranged in 1515, when Maximilian married his grandson Ferdinand and granddaughter Mary to the children of King Ladislaus of Bohemia and Hungary. This arrangement provided the legal claims to reunite Hungary and Bohemia with the Habsburg lands in 1526.

But Maximilian's attempts at building stronger institutions of rule in his own inherited lands led to increasing opposition, including open rebellion in some territories. Even the citizens of Innsbruck resented the burden of debts run up by the often cash-poor Maximilian. At the beginning of 1519 they finally refused to accept his credit, or to find stalls for his horses. In disdain he left the city for Vienna but sickened along the way and died on January 12. As a result, his magnificent tomb in Innsbruck lies empty; his body is buried in Wiener Neustadt, while his heart lies in Bruges, next to the body of his first wife, Mary.

Maximilian enjoys lasting fame as a well-rounded Renaissance prince. He was a patron of the arts and new sciences at the summit of the German Renaissance. His portrait by Albrecht Dürer is the most famous image of the monarch. Skilled and literate in several languages, he himself helped to produce two autobiographical epic poems *(Theuerdank* and *Weisskunig),* a hunting manual, and other works, including the *Ambraser Heldenbuch (Ambray Book of Heroes,* a compilation manuscript of courtly literature named after Castle Ambras). Sometimes called "the last knight," he was a great promoter of tournaments, drawing on the chivalric traditions of the court of Burgundy and continuing the

Order of the Golden Fleece. Maximilian's idea of the Holy Roman Empire of the German nation ended the Middle Ages and looked forward to the attempt at universal empire by his successor, his grandson Charles V.

See also **Frederick III; Hartmann von Aue**

Further Reading

Benecke, Gerhard. *Maximilian I (1459–1519): An Analytical Biography.* London: Routledge and Kegan Paul, 1982.
Wiesflecker, Hermann. *Kaiser Maximilian I.: Das Reich, Österreich und Europa an der Wende zur Neuzeit.* 5 vols. Vienna: Verlag für Geschichte und Politik, 1971–1986.

BRIAN A. PAVLAC

MECHTHILD VON HACKEBORN
(1241–1298/1299) A Cistercian sister of the Helfta community, Mechthild von Hackeborn's mystical visions were recorded in the *Liber specialis gratiae (Book of Special Grace).* At age seven, Mechthild entered the Rodersdorf cloister, where her sister Gertrud already resided. After the community had relocated to Helfta, Mechthild served in the capacities of magistra and cantrix. In 1261 the five-year-old Gertrud von Helfta *(die Große)* was given into her charge. Bedridden the last eight years of her life, Mechthild revealed her visions at this time to Gertrud and at least one other sister at Helfta, who recorded them without her knowledge; however, Mechthild did approve portions of the account before her death.

The original German version of Mechthild's visions has not survived. There are more than 250 contemporaneous and subsequent Latin and vernacular manuscript versions of the *Liber specialis gratiae,* but only one manuscript contains all seven books. Rich in allegory, the seven parts chronicle Mechthild's life and death, her visions, the special graces she experienced, her teachings concerning the true devotion to God and the virtuous life, and fragments of a correspondence with a female friend. In contrast to the *Fließendes Licht der Gottheit (Flowing Light of the Godhead)* of Mechthild's somewhat older namesake at Helfta, Mechthild von Magdeburg, the descriptions and observations found in the *Liber specialis gratiae* are based on liturgy, scripture, and the writings of the church fathers; however, like the *Fließendes Licht*, the *Liber* exhibits originality in imagery, language, and style. Of special note is Mechthild's description of the devotion to the Sacred Heart of Christ *(Herz-Jesu-Verehrung),* which she and Gertrud die Große promoted at Helfta.

See also **Gertrud von Helfta; Mechthild von Magdeburg**

Further Reading

Bynum, Caroline Walker. "Women Mystics in the Thirteenth Century: The Case of the Nuns of Helfta." In *Jesus as Mother: Studies in the Spirituality of the High Middle Ages.* Berkeley: University of California Press, 1982, pp. 170–262.

Finnegan, Jeremy. "Saint Mechtild of Hackeborn: *Nemo Communior.*" In *Medieval Religious Women,* vol. 2. *Peace Weavers,* ed. Lillian Thomas Shank and John A. Nichols. Kalamazoo, Mich.: Cistercian Publications, 1987, pp. 213–221.

Finnegan, Mary Jeremy. *The Women of Helfta.* Athens: University of Georgia Press, 1991 [first published 1962 as *Scholars and Mystics*].

Haas, Alois Maria. "Mechthild von Hackeborn. Eine Form zisterziensischer Frauenfrömmigkeit." In *Die Zisterzienser. Ordensleben zwischen Ideal und Wirklichkeit.* Ergänzungsband, ed. Kaspar Elm. Cologne: Rheinland-Verlag, 1982, pp. 221–239; rpt. "Themen und Aspekte der Mystik Mechthilds von Hackeborn." In *Geistliches Mittelalter,* ed. Alois Maria Haas. Dokimion 8. Freiburg, Switzerland: Universitätsverlag, 1984), pp. 373–391.

Halligan, Theresa, ed. *The Booke of Gostlye Grace of Mechthild of Hackeborn.* Toronto: Pontifical Institute of Mediaeval Studies. 1979.

Lewis, Gertrud Jaron. *Bibliographie zur deutschen Frauenmystik des Mittelalters.* Berlin: Schmidt, 1989, pp. 184–195.

Paquelin, Ludwig, ed. "Sanctae Mechthildis Virginis Ordinis Sancti Benedicti Liber specialis gratiae." In *Revelationes Gertrudianae ac Mechthildianae,* vol. 2. Poitiers: Oudin, 1877, pp. 1–422.

Schmidt, Margot. "Mechthild von Hackeborn." In *Die deutsche Literatur des Mittelalters: Verfasserlexikon,* 2d ed., ed. Kurt Ruh. Berlin: de Gruyter, 1987, vol. 6, cols. 251–260.

DEBRA L. STOUDT

MECHTHILD VON MAGDEBURG

(ca. 1207–ca. 1282) Beguine, visionary, and mystic, known to us through her sole book, *Das fließende Licht der Gottheit (The Flowing Light of the Godhead).* Biographical information gleaned or inferred from her book and its introductory material written in Latin by others indicates that she was born to a family of lower nobility near Magdeburg. She experienced her first vision at age twelve and left home about 1230 to take up the life of a Beguine in Magdeburg, returning home occasionally perhaps because of sickness or troubles caused by her book. Just as she criticized the deportment of some Beguines, male and female religious, clergy, the pope, and others, she, too, was subjected to criticism and even threats. Equally evident, however, is the support she received, especially from the Dominicans, whose order she praised. Baldwin, her brother, was received into this order, became subprior of the Dominican house in Halle, and was esteemed for virtue and learning. Another Dominican, Heinrich von Halle, was her spiritual adviser for many years and helped her edit (and, no doubt, circulate) incomplete versions of her book. About 1270 she entered the Cistercian convent at Helfta, renowned, under the leadership of Gertrud von Hackeborn, for its thriving spiritual life and devotion to learning, as witnessed by the writings of Mechthild von Hackeborn and Gertrud (the Great) von Helfta. Here Mechthild was sheltered from the trials of the unprotected life of a Beguine but, if we can believe her, was more revered from a distance than accepted into the community. With her health weakening and her sight failing, she completed the seventh and final section of her book. Her death is described in Gertrud of Helfta's *Legatus divinae pietatis*.

The original text of her book, written in Middle Low German with some Middle German characteristics, has been lost. A Middle High German version of the complete work translated about 1345 under the direction of Heinrich von Nördlingen in Basel survives in a manuscript at Einsiedeln ("E") and provides the principal textual basis for the study of Mechthild. Parts and short fragments have been discovered in other manuscripts. A Latin translation of the first six books of the Middle Low German original, probably the work of Dominicans in Halle, has come down to us preceded by a lengthy prologue justifying the book and its author.

Das fließende Licht can be described as confessional, visionary-revelatory, mystical, poetic, and devotional. It was written, we are told, by divine command to bear witness to the unusual divine favors bestowed on its author. Mechthild describes her visions, some global and some personal in scope, as well as her ecstatic mystical experiences of union. She prophesies, exhorts, criticizes, and teaches, using a rich variety of literary and nonliterary forms of expression, from highly lyrical courtly modes with their concomitant conventions to didactic expositions of moral and ascetical truths. She avails herself of prose, verse, and, most distinctively, colon rhyme—a short, verselike unit ending in rhyme or, more frequently, assonance. Much of this colon rhyme has been lost in the Middle High German version.

Because she knew little or no Latin, Mechthild acquired her knowledge of theology and spiritual traditions secondhand through instruction and the liturgy. The theological content of her book gives striking evidence of the care given religious education by her spiritual teachers and advisers, but more especially to Mechthild's own intellectual gifts and intuitive spiritual receptivity. Among the influences perceptible in her book are the Song of Songs, Augustine, Bernard of Clairvaux, Hugh and Richard of St. Victor, and Joachim of Fiore. More important, however, Mechthild's book must be seen as unique in its conception, without discernible predecessors or successors.

See also **Bernard of Clairvaux; Gertrud von Helfta**

Further Reading

Bynum, Caroline Walker. "Women Mystics in the Thirteenth Century: The Case of the Nuns of Helfta." In Bynum. *Jesus as Mother—Studies in the Spirituality of the High Middle Ages*. Berkeley: University of California Press, 1982, pp. 170–262.

Franklin, James C. *Mystical Transformations: The Imagery of Liquids in the Work of Mechthild von Magdeburg*. Rutherford, N.J.: Fairleigh Dickinson University Press, 1978.

Galvani, Christiana Mesch, trans. *Flowing Light of the Divinity*. New York: Garland, 1991.

Haug, Walter. "Das Gespräch mit dem unvergleichlichen Partner: Der mystische Dialog bei Mechthild von Magdeburg als Paradigma für eine personale Gesprächsstrutkur." *Poetik und Hermeneutik* 11 (1984): 251–279.

Lewis, Gertrud Jaron. *Bibliographie zur deutschen Frauenmystik des Mittelalters*. Berlin: Schmidt, 1989, pp. 164–183 [bibliography].

Neumann, Hans. "Mechthild von Magdeburg." In *Die deutsche Literatur des Mittelalters: Verfasserlexikon*. 2d ed, vol. 6. Berlin: de Gruyter, 1987, cols. 260–270.

Neumann, Hans, ed. *Mechthild von Magdeburg. Das fließende Licht der Gottheit*. 2 vols. Munich: Artemis, 1990.

Schmidt, Margot. "*Minne du gewaltige Kellerin*: On the Nature of *minne* in Mechthild of Magdeburg's *fliessendes licht der gottheit*." *Vox Benedictina* 4 (1987): 100–125.

Scholl, Edith. "To Be a Full Grown Bride: Mechthild of Magdeburg." In *Medieval Religious Women. vol. 2.: Peace Weavers*, ed. John A. Nichols and Lillian Thomas Shank. Kalamazoo, Mich.: Cistercian, 1987, pp. 223–238.

Tax, Petrus. "Die große Himmelsschau Mechthilds von Magdeburg und ihre Höllenvision." *Zeitschrift für deutsches Altertum* 108 (1979): 112–137.

Tobin, Frank. *Mechthild von Magdeburg— A Medieval Mystic in Modern Eyes.* Columbia, S.C.: Camden House, 1995.

von Balthasar, Hans Urs. "Mechthilds kirchlicher Auftrag." In *Das fließende Licht der Gottheit,* trans. Margot Schmidt. 1955. 2d ed. Stuttgart-Bad Canstatt: F. Frommann, 1995, pp. 19–45.

FRANK TOBIN

MEIR B. BARUKH OF ROTHENBURG
(ca. 1220 – 1293) Meir b. Barukh, known as "*MaHRaM*' (*moreinu ha-rav Meir*, "our teacher Rabbi Meir"), was born in Worms ca. 1220 (not 1215; see Urbach, pp. 407–8). His father was a rabbi in Worms and an important scholar, as were many other members of his family. Meir's teachers included his father, and in Würzburg the renowned Isaac b. Moses of Vienna, author of the halakhic work *Or zarua'*, and others. He also learned in yeshivot in France, where he copied responsa and talmudic commentaries that he later used in his own work. If the lamentation Meir wrote about the burning of books refers to the burning of the Talmud in Paris in 1242, then he may have been an eyewitness to that event and returned to Germany shortly thereafter. It is uncertain when he went to Rothenburg, the city most connected with his name, but probably soon after his return from France. He served also as rabbi in several other communities. After the death of his father (1276 or 1281), Meir went to Worms to replace him there. He had a *beit midrash*, or yeshivah, attached to his house there, with a "winter house" (i.e., heated, apparently) and rooms for the students to sleep. According to the information he himself wrote about this, the number of students was not large, even though his yeshivah was certainly the most famous one in Germany. His main students were er b. Yeḥiel, Mordecai b. Hillel, Samson b. Ṣaddoq, Ḥayyim b. Eliʿezer (grandson of Isaac, author of *Or zarua'*), and others, all outstanding scholars in their own right.

Meir was not, as Graetz had assumed, appointed "chief rabbi" of Germany (indeed, no such position existed); however, he was widely regarded as the foremost talmudic and legal authority, to whom rabbis not only from Germany but also France and other lands turned for decisions. Because of the large number of requests received, he even had to write his answers on the eve of holidays and the eve of Yom Kippur (see Urbach, p. 421). He was independent in his views and did not refrain from strongly disagreeing with those whose position he considered to be wrong (the story told by Urbach, p. 412, bottom, is not entirely accurate, however; see the text of the respon-sum ed. Bloch, p. 188, No. 81; it is understandable that the author whom Urbach cites thought that the bride's father was French, since the Amsterdam manuscript in fact reads "Roda," probably Dreux in France, cf. Gross, *Gallia Judaica*, p. 184, for similar spellings).

He used his authority to forestall enactments (*taqqanot*) that he thought would create a burden on people, such as the attempt by some communities to allot a portion of the taxes to property, something that Meir said had never been done in all the kingdom; rather, taxes were collected only on buying and selling, and were not collected at all from the poor (*She'elot u-teshuvot*, ed. Prague, No. 541, second part of the question; cf. ed. Bloch, p. 209, No. 141, where he advised more cautiously that they investigate the custom throughout Germany and act accordingly, but in general the opinion agrees with that of the previous question).

The rapidly deteriorating situation of the Jews in Germany in the latter half of the thirteenth century resulted in many Jews leaving to move to other towns under different overlords or leaving the empire altogether. Some followed earlier French rabbis to settle in Palestine. Meir himself finally decided upon this plan. Emperor Rudolph issued a decree in December of 1286 prohibiting any Jew from going across the sea without his permission or that of their overlord (text in Guido Kisch, *The Jews in Medieval Germany* [Chicago, 1949], p. 130, in which book, incidentally, Meir is not mentioned). Meir and his entire family also decided to leave for Palestine in spite of the royal decree, but on the way they encountered the bishop of Basel, who had with him an apostate Jew who recognized the rabbi and informed the bishop. Meir was arrested and turned over to the emperor, who imprisoned him in the castle at Ensisheim. According to Urbach (p. 424), the place where Meir was caught, in the mountains of Lombard, was a transition point for those going on to Palestine, and Meir was arrested not only for transgressing the decree but for leading others seeking to leave. By 1288 the German Jewish communities had raised a substantial ransom, which they offered for Meir's release. According to Solomon Luria (commentary *Yam shet Shelomoh on Giṭṭin* ch. 4. 6), the rabbi refused the ransom, sayingthat a captive should not be redeemed for more than his worth (lest this encourage capturing other Jews). In his "ethical testament," Judah, the son of Asher b. Yeḥiel, relates that the emperor held Asher responsible for the collection of the ransom money, and when Meir died in prison before the ransom could be paid, Asher decided to flee Germany. From the prison at Ensisheim Meir was apparently

moved to the castle at Wasserburg, where his students were able to visit him, and one of them, the aforementioned Samson b. Ṣaddoq, regularly administered to his needs and recorded his customs in a book that he later wrote. Meir continued also to write responsa from prison, in spite of his lack of books and even sufficient paper. He died in captivity in 1293.

His works include more than a thousand responsa; aside from the volumes published under his name, many are found in the writings of his students and elsewhere, such as in the responsa of Ibn Adret (*She'elot u-teshuvot* I, Nos. 829–78; possibly others there). In addition, he composed *tosafot* (additional commentaries) on several tractates; all of those on *Yoma* in standard editions of the Talmud are by him. He is known also to have written commentaries on the Talmud (on *Yevamot* was published in 1986), and his commentaries on the *mishnayot* of Neg'im and *Ohalot* have been published, as well as fragments from commentaries on parts of the order of Ṭehorot. His customs (*minhagiym*), chiefly on religious matters and holidays, are found in *Sefer ha-Tashbaṣ* of his student Samson b. Ṣaddoq; in a collection by his student Moses Sheneur, published as 'Al ha-kol (Berditchev, 1908); in Moses "Parnas" of Rothenburg, *ha-Parnas* (Vilna, 1865); and in a modern edition, *Sefer minhagiym de-vei MaHaRaM*, ed. S. Elfenbein (New York, 1948). He also wrote some twenty eulogies and religious poems that have survived.

See also **Asher b. Yeḥiel; Ibn Adret, Solomon**

Further Reading

Works by Meir b. Barukh
She'elot u-teshuvot (Cremona, 1557/8).

She'elot u-teshuvot (Prague, 1608; revised ed. by Moses Bloch, Pressburg, 1895, Budapest, 1896).

She'elot u-teshuvot, ed. Raphael N. Rabbinovicz (Lvov, 1860).

Sefer sha'arei teshuvot, ed. Moses Bloch (Berlin, 1891); according to mss. (additional responsa were published by Y. Kahana in *Sinai* [1943] and later, and as offprint in a limited edition [Jerusalem, 1957]; also in Solomon Wertheimer, *Ginzei Yerushalayim*, part 3 [Jerusalem, 1902], and by M. Hirschler in *Sinai 55* [1965]: 317–22).

Work on Meir b. Barukh

Urbach, Ephraim E. *Ba'aley ha-tosafot* (Jerusalem, 1968), ch. 10.

NORMAN ROTH

MEISTER ECKHART (ca. 1260–1327/1328) Dominican theologian, preacher, administrator, and mystic. The title *meister,* a corruption of the Latin *magister* (teacher) refers both to his having received the highest academic degree then attainable and to his professional duties at the University of Paris. He was born in Thuringia, possibly in a village called Hochheim, of which there are two, one near Erfurt and one near Gotha. One document refers to him as *de* (from, of) Hochheim, but some scholars consider this a familial rather than a geographical designation and use it to bolster the claim that Eckhart was of noble origin. He most likely entered the Order of Preachers (Dominicans) at the priory in Erfurt at about the age of fifteen. Possibly he received his early training in the arts at Paris and was witness to Bishop Stephen Tempier's condemnation of 219 articles of theology including several taught by Thomas Aquinas (d. 1274), the Dominican order's most distinguished theologian. At any rate, Eckhart is documented in Paris lecturing on Peter Lombard's *Sentences* in 1293–1294. Prior to this he had absolved the various stages of Dominican formation: one year novitiate, two years studying the order's constitutions and the divine office, about five years studying philosophy, with three additional years devoted to theology. Eckhart was no doubt also among those chosen for further study, very likely at the order's *studium generale* (early form of university) in Cologne, where he might have had direct contact with Albert the Great. After lecturing in Paris Eckhart advances rapidly within the order. He is prior in Erfurt 1294–1298, professor in Paris 1302–1303, provincial of the newly formed German Dominican province of Saxony 1303–1311, and again professor in Paris 1312–1313. There followed several years of preaching in the vernacular, to Beguines and nuns among others, in Strasbourg and then later in Cologne, where he might also have had professorial duties at the *studium generale*.

In 1325 the first clouds appear when some of Eckhart's teachings are investigated as to their orthodoxy. Eckhart is cleared, but the following year Henry of Virneburg, archbishop of Cologne, begins inquisitorial proceedings against him. Eckhart responds to lists of suspect theses taken from a broad selection of his Latin and German works and, on January 24, 1327, citing delays and the public scandal the proceedings are causing, appeals to the pope. On February 13 he protests his innocence from the pulpit of the Dominican church in Cologne and soon thereafter travels to Avignon, where a papal commission begins an investigation. On March 27, 1329, some time after Eckhart's death, a papal bull, *In agro dominico*, definitively ends the investigation. In it seventeen articles are condemned as heretical, two of which Eckhart claimed never to have taught. Eleven others are judged to be evil sounding but capable of an orthodox interpretation. The bull states that Eckhart, before his death, recanted the articles and anything else that might have caused error in the minds of his audience *quoad illum sensum*. In other words, he recanted a heretical interpretation of his words, not the words themselves.

Eckhart's writings can be divided into Latin works (professional theological treatises, learned commentaries on scripture, and some sermons or sermon outlines) and German works (spiritual tracts and, especially, sermons). Because of

Eckhart's sad fate, his Latin works were generally forgotten and only rediscovered in the late nineteenth century. His German works became mixed with those of other spiritual authors or were often passed on with false or no attribution. As a result, the task of creating a reliable critical edition of the German works begun by Josef Quint in 1936 is just now nearing completion. Disagreement still remains concerning the authenticity of many German sermons not yet included in the critical edition, and discussion of their chronology has just begun. Eckhart is admired both for the brilliance of his mystical thought and for his virtuosity in expressing it. The first admirers of Eckhart after his rediscovery in the nineteenth century, because of their unfamiliarity with medieval philosophy and theology, made uninformed judgments about his originality in thought and language. Although scholars still view him as an original thinker, he is now recognized as being original within the context of the already well-developed system of scholastic thought. His mysticism has been termed speculative to indicate both its imbeddedness in scholastic philosophy and theology as well as the fact that he does not talk about mystical union in terms of personal experience. Rather, he describes the metaphysical constitution of both the human soul and God's nature that makes union possible. For Eckhart mystical union between God and the soul rests on their metaphysical oneness. Eckhart sees creatures as differing from God, but they differ only through the nothingness limiting the being that they possess; and being is God. Eckhart distinguishes between two kinds of being in creatures: formal or limited being, which constitutes them in existence separate from God, and virtual being—the being of creatures in the mind of God existing from eternity. The virtual being of creatures at one with God's being is their more real and vital being. Their formal being is a mere shadow by comparison. This distinction between formal

and virtual being in creatures provides the context for understanding most of Eckhart's characteristic doctrines. Thus, for example, he urges us to become as poor in spirit as we were (in the mind of God) before we were (formally existing). In other words, we are to "reduce" our existence to existence in God. So, too, in becoming the just man, we do so by uniting completely with justice, which is identical with God's being. Through our oneness with God's being the birth of the Son takes place in us, as it does in Bethlehem, and united with this divine action we become both the begotten (Son) and the "begetter" (Father). The human intellect, that faculty most essential in establishing our likeness with God, is in its purely spiritual activity the spark of the soul in which we most throw off the confines of our creatureliness and imitate divine activity. And through detachment, a key term in Eckhart's mystical asceticism, the creature frees himself from his own specific self or formal being, which is in essence the limiting factor separating us from God, to become whole or one with him.

The startling vigor of Eckhart's thought is matched by the power and artfulness with which he expresses it. Though the Latin works show skillful manipulation of language, it is his German works, especially the sermons, that display a rich variety of linguistic artistry, some of it best termed rhetorical and some clearly poetic. Often he overcomes the limitations of the young vernacular's ability to express his rarefied mysticism by placing a key term in a variety of juxtaposed contexts in the manner of a leitmotif and thus gradually reveals to his audience the treasures it contains. He employs such figures as accumulation, antithesis, parallelism, hyperbole, chiasmus, and paradox to great advantage. Word games and original verbal strategies of other kinds abound.

Eckhart influenced most immediately John Tauler and Henry Suso, Dominican mystics of the next generation, and less clearly their Flemish contemporary John (Jan van) Ruusbroec. From the library of the Swiss cardinal Nicholas of Cusa (Cusanus), Latin works by Eckhart have come down to us with comments by the cardinal scribbled in the margins. Cusanus shows much affinity in thought with Eckhart and defended him against the attacks of the Heidelberg theologian Johannes Wenck. The baroque poet Johann Scheffler (Angelus Silesius) was certainly touched by Eckhartian ideas, but, as in the case of many other authors and works of the reformation period and beyond, whether the influence was direct or indirect is impossible to tell. In more modern times the philosophers Hegel, Schelling, and Baader all admired his thought, though until the mid–twentieth century much of this admiration was based on misunderstandings arising from ignorance about Eckhart's own intellectual context. The last forty years have seen great progress in understanding this exhilarating mystic, though much of his uncharted profundity remains to be explored.

See also Jan van Ruusbroec; Nicholas of Cusa; Peter Lombard; Seuse, Heinrich

Further Reading

Colledge, Edmund, and Bernard McGinn, trans. *Meister Eckhart: The Essential Sermons, Commentaries, Treatises, and Defense*, New York: Paulist, 1981.

Koch, Josef. "Zur Analogielehre Meister Eckharts." 1959; rpt. in Josef Koch. *Kleine Schriften*, vol. 1. Rome: [n.p.], 1973, pp. 367–409.

Largier, Niklaus. *Bibliographie zu Meister Eckhart*. Freiburg: Universitätsverlag, 1989 [bibliography].

McGinn, Bernard. "Eckhart's Condemnation Reconsidered." *Thomist* 44 (1980): 390–414.

——. "The God Beyond God: Theology and Mysticism in the Thought of Meister Eckhart." *Journal of Religion* 61 (1981): 1–19.

——. "Meister Eckhart on God as Absolute Unity." In *Neoplatonism and Christian Thought*, ed. Dominic J. O'Meara. Albany: State University of New York Press, 1982, pp. 128–139.

——, ed., *Meister Eckhart and the Beguine Mystics*. New York: Continuum, 1994.

McGinn, Bernard, Frank Tobin, and Elvira Borgstadt. *Meister Eckhart: Teacher and Preacher*. New York: Paulist, 1986.

Meister Eckhart. *Die deutschen und lateinischen Werke*, ed. Josef Quint. Stuttgart: Kohlhammer, 1936ff.

Ruh, Kurt. *Meister Eckhart: Theologe, Prediger, Mystiker*. Munich: Beck, 1985.

Schürmann, Reiner. *Meister Eckhart: Mystic and Philosopher*. Bloomington: University of Indiana Press, 1978.

Smith, Cyprian. *Meister Eckhart: The Way of Paradox*. London: Darton, Longman and Todd, 1987.

Tobin, Frank. *Meister Eckhart: Thought and Language*. Philadelphia: University of Pennsylvania Press, 1986.

Walshe, M. O'C. *Meister Eckhart: Sermons and Treatises*. Rockport, Me.: Element, 1992.

FRANK TOBIN

MENA, JUAN DE (1411–1456)
Secretary and chronicler of Juan II of Castile and one of the outstanding poets of his time. Author of two long narrative poems, *La coronación del marques de Santillana* (c.1438), and his masterpiece, *El laberinto de Fortuna* (1444); an allegorical debate, *Coplas de los pecados mortales* (also known as *Debate de la Razón contra la Voluntad*), left incomplete at his death; and some fifty shorter compositions typical of the courtly verse of his day: queries and responses to other poets, occasional pieces, riddles, love poems, and satiric verse. His prose works include a prologue and commentary to his *Coronación; La llíada en romance*, a translation of the *Ilias latina*, with prologue (c. 1442); *Tratado de amor* (c. 1444); *Tratado del título de duque* (1445); a prologue to Alvaro de Luna's *Libro de las virtuosos e claras mugeres* (c. 1446); and the fragmentary *Memorias de algunos linajes antiquas é nobles de Castilla* (1448).

Reliable data on Mena's life is sparse. He was born in late December 1411 in Córdoba, and was named alderman (*veinticuatro*) there possibly as early as 1435. In his *Memorias* he traces the Mena lineage to the valley of Mena in La Montaña. Vatican archival documents place him in Florence in 1442–1443 at the court of Pope Eugene IV, from whom he unsuccessfully sought ecclesiastical benefices in Córdoba. He was appointed secretary for Latin and royal chronicler by King Juan II of Castile probably in the mid-1440s, although the earliest extant document which refers to him with either of these titles is his own *Memorias* (1448). He married Marina Méndez, some twenty years his junior, around 1450. Upon the death of King Juan II in 1454 he remained in the service of King Enrique IV; he died in Torrelaguna in 1456, leaving no descendants.

The poet's first editor, Hernán Núñez, supplies additional biographical data that cannot be corroborated: that he was the son of Pedrarias and of a sister of Ruy Fernández de Peñalosa, lord of Almenara and *veinticuatro* of Córdoba; that both parents died when he was very young; that he began his studies in Córdoba and continued them in Salamanca; and that he was married in Córdoba to a sister of García de Vaca and Lope de Vaca. Other early biographical accounts derive from Núñez, although they differ in some particulars.

Throughout his adult life Mena divided his time between Córdoba and the royal court. He was a loyal supporter of King Juan II and an unabashed admirer of Alvaro de Luna; at the same time, his friendship with the Marquis of Santillana transcended the political turmoil of the time and survived the Marquis's disaffection with the crown and the *condestable*.

El laberinto de Fortuna (popularly called *Las trescientas*), a narrative poem of 297 *arte mayor* stanzas, was presented to King Juan II in February 1444. The poet inveighs against capricious Fortune, and is forthwith transported in a visionary journey to her palace. There he is met by Providence, who will serve as his guide. Providence shows him the three wheels of Fortune corresponding to the past, present, and future, each with seven circles governed by the seven planets. The wheel of the unknowable future remains veiled, but the poet will be permitted to see those of the past and the present.

The main body of the poem (stanzas 61–238) recounts the histories of exemplary figures (exalted and condemned) in each of the seven circles. The first four circles (Diana, Mercury, Venus, and Phoebus) stress figures from the past and ethical concerns, while the last three (Mars, Jupiter, and Saturn) emphasize the present (and, by extension, the recent past). Here Fortune holds sway; only Alvaro de Luna has been able to conquer her, and the king must emulate his example if he is to attain the greatness foretold for him.

The work concludes with Providence's prophecy of future glory for the king, whose fame will eclipse that of his ancestors; the vision fades, however, before the poet can inquire of his guide as to the particulars of the king's future accomplishments. His task is clear: he must put an end to civil strife ("las guerras que vimos de nuestra Castilla," 141b) and unite the warring factions in a final push to victory over the Muslims (the "virtuosa, magnífica guerra" of 152a).

Mena drew selectively and deftly from a wide variety of sources. His allegorical construct owes much to such works as *Anticlaudianus*, *Roman de la rose*, and Dante's *Divine Comedy*, though he appears to have made his own contribution to the symbology of Fortune in the concept of the three wheels. He knew and utilized Latin epic poets (Virgil, Lucan, Statius) and relied heavily on Ovid's *Metamorphoses* for Greco-Roman mythology.

The language of the *Laberinto* is a language of poetic innovation. It is characterized by an abundance of neologisms coined from Latin roots, a tendency toward Latinate morphology and syntax, and the extensive use of a wide variety of rhetorical devices. Yet the poet does not hesitate to juxtapose a vulgar, archaic vernacular word and an elegant Latinism: "*fondón* del *çilénico* çerco segundo" (at the deepest bottom of the second celaenic [i.e., Meraniel] circle) (92b) or "con *túrbido* velo su *mote* cubría" (with turbid veil covered their riddle 57d). The result is a compendium of tragic, satiric, and comedic styles consistent with principles enunciated earlier by the poet (*Coronación*, prologue).

La coronación del marqués de Santillana was composed to celebrate Santillana's victory over the Moors in the Battle of Huelma in 1438. It consists of fifty-one octosyllabic *coplas reales*, accompanied by the author's extensive prose commentary in which he explicates each stanza, clarifying classical allusions and glossing his neologisms. Mena coined the term *calamicleos* (from the Latin *calamitas* and Greek *cleos*) to describe the work, "a treatise on the misery of evildoers and the glory of the good." The poet describes his allegorical journey through the valleys of Thessaly, where he contemplates the fate of figures from antiquity such as Ninus of Babylon (armless in punishment for his failure to raise his arms in defense of his city) and Jason (afire in punishment for his lust). He then makes his way through a forest of knowledge and ascends Mt Parnassus, reaching a place reserved for those who have attained fame through their works: Solomon, David, Homer, Lucan, Virgil, Seneca, and others. Under a canopy, attended by the immortal authors and the Muses, is the Marquis of Santillana; the poet watches as he receives the laurel crown from four maidens who represent the cardinal virtues, and exhorts the goddess Fame to spread the news of the event worldwide.

Stanza 42 and its commentary reveal that Santillana is being recognized for his diligence, loyalty, and valor in the service of the king against the Muslims rather than for his accomplishments as a writer. By implication, the poet's condemnation of those being punished for cowardice or irresponsibility could be extended to some of his contemporaries; the example of Santillana (like that of Alvaro de Luna in *Laberinto*) is worthy of emulation.

In *Coplas de los pecados mortales*, the poet invokes the Christian muse, disavowing the "dulçura enponzoñada" of his earlier works and ruing time misspent in the study of pagan antiquity. Written in octosyllabic *arte menor* stanzas and structured as an allegorical debate between Reason and the Seven Deadly Sins, represented as seven faces of Will, the work leaves off at Stanza 106, during the debate between Reason and Anger. An indication of the work's reception in its own time are the continuations of it written by Gómez Manrique, Pero Guillén de Segovia, and Fray Jerónimo de Olivares.

Mena's earliest prose work is probably his commentary to the *Coronación*. There he cultivates several styles, ranging from elaborate Latinate through simpler narrative to direct didactic. The *Ilias latina* is his translation of an abridged version of the Homeric epic in 1,070 Latin hexameters. *Tratado de amor*, in relatively straightforward didactic style, reveals some of the author's subtle humor as he concentrates on "el amor no lícito e insano" and devotes almost equal attention to that which engenders it as to that which repels it. *Tratado sobre el título de duque* purports to trace the origins, rights, privileges, insignia, and prerogatives of dukes but serves as a vehicle for the poet's praise of the duke of Medina Sidonia and count of Niebla, Juan de Guzmàn, to whom it is dedicated. In his brief prologue to Alvaro de Luna's *Libro de las virtuosas e claras mugeres*, Mena renders thanks at the behest, he says, of many well-born ladies to Alvaro for his defense of their honor; finally, the fragmentary *Memorias de algunos linages antiguos é nobles de Castilla* are brief sketches of the historical and geographical origins of fourteen lineages, including his own.

Mena's works—particularly the *Laberinto*—were well known to his contemporaries and to posterity. He was cited extensively by Elio Antonio de Nebrija and Juan del Encina, annotated by Hernán Núñez and Francisco Sánchez de las Brozas, and his influence can be found throughout the sixteenth century (in Cristóbal de Castillejo and Fernando de Herrera, for example), and into the seventeenth (Luis de Góngora). The point of departure for modern Mena scholarship is Lida de Malkiel's monumental study (1950).

See also **Luna, Álvaro de**

Further Reading

Deyermond, A. D. "Structure and Style as Instruments of Propaganda in Juan de Mena's *Laberinto de Fortuna,*" *Proceedings of the Patristic, Medieval, and Renaissance Conference* 5 (1980), 159–67.

Gericke, P. O. "The Narrative Structure of the *Laberinto de Fortuna*" *Romance Philology* 21 (1968), 512–22.

Lida de Malkiel, M. R. *Juan de Mena, poeta del prerrenaci-miento español* 2d ed. Mexico City, 1984.

Mena, J. de. *Obras completas.* Ed. M. A. Pérez Priego. Barcelona, 1989.

——. *Tratado sobre el título de duque.* Ed. L. Vasvari Fainberg. London, 1976.

PHILIP O. GERICKE
COLBERT I. NEPAULSINGH

MÉZIÈRES, PHILIPPE DE (1327–1405) Born in Mézières in Picardy, Philippe was a soldier of fortune, then an advocate on the diplomatic and political levels of a crusade to regain Jerusalem for Christendom. He founded the chivalric Order of the Passion of Jesus Christ, was chancellor of Cyprus under Peter I, was a citizen of Venice, knew popes Urban V and Gregory XI and was a friend of Petrarch, and served as counselor to Charles V of France from 1373 until 1380, when he withdrew to the convent of the Celestines in Paris. Here, he wrote the major part of his work, in both French and Latin prose, remaining at the convent until his death. His first known work is the Latin *vita* (1366) of his spiritual adviser, Peter Thomas. He wrote on the feast of Mary's Presentation at the Temple, achieving celebration in the West of this originally eastern feast. Three of his treatises depict the order he had founded: *Nova religio milicie Passionis Jhesu Christi pro acquisicione sancte civitatis Jherusalem et Terre Sancte,* extant in two versions written in 1368 and 1384, respectively, but copied together in the only surviving manuscript; the *Sustance de la chevalerie de la Passion de Jhesu Crist en françois* (ca. 1389–94); and the *Chevalerie de la Passion de Jhesu Crist,* written in 1396 shortly before the Battle of Nicopolis. The *Livre sur la vertu du sacrement de mariage* (1384–89) contemplates the mystical union of Christ with the church and the human soul and includes the famous exemplum of "patient Griselda," translated by Philippe from the Latin of his friend Petrarch. The *Songe du vieil pèlerin,* an allegorical pilgrimage finished in 1389, points out the evils of the world and suggests remedies. His 1395 letter to Richard II of England urges the king to wed Isabella of France as a means to European peace. All of Philippe de Mézières' major works urge the social and political stability of Europe necessary for his long-sought but never to be realized crusade.

See also **Charles V the Wise; Petrarca, Francesco; Richard II**

Further Reading

Mézières, Philippe de. *Campaign for the Feast of Mary's Presentation,* ed. William E. Coleman. Toronto: Pontifical Institute of Mediaeval Studies, 1981.

——. *Letter to King Richard II,* ed. and trans. G.W. Coopland. New York: Harper and Row, 1976.

———. *Le songe du vieil pèlerin,* ed. G.W. Coopland. 2 vols. Cambridge: Cambridge University Press, 1969.

———. *La sustance de la chevalerie de la Passion de Jhesu Crist en françois: Philippe de Mézières and the New Order of the Passion,* ed. Abdel Hamid Hamdy. 3 vols. Alexandria: Alexandria University Press, 1964–65. [Transcription of Ashmole 813.]

———. *Vita sancti Petri Thomae,* ed. Joachim Smet. Rome: Institutum Carmelitanum, 1954.

Iorga, Nicolae. *Philippe de Mézières (1327–1405) et la croisade au XIVe siècle.* Paris: Bouillon, 1896.

JOAN B. WILLIAMSON

MICHAEL SCOT (c. 1175 or 1195–1235 or 1236)

Though famous as an astrologer and magician, Michael Scot (or Scott) is chiefly important as a scientific translator. He was born in Scotland but went to Spain, where he learned enough Arabic to make Latin translations of numerous scientific and philosophical works, sometimes with a collaborator. The earliest of these works was al-Bitruji's defense of the Aristotelian astronomical model (Toledo, 1217), to which Aristotle's *De caelo* was a natural sequel, together with Averroës's major commentary on it. Equally important were Scot's translations of Aristotle's *History of Animals* and several related biological works. In addition to these major translations, which undoubtedly are the work of Scot, many others have been attributed to him (Minio-Paluello 1974). Like other Latin translations of Aristotle from Arabic, Scot's were replaced within a century by better versions from the original Greek, but his were the ones from which thirteenth-century scholastics worked.

By 1220, Scot had moved to Italy, where he remained until his death. His success as a translator gained him the patronage of the papacy, through which he secured several ecclesiastical benefices in England and Scotland (1224–1227); the income from these sinecures, which he never visited, apparently supported him for the rest of his life. From the papal letters of recommendation we learn that Scot was a priest and held a university degree (*magister*). Although some scholars have supposed that he studied and taught at Paris, his association with Bologna is better documented, for he was living there in 1220–1221 and predicted the future of the Lombard League for officials of Bologna in 1231.

Scot's most famous patron was Emperor Frederick II. A later generation (e.g., Salimbene, c. 1221–1290) would remember Scot as "astrologer to the emperor," although it is not clear whether Frederick retained Scot at court or only consulted him occasionally. Certainty Frederick and Scot conversed from time to time, as Scot repeatedly recalled with pride. In 1232, Scot translated Avicenna's treatise on animals for Frederick, who used it in his own work on falconry.

Scot also dedicated his most ambitious work to Frederick. This was an untitled trilogy on astrology to which he devoted his last years. The first book, *Liber introductorius,* is a rambling introduction to astrology that is addressed to amateurs with little background in science. Scot fleshes out the dry bones of professional astrology with examples, digressions, and encyclopedic information that make this work more lively and engaging, though less useful, than its predecessors. The second book, *Liber particularis,* adds more advanced explanations, including some given in response to questions asked by Frederick. The third book, *Liber physionomiae,* deals with living creatures, notably mankind, and shows especially how human character can be deduced from physical signs. An abridged version of the last book was immensely popular (it was printed about forty times), but the rest remains unpublished except for excerpts. Unlike other scholastics, Scot wrote for nonspecialists; he was remarkable not so much for his learning as for his willingness to display and exaggerate it. His contemporaries were duly impressed and regarded him as a magician, but in the next generation, Roger Bacon and Albertus Magnus insisted that he was a charlatan, and Dante put Scot in hell as a diviner (*Inferno,* 20.115–117).

See also **Frederick II**

Further Reading

Haskins, Charles Homer. *Studies in the History of Mediaeval Science,* 2nd ed. Cambridge, Mass.: Harvard University Press, 1927, pp. 272–298.

Kay, Richard. "The Spare Ribs of Dante's Michael Scot." *Dante Studies,* 103, 1985, pp. 1–14.

Minio-Paluello, Lorenzo. "Michael Scot." In *Dictionary of Scientific Biography,* ed. Charles Coulston Gillespie. New York: Scribner, 1974, Vol. 9, 361–365.

Thorndike, Lynn. *Michael Scot.* London: Nelson, 1965.

RICHARD KAY

MOLINA, MARÍA DE (c. 1270–1321)
Queen of Castile María (c. 1270–1321) was the wife of Sancho IV (r.1284–1295) and the mother of Fernando IV (c.1295–1312). As the daughter of Alfonso de Molina and Mayor Téllez de Meneses, she was a niece of Fernando III and a first cousin of Alfonso X. In June 1282 at Toledo she married Infante Sancho, the son and heir of Alfonso X, even though they were related within the prohibited degrees of kindred. Threatening them with excommunication and interdict, Pope Martin IV ordered them to separate in 1283, but they would not do so. Inasmuch as they lacked a papal dispensation, their enemies regarded the marriage as invalid and their children as illegitimate. María was crowned with Sancho IV at Toledo in April 1284. She seems to have been an active counselor to her husband, but her powerful presence in Castilian politics was particularly felt after his death in 1295.

As guardian of their firstborn, Fernando IV, her responsibility was to protect his person and to repel those who challenged his right to the throne. Her brother-in-law, Infante Juan, denied Fernando IV's claims on the grounds that he was illegitimate. Alfonso de la Cerda, as the son of Fernando de la Cerda, Alfonso X's eldest son, alleged that he had a better right to rule. She also had to contend with Sancho IV's uncle, Infante Enrique, who, after long years in exile in Italy, returned home and now demanded the right to act as regent for the boy king. María skillfully won over the towns of the realm, who formed their *hermandades* (military and religious fraternities) in defense of their liberties and the rights of Fernando IV. Through her impassioned appeal the *cortes* (parliament) of Valladolid in 1295 recognized him as king, giving María custody of his person and naming Enrique as guardian of the realm. In the turmoil of the next few years she succeeded in keeping her son's domestic enemies at bay and eventually made peace with his external enemies, Portugal and Aragón. She then arranged his betrothal to Constanza, daughter of King Dinis of Portugal. When Fernando came of age in 1302 he wished to be free of his mother's control and so there followed a period of estrangement. Though forced to withdraw into the background, she later endeavored to induce the nobles to abandon their hostility toward her son.

After the sudden death of Fernando IV in 1312 and of Queen Constanza in 1313, María de Molina emerged once more as a central figure in Castilian politics, championing the cause of her grandson, Alfonso XI (r. 1312–1350), then an infant. Summoned to determine who should be regent, the cortes of Palencia in 1313 were unfortunately divided, some acknowledging her brother-in-law, Infante Juan, while others accepted María and her son, Infante Pedro. After a year of diplomatic, political, and military maneuvering, María took the lead in persuading the infantes to collaborate.

The cortes of Burgos in 1315 acknowledged the unified regency, entrusting María with custody of the king. She successfully maintained the unity of the regency, despite the tensions between Juan and Pedro, but after both men died on the plains of Granada in 1319, her skill was tried to the utmost. Her son Felipe, Juan's son Juan, and Infante Juan Manuel, the distinguished writer, now all demanded a share in the regency. Insisting that nothing could be done without the consent of the cortes, she summoned them to Valladolid in 1321, but she fell gravely ill. After making her will on 29 June, she died the next day and was buried in the Cistercian nunnery in Valladolid. By her marriage to Sancho IV she had several children: Fernando IV, Alfonso, Enrique, Pedro, Felipe, and Beatriz. A truly remarkable woman, she deserves to be ranked among those who most effectively governed medieval Castile. In many respects both Fernando IV and Alfonso XI owed their thrones to her.

See also **Alfonso X, El Sabio, King of Castile and León; Dinis, King of Portugal; Fernando III, King of Castile; Juan Manuel**

Further Reading

Gaibrois de Ballesteros, M. *Doña María de Molina*. Madrid, 1936.

JOSEPH F. O'CALLAGHAN

MÖNCH VON SALZBURG, DER (fl. 2d half of the 14th c.)

Known variously as Hermann, Johanns, or Hans in the over one hundred manuscripts in which his songs are transmitted, the Monk of Salzburg was the most prolific and popular German singer of the fourteenth century. His six polyphonic pieces are the earliest surviving part-songs in German. His forty-nine secular and fifty-seven religious songs represent nearly every genre current in fourteenth-century German singing, including the hymn, the sequence, the new year's song, the alba, the drinking song, and the *Leich* (lay).

Virtually nothing is known about his life except that he moved in the courtly circles of the archbishop of Salzburg, Pilgrim II von Puchheim (r. 1365–1396).

His melodies fall between those of two dominant medieval German genres, *Spruchdichtung* and *Meistergesang*. Some reflect the traditional German e-based modalities (phrygian), though many tend toward the modern major, beginning on E or B-natural and ending on C. The songs are frequently adorned with richly textured preludes, interludes, and postludes. He sometimes favors *melissmas* at the beginning and end of lines and makes frequent use of refrains. "Josef, liber neve min" (Joseph, My Dear Nephew), a German Christmas song still sung today, is attributed to him in one of the manuscripts.

The monk's secular poetry combines themes of the courtly lyric and folk songs, earthy but sometimes simple and affecting, with strong reminiscences of the rhetoric of *Minnesang* and of the Neidhart tradition. His religious songs, some translations of Latin hymns, are closely akin to and probably influenced the songs of the Meistersinger in the fifteenth century. The most gifted German-language lyric singer of the next generation, Oswald von Wolkenstein, was indebted to the monk in both text and melody.

See also **Neidhart; Oswald von Wolkenstein**

Further Reading

Meyer, Friedrich Arnold, and Heinrich Rietsch. *Die Mondsee-Wiener Liederhandschrift und der Mönch von Salzburg*. Berlin: Mayer and Müller, 1896 [texts and melodies of the secular songs].

Spechtler, Franz Viktor, ed. *Die geistlichen Lieder des Mönchs von Salzburg*. Berlin: de Gruyter, New York, 1972 [texts and melodies of his religious songs].

Wachinger, Burghart. *Der Mönch von Salzburg: Zur Überlieferung geistlicher Lieder im späten Mittelalter*. Tübingen: Niemeyer, 1989.

PETER FRENZEL

MORTON, ROBERT (1430?–1497?)

Composer documented as a "chappellain angloix" at the Burgundian court chapel choir from 1457 to June 1475, though until 1471 he occupied the relatively humble position of "clerc" within that institution. He was certainly a priest by 1460; and he was still alive in March 1479, when he resigned the parish of Goutswaard Koorndijk in the diocese of Utrecht. There seems a good case for identifying him with the Robert Morton who had studied at Oxford, later becoming master of the rolls (January 1479) and bishop of Worcester (1486–97), under the patronage of his brother, Cardinal John Morton. His Burgundian career coincides with the years when the family was in political difficulties; his disappearance from the continental records just precedes the real political career of Bishop Robert Morton, and it coincides with a diplomatic visit to Burgundy by the newly reestablished John Morton.

Twelve songs are ascribed to Morton. Four are of contested authorship. But the other eight, all setting French rondeau texts, include two of the most widely copied and quoted songs of their generation: *Le souvenir de vous me tue* (fourteen sources) and *N'aray je jamais mieulx quej'ay* (fifteen sources). His *Il sera pour vous combatu*, built over the famous *L'homme arm–* tune and perhaps one of the earliest known settings of it, pokes fun at a colleague in the Burgundian choir, Simon Le Breton, possibly on the occasion of his retirement in 1464. The anonymous rondeau *La plus grant chiere que jamais* describes a visit to Cambrai by Morton and another famous song composer, Hayne van Ghizeghem.

Morton's music appears in none of the few surviving English song sources, but it is in continental manuscripts copied as far afield as Florence, Naples, the Loire Valley, and Poland. The theorist Tinctoris praised Morton as one of the most famous composers of his day.

Further Reading

Primary Sources

Atlas, Allan, ed. *Robert Morton: The Collected Works.* Masters and Monuments of the Renaissance 2. New York: Broude, 1981.

Secondary Sources

Emden, Alfred B. *A Biographical Register of the University of Oxford to* A.D. *1500.* 3 vols. Oxford: Clarendon, 1957

Fallows, David. "Morton, Robert." NGD 12:596–97.

DAVID FALLOWS

MOSER, LUCAS (fl. ca. 1431/1432)

The reputation of the painter Lucas Moser rests on a single work, the altarpiece with scenes from the life of Mary Magdalene in the former chapel of the Virgin (now the parish church) in Tiefenbroon, near Pforzheim in southwestern Germany. An inscription dates the work 1431 or 1432—the last digit is hard to read with clarity—and names "Lucas Moser, painter from Weil," a nearby town, as its author. Apart from this brief mention, nothing is known of the artist's life or career, and attempts to link him with documentary mentions of painters named Lucas in this area and with other works have not been widely accepted. Even the attribution of the Magdalene altar to Moser was disputed in a highly controversial book on the altarpiece published by Gerhard Piccard in 1969. Considering the inscription as a nineteenth-century forgery, Piccard assigned the work to a follower of the Sienese painter Simone Martini and argued that it had been made for the church of the Magdalene at Vézelay in Burgundy. Piccard's book, which received much publicity in advance of its publication, occasioned numerous rebuttals afterward, many of them based on new art historical or technical work. Current consensus holds that the inscription is not modern; that the altarpiece was made for its present position, where its unusual shape reflects that of the wall painting underneath, which it replaced; and that the coats-of-arms, which may have been added very slightly later, represent the patrons of the work, Bernhard von Stein and his wife, Agnes (Engelin) Maiser von Berg.

The central part of the altarpiece is occupied by episodes from the life of Mary Magdalene as told in the *Legenda aurea*. At the left, the saint and her companions, set adrift by pagans in a rudderless boat, approach the coast of Marseille, portrayed here in a recognizable view. In the center, the saint's companions are asleep below, while in the attic room above, the Magdalene appears to the ruler's wife in her sleep to ask her to intervene with her husband on behalf of the Christians. In the final scene, angels deliver the saint, clothed only in her hair after long years in the desert, to a church where the Bishop Maximinus administers her the last rites. In the unusual arched upper panel, the Magdalene washes the feet of Christ, while bust-length figures representing Christ as the Man of Sorrows in the midst of the Wise and Foolish Virgins fill the long, horizontal predella below. On feast days the unusually narrow wings would have been opened to reveal the siblings of the Magdalene, Saints Martha and Lazarus, painted on their insides, flanking a sculpted figure of the Magdalene (now replaced) at the center of the shrine.

Moser's style provides some clues to his early training. His individualized head types, exceptional interest in detail, and use of disguised symbolism indicate knowledge of Flemish painting. Charles Sterling sees Moser as "a close follower of Robert Campin" and notes particularly the use of a continuous background across the four scenes of the center of the altarpiece, a device the Fleming had used as early as about 1420 (1972: 19–22). Sterling also suggests the influence of Flemish and Franco-Flemish manuscript illumination and the possibility of a trip to Provence. What is clear is that Moser's only known work is a masterpiece in both its style and its virtuoso handling of material and technique.

Further Reading

Haussherr, Rainer. "Der Magdalenenaltar in Tiefenbronn: Bericht über die wissenschaftliche Tagung am 9. und 10. März 1971 im Zentralinstitut für Kunstgeschichte in München." *Kunstchronik* 24 (1971): 177–212.

Köhler, Wilhelm. Review of Gerhard Piccard, *Der Magdalenenaltar des 'Lucas Moser' in Tiefenbronn. Zeitschrift für Kunstgeschichte* 35 (1972): 228–249.

Piccard, Gerhard, *Der Magdalenenaltar des 'Lucas Moser' in Tiefenbronn: Ein Beitrag zur europäischen Kunstgeschichte.* Wiesbaden: Harrossowitz, 1969.

Richter, Ernst-Ludwig. "Zur Rekonstruktion des Tiefenbronner Magdalenen-Altars." *Pantheon* 30 (1972): 33–38.

Sterling, Charles. "Observations on Moser's Tiefenbronn Altarpiece." *Pantheon* (1972): 19–32.

JOAN A. HOLLADAY

MOSES BEN NAḤMAN Moses ben Naḥman (Naḥmanides), rabbi of the Jewish community of Girona during the middle decades of the thirteenth century, was a leader of Iberian Jewry during his lifetime, and one of the most distinguished intellectual and spiritual figures in all of medieval Jewry. Like so many Iberian Jewish luminaries, Naḥmanides is striking for the remarkable range of his intellectual abilities and achievements. He was a master of Jewish law, mentoring important students and composing important *novellae* to major Talmudic tractates. He was, at the same time, a keen student of the Bible, composing an extensive commentary on the Pentateuch that is rich in exegetical insight and is still widely studied. He was one of the leaders in the rapidly developing school of Spanish Jewish mysticism, rather conservative in his approach to the explosive issues associated with the new mystical speculation but extremely important for the more traditional prestige and acumen that he brought to bear on the development of mystical teachings. His remarkable command of the Hebrew language in all its styles linked him to earlier tendencies in Iberian Jewry. The account that he composed of his public disputation with a former Jew, Pablo Christiani, who had become a Dominican friar, is a masterpiece of narrative art and one of the most effective Jewish polemical treatises of the Middle Ages.

That famous disputation highlights the public career of Naḥmanides. Prior to this engagement the rabbi was already known to King Jaime I of Aragón. In the face of the missionizing assault of the Dominicans, Rabbi Moses ben Naḥman was chosen as the Jewish spokesman for the encounter. Essentially the carefully contrived disputation involved an effort by the Dominican spokesman to prove to the Jews, from materials including both commentary on the Bible and rabbinic dicta, the truth of key Christian doctrines, most importantly the Christian claim that the promised Messiah had already appeared.

The role of the Jewish spokesman was to be limited to rebuttal of the Christian use of rabbinic texts only, with no allowance for Jewish negation of Christian teachings. Whether or not the limited parameters of Jewish rebuttal were in fact rigidly maintained is not altogether certain. In his brilliant narrative account of the disputation, Naḥmanides portrays himself as ranging far and wide in direct attack on central tenets of Christianity and on fundamental characteristics of Christian society. While modern researchers have questioned the reliability of these aspects of Naḥmanides' narrative, it is clear that the rabbi of Girona composed a captivating account of his public encounter and, in the process, provided his Jewish readers with appealing argumentation for the superiority of the Jewish faith.

The publication of Naḥmanides' narrative aroused the ire of ecclesiastical leadership and produced calls for punishment of the aged rabbi of Girona. The king of Aragón, who is portrayed most sympathetically in Naḥmanides' narrative, proved an effective supporter, although by 1267 Naḥmanides had made his way to the Holy Land. It is by no means clear whether this move reflects the pressures brought to bear against him or whether it resulted from his personal religiosity. He exercised leadership briefly within the Jewish community of Jerusalem, and died shortly thereafter.

See also **Jaime (Jaume) I of Aragón-Catalonia**

Further Reading

Baer, Y. *A History of the Jews in Christian Spain.* 2 vols. Trans., by L. Schoffman et al. Philadelphia, 1961–66.

Chazan, R. *Barcelona and Beyond: The Disputation of 1263 and Its Aftermath.* Berkeley, 1992.

Twersky, I. (ed.) *Rabbi Moses ben Naḥman (Ramban): Explorations in His Religious and Literary Virtuosity.* Cambridge, Mass., 1983.

Wolfson, E. R. " 'By Way of Truth': Aspects of Nahmanides' Kabbalistic Hermeneutic." *Association for Jewish Studies Review* 14 (1989), 103–78.

——. "The Secret of the Garment in Naḥ manides." *Daat* 24 (1990), Eng. sec., xxv–xlix.

MULTSCHER, HANS (ca. 1400–before March 13, 1467)

Working in stone, wood, and metal, Multscher was Ulm's foremost sculptor during the mid–fifteenth century. Originally from the countryside near Leutkirch in the Allgäu, he moved to Ulm by 1427, when he was accepted as a freeman, married Adelheid Kitzin, daughter of a local sculptor, and became a citizen. Since he already owned a house in Ulm, Multscher may have arrived a few years earlier. Where and with whom he trained are unknown. Artistic influences in his work suggest he traveled to the Rhineland, Burgundy, and the Low Countries during his *Wanderjahr* (year as a journeyman).

Multscher's large workshop produced both single figures and complex retables with painted panels. His name is inscribed on the Karg Altar of 1433 in the cathedral of Ulm, whose statues were destroyed during the Protestant iconoclasm of 1531. Multscher signed the painted wings of the large Wurzbach Altar from 1437, portions of which are in Berlin (Germäldegalerie). This altarpiece may have been executed for the Church of the Assumption of the Virgin (St. Maria Himmelfahrt) in Landsberg am Lech, where the large stone Madonna and Child remains. Between 1456 and 1459 Multscher and his workshop prepared the high altar of the parish church at Sterzing (Vipiteno) in South Tyrol; the remnants of this altar, which was dismantled in 1779, are divided among the church and the Museo Multscher in Sterzing, the Ferdinandeum in Innsbruck, the Bayerisches Nationalmuseum in Munich, and a private collection in Basel. These works form the basis for other attributions. Although Multscher is often cited as a painter, there is little evidence that his personal involvement extended beyond his roles as workshop head, master designer, and sculptor of some of the statues.

The artist introduced a greater sense of realism into southern German art. At a time when the lyrical Soft Style with its Beautiful Virgins, gracefully curved poses, and elongated proportions was popular, Multscher developed solid, more naturalistic figures that display the general influence of Netherlandish post-Sluterian sculpture. The Landsberg Madonna and Child from 1437 still includes hints of the Soft Style with its swaying stance, yet her inherent stability, the clear treatment of the deeply cut drapery folds, and the marvelously animated Christ Child who squirms in Mary's grasp reveal Multscher's new aesthetic sensibilities. Using this and related works, scholars have attributed to Multscher several slightly earlier projects. The most significant of these are the images of Charlemagne and other figures made circa 1427–1430 to adorn the eastern window of Ulm's city hall (the originals are now in the Ulmer Museum), the life-size Man of Sorrows from 1429 above the western entry to the cathedral of Ulm, and the alabaster Trinity group from circa 1430 in the Liebieghaus in Frankfurt. The half-nude Christ evocatively displays his wounds to all who enter the cathedral. Its spirit recalls similar Christ figures by both Claus Sluter and the Master of Flémalle. Related to the Man of Sorrows is the slightly later model for the tomb of Duke Ludwig the Bearded of Bavaria (1435, now in the Bayerisches Nationalmuseum, Munich). Employing fine Solnhofen limestone rather than the coarser sandstone that he typically used, Multscher devised a highly detailed scene of Ludwig kneeling before the Holy Trinity. The tomb, intended for Ingolstadt, was never executed.

In the ensuing decades Multscher and his shop supplied numerous Madonnas, crucifixions, and other religious figures for churches near Ulm. His most notable creations include the tomb effigy of Countess Mechthild von Württemberg-Urach (1450–1455), now in the Stiftskirche in Tübingen; the bronze reliquary bust (ca. 1460) in the Frick Collection in New York; the life-size wooden *Palmesel* (palm donkey, 1456, Ulm Museum), which was made initially for the church of St. Ulrich and Afra in Augsburg, and the now divided Sterzing High Altar. The latter was made in Ulm and then transported to Sterzing, where Multscher and several assistants spent about seven months erecting the altarpiece in 1458 and early 1459.

See also **Sluter, Claus**

Further Reading

Baxandall, Michael. The Limewood Sculptors of Renaissance Germany. New Haven, Conn.: Yale University Press, 1980, pp. 12–13, 245–247.

Beck, Herbert, and Maraike Bückling. Hans Multscher: Das Frankfurter

Trinitätsrelief, Ein Zeugnis spekulativer Künstlerindividualität. Frankfurt: Fischer Taschenbuch Verlag, 1988.

Grosshans, Rainald. "'Hans Multscher hat das werk gemacht': die Flugel des 'Wurzachet Altars' und ihre Restaurierung." Museums Journal (Berlin) 10 (1996): 78–80.

Reisner, Sabine, and Peter Steckhan. "Ein Beitrag zur Grabmalvisier Hans Multschers für Herzog Ludwig den Bärtigen." In Das geschnitzte und gemalte bild auf den altaren stehen ist nutzlich und christenlich: Aufsätze zur süddeutschen Skulptur und Malerei des 15. und 16. Jahrhunderts, ed. Rupert Schreiber. Messkirch: A. Gmeiner, 1988, pp. 9–74.

Schädler, Alfred. "Bronzebildwerke von Hans Multscher." In Intuition und Kunstwissenschaft: Festschrift Hanns Swarzenski zum 70. Geburtstag am 30. August 1973, ed. Peter Bloch. Berlin: Gebrüder Mann, 1973, pp. 391–408.

Theil, Edmund. Der Multscher-Altar in Sterzing. Bozen: Athesia, 1992.

Tripps, Manfred. "Hans Multscher: Seine Ulmer Schaffenszeit 1427–1467." Dissertatin, Heidelberg University, 1966–1967. Weissenhorn: A. H. Konrad, 1969.

——. Hans Multscher: Meister der Spätgotik, sein Werk, seine Schule, seine Zeit. Leutkirch: Heimatpflege Leutkirch, 1993.

JEFFREY CHIPPS SMITH

N

NARDO DI CIONE (died c. 1336) The Florentine painter Nardo di Cione, with his brothers Andrea (called Orcagna) and Jacopo, dominated painting in Florence in the decades following the black death of 1348. Nardo's date of birth is not known. His name appears for the first time in 1346–1348 in a list of members of the guild of doctors and apothecaries, the guild to which the painters belonged. By then his reputation was already established, for c. 1348, when the authorities of Pistoia asked the Florentines for the names of their best painters to execute the high altarpiece for Pistoia's church of San Giovanni Fuorcivitas, Nardo was recommended along with Orcagna. At this time the brothers were living in the parish of San Michele Visdomini and may have shared a workshop. In the 1350s and the first half of the 1360s Nardo lived in the center of Florence, but not always in the same parish as Orcagna, although the two of them may have continued to work together. In 1356 Nardo signed a panel of the Madonna which hung in the offices of the Gabella dei Contratti but which no longer survives. And in 1363 he was paid for painting "the vault and other things" in the oratory of the confraternity of the Bigallo; only fragments of this work remain. These are the only two works to which his name can positively be attached. Nardo made his will in 1365, and by May 1366 he had died. Apart from a bequest to the Bigallo, he left his money and possessions to be divided equally among his three brothers—Andrea, Jacopo, and Matteo. Since no wife or children are mentioned, Nardo was probably a bachelor. These few facts are all we have for a working life that can be documented over some twenty years. Although most of Nardo's painting seems to have been for locations in Florence, he may also have worked elsewhere. At an unknown date the Pistoian painter Bartolommeo Cristiani entered into an agreement whereby whenever he worked outside Florence, Nardo would help him. In an altarpiece now in Prague the presence of Saint Ranieri, a patron saint of Pisa, suggests that Nardo may have painted it for a church in that town.

Nardo is credited with about a dozen surviving works comprising frescoes, altarpieces, and small-scale devotional panels. In reconstructing an oeuvre for him, Offner (1960) relied on stylistic evidence provided by the frescoes in the Strozzi Chapel in Santa Maria Novella (Florence), which Ghiberti, writing in the mid-fifteenth century, ascribed to Nardo. Here, on three walls, Nardo represented the Last Judgment with a scene of heaven and a hell in which the imagery is derived from Dante's description in the *Inferno*. The frescoes are probably contemporary with the altarpiece in the same chapel that Orcagna painted between 1354 and 1357. The decoration of the Strozzi Chapel exemplifies the Florentine taste in art after mid-century, a taste that departed in some ways from the more naturalistic style pioneered by Giotto. Spatial illusionism is rejected in favor of more abstract two-dimensional effects. The saints of Nardo's *Paradise,* for example, are stacked up tier on tier, like, as one writer said, a football crowd. Medieval conventions of scale, in which a figure's place in the hierarchy of the holy is indicated by his size, are strictly followed. God's divinity and the otherworldly piety of the saints tend to be emphasized at the expense of their humanity. The holy figures appear self-absorbed, preserving their distance from each other and from the spectator. Some of these characteristics may be seen in Nardo's large-scale panel of the Virgin and saints belonging to the New York Historical Society and his altarpiece with three saints in the National Gallery, London.

This reversion to what have been seen as archaizing modes of representation that draw on late thirteenth-century formulas has been explained in terms of the unsophisticated and conservative taste of a new bourgeois class in Florentine society (Antal 1948) and the psychological effects of the black death (Meiss 1951). However, Nardo's art evinces less obviously than Orcagna's the somber, pessimistic mood that Meiss identified in the art of Florence and Siena after 1348. Nardo's style is more lyrical and less austere than that of his brother; his color combinations are more harmonious, and the facial expressions of his saints are less intimidatingly severe. His stylistic origins lie in the decorative taste of Florentine painters such as Bernardo Daddi and the Sienese school as exemplified in the sumptuous work of Simone Martini. Bright enamel colors are juxtaposed with opulent brocades and patterned floors, as in the polyptych in Prague and the two panels with saints in the Alte Pinakothek in Munich. Nardo's Madonnas in Prague, Washington, and Minneapolis have a distinctive beauty that led Offner to describe him as "the most romantic artist of his age." The delicate *sfumato* modeling of pale flesh tones enlivened with rose-pink on the cheeks and lips, and of blond hair draped with diaphanous veils, is achieved by a patient application of successive layers of semitransparent glazes. The consummate care that Nardo lavished on his paintings—in the preparation of the panel, the detailed underdrawing, the meticulous application of paint and the painstaking execution of *sgraffito* and gilded punchwork—make him possibly the finest craftsman among *Trecento* painters. As a result, his works are remarkably well-preserved.

Nardo's reputation has fared less well. History has been unfair to Nardo. He has suffered from standing in the shadow of his more famous brother, Orcagna. Vasari must share some of the responsibility for this: he got the artist's name wrong (calling him Bernardo), relegated Nardo to the role of assistant in Orcagna's workshop, and credited to Nardo inferior works that were actually by others. Even now, despite Offner's study, Nardo has yet to receive the attention that is his due.

See also **Daddi, Bernardo; Martini, Simone; Orcagna, Andrea di Cione**

Further Reading

Antal, Frederick. *Florentine Painting and Its Social Background: The Bourgeois Republic before Cosimo de' Medici's Advent to Power— XIV and Early XV Centuries.* London: K. Paul, 1948.

Meiss, Millard. *Painting in Florence and Siena after the Black Death.* Princeton, N.J.: Princeton University Press, 1951.

Offner, Richard. *A Critical and Historical Corpus of Florentine Painting,* Section 4, Vol. 2, Nardo di Cione. New York: College of Fine Arts, New York University, 1960.

Pitts, Frances Lee. "Nardo di Cione and the Strozzi Chapel Frescoes: Iconographic Problems in Mid-Trecento Florentine Painting." Dissertation, University of California, Berkeley, 1982.

BRENDAN CASSIDY

NEBRIJA, ELIO ANTONIO DE (c. 1441–1522), Spain's leading pre-Renaissance humanist was born Antonio Martínez de Cala e Hinojosa in the Andalusian town of Lebrija. Opinion is divided concerning the year of his birth. In the prologue to his undated Latin-Spanish dictionary he gives his age as fifty-one and states that he was born in the year prior to the battle of Olmedo (1444). However, other observations in the same prologue concerning the age at which he went to Italy, the length of his stay there and of his subsequent service to Alonso de Fonseca, archbishop of Seville, have led some specialists to place Nebrija's date of birth in 1441.

At the age of nineteen Nebrija left for Italy to study in the Spanish College of San Clemente in the University of Bologna, where he was exposed to the writings of Lorenzo Valla and to his critiques of the medieval system of teaching Latin grammar. Nebrija was appalled at the state of Latin instruction in the University of Salamanca, by the teaching manuals employed (typified by the highly popular verse *Doctrinale* of Alexander de Villadei), which stressed rote memorization of paradigms, and by the lack of attention paid to classical authors. Nebrija returned to Spain determined to introduce the reforms advocated by Valla. In 1476 he took possession of the chair of Latin grammar at Salamanca, where he remained until 1487, when he entered the service of his former student Juan de Zúñiga, master of the Order of Alcántara and future cardinal archbishop of Seville. The years spent with Zúñiga were among Nebrija's most productive. At the beginning of the sixteenth century, Nebrija joined the group headed by Cardinal Cisneros, that was preparing the edition of the *Biblia Poliglota* at the newly created University of Alcalá. Nebrija's insistence on applying strict philological criteria to the text of the Latin Bible brought him into conflict with the group's theologians. After Cisneros lent them his support, Nebrija chose to withdraw from the project and returned to the University of Salamanca where he held various chairs. In 1513 Nebrija failed in his bid to win the chair of prima de gramática. Embittered, he left Salamanca. In 1514 Cisneros granted the ageing Nebrija the chair of rhetoric at Alcalá de Henares, which he occupied until his death on 2 July 1522.

Nebrija can be described as Spain's first linguist, perhaps best known today for his studies of Latin, Greek, Hebrew, and the Castilian vernacular. Despite his pioneering work on Castilian, Latin seems to have been Nebrija's primary concern as a linguist. His first major book was *Introductiones Latinae* (1481), a direct result of Nebrija's concern with the quality of Latin teaching at Salamanca and his belief that *grammatica*, the acquisition of Latin, was the key to all other scholarly disciplines. *Introductiones* was designed as a clear and systematic pedagogical manual for university students, with which Nebrija sought to reintroduce into Spain classical models and the pre-medieval grammatical theory of Donates and Priscian. This work was an instant success. It was revised and reedited several times during Nebrija's life and frequently reprinted (often under different titles) throughout the sixteenth century in Spain and elsewhere. At the insistence of Queen Isabel, Nebrija published around 1488 (apparently reluctantly) a bilingual Latin and Spanish version of this manual. *Introductiones* became the basic manual for university teaching of Latin in Spain and was one of the books most often exported to the New World during the colonial period. Throughout his career Nebrija published a series of *Repetitiones*, formal university lectures dealing with the pronunciation of Latin, Greek, and Hebrew.

Within the intellectual framework of late-fifteenth-century Spain, Nebrija's Latin-Spanish (1492) and Spanish-Latin dictionaries (c. 1495) as well as his *Gramática de la lengua castellana* (1492) represent major innovations. In all likelihood the two dictionaries were designed to provide access to Latin rather than to constitute repositories of contemporary Spanish. They may well represent the fruits of an announced larger "*obra de vocablos*," which was to include lexicons of civil law, medicine, and the Scriptures (his *Ius Civilis Lexicon* of 1506 and his *Lexicon illarum vocum quae ad medicamentariam artem pertinent* appended to a 1518 edition of a Latin translation of Dioscorides). The Spanish-Latin dictionary was the first systematic and comprehensive work in which Spanish was the source language. Both dictionaries, in many respects quite modern in their lexicographic principles, were revised by Nebrija and underwent several editions. The Latin materials served other early sixteenth-century lexicographers in the preparation of bilingual dictionaries involving Catalan, French, and Sicilian.

According to its prologue, Nebrija published his *Gramática de la lengua castellana* to fix and stabilize the Spanish language in order to prevent its further decay, to facilitate the acquisition of Latin grammar, and to provide a means of learning Spanish for those peoples over whom Spain would one day rule. Within a framework of Latin grammatical theory, Nebrija examines the linguistic facts of Spanish, with emphasis on form rather than on function. The *Gramática* treats orthography and pronunciation, prosody, etymology (that is, morphology), the syntax of the ten parts of speech, and closes with an overview of Spanish for the second-language learner. Motivated by the belief that standardized spelling would contribute to language stability, Nebrija published a second spelling treatise in 1517 under the title *Reglas de orthographía en la lengua castellana*, essentially a resume of book 1 of the *Gramática castellana*. Nebrija's *Gramática* was not reprinted until the eighteenth century and did not seem to have much impact on the work of other sixteenth- and seventeenth-century

Spanish grammarians, many of whom may not even have known this work.

In addition to his activities in the realm of language studies, Nebrija composed Latin verse and prepared in that language commentaries on Scripture, rhetorical treatises, works of historiography, geography, and cosmography, as well as editions of and commentaries on the writings of other humanists. Unfortunately, hardly any of these works is available in a modern edition (for titles, see Odriozola).

Further Reading

Braselmann, P. *Humanistische Grammatik und Volkssprache. Zur "Gramática de la lengua castellana" von Antonio de Nebrija*. Düsseldorf, 1991.

García de la Concha, V., ed. *Nebrija y la introduction del Renacimiento en España*. Salamanca, 1983.

Nebrija, A. de A. *Gramática de la lengua castellana*. A. Quilis, 3d ed. Madrid, 1989.

Odriozola, Antonio. "La caracola del bibliófilo nebrisense," *Revista de bibliografía nacional* 7 (1946) 3–114.

Rico, F. *Nebrija frente a los bárbaros*. Salamanca, 1978.

STEVEN N. DWORKIN

NEIDHART (fl. ca. 1215–1230) A Middle High German poet of some renown, there is no documentary evidence of Neidhart's name or of his origins. Under the title "Lord" *(her) nithart*, the so-called large ("C") and the small ("A") *Minnesang*-manuscripts at Heidelberg University Library record the stanzas attributed to him. The singer is apostrophized as der *von Riuwental* (the one from the Riuew Valley) in the *Summer Songs (Sommerlieder)* and the defiantly stated "response-verses" *(Trutzstrophen)* of the *Winter Songs (Winterlieder)*. This explains the name Neidhart von Reuental, a term especially used by earlier scholars. Both names can also be interpreted allegorically (*nithart* is a medieval name for the devil); *riuwental* taken literally reads as "valley of grief"). The only indication for dating Neidhart's poems is through an allusion in "Wolfram von Eschenbach's courtly novel *Willehalm* (l. 312,12; written ca. 1215), as well as references to contemporary political events or personalities in his songs (Archbishop Eberhard II of Salzburg, Duke Friedrich II of Austria). These clues lead to the conclusion that Neidhart may possibly have lived from circa 1190 to 1240. The author's occupation and social rank are just as unknown, although, like Walter von der Vogelweide, he was probably a professional poet. It is almost certain that Neidhart spent part of his early literary career in the area of Bavaria/Salzburg, which he was forced to leave for some unknown reason—possibly due to losing his patron and/or audience, as can perhaps be discerned in changes in his literary style. There are no definite clues that Neidhart might have belonged to the Wittelsbach court of Ludwig I the Kelheimer. On the other hand, Winter Song No. 37 directly addresses Archbishop Eberhard II of Salzburg. Later on Neidhart sang in the vicinity of the Babenberg court of Friedrich II the Valiant (der Streitbare) in Vienna. This may also have been the setting for a literary argument with Walter von der Vogelweide and his concept of *Minnesang* (see Song L 64,31). The writers of subsequent generations (Rubin, Der Marner, Hermann Damen) regarded Neidhart as a good example and "master." The special form of his poetry developed into a separate lyrical genre in the late Middle Ages, while the content partly underwent strong changes. These later poems were passed on under the name *ain nithart* (a Neidhart) in the manuscripts (these songs, regarded largely as imitations following the nineteenth-century scholar Moritz Haupt, have come to be put under the term "pseudo-Neidhart" by researchers). During the last stage of this reception Neidhart became the hero of the *Schwankroman Neidhart Fuchs Schwankerzählungen und Lieder*

(*Neidhart Fox's Comical Tales and Songs,* published 1491/1497, 1537, und 1566), and many Neidhart plays, which belong to the oldest existing secular plays written in German. Altogether the numerous manuscripts (from the end of the thirteenth to the fifteenth century) record about 140 songs under the name of Neidhart, of which, however, only 66 are considered to be authentic. In the field of *Minnesang*, well-preserved songs form the major exception, even though they were recorded mostly only at a later period (about 68 tunes in all).

As far as form and content are concerned, Neidhart's songs, often described as "rustic/rural poetry" *(dörperlich)*, can be divided into Summer Songs and Winter Songs (according to the varying introductory natural settings) and *Schwanklieder* (comic songs). The Summer Songs, divided into scenes, render simple verse forms that have been worked out in detail *(raien)*, while their content forms a clear contrast to traditional *Minnesang*. The plot is shifted from the courtly to the rural realm, the "Knight," or Ritter von Riuwental, is exposed to the unconcealed sexual desires of the farmer's daughters and wives. Whereas the mother, who is the representative of socially accepted moral conventions, warns her daughter of the consequences of having an affair with the impoverished knight—in the so-called *Songs of the Aged (Altenlieder)* the positions of mother and daughter are reverse—the girl struggles to participate in the summer dance and thus also to gain the opportunity of a rendezvous. In the Sommer Songs, thought by some to be later, there are frequently statements on the unsatisfactory position of the singer and the loss of *vreude* (happiness) in courtly society (demonstrated via the theme of Engelmar's mirror theft). The Winter Songs, structured by stollen, require an intimate acquaintance with form and content of "classical" *Minnesang* to be understood, since the patterns of content and representation in *Minnesang* are constantly referred to in quotations and opposed to the so-called *dörper,* or farmer-stanzas. They portray the threat posed to the singer by rural upstarts, who arrogate aristocratic clothing and lifestyles to themselves, and, even though they adopt only the superficial forms of courtly culture, but not its actual contents, alienate the singer from his *vrouwe* "lady" (who turns out to be a "farmer's daughter" or, in the so-called *werlt-süeze,* or "wordly delight" songs, "Hure Welt"/Whore World). In the *Schwanklieder* the knight Neidhart is promoted to the role of ever-victorious enemy of the physically and intellectually inferior peasants. According to massive tradition as well as extraliterary evidence, the Neidhart-*Lieder* (songs) with their transformations of content enjoyed sustained popularity from the thirteenth to the sixteenth century. Only in recent times has research begun to refrain from continuing the debate about authenticity and to accept instead the genre of the "Neidharts" in the fullness of its tradition and history.

See also **Wolfram von Eschenbach**

Further Reading

Bennewitz, Ingrid. *Original und Rezeption. Funktionsund überlieferungsgeschichtliche Studien zur Neidhart-Sammlung R.* Göppingen: Kümmerle, 1987.

Beyschlag, Siegfried, ed. *Die Lieder Neidharts.* Darmstadt: Wissenschaftliche Buchgesellschaft, 1975.

Fritz, Gerd, ed. *Abbildungen zur Neidhart-Überlieferung I. Die Berliner Neidhart-Hs. R und die Pergament-Fragmente Cb, K, O und M.* Göppingen: Kümmerle, 1973.

Haupt, Moriz, ed. *Neidhart von Reuenthal.* Leipzig, 1864. 2d ed. Edmund Wießner. Leipzig 1923; rpt. ed. Ingrid Bennewitz, Ulrich Müller, and Franz V. Spechtler. Stuttgart: Hirzel, 1986.

Herr Neidhart diesen Reihen sang. Die Texte und Melodien der Neidhartlieder mit 'Übersetzungen und Kommentaren, ed. Siegfried Beyschlag and Horst Brunner. Göppingen: Kümmerle, 1968.

Holznagel, Franz-Josef. *Wege in die Schriftlichkeit. Untersuchungen und Materialien zur Überlieferung der mittelhochdeutschen Lyrik.* Tübingen: Francke, 1995.

Jöst, Erhard, ed. *Die Historien des Neithart Fuchs. Nach dem Frankfurter Druck von 1566.* Göppingen: Kümmerle, 1980.

Margetts, John, ed. *Neidhartspiele.* Graz: Akademische Druck- und Verlagsanstalt, 1982.

Schweikle, Günther. *Neidhart.* Stuttgart: Metzler, 1990.

Simon, Eckehard. *Neidhart v. Reuental. Geschichte der Forschung und Bibliographie.* The Hague: Mouton, 1968.

Wenzel.Edith, ed. *Abbildungen zur Neidhart-Überlieferung II. Die Berliner Neidhart-Hs. c (mgf779).* Göppingen: Kümmerle, 1975.

INGRID BENNEWITZ

NICHOLAS III, POPE (c. 1225–1280, r. 1277–1280) Pope Nicholas III (Giovanni Gaetano Orsini) was the son of Matteo Rosso Orsini, senator in 1244 and 1246. Nicholas had been created cardinal priest of Saint Nicholas in Carcere Tulliano in 1244 and succeeded John XXI as pope in 1277 after a vacancy of seven months, in the face of strongly voiced opposition from Charles of Anjou, then senator of Rome. Charles's term as senator expired in September 1278. Nicholas prevented its renewal and, in the bull *Fundamenta militantis Ecclesie,* specified that any emperor, king, prince, marquis, duke, or baron could become senator only with express permission from the pope, and never for more than one year; Romans could become senator without problems. Nicholas (as an Orsini) was then elected senator himself, but he exercised power through deputies, all Roman nobles.

Rudolf of Hapsburg was negotiating to come to Italy for his coronation when Nicholas became pope. Nicholas agreed to receive Rudolf in return for the cession of the Romagna to the papal state (1278). The province, influenced by the

Ghibelline leader Guido da Montefeltro, proved difficult to pacify, despite conciliatory measures including a temporary recall of the exiled Ghibelline faction to Bologna. Nicholas finally requested help from Charles of Anjou but died before order was restored in the Romagna.

Ptolemy of Lucca accused Nicholas of aspiring to establish an Orsini kingdom based on the Romagna. This has been seen as either an attempt to counterbalance the Angevin power, which was encircling the papacy, or an Angevin fiction designed to bring Nicholas into disrepute. Probably it was neither: Charles manifested no intention of attacking the papal state. The coolness between him and Nicholas shown in his opposition to Nicholas's election, in the ending of Charles's tenure of the senate, and subsequently in the termination of Charles's papal vicariate in Tuscany has been exaggerated, notably by Giovanni Villani. Although Charles probably distrusted the Orsini, he continued to receive support from the papacy in the south and sent support to the pope further north. Dante's story that Nicholas was persuaded by Byzantine gold, offered by John of Procida, to transfer Sicily from the Angevins to the Aragonese seems unfounded.

However, Dante justifiably denounced Nicholas for unprecedented nepotism. Nicholas created three Orsini cardinals. One nephew was papal vicar in the Romagna; another nephew was papal legate there; in Tuscany, a brother was senator twice; and so on.

Before his election Nicholas had been cardinal protector of the Franciscans. As pope, he issued the bull *Exiit qui seminat*, which was based on the *Apologia pauperum* of Saint Bonaventura and was intended as a definitive statement on the problem of Franciscan poverty—on which it (unsuccessfully) forbade further discussion.

Nicholas began an artistic revival in Rome that was carried on by his successors. He extended and embellished Innocent III's palace on the Vatican, rebuilt the Sancta Sanctorum chapel (the only part of the medieval Lateran palace now surviving), and started improvements at Saint Peter's and Santa Maria in Aracoeli.

See also **Dante Alighieri; Ptolemy of Lucca, Villani, Giovanni**

Further Reading

Editions

Nicholas III. *Les registres*, ed. Jules Gay. Paris: A. Fontemoing, 1898–1938.

Ptolemy of Lucca. *Historia ecclesiastica*. In *Return Italicarum Scriptores*, ed. L. A. Muratori, Vol. 3. Milan: Societatis Palatinae, 1723–1751.

Critical Studies

Davis, Charles T. "Roman Patriotism and Republican Propaganda: Ptolemy of Lucca and Pope Nicholas III." *Speculum*, 50, 1975, pp. 411–433.

Demski, Augustin. *Papst Nikolaus III: Eine monographie*. Münster: H. Schöningh, 1903.

Léonard, Émile G. *Les Angevins de Naples*. Paris: Presses Universitaires de France, 1954. (See especially pp. 124–128.)

Partner, Peter. *The Lands of Saint Peter: The Papal State in the Middle Ages and the Early Renaissance*. London: Eyre Methuen, 1972, pp. 268–277.

Sternfeld, Richard. *Der Kardinal Johann Gaetan Orsini (Papst Nikolaus III.) 1244–1277: Ein Beitrag zur Geschichte der römischen Kurie im 13. Jahrhundert*. Berlin: E. Ebering, 1905.

CAROLA M. SMALL

NICHOLAS OF CUSA (1401–1464)

Most important German thinker of the fifteenth century (Latin, Nicolaus Cusanus), ecclesiastical reformer, administrator, and cardinal. His lifelong effort, as canon law expert at church councils, as legate to Constantinople and later to German dioceses and houses of religion, in his own diocese, and even in the papal curia was to reform and unite the universal and Roman Church. This active life finds written expression in several hundred Latin sermons and more theoretical background in his writings on ecclesiology, ecumenism, mathematics, philosophy, and theology. Curious and open-minded, learned and steeped in the Neoplatonic tradition, well aware of both humanist and scholastic learning, yet self-taught in philosophy and theology, Nicholas anticipated many later ideas in mathematics, cosmology, astronomy, and experimental science while constructing his own original version of systematic Neoplatonism. A whole range of earlier medieval writers influenced Nicholas, but his important intellectual roots are in Proclus and Pseudo-Dionysius. In spite of his significance few later thinkers, apart from Giordano Bruno, understood or were influenced by him until the late nineteenth century.

Born in Kues (between Koblenz and Trier), Nicholas studied liberal arts (and perhaps some theology) at Heidelberg (1416–1417) and canon law at Padua, where he earned his *doctor decretorum* (1423) and made initial contacts with Italian humanists and mathematicians. He studied and taught canon law at Cologne (1425), where Heimericus de Campo introduced him to the ideas of Albertus Magnus, Ramon Llull, and Pseudo-Dionysius. He soon ended his formal schooling and became secretary, then chancellor, to the archbishop of Trier. He refused chairs of canon law at Louvain in 1428 and 1435, preferring administrative work in the church. As an expert at the Council of Basel (1432–1438), he wrote on the Hussites, papal authority, and reform of the calendar. His important conciliarist treatise, *De concordia catholica* (*On Catholic Harmony*, 1433), stressed the principles of representation and of consent of the governed and embodied his lifelong commitment to bring harmony and unity out of conflict and diversity.

In 1437 Nicholas changed his support from the conciliarists to the pope to better work for unity. He traveled in the delegation to Constantinople seeking to reunite Greek and Roman churches. Ordained a priest by 1440, he traveled as legate to Germany for the next ten years on behalf of the papal cause, and was named (1448) and made (1450) cardinal. He was appointed bishop of Brixen in Tyrol the same year, but traveled to Germany and the Low Countries to preach the jubilee year and issue edicts of reform. His efforts to reform his own diocese led to enmity with the local archduke; twice Nicholas had to flee to Rome. After 1458 he remained in the papal curia of Pius II at Rome. Nicholas died in 1464 en route to Ancona from Rome.

His important masterpiece of 1440, *On Learned Ignorance (De docta ignorantia),* was the foundation for his writings over the next quarter century. While fully engaged in practical ecclesiastical affairs, Nicholas also wrote some twenty philosophical/theological treatises and dialogues, plus ten works on mathematics, focusing on the problem of squaring the circle and on using mathematics in philosophical theology. The three books of *On Learned Ignorance* expound his central ideas about God, the universe, and Christ. Nicholas was to extend, expand, and modify these speculations in later writings.

"Learned ignorance" is so called because it involves acknowledging the limits of human knowledge when we seek to know what God is (or, indeed, what the exact essence of anything amounts to). Our rational knowledge is a kind of conceptual measuring designed for the finite realm of more and less, but unable to reach the absolute maximum and thus inadequate for measuring the infinite God. There is no humanly conceivable proportion between God and creatures. Yet for Nicholas, we are supposed to move in ignorance beyond reason's inadequacies in hopes of touching God *(incomprehensibiliter comprehendere)* through a kind of intellectual-mystical vision wherein all things are one. Since God's fullness comprises everything, Nicholas invokes the idea of the coincidence of opposites *(coincidentia oppositorum)* as the ontologicai correlative of learned ignorance. By limiting the principle of contradiction to the realm of finite creatures and their differences, we recognize that in divinity all opposites coincide in the transcendent infinite oneness. The lack of resemblance between God and creatures means that all our knowledge of God must be metaphorical.

Nicholas's later writings propose conjectural metaphors for exploring the limits of our knowledge and at the same time seeking the God beyond. Of particular import are *De coniecturis: On conjectures* (ca. 1442), where Nicholas proposes a hierarchical Neoplatonic ontology as a speculative conjecture (while pointing out that all our conceptual knowledge is provisional or conjectural) and *Idiota de mente: The Layman—About Mind* (1450), which parallels our minds' creation of a conceptual universe and the divine mind's creation of the actual world. In *De visione Dei: The Vision of God* (1453), Nicholas proposes an all-seeing icon to hold together for imagination and thought how our striving to see God is one with God's seeing us.

De possest: On Actualized Possibility (1460) and *De li non aliud: On the Not-other* (1461–1462) work out two descriptions, or "names," of God. The first stresses how in God all possibilities are real or actually exist; thus in God possibility and actuality coincide. The second is concerned to express how God is and is not present to created things—intimately connected ("not other than") yet never identical with (*not* "nothing else but") creatures in space and time. Each of these metaphors and, indeed, all of Nicholas's later writings are calculated to initiate dialectical thinking so that one may move from thinking of God and creatures as exclusive and exhaustive alternatives to seeing them as identified, yet not identical. God is to be seen as both all and nothing of created things; creatures are limited images of the divine infinite oneness that they cannot resemble yet for which they ceaselessly strive.

See also **Albertus Magnus; Llull, Ramón**

Further Reading

The Catholic Concordance, trans. Paul E. Sigmund. Cambridge: Cambridge University Press, 1991.

De ludo globi = The Game of Spheres, trans. Pauline Moffitt Watts. New York: Abaris, 1986.

Duclow, D. F. "Nicholas of Cusa." In *Dictionary of Literary Biography: Medieval Philosophers,* vol. 115, ed. J. Hackett. Detroit: Bruccoli Clark, 1992.

Flasch, K. *Nikolaus von Kues: Geschichte einer Entwicklung.* Frankfurt am Main: Klostermann, 1998.

Haubst, R. *Streifzuege in die cusanische Theologie.* Münster: Aschendorff, 1991.

—— et al., eds. *Mitteilungen und Forschungsbeiträge der Cusanus-Gesellschaft.* Mainz: Mattias-Grünewald, 1961 ff. [Cusanus journal, bibliographies in vols. 1, 3, 6, 10, 15].

Hopkins, Jasper, trans. *Nicholas of Cusa on Learned Ignorance.* Minneapolis: Banning, 1985.

Hopkins, J. *A Concise Introduction to the Philosophy of Nicholas of Cusa,* 3d ed. Minneapolis: Banning, 1986.

Idiota de mente = The Layman, about Mind, trans. Clyde Lee Miller. New York: Abaris, 1979.

Jacobi, K. ed. *Nikolaus von Kues: Einführung in sein philosophisches Denken.* Freiburg: Alber, 1979.

The Layman on Wisdom and the Mind, trans. M.L. Fuhrer. Ottawa: Dovehouse, 1989.

Li non aliud. English & Latin. Nicholas of Cusa on God as not-other, trans. Jasper Hopkins. 2d ed. Minneapolis: Banning, 1983.

Nicola de Cusa Opera Omnia, Heidelberg Academy Edition. Lepzig/Hamburg: Miner, 1932 ff.

Nicholas of Cusa's Metaphysic of Contraction, trans. Jasper Hopkins. Minneapolis: Banning, 1983.

Nicholas of Cusa: Selected Spiritual Writings, trans. H. Lawrence Bond. New York: Paulist, 1997.

Opera. 3 vols., ed. Jacques LeFevre d'Etaples. Paris: J. Blade, 1514; rpt. Frankfurt: Minerva, 1962.

CLYDE LEE MILLER

NICHOLAS OF VERDUN (ca. 1150–ca. 1210)

A goldsmith and enamelist active in the late twelfth and early thirteenth centuries, Nicholas is known for the stylistic originality of his work. Two dated works inscribed with his name exist: the ambo, or pulpit, dated 1181 (and remodeled into an altarpiece in 1330), from the Augustinian Abbey of Klosterneuburg near Vienna, and the shrine of the Virgin in Tournai Cathedral, dated to 1205. The shrine of the Three Kings in Cologne Cathedral, usually dated to the 1190s, is also partially attributed to Nicholas. This large reliquary was built to house the relics of the Three Magi, which Archbishop Rainald von Dassel had received from Emperor Frederick Barbarossa in 1164. After Nicholas's creation of the shrine, the Magi, as examples of both the first Christian pilgrims and the first Christian kings, became closely associated with theories of German kingship and also with the city of Cologne, their crowns appearing on its coat of arms by the end of the thirteenth century.

In technical details and certain stylistic features, Nicholas's work is related to the general tradition of metalwork in the Rhine and Meuse valleys, a region known in the twelfth century for its sophistication. His work is particularly closely related to the Heribert Shrine, considered the major achievement in metalwork from this area in the second half of the century. As with other Mosan artists, Nicholas was accomplished in creating both champlevé (decorative enamel filling) plaques, such as those found on the Klosterneuburg ambo, and three-dimensional figures, which are found on the Three Kings' Shrine and that of the Virgin. In addition to reflecting Mosan traditions, Nicholas's work, both two- and three-dimensional, shows a new interest in the natural proportioning of the human body, the fall of cloth garments over it, and a type of soft drapery fold called *Muldenfaltenstil* (trough fold style), which is smoothly curved and unlike the angular, inorganic drapery found in Romanesque art. This drapery style, perhaps first appearing in Nicholas's work, becomes extremely popular in the years around 1200 in a variety of other works, including cathedral sculpture, such as that at Bamberg Cathedral, stained glass, and manuscripts. The sources for these components of Nicholas's art are a matter of controversy with contemporary Byzantine art, Ottonian art, early Christian art, and even Roman minor arts cited as possible works Nicholas may have studied to acquire classicizing elements.

In spite of great stylistic innovation, there is evidence that Nicholas had the help of theologians in designing the complex iconographies of his shrines. A plaque of the Mouth of Hell from the Klosterneuburg ambo features a sketch of the Three Marys at the Tomb on the back. This is believed to represent a trial composition whose subject was later modified by the theological advisers to better accommodate the typological meaning of the whole ambo. The complex relationships between the Three Magi and contemporary kings implied by the images of the Three Kings' Shrine are also thought to reflect the ideas of theologians, in this case persons associated with Cologne Cathedral.

Further Reading

Dahm, Frederick. *Studien zur Ikonographie des Klosterneuburger Emailwerkes des Nicholaus von Verdun.* Vienna: VWGO, 1989.

Ornamenta Ecclesiae: Kunst und Künstler der Romanik in Köln, ed. Anton Legner. 3 vols. Cologne: Schnütgen Museum, 1985, vol. 2, pp. 216–224, 447–455.

Swarzenski, Hans. "The Style of Nicholas of Verdun: Saint Armand and Reims," in

Gatherings in Honor of Dorothy R. Miner, ed. U. E. McCracken et al. Baltimore: Walters Art Gallery, 1974, pp. 111–114.

SUSAN L. WARD

NICOLAUS GERHAERT VON LEYDEN (d. 1473)

A sculptor whose few surviving documented works are dispersed from Trier and Strasbourg to Vienna, Nicolaus Gerhaert von Leyden remains relatively unknown today even though his style influenced late Gothic sculpture throughout Germany. Of the surviving stone carvings attributed to him or to his school, only five are authenticated by documents or signatures. The earliest to display his new inner dynamism and portrait realism is the signed tomb effigy of Archbishop Jacob von Sierck, dated 1462, now in the Diocesan Museum in Trier. Originally the upper half of a two-tiered tomb with his decaying corpse below, the deeply cut effigy was undoubtedly made by a mature artist. His stay in Strasbourg, where Nicolaus was mentioned frequently in documents from 1463 to 1467 and where he became a citizen in 1464, is the best-documented and most productive period of his life. Here he was commissioned in 1464 to create the portal of the Neue Kanzlei (New Chancellery), on which busts appeared as if looking down from a window; only two heads survive: the so-called Bärbel von Ottenheim in the Liebieghaus Museum in Frankfurt and Count Jacob von Hanau-Lichtenberg in the Musée de l'Oeuvre NotreDame in Strasbourg. The Epitaph of Conrad von Busnang in the Chapel of St. John in the cathedral at Strasbourg, signed and dated 1464, provides the only comparison for Madonna statues attributed to his circle. In 1465–1467 he worked on the carved wood high altar for the Constance Minster that was later destroyed. His best-known work, the signed Crucifix for the Old Cemetery in Baden-Baden, now in the Stiftskirche there, was dated 1467. In the same year, in response to the second invitation of Emperor Frederick III, Nicolaus went to Vienna and Wiener Neustadt, where he was responsible for the tomb lid of the Emperor in the Apostle's Choir of St. Stephen in Vienna. Nicolaus died in 1473 and was buried in Wiener Neustadt. There are fewer documents from these last years, and they provide less certitude in regard to the extent of his work.

In spite of the widespread destruction of Netherlandish sculpture of the fifteenth century and a lack of study of French work of the same time, the stylistic origins of Nicolaus are generally agreed to lie in the Flemish-Burgundian region. The individualism of his portrait heads derives from those of Claus Sluter at Dijon, and his knowledge of the late work of Jan van Eyck is also generally accepted. His busts from the Chancellery at Strasbourg are often compared to the earlier figures above the entrance to the house of Jacques Coeur in Bourges. The new dynamism he infused into his figures together with their physical expressiveness and the drapery expanding into the surrounding space characterize his contribution to the new style. These characteristics also appear in the works of the Masters E.S. and Martin Schongauer, both working in the Rhineland at approximately the same time as Nicolaus; the engravings of these artists are partly responsible for the rapid spread of his style in the late fifteenth century.

The most convincing unsigned and undocumented work attributed to Nicolaus is the bust of a Meditating Man in the Strasbourg museum, assumed to be a self-portrait, also from the New Chancellery. The Crucifixion Altar in Nördlingen and the Virgin of Dangolsheim in Berlin are frequently considered his early work or that of a sculptor close to him.

See also **Frederick III, Schongauer, Martin; Sluter, Claus**

Further Reading

Müller, Theodor. *Sculpture in the Netherlands, Germany, France and Spain 1400 to 1500.*

Pelican History of Art 25. Harmondsworth: Penguin, 1966, pp. 79–87.

Recht, Roland. *"Nicolas de Leyde et la sculpture à Strasbourg (1460–1525)."* Ph.D. diss., Université des Sciences Humaines de Strasbourg, 1978. Strasbourg: Presses Universitaires de Strasbourg, 1987, pp. 115–151, 341–345.

MARTA O. RENGER

NILUS OF ROSSANO (c. 910–1004)

Nilus of Rossano (Neilos) is perhaps the best-known representative of Greek monasticism in medieval Italy before the Great Schism. The chief source for his biography is an anonymous eleventh-century *Life of Saint Nilus the Younger,* an impressive document of Italo-Greek monastic ideals; despite the exemplary import of the incidents chosen for narration, it seems in outline to be factually accurate. According to this account, Nilus was born to an aristocratic family in Rossano, an important eastern Roman (Byzantine) administrative center in eastern Calabria, received a good religious education, and was orphaned at an early age. At the age of thirty, he abandoned the world (he had sired a daughter, perhaps out of wedlock) for an ascetic life in the mountainous border region of the Mercurion and there came under the influence of Fantinus the Younger and other holy fathers. To evade a gubernatorial ban on his becoming a monk, he took the habit at a Greek monastery in the Lombard principality of Salerno. Nilus then returned to Fantinus's lavra (colony of anchorites). Living first there and then in a nearby cave, he learned and later taught calligraphy. During this time he also traveled to Rome to visit the tombs of the apostles and to consult books whose identity, regrettably, is unknown.

Arab raids caused Nilus to retreat in the late 940s to one of his properties near Rossano, where together with some of his students he founded a monastery of his own. He resided here as a penitent for the next quarter-century, achieving more than local repute as a holy man and miracle worker. He is said to have declined being named bishop of Rossano and to have obtained from the emir of Palermo the liberation of three of his monks who had been captured and enslaved. Around 980, fleeing further Arab incursions and his own growing fame, Nilus and his comrades left the eastern empire for good and were welcomed in the Latin west by the Lombard prince of Capua, Pandulf Ironhead. At the behest of Pandulf's successor Landulf IV, Abbot Aligern of Monte Cassino installed them in 981 at the abbey's daughter house at Vallelucio (now Valleluce), where they participated to a limited extent in the life of the neighboring Benedictine community. Here Nilus composed an office for Saint Benedict and probably some of his other poetry.

After Aligern's death, relations between the two groups soured, and in 994 and 995 Nilus founded a new monastery at tiny Serperi (now Sèrapo) in the duchy of Gaeta. From here he made journeys to Rome, where he failed to persuade his fellow Rossanese, John Philagathus, to renounce the papacy he had assumed in 997 after the ouster from the city of the imperially selected incumbent, Gregory V; and where, too, after John had been deposed and later blinded, Nilus attempted in an interview with the emperor Otto III to have the former antipope released to his custody. In 1004, the aged Nilus left Serperi and, staying at a small Greek monastery in the Alban hills not far from Rome, obtained land for a new foundation from Gregory I, count of Tusculum. Nilus died there shortly after his monks had arrived at the nearby site and begun work on what would become the famous Greek abbey of Grottaferrata.

Nilus's surviving verse, all in his native Greek, is not a large body of work. Specimens of his scribal work and that of his students also survive, however. His correspondence does not survive, apart from brief summaries and extracts (mostly in the *Life,* a partly eyewitness account sometimes ascribed to his companion and successor Bartholomew of Grottaferrata). To Nilus himself has been ascribed, on very slender grounds, the commentary of Nilus the Monk on the *Perí stáseon* (*On Issues*) of the ancient Greek rhetorician Hermogenes.

Further Reading

Editions

Gassisi, Sofronio, ed. *Poesie di San Nilo Iuniore e di Paolo monaco, abbati di Grottaferrata, nuova edizione con ritocchi ed aggiunte.* Innografi Italo-Greci, Fasc. 1. Rome: Tipografia Poliglotta della S. C. de Prop. Fide, 1906.

Giovanelli, Germano, ed. *Bíos kaí politeia toû hosíou patròs hemôn Neílou toû Néou.* Grottaferrata: Badia di Grottaferrata, 1972. (Bartholomew, Saint, Abbot of Grottaferrata, ascribed author.)

Translations

Giovanelli, Germano, trans. *Vita di S. Nilo, fondatore e patrono di Grottaferrata.* Grottaferrata: Badia di Grottaferrata, 1966.

Romano, Roberto, trans. "S. Nilo di Rossano, *Kondakion per S. Nilo di Ancira.*" *Italoellenika,* 5, 1994–1998, pp. 401–405.

Manuscripts

Caruso, Stefano. "Un tabù etico e filologico: La mutilazione *verecundiae gratia* del Cryptensis B.b II (Bìos di Nilo da Rossano)." *PAN: Studi dell' Istituto di filologia latina "Giusto Monaco,"* 15–16, 1998, pp. 169–193.

D'Oria, Filippo, "Attività scrittoria e cultura greca in ambito longobardo (note e spunti di riflessione)." In *Scrittura e produzione documentaria nel Mezzogiorno longobardo: Atti del convegno internazionale di studio (Badia di Cava, 3–5 ottobre 1990),* ed. Giovanni Vitolo and Francesco Mottola. Cava dei Tirreni: Badia di Cava, 1991, pp. 131–167. (See especially pp. 135–144.)

Gassisi, Sofronio, "I manoscritti autografi di S. Nilo Iuniore, fondatore del monastera di S. M. di Grottaferrata." *Oriens Christianus,* 4, 1904, pp. 308–370.

Critical Studies

Atti del Congresso Internazionale su s. Nilo di Rossano (28 settembre–1 ottobre 1986). Rossano and Grottaferrata: n.p., 1989.

Follieri, Enrica. "Per una nuova edizione della Vita di san Nilo da Rossano." *Bollettino della Badia Greca di Grottaferrata,* n.s., 51, 1997, pp. 71–92.

Luzzatti Laganà, Francesca. "Catechesi e spiritualità nella Vita di S. Nilo di Rossano: Donne, ebrei e `santa follia.'" *Quaderni Storici,* 93, 1996, pp. 709–737. (Year 31, number 3.)

Romano, Roberto. "Il commentario a Ermogne attribuito a S. Nilo di Rossano." *Epeterìs Hetaireías Byzantinôn Spoudôn,* 47, 1987–1989, pp. 253–269.

Rousseau, Olivier. "La visite de Nil de Rossano au Mont-Cassin." In *La chiesa greca in Italia dall'VII al XVI secolo: Atti del convegno storico interecclesiale (Bari, 30 apr.-4 magg. 1969),* Vol. 3. Italia Sacra, 20–22. Padua: Antenore, 1973, pp. 1111–1137.

Sansterre, Jean-Marie. "Les coryphées des apôtres, Rome et la papauté dans les *Vies* des saints Nil et Barthélemy de Grottaferrata." *Byzantion,* 55, 1985, pp. 516–543.

——. "Otton III et les saints ascètes de son temps." *Rivista di Storia della Chiesa in Italia,* 43, 1989, pp. 377–412. (See especially pp. 390–396.)

——. "Saint Nil de Rossano et le monachisme latin." *Bollettino della Badia Greca di Grottaferrata,* n.s., 45, 1991, pp. 339–386.

JOHN B. DILLON

NOTKER LABEO (ca. 950–1022)   Also known as Notker III and Notker Teutonicus (Notker the German), Notker Labeo (the lip) was a St. Gall monk and teacher best known for his Old High German translation-commentaries of Latin classroom texts. In a letter to Bishop Hugo of Sitten (ca. 1019–1020), Notker refers to the vernacular translation project on which he has embarked as something uncommon and revolutionary and notes that it may even shock his reader. He argues, however, that students can understand texts in their mother tongue much more easily than in Latin. Notker's translation method adopts contemporary glossing practices (syntactical, morphological, and lexical) and develops and integrates them into a continuous Latin/German text. First Notker often rearranges the word order of the original Latin into a variant of the so-called natural order, the *ordo naturalis,* a current pedagogic word order that roughly corresponds to a subject-verb-object typology. He then expands on the text with additional classroom commentary—either his own or culled from other sources—by providing synonyms, supplying any implied subjects or objects, expounding rhetorical figures and etymologies, and interpreting mythological figures. Finally Notker appends his Old High German translation, which is sprinkled with further explanation in the vernacular and occasional Latin terms, a kind of mixed prose (*Mischsprosa*).

In his letter to the bishop, Notker also includes a list of works he had finished, thereby providing us with a fairly accurate account of his corpus: Boethius, *De consolatione Philosophiae (On the Consolation of Philosophy)*; Martianus Capella, *De nuptiis Philologiae et Mercurii* (On the Marriage of Philology and Mercury); Boethius's Latin versions of Aristotle's, *De categoriis* (Categories) and *De interpretatione* (On Interpretation), and, his most popular work, the Psalter (together with the *Cantica* and three catechistic texts). He also refers to several of his own classroom compositions, which contain translations of technical terms and/or examples in Old High German; among these are thought to be *De arte rhetorica* (On the Art of Rhetoric), *Computus* (Calculating the Calendar), *De definitione* (On Definition), *De musica* (On Music), *Partibus logicae* (On the Parts of Logic), and *De syllogismis* (On Syllogisms). A few Latin treatises produced in the St. Gall school may also have been compiled by him: *De dialectica* (On Dialectics), *Distributio* (Logic), and *The*

St. Gall Tractate. Other translations listed by Notker have not survived: *Principia arithmetica* (Arithmetic Principles, by Boethius?), *De trinitate* (On the Trinity, by Boethius or Remigius of Auxerre?), Gregory the Great's *Moralia in Iob* (Moral Deliberations on the Book of Job), and Cato's *Distichs*, Vergil's *Bucolica*, and Terence's *Andria*. Notker's work did not find great resonance, and only the Psalter and several of the minor treatises are preserved outside of St. Gall.

Notker's late-tenth-century Alemannic marks an important transition period in the history of the German language. The extant eleventh-century St. Gall copies of his texts are recorded with a fairly consistent spelling, which modern scholars have interpreted to reflect guidelines that Notker imposed on the St. Gall scribes. They include the *Anlautgesetz* (devoicing initial voiced stops /b d g/ following a voiceless consonant and/or a pause and in compounds) and the use of the acute and circumflex accents to mark word and/or sentence stress and vowel length. Notker's lexicon has also received considerable scholarly attention, owing to the many new words he coined to render into Old High German the highly complex Latin terminology he was translating.

See also **Gregory I, Pope; Martianus Capella**

Further Reading

Colemnan, Evelyn S. "Bibliographie zu Notker III. von St. Gallen," in *Germanic Studies in Honor of Edward H. Sehrt*. Coral Gables, Fl.: University of Miami Press, 1968, pp. 61–76.
——. "Bibliographie zu Notker III. von St. Gallen: Zweiter Teil," in *Spectrum medii aevi. Göppingen: Kümmerle, 1983, pp. 91–110.*
De nuptiis Philologiae et Mercurii: Konkordanzen, Wortlisten und Abdruck des Textes nach dem Codex Sangallensis 872, ed. Evelyn S. Firchow. Hildesheim: Olms, 1999.
Ehrismann, Gustav. *Geschichte der deutschen Literatur bis zum Ausgang des Mittelalters*. Munich: Beck, 1932, pp. 416–458.

Hellgardt, Ernst. "Notker des Deutschen Brief an Bischof Hugo von Sitten," in *Befund und Deutung.* Tübingen: Niemeyer, 1979, pp. 169–192.

——. "Notker Teutonicus: Überlegungen zum Stand der Forschung." *Beiträge zur Geschichte der deutschen Sprache und Literatur* 108 (1986): 190–205 and 109 (1987): 202–221.

King, James, and Petrus Tax, eds. *Die Werke Notkers des Deutschen, Altdeutsche Textbibliothek.* 10 vols. Tübingen: Niemeyer, 1972–1996.

Notker der Deutsche. *De interpretatione: Boethius' Bearbeitung von Aristoteles' Schrift Peri hermeneias: Konkordanzen, Wortlisten und Abdruck des Textes nach dem Codex Sangallensis 818,* ed. Evelyn S. Firchow. Berlin: de Gruyter, 1995.

Notker der Deutsche von St. Gallen. Categoriae: Boethius' Bearbeitung von Aristoteles' Schrift Kategoriai: Konkordanzen, Wortlisten und Abdruck der Texte nach den Codices Sangallensis 818 and 825, ed. Evelyn S. Firchow. Berlin: de Gruyter, 1996.

Notker-Wortschatz, eds. Edward H. Sehrt und Wolfram K. Legner. Halle (Saale): Niemeyer, 1955. Sehrt, Edward H. *Notker-Glossar.* Tübingen: Niemeyer, 1962.

The St. Gall Tractate: A Rhetorical Guide to Classroom Syntax, eds. and trans. Anna Grotans and David Porter. Columbia, S.C.: Camden House, 1995.

Schröbler, Ingeborg. *Notker III. von St. Gallen als Übersetzer und Kommentator von Boethius' De consolatione Philosophiae.* Tübingen: Niemeyer, 1953.

Sonderegger, Stefan. *Althochdeutsch in St. Gallen.* St. Gallen: Ostschweiz, 1970.

——. *Althochdeutsche Sprache und Literatur,* 2d ed. Berlin: de Gruyter, 1987.

——. "Notker III. von St. Gallen," in *Die deutsche Literatur des Mittelalters: Verfasserlexikon,* vol. 6., 2d ed. Berlin: de Gruyter, 1987, cols. 1212–1236.

Tax, Petrus W. "Notker Teutonicus," in *Dictionary of the Middle Ages,* vol. 9. New York: Scribner's, 1987, pp. 188–190.

ANNA A. GROTANS

O

OCKEGHEM, JOHANNES (ca. 1420–1497) Franco-Flemish composer, active mainly in France. According to recently discovered documents, he was born in Saint-Ghislain, a village near Mons in the Belgian province of Hainaut. His career is first traced in Antwerp, where he was a singer at the church of Notre-Dame in 1443/44. From 1446 to 1448, he was singer in the chapel of Charles I, duke of Bourbon, at Moulins. He became a member of the French royal chapel under Charles VII ca. 1450 and continued to serve that institution under Louis XI and Charles VIII. Named as first chaplain in 1454, he was subsequently cited as master of the chapel (1464) and counselor to the king (1477). In 1459, Charles VII, who was hereditary abbot of Saint-Martin of Tours, appointed Ockeghem to the important post of treasurer of Saint-Martin. Sometime before 1472, possibly in 1464, he was ordained a priest at Cambrai. The only journey he is known to have undertaken outside France and the Low Countries is one to Spain in 1470. In 1484, he revisited his native country when he and other members of the royal chapel traveled to Damme and Bruges in Flanders. He eventually retired to Tours, where he died on February 6, 1497.

Among his pupils may have been Antoine Busnoys, a cleric at Saint-Martin of Tours in 1465 and subsequently singer in the chapel of Charles the Bold, duke of Burgundy. Busnoys honored Ockeghem in his motet *In hydraulis*, calling him the "true image of Orpheus." At Cambrai, Ockeghem met Guillaume Dufay, his greatest musical contemporary, who in 1464 entertained him at his house. The Flemish music theorist Johannes Tinctoris dedicated his treatise on the modes (1476) jointly to Ockeghem and Busnoys, and in his treatises on proportions and counterpoint he cited Ockeghem as "the most excellent of all the composers I have ever heard." In his last treatise, *De inventione et usu musicae* (ca. 1481), Tinctoris describes him not only as a distinguished composer but as the finest bass singer known to him.

Ockeghem's personal appearance and manner, as well as his musicianship, were often praised by his contemporaries. Guillaume Crétin wrote a *Déploration surle trespas de feu Okergan*, praising his "subtlety" and calling on his mourning colleagues, led by Dufay and Busnoys, to sing his music, including his "exquisite and most perfect Requiem Mass." The poet Jean Molinet also wrote a *déploration* on his death, which was set to music by Josquin des Prez, the great master of the next generation of French composers. An *epitaphium* for Ockeghem by Erasmus of Rotterdam was set by Johannes Lupi in the 16th century.

Ockeghem composed in all genres, but his most important works are his fourteen Masses. A single Credo and only five motets by him are known, but they are each highly individual works. Twenty-two secular songs, all but one in French, come down to us. The exception is a Spanish song, probably a memento of his visit to Spain.

In his time and throughout subsequent centuries, Ockeghem was renowned for his contrapuntal skill, especially in canonic writing. His masterpiece in this technique is his *Missa prolationum*, consisting almost entirely of double canons at all intervals within the octave, and in four different "prolations" (meters) simultaneously. Almost legendary in his time was a thirty-six-voice canon mentioned by Crétin and others, the identity of which remains controversial. His Requiem Mass, which may have been written on the death of Charles VII (1461), is the earliest surviving example of its kind.

The most distinctive features of Ockeghem's music are its varied, unpredictable rhythms and long-breathed, overlapping phrases. Its texture of equally important though highly independent melodic lines and its exploration of the bass register are progressive features, but in many respects its unpredictable, "mystical" character, which virtually defies analysis, evokes a Late Gothic spirit rather than displaying the clarity of the emerging Renaissance style of his contemporaries.

See also **Busnoys, Antoine; Charles VII; Dufay, Guillaume; Louis XI**

Further Reading

Ockeghem, Johannes. *Collected Works*, ed. Dragan Plamenac and Richard Wexler. 3 vols. N.p.: American Musicological Society, 1947–92.

Goldberg, Clemens, *Die Chansons Johannes Ockeghems*. Laaber: Laaber, 1992.

Lindmayr, Andrea. *Quellenstudien zu den Motetten von Johannes Ockeghem*, Laaber: Laaber, 1992.

Perkins, Leeman L. "The *L'homme armé* Masses of Busnoys and Ockeghem: A Comparison. "*Journal of Musicology* 3 (1984): 363–96.

Picker, Martin. *Johannes Ockeghem and Jacob Obrecht: A Guide to Research*. New York: Garland, 1988.

Sparks, Edgar H. *Cantus Firmus in the Mass and Motet, 1420–1520*. Berkeley: University of California Press, 1963.

Thein, Wolfgang. *Musikalischer Satz und Textdarbeitung im Werk von Johannes Ockeghem*. Tutzing: Schneider, 1992.

MARTIN PICKER

OCKHAM, WILLIAM OF (William Occam; ca. 1285–1347) Born in Ockham in Surrey, England, William entered a Franciscan convent at an early age. In 1306, he was ordained subdeacon at Southwark in London and began his education at Oxford, where he lectured on Peter Lombard's *Sententiae* from 1317 to 1319. John Luttrell, the chancellor at Oxford, opposed Ockham's views. Pope John XXII called him to Avignon in 1323/24. A committee investigated Ockham's works and censured fifty-one propositions but did not formally condemn him. In 1327, he met Michael of Cesena, the minister-general of the Franciscan order and leader of the Spiritual Franciscans. Cesena requested Ockham to examine John XXII's constitutions on Franciscan poverty. Ockham declared them full of error and the following year fled Avignon with Cesena and others. He was excommunicated in 1328. He joined the emperor Louis of Bavaria in his dispute with the pope and in 1330 settled at the Franciscan convent in Munich. In 1331, Ockham was expelled from the order and sentenced to imprisonment. He died in Munich in 1347, still under Louis's protective care.

Ockham's writings fall into three stages corresponding to his major residences: Oxford (1306/07–23), Avignon (1323–28), and Germany (1330–47). At

Oxford and Avignon, his writings include his commentary on the *Sententiae*, later published in two parts: the *Ordinatio*, his lectures on the first book, and the *Reportatio*, comprising notes taken at his lectures. He also composed commentaries on Aristotle's *Organon*; *Summa logicae*, his major statement on logic; seven quodlibetals; and treatises on the Body of Christ, on the eucharist, and on predestination. After his departure from Avignon in 1328, he wrote works against the Avignon papacy, the chief ones being *Opus nonaginta dierum*, about papal errors regarding poverty; *Dialogus inter magistrum et discipulum* (1333–47); eight *quaestiones* on papal authority (1340); and a treatise on the respective powers of emperor and pope (ca. 1347).

Ockham was principally a theologian, vigorously exploring the philosophical limits of each epistemological, logical, or metaphysical issue, often to see more clearly the theological application. He rejected the older Platonic Realism and the *via antiqua* of the Aristotelians to pursue a *via moderna*, a path of demonstration and the near-autonomy of faith. He insisted upon a method of economy of explanation, later termed "Ockham's razor." With the nominalists, he contested the reality of universals and affirmed the fundamental reality of particulars for the human mind. His own solution to the relationship between universals and particulars is often called "conceptualist" instead of "nominalist," because he viewed concepts not merely as creatures of the mind but rather as entities identical with the abstractive cognition by which the mind considers individual objects in a certain way. With Duns Scotus, he asserted the utter transcendence and unique necessity and freedom of God in contrast with the contingency of all else, including so-called natural and moral laws. He argued the distinction between God's absolute power and that of his ordained power, manifest in his decrees, by which God limits himself to operate within ordi-

nations he established. Ockham also contributed to medieval and early-modern political theory and ecclesiology. He influenced conciliarism, and his theological legacy reached to Pierre d'Ailly, Gabriel Biel, and Martin Luther. He attacked the wealth of the church, challenged the notions of papal infallibility and plenitude of power, upheld the right of imperial election apart from papal interference, and conceded to the emperor the responsibility to depose a heretical pope. He maintained that the papacy was not established by Christ, that the general council was superior to the papacy, but that the pope possessed an ordinary executive authority unless he were heretical.

See also **D'ailly, Pierre; Duns Scotus, John**

Further Reading

Ockham, William of. *Opera philosophica*, ed. Philotheus Boehner et al. 3 vols. St. Bonaventure: Editiones Instituti Franciscani Universitatis S. Bonaventurae, 1974–85.

———. *Opera theologica*, ed. Gedeon Gá et al. 10 vols. St. Bonaventure: Editiones Instituti Franciscani Universitatis S. Bonaventurae, 1967–86.

———. *Opera politica*, ed. Jeffrey G. Sikes et al 3 vols. Manchester: University of Manchester Press, 1940–.

———. *William of Ockham. Philosophical Writings: A Selection*, ed. and trans. Philotheus Boehner. rev. ed. Stephen F. Brown. Indianapolis: Hackett, 1990.

Adams, Marilyn McCord. *William Ockham.* 2 vols. Notre Dame: University of Notre Dame Press, 1987.

Baudry, León. *Guillaume d'Occam: sa vie, ses œuvres, ses idées sociales et politiques*. Paris: Vrin, 1949, Vol. 1: *L'homme et les œuvres*.

Boehner, Philotheus. *Collected Articles on Ockham*, ed. Eligii M. Buytaert. St. Bonaventure: Franciscan Institute, 1958.

McGrade, Arthur Stephen. *The Political Thought of William of Ockham: Personal and Institutional Principles.*

London: Cambridge University Press, 1974.

Moody, Emest A. *The Logic of William Ockham.* London: Sheed and Ward, 1935.

H. LAWRENCE BOND

OFFA (r. 757–96) King of Mercia in 757, after ousting another claimant. By the time of his death on 28 July 796 Offa also held sway over Sussex, Kent, and East Anglia. His daughters married rulers of Wessex and Northumbria, thus extending his sphere of influence. He clashed with the Welsh, which probably led him to construct the dike that bears his name. Running along much of the nearly 150 miles of the Welsh frontier, from the Severn estuary to a few miles south of the Dee estuary, Offa's Dyke is the longest earthwork in Britain. It could have been planned in one season and completed in the next; if this was indeed so, it is testimony to the organizational and coercive power that made him the leading English ruler of his day.

Offa utilized the church to enhance his power. He persuaded Pope Hadrian to sanction the creation of a new archdiocese at Lichfield in 787, only a few miles from his palace at Tamworth, thus effectively neutralizing the hostile archbishop of Canterbury. Probably imitating Charlemagne, he had his son, Ecgfrith, consecrated as his successor in 787, the first royal anointing in English history.

Offa seems to have had extensive trade contacts with the Carolingian realm, which in turn appears to have made monetary reform possible. His silver penny, influenced by a Carolingian model, was the basis of the English coinage until the reign of Henry III. He appreciated the coin's potential for symbolism; many bear his name and a finely wrought effigy, and some even carry the likeness of his wife, Cynethryth, a practice drawn either from Byzantine Italy or even late-imperial Rome.

The poems *Beowulf* and *Widsith*, a tribute list known as "The Tribal Hidage"— even the origin of a system of burghal defense later associated with Alfred the Great of Wessex—have been associated with Offa. Much more research will be needed, however, before a balanced assessment of the cultural and social contributions of his reign can be made.

Though his achievements did not long survive him, he was regarded as a great figure in the Middle Ages. Alfred claimed to have adopted and modified his laws; a sword reputed to be his was still treasured two centuries after his death; a 14th-century *Life* was composed by the monks of St. Albans, who revered him as their founder. An imitator rather than an innovator; his image of greatness derived from his longevity, ruthlessness, and astute ability to exploit the imagery of rulership. Apart from the dike little evidence of his power survives; the Mercian archives are lost, as is his burial place. His palace at Tamworm probably lies under the parish churchyard and so cannot be excavated.

Further Reading

Blunt, Christopher E. "The Coinage of Offa." In *Anglo-Saxon Coins: Studies Presented to F.M. Stenton on the Occasion of His 80th Birthday*, ed. R.H.M. Dolley. London: Methuen, 1961, pp. 39–62.

Brooks, Nicholas. "The Development of Military Obligations in Eighth- and Ninth-Century England." In *England before the Conquest: Studies in Primary Sources Presented to Dorothy Whitelock*, ed. Peter Clemoes and Kathleen Hughes. Cambridge: Cambridge University Press, 1971, pp. 69–84.

Hart, Cyril. "The Kingdom of Mercia." In *Mercian Studies*, ed. Ann Dornier. Leicester: Leicester University Press, 1977, pp. 43–61.

Keynes, Simon. "Changing Faces: Offa, King of Mercia." *History Today* 40/11 (November 1990): 14–19.

Levison, Wilhelm. *England and the Continent in the Eighth Century.* Oxford: Clarendon, 1946.

Noble, Frank. *Offa's Dyke Reviewed.* Ed. Margaret Gelling. BAR Brit. Ser. 114. Oxford: BAR, 1983.

Stenton, F.M. "The Supremacy of the Mercian Kings." In *Preparatory to Anglo-Saxon England*, ed. Doris M. Stenton. Oxford: Clarendon, 1970, pp. 48–66.

Wormald, Patrick. "The Age of Offa and Alcuin." In *The Anglo-Saxons*, ed, James Campbell. Oxford: Phaidon, 1982, pp. 101–31.

Wormald, Patrick. "In Search of King Offa's "Law-Code." In *People and Places in Northern Europe 500—1600: Essays in Honour of Peter Hayes Sawyer*, ed. Ian Wood and Niels Lund. Woodbridge: Boydell, 1991, pp. 25–45.

DAVID A.E. PELTERET

ÓLÁFR TRYGGVASON (r. 995-999/1000)

Óláfr Tryggvason was king of Norway 995–999/1000. He was the son of Tryggvi Óláfsson, grandson of Haraldr hárfagri ("fair-hair") Hálfdanarson, a petty king of Viken or the Upplands.

Before Óláfr Tryggvason became king, he led great Viking raids to England, Scotland, and Ireland. The *Anglo-Saxon Chronicle* for the years 991 and 994 states that Óláfr led a large Viking fleet to attack the eastern and southern coast of England. In both cases, the English king paid large amounts of silver, "Danegeld," to buy off the Vikings.

Just before Óláfr Tryggvason went to Norway, controversy arose in Trøndelag between Earl Hákon, who was the actual ruler of the country, and the Tronds. According to *Heimskringla*, the earl constantly abused their wives and daughters, "and the farmers began to grumble just as the Tronds are wont to do over anything which goes against them" (*Heimskringla* 1:343). One of the rich peasants who had refused to give up his wife to the earl gathered the farmers and set out against Hákon. The earl fled and was killed by his own slave, Karkr, while escaping. Óláfr Tryggvason, who was on his way to Niðaróss (Trondheim), inadvertently encountered one of the earl's sons and killed him in battle; the two other sons fled. Óláfr was chosen king by the people of Trøndelag at the Eyraþing. After that, he traveled throughout the country and was made king of all Norway. In 996, Óláfr was in Vikin (Viken), and from there he carried out his plans to introduce Christianity in Norway and to secure complete control over the country.

With the help of his paternal relatives, he succeeded in making the farmers of Viken accept the new faith in 996/7. Those who refused or disagreed with him, "he dealt with hard; some he slew, some he maimed, and some he drove away from the land" (*Heimskringla* 1:362). Gradually, his actions led to a conflict between the king and the farmers. In the summer of 997, he went to the southwestern part of the country, made the Rogalenders embrace the new faith, and secured their support by marrying his sister to one of the chieftains there, Erlingr Skjálgsson, at Sóli (Sole). In the west, he introduced Christianity through the support of his maternal relatives while securing control over this province. The introduction of Christianity in these provinces, the west, and Viken, was facilitated by long-lasting contact with Christian western Europe, especially the British Isles.

In the fall of 997, Óláfr Tryggvason, went to Trøndelag. There and in the north, paganism was stronger than in the other provinces. Óláfr Tryggvason met with strong opposition from the farmers and was forced to acquiesce. He returned one year later, killed the leader of the farmers, Járn-Skeggi, and made the Tronds embrace the new faith. Some of the rich farmers refused to accept the new order. They fled and went to Sweden, joining Eiríkr, son of Earl Hákon. Óláfr Tryggvason tried to secure control over Trøndelag and the good-will of the Tronds by marrying Guðrún, Járn-Skeggi's daughter. He did not succeed; Guðrún attempted to murder him on their wedding night. In 999, he made the people of Háleygjaland (Hålogaland) accept Christianity. Thus, he had christianized the entire coastal area of Norway. Óláfr Haraldsson later christianized the interior.

But it was not only in Norway that Óláfr Tryggvason tried to spread Christianity. His pressure on the Icelandic chieftains was undoubtedly one of the main reasons why the Icelanders accepted the new faith at the Alþingi in 999/1000. He also made the Greenlanders accept Christianity.

Óláfr Tryggvason's strengthening of the power of the king involved not only an expansion of the king's territorial control over the country, but also an attempt to develop the internal organization of the kingdom. It was most likely Óláf Tryggvason who introduced the office of district governor, a service rendered by a chieftain who received royal land in return. He was also the first Norwegian king to mint coins.

Óláfr Tryggvason died in the battle of Svǫlðr (Svold) in 999/1000, where he fought the Danish king Sven Haraldsson (Forkbeard), who had been forced to give up Viken, the Swedish king who wanted control of Gautaland, and Eirikr, son of Earl Hákon.

Further Reading

Literature

Finnur Jónsson, ed. Heimskringla. 4 vols. Samfund til udgivelse af gammel nordisk litterarur, 23. Copenhagen: Møller, 1893–1901.

Koht, Halvdan. "The Scandinavian Kingdoms Until the End of the Thirteenth Century." In The Cambridge Medieval History 6. Ed. J. R. Turner et al. Cambridge: Cambridge University Press, 1929, pp. 362–92.

Baetke, Walter. Christliches Lehngut in der Saga-religion. Das Svolder-Problem. Zwei Beiträge zur Saga-kritikk. Berichte über die Verhandlungen der sächsischen Akademie der Wissenschaften zu Leipzig. Philol.-hist. Klasse, 98.6. Berlin: Akademie-Verlag, 1951.

Ellehøj, Svend. "The Location of the Fall of Olaf Tryggvason." Arbók hins íslenzka fornleifafélags, Fylgirit (1958), 63–73

Gunnes, Erik. Rikssamlingogkristning 800–1177. Norges historie, 2. Oslo: Cappelen, 1976.

Andersen, Per Sveaas. Samlingen av Norge og kristningen av landet, 800–1130. Handbok i Norges historie 2. Bergen: Universitetsforlaget, 1977.

Helle, Knut. "Norway in the High Middle Ages: Recent Views on the Structure of Society." Scandinavian Journal of History 6 (1981), 161–89.

Birkeli, Fridtjov. Hva vet vi om kristningen av Norge? Oslo: Universitetsforlaget, 1982.

Bagge, Sverre. Society and Politics in Snorri Sturluson's Heimskringla. Berkeley and Los Angeles: University of California Press, 1991.

JÓN VIÐAR SIGURÐSSON

OLIVER OF PADERBORN (d. 1224)

Oliver of Paderborn (North Rhine-Westphalia) appears as the scholastic at Paderborn in the waning years of the twelfth century. His reputation was such, however, that by 1202 he had been appointed scholastic at Cologne Cathedral. In 1207 we find him in Paris, where he acted as the mediator between a canon from Reims and the monastery of St. Remy. Presumably, he had been attending the schools of Paris at the time. The following year, he appears in southern France, apparently as a preacher against the Albigensians. At this time, he established his lifelong friendship with Jacques de Vitry and Robert de Courçon, both of whom became well-known preachers of the Fifth Crusade in France.

In the papal encyclical Quia maior nunc of May 1213, Oliver was named as one of several crusade-preachers for Germany, with specific duties in the ecclesiastical province of Cologne. Assisting him was *magister* (master) Hermann, dean of St. Cassius's Church in Bonn. Over the next four years, he and his colleagues criss-crossed Germany, convening assemblies of people and exploiting every opportunity to present their message and enlist support for the crusade. They were armed with letters of indulgence with which to entice and reward participants. Following the Fourth Lateran Council in Rome (at which Oliver was also present), he and the other preachers were also charged with collecting the half-tithe that Innocent III had imposed on the clergy as a means of providing financial support for the crusade.

In the summer of 1217 the first company of warriors departed by ship from the Lower Rhine. Among them was Oliver himself, who played a viral role in the campaign against Damietta in the Nile delta. His *Historia* of this event and his other writings and letters make him the best known of the German preachers. Only after the fall of Damietta to the Muslims on September 8, 1221, did Oliver return to Cologne, where he appears again in the spring of 1222.

In 1223 Oliver was elected bishop of Paderborn. He never really occupied the office, however, having first resumed his role as crusade-preacher in 1224, and shortly thereafter being elevated to the cardinal-bishopric of St. Sabina. One sees the influence of his fellow German, Conrad of Urach, and perhaps also of Cardinal Robert de Courçon, in this appointment. Like Conrad, however, Oliver lived but a short time after donning the cardinal's hat; he died the same year.

See also **Conrad of Urach**

Further Reading

Hoogeweg, Hermann. "Der Kölner Domscholaster Oliver als Kreuzprediger." *Westdeutsche Zeitschrift für Geschichte und Kunst* 7 (1888): 237ff.

——. *Die Schriften des Kölner Domscholasters, späteren Bischofs von Paderborn und Kardinalbischof von S. Sabina Oliverus.* Stuttgart: Litterarischer Verein, 1894.

——. "Die Kreuzpredigt des Jahres 1224 in Deutschland mit besonderer Rücksicht auf die Erzdiözese Köln." *Deutsche Zeitschrift für Geschichtswissenschaft* 4 (1890): 54ff.

Pixton, Paul B. "Die Anwerbung des Heeres Christi: Prediger des Fünften Kreuzzuges in Deutschland." *Deutsches Archiv* 34 (1978): 166–191.

PAUL B. PIXTON

ORCAGNA, ANDREA DI CIONE (d. 1368)

Andrea di Cione, known as Orcagna, belonged to an extended family of Florentine artists, among whom he and his brother Nardo are best-known to modern scholars. Both artists were also well-known in their own time. Indeed, in a list identifying the six most prominent painters of Florence, compiled in 1349 (near the midpoint of Andrea's career), Andrea and Nardo occupy the third and fourth positions, respectively.

Over the course of his career Orcagna worked as a painter, sculptor, and architect, but he was trained as a painter and identifies himself as such even on the great sculptured tabernacle in Or San Michele (Orsanmichele). Thanks to the efforts of Kreytenberg and others, who have pieced together the extant documents and the known works, we now have a relatively comprehensive picture of Orcagna's career. We know that he matriculated in the Florentine painters' guild (part of the larger Arte dei Medici e Speziali) sometime between 1343 and 1346. We also know that he joined the guild of builders and masons in 1352. Between 1343 and 1360 Orcagna executed paintings and sculptures for many important civic and ecclesiastical sites in Florence, including the city's prison, the city grain market of Or San Michele, and the great mendicant churches of Santa Croce and

Santa Maria Novella. At Santa Maria Novella, he was involved in the decoration of the Cappella Maggiore, one of the most important commissions of the day. Beginning in 1357 Orcagna participated in the ongoing planning of the cathedral of Florence; and in 1358 he was appointed *capomaestro* of the masons' workshop for the cathedral in Orvieto.

Orcagna's presumed early works include the great fresco of the *Triumph of Death, the Last Judgment, and Hell* for the nave of the church of Santa Croce, which was attributed to him following Ghiberti's testimony and is now generally held to have been painted in 1344–1345. Another early work is a frescoed roundel depicting the *Expulsion of the Duke of Athens* (now in the Palazzo Vecchio), painted for the entry hall of Florence's prison, the *carcere delle Stinche*. This fresco, which has been attributed to Orcagna on stylistic grounds, was possibly commissioned as early as 1343–1344, immediately after the expulsion from Florence of the infamous duke of Athens, Walter of Brienne. It is a permanent version of the type of ephemeral defamatory images (*pitture infamate*) commonly commissioned by Italian cities to be painted on the facades of public buildings. In Orcagna's painting, realistic details, including a remarkably accurate portrait of the Palazzo Vecchio as it appeared during the rule of the duke of Athens, are unified in an abstract narrative structure to produce an effect of reality within a timeless image of the triumph of virtue over tyranny.

Until relatively recently, scholars of art history generally associated Orcagna with a retrogressive style of painting that supposedly took hold in Florence after the black death. In fact, Meiss (1951) considered Orcagna's great altarpiece *Christ with Saints Thomas and Peter*, made for the Strozzi Chapel in Santa Maria Novella, an example of this style. Although Meiss's study remains a powerfully persuasive piece of *eckphrasis*, his assessment of Orcagna's style as the repository of a general cultural psychology has been challenged by scholars who have looked less to the history of style and more to the circumstances of individual commissions to explain the formal characteristics of Orcagna's work. In this process, paintings like the Strozzi altarpiece have emerged as highly sophisticated visual structures. In his work for the Strozzi Chapel, Orcagna manipulated space and form to evoke a sacred vision, which appears in the midst of a panoramic view of the *Last Judgment* painted by his brother Nardo on the surrounding walls.

One of Orcagna's most important commissions was the richly decorated marble tabernacle for Or San Michele, designed and executed between 1352 and 1360. The site—on the main street leading from the Duomo to the Palazzo Vecchio—was not only the city's grain market but also a nexus of power. Or San Michele served as the center of devotion for the city's guilds, and Orcagna's tabernacle was commissioned by the Compagnia della Madonna di Orsanmichele to enshrine a miracle-working image of the Madonna that had made the site the center of a popular cult. Actually, the object enshrined in Andrea's tabernacle was a newly painted image commissioned in 1346 by the *compagnia* from Bernardo Daddi. The tabernacle itself is a freestanding marble structure, inlaid with stone and gold glass and covered with relief sculptures, including scenes from the *Life of the Virgin*. The structure is neatly tied, both thematically and visually, to the surrounding loggia, with a crowning figure of Saint Michael (San Michele), rising to nearly touch one of the bosses of the vaulting. As Cassidy (1992) has shown, the tabernacle was also engineered to meet the needs of the cult, with movable screens which normally shrouded the image of the Virgin but which could be raised to reveal the icon on Sundays, feast days, and other significant occasions. It was in connection with this commission that Orcagna, a painter, became a member of the guild of masons and stone workers; and it was presumably through this project, for which he must have assembled a workshop of skilled masons and sculptors, that he established his credentials as an orchestrator of architectural decoration.

See also **Daddi, Bernardo; Nardo di Cione**

Further Reading

Belting, Hans. "Das Bild als Text: Wandmalerei und Literatur im Zeitalter Dantes." In *Malerei und Stadtkultur in der Dantezeit: Die Argumentation der Bilder,* ed. Hans Belting and Dieter Blume. Munich: Hirmer, 1989.

Boskovitz, Miklós. "Orcagna in 1357— and in Other Times." *Burlington Magazine,* 113, 1971, pp. 239–251.

Cassidy, Brendan. "The Assumption of the Virgin on the Tabernacle of Orsanmichele." *Journal of the Warburg and Courtauld Institutes,* 51, 1988a, pp. 174–180.

——. "The Financing of the Tabernacle of Orsanmichele." *Source,* 8, 1988b, pp. 1–6.

——. "Orcagna's Tabernacle in Florence: Design and Function." *Zeitschrift für Kunstgeschichte,* 55, 1992, pp. 180–211.

Cole, Bruce. "Some Thoughts on Orcagna and the Black Death Style." *Antichità Viva,* 22(2), 1983, pp. 27–37.

Giles, Kathleen Alden. "The Strozzi Chapel in Santa Maria Novella: Florentine Paintings and Patronage, 1340–1355." Dissertation, New York University, 1977.

Kreytenberg, Gert. "L'enfer d'Orcagna: La première peinture monumentale d'après les chants de Dante." *Gazette des Beaux Arts,* 6(114), 1989, pp. 243–262.

——. "Bemerkungen zum Fresko der Vertreibung des Duca d'Atene aus Florenz." In *Musagetes: Festschrift für Wolfram Prinz zu seinem 60. Geburtstag am 5. February 1989.* Berlin: Gebr. Mann Verlag, 1991, pp. 151–165.

——. "Image and Frame: Remarks on Orcagna's Pala Strozzi." *Burlington Magazine,* 134, 1992, pp. 634–638.

——. *Orcagna's Tabernacle in Orsanmichele, Florence.* New York: Abrams, 1994.

——. "Orcagnas Fresken im Hauptchor von Santa Maria Novella und deren Fragmente." *Studi di Storia dell'Arte,* 5–6, 1994–1995, pp. 9–40.

Meiss, Millard. *Painting in Florence and Siena after the Black Death.* Princeton, N.J.: Princeton University Press, 1951.

Padoa Rizzo, Anna. "Per Andrea Orcagna pittore." *Annali della Scuola Normale Superiore di Pisa,* Series 3, 11(3), 1981, pp. 835–893.

Paoletti, John T. "The Strozzi Altarpiece Reconsidered." *Memorie Domenicane,* 20, 1989, pp. 279–300.

Rash Fabbri, Nancy, and Nina Rutenberg. "The Tabernacle of Orsanmichele in Context." *Art Bulletin,* 63, 1981, pp. 385–405.

Taylor-Mitchell, Laurie. "Images of Saint Matthew Commissioned by the Arte del Cambio for Orsanmichele in Florence: Some Observations on Conservatism in Form and Patronage." *Gesta,* 31, 1992, pp. 54–72.

C. Jean Campbell

ORESME, NICOLE (ca. 1320/25– 1382) A writer known mainly for his mathematical, scientific, and economic treatises and for his vernacular translations of Aristotle. Educated in arts and theology at the Collège de Navarre in Paris, Oresme was in 1356 appointed its grand master. During this period, his long association with the royal family began; he may have been tutor of John II's son, the future Charles V. Partly because of his royal connections, Oresme obtained church offices, becoming canon at Rouen (1362), canon at the Sainte-Chapelle (1363), dean of the cathedral of Rouen (1364), and bishop of Lisieux (1377).

Oresme's writings demonstrate his wide learning. His mathematical and scientific works, such as *De proportionibus proportionum*, *De configurationibus qualitatum et motuum*, and *De commensurabilitate vel incommensurabilitate motuum celi*, are important for their treatment of fractional exponents, their graphic representation of mathematical functions, and their sophisticated discussions of mechanics and astronomy. Oresme also used his learning, in such treatises as *Contra judiciarios astronomos*, *Livre de divinacions*, and De *causis mirabilium*, to attack the "misuse" of science, especially by the astrologers.

Certain of Oresme's works were written explicitly for the royal family. His economic treatise, *De mutationibus monetarum*, was composed during the 1350s for John II. In the late 1360s, Charles V asked Oresme to translate the Latin versions of four Aristotelian texts, the *Ethics*, the *Politics*, the pseudo-Aristotelian *Economics*, and *De caelo et mundo*. Oresme's vernacular translations helped to create a flexible French prose and to expand the French vocabulary, introducing as many as 1,000 new words.

Oresme has often been seen as anticipating modernity: in certain ways, his astronomy foreshadows Copernicus, Galileo, and Kepler, and his mathematics Descartes; his economics may anticipate Gresham's Law. But Oresme is perhaps most impressive in his ability to summarize and synthesize logically and intelligently, all the while advancing the important theories of his age.

See also **Charles V the Wise**

Further Reading

Oresme, Nicole. De *proportionibus proportionum and Ad pauca respicientes*, ed. and trans. Edward Grant. Madison: University of Wisconsin Press, 1966.
——. *Le livre de politiques d'Aristote*, ed. Albert Douglas Menut. Philadelphia: American Philosophical Society, 1970.
——. *Nicole Oresme and the Medieval Geometry of Qualities and Motions: A Treatise on the Uniformity and Difformity of Intensities Known as Tractatus de configurationibus qualitatum et motuum*, ed. and trans. Marshall Clagett. Madison: University of Wisconsin Press, 1968.
Hansen, Bert, ed. and trans. *Nicole Oresme and the Marvels of Nature: A Study of His De causis mirabilium with Critical Edition, Translation, and Commentary*. Toronto: Pontifical Institute of Mediaeval Studies, 1985.
Menut, Albert Douglas. "A Provisional Bibliography of Oresme's Writings." *Mediaeval Studies* 28 (1966): 279–99; supplementary note, 31 (1969): 346–47.

STEVEN F. KRUGER

OSWALD VON WOLKENSTEIN (1376 or 1377–1445) No other medieval German poet is better known to us today than the South Tyrolean Oswald von Wolkenstein. Apart from amazingly concrete autobiographical references contained in his large oeuvre of 133 songs, the poet also left a vast number of historical traces in more than one thousand still extant documents. Even though the poetic statements about his own life have often to be taken as tongue-in-cheek and as topical in nature, recent research by Anton Schwob and others who have studied the archival material has confirmed most of Oswald's claims in his songs regarding his personal experiences. Born as the second son of an aristocratic South Tyrolean family, Oswald had to struggle for many years to establish his own existence both on the local and the international level. In 1401 he participated in a military campaign in Italy of the German King Ruprecht of the Palatinate; in 1410 he went on a pilgrimage to the Holy Land; between 1413 and 1415 he served Bishop Ulrich of Brixen and subsequently joined the diplomatic service of King Sigis-mund, with whom he traveled through western Europe. In

1417 Oswald married Margaretha von Schwangau and thus gained the rank of an imperial knight. In 1420–1421 he participated in one of the several wars against the always victorious Hussites, but in one of his songs ("Kl[ein]. [no.] 27") Oswald ridiculed the opponents. In the following years the poet was involved in many struggles and military conflicts with his neighbors, both peasants and aristocrats, and so also with the duke of Tyrol, Frederick IV of Habsburg. A major bone of contention was the castle Hauenstein in Seis am Schlern, to which Oswald had only a partial claim but which he took in his total possession after his marriage. At one point he even ended up in the ducal prison (1421–1422) and had to pay a huge ransom to be released. Although Oswald's power position improved over the next years to some degree, he was imprisoned again in 1427 and then had finally to submit under the centralized government of Duke Frederick. In 1429 Oswald joined the secret but highly influential court of justice, Feme, which was active all over Germany, and he also managed to consolidate his power base back home through manifold political connections and public services. In recognition of his accomplishments as diplomat and imperial servant, Oswald was inducted into the Order of the Dragon in 1431. In 1432 King Sigismund, while he stayed in northern Italy, called him into his service again and soon after sent him as one of his representatives to the Council of Basel. In 1433 Oswald probably witnessed the coronation of Sigismund as emperor at the hand of Pope Eugene IV in Rome. In 1434 Oswald participated in the imperial diet of Ulm, where Sigismund commissioned him to collect fines and taxes in South Tyrol and also confirmed his rank as imperial knight. After the death of Duke Frederick, Oswald and his allies successfully organized opposition against the Habsburgians in South Tyrol, as they could influence and dominate the young successor, Duke Sigmund, at that

time still under age, for several years. Ultimately, however, the landed gentry, and so the Wolkenstein family, increasingly lost ground and had to submit to the centralized government, the growing weight of the urban class, and even the economic power of the peasants.

Whereas Oswald's political career sheds significant light on the political and economic history of the early fifteenth century, his poetic production has earned him greatest respect among modern philologists and musicologists since the full rediscovery of this amazing literary personality as of the early 1960s. In contrast to most other medieval poets Oswald created his songs for personal reasons and commissioned his first personal collection of his works in 1425, manuscript A, to which he added songs until 1436, perhaps even 1441. In 1432 the second collection was completed, manuscript "B," in which Oswald also incorporated a stunning portrait of himself created by the Italian Renaissance painter Antonio Pisanello or one of his disciples while the poet was staying in Piacenza, Italy, in the entourage of King Sigismund. Both manuscripts were most likely produced in Neustift, near Brixen, and contain melodies for many of the songs. In 1450 Oswald's family had another copy of his songs made in a paper manuscript ("c"—by convention, paper manuscripts are listed by lowercase, parchment by uppercase letters), which is almost identical with manuscript "B" but lacks the notations.

Although twenty of Oswald's more traditional songs were also copied in a number of other song collections all over Germany throughout the fifteenth and sixteenth centuries (the last one in 1572), the poet was soon forgotten after his death, probably because his most important songs were too autobiographical and idiosyncratic, and also too innovative for his time. Some of the texts contain surprisingly erotic elements and seem to reflect Oswald's private experiences with his wife. His prison songs and his dawn songs are unique for his time, and so the various polyglot songs in which he combined a string of languages to present his own linguistic mastership. On the one hand Oswald demonstrated a thorough familiarity with conventional German courtly love song, or *Minnesang*; on the other he introduced melodies and poetic images from French, Flemish, and Italian contemporaries. Many of Oswald's songs are polyphonic and reflect an amazing variety of musical forms, such as the *caccia* (hunt, Kl. 52), or the *lauda* (praise, Kl. 109).

Hardly any other poet before him had such an excellent command of the broadest range of lyrical genres, as his oeuvre contains marriage songs, spring songs, prison songs, war songs, autobiographical songs, travel songs, dawn songs, Marian hymns, calendar songs, Shrovetide songs, songs about city life, songs in which he criticized both the rich merchants and the arrogant courtiers, various religious songs, and repentance songs.

Oswald was also a master of onomatopoetic expressions, such as in his Kl. 50, where the arrival of spring is vividly conveyed through the imitation of birdsongs. He seems to have learned much both from the Middle High German Neidhart tradition and from the Middle Latin tradition of boisterous and vivacious love songs as in the *Carmina Burana*. In addition, the Italian trecento (thirteenth-century) poets Cecco Angiolieri, Giannozzo, and Franco Sacchetti might have provided Oswald with important poetic models, but in his many old-age songs we also discover possible influences from the French poet Charles d'Orléans. Moreover, some scholars have suggested François Villon as a possible source for Oswald's autobiographical songs. Considering Oswald's extensive travels throughout western and southern Europe, Spanish and Flemish poetry also might have had a considerable impact on his work, as he adapted his models by way of *contrafacture* (use of secular melody in religious song). Recently we have also learned that contemporary folk poetry, proverbs, and perhaps specific legal formulas can be discerned in Oswald's language. Even narrative epics such as the Old Spanish *El Cid* and the Italian *Decamerone* by Boccaccio might have influenced him in his compositions. Finally, the poet also translated several Latin sequences that were usually performed during the liturgy.

Oswald's poetic genius transformed all these sources and models into highly individual poetic expressions. We will probably never reach a full understanding of which elements the poet borrowed from his predecessors and contemporaries, but we know for sure that Oswald had an extremely open mind for novel ideas and thoroughly enjoyed experimenting with a wide variety of poetic genres, styles, and images. He was one of the first medieval German poets to correlate closely text and melody and also created astoundingly polyphonic effects typical of *Ars nova* and the Italian trecento culture. Curiously, though, Oswald does not seem to have been in contact with humanists and Renaissance writers, even though he once refers to Petrarch (Kl. 10, 28), whose concept of man's sinfulness seems to have influenced Oswald's religious thinking. In this regard the poet is quite representative of his own time, as he still lived in the medieval tradition and yet also opened his mind to many new approaches to music (*Ars nova*) and poetry.

Oswald's oeuvre can be located at the crossroads between the late Middle Ages and the Renaissance, as the poet belonged to neither cultural period yet shared elements with both. His songs already reflect a strong sense of the modern individual with the emphasis on personal experiences, ideas, needs, and desires, but they are, at the same time, deeply drenched in the medieval concept of human sinfulness and of life as nothing but a transitional period here on earth.

See also **Charles d'Orléans; Neidhart**

Further Reading

Classen, Albrecht. "Oswald von Wolkenstein," in *German Writers of the Renaissance and Reformation 1280–1580*, ed. James Hardin and Max Reinhart. Detroit: Gale, 1997, pp. 198–205.

Die Lieder Oswalds von Wolkenstein, ed. Karl Kurt Klein et al., 3d. ed. Tübingen: Niemeyer, 1987.

Jahrbuch der Oswald von Wolkenstein Gesellschaft, 1ff. (1980/1981ff.).

Joschko, Dirk. *Oswald von Wolkenstein. Eine Monographie zu Person, Werk und Forschungsgeschichte.* Göppingen: Kümmerle, 1985.

Oswald von Wolkenstein. *Sämtliche Lieder und Gedichte*, trans. Wernfried Hofmeister. Göppingen: Kümmerle, 1989 [modern German trans.].

Schwob, Anton. *Oswald von Wolkenstein. Eine Biographie*, 3d ed. Bozen: Athesia, 1979.

——. *Die Lebenszeugnisse Oswalds von Wolkenstein. Edition und Kommentar. Bd. 1, 1382–1419, Nr. 1–92.* Vienna: Böhlau, 1999.

Spicker, Johannes. *Literarische Stilisierung und artistische Kompetenz bei Oswald von Wolkenstein.* Stuttgart: Hirzel, 1993.

ALBRECHT CLASSEN

OTFRID (ca. 800–ca. 875)   A monk of the abbey of Weißenburg (now Wissembourg in Alsace), Otfrid is the author of a remarkable poem based on the four gospels, completed by about 870 and preserved in four manuscripts, three of them complete or nearly so. The famous Vienna manuscript was carefully corrected, and perhaps written in part, by Otfrid himself.

Otfrid composed the poem in a new, stress-based strophic verse form with two long lines per strophe. Each long line contains two half lines joined by rhyme or at least assonance at the caesura (audible break at the middle of a line). Thus the Lord's Prayer begins:

Fáter unser gúato, bist drúhtin thu gim‡ato
in hímilon io hóher, uuíh si námo thiner.

Biquéme uns thinaz ríchi, thaz hoha hímilrichi,
thára uuir zua io gíngen ioh émmizigen thíngen.

Our Father good, thou art a kindly king
so high in the heavens, holy be thy name.
Thy kingdom come to us, the high kingdom
  of heaven,
toward which may we always strive and
  firmly
believe. (2,22,27-30)

All four manuscripts show the caesura and use initials, indentation, and rhythmic accents to explicate and show off the new verse form. Otfrid describes the meter and his spelling innovations in a letter to archbishop Liutbert of Mainz (included in two manuscripts), where his pride of invention is everywhere apparent. Suggestions that Otfrid merely modified an existing German verse form are therefore unlikely. Neither did Otfrid slavishly imitate Latin hymnody of the period: though some contemporary Latin hymns also show assonance, rhyme, and/or alternating stress, the overall effect of his poem is quite different. Otfrid's verse form was quickly used in several other Old High German and early Middle High German poems and seems the likely basis for the couplets of the Middle High German courtly epics.

Otfrid portrays the life of Christ as described in the four gospels, but his work is not merely a verse translation. After many narrative sections, he includes passages for reflection, labeling them *mystice*, or in a mystical sense. As in Germanic alliterative verse, Otfrid constantly repeats and restates ideas and phrases, often for the sake of the rhyme or the rhythm. His writing seems prolix; in the passage above, he uses thirty words where the alliterating Old Saxon Heliand has twenty-one and the prose Weißenburg Catechism only thirteen.

Otfrid's attention to meter and orthography suggests that the poem was meant to be read aloud or even chanted (one manuscript has some neums, an early form of musical notation), but it could have had no place in the Latin liturgy of the time.

The dialect of the poem is Southern Rhenish Franconian, though in part because of Otfrid's orthographic innovations, it differs slightly from that of other Weißenburg documents.

Further Reading

Haubrichs, Wolfgang. "Otfrid von Weißenburg: Übersetzer, Erzähler, Interpret. . . ." in *Übersetzer im Mittelalter*, ed. Joachim Heinzle et al. Wolfram-Studien 14. Berlin: Schmidt, 1996, pp. 13–45.

Kleiber, Wolfgang. *Otfrid von Weißenburg: Untersuchungen zur handschriftlichen Überlieferung und Studien zum Aufbau des Evangelienbuches*. Bern: Francke, 1971.

Murdoch, Brian O. *Old High German Literature*. Boston: Twayne, 1983.

Patzlaff, Rainer. *Otfrid von Weißenburg und die mittelalterliche versus-Tradition*. Tübingen: Niemeyer, 1975.

Schweikle, Gunther. "Die Herkunft des althochdeutschen Reimes: Zu Otfried von Weißenburgs formgeschichtlicher Stellung." *Zeitschrift für deutsches Altertum und deutsche Literatur* 96 (1967): 166–212.

LEO A. CONNOLLY

OTTO I (912–973) King of Germany 936–973 and emperor 962–973, Otto (the Great) was a member of the Liudolfing, or Saxon, dynasty, born in 912 to the future Henry I and his wife, Mathilda. Little is known of his early years. In 930 Otto married Edith, the half sister of King Aethelstan of Wessex, beginning a policy of marriage to foreign princesses that became the norm in Germany. He was almost certainly designated at that time as the next king. After his father's death, Otto was acclaimed by the nobles and crowned in Aachen on August 7, 936, reviving the coronation ritual that Henry I had foregone. This is the first sign of

Otto's new view of kingship, marked by a policy of systematically increasing the gap between king and dukes and rejecting the rule by personal pacts that had characterized his father's reign. Perhaps this attitude helped provoke the civil wars of 937–941, as nobles took advantage of an unestablished king to settle old feuds and reduce royal rights. The two most important rebels were Otto's elder half brother Thankmar (who deeply resented that Henry I had declared his first marriage to Thankmar's mother invalid) and his younger brother Henry, who was supported by their mother, Mathilda. This has been hailed as resistance against a new Ottonian principle that the realm could not be divided as it had been by Merovingians and Carolingians; the truth was that Henry I had not had enough control of the kingdom to make a division possible, although he did divide his personal lands and treasure among his sons. The period of rebellion concluded with Thankmar's death and the submission of the other important rebels. Henry was forgiven and, in 947, given the duchy of Bavaria.

Otto continued his father's vigorous eastern and northern policy. Margraves Hermann Billung and Gero, acting with Otto's support, won a series of victories against the Slavs, gaining territory that Otto strove to pacify with an active policy that included both the establishment of fortified garrison outposts and active royal activity in missionary enterprises. The latter included the erection of several bishoprics—Brandenburg and Havelberg in 948; Oldenburg, Merseburg, Meissen, and Zeitz later in 968—at which time Otto's beloved monastic foundation of Magdeburg was also elevated to an archbishopric with authority over much of the eastern frontier. The success of the Ottonian eastern policy culminated in a series of victories in 955. On August 10 of that year, Otto decisively defeated a Magyar coalition at the battle of Lechfeld near Augsburg, an event that marked the end of Magyar raiding in Germany. This was followed by a victory over the Slavs at Recknitz on October 16th. Further campaigns led to the subjection of the Slavs between the middle Elbe and the middle Oder by 960, as well as making Bohemia and Poland tributary to the German king.

From an early period Otto had imperial ambitions. He took advantage of the disorders caused by Bangor's seizure of power in Lombardy to establish a foothold in Italy in 951. Otto accepted Bangor's submission and reinstated him as subking. To strengthen his personal control of Lombardy, though, the widower Otto married Adelheid, the widowed queen of the Lombards. At that time, Otto requested that the pope crown him as emperor, but the pope refused, probably from fear of a strong German presence in Italy. Otto had to cut short his time in Italy, returning to Germany to deal with the revolt of his eldest son, Liudulf, who apparently felt threatened by Otto's new marriage alliance. In 961, though, Pope John XII appealed for Otto's help against his enemies. Otto responded swiftly with a second expedition to Italy. He prepared for a long campaign, taking the precaution of having the six-year-old Otto II, his eldest son by Adelheid, elected and crowned as king, and establishing a regency in Germany. The pope's enemies fled before Otto's army, and John XII crowned Otto I as emperor on February 2, 962, reviving the imperial title that had fallen in abeyance early in the century, and creating a link to the prestige of Charlemagne.

The imperial coronation led to a major shift in Otto's interests, leading him to spend ten of the last twelve years of his life in Italy. John XII soon realized that Otto was exerting much more direct domination over Italian affairs than he had bargained for. The pope therefore took part in a conspiracy aimed at ending Ottonian involvement in Italy, which led Otto to drive John from Rome and arrange his deposition. Otto then set up a new pope

of his own choice, initiating almost a century of German control of the papacy. Imperial interests also led to campaigns in southern Italy from 966 on, especially with the goal of gaining Byzantine recognition of Otto's imperial title.

Otto I was an even more peripatetic ruler than most of his contemporaries, ruling largely through verbal orders during constant travels throughout his realm. He received little formal education, learning to read only in 946, while mourning for his first wife, Edith. Despite this, Otto established a particularly strong and secure kingdom, thanks especially to his military successes, the wealth acquired through exploitation of the newly found silver mines at Goslar, and his alliance with the church, particularly with German monasteries. Beginning in the 940s, Otto gradually replaced the dukes of Germany with members of the Ottonian family, who on the whole proved to be loyal supporters of the throne. His personal prestige and close kinship to the top families in western Europe allowed Otto to act as mediator in Burgundy and in France between the last Carolingians and the rising Capetian (French kings, tenth to fourteenth century) family. By the time of Otto's death at Memleben on May 7, 973, his German-based empire was the strongest state in Europe, a position it held for the next century. He is buried in the church he founded at Magdeburg, beside his wife, Edith.

See also **Charlemagne; Henry I of Saxony; Otto II**

Further Reading

Althoff, Gerd, and Hagen Keller. *Heinrich I. und Otto der Große: Neubeginn und karolingisches Erbe.* Göttingen: Muster-Schmidt, 1985.

Leyser, Karl. *Communications and Power in Medieval Europe: The Carolingian and Ottonian Centuries*, ed. Timothy Reuter. London: Hambledon Press, 1994.

Reuter, Timothy. *Germany in the Early Middle Ages, 800–1056*. London: Longman, 1991.

PHYLLIS G. JESTICE

OTTO II (955–983) King 961–983, emperor 967–983, sole ruler of the German Empire from 973, Otto II was born in 955 to Otto I and his second wife, Adelheid. His father arranged for the six-year-old Otto's election and coronation as king of the Germans in May 961, before setting out on his second Italian expedition. To secure the imperial title to his dynasty, the elder Otto further arranged to have his son crowned co-emperor on Christmas Day 967; Otto II was the last western emperor to receive imperial coronation in his father's lifetime. Despite these honors, the future Otto II was not given an independent position even after he came of age, and has left only twenty-seven extant documents from the twelve years of his official shared rule with Otto I. At his father's death in 973, the eighteen-year-old Otto was accepted as ruler without opposition.

The early years of Otto II's reign were occupied by a series of rebellions in Bavaria and Lotharingia. These rebellions were provoked by an attempt Otto made in 974 to reduce the power of his overly mighty cousin, Henry II "the Quarrelsome" (the nickname is not contemporary), duke of the semiautonomous duchy of Bavaria. Henry's defeat in 976 gave Otto the opportunity to reorganize the southern duchies, weakening Bavaria by turning its province of Carinthia into a separate duchy. Henry, unsatisfied with his position, led a second uprising in 976–977, and Bavaria was pacified only with Henry's imprisonment in 978.

Otto II's early military campaigns were successful, as Otto continued the strong eastern and northern policies of his father and grandfather. A victory over the Danes in 974 led to an expansion of German efforts to evangelize in the north. He also

Emperor Otto receives the homage of the nations. Gospels of Emperor Otto (II or III), also called "Registrum Gregorii." Ottoian art, 10th. © Erich Lessing/Art Resource, New York.

invaded Bohemia several times, returning it to its earlier tributary status after its ruler had seceded by joining with Henry the Quarrelsome in the rebellions of 974–977. On the western front, though, Otto was unable to play as strong a role as his father had. An effort of the French King Lothar to gain control of Lotharingia in 978 caught Otto by surprise, forcing him to flee Aachen before the French army. Otto quickly retaliated with a raid that penetrated France to the gates of Paris, but that accomplished little besides salving Otto's pride.

In 972, Otto II had married the Byzantine princess Theophanu, a marriage arranged by his father to enhance the prestige of the Ottonian dynasty. Contemporary sources suggest that Theophanu exerted a very strong influence on Otto, including the belief that the empress's "childish advice" led to Otto's disastrous campaign in southern Italy in 982. In reality, the southern campaign needs little explanation. Otto decided in 981 on the conquest of southern Italy, split at that time among Saracens, Greeks, and Lombards. He probably planned the campaign as an extension of imperial policies begun by Otto I, who had conducted several inconclusive campaigns in the region. Otto II's army was, however, decisively defeated by a Saracen force at the battle of Cotrone (Cap Colonne) on July 13, 982. Almost the entire German army was destroyed; Otto himself escaped only by swimming his horse out to a Greek ship in the bay, then disguising his identity until he reached safety. The Saracen army was too badly weakened to press its advantage, so the battle had little effect on the balance of power in Italy. This defeat, though, dealt a severe blow to Otto's prestige. The Slavs responded to news of the German defeat with an uprising in the summer of 983. A Slavic confederation devastated the German border, destroyed the bishoprics of Havelberg and Brandenburg, and burned Hamburg, reversing most of Otto I's successes in Slavic territory. Perhaps the seriousness of the political situation can be seen in the feet that Otto II summoned an imperial diet at Verona on May 27, 983, where he had his three-year-old son Otto III elected to the German kingship, then sent the child on to Aachen to be crowned. Otto II remained in Italy, trying to subject Venice to imperial control. He died of malaria in Rome on December 7, 983, at the age of twenty-eight, and is the only emperor to be buried in St. Peter's Basilica.

Otto II appears to have been dominated and overshadowed throughout his life by people of stronger character, first his father, then his wife Theophanu, and also by his counselors, especially the loyal and talented Archbishop Willigis of Mainz. Physically Otto was not as impressive as his father; the exhumation of his body in 1609 revealed that he was a small man, and eleventh-century sources describe him as a redhead. Certainly his reputation has suffered by comparison to his great father and

exotic son. In general, his reign is best seen as one of consolidation and growing sophistication. Unlike his predecessors, Otto II was well educated. His love of luxury and ostentation was notorious, although this perhaps should be taken more as a sign of the enormous wealth the Ottonians were able to command than of character weakness. His reign saw advances in the imperial chancery and greater cooperation between the German and Italian parts of the empire. It also saw a closer identification with the ancient Roman Empire and the city of Rome, setting aside the Byzantine emperor's claim to be the only true successor of the caesars. Otto's chancery in 982 adopted for the first time the title Roman empire (*imperator Romanorum augustus*) as the designation of a German emperor, a title that became standard to Otto's successors. Despite his reverses in Italy and on the Slavic frontier, Otto left a firmly established realm, increasingly self-assured and international, to his son.

See also **Otto I, Otto III**

Further Reading

Beumann, Helmut. *Die Ottonen.* Stuttgart: Kohlhammer, 1987.
Reuter, Timothy. *Germany in the Early Middle Ages, 800–1056.* London: Longman, 1991.

PHYLLIS G. JESTICE

OTTO III (980–1002) King of the Germans, 983–1002, emperor 996–1002, Otto III was the most flamboyant and controversial of the German emperors. He was born in 980, the only son of Emperor Otto II and the Byzantine princess Theophanu. Otto II continued his own father's policy of assuring Ottonian rule by having the young Otto elected king at Verona, May 27, 983. He then dispatched the three-year-old Otto to Aachen for coronation on Christmas 983. This was several weeks after Otto

II's death in Italy but before the news had reached the north.

A series of informal regents governed the empire for most of Otto's short life. By German custom, the young king's proper guardian was his closest adult male relative, Duke Henry II the Quarrelsome of Bavaria. Henry, though, soon tried to supplant his charge, claiming the kingship in his own name. Archbishop Willigis of Mainz, though, threw his support behind Otto III, summoning the young king's mother, Theophanu, and grandmother Adelheid from Italy to help him preserve Otto's rights. After a period of intense political maneuvering, Henry surrendered Otto to the two empresses on June 29, 984. Theophanu assumed the regency for her son. After her death in 991, Adelheid directed affairs until Otto III formally came of age in September 994.

Otto's role during his childhood was strictly symbolic. In 986 he was sent on a campaign against the Slavs—not to fight but so Mieszko of Poland could join the host and do homage. For the most part, though, Otto was not very visible in German affairs until he came of age. He was very well educated. His main tutor was Bernward, the future bishop of Hildesheim, but he also received instruction in Greek from his mother's friend John Philagathos, a southern Italian. After coming of age, Otto continued his education with the most learned man of the age, Gerbert of Aurillac.

Rome during Otto's minority had fallen into the hands of the local noble Crescentius II. Pope John XV asked for Otto's help in 995, leading to Otto's first Italian expedition. John died before his arrival, so Otto forced the Roman Church to accept his own cousin Bruno of Carinthia as pope, who took the name Gregory V. Gregory then crowned Otto as emperor on May 21, 996. The imposition of a German pope shows Otto's early determination to control Rome. This marked a new departure, since Gregory was the first non-Roman pope since the Byzantine

emperors had appointed Greeks to the office in the seventh century. Gregory was soon driven from the city, forcing Otto to return and reinstate him in 998. This time Otto secured Rome by having Crescentius executed, and had Crescentius's antipope (none other than Otto's former tutor, John Philagathos) blinded and imprisoned. Afterward, Otto stayed in Rome, having decided to make the city the capital of his empire. He had a palace built for himself on the Aventine. This has been taken as evidence of Otto III's grandiose plan to create a new Roman empire. Certainly Otto greatly developed the idea of a western empire, but it was not inextricably linked to Rome. At first he wanted to set up Aachen as a "new Rome," placing the focus of the empire in the north. It is probable that political instability in Italy made Otto decide to stay closer, where he could intervene effectively in affairs. Naturally enough, this made him very unpopular with the Romans, who revolted in early 1001, besieging Otto for a time in his own palace. Otto sent for more troops and was preparing an attack on Rome at the time of his death.

The earlier Ottonians had ruled almost entirely by means of continual travel throughout their realm. The decision to reside in a permanent capital thus marked another new departure. It forced Otto to develop a larger bureaucracy and enabled him to acquire a larger and more glittering court. For a time Otto's aunt, Abbess Mathilda of Quedlinburg, acted as regent in Germany, but after her death the emperor relied ever more on bishops to perform the work of government, laying the groundwork for the "imperial Church system" of the late Ottonians and Salians. In Rome itself, Otto created a hierarchy of court officials, elaborate by German standards, most of whom had Greek titles in emulation of the Byzantine court. Otto also insisted on a higher degree of ceremony than had been known to earlier German rulers, modeled on Byzantine practice.

Otto clearly saw his role as emperor in terms of leadership over the Christian world, assuming the titles "servant of Jesus Christ," and "servant of the apostles." This strong development of the imperial idea was already visible in 996 with Otto's appointment of the first German pope; after Gregory V's death in 999, the emperor continued his effort to control the papacy by appointing his former tutor Gerbert of Aurillac, who took the name Sylvester II. The two cooperated closely, even declaring the Donation of Constantine to be invalid, Otto appears to have been personally pious; he was close to both St. Nilus and St. Romuald of Ravenna; Bruno of Querfurt claims that the emperor even swore an oath to abdicate and retire to the wilds of Poland as a hermit. While this is unlikely, Otto did take very seriously his duty toward the church. In 1000 he made a pilgrimage to the tomb of the martyred Bishop Adalbert of Prague in Gniezno, arranging at that time for Gniezno to become the archbishopric of Poland. He went on from there to Aachen, where he had Charlemagne's grave opened, taking the pectoral cross from the body. Certainly this was in part the effort of an upstart Ottonian to associate himself with the prestige of the Carolingian dynasty. It is very likely that the tomb opening was also the first step in a project to canonize Charlemagne, perhaps the best example of Otto III's belief in the divine nature of the empire (*imperium*). He also planned to continue the family alliance with the Byzantine emperors, arranging to marry the porphyrogenita (female successor) Theodora, but she arrived in Italy only at about the time of Otto's death.

Otto III's history, though, is one of largely unrealized potential. He died unexpectedly on January 24, 1002, at the age of twenty-one.

See also **Charlemagne; Otto II; Romuald of Ravenna, Saint**

Further Reading

Althoff, Gerd. *Otto III*. Darmstadt: Wissenschaftliche Buchgesellschaft, 1996.

Beumann, Helmut. *Die Ottonen*. Stuttgart: Kohlhammer, 1987.

Leyser, Karl J. *Medieval Germany and Its Neighbours 900–1250*. London: Hambledon, 1982.

PHYLLIS G. JESTICE

OTTO IV (1175/1182–May 19, 1218) Emperor and sometime ally of Pope Innocent III (1198–1216), Otto's reign was a time of chaos after the premature death of Henry VI. Leader of the Welf house and son of Henry the Lion, Otto was involved in a civil war for control of the empire with candidates of the rival Hohenstaufen house, Philip of Swabia and Frederick II. The struggle for control of the imperial crown had international implications and involved the princes of Germany, the kings of England and France, and the pope. Otto would ultimately lose the struggle to maintain control of the empire to Frederick.

The unexpected death of Henry in 1197 left the empire in a difficult situation because his heir, Frederick, was only three years old. It also offered the papacy the opportunity to break free from encirclement by the Hohenstaufen, an opportunity Innocent would exploit by playing one side against the other in the civil strife in Germany or by acting as referee between them. The situation was complicated by shifting alliances both inside and outside the empire. Frederick was first supported by the Staufen, including his uncle, Philip of Swabia. But Philip, motivated by the activities of forces opposed to his family, presented himself as king and was crowned at Mainz in September 1198. He also revived the alliance between his family and the Capetian dynasty, headed by Philip Augustus, to improve his position in Germany and Europe. The anti-Staufen forces inside Germany, supported by King

Richard I of England, did not stand idly by but promoted a Welf candidate. The eldest son of Henry the Lion was still on crusade, and therefore the younger son, Otto, became the anti-Staufen candidate.

Otto, who had been raised at the court of his uncle, Richard I, and had been made count of Poitou and duke of Aquitaine in 1190 and 1196, respectively, made the most of his opportunity. He was crowned before Philip by the proper ecclesiastic, the archbishop of Cologne, and in the right place, Aachen. His election also carried great weight because he was elected by those traditionally empowered to choose the king. Indeed, the nature of his election was of great importance to Innocent, who would involve himself in the succession crisis because of the close ties of empire and papacy and because of papal claims to superior jurisdiction. Innocent, suspicious of the Hohenstaufen family and fearful of their territorial gains in northern and southern Italy, came to support Otto. This was critical to the king's success because his situation in Germany was weak despite having been elected by the right people and crowned in the right place, and because his greatest international ally, Richard, died in early 1199. To maintain papal support, Otto made important territorial concessions to the pope in Italy.

Otto's difficulties did not end, however, even though he had papal support, which was reinforced by Otto's concessions. Despite his excommunication, Philip managed to increase his power in Germany in the opening decade of the thirteenth century. He managed to increase support among the bishops of the empire, including the very important archbishop of Cologne, Adolf. Perhaps motivated by hostility to Rome, many princes also came to support Philip. By 1207 the papal curia had come to support Philip's claim to the imperial dignity and kingship in Germany, and in the following year the pope himself recognized Philip as king. Negotiations over territory

in Italy and the imperial coronation were held between Philip and the pope, but they made little headway before Philip was murdered by Otto of Wittelsbach over Philip's broken engagement to Otto's daughter.

In 1208, fortunes once again turned for Otto, and he now received widespread support in Germany. He was elected king by the German princes a second time in November in Frankfurt and was victorious over French attempts to establish a rival king. To further strengthen his position in Germany, Otto was betrothed to Philip's daughter Beatrix. He was then crowned emperor by Innocent in Rome in October 1209, after renewing his promises to respect papal territory in Italy and also to refrain from intervening in Sicilian affairs.

Otto's success, however, seems to have gotten the better of him and, following the advice of his ministerials, he decided to extend his authority in Italy. He sought to expand his rights into papal lands, and thus alienated an important ally and created a dangerous opponent, Innocent. He further raised the ire of the pope by occupying Tuscany and invading the Hohenstaufen kingdom of Sicily. His invasion and conquest of Sicily in November 1210 led to the very encirclement by a German ruler that Innocent had struggled to prevent. Otto's actions also led Innocent to excommunicate the emperor in the autumn of 1210, and in the spring of 1211 Innocent released Otto's vassals from their oaths to the emperor.

Otto's difficulties were not limited to the opposition from the pope. To secure his position in Germany, Otto married Beatrix in 1212, but she died shortly after their marriage. He faced revolts in northern Italy, where opposition to German domination had existed for more than a generation, and in Germany, where the nobility had been released from their obligation of loyalty by the pope. He faced a rival king because Frederick followed him to Germany, where the princely opposition to Otto, with papal support, crowned

Frederick king at Mainz. Frederick was able to gain a solid foothold in southern Germany, thus undermining Otto's authority and blocking his access to Italy. And both Frederick and Otto benefited from their alliances with the kings of France and England.

Otto's alliance with King John, however, would prove his undoing. Fearing that Philip Augustus would take English territory in France, John invaded with his nephew and ally Otto, who hoped to weaken French support for his Hohenstaufen rival. First John was defeated on the Loire and then, on July 27, 1214, Otto was disastrously defeated at the Battle of Bouvines. His supporters melted away after the defeat, and Frederick went on the offensive in the empire, imposing himself on Otto's remaining allies. Otto was formally deposed the following July and was confined to his personal lands in Brunswick until his death on May 19, 1218.

See also Frederick II; Henry the Lion; Innocent III, Pope

Further Reading

Abulafia, David. *Frederick II: A Medieval Emperor*. Oxford: Oxford University Press, 1988.

Duby, Georges. *The Legend of Bouvines: War, Religion and Culture in the Middle Ages*, trans. Catherine Tihanyi. Berkeley: University of California Press, 1990.

Haverkamp, Alfred. *Medieval Germany, 1056–1273*. 2d ed., trans. Helga Braun and Richard Mortimer. Oxford: Oxford University Press, 1992.

MICHAEL FRASSETTO

OTTO OF FREISING (ca. 1112–1158) The most important historian of the twelfth century, Otto of Freising was well placed to write his works of history. He was born into the most prominent families in the empire and was related to the imperial Salian and Staufen lines. His father was Leopold III of Austria and his mother was Agnes, daughter of Henry IV and whose first husband was Frederick I, duke of Swabia. Otto was thus half brother of Conrad III and uncle of Frederick I Barbarossa. His ecclesiastical career began while he was still a child, when he became provost of the house of canons at Klosterneuburg (near Vienna). In 1127 or 1128, Otto journeyed to France to study with the great masters at Paris, including Hugo of St. Victor, Gilbert de la Porrée, and, probably, Peter Abelard. He left Paris in 1133 and on his way home joined the Cistercian abbey at Morimond. He was later elected bishop of Freising, before the canonical age and as the result of family influence. He participated in the Second Crusade (1147—1148) and, while en route to a Cistercian general chapter, died in Morimond in 1158.

Otto is best known for two historical works, *The Two Cities* and *The Deeds of Frederick Barbarossa*. The first of the two, is the more pessimistic but also the more philosophical work. Written between 1143 and 1146, *The Two Cities* is a world chronicle that tells the tale of salvation history that was heavily influenced by the work of St. Augustine. The first seven books outline the history of the world from creation to 1146. Otto's history describes the struggles of good and evil and praises the monks, the true representatives of the City of God on earth. *The Two Cities* also is a history of the *translatio imperii*, describing the transfer of universal power from the Greeks to the Romans to the Franks and ultimately to the Germans. It was in the Christian empire of the Germans that Otto saw the possibility of the existence of the City of God on earth, but the troubled times facing the empire from the time of Henry IV to Conrad III left him with little hope. The eighth, and final, book of *The Two Cities* is thoroughly eschatological and describes the coming of Antichrist, the Final judgment, and establishment of the heavenly Jerusalem. Otto's somber perspective is not continued, however, in his other great work, *The Deeds of Frederick Barbarossa*. Completing the first two books before his death in 1158, Otto followed the plan outlined in a letter requested by Otto from his sponsor, Barbarossa himself. The first book details the events of the tumultuous reigns of Barbarossa's predecessors, and the second describes the first four years of the reign of Barbarossa, a time of peace and glory for the empire. Although *Deeds* overlooks matters unfavorable to the Staufen line, misrepresents the state of the realm at Barbarossa's ascension, and overstates his successes in Italy, it remains the most important source for events in the early years of Barabarossa's reign.

See also **Frederick I Barbarossa; Henry IV Emperor**

Further Reading

Otto of Freising. *Chronica sive Historia de Duabus Civitatibus*, ed. A. Hofmeister. Monumenta Germaniae Historica Scriptores Rerum Germanicarum 40. Hannover: Hahn, 1912.

Otto of Freising and Rahewin. *Gesta Friderici Imperatoris*, ed. G. Waitz. Monumenta Germaniae Historica Scriptores Rerum Germanicarum 46. Hannover: Hahn, 1912.

Otto of Freising. *The Two Cities, by Otto, Bishop of Freising*, trans. Charles Christopher Mierow. New York: Columbia University Press, 1928.

Otto of Freising and his continuator, Rahewin. *The Deeds of Frederick Barbarossa*, trans. Charles Christopher Mierow with Richard Emery, 1953; rpt. Toronto: University of Toronto Press, 1994.

MICHAEL FRASSETTO

P

PACHER, MICHAEL (ca. 1430/1435–1498) Born in the Puster valley in south Tyrol, the painter and wood carver Michael Pacher was one of those rare double talents of the late Middle Ages whose reputation reached well beyond his native region. Contemporary documents reveal, however, that he was primarily a painter, like Friedrich Pacher, who is presumed to be a relative. Thus, in spite of his astounding professional activity as a sculptor, most of his religious works comprise panel paintings and frescoes, including the vault paintings in the old sacristy at the cloister Neustift from about 1470. By 1467 at the latest he directed a workshop in Bruneck.

Pacher's importance lies in his adaptation of new artistic forms from Italy, the Netherlands, and southern Germany, which, in combination with his Alpine piety, he transforms into a new pictorial language. A clear understanding of Mantegna's frescoes in Padua and Mantua with their bold foreshortening and deep spaces constructed in virtuoso perspective is already apparent in four early panel paintings preserved from an otherwise lost altar dedicated to Thomas Becket (about 1460; Graz, Joanneum). In the altarpiece of the church fathers from Neustift near Brixen (1482–1483; Munich, Alte Pinakothek), he developed these pictorial techniques fully, setting the monumental figures under diagonally arranged trompe l'oeil baldachins (realistic figures) that seem to spring out of the paintings. Realistic, portraitlike facial features characterize the four small panels with the apostles and the helpers in need that were located at Wilten after 1820 (about 1465; now divided among the Österreichische Galerie in Vienna, the Museum Ferdinandeum in Innsbruck, and a private collection in the United States). No trace remains of a documented altarpiece, probably dedicated to the Archangel Michael, made for the parish church in Bozen between 1481 and 1484.

Of four Virgin altarpieces, all with richly sculptured shrines, three are fragmentarily preserved. An enthroned Madonna from 1462–1465 in the parish church of St. Lorenz near Bruneck, probably accompanied by the figures of St. Michael (Munich, Bayerisches Landesmuseum) and St. Lawrence (Innsbruck, Museum Ferdinandeum), has lasted through the centuries, although without the original shrine structure. Single panels from the wings, which were painted on both sides, are now housed in Munich (Alte Pinakothek) and Vienna (Österreichische Galerie). Pacher set a Coronation of the Virgin, composed as a scene rather than a stiff row of saints, into the center of the polyptych at Gries near Bozen (1471–1475); polychromed and gilded reliefs occupy the wings of the chapel-like shrine. Pacher's representation of the coronation before a gold brocade curtain supported by angels is based on Hans Multscher's altar in Sterzing. The contract mentions guard figures, which would have flanked the shrine; these, along with the painted wing panels, have disappeared. The masterpiece among Pacher's altars is the double triptych in the choir of the pilgrimage church at St. Wolfgang in the Salzkammergut; the contract is dated 1471, the execution between 1475 and 1481. With this work Pacher set the artistic standards against which other paintings and sculptures of the last phase of the late Gothic are measured. Here this "genius among altar sculptors of south Tyrol" (Paatz 1963: 44, my trans.) developed his own artistic language in the shimmering gold coronation set onto a stage under a filigreed tracery superstructure that reaches up to the vaults, in the imposing figures of the church's patron and St. Benedict, in the militant knight-saints at the sides of the shrine, and in the accompanying painted cycles with scenes from the lives of Christ, the Virgin, and St. Wolfgang. Probably the largest of Pacher's Virgin altars was that commissioned for the Franciscan church in Salzburg in 1484 and finished in 1498. This structure, greater than seventeen meters, was dismantled in the baroque period; its enthroned Madonna, later inserted into an altar by Fischer von Erlach, and several panels are preserved (Vienna, Österreichische Galerie). The extraordinary sum of 3,300 Rhenish gold florins was likely the highest paid for an altarpiece of this period. Pacher died in 1498, shortly before its completion.

See also **Multscher, Hans**

Further Reading

Egg, Erich. *Gotik in Tirol: Die Flügelaltäre.* Innsbruck: Haymon-Verlag, 1985, pp. 177–189.

Evans, Mark. "Appropriation and Application: The Significance of the Sources of Michael Pacher's Altarpieces," in *The Altarpiece in the Renaissance,* ed. Peter Humphrey and Martin Kemp. Cambridge: Cambridge University Press, 1990, pp. 106–128.

Goldberg, Gisela. "Late Gothic Painting from South Tyrol: Michael Pacher and Marx Reichlich." *Apollo* 116 (1982): 240–245.

Hempel, Erhard. *Michael Pacher.* Vienna: A. Schroll, 1931.

Koller, Manfred, and Norbert Wibiral. *Der Pacher-Altar von St. Wolfgang: Untersuchung, Konservierung, Restaurierung 1969–1976.* Studien zu Denkmalschutz und Denkmalpflege 11. Vienna: Hermann Böhlaus Nachfolger, 1981.

Michael Pacher und sein Kreis: Bin Tiroler Künstler der europäischen Spätgotik (1498–1998). Bozen: Südtiroler Landesregierung, 1998.

Paatz, Walter. "Süddeutsche Schnitzaltäre der Spätgotik." *Heidelberger kunstgeschichtliche Abhandlungen. Neue Folge* 8 (1963): 44–54.

Rasmo, Nicolo. *Michael Pacher.* London: Phaidon, 1971.

BRIGITTE SCHLIEWEN

PADILLA, MARÍA DE (d. 1361) The daughter of a Castilian family of the lesser aristocracy, María de Padilla became Pedro I's favorite in 1352, shortly after meeting through the Pedro's chief minister Juan Alfonso de Alburquerque. María was a member of the household staff of Alburquerque's wife, Isabel de Meneses. In spite of two subsequent marriages, Pedro's attachment to María was the most enduring relationship of his life. It lasted, with brief interruptions, until her death in 1361.

María's reputation has remained largely unscathed, in spite of Pedro's many excesses. Contemporary sources generally praise her for her beauty and charm, and for attempting to soften Pedro's harshness. A notable exception is the collection of anti-Pedro ballads, *Romancero del rey don Pedro,* in which she is portrayed as cruel and vengeful. In Romance 9, for example, she is held responsible for breaking up Pedro's marriage to Blanche de Bourbon in 1353. Jealousy leads María to hire a Jewish necromancer to put a spell on a gem-encrusted belt that Blanche gave the king to wear on their wedding night. As Pedro puts it on, the belt turns into a snake; the king, horrified, flees from his bride.

Pedro's refusal to live with his French wife, and his attachment to María, served as a political excuse for his enemies and resulted in the alienation of Albur querque. At the same time, María's relatives gained ascendancy at court and replaced Alburquerque and his circle. Juan Fernández de Henestrosa, an uncle, became *camarero mayor mayordomo mayor*, and *canciller mayor*. María's brother Diego García de Padilla owed his election as Master of the Order of Calatrava to Pedro's influence. He later became the king's *mayordomo mayor*. A half-brother of María received the *encomienda mayor* of the Order of Santiago, while another relative, Juan Tenorio, became *repostero mayor*.

María, with Pedro's financial support, founded the monastery of Santa Clara at Astudillo in 1354 which, together with an earlier cession of Huelva, constituted the only significant settlement the king made on her.

María died in July 1361. She bore Pedro four children: three daughters and a son. Immediately after her death Pedro proclaimed María queen of Castile and ordered a royal burial at the monastery at Astudillo. The following year, Pedro hastily assembled a meeting of the *cortes* at Seville to declare their son Alfonso, then two years old, heir to the Castilian throne. Upon the child's death the following year, Pedro designated his first daughter Beatriz his heir. He also insisted that he and María had been legally wed and had her remains transferred and buried in the royal chapel at Seville. The Trastamáran usurpation of the Castilian throne in 1369 made Pedro's succession arrangements moot. However, Pedro's line eventually returned to the throne when his granddaughter Catherine of Lancaster, daughter of his and María's second child Constanza and John of Gaunt, duke of Lancaster, wed Enrique III of Castile.

See also **Pedro I the Cruel, King of Castile**

Further Reading

Romancero del rey don Pedro, 1368–1800. Ed. Antonio Pérez de Gómez. Valencia, 1954.

CLARA ESTOW

PAOLO DA FIRENZE (d. September 1419) The composer Paolo da Firenze (Tenorista, Magister Dominus Paulus Abbas de Florentia) was born sometime in the latter half of the fourteenth century and became a Camaldolese monk; he died in the order's monastery of San Viti (Arezzo). He was a member of the final generation of Italian *Trecento* composers and is a connecting figure between Francesco Landini of the earlier generation and Andrea da Firenze of his own, both of whom he seems to have known well. Paolo is supposed to have accompanied one patron, Cardinal Angelo Acciaiuoli, to Rome c. 1404; and one of his madrigals, *Godi, Firençe* (with a text from Dante's *Commedia: Inferno,* 26), was clearly composed to celebrate Florence's conquest of Pisa in 1406.

Paolo was not only an active and admired composer but a learned and distinguished music theorist. Though the issue is hotly contested, some scholars have argued that he played a crucial role in assembling the famous Squarcialupi Codex. If so, it is ironic that, although his supposed portrait appears in the codex, the place reserved for his own musical works was left as seventeen blank folios; his surviving works are preserved in other Tuscan manuscripts.

These works comprise, beyond two scant Latin liturgical pieces, a sizable body of Italian vocal music. Attributed with relative certainty are twenty-two *ballate*, variously for two or three voices; and eleven madrigals, all for two voices. There are also two more *ballate* that survive as fragments; and thirteen other *ballate*, variously for two or three voices, which are preserved in one manuscript where the attributions of his name have been erased, leaving us uncertain as to their authenticity.

On the one hand, Paolo impresses for his conservatism. He is unusual in clinging to the madrigal, an older form bypassed by most musicians of his generation. In both, of his vocal forms, Paolo generally seems to continue the traditions of his older colleague, Landini. On the other hand, Paolo's writing clearly shows an assimilation not only of more progressive Italian styles but also of some influence from French styles of the late *ars nova*. Though his vocal lines are simple and clearly Italianate in tradition, he attempts to go beyond earlier flexibility and construct compositions with an overall logic of motivic development. His two liturgical works also show him combining Italianate vocal lines with *cantus firmus* material after the French polyphonic manner. He seems to have known something of Johannes Ciconia and Ciconia's work. Paolo belongs to a trend that envisioned a fusion of French and Italian elements at the dawn of the *Quattrocento*.

See also Ciconia, Johannes; Landini, Francesco

Further Reading

Becherini, Bianca. "Antonio Squarcialupi e il codice Mediceo Palatino 87." In *L'Ars nova italiana del Trecento: Primo convegno internazionale 23–26 luglio 1959*, ed. Bianca Becherini. Certaldo: Centro di Srudi sull'Ars Nova Italiana del Trecento, 1962, pp. 140–180.
Corsi, Giuseppe. *Poesie musicali del Trecento*. Bologna: Commissione per i Testi di Lingua, 1970.

Fischer, Kurt von. *Studien zur italienischen Musik des Trecento und frühen Quattrocento*. Bern: P. Haupt, 1956.
——. "Paolo da Firenze und der Sqnarcialupi-Kodex (I-Fl 87)." *Quadrivium*, 9, 1968, pp. 5–29.
Fischer, Kurt von, and F. Alberto Gallo, eds. *Italian Sacred Music*. Polyphonic Music of the Fourteenth Century, 12. Monaco: Éditions de L'Oiseau-Lyre, 1976.
Königsglow, Annamarie von. *Die italienischen Madrigalisten des Trecento*. Würzburg: Triltsch, 1940.
Li Gotti, Ettore, and Nino Pirrotta. "Paolo Tenorista fiorentino, extra moenia." In *Estudios dedicados a Mendénez Piáal*, Vol. 3. Madrid, 1952, pp. 577–606.
Marrocco, William Thomas, ed. *Italian Secular Music*. Polyphonic Music of the Fourteenth Century, 9. Monaco: Éditions de L'Oiseau-Lyre, 1975.
Pirrotta, Nino. "Paolo da Firenze in un nuovo frammento dell'Ars Nova." *Musica Disciplina*, 10, 1956, pp. 61–66.
——. ed. *Paolo Tenorista in a New Fragment of the Italian Ars Nova*. Palm Springs, Calif.: Gottlieb, 1961.
Pirrotta, Nino, and Ursula Günther, eds. *The Music of Fourteenth-Century Italy*, Vol. 6. Corpus Mensurabilis Musicae, 8(6). Rome: American Institute of Musicology, n.d.
Seay, Albert, "Paolo da Firenze: A Trecento Theorist." In *L'Ars nova italiana del Trecento: Primo convegno internazionale 23–26 luglio 1959*, ed. Bianca Becherini. Certaldo: Centro di Studi sull'Ars Nova Italiana del Trecento, 1962, pp. 118–140.
Wolf, Johannes. "Florenz in der Musikgeschichte des 14. Jahrhunderts." *Sammelbände der Internationalen Musikgesellschaft*, 3, 1901–1902, 599–646. (Leipzig.)

JOHN W. BARKER

PASCHAL II, POPE (d. 1118, r. 13 August 1099–21 January 1118) Pope Paschal II (Rainerius) was born of a noble family at Bieda, south of Faenza in central Italy; his parents were Crescentius and Alfatia. While still a young boy, he was put into a Benedictine monastery. A general belief that he entered the monastery at Cluny was dismissed by Odericus, who confirmed that the monastery was Vallombrosa, between Florence and Arezzo. Rainerius was highly esteemed by his superiors and at age twenty was sent to Rome, where he gained the trust and favor of Pope Gregory VII, who made him cardinal priest of San Clemente. Under Urban II, Rainerius served as legate to Spain. He later became abbot of San Lorenzo Fuori le Mura. His intellectual and spiritual qualities made him an excellent candidate for the papacy and helped secure his election to succeed Pope Urban II. He was highly educated, a promoter of learning and culture; he was also pious, merciful, and forgiving. It was reported that during the conclave, when he realized that the consensus was turning toward him, he attempted to avoid being elected by fleeing, deeming himself unworthy of such an important position.

His pontificate as Paschal II was to prove very difficult because of the struggle between church and the state over the right of investiture for major church offices, but it also saw the initial signs of emancipation of the church from the state, which Gregory VII had worked so hard to achieve. Throughout his reign, Paschal had to fight on many fronts: against the antipopes, the German kings, and the Roman nobles. Paschal also strenuously fostered the crusade movement.

During Paschal's reign, settlements were made between Saint Anselm and Henry I of England and with Philip I of France; but there was a constant struggle with the German king Henry IV, who persistently encouraged and supported the elections of antipopes, in order to undermine the authority of the legitimately elected pope. There was a whole succession of antipopes. At the death of the antipope Guibert of Ravenna (Clement III) in 1100, Theoderic became antipope after a mock election in Saint Peter's (1101–1102); then came the antipopes Albert (1102) and Sylvester IV (1105–1111). Henry IV was excommunicated by Paschal in 1302 but restored himself

to the pope's favor by promising to lead a crusade, although he never fulfilled this promise. In 1104, Henry IV's young son, Henry V, spurred on by disappointed princes, rebelled against his father. Weary of the constant struggle with the king, Paschal made an agreement with his rebellious son. The elder Henry resigned his power at Ingelheim on 31 December 1105, and his son was solemnly crowned emperor at Mainz on 1 February 1106. While the dethroned monarch was getting ready to fight back, he fell ill and died in August 1106.

The struggle between papacy and empire found no resolution with Henry V. From the beginning of his reign, the younger Henry proved just as determined as his father not to give up the right of investiture. Paschal II and Henry V met at Sutri in 1110. Initially, Henry showed willingness to renounce the right to investiture, while the pope committed himself to giving back all lands and rights received from the German crown by the church. However, these conditions were rejected by the German bishops, who considered that they were being deprived of all temporal power. Henry V fled Rome and took the pope with him as a prisoner, until Paschal conceded the right of investiture to the king. Despite the strong opposition of the Roman curia, Paschal crowned Henry V emperor in Saint Peter's on 13 April 1111, as part of their agreement. In September 1112, the emperor was excommunicated by the French bishops because of his capture of the pope and his extortion of the concession regarding investiture. Paschal subsequently confirmed the emperor's excommunication.

While struggling to achieve peace with the empire, Paschal had to fend off revolts in Rome itself. The Corsi family supported the third antipope, and Paschal retaliated by destroying their stronghold on the Capitoline hill.

Soon after his election to the papacy, Paschal, following the lead of his predecessors, congratulated the crusaders for their successes in Palestine and then urged bishops and soldiers to hasten to their help.

Although the relationship between papacy and empire was exceedingly tumultuous during his reign, Paschal's diplomatic accomplishments were instrumental in bringing a conclusion to the investiture controversy; his pontificate opened the way to the concordat that Pope Calixtus II concluded at Worms in 1122.

See also **Gregory VII, Pope; Henry I; Henry IV, Emperor; Urban II, Pope**

Further Reading

Cantarella, Glauco Maria. *Pasquale II e il suo tempo.* Naples: Liguori, 1997. *Enciclopedia Cattolica.* Florence: Sansoni, 1950.
Mann, Horace K. *The Lives of the Popes in the Middle Ages.* London: Kegan Paul, Trench, Trubner; Saint Louis, Mo.: Herder, 1925.
Morrison, Karl F. *Tradition and Authority in the Western Church, 300–1140.* Princeton, N.J.: Princeton University Press, 1969.
The New Catholic Encyclopedia, 2nd ed. Detroit, Mich.: Thomson-Gale, 2003.
Strayer, Joseph R., ed. *Dictionary of the Middle Ages.* New York: Scribner, 1983.

ALESSANDRO VETTORI

PAUL THE DEACON (c. 720–c. 799) Paul the Deacon (Paulus Diaconis) was the son of Warnefrid and was probably born at Cividale in Friuli. Paul was educated by the grammarian Flavianus, joined the royal court at Pavia, and became tutor to Adelperga, a daughter of the last independent Lombard king, Desiderius (r. 756–774). When Adelperga's husband, Arichis, was made duke of Benevento in 758, Paul became a part of the literary circle that developed at Benevento. There, in 763, Paul wrote his first poetic work (dedicated to Adelperga), followed by a prose continuation (also dedicated to Adelperga) of Eutropius's *Historia Romanum.*

After Charlemagne's defeat of the Lombards and his assumption of the Lombard crown in 774, Paul retired to the Benedictine monastery at Monte Cassino, where he remained until 783. He then left to seek the court of Charlemagne, ostensibly to plead on behalf of a brother, Arichis, who had been taken prisoner after participating in an unsuccessful revolt in northern Italy in 776. Paul remained at Charlemagne's court for two or three years before returning to Monte Cassino, where he continued to live and write until his death.

Paul is an important figure both in Italian letters and in the early Carolingian renaissance. He wrote in verse and in prose on secular and religious subjects. While he was at Aachen, in addition to a number of literary efforts that were primarily liturgical and homiletic, he composed in honor of the Carolingians a *History of the Bishops of Metz* (*Historia episcoporum Metensium*); after returning to Monte Cassino he produced a number of other works including his last and most important, *History of the Lombards* (*Historia Langobardorum*). This last work, which was never finished, covers the story of the Lombards from their semilegendary beginnings through the reign of King Liutprand (712–744). Paul's history is a typical eighth-century product, relying heavily on the materials available to him: Pliny; Isidore; Gregory of Tours; a work on the Lombards (now lost) by Secundus of Nun from Trent, who was a member of the court circle of King Agilulf (r. 590–616); Bede; and several much shorter and less reliable Lombard chronicles—an interesting commentary on the literary materials available at Monte Cassino in the late eighth century.

See also **Charlemagne; Gregory of Tours; Isidore of Seville, Saint; Wyclif, John**

Further Reading

Belting, Hans. "Studien zum beneventanischen Hof im 8. Jahrhundert." *Dumbarton Oaks Papers,* 16, 1962.

Bethmann, L., and G. Waitz, eds. *Pauli Historia Langobardorum.* Monumenta Germaniae Historica, Scriptores Rerum Langobardicarum et Italicarum, Saec. VI–IX. Hannover: Hahn, 1878.

Goffart, Walter. *Narrators of Barbarian History: Jordanes, Gregory of Tours, Bede, and Paul the Deacon.* Princeton, N.J.: Princeton University Press, 1988.

Paul the Deacon. *History of the Lombards,* trans. William Dudley Foulke. Philadelphia: University of Pennsylvania Press, 1974.

KATHERINE FISCHER DREW

PECOCK, REGINALD (early 1390s-ca. 1460) Theologian, religious educator, and bishop tried for and convicted of heresy. Pecock was a fellow of Oriel College, Oxford (ca. 1414–24); rector of St. Michael's, Gloucester (1424–31); rector of St. Michael Royal (also called St. Michael in Riola) and master of Whittington College (1431–44); bishop of St. Asaph (1444–50); and bishop of Chichester (1450–58). He was unusual in that he tried to bring the Lollards out of error by means of logical persuasion in vernacular treatises, especially in his *Repressor of Over Much Blaming of the Clergy.* Ironically the legal ground for his trial may have been an ecclesiastical statute originally designed to suppress Lollardy, not only because he wrote in English but also because he stressed the authority of reason, and particularly of syllogistic logic, over that of the church doctors, of the scriptures, and sometimes of the church itself.

Pecock's position on these issues was not as extreme as his accusers asserted, but enough evidence was found in his works (many of which, he pointed out, had circulated without his approval) to convict him of heresy in 1457. Upon conviction he was offered the choice of recanting or being burned at the stake. He publicly abjured and handed over fourteen of his books, which were consigned to flames. Although he was reinstated in his bishopric for one more year, his enemies were soon able to remove him from office and have him placed under restrictive house arrest at Thorney Abbey in 1459. Not long after, perhaps within a year or so, he died there.

Pecock wrote or planned to write some 30 to 50 books in Latin and English, but only a few have survived. We know of at least some of those that perished by their mention in the surviving works, which in probable chronological order are these: *The Rule of Christian Religion* (ca. 1443); *The Donet* (ca. 1443–49); *The Poor Men's Mirror* (an extract of part 1 *of The Donet*); the "Abbreviatio Reginaldi Pecok" (ca. 1447); *The Folewer to the Donet* (ca. 1453–54); *The Repressor of Over Much Blaming of the Clergy* (written ca. 1449, published ca. 1455); and *The Book of Faith* (ca. 1456).

Pecock's extant English treatises are notable for their prose style, which is strongly shaped by the attempt to render theological and philosophical concepts in a relatively nonlatinate English, leading to frequent neologisms (e.g., *un-away-fallable; folewer* for "sequel"; *eendal* and *meenal for* "pertaining to ends" and "pertaining to means"). His language is often abstract and syntactically complex, especially in his expositions of logical arguments. He thoroughly reorganized the standard religious instructional topics (vices and virtues, sacraments, articles of faith, etc.) into a nontraditional arrangement of 31 virtues. Not surprisingly, given the destruction of many of his books and the dense, complex style of those few that survived, Pecock's works had little influence on later writers. Nonetheless, they remain worthy of study for what they reveal about the capacities of late ME prose as a medium for philosophical discourse and the degree to which 15th-century English religious instruction could—and could not—diverge from institutionally approved form and content.

Further Reading

Primary Sources

Babington, Churchill, ed. *The Repressor of Over Much Blaming of the Clergy.* 2 vols. Rolls Series. London: Longman, Green, Longman, & Roberts, 1860.

Greet, William Cabell, ed. *The Reule of Crysten Religioun.* EETS o.s. 171. London: Humphrey Milford, 1927.

Hitchcock, Elsie Vaughan, ed. *The Donet* and *The Folewer to the Donet.* EETS o.s. 156, 164. London: Humphrey Milford, 1921–24.

Morison, John L., ed. *The Book of Faith.* Glasgow: Maclehose, 1909.

Secondary Sources

New *CBEL* 1:665–66, 805.

Brockwell, Charles W., Jr. "Answering the 'Known Men': Bishop Reginald Pecock and Mr. Richard Hooker." *Church History* 49 (1980): 133–46.

Patrouch, Joseph F., Jr. *Reginald Pecock.* New York: Twayne, 1970.

LARA RUFFOLO

PEDRO ALFONSO, OR PETRUS ALFONSI

Moisés Sefardí, a noted Jew from Huesca, adopted the name Pedro Alfonso when he was baptized on 29 June 1106, with King Alfonso I el Batallador serving as godfather. Pedro Alfonso probably left the Iberian Peninsula soon after his baptism; a few years later he was located in England as a *magister* of liberal arts, where he likely contributed to the diffusion of Arabic science, especially astronomy and calculus, around the monastery of Malvern. Whether he was the physician to both Alfonso I and Henry I of England, as is often claimed, is not certain.

The preserved literary production of Pedro Alfonso is in Latin, and can be separated into three fields of interest: apologetic, scientific, and didactic literature. As a response to the scandal caused by his conversion, he wrote *Diálogos contra los judíos,* in which two characters, Pedro and Moisés, represent the author before and after his baptism. Throughout the work's twelve chapters, Pedro turns to a wide variety of medical, cabbalistic, and theological arguments to show Moisés the error of his ways. At the latter's insistence, in the fifth chapter Pedro traces a broad critical panorama of Islam. If the *Diálogos* enjoyed especially wide distribution, as the more than seventy preserved manuscripts dispersed throughout European libraries prove, the repercussions of this chapter were even greater.

Very few of Pedro Alfonso's scientific works are preserved, and only some incomplete *Tablas astronómicas* can be attributed to him with surety. These tablas are preceded by a curious preliminary text titled "Carta a los estudiosos franceses", which seems to have been motivated by a stay in France, and which becomes an important document with regard to the author's position on the cultural renaissance of the twelfth century. In the letter, Pedro Alfonso criticizes European intellectuals for their bookish culture, far removed from the world of scientific practice. He also addresses the traditional division of the liberal arts, positioning himself among those partial to the quadrivium, which includes the study of medicine; in the trivium only the study of dialectics is saved from the author's condemnation, but is still only regarded as a supplementary subject.

Pedro Alfonso's name has become unquestionably most associated with the *Disciplina clericalis,* a combination of exempla (thirty-four total), comparisons, proverbs, and so on—all focusing on the indoctrination of students as the title indicates. For the subject's organization, the author likely found inspiration in the books of the Bible, Hebrew religious texts, and mixed genres of oriental origin. The dialogue between anonymous characters (father-son, teacher-disciple) creates a frame that reaches its maximum development between examples 9 and 17. The subject matter—knowledge of self and of neighbor, but always remembering the fear of God—corresponds to other similar works of oriental literature.

The most popular stories, though, deal with misogynistic themes, and are closer to the *fabliaux* in their narrative scheme. Medieval preachers turned to the *Discliplina clericalis* frequently, explaining its wide diffusion and its importance in the origins of the novel. Because it was written in Latin, the *Disciplina clericalis* became the first pathway through which oriental narrative began to circulate in the West.

Further Reading

Alfonso, Pedro. *Disciplina clericalis*. Intr. M. J. Lacarra, tran. E. Ducay. Zaragoza, 1980.
Reinhardt, K., and H. Santiago-Otero, *Biblioteca bíblica ibérica medieval* Madrid, 1986, 250–58.

MARÍA JESÚS LACARRA

PEDRO I THE CRUEL, KING OF CASTILE (1334–1369) Born 30 August 1334 in Burgos, Pedro was the only legitimate child and heir of Alfonso XI of Castile (1312–1350). His mother was María daughter of King Afonso IV of Portugal. One of the most controversial kings of the Castilian Middle Ages, he is the only one who came to be known by the sobriquet of "the Cruel" for the many acts of violence associated with the last stages of his rule. Aside from the personal excesses that inspired this reputation, Pedro's reign (1350–1369) is distinctive for a number of other reasons.

His subjects experienced the full economic and demographic effects of the first wave of the Black Death that hit Castile from 1348 to 1350. He led an aggressive war of expansion against Aragón that lasted, intermittently, from 1357 until the end of the reign. His policies and alliances contributed to the involvement of international troops in the peninsular conflict, making Spain, from 1366 to 1369, the main theater for the larger military conflict known as the Hundred Years' War. His treatment of the aristocracy and his poor relations with the Castilian Church and the Avignon papacy alienated a substantial portion of his most important subjects, causing many to side with his chief rival, his half-brother Enrique de Trastámara, during the Castilian civil war of 1366–1369. The reign ended violently with Pedro's death and the usurpation of the throne by Enrique.

Coming to the throne 28 March 1350 shortly before his sixteenth birthday, Pedro spent the first two years under the influence of Juan Alfonso de Alburquerque, a Portuguese nobleman who had been in the service of Queen María, and had become Pedro's first minister. Under the auspices of Alburquerque, Pedro convened the Cortes of Valladolid in 1351, the only such meeting for which we have any detailed records for the entire reign. Through a series of measures redacted during these proceedings, Pedro attempted to remedy some of the economic consequences of the plague such as the abandonment of arable lands, and the steep rise in the cost of living. At the same time, the *cuadernos de cortes* (records of the courts) reveal Pedro's interest in a healthy royal treasury and an effective system of tax-collection. This concern with sound finances remained a constant feature of his reign, and resulted in the unpopular appointment of Samuel Halevi, a Jew, as his chief treasurer and the extensive use of Jews as tax-farmers. These measures, for which Pedro was severely criticized, served as evidence to his detractors of the king's presumed philojudaism, a quality almost as objectionable as his cruelty.

From the early days of his reign, Pedro also had to contend with an endemic feature of Castilian medieval politics, a restless and rebellious aristocracy. In his particular case, the situation was aggravated by the existence of a rival group of wealthy and influential individuals composed of the bastard children of Alfonso XI and his mistress Leonor de Guzmán, their allies, and retainers who challenged Pedro's authority almost from the beginning of the reign. Pedro reacted to these challenges in an increasingly suspicious and retaliatory manner.

In 1353 Pedro married the French princess Blanche de Bourbon and abandoned her two days after the wedding. It is likely that Blanche's sponsor, the French crown, was not able to fulfill the financial obligations of the marriage contract, and that Pedro left her for that reason. The more popular yet unverifiable reason given to explain the king's actions states that he abandoned Blanche because he could not bear to be away from the woman he loved, María de Padilla, whom he had met in 1352.

Whatever his motives, Pedro's refusal to cohabit with Blanche served to alienate his mother and Alburquerque, the principal architects of the marriage contract with the French, and gave his half-brothers a pretext for rebellion. As the minister and the bastards became allies, they were joined by other prominent Castilians displeased with the king's behavior. Outnumbered, Pedro gave himself up to the rebels at Toro only to escape after a month to begin a slow but successful campaign against them. With the capitulation of Toledo in 1355 and Toro in 1356, the main centers of antiroyal activity, Pedro succeeded in defeating the first serious challenge to his authority.

Shortly after this victory, Pedro went to war against Aragón, seeking redress over several territorial and dynastic grievances. Pedro IV was soon joined by Enrique de Trastámara, who had escaped from Castile before Pedro's victory at Toro, and other Castilians who had fled fearing the king's justice while Pedro counted on the support of Pedro's hated half-brother Ferrán. Pedro experienced several successes at Tarazona (1357); Guardamar (1359); Calatayud (1362); Teruel; Segorbe and Murviedo (1363); Alicante, Elche, Denia (1363), and Orihuela (1365); but he was never able to win a decisive victory. Several truces and peace efforts mediated by papal legates did not succeed in bringing a lasting peace between the two kingdoms.

Meanwhile, from the conspiracy at Toro onward Pedro had turned increasingly against those he suspected of treason. He eliminated many of his former allies; several of his half-brothers, among them Fadrique; and his aunt Leonor and her son Juan, and he was believed responsible for the death of his wife Blanche in 1361.

Pedro's policies, Enrique de Trastámara's ambitions, Pedro's predicament, and even the politics of Navarre all contributed to the participation of the French in peninsular affairs, beginning in 1360. The French crown agreed to sponsor Enrique's ambitions by commissioning Bertrand du Guesclin and an army of mercenaries to fight in Castile. When they entered the kingdom in 1366, Pedro was forced to flee in search of outside help, which he finally secured from Edward the Black Prince in Bordeaux. The ensuing battle at Nájera on 13 April 1367 was a resounding, albeit shortlived, victory for Pedro. His alliance with the English collapsed when the Castilian would not meet the terms of their agreement and, as the Black Prince's troops withdrew from the peninsula, Enrique and Guesclin returned in 1368 and received the support of several important regions.

Pedro determined to meet his enemy in the vicinity of Toledo. At the Battle of Montiel on 14 March 1369 Enrique and the French soundly defeated Pedro's scattered army. Pedro, who had fled to a nearby fortress, tried to buy his freedom from Guesclin. Some days later, believing that the French captain had accepted his terms, Pedro went to Guesclin's tent where, within a few minutes, Enrique arrived. He killed Pedro with a dagger, after a short struggle on 23 March 1369. Through this fratricide Enrique became uncontested king of Castile, a title he began to use when he first entered the kingdom alongside the French in 1366.

In addition to his marriage to Blanche de Bourbon, Pedro is said to have married

María de Padilla—at least he claimed this following her death in 1361 in order to declare their four children (three daughters and a son, the youngest) legitimate heirs to the throne. Shortly after his marriage to Blanche, he had also wed Juana de Castro, but this marriage was just as ephemeral as his first and left no children. Eventually Pedro's line returned to the Castilian throne when his granddaughter, Catherine of Lancaster, daughter of John of Gaunt and Pedro and María's second daughter Constanza, married the future Enrique III of Castile.

See also **Padilla, María de**

Further Reading

Díaz Martín, L. V. *Itinerario de Pedro I de Castilla.* Valladolid, 1975.
López de Ayala, P. *Crónica del rey don Pedro.* Biblioteca de Autores Españoles, vol. 66. Madrid, 1953.
Sitges, J. B. *Las mujeres del rey Don Pedro I de Castilla.* Madrid, 1910.

CLARA ESTOW

PEDRO III, KING OF ARAGÓN (1240–1285) Pedro III the Great, Pere III of Aragón, Pere II of Catalonia, Pere I of Valencia, and Pere I of Sicily, "was the troubadour-warrior ruler of the realms of Aragón (1276–1285) and liberator-conqueror of Sicily. He was born at Valencia, two years after that Islamic city fell to his father Jaime the Conqueror, of Jaime's second wife Violante of Hungary. Jaime named him heir to Catalonia in 1253, procurator or vice-regent there at seventeen in 1257, and—at the death of Jaime's son Alfonso by his first wife in 1260—procurator of the Catalonia, Aragón, and Valencia realms. (Pedro's brother Jaime became procurator of the Balearics, Roussillon, and Cerdanya.) In 1262 Pedro married Constance, the daughter and heiress of Manfred, the Hohenstaufen ruler of Sicily-Naples. Besides four sons and two daughters by

his mistresses María and Agnés Zapata, he had four sons (Including his successors Alfonso II and Jaime II, and Frederico III of Sicily), and two daughters (Queen Vio lante of Naples and Isabel Queen of Portugal).

Although his formal reign lasted only nine years versus his famous father's sixty-three, the Infante Pedro enjoyed a fifteen-year public career as procuratorial co-ruler and soldier before his coronation. He restored feudal order as a teenager, plunged into Mediterranean Ghibelline politics during negotiations for his marriage, championed Occitan refugees after such troubles as the 1263 Marseilles revolt, captained the first phase of the Murcian Crusade in 1265–1266, replaced his father at home during Jaime's abortive Holy Land Crusade in 1269 (and intervened in the Urgell wars of 1268), and prepared an invasion army to seize Toulouse in 1271. Relations with his father deteriorated in 1272, with Pedro stripped of all offices and revenues; reconciliation came the following year. When the northern Catalan nobles revolted, Pedro captured and drowned their leader, his bastard brother Ferran Sanxis. During a diplomatic visit to Paris, he met Philippe the Bold. His greatest test came in 1275–1277, when the Mudéjars of Valencia with Maghribian support revolted and nearly recovered their land. Pedro had one thousand horsemen and five thousand foot soldiers at first, but soon had to assume the entire responsibility when his father died on the field (27 July 1276). Burying Jaime provisionally at Valencia and deferring his coronation at Zaragoza to 17 November, Pedro grimly set about conquering much of Valencia "a second time," as the contemporary memoirist Ramón Muntaner puts it. Meanwhile his brother Jaume II of Mallorca received the Balearics, Cerdanya, Montpellier, and Roussillon.

With the Mudéjar headquarters at Montesa castle fallen (September 1277), Pedro began a vigorous domestic and international program. He demanded tribute from Tunis, harrying it through his admiral Conrad Llanca, pressured Jaime II of Mallorca into accepting vassalage, and moved strongly against the still-rebellious northern barons, ending their six-year war by his siege of Balaguer (1281) and winning their support by his clemency. By holding as "guest hostages" the Infantes de la Cerda, he dominated the Castilian succession crisis. His negotiations with Philippe the Bold at Toulouse in 1281, and his treaties of Campillo and Ágreda with Alfonso X and the Infante Sancho of Castile that year, stabilized his peninsular situation. He established understandings with Byzantium, England, Genoa, Granada, Portugal, and the papacy, and was finally ready for his life's coup: to foil the Angevin power that had absorbed Occitania and taken over Sicily-Naples, and to assume the Hohenstaufens' Sicilian kingdom and Ghibelline leadership in the western Mediterranean.

Massing his naval and military strength, he simulated a crusade against Tunis, actually taking Collo there; the pope refused crusade title or aid. Previously in contact with the Sicilians, Pedro now supported the Sicilian Vespers revolt of 30 March 1282. He moved eight hundred knights and fifteen thousand foot soldiers by sea to Trapani, receiving the crown of Sicily-Naples at Palermo and starting a twenty-year war. A succession of naval victories by his admirals, especially Roger de Llúria, established the Catalans as the dominant maritime power of the western Mediterranean after Genoa. Besides Sicily and much of the Italian mainland, Pedro also took Malta and Tunisian Djerba island.

Meanwhile Pope Martin IV, feudal lord of Sicily and proponent of its Angevin king Charles of Anjou, excommunicated Pedro in November 1282, deposed him in March 1283, and transferred all his realms to the son of Philippe the Bold of France, Charles of Valois, in February 1284. The Catalans supported their king,

but the Aragónese had been ill-disposed toward the Sicilian adventure from the start. In that long and bloody war, one episode stands out—the Challenge (*desafiament*) of Bordeaux. Anjou offered to settle the war by personal combat with Pedro, but instead arranged a trap for his arrival at English Bordeaux; Pedro still appeared, met the challenge, and escaped, to the edification of Europe's chivalric classes (1283). More formidably, a papal crusade to set Valois during Pedro's reign saw an army of 118,000 foot and 7,000 horse under Philippe the Bold sweep into Catalonia. Pedro delayed this greatest army since ancient Rome at Girona until Llúia's fleet from Sicily could arrive to destroy the French naval flank and logistics, ending the invasion (September 1285). Pedro suppressed a plebeian revolt in Barcelona under Berenguer Oller that same year, negotiated a major commercial treaty with Tunis, and mounted a punitive amphibious expedition against his traitorous brother on Mallorca, but died on the road to join the fleet.

The contemporary memoirist Bernat Desclot calls Pedro "a second Alexander" for his generalship. Dante lauds him as "the heavy-sinewed one [who] bore in his life the seal of every merit"; and he appears both in Boccaccio's *Decameron* and Shakespeare's *Much Ado about Nothing*. Pedro was a troubadour (two of his poems survive) and their patron. He presided over a constitutional revolution (Aragón's Privilege of Union, Catalonia's *Recognoverunt proceres* annual parliament) in 1283–1284. He stabilized coinage with his silver croat, and maritime law with his restructured *Llibre del Consolat* (1283). He protected Jews and gave them important posts in his administration. As a politician and diplomat he is thought superior to his great father, and he presided over a commercial, literary, and architectural flowering in Catalonia.

See also **Jaime II; Philip III the Bold**

Further Reading

Soldevila, F. *Pere el Gran.* 2 parts in 4 vols. Institut d'Estudis Catalans, Memòries de la Secció Històrico-arqueològica. Vols. 11, 13, 16, 22. Barcelona, 1950–1962.

———. *Vida de Pere el Gran i d'Alfons el Liberal.* Barcelona, 1963. XI Congres de Història de la Corona d'Aragó. 3 vols. Palermo, 1983–84.

ROBERT I. BURNS, S. J.

PEGOLOTTI, FRANCESCO DI BALDUCCIO (born c. 1280s) Francesco di Balduccio Pegolotti was a Florentine factor for the great Bardi banking house in the first half of the fourteenth century, until its failure in 1347. His name appears in 1310 in the firm's payroll for the branch in Florence, at a rate which suggests that he already had considerable experience. His work was rewarded with promotions to positions of greater importance. In 1315, he negotiated trade rights for Florentines in Antwerp. From 1318 to 1321, as director of the firm's English office, he had duties that included financial transactions to help finance the English king, private business, and transferral of the tithes collected in England to the papal curia. Pegolotti next moved to Cyprus, where he remained until 1329; again, his job involved diplomacy, handling papal monies, and handling monies for individual merchants. He returned to Florence in order to hold civic office but then moved back to the east by 1335. In 1340, he returned again to Florence, for the last time. The last known mention of him is in 1347, when he was one of the civic officials overseeing the liquidation of the assets of the bankrupt Bardi firm.

Pegolotti is best known not for his service to the Bardi but for the compilation of his observations on trade now known as *La practica della mercatura.* The oldest known manuscript, from 1472, is a copy made by Filippo di Niccolaio Frescobaldi in the Riccardian Library in Florence.

The manuscript has evident inaccuracies, which can be attributed to the copyist; these include misreadings that arose when the copyist was trying to expand the original abbreviations, and chapters that are out of place. Internal evidence, such as the mention of current kings, helps to show that the material in the *Practica* was collected throughout Pegolotti's career with the Bardi, and also that it was not written down all at one time.

The *Practica* is one of a "genre" of documents called merchant manuals. It is by far the best-known because historians have used Pegolotti's discussion of the route to Cathay as proof that Europeans had knowledge of and easy access to the Silk Road. The data come from Pegolotti's experience and from documents he collected that had something to do with his work—such as a list of brokerage fees charged in Pisa, quoted from the *Breve dell' Ordine del Mare* of 1323. The section on Cathay is almost certainly based on information Pegolotti collected rather than on personal experience. The manual contains information on conversions for weights, measures, and currencies between various places, as well as discussions of other topics such as the steps involved in producing the most important commodities of a particular region and the expenses involved in producing coins. The *Practica* is among the earliest known merchant manuals, but it is possible that Pegolotti borrowed some of his material from still earlier manuals, just as later manuals would borrow from his. This type of book probably functioned as an exemplar to teach apprentices how international trade worked, not as a reference for absolute values or information.

Further Reading

Borlandi, Antonia, ed. *Il manuale di mercatura di Saminiato de' Ricci.* Genoa: Di Stefano, 1963.

Borlandi, Franco, ed. *El libro di mercatantie et usanze de' paesi.* Turin: S. Lattes, 1936.

Cessi, Roberto, and Antonio Orlandini, eds. *Tarifa zoè noticia dy pexi e mesure di luoghi e tere che s'adovra mercadantia per el mondo.* Venice, 1925.

Ciano, Cesare, ed. *La pratica di mercatura datiniana.* Milan: Giuffrè, 1964.

Dotson, John, trans. and ed. *Merchant Culture in Fourteenth-Century Venice: The Zibaldone da Canal.* Binghamton, N.Y.: Center for Medieval and Renaissance Studies, 1994.

Pagnini del Ventura, Giovanni Francesco. *Della decima e di varie altre gravezze imposte dal comune di Firenze: Della moneta e della mercatura de' fiorentini fino al secolo XVI,* Vol. 3, *La pratica della mercatura* (by Balducci Pegolotti); Vol. 4, *La pratica della mercatura* (by Giovanni di Antonio da Uzzano). Lisbon, 1765–1766. (Reprint, Bologna: Forni, 1967.)

Pegolotti, Francesco Balducci. *La pratica della mercatura,* ed. Allen Evans. Cambridge, Mass.: Medieval Academy of America, 1936.

Stussi, Alfredo, ed. *Zibaldone da Canal: Manoscritto mercantile del sec. XIV.* Venice: Comitato per la Pubblicazione delle Fonti Relative alla Storia di Venezia, 1967.

ELEANOR A. CONGDON

PEIRE CARDENAL (ca. 1180–ca. 1272) One of the most prolific troubadours and the longest-lived, Peire Cardenal composed *sirventes,* or satires, on moral and religious subjects. He left some ninety-six poems. Born in Le Puy, he was employed as a clerk by Raymond VI of Toulouse and frequented the courts of Les Baux, Rodez, Auvergne, and (according to his *vida)* of Aragon. He may have died in Montpellier.

As a satirist, Peire is distant from Marcabru but closer to Bertran de Born, whom he imitated in a number of compositions, sometimes equaling the sting of Bertran's invective, on other occasions echoing his technique of martial description the better to express his disapproval of Bertran's eagerness for combat. Peire imitated the metrical and musical form of preceding compositions in at least 80 percent of his own songs, exploring the possibilities of an increasingly strict sense of contrafacture with impressive technical inventiveness.

As a moralist, Peire praises good actions and blames the bad but laments that he is understood by no one, as though he spoke a foreign language. He tells a fable, *Una ciutatz fo,* in which rain falls on a city and drives everyone mad except one man who has been sheltered; when he goes out into the street, he sees that everyone else is crazy, but they think him mad and drive him away. Thus, worldly spirits reject the man who hears the voice of God. In a few poems, Peire criticizes the worldly love sung by other troubadours and anticipates the *dolce stil nuovo* with his claim that *fin'amors* is born in a *franc cor gentil,* "a noble, gentle heart."

During the extended period of the Albigensian Crusade (1209–29), Peire expressed vigorous anticlericalism at the expense of Dominican inquisitors and severely criticized the French army led by Simon de Montfort. He did not, however, defend the cause of the Albigensians, regarded as heretics by the church, but rather championed the political cause of the counts of Toulouse, whose lands were invaded by the crusaders. In his religious poems, he expresses an orthodox belief in Catholic doctrine.

See also **Marcabru; Simon de Montfort, Earl of Leicester**

Further Reading

Peire Cardenal. *Poésies complètes du troubadour Peire Cardenal,* ed. René Lavaud. Toulouse: Privat, 1957.

Marshall, John Henry. "Imitation of Metrical Form in Peire Cardenal." *Romance Philology* 32 (1978): 18–48.

Riquer, Martín de, ed. *Los trovadores: historia literaria y textos.* 3 vols. Barcelona: Planeta, 1975, Vol. 3, pp. 1478–518.

Wilhelm, James J. *Seven Troubadours: The Creators of Modern Verse.* University Park: Pennsylvania State University Press, 1970, pp.173–95.

WILLIAM D. PADEN

PEÑAFORT, RAMÓN DE (c. 1180–1275) Ramón de Peñafort was the greatest canon lawyer of his century, third master general of the Dominicans, and architect of the century's novel program for proselytizing Muslims and Jews. Born at his father's castle or seignorial residence of Peñafort at Santa Margarida del Penedes, Ramón presumably received his arts education at the cathedral of Barcelona, where he became a cleric and *scriptor* in 1204. A decade later he undertook legal studies at the University of Bologna and subsequently taught there. By 1223 he was back at Barcelona Cathedral as provost canon of its chapter. He soon left all to become a Dominican mendicant, presumably at Barcelona's Santa Caterina priory. He is thought to have assisted Cardinal Jean d'Abbeville, the papal legate, in his travels across Spain beginning in 1228 to reinforce the reforms of the Fourth Lateran Council; he was certainly at Zaragoza in 1229 to decide the annulment of the marriage between Jaime I and Leonor of Castile. In 1230 he was called to Rome as papal chaplain and confessor. Pope Gregory IX commissioned him there to construct the *Decretals,* promulgated in 1234; with Gratian's *Decretum,* this systematization of a century's laws in some two thousand sections remained the code of the church until the twentieth century. Ramón then refused the metropolitanate of Tarragona, and in 1236 returned to the Barcelona priory. Continuously involved in important canonical cases there, he was active at the parliament (*corts*) of Monzón in 1236, was delegated to lift the papal excommunication from Jaime I (whose friend and counselor he was), and became involved in the dismissal of Tortosa's bishop and the provision of Huesca's and Mallorca's bishops. The Dominican chapter general elected him head of the order in 1238. He left a lasting mark especially by his revision of their constitutions and his integration of the order's nuns before suddenly resigning in 1240.

Returning to Santa Caterina priory, he spent the next thirty-five years there on massive missionary projects and in most of the Crown of Aragón's religious crises. He was active against heresy, persuading King Jaime to allow the Inquisition; he was regularly counselor to the king; and he adjudicated important public quarrels. Ramón's main preoccupation was with the founding of language schools for intrusive missionary disputation with Muslims and Jews, and with devising a program of persuasive confrontation and handbooks of polemical argumentation. He opened an Arabic language and disputation center at Tunis in 1245 and at Murcia in 1266. He persuaded Thomas Aquinas to construct his masterwork, *Contra gentiles,* for these missions.

Through the school centers, compulsory sermons in mosques and synagogues, the public disputation of 1263 in Barcelona, censorship of rabbinic books, and the aggressive labors of Dominicans like Pau Cristià and Ramon Martí, Ramón helped turn Mediterranean Spain into a stormy laboratory for the new rationalist-confrontational missionary methods. This was part of the wider mendicant effort to convert India, China, and Islamic countries by polemical dialogue. Jeremy Cohen argues for an even more revolutionary orientation in Ramón's vision: a conviction that Talmudic Judaism was antibiblical, depriving Jews of their right by Christian teaching to practice their faith in Christian lands. Contemporary hagiographers stress instead Ramón's mission to the Muslims of Spain, and he himself reported euphorically on the successful conversion of many. The roots of these movements, and the inevitability of their ultimate failure, have been more recently discussed by authors such as Robert Burns, Jeremy Cohen, and Dominique Urvoy.

Throughout all his activity in public life, missionary disputation, or Dominican administration, Ramón remained a scholar on the cutting edge of

Roman and canon law. His legal publications multiplied from the start of his career at Bologna to his last year of life in Barcelona. The writings circulated throughout Europe and had immense influence. The most important were his *Summa iuris canonici*, written at Bologna; his *Summa de casibus poenitentiae* (or *Summa de confessoribus*), written in 1222–1225 but redone in 1234–1236; his *Decretales*, written between 1230 and 1234; and the Dominican constitutions. Some sermons and letters, as well as legal responses (*dubitalia*) survive. The *Decretales* had as great an influence on national codes, like Alfonso el Sabio's *Siete Partidas*, as his confessors' handbook had on the ethical and behavioral life of Christendom. Though a Tarragona Council presented a special report and petition for his canonization in 1279, that honor came only in 1601.

See also **Gratian; Jaime (Jaume) I of Aragón-Catalonia; Martí, Ramón**

Further Reading

Burns, R. I. "Christian-Islamic Confrontation in the West: The Thirteenth-Century Dream of Conversion." *Amer can Historical Review* 76 (1971), 1386–1434.
Rius Serra, J. *San Raimundo de Peñafort: diplomatario.* Barcelona, 1954.

ROBERT I. BURNS, S. J.

PEPIN Frankish leaders of the Carolingian family. Among Charlemagne's ancestors, three named Pepin were especially distinguished by their political authority among the Franks. Pepin I of Landen (Pepin the Old or the Elder; d. ca. 640) founded the family of the Arnulfings or the Pippinids, later known as the Carolingians, through the arranged marriage of his daughter, Begga, to Ansegisel, the son of Arnulf of Metz (d. ca. 645). Pepin was named mayor of the palace (*major domus*) of Austrasia by the Merovingian king Clotar II of

Neustria (r. 584–629), for having assisted the monarch to unite the kingdoms of Austrasia and Neustria. During his mayoralty, the office grew into the most powerful position in the Frankish territories, equaling or surpassing the royal throne in importance.

After the murder of Pepin's son and successor, Grimoald in 656, the Pippinids lost control of the Austrasian mayoralty; but in 687, Pepin II of Heristal, duke of Austrasia and Grimoald's nephew, led the Austrasian army to victory over the Neustrians and became mayor of the palace in both regions. From this post, he gradually strengthened his authority over all the Merovingian kingdoms, through his support of the church, manipulation of ecclesiastical posts, and military campaigns.

Pepin III (the Short; d. 768) and Carloman I (d. 754), grandsons of Pepin II, each inherited half the Frankish territories on the death in 741 of their father, Charles Martel, mayor in the united realm. The two brothers cooperated closely in governing their lands; in 743, they together placed another Merovingian, Childeric III, on the royal throne, empty since 737. In 747, however, Carloman felt called to a religious life and abdicated; Pepin became mayor of the entire kingdom. Having deposed Childeric, a move supported by Pope Zachary I, Pepin was acclaimed king in November 751. During a visit to Francia in 754, Pope Stephen II anointed the new monarch along with his wife and sons, Charles (later Charlemagne; 742–814) and Carloman II (d. 771). In recognition of the hope that the new monarchy would protect the Roman church, the pope used the occasion to name Pepin and his sons "patricians of the Romans."

As ruler of the Franks, Pepin III oversaw reform of the secular government and, with the aid of the Irish missionary Boniface, of the ecclesiastical organization. His efforts in the latter regard, especially, provided the foundation for the cultural and intellectual revival known as the Carolingian renaissance, under Pepin's son Charlemagne.

See also **Charlemagne; Charles Martel; Pepin III the Short**

Further Reading

Hlawitschka, Eduard. "Die Vorfahren Karls des Grossen." In *Karl der Grosse: Lebenswerk und Nachleben*, ed. W. Braunfels et al. 5 vols. Dusseldorf: Schwann, 1965, Vol. 1, pp. 51–82.

McKitterick, Rosamond. *The Frankish Kingdoms Under the Carolingians, 751–987*. London: Longman, 1983.

Miller, David Harry. "Sacral Kingship, Biblical Kingship, and the Elevation of Pepin the Short." In *Religion, Culture, and Society in the Early Middle Ages: Studies in Honor of Richard E. Sullivan*, ed. Thomas F.X. Noble and John J. Contreni. Kalamazoo: Medieval Institute, 1987.

Noble, Thomas F.X. *The Republic of St. Peter: The Birth of the Papal State, 680–825*. Philadelphia: University of Pennsylvania Press, 1984.

Riché, Pierre. *The Carolingians: A Family Who Forged Europe*, trans. Michael I. Allen. Philadelphia: University of Pennsylvania Press, 1993.

CELIA CHAZELLE

PEPIN III THE SHORT (714–768), Pepin III, called "the Short" by later historians, played a key role in establishing the Carolingian family as the predominant force in the west. In 741 Pepin and his brother Carloman succeeded their father, Charles Martel, as joint holders of the office of mayor of the palace, an office that had been successfully exploited by Charles Martel (in 714–741) and his father, Pepin II of Herstal (in 687–714), to the point where they exercised real power at the expense of the Merovingian kings of the Franks whom they supposedly served. From 741 to 747 Pepin III and Carloman acted jointly to withstand threats to their position, especially from

the dukes of Bavaria, Aquitaine, and Alemannia who were seeking to escape Frankish overlordship. They strengthened their ties with the church by supporting the missionary and reforming efforts of the Anglo-Saxon monk Boniface, acting in Francia under papal auspices.

In 747 Carloman withdrew from his office to become a monk. Pepin assumed sole power and soon decided to assume the royal office. To legitimatize this bold act against the claims of the Merovingian dynasty, he sought and received the approval of Pope Zacharias I (r. 741–752). In 751 Pepin deposed the last Merovingian king and had himself elected king by the Frankish magnates and anointed by a bishop, an innovation in Frankish history that gave a sacramental character to the royal office.

Pepin's accession to the royal office soon led to his involvement in Italian affairs. By the mid-eighth century a crisis had developed in Italy as a result of the decline of Byzantine power. The papacy, which had established control over the territory around Rome, was challenged by the Lombards, who in 751 seized Byzantine territories around Ravenna (called the Exarchate) and threatened Rome. Pope Stephen II (r. 752–757) turned to Pepin for protection and in late 753 traveled to Francia to negotiate with him. The result was a promise by Pepin to protect the pope and his Roman subjects and to restore to the papacy territories that Stephen claimed the Lombard had illegally seized. In return, Stephen reanointed Pepin and his sons and invested them with the title *patricius Romanorum*, which implied a role as protector of the Romans. Pepin made good his promise by conducting successful military campaigns against the Lombards in 755 and 756. He forced the Lombards to surrender to the papacy considerable territories legally belonging to the Byzantine empire. This "Donation of Pepin," coupled with the territory around Rome that the papacy already controlled, formed the basis of an independent papal state stretching across the Italian peninsula from Rome to Ravenna. During the remainder of his reign Pepin honored his role as protector of the papacy and the "republic of Rome" by using diplomatic means to restrain the Lombards.

As king of the Franks, Pepin was mainly concerned with solidifying and expanding the power and prestige of the royal office. He effectively used force to increase the Franks' control over Bavaria and Aquitaine and to ward off attacks by the pagan Saxons. He took the lead in promoting reform of the church, a role that gave substance to his claim to rule as an agent of God promoting the true faith. The expanding influence of the Franks in Italy and southern Gaul led to diplomatic exchanges with the Byzantine empire and the Abbasid caliphs of the Muslim world. By the end of his reign, the first Carolingian king of the Franks had expanded the position of his people to the status of a major power.

See also **Charles Martel; Stephen II, Pope**

Further Reading

Editions and Translations

Capitularia regum Francorum, ed. Alfred Boretius and Victor Krause. Monumenta Germaniae Historica, Leges, 2(1–2). Hannover: Hansche Buchhandlung, 1883–1897, Vol. 1, pp. 24–43.

Carolingian Chronicles: Royal Frankish Annals and Nithard's Histories, trans. Bernhard Walter Scholz with Barbara Rogers. Ann Arbor: University of Michigan Press, 1970, pp. 37–47.

Codex Carolinus, ed. Wilhelm Gundlach: Monumenta Germaniae Historica, Epistolae Merowingici et Karolini, 1. Berlin: Weidemann, 1892, pp. 469–558, 649–653.

Concilia aevi karolini, ed. Albert Werminghoff. Monumenta Germaniae Historica, Concilia, 2(1–2). Hannover and Leipzig: Hahnsche Buchhandlung, 1896–1898, pp. 1–73.

The Fourth Book of the Chronicle of Fredegar; with its Continuation, trans. J. M. Wallace-Hadrill. Medieval Classics. London and New York: Nelson, 1960, pp. 96–122. (Latin text with English translation.)

Die Urkunden der Karolinger, Vol. 1, *Die Urkunden Pippins, Karlomanns und Karls des Grossen,* ed. Engelbert Mühlbacher. Monumenta Germaniae Historica, Diplomatum Karolinorum, 1. Hannover: Hahnsche Buchhandlung, 1906, pp. 1–60.

Critical Studies

Affeldt, Werner. "Untersuchungen zur KönigshebungPippins." *Frühmittelalterliche Studien,* 14, 1980, pp. 95–187.

Hahn, Heinrich. *Jahrbücher des fränkischen Reiches, 741–752.* Berlin: Duncker und Humblot, 1863.

Halphen, Louis. *Charlemagne and the Carolingian Empire,* trans. Giselle de Nie. Europe in the Middle Ages, 3. Amsterdam: North-Holland, 1977, pp. 3–39.

Kempf, Friedrich, et al. *Handbook of Church History,* Vol. 3, *The Church in the Age of Feudalism,* ed. Hubert Jedin and John Dolan, trans. Anselm Biggs. New York: Herder and Herder; London: Burns and Oates, 1969, pp. 3–25.

Noble, Thomas F. X. *The Republic of Saint Peter: The Birth of the Papal State, 680–825.* The Middle Ages. Philadelphia: University of Pennsylvania Press, 1984, pp. 1–122.

Oelsner, Ludwig. *Jahrbücher des fränkischen Reiches unter König Pippin.* Leipzig: Duncker und Humblot, 1871.

Riché, Pierre. *Les carolingiens: Une famille qui fit l'Europe.* Paris: Hachette, 1983, pp. 71–103.

RICHARD E. SULLIVAN

PÉROTIN (Pérotinus; fl. late 12th–early 13th c.) Because he composed liturgical vocal polyphony at Notre-Dame for two, three, and four parts (each part sung by a soloist) and employed the rhythmic modes, sophisticated devices of repetition and voice exchange, unprecedented length, and important notational innovations, Pérotin was the most significant musical figure of the early 13th century. His achievements profoundly influenced the course of Western music. The music theorists Johannes de Garlandia and Anonymous 4 mention "Magister Pérotinus," but only the latter lists seven of his musical compositions and chronologically places him as "the best discantor" among other singers, composers, and notators working in Paris from the late 12th to late 13th century. Anonymous 4 credits Pérotin with the polyphony found today at the beginning of each of the three major extant Notre-Dame sources *(W1, F,* and *W2):* the Graduals *Viderunt omnes* and *Sederunt principes*, both for four voices, and adds to the list three-part polyphony for the Alleluia *Posui adiutorium* and Alleluia *Narivitas*, and three conductus, the three-part *Salvatoris hodie*, the two-part *Dum sigillum*, and the monophonic *Beam viscera*. On the basis of stylistic affinity with these works, several other works in the Notre-Dame sources have been credited to him. Anonymous 4's statement that Pérotin made many clausulae and edited, revised, or shortened Léonin's *Magnus liber organi* has led many to attribute to him one or more of the series of independent discant clausulae that survive in *W1* and *F.*

Petrus, succentor (subcantor) of the cathedral ca. 1207–38, has been proposed as the most probable identity for Anonymous 4's *"Pérotinus optimus discantor,"* partly because responsibility for the daily services at the cathedral would have fallen to the succentor rather than the cantor, whose post had become largely administrative. Petrus' dates seem to correlate with Anonymous 4's description of Léonin's *Magnus liber organi*, which he stated was in use until the time of Pérotin, while Pérotin's "book or books" were used in the cathedral of Notre-Dame in Paris up to Anonymous 4's own time, probably the 1280s. Hans Tischler and others have maintained, however, that Pérotin lived ca. 1155/60–1200/05, largely on the basis that ordinances issued in 1198 and 1199 by Odo de Sully, bishop of Paris, sanctioned performance of three-

and four-part organum at Notre-Dame during Christmas Week. That Pérotin's composition of the four-part polyphony for *Viderunt omnes* and *Sederunt principes* might have elicited these decrees can only be conjectured. The dating of Pérotin's polyphony is particularly important to a history of the musical style of the period. If it dates generally before 1200, that would mean that the rhythmic modes and their notation as well as the discant clausula and consequently the early motet were well advanced at the very beginning of the 13th century.

See also **Léonin; Philip the Chancellor**

Further Reading

Pérotin. Works, ed. Ethel Thurston. New York: Kalmus, 1970. Tischler, Hans. "Pérotinus Revisited." In *Aspects of Medieval and Renaissance Music: A Birthday Offering to Gustave Reese*, ed. Jan LaRue. New York: Norton, 1966, pp. 803–17.

Wright, Craig. *Music and Ceremony at Notre Dame of Paris, 500 –1550*. Cambridge: Cambridge University Press, 1989, pp. 288–94.

SANDRA PINEGAR

PETER COMESTOR (ca. 1000– 1178) Born in Troyes, Peter became in 1147 dean of the cathedral there. Sometime before 1159, he went to Paris, where he studied under Peter Lombard and later taught theology. He became chancellor of the cathedral of Notre-Dame between 1164 and 1168. He died in 1178 and was buried at the abbey of Saint-Victor. Although known primarily for the *Historia scholastica*, Peter wrote other works, including some 150 sermons, the *Summa de sacramentis* (based on Peter Lombard's *Sententiae)*, some *quaestiones*, and commentaries on the Gospels, as well as glosses on the *Glossa ordinaria*, on the *Magna glossatura* of Peter Lombard, and perhaps on Lombard's *Sententiae*. The *Historia scholastica*, used in the schools and later in the university curriculum, was a narrative presentation of biblical history from Creation through the life of Jesus. Peter here sought to counteract what he saw as the destruction of the connected literal-historical sense of the text through the practice of a spiritual exegesis that tended to divide the text into brief "fragments" for symbolic interpretation. Peter not only drew upon traditional patristic authors for the historical sense; he also used Josephus's *Jewish Antiquities* and the commentaries on the *Octateuch* by Andrew of Saint-Victor. In a practical way, Peter continued the emphasis on reading Scripture according to the literal-historical sense that had been established at the abbey of Saint-Victor by Hugh of Saint-Victor.

See also **Andrew of Saint Victor; Hugh of Saint-Victor; Peter Lombard**

Further Reading

Peter Comestor. *Historia scholastica; Sermons.* PL 198.1045–844.
——. *Summa de sacramentis*, ed. Raymond M. Martin. In *Maître Simon et son groupe: De sacramentis*, ed. Heinrich Weisweiler. Louvain: "Spicilegium Sacrum Lovaniense," 1937, appendix.
Smalley, Beryl. *The Study of the Bible in the Middle Ages.* 3rd ed. Oxford: Blackwell, 1983.

GROVER A. ZINN

PETER LOMBARD (ca. 1100–1160) The "Master of the *Sentences*" born and educated in Novara, Lombardy, arrived in Paris via Reims (ca. 1135) with a letter of recommendation from Bernard of Clairvaux to Abbot Gilduin of Saint-Victor. While he apparently never taught at the abbey, Peter did preach there, and he maintained close ties with Saint-Victor throughout his life.

The Lombard soon made himself a reputation as a formidable theologian. By 1142–43, he had the dubious dis-

tinction of being named by Gerhoch of Reichersberg as a dangerous innovator; in 1148, he was summoned by Pope Eugenius III to the Consistory of Reims to help judge the orthodoxy of another innovator, Gilbert of Poitiers, whose christology Peter found lacking. Teaching at Notre-Dame by 1143, he was a canon by 1145 and steadily rose in rank (subdeacon by 1147, deacon by 1150, archdeacon by 1157). In 1158, his years of service were crowned by his election as bishop of Paris; this honor was shortlived, as he died in 1160.

The earliest works of the Lombard are his commentaries on the Psalms (before 1138) and on the epistles of Paul (by 1142). Though Herbert of Bosham reports that Peter meant them for his personal edification only and that he never finished them, they were swiftly and widely circulated, often even replacing the marginal-interlinear glosses for the Psalms and epistles in the *Glossa ordinaria*. Known as the *Magna glossatura*, they became the most frequently cited works of Scripture exegesis in the Middle Ages. Peter based his two commentaries on a close reading of Anselm of Laon's glosses and Gilbert of Poitiers's biblical commentaries. He kept the *Glossa's* patristic and Carolingian base, took over Gilbert's organization scheme and hermeneutic principles, and consistently worked out doctrinal positions and current theological issues in connection with the scriptural text.

Even more central to the history of medieval theology and philosophy is the Lombard's *Quattuor libri sententiarum*, or the *Sententiae*. Sentence collections proliferated in the 12th century, as theologians strove to systematize and professionalize their field. Peter Lombard's *Sententiae* (1155–57) became an instant and enduring success throughout Europe (legislated into the theological curriculum of the University of Paris in 1215) and remained without serious competition until replaced by the *Summa* of Thomas

Aquinas in the 16th century. It was second only to the Bible in importance in theological training; hundreds of theologians wrote commentaries on the *Sententiae*. The reasons for its success have recently been set forth in a effort to restore the luster to the Lombard's tired reputation. Its comprehensive coverage of topics, logical order, lack of dependence on or promotion of any elaborate philosophical system, sensitivity to the need for clarity and consistency in theological language, and readiness to address controversial issues while acknowledging contemporary consensus, all ensured the utility of the *Sententiae* to generations of theologians and philosophers. In addition, Peter's christology avoided many of the semantic pitfalls that plagued contemporary theologians; his Trinitarian views were solemnly ratified at the Fourth Lateran Council in 1215.

See also **Anselm of Laon; Aquinas, Thomas; Bernard of Clairvaux**

Further Reading

Peter Lombard. *Commentariu sin psalmos davidicos.* PL 191.55–169.
——. *Collectanea in omnes b. Pauli epistolas.* PL 191.1297–696 and PL 192.9–520.
——. *Sententiae in IV libris distinctae,* ed. Ignatius Brady. 3rd ed. rev. In *Spicilegium Bonaventurianum.* Grottaferrata: Editiones Collegii S. Bonaventurae ad Claras Aquas, 1971–81,Vols. 4–5.
——. *Sermons* (printed under the name of Hildebert of Lavardin). PL 171.339–964. [See list in J. de Ghellinck, "Pierre Lombard." In *Dictionnarie de théologie catholique.* Vol. 12 (1935), cols. 1961–62.]
Bertola, Ermenegildo. "Pietro Lombardo nella storiografia filosofica medioevale." *Pier Lombardo* 4 (1960): 95–113.
Colish, Marcia L. *Peter Lombard.* Leiden: Brill, 1993.
——. "Systematic Theology and Theological Renewal in the Twelfth Century." *Journal of Medieval and Renaissance Studies* 18 (1988): 135–56.
——. "From *sacra pagina* to *theologia*: Peter Lombard as an Exegete of Romans." *Medieval Perspectives* 7 (1991): 1–19.
——. "*Psalterium Scholasticorum*: Peter Lombard and the Emergence of Scholastic Psalms Exegesis." *Speculum* 67 (1992): 531–48.
Delhaye, Philippe. *Pierre Lombard: sa vie, ses œuvres, sa morale.* Montreal: Institut d'Études Medievalès, 1961.

THERESA GROSS-DIAZ

PETER OF POITIERS (d. 1205)   Master in theology at Paris from ca. 1167, successor (1169) to the chair in theology held by Peter Comestor, and chancellor of the schools of Paris from 1193. Peter of Poitiers (to be distinguished from another contemporary Peter of Poitiers, a regular canon of the abbey of Saint-Victor at Paris) was a leading figure in the Parisian schools in the last third of the 12th century. A student under Peter Lombard and a strong supporter of the Lombard's theology when it came under attack in the last decades of the 12th century, Peter of Poitiers was a determined advocate of the usefulness of dialectics in theology.

He was also influenced by the Victorine tradition, represented by Hugh and Richard of Saint-Victor, Peter Comestor, and Peter the Chanter, that emphasized both historical study and the importance of biblical allegory. Four of Peter's works reveal these influences and also Peter's distinctive contributions to theological, historical, and exegetical-homiletic studies in the schools of Paris.

Peter's *Sententiarum libri quinque* (probably before 1170) is modeled directly on the dialectical method as used by Peter Lombard in his *Quattuor libri sententiarum* and also draws upon its content. Peter's work is not, however, a commentary on the Lombard's but is his own formulation of a "compendium of theology" to instruct those who are beginning the study of Scripture. Peter's faithfulness to the Lombard's thought earned him the distinction of being included with the Lombard, Gilbert of Poitiers, and Abelard as one of the "four labyrinths of France" in Walter of Saint-Victor's antidialectical polemic.

Three of Peter's works on scriptural interpretation deserve mention. *Allegoriae super tabernaculum Moysis* explicates the four senses of scriptural interpretation (history, allegory, tropology, and anagogy) and presents a detailed allegorical interpretation of the materials, construction, associated objects, and other aspects of the Tabernacle of Moses. *Compendium historiae in genealogia Christi* is a work of historical explication in service of biblical exegesis. By means of a grand genealogical schematic, with accompanying text, extending from Adam and Eve to Jesus Christ, Peter sketched out the essentials of biblical history for beginning students. Tradition held that he was the first to draw genealogical "trees" on animal skins and hang them on classroom walls in order to instruct students. Finally, *Distinctiones super psalterium* is part of a move within the schools to make resources for biblically based preaching more accessible to students and preachers. The *Distinctiones* takes a word from a psalm and gives a set of meanings, the *distinctio*, all supported by references to other passages of Scripture. Thus, the reader had ready at hand a compendium of many symbolic interpretations of such words as "bed," "fire," or "stone." Some manuscripts present the work as a continuous prose text; others have a schematic structure, with the "key word" in the margin and a series of red lines connecting with the meanings. Such a handbook would be of great use to preachers searching for allegories, and Peter's book is similar in its intent to Peter the Chanter's *Summa Abel* and Praepositinus of Cremona's *Summa super psalterium*.

See also **Hugh of Saint-Victor; Peter Comestor; Peter Lombard**

Further Reading

Moore, Philip S. *The Works of Peter of Poitiers, Master in Theology and Chancellor of Paris (1193–1205)*. Notre Dame: University of Notre Dame Press. 1936.

—— and James Corbett, eds. *Petri Pictaviensis Allegoriae super tabernaculum Moysis*. Notre Dame: University of Notre Dame Press, 1938.

—— and Mathe Dulong, eds. *Pern Pictaviensis Sententiarum libri quinque*. Notre Dame: University of Notre Dame Press, 1943, Vol. 1.

——, Joseph N. Garvin, and Marthe Dulong, eds. *Petri Pictaviensis Sententiarum libri quinque*. 2 vols. Notre Dame: University of Notre Dame Press, 1950.

GROVER A. ZINN

PETER THE CHANTER (d. 1197) Born near Beauvais, Peter studied at Reims and by ca. 1173 was a master in theology in the schools of Paris. In 1183, he was named chanter of the cathedral of Notre-Dame in Paris. Peter was judge delegate for the pope on a number of occasions, including the divorce trial of Philip II Augustus (1196). He was elected dean of the cathedral of Reims in 1196, but he became ill and was unable to take the position. He entered the Cistercian abbey of Longpont as a monk and died there.

As a teacher in the schools, Peter exerted a remarkable influence on both students and peers. He was at the center, with Peter Comestor and Stephen Langton, of what Beryl Smalley (following Grabmann) called the "biblical moral school," a group of masters in the late 12th-century schools who followed the emphasis on biblical study developed at the abbey of Saint-Victor by Hugh, Richard, and Andrew of Saint-Victor.

While most masters of the day commented only on the Psalms and Gospels, Peter, like Stephen Langton, commented on all the books of the Old and New Testaments. Moreover, Peter was critical of those masters who devoted themselves to seeking out details of the text and its interpretation rather than focusing on the important matters of moral teaching and behavior.

In addition to his lectures on Scripture (which were taken down as *reportationes* by his students), the Chanter devoted much of his time to lecturing and disputing on moral questions; he found the 12th-century church desperately lacking when compared with gospel injunctions and Paul's teaching. Dedicated to testing present practice against the straightforward teaching of Scripture, he was, however, a realist who saw that seriously embracing scripturally based reform could lead to criticism of accepted practices in the church of his day. He raised and resolved hundreds of moral "questions," which were incorporated in his *Summa de sacramentis et animae consiliis*. The questions, with numerous exempla to illustrate situations and conclusions, were grouped according to the sacraments of the church (baptism, confirmation, extreme unction, consecration of churches, the eucharist, and penance). All systematization seems to have given way in the section on penance, for it is a vast collection of case after case for analysis and resolution. Peter's *Verbum abbreviation* is also directed toward moral concerns, this time with copious citations of passages from "authorities" (Scripture, Christian writers, classical authors) and exempla to discourage vice and promote virtue. Although Peter was recognized as a preacher, no sermons have survived. He was tireless in his devotion to ecclesiastical duties and to the work of a master in lecturing on Scripture, posing questions for resolution through disputation, and providing in his writings the outcome, in a text, of his labors in the classroom.

See also **Peter Comestor; Stephen Langton**

Further Reading

Peter the Chanter. *Summa de sacramentis et animae consiliis*, ed. Jean-Albert Dugauquier. 3 vols. in 5. Louvain: Nauwelaerts, 1954–67.

——. *Verbum abbreviation*. PL 205.1–554. [Short version.]

Baldwin, John W. *Masters, Princes, and Merchants: The Social Views of Peter the Chanter and His Circle*. 2 vols. Princeton: Princeton University Press, 1970.

Smalley, Beryl. The *Gospels in the Schools* c. *1100–c. 1280*. London: Hambledon, 1985, pp. 101–18.

——. *The Study of the Bible in the Middle Ages*. 3rd ed. rev. Oxford: Blackwell, 1983, chap. 5.

GROVER A. ZINN

PETER THE VENERABLE (1092/94–1156) Born into the noble Montbossier family in Auvergne, Peter was dedicated by his mother as a child oblate to the Cluniac monastery of Sauxillanges, where he was educated. He became a monk of Cluny not long before 1109. Four of his six brothers also entered ecclesiastical careers; one became archbishop of Lyon while the other three were abbots of Vézelay, La Chaise-Dieu, and Manglieu. Peter served as prior of Vézelay and of Domène before being elected abbot of Cluny in 1122. He proved to be a skillful administrator of a vast monastic organization comprising over 1,000 dependent monasteries and priories; he was also an influential ecclesiastical leader, had scholarly interests, and was a strong defender of Cluniac customs against Cistercian criticisms. His extensive correspondence with notables throughout the western church (193 extant letters) is a rich source of information about various matters, both ecclesiastical and secular, including the world of learning and spirituality. Although Peter and Bernard of Clairvaux were in opposition on matters of monastic discipline and practice, they remained friends throughout life, as their letters reveal. Peter's health was never good, and he probably suffered from malaria on several occasions and from chronic bronchitis.

Peter's election to the abbacy of Cluny came at a time when the order needed a firm hand, following the disastrous abbacy of Pons de Melgeuil and the brief four-month abbacy of Hugues II. Monastic discipline was lax; finances needed attention; the large sprawling Cluniac order needed an effective leader. Peter rose to the occasion. He began to enforce a more strict discipline, attended to finances, and traveled often to deal with problems within the order. He was moderate in demands, conservative in outlook, conciliatory in approach, and thoughtful in controversy. Peter became enmeshed in the controversy between Cistercians and Cluniacs, which was marked by heated exchanges on both sides. Peter's Letter 28, a response (if not directly, at least in effect) to Bernard of Clairvaux's *Apologia ad Guillelmum* as well as the general Cistercian attack on Cluniac laxity in discipline and departure from the *Rule* of St. Benedict, is a carefully reasoned defense of the Cluniac way of life and offers one of the best sources for understanding both the conflict and the Cluniac point of view. Peter was no idle defender of the *status quo*, however; he actively reformed and strengthened Cluniac discipline.

Peter wrote against both heresy (the Petrobrusians [*Tractatus adversos Petrobrusianos haereticos*]) and non-Christian religions (Judaism [*Adversos Judaeorum inveteratum duritiem*] and Islam [*Epistola de translatione sua; Summa totius haeresis Saracenorum*]), After a journey to Spain in 1142, he commissioned a translation of the Qur'an, the first into Latin, and other Arabic texts, so that he might better understand Islam in order to refute it with reason rather than force. In writing against Judaism, he respected the Hebrew version of Scripture and argued without special pleading from Christian Scripture, i.e. the New Testament.

In addition to his numerous journeys in France, Peter traveled to England (1130 and 1155), Spain (1142; perhaps 1124 and 1127), and Rome (1139 [Lateran Council], 1144,1145,1147,1151–52,1154). He extended the hospitality of Cluny to Peter Ab–lard after Ab–lard's condemnation at Sens in 1140. Peter the Venerable wrote to H–lo+se a sensitive letter giving a detailed account of Ab–lard's last days. In addition to the works mentioned above, his writings include sermons, liturgical texts (including an Office of the Transfiguration), hymns, and a treatise recounting holy lives (De *miraculis*). He was an exemplar of the best of the Benedictine tradition.

See also **Abélard, Peter; Bernard of Clairvaux; Héloïse**

Further Reading

Peter the Venerable. *Opera omnia.* PL 189.61–1054.
——. *The Letters of Peter the Venerable,* ed. Giles Constable. 2 vols. Cambridge: Harvard University Press, 1967.
Constable, Giles, ed. *Petrus Venerabilis, 1156–1956: Studies and Texts Commemorating the Eighth Centenary of His Death.* Rome: Herder, 1956.
Knowles, David. *The Historian and Character.* Cambridge: Cambridge University Press, 1963, pp. 50–75.

GROVER A. ZINN

PETRARCA, FRANCESCO (20 July 1304–19 July 1374) It is a critical commonplace to refer to Dante Alighieri as the "last medieval man" and to Petrarch (Francesco Petrarca) as the "first modern man," but this tends to obscure the many distinctly "medieval" aspects of Petrarch's works. To be sure, Petrarch does anticipate certain characteristics that are central to our (modern) understanding of the changeover in attitudes in the passage from the Middle Ages to the Renaissance: the emphasis on the individual and on secular matters; the minute investigation of the human psyche; the imitation of classical literary forms, style, and language; the understanding of discrete periods in history; and the interest in travel undertaken to see and experience the world. While all these characteristics suggest Petrarch's desire to escape the narrow frame of the religiously and morally proper medieval world, he repeatedly and simultaneously gives evidence of his longing to embrace that same world and its precepts. This constant state of tension is what defines Petrarch's so-called modern sensitivity and allows us, his readers, to identify with him and his seemingly contradictory aspirations; and this sentiment is aptly presented, over and over, in the *Canzoniere*. We find it in the poems themselves, as in the final verses of *canzone* 264 (*I' vo pensando*): *ché co la morte a latol cerco del viver mio novo consiglio, le veggio 'l meglio et al peggior m'appiglio* (verses 136–136), of which the final verse is a direct and sympathetic translation from Ovid (*Metamorphoses*, 7.20–21). Or we note how Petrarch has ordered the poetic universe of the *Canzoniere* by juxtaposing poems that praise, alternately, his love of earthly things and his profound repentance for such an attitude, as, for example, in the positioning of the two sonnets *Benedetto sia 'l giorno, e' l mese, e l'anno* (61) and *Padre del ciel, dopo i perduti giorni* (62).

In all of Petrarch's works, we recognize the acute eye of the intellectual who carefully observes himself and the world around him and attempts to make some sense of the fragile human condition and its immediate and ultimate purpose within the great order of the cosmos. It is in this unprecedented focus on his own personal situation that we may observe Petrarch's genius and the human drama played out on a small yet universal stage.

While most of his works are ultimately about himself and are thus full of interesting though stylized and carefully crafted bits of autobiographical information, Petrarch did write, late in his life, a *Letter to Posterity* (the Latin title is *Ad posteros* or *Posteritati*), to future generations who

might be curious to learn more about him and his life. This fragmentary epistle was first composed in 1367 and was revised in 1370–1371, yet the latest event recounted is from 1351. In the letter, Petrarch intends to speak about himself, his interests, his outlook—in short, about his personality. What strikes the modern reader is the egotism that pervades the letter, the dramatic departure from the more humble attitude generally adopted by medieval authors who were less likely to put themselves and their accomplishments on display in such a self-centered and self-serving way. Although idealized, conventional portraits are common in works of medieval literature and although the *vidas* of the troubadours and Dante's *Vita nuova* present so-called personal data as historical facts, the authorial "I" and the empirical "I" remain distinctly separate persons. With Petrarch, however, we see a dramatic change in the attitude toward autobiography, such that we know more about this fourteenth-century author than about virtually any other person of his age, precisely because the author himself decided that this would be the case. To make sure that we would know about him, Petrarch compiled large collections of letters, made copious annotations on his manuscripts, and left us other pieces of evidence that allow us see and understand his life as he wanted it to be recorded and remembered. Thus, in the *Letter to Posterity*, Petrarch fashions his own identity, creates his own historical persona, and delineates his role in the events of his time. From other, independent documents we are able to judge the accuracy of the *Letter to Posterity*, and we may conclude that he was a master of self-promotion, acutely aware of his particular place in history. For this reason, we may view him as a precursor of humanistic attitudes on the individual that would emerge in the next centuries.

In the *Letter to Posterity*, Petrarch describes himself as modest and even tempered, as one who prefers sacred literature to vernacular poetry, who is acutely aware of the greatness of antiquity to the impoverished state of his own age, who yearns for the tranquil life of the country and disparages the hectic pace of urban society. While he notes that in his youth he had been overwhelmed by a powerful love, he declares that this is a thing of the past. Despite his voluminous literary production in both Latin and Italian, Petrarch refers only to his works in Latin—his epic poem *Africa*, his treatise on the solitary life (*De vita solitaria*), and his pastoral poems (*Bucolicum carmen*)—for they are the reason for his coronation as poet laureate in Rome atop the Capitoline Hill. As Petrarch tells the story, on the same day (1 September 1340), he received invitations for coronations from the chancellor of the University of Paris and from the Roman senate; to have chosen Paris would have been to give precedence to scholastic culture, and thus his choice of Rome was intended to help restore the ancient glory of that city.

In the *Letter to Posterity*, Petrarch also speaks about his family and friends, his personal habits, his travels, the cities where he lived, and the benefits—for work and mind—of his "transalpine solitude." The last few sentences of the letter speak of Petrarch's affection for Jacopo da Carrara the Younger, ruler of Padua; and while Petrarch would have liked to reside permanently in Padua, Jacopo's untimely death in December 1350 made that impossible. Petrarch notes: "I could stay no longer [in Padua], and I returned to France, not so much from a desire to see again what I had already seen a thousand times as, like a sick man, to be rid of distress by shifting position." This sentence represents perfectly Petrarch's carefully constructed *persona*: he is the restless traveler, the seeker of old manuscripts, the frequenter of ancient sites in an attempt to recapture something of their past glory. The image of the sick man who tries to assuage his pain by shifting position recalls Saint Augustine's image of the sick

woman, who, in allegorical terms, represents the unquiet human soul that will find its peace only in God (*Confessions*, 6.16); however, here Petrarch's frame of reference is limited to earthly life. In this passage, we also observe the drama of his own internal conflict as one caught between earthly attractions and spiritual aspirations, one who, profoundly discontent with his own age, but powerless to change it, dreams of a past grandeur and of a better future time. His confessional work, the *Secretum*, in which Augustine is one of the interlocutors, is concerned with this same conflict.

Life and Works

Petrarch was born in Arezzo to Pietro di Parenzo and Eletta Canigiani. His father, usually called Ser Petracco, was a notary who had migrated to Florence from his hometown of Incisa in the Arno River valley. During the tumultuous early years of the fourteenth century, he made some political enemies in Florence and was exiled on false charges of corruption in public office in October 1302—some nine months after the expulsion of Dante Alighieri on similar grounds. Early in 1305, Petrarch and his mother moved to Incisa, where his brother Gherardo was born in 1307. After six years in Incisa, the family moved to Pisa (1311), where Francesco may have seen Dante among a group of fellow Florentine exiles. In 1312, Ser Petracco resettled his family in Carpentras in southern France, where he was associated with the papal court of Clement V in Avignon. In Carpentras, Francesco began his study of grammar and rhetoric with Convenevole da Prato and became friends with Guido Sette, a boy his own age whose family had moved to France from Genoa. In 1316, Ser Petracco decided that Petrarch should become a lawyer and sent him to the University of Montpellier. During this period his mother died, and to commemorate the sorrowful occasion Petrarch composed his earliest surviving work, an elegiac poem

Altichiero da Zevio (1330–1385). Francesco Petrarca, poet. Detail from the Burial of Saint Lucia. Fresco (1479–1381).
© Erick Lessing/Art Resource, New York.

in thirty-eight Latin hexameters. In 1320, Francesco went, together with his brother and Guido Sette, to Bologna to continue his legal studies, and although he excelled academically, he came to realize that the legal profession was not for him. Nevertheless, the years in Bologna were important in his literary and cultural development, for he befriended a number of other Students and became familiar with the Italian lyric tradition. On the death of his father in April 1326, he returned to Avignon.

On Good Friday, 6 April 1327, in the Church of Saint Clare in Avignon, Petrarch first saw and immediately fell in love with the woman whom he would call Laura. This passion would provide inspiration for his poetic imagination for his entire life. Many poems contained in the evolving collection known as the *Rerum vulgarium fragmenta* or *Canzoniere* celebrate his love for her, as well as her symbolic meaning. Her name, Laura—like that of Dante's Beatrice ("one who gives blessedness or salvation")—was significant in that it suggested the evergreen laurel tree, sacred to Apollo, and thus the

laurel crown of poetic glory. Throughout the *Canzoniere*, Petrarch engages in elaborate wordplay based on "Laura," using such puns as *l'aura* ("the breeze") and *aureola* ("golden") to reiterate her importance.

In 1330, Petrarch and his brother Gherardo had almost dissipated their inheritance. Refusing to follow law or medicine as a profession, Petrarch had to find other employment. Fortunately, he had befriended the bishop of Lombez, Giacomo Colonna, who recommended Petrarch to his brother Cardinal Giovanni Colonna, who in turn offered Petrarch a position as personal chaplain in his household. At Giacomo Colonna's residence in the summer of 1330, Petrarch met and became friends with two other young men: Lello di Pietro Stefano dei Tosetti from Rome (whom Petrarch nicknamed "Lelius") and Ludwig van Kempen ("Socrates") from Flanders, who served as chanter in Cardinal Colonna's chapel. These and other close friends would be very important to Petrarch throughout the course of his life.

As a member of the cardinal's staff, Petrarch was able to travel and meet many people. In 1333, he traveled to Paris and, from there, to Ghent, Liège, Aix-la-Chapelle, Cologne, and Lyon. During these travels he began his lifelong pursuit of manuscripts containing works by classical authors, discovering at Liège, for example, some of Cicero's orations (*Pro Archia*). Also in 1333, in Avignon, Petrarch met the Augustinian monk Dionigi da Borgo San Sepolcro, who introduced him to the works of early Christian writers, especially Saint Augustine, and who gave Petrarch his copy of the *Confessions*. In a letter to Dionigi (*Familiares*, 4.1, dated 26 April 1336), Petrarch gives an account of his and his brother Gherardo's ascent of Mont Ventoux. In it he relates, in thinly veiled allegorical language, how rapidly Gherardo arrives at the summit (signifying the benefits of his monastic vocation) but how difficult his own climb is (signifying the attraction of earthly things). Finally, arriving at the summit and overwhelmed by the majesty of the view, Petrarch opens his copy of Augustine's *Confessions* and reads the following morally oriented monitory sentence: "And men go about wondering at mountain heights and the mighty waves of the sea and broad flowing streams and the circuit of the sea and the wheeling of the stars: and to themselves they give no heed" (10.8.15). The relevance of these words to Petrarch's own situation and their call to introspection are obvious: it is always more difficult to ascend the steep path to the good than it is to wander around in the valleys looking for an easy route to happiness. This intensely Augustinian moment demonstrates the great influence that the saint had on Petrarch, not only in literature but also in life.

In January 1335, thanks to a recommendation by Cardinal Colonna, Petrarch was named by Pope Benedict XII to a canonry in the cathedral of Lombez, an appointment that supported him financially but did not require his residence. Sometime before this appointment, Petrarch had written a long letter in Latin verse to Pope Benedict XII encouraging Benedict to return to Rome. This is the first indication we have of Petrarch's firm belief in the preeminence of Rome as the rightful seat of both the papacy and the empire. Petrarch first journeyed to Rome, as a guest of the Colonna family, late in 1336, and that visit determined his attitude toward the classical past. In a letter to Cardinal Giovanni Colonna, dated 15 March 1337 (*Familiares*, 2.14), he recounts his first impressions of Rome: "No doubt I have accumulated a lot of matter to write about later, but at present I am so overwhelmed and stunned by the abundant marvels that I shouldn't dare to begin.... Rome was greater than I thought, and so are its remains. Now I wonder not that the world was ruled by this city but that the rule came so late."

Petrarch's enthusiasm for Rome is complemented by his patriotism for Italy in general; for example, in *canzone* 128 of the *Canzoniere*, *Italia mia, benché 'l parlar sia indarno*, he laments Italy's abject, strife-torn condition; issues a call to arms (verses 93–96); and concludes with an urgent plea for peace, *i' vo gridando: Pace, pace, pace* (verse 122).

Shortly after his return to Avignon in 1337, Petrarch purchased property and a house in Vaucluse along the Sorgue River, and this became his resort of peace and solitude: *transalpina solitudo mea jocundissima* ("My most delightful transalpine solitary refuge"). In this *locus amoenus* he found the time to read, meditate, write, and entertain close friends. Vaucluse represented for Petrarch the Ciceronian ideal of *ottum,* the leisure to pursue one's interests without having to attend to the concerns of everyday life. A new acquaintance of his in Vaucluse was Philippe de Cabassoles, bishop of Cavillon, to whom Petrarch would later dedicate his Latin treatise *De vita solitaria (On the Solitary Life)*.

During this period of meditative leisure, Petrarch began several of his works, some of classical inspiration: the treatise on the lives of famous men, *De viris illustribus*; his epic poem on the deeds of Scipio Africanus, *Africa*; his collection of Italian poems, the *Canzoniere* or *Rerum vulgarium fragmenta*; and the *Triumph of Love*, the first of the *Trionfi*—six allegorical poems in *terza rima*, based on the descriptions of ancient triumphal pageants. Petrarch would continue to revise most of these works for the rest of his life. The evolution of the *Canzoniere* can be traced through extant manuscripts, some in Petrarch's own hand, that disclose the successive forms of the collection; this would culminate in the version in the Vatican Library, Codex Lat. 3195. Although he divided his time at Vaucluse between Latin and Italian works, Petrarch clearly indicated his preference for the former. On 1 September 1340 he received two invitations to be crowned poet laureate: one letter came from the chancellor of the University of Paris and the other from the Roman senate. Because we know that Petrarch carefully planned the sequence of events leading to these invitations, we can appreciate the coyness with which he reports his careful weighing of these offers, his asking advice from Cardinal Colonna, and his eventual (but foregone) decision to accept the invitation from Rome. Petrarch was familiar with the coronation of poets in antiquity and with a recent revival of that tradition (the coronation of Albertino Mussato in Padua in 1315). This signal honor would, he thought, ensure his fame for posterity and, just as important, reestablish Rome as the locus for culture in the world. To ascertain his worthiness for this honor, he voluntarily underwent a rigorous examination by his sponsor, King Robert of Anjou of Naples. On 8 April 1341, in the palace of the senate on the Capitoline, Petrarch was crowned poet laureate and delivered an oration, in which he spoke of the poet's responsibility and rewards as well as the nature of the poet's profession. The *Coronation Oration* is a wonderful combination of medieval homily and classical rhetoric; in it Petrarch begins with a citation from Virgil's *Georgics* (3.291–292), interrupts it with a recitation of the *Ave Maria*, and then immediately returns to the Virgilian passage. The remainder of the oration contains numerous citations from Virgil, Ovid, Cicero, Horace, and other classical authors. The fame that Petrarch achieved in this single event was immeasurable; indeed, he was now a celebrity, one who was in demand as an honored guest in cities throughout Europe and was cheered wherever he went. This was, in many ways, the beginning of what we might call the cult of personality that Petrarch cultivated and shaped for himself. After leaving Rome, Petrarch spent time in Parma as a guest of the Correggio family and finished a draft of his *Africa*. When he returned to Provence, he began

to study Greek with the Calabrian monk Barlaam, but without mastering much beyond a very elementary level.

The year 1343 was important for Petrarch. At the papal court in Avignon, he met Cola di Rienzo, who would later become the Roman "tribune of the people." In February, Robert of Anjou died. In April, Petrarch's brother Gherardo became a Carthusian monk, and this led Petrarch to reexamine his own life and goals. In 1343, his illegitimate daughter, Francesca, was born. From these troubling events emerged his soul-searching imaginary dialogue with (Saint) Augustine—the *Secretum*—as well as his *Seven Penitential Psalms* and his treatise on the cardinal virtues, the *Rerum memorandarum libri*. In form and content, the *Secretum* is based on classical and early Christian models, especially Augustine's *Confessions*. Whereas in his work the saint achieves a relative peace, Petrarch is constantly tormented by the unresolved conflict between spiritual aspirations and worldly concerns. Despite the sound Christian advice imparted by the character Augustinus to Franciscus and the insistent call to meditate on death in order to prepare one's soul for the afterlife, Franciscus cannot easily abandon his earthly pursuits, nor does he really wish to. The lack of resolution at the end of the three-day dialogue suggests not so much Petrarch's lack of faith as his very human reluctance to abandon immediate worldly pursuits in favor of distant eternal rewards.

During the next few years, Petrarch traveled frequently: to Naples (in 1343), Parma (1344–1345), and Verona (1345). In the Capitular Library in Verona, he found and transcribed the manuscript of Cicero's letters to Atticus, a discovery that encouraged him to begin his own series of letters addressed to classical authors. After returning to Vaucluse in 1346, Petrarch began work on his treatise on the solitary life, *De vita solitaria*, which he subsequently dedicated to Philippe de

Cabassoles. In 1347, Petrarch was happy to receive news of a revolution in Rome and the nomination of Cola di Rienzo to the position of tribune (essentially, dictator), for in these events he saw some signs of the old Roman grandeur. In letters to Cola and the Roman people, Petrarch encouraged them in their battle for liberty. However, Cola's excesses and megalomania would gradually undermine his position and destroy Petrarch's faith in him. After imprisonment in Avignon on charges of heresy, Cola returned to Rome as a senator, only to meet his death at the hands of the Roman people in 1354.

In 1347–1348, the time of the black death, Petrarch was in Verona and in Parma, where news of Laura's death (6 April 1348) came to him in a letter from his old friend "Socrates." The date of Laura's death and that of his first meeting with her, exactly twenty-one years before in 1327, would provide the basic chronological structure for a series of "anniversary" poems in the *Canzoniere*. The disastrous effects of the plague, which resulted in the deaths of several friends (e.g., Cardinal Colonna and Franceschino degli Albizzi), led Petrarch to write the *Triumph of Death* (*Triumphus mortis*).

His discovery of Cicero's letters in Verona in 1345 gave Petrarch the idea of collecting his own letters, and by 1350 he was actively engaged in this project, which would lead to the formation of the *Familiares* (twenty-four books), *Seniles* (seventeen books), *Sine nomine* (nineteen letters), and *Epistolae metricae* (three books). For the jubilee year of 1350, Petrarch traveled to Rome, stopping on the way in Florence, where he met Giovanni Boccaccio for the first time. Among Petrarch's many admirers in Florence were Boccaccio, Zanobi da Strada, Francesco Nelli, and Lapo da Castiglionchio. Always searching for manuscripts, Petrarch found in Lapo's library a copy of Quintilian's *Institutes* and some of Cicero's orations. After his Roman pilgrimage, Petrarch spent time in Parma

and Padua. The Florentine republic offered him a teaching post at the university there, and the pope summoned him to return to Avignon. In 1351–1352, Petrarch was once again working in Vaucluse on *De viris illustribus* and the *Canzoniere*. In 1353, during his last months in Vaucluse, Petrarch was involved in an extended and intense debate with one of the pope's doctors over the relative merits of medicine and poetry, and this discussion resulted in the *Invective contra medicum*, in which Petrarch defends the supremacy of the liberal arts over the lower mechanical arts and praises poetry as the highest form of wisdom.

During 1353–1361, Petrarch lived for the most part in Milan, as a guest of the Visconti family and with the special support of Archbishop Giovanni Visconti. Despite the criticism he received from his friends for living under a despot, Petrarch was pleased with his circumstances, for he was able to do virtually anything he wanted. One project he began there became his longest work, *De remediis utriusque fortune*, a moral treatise in two books, the first dealing with the perils of good fortune and the second with the dangers of its opposite, adverse fortune. The form of *De remediis* is a series of dialogues between personified qualities; for example, in Book I, Joy and Hope—the children of Prosperity—argue against Reason; and in Book II, Reason's opponents are Sorrow and Fear, the offspring of Adversity. It was in Milan that Petrarch met Emperor Charles IV, whom he encouraged to reestablish the empire with Rome as its capital. These dealings with Charles, undertaken on behalf of the Visconti, allowed Petrarch to travel to Basel and Prague. In 1361, the Visconti sent him to Paris, where he delivered an oration, in Latin, in the presence of King John of France and John's court. Petrarch's eight years in Milan marked the longest nearly continuous residency of his life. Moreover, they were productive years, allowing him to complete *De remediis* and to make great progress in his compilation of the *Canzoniere* and the *Familiares*.

After his move to Padua in the summer of 1361, Petrarch received the sad news of the deaths of his illegitimate son Giovanni (who died in the plague in Milan) and of his old friends "Socrates" and Philippe de Vitry. However, he enjoyed frequent correspondence and encounters with Boccaccio, who often supplied him with copies of rare manuscripts (e.g., Augustine's *Expositions on the Psalms,* Varro's *De lingua latina,* the life of Peter Damian). In May 1362, Petrarch had an opportunity to advise Boccaccio, who had been terrified by a visit from a fanatical monk representing the late Pietro Petroni of Siena. Informed that he did not have long to live and that he should renounce the study of poetry, Boccaccio thought first to dispose of all his books, but Petrarch dissuaded him and encouraged him to continue his studies. However, Petrarch said that he would gladly buy Boccaccio's books if Boccaccio had a change of heart. Petrarch's love of books, and his zeal in collecting them, enabled him to amass what was at the time perhaps the largest private library in Europe. Recognizing the value of his collection, Petrarch reached a formal agreement with the *maggior consiglio* of Venice whereby he would give his library to Venice in exchange for a suitable house there and the assurance that his books would not be dispersed. Petrarch's collection thus formed the basis for the Biblioteca Marciana in Venice. In Venice, Petrarch enjoyed visits from Boccaccio and numerous other friends; he also was gladdened by the birth of his grandchildren (Eletta and Francesco) and saddened by the death of his friends "Laelius" and Francesco Nelli.

Around 1366, Petrarch employed Giovanni Malpaghini as a scribe for the tedious task of copying the *Familiares* and the *Canzoniere.* In 1367, during a journey to Pavia by canal barge, Petrarch was able to respond to accusations lodged against him a year previously by four Aristotelian philosophers (Leonardo Dandolo, Tommaso Talenti, Zaccaria Contarini, and Guido da Bagnolo) who claimed that he was "a good man, but uneducated." In his response, the invective *De sui ipsius et multorum ignorantia* (*On His Own Ignorance and That of Many Others*), Petrarch gives clear evidence of the changeover from the outmoded ideas of scholastic philosophy to the new humanism; in particular, he argues that the source of knowledge lies not in pseudoscientific syllogistic arguments but rather in a profound intuitive awareness of the self.

In 1368, Petrarch, having been given some land near Arquà (some 10 miles, or about 16 kilometers, southwest of Padua)—initiated the construction of a house, which was finished in 1370. Among his possessions were a lute and a painting of the Madonna by Giotto, both of which have disappeared. Failing health prevented him from undertaking some highly desired trips to Rome and Avignon. His last works include a translation into Latin of Boccaccio's story of Griselda (*Decameron*, 10.10) and the *Invective against the Man Who Maligned Italy* (*Invectiva contra eum qui maledixit Italie*). The motivation for the *Invective* was an anonymous letter written by a Frenchman (Jean de Hesdin) that praised the French and spoke ill of Italy. As for the tale of patient Griselda, Petrarch was so taken by its value as a moral example that he wanted to make it available to readers who did not know Italian, and his translation was Chaucer's model for the Clerk's Tale in the *Canterbury Tales.* In his last years, Petrarch went on several diplomatic missions for Francesco da Carrara; he wrote letters and continued to work on the definitive versions of the *Canzoniere, Trionfi,* and *De viris illustribus* as well as on the compilations of his letters. During the night between 18 and 19 July 1374, Petrarch died. He was buried on 24 July in a marble tomb in the parish church at Arquà.

The Vernacular Works

Although the *Letter to Posterity* says virtually nothing about his Italian works, Petrarch obviously considered them of great importance, for he was continuously revising them up to the very end of his life. If what he says in the *Letter to Posterity* is truly indicative of the way he wanted to be remembered, then it is a great irony, for his fame today rests primarily on his Italian poetry, which proved so influential during the Renaissance, particularly in France, Spain, and England. The composition of the *Canzoniere* was attended to with great care: its 366 poems are divided into two major sections—*In vita di madonna Laura* and *In morte di madonna Laura*—beginning with the secular sonnet *Voi ch'ascoltate in rime sparse il suono* ("You who hear the sound in scattered rhymes") and ending with the religious ode to the Virgin *Vergina bella, che di sol vestita* ("Beautiful Virgin, clothed with the sun"). A large variety of subjects and themes—amorous, political, artistic, moral, and religious—are treated; nevertheless, the truly remarkable feature of the collection is Petrarch's obsessive attention to the presentation of his own poetic persona. Many poems in the *Canzoniere* are characterized by stylized, conventional attitudes toward love and by the presentation of a pensive, introspective lover, and these features were imitated widely in the Renaissance. This combination of psychological and poetic conceits would come to constitute what we generally refer to today as Petrarchism. Although Petrarch was not the inventor of the sonnet, he brought it to such perfection that this fourteen-line metrical form has become known as the Petrarchan sonnet. The six allegorical *Triumphs* (*Trionfi*), which relate the progress of the soul in relation to love, chastity, death, fame, time, and eternity, had a major impact on Renaissance literature, art, and pageantry.

The Latin Works

Petrarch's literary production in Latin encompasses a number of major themes that highlight his crucial place in the history of western civilization. On the one hand, his treatises on fortune (*De remediis utriusque fortune*) and on the monastic life (*De otio religioso*) are distinctly medieval in flavor and conception. On the other hand, there is a definite, forward-looking "Renaissance" cast to many of the Latin works. Petrarch consciously attempted to revive classical genres and patterns in the epic poem *Africa* and in the series of famous lives (*De viris illustribus*) and events (*Rerum memorandarum libri*). His treatise on the solitary life, *De vita solitaria*, is a well-reasoned defense of the Ciceronian ideal of studious leisure (*otium*), which he tried to follow in his own life. He took the cue from classical examples in his collections of letters, in his invectives, in his pastoral poems (*Bucolicum carmen*), and in his dialogue with Augustine (*Secretum*).

See also Boccaccio, Giovanni; Chaucer, Geoffrey; Dante Alighieri; Robert of Anjou

Further Reading

Editions and Translations of Petrarch

Il Bucolicum carmen e i suoi commenti inediti, ed. Antonio Avena. Padua: Società Cooperativa Tipografica, 1906. (Reprint, Bologna: Forni, 1969.)

Canzoniere, ed. Gianfranco Contini. Turin: Einaudi, 1968.

Canzoniere, 2 vols, ed. Ugo Dotti. Rome: Donzelli, 1996.

Canzoniere, ed. Marco Santagata. Milan: Mondadori, 1996.

Il "De otio religioso," ed. Giuseppe Rotondi. Vatican City: Biblioteca Apostolica Vaticana, 1958.

De viris illustribus, ed. Guido Martellotti. Florence: Sansoni, 1964.

De vita solitaria, Buch I: Kritische Textausgabe und Ideengeschichtlicher Kommentar, ed. K. A. E. Enenkel. Leiden: Brill, 1990.

Epistolae de rebus familiaribus et varie, 3 vols, ed. G. Fracassetti. Florence: Le Monnier, 1859.

Invective contra medicum, ed. P. G. Ricci. Rome: Edizioni di Storia e Letteratura, 1950.

Letters from Petrarch, trans. Morris Bishop. Bloomington: Indiana University Press, 1966.

Letters of Old Age: Rerum Senilium Libri XVIII, 2 vols., trans. Aldo S. Bernardo, Saul Levin, and Reta A. Bernardo. Baltimore, Md.: Johns Hopkins University Press, 1992.

Letters on Familiar Matters (Rerum familiarum libri) I—XVI, trans. Aldo S. Bernardo. Baltimore, Md.: Johns Hopkins University Press, 1982.

Letters on Familiar Matters (Rerum familiarum libri) XVII–XXIV, trans. Aldo S. Bernardo. Baltimore, Md.: Johns Hopkins University Press, 1985.

The Life of Solitude, trans. Jacob Zeitlin. Urbana: University of Illinois Press, 1924.

Lord Morley's "Tryumphes of Fraunces Petrarcke": The First English Translation of the "Trionfi," ed. D. D. Carnicelli. Cambridge, Mass.: Harvard University Press, 1971.

Petrarch: The Canzoniere or Rerum vulgarium fragmenta, trans. Mark Musa. Bloomington: Indiana University Press, 1996.

Petrarch's Africa, trans. Thomas G. Bergin and Alice S. Wilson. New Haven, Conn.: Yale University Press, 1977.

Petrarch's Book without a Name: A Translation of the Liber Sine Nomine, trans. Norman P. Zacour. Toronto: Pontifical Institute of Mediaeval Studies, 1973.

Petrarch's Bucolicum Carmen, trans. Thomas G. Bergin. New Haven, Conn.: Yale University Press, 1974.

Petrarch's Letters to Classical Authors, trans. Mario Cosenza. Chicago, Ill.: University of Chicago Press, 1910.

Petrarch's Lyric Poems: The "Rime Sparse" and Other Lyrics, ed. and trans. Robert M. Durling. Cambridge, Mass.: Harvard University Press, 1976.

Petrarch's Remedies for Fortune Fair and Foul, 5 vols., trans. Conrad H. Rawski. Bloomington: Indiana University Press, 1991.

Petrarch's "Secretum" with Introduction, Notes, and Critical Anthology, trans. Davy A. Carozza and H. James Shey. New York: Peter Lang, 1989.

Petrarch's "Songbook," "Rerum vulgarium fragmenta": A Verse Translation, trans. James Wyatt Cook. Binghamton, N.Y.: Medieval and Renaissance Texts and Studies, 1995.

Prose, ed. G. Martellotti, P. G. Ricci, E. Carrara, and E. Bianchi. Milan and Naples: Ricciardi, 1955.

The Renaissance Philosophy of Man, ed. Ernst Cassirer, Paul Oskar Kristeller, and John Herman Randall, Jr. Chicago, *Ill.*: University of Chicago Press, 1948. (Contains the following translations: *A Self-Portrait; The Ascent of Mont Ventoux; On His Own Ignorance and That of Many Others; A Disapproval of an Unreasonable Use of the Discipline of Dialectic; An Averroist Visits Petrarca. Petrarca's Aversion to Arab Science; A Request to Take Up the Fight against Averroes.*)

Rerum familiarium: Libri I—VIII, trans. Aldo S. Bernardo. Albany: State University of New York Press, 1975.

Rerum memorandarum libri, ed. Giuseppe Billanovich. Florence, 1945.

Rime disperse, ed. and trans. Joseph A. Barber. New York: Garland, 1991.

Rime disperse, ed. Angelo Solerti. Florence: Sansoni, 1909.

Rime, Trionfi, e Poesie Latine, ed. F. Neri, G. Martellotti, E. Bianchi, and N. Sapegno. Milan and Naples: Ricciardi, 1951.

Salmi penitenziali, ed. Roberto Gigliucci. Rome: Salerno Editrice, 1997.

Secretum, ed. Ugo Dotti. Rome: Archivio Guido Izzi, 1993.

Sine nomine: Lettere polemiche e politiche. Bari: Laterza, 1974.

Trionfi, Rime estravaganti, Codice degli abbozzi, ed. Vinicio Pacca and Laura Paolino. Milan: Mondadori, 1996.

The Triumphs of Petrarch, trans. Ernest Hatch Wilkins. Chicago, Ill.: University of Chicago Press, 1962.

Critical Studies

Amaturo, Raffaele. *Petrarca.* Bari: Laterza, 1971.

Baron, Hans. *Petrarch's "Secretum": Its Making and Its Meaning.* Cambridge, Mass.: Harvard University Press, 1985.

Bernardo, Aldo S. *Petrarch, Scipio, and the "Africa": The Birth of Humanism's Dream.* Baltimore, Md.: Johns Hopkins University Press, 1962.

——. *Petrarch, Laura, and the Triumphs.* Albany: State University of New York Press, 1974.

Bishop, Morris. *Petrarch and His World.* Bloomington: Indiana University Press, 1963.

Bosco, Umberto. *Francesco Petrarca.* Bari: Laterza, 1961.

Cosenza, Mario Emilio. *Francesco Petrarca and the Revolution of Cola di Rienzo,* 2nd ed. New York: Italica, 1986. (With new introduction and bibliography by Ronald G. Musto. Originally published 1913.)

Dotti, Ugo. *Vita di Petrarca.* Bari: Laterza, 1987.

Forster, Leonard. *The Icy Fire: Five Studies in European Petrarchism.* Cambridge: Cambridge University Press, 1969.

Foster, Kenelm. *Petrarch: Poet and Humanist.* Edinburgh: Edinburgh University Press, 1984.

Francesco Petrarca, Citizen of the World, ed. Aldo S. Bernardo. Padua and Albany: Antenore and State University of New York Press, 1980.

Francis Petrarch, Six Centuries Later: A Symposium, ed. Aldo Scaglione. Chapel Hill and Chicago, Ill.: University of North Carolina and Newberry Library, 1975.

Hainsworth, Peter. *Petrarch the Poet: An Introduction to the Rerum Vulgarium Fragmenta.* New York and London: Routledge, 1988.

Jones, Frederic J. *The Structure of Petrarch's "Canzoniere": A Chronological, Psychological, and Stylistic Analysis.* Cambridge: D. S. Brewer, 1995.

Kennedy, William J. *Authorizing Petrarch.* Ithaca, N.Y.: Cornell University Press, 1994.

Mann, Nicholas. *Petrarch.* Oxford: Oxford University Press, 1984.

Mazzotta, Giuseppe. *The Worlds of Petrarch.* Durham, N.C.: Duke University Press, 1993.

Nolhac, Pierre de. *Petrarque et l'humanisme,* 2 vols. Paris: Champion, 1907.

Petrarch's "Triumphs": Allegory and Spectacle, ed. Konrad Eisenbichler and Amilcare A. Iannucci. Ottawa: Dovehouse, 1990.

Rico, Francisco. *Vida u obra de Petrarca.* Chapel Hill: University of North Carolina Press, 1974.

Shapiro, Marianne. *Hieroglyph of Time: The Petrarchan Sestina.* Minneapolis: University of Minnesota Press, 1980.

Sturm-Maddox, Sara. *Petrarch's Metamorphoses.* Columbia: University of Missouri Press, 1985.

——. *Petrarch's Laurels.* University Park: Pennsylvania State University Press, 1992.

Trinkaus, Charles. *The Poet as Philosopher: Petrarch and the Formation of Renaissance Consciousness.* New Haven, Conn.: Yale University Press, 1979.

Whitfield, J. H. *Petrarch and the Renascence.* Oxford: Blackwell, 1943.

Wilkins, Ernest Hatch. *The Making of the Canzoniere and Other Petrarchan Studies.* Rome: Edizioni di Storia e Letteratura, 1951.

——. *Studies in the Life and Works of Petrarch.* Cambridge, Mass.: Medieval Academy of America, 1955.

——. *Petrarch's Eight Years in Milan.* Cambridge, Mass.: Medieval Academy of America, 1958.

——. *Petrarch's Later Years.* Cambridge, Mass.: Medieval Academy of America, 1959.

——. *Life of Petrarch.* Chicago, Ill.: University of Chicago Press, 1961.

——. *Studies on Petrarch and Boccaccio.* Padua: Antenore, 1978.

CHRISTOPHER KLEINHENZ

PETRUS DE DACIA (ca. 1230–1289)

Petrus de Dacia is called Sweden's first author. While studying at the *studium generale* of the Dominicans in Cologne (1267–1269), Petrus visited the nearby village of Stommeln, where he met the German beguine Christina of Stommeln in 1267. As Christina's confessor, he often witnessed her remarkable and even terrifying experiences: ecstasies, stigmatizations, and visions that convinced him that Christina was a saint capable of showing him the right way to God. In 1269–1270, when studying in Paris, Petrus began the correspondence with Christina that continued until his death. In 1270, he returned to Sweden, revisiting Stommeln on his way home, and in 1271 he was appointed lector of the Dominican convent of Skanninge. Not earlier than 1277, he was transferred to Västerås, where he became lector and then prior, until 1280, when he was made lector of the convent of Visby in his native island of Gotland. In 1279, while staying a month in Cologne, he again paid several visits to Christina. Having become prior in Visby, he was also appointed *socius* of the provincial for the General Chapter at Bordeaux in summer 1287. On his way home from Bordeaux, Petrus met Christina at Stommeln for the last time. In a letter of September 9, 1289, Christina was informed that Petrus had died during the Lent of that year.

Two literary works in Latin by Petrus are known, both in the *Codex Juliacensis* from about 1300, now in the Bischöfliches Diözesanarchiv in Aachen. In the *Vita Christinae Stumbelensis* ("Life of Christina of Stommeln"), Petrus describes his visits to Stommeln and his strong emotional reactions to Christina's mystical experiences. The book also contains their correspondence and a biography of Christina written by the parish priest of Stommeln, who used to read and translate Petrus's letters to Christina and write down her letters. Although Petrus was deeply attached to Christina, he repeatedly emphasizes that their love is a spiritual one, having Christ for its true object.

Petrus's other known work is *De gratia naturam ditante sive De virtutibus Christinae Stumbelensis* ("On Grace Enriching Nature, or On the Virtues of Christina of Stommeln"). It consists of a poem of forty-three hexameters praising Christina's virtues and a long theological treatise commenting on each word of the poem. The greater part of this work is lost. Petrus exploits his philosophical and theological learning to find theoretical explanations of Christina's behavior. The work presents few original thoughts, being mainly a compilation of the ideas of Petrus's masters in Cologne and Paris, Albertus Magnus and Thomas Aquinas.

Further Reading

Editions

Petrus de Dacia. *Vita Christinae Stumbelensis.* Ed. Johannes Paulson. Scriptores Latini Medii Aeui Suecani, 1. fasc. 2. Gothenburg: Wettergren & Kerber, 1896.

Petrus de Dacia. *De gratianaturam ditante sive De virtutibus Christinae Stumbelensis.* Edition *critique avec une introduction par Monika Asztalos.* Acta Universitatis Stockholmiensis. Studia Latina Stockholmiensia, 28. Stockholm: Almqvist & Wiksell, 1982 [review by Eva Odelman in *Archivum Latinitatis Medii Aevi,* 43 (1984), 166–76]; [a new edition of Petrus's letters with a Swedish translation is being prepared by Monika Asztalos].

Literature

Schück, Henrik. *Vår förste författare. En själshistoria från medeltiden.* Stockholm: Geber, 1916.

Lehmann, Paul. *Skandinaviens Anteil an der lateinischen Literatur und Wissenschaft des Mittelalters.* 1. Stück. Sitzungsberichte der Bayerischen Akademie der Wissenschaften. Philosophisch-historische Abteilung, jahrgang 1936, Heft 2. Munich: Bayerische Akademie der Wissenschaften, 1936, pp. 44–47.

Gallén, jarl. *La province de Dacie de l'ordre des Frères Prêcheurs. 1: Histoire générale jusqu'au grand schisme.* Helsinki: Söderström, 1946.

Olsen, T. D. "Petrus de Dacia." *New Catholic Encyclopedia.* New York: McGraw-Hill, 1967, vol. 11, p. 247.

Lindroth. Sten. *Svensk lärdomshistoria.* 4 vols. Stockholm: Norstedt, 1975–81. vol. 1, pp. 64–71.

Nieveler, Peter. *Codex luliacensis. Christina von Stommeln und Petrus von Dacien, ihr Leben und Nachleben in Geschichte. Kunst und Literatur.* Veröffentlichungen des Bischöflichen Diözesanarchivs Aachen, 34. Mönchengladbach: Kühlen, 1975.

Asztalos, Monika. "Les lettres de direction et les sermons épistolaires de Pierre de Dacie." In *The Editing of Theological and Philosophical Texts from the Middle Ages: Acts of the Conference Arranged by the Department of Classical Languages, University of Stockholm, 29–31 August 1984.* Ada Universitatis Stockholmiensis.

Studia Latina Stockholmiensia, 30. Stockholm: Almqvist & Wiksell, 1986, pp. 161–84.

Den Svenska Litteraturen. 1: Från fomüd till frihetsid 800–1718. Stockholm: Bonnier, 1987, pp. 66–71.

EVA ODELMAN

PHILAGATHUS OF CERAMI (d. 1154 or later)

Greek prose in medieval Italy reaches a high point with the sermons of the twelfth-century Siculo-Calabrian monk Philagathus. He is conventionally called "of Cerami," although it is not clear whether the designation *Keramítes* refers to Cerami in Sicily or to some other place, or is instead a classicizing version of the demotic surname *Kerameüs* ("Potter"). Until fairly recently, he was known as Theophanes Cerameus, thanks to a misattribution in one branch of a later Byzantine redaction that converted his sermon collection into a homiliary organized according to the liturgical calendar, and his work was at times presented as that of a ninth- or eleventh-century writer into which more recent material had been inserted. In his Italo-Greek manuscripts he is styled "the philosopher" (and therefore is sometimes so identified in library catalogs) and is also often called Philippus (perhaps his baptismal name) rather than Philagathus. Of his approximately ninety surviving sermons, only thirty-eight have a modern critical edition; the remainder either must be read in texts descended from the very defective *editio princeps* of Francesco Scorso (1644) or are still unpublished. Even so, these cultured and rhetorically accomplished productions have earned a considerable reputation for artistic excellence.

To the extent that they can be localized with certainty, Philagathus's early associations are Calabrian. After entering religion at an unidentified church of Saint Andrew, he trained at the Nea Hodegetria monastery near Rossano, later known as the Patír or the Patirion, for whose founder, Bartholomew of

Simeri (d. 1130), he gave a commemorative sermon. Philagathus preached in Rossano proper; in Reggio; and in Sicily, at Messina, Taormina, Troina, and especially Palermo, where at least one of his sermons was delivered before King Roger II in the predecessor of today's cathedral. His sermon in Roger's Palatine Chapel (seemingly after 1140 but sometimes assigned to the chapel's consecration in 1140) contains the earliest extended description of this renowned monument.

Although Philagathus has been called a court preacher, it might be more accurate to call him a preacher whose distinction led to appearances at court. The venues of most of his sermons are not fully known. He was still active during the reign of William I (1154–1166). An allegorical commentary on the *Aethiopica* of Heliodorus (an ancient Greek novel used by Philagathus in at least one sermon), recently thought to be his, has now been shown to be much older. The attributions to him of the anonymous *Life* of Bartholomew of Simeri, of a grammatical textbook now lost, and of a verse introduction to the fables of Symeon Seth (one form of the Greek "mirror of princes" *Stephanites and Ichnelates*) are all very dubious.

Further Reading

Editions

Caruso, Stefano, ed. "Le tre omilie inedite 'Per la domenica delle palme' di Filagato da Cerami." *Epeterìs Hetaireías Byzantinôn Spoudôn,* 41, 1974, pp. 109–127.

Patrologia Graeca, 132, cols. 9–1078. (Scorso's edition and Latin translation of sixty-two sermons.)

Rossi Taibbi, Giuseppe, ed. *Filagato da Cerami: Omelie per i vangeli domenicali e le feste di tutto l'anno,* Vol. 1, *Omelie per le feste fisse, Istituto siciliano di studi bizantini e neoellenici.* Testi, 11. Palermo: Istituto Siciliano di Studi Bizantini e Neoetenici, 1969.

Translations

Gaşpar, Cristian-Nicolae. "Praising the Stylite in Southern Italy: Philagathos of Cerami on Saint Symeon the Stylite." *Annuario dell'Istituto Romeno di Cultura e Ricerca Umanistica*, 4, 2002, pp. 93–108.

Lavagnini, Bruno. *Profilo di Filagato da Cerami: Con traduzione della Omelia XXVII pronunziata dal pulpito della Cappe Palatina in Palermo*. Palermo: Accademia Nazionale di Scienze, Lettere, e Arti già del Buongusto, 1992. (Reprinted in *Bollettino della Badia Greca di Grottaferrata*, n.s., 44, 1990, pp. 231–244, issued in 1993.)

Manuscript

Rossi Taibbi, Giuseppe. *Sulla tradizione mano-scritta dell'omiliario di Filagato da Cerami*. Istituto Siciliano di Studi Bizantini e Neoellenici, Quaderni, 1. Palermo: Istituto Siciliano di Studi Bizantini e Neoellenici, 1965.

Critical Studies

Acconcia Longo, Augusta. "Filippo il filosofo a Costantinopoli." *Rivista di Studi Bizantini e Neoellenici*, n.s., 28, 1991, pp. 3–21.

Foti, Maria Bianca. "Culture e scrittura nelle chiese e nei monasteri italo-greci." In *Civiltà del Mezzogiorno d'Italia: Libro, scrittura, documento in età normanno-sveva—Atti del convegno dell'Associazione Italiana dei Paleografi e Diplomatisti (Napoli–Badia di Cava dei Tirreni, 14–18 ottobre 1991)*, ed. Filippo D'Oria. Cultura Scritta e Memoria Storica, 1. Salerno: Carlone, 1994, pp. 41–76. (See especially pp. 65–67.)

Garzya, Antonio. "Per la cultura politica nella Sicilia greconormanna." In *Percorsi e tramiti di cultura*. Naples: M. D'Auria, 1997, pp. 241–247.

Houben, Hubert. "La predicazione." In *Strumenti, tempi, e luoghi di comunicazione nel Mezzogiorno normanno-svevo: Atti delle undecime Giornate normanno-sveve, Bari, 26–29 ottobre 1993*, ed. Giosuè Musca and Vito Sivo. Bari: Dedalo, 1995, pp. 253–273.

Kitzinger, Ernst. "The Date of Philagathos' Homily for the Feast of Saints Peter and Paul." In *Byzantino-Sicula*, Vol. 2, *Miscellanea di scritti in memoria di Giuseppe Rossi Taibbi*. Istituto Siciliano di Studi Bizantini e Neoellenici, Quaderni, 8. Palermo: Istituto Siciliano di Studi Bizantini e Neoellenici, 1975, pp. 301–306.

Lucà, Santo. "I Normanni e la 'ritmica' del sec. XII." *Archivio Storico per la Calabria e la Lucania*, 60, 1993, pp. 1–91. (See especially pp. 69–79, 86–87.)

Perria, Lidia. "La clausola ritmica nella prosa di Filagato da Cerami." *Jahrbuch der österreichischen Byzantinistik*, 32 (*Akten des XVI. Internationalen Byzantinistenkongress, Wien, 4.–9. Oktober 1981*), part 3, 1982, pp. 365–373.

JOHN B. DILLON

PHILIP II AUGUSTUS (1165–1223)

King of France, 1180–1223. Philip II was the first great architect of the medieval French monarchy. Building upon the accomplishments of Louis VI and Louis VII, he began the process of converting feudal into national monarchy, expanding the crown's political and geographical influence, by his death in 1223, far beyond what they had been at his accession in 1180.

As was common in the case of kings ascending as children to the throne, Philip was initially dominated by powerful relatives, in his case the influential and wealthy ruling family of Champagne. His early struggle to assert royal influence was supported by his father's rival, Henry II of England, who denied himself the pleasure of taking advantage of the fifteen-year-old king's apparent weakness. A few years later, Henry probably wished that he had not been so honorable, since Philip utilized the traditional patricidal conflict traditional in the Angevin family against his former protector. This policy saw the French king triumphant over his father's ancient adversary and his sons by 1204, when the luckless King John saw the Angevin territories in France dissolve. By the end of his reign, Philip II had increased his territory nearly fourfold. The English loss of territory north of the Loire augmented the French ruler's lands, but he also added to his acquisitions by the forfeitures of contumacious vassals, by political duplicity, by cleverly arranged marriages, and by manipulation of the confusion over land possession arising from the Albigensian Crusade. Philip Augustus was not a great military leader; he was an astute politician.

Philip was the founder of the centralized bureaucratic state. He chose bourgeois administrators, as well as men from the lower nobility, to run his kingdom, men whose primary loyalty was to their king rather than to their class or to their families. Their offices were remunerated by salary rather than farmed. Philip used feudal rights to enhance his royal position; in his reign, the authority of the king began shifting slowly from his rights exercised as feudal suzerain to his rights exercised as sovereign; he was becoming less a private, feudal lord than a public figure of authority. This obviously contributed to a decline in the functional importance of the feudal structure (it was never a feudal *system*), as did the growing commutation of lord-vassal relationships from mutually exchanged personal obligations into money payments. The administrators of Philip's domains, *baillis* and *prévôts*, were essentially estate managers, men with wide-ranging fiscal, judicial, military, and other responsibilities. Philip's financial administration improved greatly, his policies based upon the model of his newly conquered province, Normandy. He also made Paris what we moderns would call the capital of France.

Philip Augustus was, then, the monarch under whom French monarchy became more a practical than a theoretical concept. His domain, larger than the fief of any vassal, was to remain the dominant power base in France in succeeding generations. As Luchaire wrote, at Philip's death "the [Capetian] dynasty was solidly established, and France founded."

See also **Henry II; John**

Further Reading

Baldwin, John W. *The Government of Philip Augustus*. Berkeley: University of California Press, 1986.

Bautier, Robert-Henri, ed. *La France de Philippe Auguste:le temps des mutations*. Paris: CNRS, 1982.

Bordonove, Georges. *Philippe Auguste*. Paris; Pygmalion, 1983.

Fawtier, Robert. *The Capetian Kings of France*. London: St. Martin, 1960.

Hallam, Elizabeth. *Capetian France, 987–1328*. London: Longman, 1980.

JAMES W. ALEXANDER

PHILIP III THE BOLD (1245–1285)
King of France, 1270–85. As a boy, Philip appears to have been easygoing and easily influenced, especially by his mother, Margueritc of Provence. As a king, he was dominated at the outset by the counsels of Pierre de la Broce, a former adviser of his father, Louis IX. Later, he came under the influence of his uncle Charles, count of Anjou. Philip became king while on crusade to Tunis with his father, who died of illness during the siege of the city. Philip is the first king whose regnal years begin with the burial of his predecessor rather than the coronation of the new king, which in his case was delayed until 1271.

Although most scholars regard Philip's reign as a hiatus in the development of the monarchy, it was marked by important events. The death, childless, of his uncle and aunt, Alphonse of Poitiers and Jeanne de Toulouse, in 1271 on the way back from crusade brought their vast holdings in the south of France into the royal domain despite the importunities of Charles of Anjou, who coveted the fiefs. The acquisition of these lands by the crown sealed the ascendancy of the French in Languedoc. Philip carried on an active foreign policy. With the support of Charles of Anjou, he briefly put forward his candidacy to the imperial throne. He made efforts to draw neighboring German principalities under French influence. He aggressively defended Capetian family interests in Castile and Aragon. And he intervened with military success in Navarre when a succession crisis there in the mid-1270s threatened French interests.

Philip was drawn into war in Spain again toward the end of his reign when the Aragonese supported the rebellion of the Sicilians against Charles of Anjou (the Sicilian Vespers, 1282). Charles's pleas for support and the blessing of the pope led to the French crusade against Aragon, an ill-fated expedition across the Pyrénées in 1285, in which the French were routed. During the retreat, Philip III himself died.

Philip was married twice: first (1262) to Isabella of Aragon, who died in 1271 on the return from the crusade to Tunis. She was the mother of Philip's son and successor, Philip IV the Fair. In 1274, Philip III married Marie de Brabant, whose party at court was responsible for bringing an end to the influence of Pierre de la Broce; charged with treason, he was executed in 1278. Philip the Fair seems always to have had a strong dislike of Marie, about whom Pierre had spread ugly rumors. These included allegations that she and her party wanted to displace the children of her husband's first marriage by her own in the line of succession and that she had even poisoned Philip IV's older brother as part of her plan. No such conspiracy was ever proved, however, and the succession proceeded smoothly even under the difficult circumstances of the crusade against Aragon.

See also **Louis IX**

Further Reading

Langlois, Charles-Victor. *Le régne de Philippe III le Hardi.* Paris: Hachette, 1887.

WILLIAM CHESTER JORDAN

PHILIP IV THE FAIR (1268–314) King of France, 1285–1314. Philip expanded royal power within the kingdom and dominated the ecclesiastical and secular affairs of western Europe. The grand-son of St. Louis, whose canonization he achieved in 1297, he imitated and attempted to surpass Louis's achievements. Served devotedly by a series of powerful ministers, he imposed his own stamp on governmental policies, instituting widespread consultation of his subjects, issuing a host of reform charters, canceling and returning taxes when the causes that prompted them ceased, and subordinating to his authority the dukes of Aquitaine/Guyenne (also kings of England) and the counts of Flanders. Attentive to matters of conscience and believing in his role as God's minister, he upheld Christian orthodoxy against Pope Boniface VIII and the Knights Templar, appealing to a general council against the pope and destroying the Templars; he obtained papal bulls forgiving him for sins he feared he might commit; he magnified the importance of the royal power to cure; in 1306, he expelled the Jews from France. Anxious to establish the full legitimacy and the glory of the Capetian house, he encouraged the reinterpretation of the Capetians' history. Upholding the highest standards of morality and publicizing his own scrupulosity, in 1314 he presided over the trial and execution of two knights charged with adultery with his own daughters-in-law, thus casting doubt on the legitimacy of his grandchildren.

Born between April and June 1268, while Louis IX was still ruling, Philip, second son of Philip III the Bold and Isabella of Aragon (d. 1271), had a troubled childhood, dominated by the scandals that erupted at court after his father's marriage in 1274 to Marie de Brabant, suspected of poisoning Philip's elder brother, who died in 1276, shortly before the death of his third brother. In 1284, Philip was knighted and married to Jeanne, heiress of Champagne and Navarre; he became king in 1285 after his father's death on a crusade against Aragon. Having extricated himself from the ill-fated venture, Philip avoided conflict for nine years, but in 1294 he precipitated war against the mighty Edward I of England, duke of Aquitaine/Guyenne. Settled in 1303, the fruitless episode strained the kingdom's finances and led to manipulation of the currency. It resulted in the marriages of Philip's sister Marguerite to Edward in 1299 and of his daughter Isabella to Edward II in 1308; the latter union would give Edward III grounds for claiming the throne of France. The war also initiated a conflict with the Flemings, Edward I's allies and Philip's subjects, which, settled in 1305, broke out again in 1312 because of the harsh peace terms Philip imposed. Clerical taxation imposed for the war occasioned Boniface VIII's controversial bull *Clericis laicos* in 1296. From then until Boniface's death in 1303, Philip and the pope were locked in sporadic but bitter struggles involving the limits of secular jurisdiction over ecclesiastics. In the spring of 1303, Philip presided over assemblies in Paris that charged Boniface with heresy and immorality; in September 1303, the pope was violently attacked in Anagni when Philip's minister Guillaume de Nogaret summoned him to submit to the judgment of a council. Clement V, the Gascon-born cardinal who became pope in 1305, was more to the king's liking; he granted Philip many privileges and in 1311 accepted the suppression of the Knights Templar, the crusading order whose assets Philip had seized in 1307, again because he believed them guilty of heresy and immorality.

Philip failed to achieve some of his ambitions. He never succeeded in placing a relative on the imperial throne; his visionary scheme after his wife's death in 1305 to become ruler of the Holy Land was abortive. The power he exercised within the kingdom led, at the end of his reign, to the formation of leagues of disgruntled subjects protesting his fiscal and monetary policies and demanding the restoration of old customs; his eldest son and successor, Louis X (r. 1314–16), issued numerous charters to pacify them, and he sacrificed Philip's minister

Enguerran de Marigny and other officials to their princely enemies at court. Philip used his three sons and his daughter to advance his own goals. Isabella married Edward II of England; Louis married Marguerite, daughter of the duke of Burgundy; Philip's wife, Jeanne, brought to the crown the county of Burgundy; Jeanne's mother, Mahaut of Artois, offered a dowry of 100,000 *livres* to persuade Philip to accept another daughter, Blanche, as the wife of his youngest son, the future Charles IV. The imprisonment of Marguerite and Blanche for adultery in 1314 was the first of a series of tragedies suffered by Philip's direct descendants. Because of the death of Louis X's posthumous son, John I, the product of a second marriage, the throne passed to Philip V (r. 1316–22); because he left no male heir, he was succeeded by Charles IV (r. 1322–28), at whose death without male heir the rule of the direct Capetians ended and the crown passed to the house of Valois.

See also **Boniface VIII, Pope; Clement V, Pope; Edward I; Jeanne of Navarre**

Further Reading

Bautier, Robert-Henri. "Diplomatique et histoire politique: ce que la critique diplomatique nous apprend sur la personnalité de Philippe le Bel." Revue *historique* 259 (1978): 3–27.

Brown, Elizabeth A.R. *The Monarchy of Capetian France and Royal Ceremonial.* London: Variorum, 1991.

———. *Politics and Institutions in Capetian France.* London: Variorum, 1991.

Favier, Jean. *Philippe le Bel* Paris: Fayard, 1978.

Strayer, Joseph R. *The Reign of Philip the Fair.* Princeton: Princeton University Press, 1980.

ELIZABETH A.R. BROWN

PHILIP VI (1293–1350) First Valois king of France, 1328–50. The son of Charles of Valois (brother of King Philip IV the Fair) and Marguerite, daughter of

Charles II of Naples, Philip did not become an important figure until he inherited the counties of Valois, Anjou, and Maine from his father in 1325. By that time, the reigning monarch was Philip's first cousin Charles IV, who had no son or surviving brother. When Charles died at the end of January 1328, he left a pregnant queen, and the French magnates named Philip of Valois regent, with the understanding that he would become king if the queen gave birth to a daughter.

When a daughter was indeed born on April 1, Philip VI became king. He was crowned at Reims late in May, and then, at the behest of an important supporter, Louis I of Flanders, he led a French army against Flemish rebels and won a resounding victory at Cassel in August.

Throughout his reign, Philip VI had to maneuver among conflicting political groupings whose ability to cause him trouble was enhanced by the existence of other descendants of St. Louis who might claim the French throne. Philip IV the Fair, Louis X, and Philip V all had grandsons who were disqualified by the decision to exclude princes whose claims were through their mothers. Two of these, Edward III of England and the future Charles II of Navarre (r. 1349–87), presented malcontents with attractive alternatives to whom to give allegiance. To avoid alienating the count of Flanders and duke of Burgundy, Philip had to rule against his friend and cousin Robert of Artois in the disputed succession to Artois, and Robert then gave his allegiance to Edward III. When Philip ruled in favor of his nephew Charles de Blois in the disputed Breton succession (1341), the opposing claimant, Jean de Montfort, also turned to Edward. Many nobles of the north and west felt more closely tied to England than to the Valois, and they disliked Philip's queen, Jeanne of Burgundy. Perhaps because of her influence, Philip tended to distrust this important regional aristocracy and to draw a disproportionately large number of his advisers from regions like Auvergne and Burgundy.

Amid growing discontent in the north and west, Philip's relations with England steadily deteriorated. The two monarchies could not resolve differences over Aquitaine, and Philip supported Scottish opposition to Edward, while the latter built up an anti-Valois coalition in the Low Countries. In 1337, the Hundred Years' War began, with the first years marked by expensive preparations and little military action. Edward then defeated the French fleet at Sluys in 1340 and gained a valuable new fighting front the next year with the disputed succession in Brittany. Always short of money, Philip gave great power to the leaders of the Chambre des Comptes, whose aggressive fiscal measures did not produce the military success needed to offset the antagonism they caused.

In 1345, the military situation began to deteriorate seriously. The English victory at Auberoche that autumn secured important gains in Aquitaine. The next year, Edward III invaded Normandy, threatened Paris, and then crushed Philip's army at Crécy. In 1347, the English in Brittany won a major victory at La Roche-Derrien, while Philip could not save Calais from capitulating to Edward III in August.

At the end of 1347, the Estates General convened in Paris and demanded governmental reforms before endorsing plans for each region to raise large taxes to pay for an effective army. Before this initiative could achieve results, France began to be ravaged by the Black Death, which eventually claimed the lives of Philip's queen and daughter-in-law and left government and society in disarray. The plague also produced a lull in the war, but when he died in August 1350, Philip left behind many problems for his son and successor, John II the Good.

See also **Edward III; Philip IV the Fair**

Further Reading

Cazelles, Raymond. *La société politique et la crise de la royauté sous Philippe de Valois.* Paris: Argences, 1958.

Henneman, John Bell. *Royal Taxation in Fourteenth Century France: The Development of War Financing, 1322–1356.* Princeton: Princeton University Press, 1971.

Viard, Jules. "La France sous Philippe VI de Valois." *Bibliothèque de l'école des Chartes* 59 (1896): 337–402.

——. "Itinéraire de Philippe de Valois." *Bibliothèque de l'école des* Chartes 74 (1913): 74–128,524–92; 84 (1923): 166–70.

JOHN BELL HENNEMAN, JR.

PHILIP THE BOLD (1342–1404) The first of the Valois dukes of Burgundy, Philip the Bold was the fourth son of King John II of France and Bonne de Luxembourg. Born at Pontoise on January 17, 1342, he fought beside his father at the age of fourteen and was captured with him at the Battle of Poitiers (1356). After he and the king secured release in 1360, he became, duke of Touraine, but he surrendered this duchy in 1363 when John II made him duke of Burgundy and first peer of France. In May 1364, the new king, Philip's brother Charles V, confirmed these titles.

After complex diplomatic maneuvering, Philip became an international figure with his marriage, in 1369, to Marguerite, daughter of the count of Flanders and heiress to five counties in northern and eastern France. The deaths of her grandmother (1382) and father (1384) brought these lands to her and Philip, but they needed military force to secure the most important of them, Flanders, which had been in rebellion since 1379. Marguerite also had a claim to the duchy of Brabant, and in 1385 she and Philip arranged the marriage of their son and daughter to members of the Wittelsbach family that ruled the counties of Hainaut, Holland, and Zeeland, thereby laying the foundations for a Burgundian state that eventually included most of the Low Countries.

Despite his expanding role in the Netherlands, Philip was above all the most powerful French prince of his generation. At the death of Charles V in 1380, he led a coalition that ousted from the regency his older brother Louis of Anjou, and he dominated the French government for the next eight years. He played an active diplomatic role in the Anglo-French war, the papal Schism, and imperial politics, and he secured the services of the French royal army to crush the Flemish rebels at Roosebeke in 1382 and to intimidate his enemy the duke of Guelders in 1388.

Philip supported his projects with vast sums drawn from the receipts of the French crown, as did his brother, John, duke of Berry. In the fall of 1388, Charles VI dismissed his uncles from the royal council at the urging of a reforming coalition of royal officials and military commanders, known as the Marmousets. Four years later, Charles VI's first attack of mental illness enabled the duke of Burgundy to regain his dominant position, which he held for another decade before gradually losing power at court to his nephew Louis of Orléns. He died near Brussels on April 27, 1404.

Besides establishing Burgundian power in the Netherlands, Philip the Bold began the tradition of lavish support for the arts by the Burgundian dukes. He also was the primary organizer of the abortive crusade of 1396 led by his eldest son, John, count of Nevers. His great achievements were to a large degree accomplished at the expense of the French taxpayers, but he gave his native land nearly twenty years of statesmanlike, if sometimes self-serving, leadership.

See also **Charles V the Wise; Charles VI**

Further Reading

Nieuwenhuysen, Andrée van. *Les finances du duc deBourgogne Philippe le Hardi (1384–1404).* Brussels: Éditions de l'Université de Bruxelles, 1984.

Palmer, John J.N. *England, France and Christendom, 1377–99.* London: Routledge and Kegan Paul, 1972.

Petit, Ernest. *Ducs de Bourgogne de la maison de Valois, I: Philippe le Hardi.* Paris: Champion, 1909.

Richard, Jean. *Les ducs de Bourgogne et la formation du duché* Paris: Les Belles Lettres, 1954.

Vaughan, Richard. *Philip the Bold: The Formation of the Burgundian State.* Cambridge: Harvard University Press, 1962.

JOHN BELL HENNEMAN, JR.

PHILIP THE CHANCELLOR (ca. 1160/85–ca. 1236)

An influential theologian, a preacher of considerable stature, and an accomplished poet, Philip was born into ecclesiastical circles: he was the illegitimate son of Archdeacon Philip of Paris and was related through his father to Bishop Étienne of Noyon (d. 1211) and Bishop Pierre of Paris (d. 1218), both of whom favored Philip's career. After studying theology and law, he appears in the historical record no later than 1211 as archdeacon of Noyon.

As chancellor of the University of Paris, a position that he held from 1217, Philip had authority over the fledgling university. Philip's chancellorship came in an era of discontent and controversy, and in a combative move early in his tenure (1219) he excommunicated the masters and students—a move that Pope Honorius III ordered him to reverse. During the strike initiated in 1229, Philip sided with the pope and the university against William of Auvergne, bishop of Paris, and Blanche of Castile, regent during Louis IX's minority. The papal bull *Parens scientiarum* of Gregory IX ended the university strike in 1231. Not long after Philip's death, Henri d'Andeli wrote a *Dit du chancelier Philippe*, in which he is associated with jongleurs, chansons, and vielle playing.

As a master of theology, Philip composed a treatise on moral theology, the *Summa de bono*, that had considerable influence on the earliest generation of Franciscan masters. It was organized into two main parts, *De bono naturae* and *De bono gratiae*, with the latter subdivided into three: *gratia gratum faciens*, *gratia gratis data*, *gratia virtutum* (both theological and cardinal). Philip is also credited with 723 sermons, which reveal a preacher vigorously calling both the clergy and the laity to a just and holy way of life.

Of the fifty-eight monophonic conductus attributed to Philip, at least twenty-one texts are confirmed as his. *Angelus ad virginem* was made famous by Chaucer: in *The Miller's Tale*, the scholarly but impoverished cleric Nicholas sings it. Medieval sources ascribe nine polyphonic conductus to Philip, and among four possible textings of conductus caudae at least Bullia *fulminante* (and its contrafact *Veste nuptiali*) and Minor *natu filiu* definitely can be counted as his; *Anima lugi lacrima* and *Crucifigat omnes* (which has two contrafacts: *Mundum renovavit* and *Curritur ad vocem*) are suspected of also being his. He penned the four known tropes to Pérotin's two great organa quadrupla: *Vide prophecie*, *Homo cum mandato dato*, *De Stephani roseo sanguine*, and *Adesse festina*. Philip and Pérotin appear to have known one another and may have collaborated. Since so many of Philip's texts were tropes or contrafacts for music that already had been composed, it would seem that he was not a composer himself. Although his defense of accumulating benefices earned him the displeasure of the Dominicans, he remained a friend of the Franciscans throughout his life and was buried in their church.

See also Blanche of Castile; Chaucer, Geoffrey; Pérotin

Further Reading

Dreves, Guido Maria, ed. *Lateinische Hymnendichter des Mittelalters.* Leipzig: Reisland, 1907. *Analecta hymnica medii aevi.* Vol. 50, pp. 528–32.

Paine, Thomas. *Associa tecum in patria*: A Newly Identified Organum Trope by Philip the Chancellor." *Journal of the American Musicological Society* 39 (1986): 233–54.

Principe, Walter H. *The Theology of the Hypostatic Union in the Early Thirteenth Century, IV: Philip the Chancellor's Theology of the Hypostatic Union*. Toronto: Pontifical Institute of Mediaeval Studies, 1975.

Steiner, Ruth. "Some Monophonic Songs Composed Around 1200." *Musical Quarterly* 52 (1966): 56–70.

Wright, Craig. *Music and Ceremony at Notre Dame of Paris 500–1550*. Cambridge: Cambridge University Press, 1989, pp. 249–99.

Wicki, Nikolaus. "La *pecia* dans la tradition manuscrite de la *Summa de bono* de Philippe le Chancelier." In The *Editing of Theological and Philosophical Texts from the Middle Ages*, ed. Monika Asztalos. Stockholm: Almqvist and Wiksell, 1986, pp. 93–104.

MARK ZIER/SANDRA PINEGAR

PHILIP THE GOOD (1396–1467) Duke of Burgundy, 1419–67. The son and successor of John the Fearless, duke of Burgundy and count of Flanders, Philip was twenty-three years old when the assassination of his father in 1419 made him the mightiest peer of France and the most important prince of the Low Countries. His reign of forty-seven years brought prosperity, prestige, and territorial expansion to his lands. He guided the ill-fated Burgundian state to the peak of its power, but its greatness, dependant on the weakness of the French monarchy, dissipated after the end of the Hundred Years' War.

An astute diplomat and judicious in the use of force, Philip sought to overcome ducal Burgundy's status as a French apanage by enmeshing it in an independent polity in the territories between France and Germany. The Treaty of Troyes (1420) allied him with Henry V of England, secured his French holdings, and allowed him to concentrate on the Low Countries. His second (1422) and third (1430) marriages secured political allies and territorial claims. Conquests of Holland (1425–33) and Luxembourg (1443), and the peaceful acquisitions of Namur (1420) and Brabant (1430) doubled the size of his lands. Philip eventually sought the crown of a restored Lotharingia from the emperor Frederick III in 1447. His failure to obtain a crown had no immediate political consequences, but it foreshadowed the doom of the Burgundian polity, which remained an overextended Franco-imperial principality in an age of emerging sovereign states. Within France, Philip provided minimal support for the government of Henry VI of England and later realigned himself with Charles VII in 1435 (Treaty of Arras). Fearing a revitalized monarchy, Philip abstained from the decisive campaigns of the Hundred Years' War and sheltered the fugitive dauphin after 1456. The failure of such efforts became manifest when his son, the future Charles the Bold, assumed control of Burgundy in 1464 and launched the *Guerre du bien publique* against Louis XI. Philip's rule thus ended as it began, with Valois France and Valois Burgundy inextricably locked in mortal conflict.

Philip's most celebrated achievement was to make chivalric culture an instrument of policy. The creation of the Order of the Golden Fleece in 1430 provided a diplomatic tool linking the nobility of his disparate territories and precluding their affiliation with any other prince. Even such ostentatious festivals as the Pheasant Banquet in 1454 had political value, for through such devices the prestige of the Valois dukes reached its zenith. Philip himself was a model of late-medieval chivalry: handsome, courageous, pious, self-indulgent, extravagant. He maintained mistresses and bastards throughout his lands yet made heartfelt, albeit unfulfilled, promises to go on crusade. He is remembered as "the Good" above all for the talented artists who gave him the accolade and immortalized Burgundy in tapestries, the paintings of van Eyck, and literature ranging from the *Cent nouvelles nouvelles* to the histories of Chastellain. He may seem less successful in retrospect than he did at the time, but Burgundy was a phantasm and Philip sustained it the best of all his line.

See also **Bedford, John Duke of; Charles VII; Charles the Bold**

Further Reading

Bonenfant, Paul. *Philippe le Bon.* Brussels: La Renaissance du Livre, 1955.
Cartellieri, Otto. *The Court of Burgundy: Studies in the History of Civilization.* New York: Askell House, 1970.
Huizinga, Johan. *The Waningofthe Middle Ages: A Study of the Forms of Life, Thought and Art in France and the Netherlands in the Dawn of the Renaissance.* London: Arnold, 1924.
Vaughn, Richard. *Philip the Good: The Apogee of Burgundy.* London: Longman, 1970.
———. *Valois Burgundy.* London: Lane, 1975.

PAUL D. SOLON

PHILIPPE DE THAÜN (fl. late 11th–early 12th c) Author of the earliest surviving scientific works in French. Philippe's Anglo-Norman dialect, which he helped establish as a literary medium, probably indicates that he was born in England, but he was of continental parentage originating in Thaon in lower Normandy, 13 miles northwest of Caen. His *Cumpoz* (probably 1113) is dedicated to an uncle, Humphrey (Honfroi) of Thaon, chaplain to Eudo Fitz-Hubert, also known as Eudo Dapifer, steward of Henry I of England, whose royal court was a center of learned activity. Philippe's two signed works, the *Cumpoz* and the *Bestiaire*, are in hexasyllabic rhymed, occasionally assonanced, couplets, but the *Bestiaire* ends with an octosyllabic lapidary. Several anonymous works have also been attributed to him.

The *Cumpoz* ("computus") is a practical treatise on the calendar that tells how to predict the dates of Easter and the movable feasts governed by Easter. The problem is reconciliation of the lunar calendar, which determines the date of Easter by its association with Passover, with the Julian solar calendar. Along with accurately detailed computational material, Philippe gives free rein to an allegorical bent in discussions of the zodiac and the names of the days and the months. He twice uses the year 1113 as an example for computing, once implying that it is the current year; in any case, the *Cumpoz* was dedicated before Eudo's death in 1120, for he is referred to as though still alive.

The *Bestiaire* (ca. 1125) is a "Book of Nature" divided into three sections: land animals and sea creatures, birds, and precious gems; it draws on traditional bestiary material from ancient myth and biblical sources. An article on a creature or stone generally opens with a physical description, often incorporating drawings with the text, followed by discussion of specific properties or habits. Allegorical commentary derived from the descriptive material then demonstrates the revelation of God in the natural world. The articles in the first two sections are arranged hierarchically, from the "kings" of each species (the lion, the eagle), which signify Christ, to the "lower" (land-bound birds, and fish), which refer to Satan; precious gems, beginning with their "king," the diamond, are associated with the powers of good. The *Bestiaire* is dedicated to Adeliza (Aaliz de Louvain), whom Henry I married in 1121; she retained the title of queen four years after Henry's death in 1135. Scholars tend to date the *Bestiaire* from early in Adeliza's marriage because of the date of the *Cumpoz.* One manuscript of the *Bestiaire* bears a rededication to Eleanor of Aquitaine, Henry II's queen, written after 1154.

The anonymous *Livre de Sibile* (1135–54), dedicated to the empress Matilda, Henry I's daughter, is a book of prophecies.

Authorship has been ascribed to Philippe primarily because the text bears striking linguistic and stylistic resemblances to the signed works; in addition, personal content in the dedication parallels information found in the rededication of the *Bestiaire* to Eleanor of Aquitaine. On the basis of less convincing evidence, two early Anglo-Norman lapidaries, the *Alphabetical* and the *Apocalyptic*, an Anglo-Norman allegorical *Desputeisun del cors e de l'arme*, and a geographical treatise, *Les Divisiuns del mund*, have also been attributed to Philippe.

See also **Eleanor of Aquitaine, Henry I**

Further Reading

Philippe de Thaün. *Le bestiaire de Philippe de Thaün*, ed. Emanuel Walberg. Paris: Plon, 1900.
——. *Li cumpoz*, ed. Émile Mall. Strasbourg, 1873.
——. *Le livre de Sibile by Philippe de Thaon*, ed. Hugh Shields. London: Anglo-Norman Text Society, 1979.
Legge, M. Dominica. *Anglo-Norman Literature and Its Background*. Oxford: Clarendon, 1963.
McCulloch, Florence. *Mediaeval Latin and French Bestiaries*. Chapel Hill: University of North Carolina Press, 1960.
Pickens, Rupert T. "The Literary Activity of Philippe de Thaün." *Romance Notes* 12 (1970–71): 208–12.
Shields, Hugh. "Philippe de Thaon, auteur du *Livre de Sibylle?*" *Romania* 85 (1964): 455–77.
——. "More Poems by Philippe de Thaon?" In *Anglo-Norman Anniversary Essays*, ed. Ian Short. London: Anglo-Norman Text Society, 1993, pp. 337–59.
Studer, Paul, and Joan Evans. *Anglo-Norman Lapidaries*. Paris: Champion, 1924.

RUPERT T. PICKENS

PIER DELLA VIGNA (c. 1190–1249)
Pier della Vigna (Petrus de Vinea) was born in Capua of obscure parentage and became a senior bureaucrat and officer of state under Emperor Frederick II. Pier had broad and enduring influence as a master of Latin documentary composition and Latin prose stylistics more generally.

Pier's education included the study of law and rhetoric, the former probably at the University of Bologna, and the latter probably at a notarial school in Capua or Bologna, since Bologna and Capua were centers for this sort of instruction. He entered Frederick's court chancery in the early 1220s, became a high-ranking judge, had major financial responsibilities, and wrote private letters for Frederick that did not go through the chancery. It is thought that his superior skill as a stylist and advocate was immediately recognized and that from the beginning of his lifelong employment in this milieu it fell to him to compose the most important and stylistically taxing documents. By 1243, he was protonotary of the imperial court and logothete—a high official with the functions of chancellor—of the kingdom of Sicily. In 1244, he and his colleague (and fellow Campanian) Thaddeus of Sessa were authorized to decide on all petitions presented to the emperor. Pier was a trusted counselor to Frederick, and Frederick's spokesman in many of the emperor's troubled dealings with the papacy and with the communes of northern Italy. Throughout Frederick's long dispute with Pope Gregory IX, Pier represented the emperor at the papal court and at the courts of foreign princes; shortly before Pope Innocent IV deposed the emperor in 1245, Pier attempted to intervene on his sovereign's behalf.

That Pier used his position to enrich himself and to advance his family is not surprising. But in this regard he does appear to have been excessively grasping and thus to have made many enemies. For reasons that are unclear, Frederick had him arrested in Cremona early in 1249, and blinded a few months later, probably in the fortress of San Miniato near Pisa. Pier's death not long afterward was believed in some quarters to have been a suicide, a view shared by Dante. Pier is one of the most memorable souls in the *Divine Comedy,* though he is identified only as "the man who held the double key to Frederick's heart" (*Inferno,* 13 58–59). It seems likely, as Stephany (1982) has argued, that the portrayal and punishment of Pier in the *Divine Comedy* were provoked by Dante's literal reading of Pier's widely admired *Eulogy* of Frederick, a composition that may have struck Dante as blasphemous and idolatrous.

One of a pair of busts of bearded males from Frederick's monumental gate at Capua (the gate was demolished in 1557 and the bust is now in the Museo Provinciale Campano) is sometimes considered a portrait of Pier. But it seems unlikely that the Hohenstaufen regime would have knowingly permitted this showpiece of imperial iconography to retain, in close proximity to the image of Frederick himself, the likeness of a man stigmatized in official documents of the early 1250s as *Petrus proditor* ("Pier the traitor"). Pier has also been identified as one of the figures in a portrait (now lost) at the emperor's palace at Naples, which supposedly showed him dispensing justice in Frederick's presence; but this too seems dubious.

Pier was famous in his lifetime as a person of high culture and as an artist in Latin prose. His production as a writer falls into several different categories. His early official letters match the style of the Roman curia at the time, a style characterized by elaborate patterns of verbal, phonic, and rhythmic ornaments and laden with biblical citations, all intended to convey honor and respect for the addressee and a solemn celebration of the status quo. The same verbal musicality and allusive citations of well-known biblical and classical texts are evident in letters of consolation, as well as occasional pieces such as the famous *Eulogy,* in which messianic proclamations about Frederick are amplified with biblical language. After

1225, when the emperor abandoned his posture of gratitude toward the papacy and began to focus on what he perceived as conflicts of interest between papacy and empire, the rhetoric of Pier's letters shifts, in certain cases, from persuasion rooted in praise and affection for the addressee to persuasion based on the points of contention between the parties. The historical circumstances of controversial events become an integral part of the persuasive strategy. For nearly thirty years, Pier would wage a polemical campaign in defense of Frederick II in an attempt to win the support of prelates and princes throughout Latin Europe. Ultimately, his choice of rhetorical approaches would always depend on his perception of the intended public and the subject matter discussed in the letter.

Although the extent of his personal contribution remains controversial, Pier was at least partly responsible for the drafting of *Liber Augustalis* (1231), the Latin version of Frederick's Constitutions of Melfi, a massive law code asserting the absolute authority of the prince in his kingdom. The language of its *Proemium* is richly ornamented and cadenced. Just as the *Eulogy* appropriates biblical language to glorify the emperor and his court, the *Proemium* invokes biblical, patristic, and Aristotelian phrases, as well as classical Roman legal phrases, to suggest the universality of imperial rule.

Collections of Pier's documents, to which were added some of his personal letters and various writings of his correspondents and others, began to be made as early as the 1270s and came to be known as the *Epistole (Letters), Dictamina (Formal Communications),* or *Summa (Treatise)* of Pier della Vigna. Circulating in several different redactions, they served into the fifteenth century and beyond as models in rhetorical instruction and were used pragmatically in many chanceries. At least 230 manuscripts are known; their quantity and quality attest to the importance that contemporaries and successive generations attached to these writings. The Florentine Guelf Brunetto Latini, writing several decades after Pier's death, commemorates this imperial official as an exemplary orator, and as such, master of Frederick and of the empire.

Pier's other surviving works and possible works include two Latin poems in rhythmical quatrains whose attribution to Pier, though early, is not certain: one on the months of the year and their properties, the other a satire on the mendicants. Most of Pier's Latin writings and the Latin texts associated with him still lack modern critical editions.

Pier is also a minor figure in early Italian literature. He was one of the court poets of the Sicilian school and is named in the manuscripts as the author of at least eight pieces. Two *canzoni* and a sonnet (the latter is part of a *tenzone* with Jacopo Mostacci and Giacomo da Lentini) are securely attributed to Pier; a third *canzone* (*Poi tanta caunoscenza*) is less certainly his. The modern editor of the Sicilian school corpus, Panvini (1962–1964, 1994), rejects, on a variety of grounds, Pier's authorship of the remainder.

See also **Dante Alighieri; Frederick II**

Further Reading

Editions: Latin Writings

Böhmer, Johann Friedrich, ed. "Die Regesten des Kaiserreichs unter Philipp, Otto IV, Friedrich II, Heinrich (VII), Conrad IV, Heinrich Raspe, Wilhelm und Richard, 1198–1272." In *Regesta imperii*, Vol. 5, ed. Julius Ficker and Eduard Winkelmann. Innsbruck: Wagner, 1881–1901. (Reprint, Hildesheim: Georg Olms, 1971.)

Casters, Louis. "Prose latine attribuée à Pierre de la Vigne." *Revue des Langues Romanes*, 32, 1888, pp. 430–452. (Critical edition of the satire against the mendicants.)

Conrad, Hermann, Thea von der Lieck-Buycken, and Wolfgang Wagner, eds. *Die Konstitutionen Friedrichs II. von Hohenstaufen für sein Königreich Sizilien. Studien und Quellen zur Welt Kaiser Friedrichs II*, 2. Cologne: Böhlau, 1973. (Edition and German translation of *Liber Augustalis*.)

Holder-Egger, O. "Bericht über eine Reise nach Italien im Jahre 1891." *Neues Archiv der Gesellschaft für Ältere Deutsche Geschichtskunde*, 17, 1892, pp. 461–524. (Poem on the months of the year, pp. 501–503.)

Huillard-Bréholles, J.-L.-A., ed. *Historia diplomatica Friderici Secundi*, 6 vols. Paris: Plon, 1852–1861. (Reprint, Turin: Bottega d'Erasmo, 1963. Official documents in chronological order.)

——, ed. *Vie et correspondance de Pierre de la Vigne, ministre de l'Empereur Frédéric II*. Paris: Plon, 1865. (Reprint, Aalen: Scientia, 1966. See Latin personal correspondence, pp. 289–404; and *Eulogy* of Frederick, pp. 425–426.)

Editions: Italian Writings

Macciocca, Gabriella, ed. *Poesie volgari di Pier della Vigna*. Tesi di Dottorato di Ricerca, Dip. di Studi Romanzi, Università degli Studi di Roma. Rome: La Sapienza, 1996.

Panvini, Bruno, ed. *Le rime della scuola siciliana*. Biblioteca dell' Archivum Romanicum, Series 1(65 and 72). Florence: L. S. Olschki, 1962–1964, Vol. 1, pp. xliii–xlix, 125–130, 412–414, 647.

——, ed. *Poeti italiani della corte di Federico II*, rev. ed. Naples: Liguori, 1994, pp. 185–192, 259.

Manuscript

Schaller, Hans Martin, with Bernhard Vogel. *Handschriftenverzeichnis zur Briefsammlung des Petrus de Vinea*. Monumenta Germaniae Historica, Hilfsmittel, 18. Hannover: Hahn, 2002.

Critical Studies

Cassell, Anthony K. "Pier della Vigna's Metamorphosis: Iconography and History." In *Dante, Petrarch, Boccaccio: Studies in the Italian Trecento in Honor of Charles S. Singleton*, ed. Aldo S. Bernardo and Anthony L. Pellegrini. Medieval and Renaissance Texts and Studies, 22. Binghamton, N.Y.: Medieval and Renaissance Texts and Studies, 1983, pp. 31–76.

Delle Donne, Fulvio. "Lo stile della cancelleria di Federico II ed i presunti influssi arabi."

In *Atti dell'Accademia Pontaniana*, n.s., 41, 1992, pp. 153–164.

——. "Le 'Consolationes' del IV libro del epistolario di Pier della Vigna." *Vichiana*, 4, 1993, pp. 268–290.

——. "Una perduta raffigurazione federiciana descritta da Francesco Pipino e la sede della cancelleria imperiale." *Studi Medievali*, Series 3, 38, 1997, pp. 737–749. (Reprinted in Fulvio Delle Donne. *Politica e letteratura nel Mezzogiorno medievale: La cronachistica dei secoli XII-XV*. Immagini del Medioevo, 4. Salerno: Cadone, 2001, pp. 111–126.)

Di Capua, Francesco. "Lo stile della Curia romana e il 'cursus' nelle epistole di Pier della Vigna e nei documenti della Cancelleria sveva." *Giornale Italiano di Filologia*, 2, 1949, pp. 97–166. (Reprinted in Francesco Di Capua. *Scritti minori*, Vol 1. New York: Desclée, 1958, pp. 500–523.)

Dilcher, Hermann. *Die sizilianische Gesetzgebung Kaiser Friedrichs II: Quellen der Constitutionen von Melfi und ihrer Novellen*. Studien und Quellen zur Welt Kaiser Friedrichs II, 3. Cologne: Böhlau, 1975. (See especially pp. 21–22, 26–27.)

Haskins, Charles Homer. "Latin Literature under Frederick II." In *Studies in Mediaeval Culture*. Oxford: Clarendon, 1929, pp. 124–147. (Reprint, New York: Frederick Ungar, 1958.)

Kantorowicz, Ernst. *Frederick the Second, 1194–1250*, trans. E. O. Lorimer. London: Constable; New York: Smith, 1931. (Reprint, New York: Frederick Ungat, 1957. See especially pp. 293–307, 663–667.)

Martin, Janet. "Classicism and Style in Latin Literature." In *Renaissance and Renewal in the Twelfth Century*, ed. Robert L. Benson, Giles Constable, and Carol D. Lanham. Cambridge, Mass.: Harvard University Press, 1982, pp. 537–568.

Meredith, Jill. "The Arch at Capua: The Strategic Use of *Spolia* and References to the Antique." In *Intellectual Life at the Court of Frederick II Hohenstaufen*, ed. William Tronzo. Studies in the History of Art, 44. "Washington, D.C.: National Gallery of Art, 1994, pp. 108–126.

Oldoni, Massimo. "Pier della Vigna e Federico." In *Federico II e le nuove culture: Atti del XXXI Convegno storico internazionale, Todi, 9–12 ottobre 1994*. Atti dei Convegni del Centra Italiano di Studi sul Basso Medioevo–Accademia Tudertina e del Centro di Studi sulla Spiritualità Medievale, n.s., 8. Spoleto: Centro Italiano di Studi sull'Alto Medioevo, 1995, pp. 347–362.

Paratore, Ettore. "Alcuni Caratteri dello stile della cancelleria federiciana." In *Atti del Convegno Internazionale di Studi Federiciani, 10–18 December, 1950: VII Centenario della morte di Federico II, Imperatore e re di Sicilia*. Palermo: A. Renna, 1952, pp. 283–313.

Schaller, Hans Martin. "Zur Entstehung der sogenannten Briefsammlung des Petrus de Vinea." *Deutsches Archiv für die Erforschung des Mittelalters*, 12, 1956, pp. 114–159.

——. "Die Kanzlei Kaiser Friedrichs II.: Ihr Personal und Sprachstil." *Archiv für Diplomatik*, 3, 1957, pp. 207–286; 4, 1958, pp. 264–327.

——. "L'epistolario di Pier delle Vigne." In *Politica e cultura nell'Italia di Federico II*, ed. Sergio Gensini. Collana di Studi e Ricerche, Centro di Studi sulla Civiltà del Tardo Medioevo, San Miniato, 1. Pisa: Pacini, 1986, pp. 95–111.

——. "Della Vigna, Pietro." In *Dizionario biografico degli Italiani*, Vol. 37. Rome: Istituto della Enciclopedia Italiana, 1989, pp. 776–784.

——. *Stauferzeit: Ausgewählte Aufsätze*. Monumenta Germaniae Historica, Schriften, 38. Hannover: Hahn, 1993. (See especially pp. 197–223, 225–270, 463–478.)

Shepard, Laurie. *Courting Power: Persuasion and Politics in the Early Thirteenth Century*. New York: Garland, 1999.

Stephany, William A. "Pier della Vigna's Self-Fulfilling Prophecies: The *Eulogy* of Frederick II and *Inferno* 13." *Traditio*, 38, 1982, pp. 193–212.

Wieruszowski, Helene. *Politics and Culture in Medieval Spain and Italy*. Storia e Letteratura, 121. Rome: Edizioni di Storia e Letteratura, 1971. (See especially pp. 432–435, 605–610.)

LAURIE SHEPARD AND JOHN B. DILLON

PIERRE MAUCLERC (ca. 1189/90–1250)

Pierre de Dreux (or de Braine), better known as Pierre Mauclerc, was a member of the distinguished Dreux family, a cadet branch of the Capetian line. He was a younger son of Louis VII's nephew Robert II, count of the small fiefs of Dreux and Braine. Although not a landless baron, Pierre's original endowment of lands from his father was small, the villas and manors of Fère-en-Tardenois, Brie-Comte-Robert, Chilly, and Longjumeau. By his marriage in 1212 to Alix, the heiress of Brittany and claimant to the English honor of Richmond, however, he became titular earl of Richmond and titular duke of Brittany (or count, in the view of French authorities unwilling to acknowledge Brittany's ducal status).

Pierre immediately set about imposing his will on the fiercely independent Breton baronage, exacting reliefs and wardships contrary to custom, despoiling or seizing seigneuries whose lords resisted, and commencing a concerted attack against the privileges of the episcopate. This last action precipitated his excommunication and, in retaliation, his expulsion of six of the seven bishops of Brittany. Although his wife died in 1221, he continued as guard *(custos)* and effective ruler of Brittany until his son came of age in late 1237.

Knighted in 1209 by Philip II Augustus, Pierre was secure in his position as ruler of Brittany as long as Philip, with whom he got along well, continued to reign. But with the old king's death in 1223, Pierre became a less trustworthy ally of the new king, Louis VIII (r. 1223–26), although he did take part in crusading expeditions against the Albigensian heretics led by Louis as prince (1219) and king (1226). His emerging lack of devotion to royal policies originated partly from his claims to land in England, claims that made him always eager to cultivate the Capetians' traditional enemy, the Plantagenêts. His own overweening ambition to be the preeminent baron in northwest Europe fueled his political maneuvering. After the death of his first wife, he aspired to the hand of the countess of Flanders in 1226 and the queen of Cyprus (who had claims in the great fief of Champagne) in 1229, only to

be thwarted by the king and the pope, who had their own interests to preserve in the disposition of the heiresses and their fiefs. He was reduced to marrying a minor baroness, Marguerite de Montaigu, in 1230; and his resentment was strong. He had already become an open rebel in 1227 because of the failure of the regent, Blanche of Castile, to submit to his influence or cede the regency of the young Louis IX. He was instrumental in 1229 in attacking the count of Champagne, a supporter of the regent whose fief Pierre coveted. He courted the favor of the English king, received military support and large subsidies from him, and rebelled against the French crown again in 1230–31 and still again briefly in 1234. In all of these efforts, his forces were soundly thrashed, though never completely eliminated, by the royal troops.

In November 1237, after his son reached majority and took over control of Brittany, Pierre succeeded in consolidating a small lordship around the nucleus of his wife's lands in the Breton-Poitevin march. His subsequent career saw him active as a crusader against the Muslims, an effort that achieved a reconciliation with the papacy (1235) if not with local clerics, whom he continued to harass whenever he was in a position to do so. He served with distinction on the crusade of Thibaut de Navarre (1239–40) and died of illness and wounds in 1250 on the return home from St. Louis's crusade.

See also **Blanche of Castile; Louis IX; Philip II Augustus**

Further Reading

Painter, Sidney. *The Scourge of the Clergy: Peter of Dreux, Duke of Brittany.* Baltimore: John Hopkins University Press, 1937.

WILLIAM CHESTER JORDAN

PIETRO ABANO (d. 1316) Pietro Abano (Pietro d'Abano) was the most important medical teacher in early fourteenth-century Padua. He was a Lombard by birth, but little is known of his life. In spite of his fame, and the fame he brought his university, he seems never to have accumulated the wealth of such successful teachers and practitioners as Taddeo Alderotti. Pietro's most famous book, *Conciliator of the Differences of the Philosophers and Especially the Physicians*, remained in use in universities well into the early modern period.

Pietro received his medical training at the University of Paris, where he would have been indoctrinated into the highest levels of scholarly debate surrounding the natural philosophy of Aristotle and Aristotle's interpreters. He returned to Italy from Paris c. 1306 to teach medicine, philosophy, and astrology at Padua. The *Conciliator*, which was completed sometime after 1310, shows his Parisian training. The book presents more than 200 disputed questions on the subject of medical philosophy and attempts to reconcile conflicts between the physiological teachings of Aristotle and the medical teachings of Galen. Pietro apparently was deeply impressed by similar attempts by Averroës and Avicenna, who adopted the Neoplatonic scheme of the ultimate reconciliation of conflicting philosophical viewpoints.

Pietro also distinguished himself as one of the early translators of Galen's works from the original Greek into Latin. Much of his writing examines the importance of medical astrology. This interest in astrology, as well as his devotion to Averroist teaching, marred his reputation in some circles.

See also Averroës, Abu 'L-Walīd Muhammad B. Ahmad B. Rushd; Avicenna

Further Reading

Olivieri, Luigi. *Pietro d'Abano e il pensiero neolatino: Filosofia, scienza, e ricerca dell'Aristotele greco tra i secoli XIII e XIV.* Padua: Antenore, 1988.

Paschetto, Eugenia. *Pietro d'Abano, medico e filosofo.* Florence: Vallecchi, 1984.

Siraisi, Nancy G. *Arts and Sciences at Padua.* Toronto: Pontifical Institute of Mediaeval Studies, 1973.

———. *Taddeo Alderotti and His Pupils: Two Generations of Italian Medical Learning.* Princeton, N.J.: Princeton University Press, 1981.

FAYE MARIE GETZ

PISANO, ANDREA (c. 1295–c. 1348 or 1349) Andrea Pisano (Andrea di Ugolino di Nino da Pontedera) is recorded as a sculptor, goldsmith, and *capomaestro* (master of works) of the cathedrals of Florence and Orvieto. Andrea was the son of a notary and is presumed to have been born in Pontedera, near Pisa. His reputation rests principally on his designs for the doors of the Baptistery in Florence (signed and dated 1330), which are considered among the greatest achievements of Tuscan *Trecento* sculpture. In this project, Andrea demonstrated that the direct narrative style and effective compositional principles of Giotto's painting could be successfully translated into the art of relief sculpture.

Though nothing is known for certain about Andrea's formative years, it is thought that he trained as a goldsmith, since the reliefs for the bronze doors, his earliest securely documented commission, exhibit attention to miniature detail and ornament as well as a high degree of competence in working with metal. Given the characteristics of his securely identifiable oeuvre, it comes as no surprise that Andrea was referred to as *orefice* (goldsmith) in 1335.

Andrea's Reliefs for the Baptistery, Florence (1330–1336)

In 1322, the Arte di Calimala (guild of importers and exporters of cloth) of Florence, the institution in charge of the decorative program of the Baptistery, had made plans for wooden doors covered with gilded metal. By 1329, the project had been revised, and the officials of the Calimala favored a more costly and technically more challenging option: doors in solid bronze. Andrea is first recorded in connection with this project in 1330, but his appointment almost certainly dates from 1329, when the Calimala sent a Florentine goldsmith to Pisa and Venice, which had a tradition of bronze casting, to examine examples of bronze doors. Though Andrea's reliefs carry the date 1330, his work did not end until late 1335: in 1330–1331 he worked on the wax models, which were cast in bronze by Venetian craftsmen in the *cire perdu* method; in 1333 the left door valve was installed; and the right wing was not completed until late 1335, owing to problems in the casting. The doors were dedicated on the feast of John the Baptist (the patron saint of the building and of Florence) in 1336; they originally adorned the east portal but were subsequently removed to the south portal to make way for Lorenzo Ghiberti's work.

Each wing comprises ten reliefs on the life of John the Baptist and four reliefs of virtues; all are set in quatrefoil frames that are, in turn, contained in rectangular fields. The general configuration of Andrea's doors was inspired by the Romanesque scheme of Bonanno's Porta San Ranieri at the cathedral in Pisa and, possibly, the Porta Regia (now destroyed) from the same building. The remarkable unity of Andrea's design, however, depends on a variety of decorative motifs, which include lions' heads that are placed at the corners of each panel, bands of studs and rosettes that unite the lions' heads, and dentiled moldings that frame each of the quatrefoils.

The iconographic program of the figural reliefs is closely related to the mosaic scenes of the life of John the Baptist in the interior of the Baptistery and to frescoes on the same theme by Giotto in the Peruzzi Chapel in Santa Croce (also in Florence). Giotto's influence is also reflected in the harmonious balance of the compositions, in which reliefs are carefully structured into planes; and in the classical economy of the narratives, which rely on the purposeful movements of concentrated groups of figures. The technique of applying figures to a plain background, a feature of Sienese metalwork of the early *Trecento*, adds to the solemnity of the compositions. Concessions were, however, made for the occasional motif of a doorway, curtain, or canopy; and in five reliefs from the left door valve, landscape is incorporated into the designs with great subtlety. The influence of Giotto's measured style in Andrea's work is tempered by a debt to French and Sienese artistic traditions: activated, spirited drapery forms, which envelope the bodies of Andrea's dignified figures, introduce a note of grace and elegance to the otherwise restrained reliefs.

That Andrea was at the height of his creative powers when he worked on the doors is clear from the precision of the finely chased details of the fire-gilt surfaces. The Calimala had, evidently, awarded this difficult commission to a mature and proficient artist, and his work would remain a benchmark for artistic excellence into the *Quattrocento*. In fact, when the Calimala set up a competition in 1400–1401, the aim was to attract an artist who could work on a second set of bronze doors that would follow Andrea's model and maintain his high standards.

Andrea as Capomaestro at Florence and Orvieto (1337–1348)

Andrea's contribution to the decoration of the *campanile* in Florence probably dates from before Giotto's death in 1337. Thereafter, Andrea succeeded Giotto as *capomaestro*, supervising work on the tower until 1341. He proceeded according to his great predecessor's plans for the lower part of the structure, which included two rows of reliefs: the lower group, within hexagonal frames, shows scenes from Genesis and practitioners of the arts, sciences, and works of man; the upper set shows the seven sacraments, the seven planets, the seven virtues, and the seven liberal arts in rhomboid frames. However, Andrea departed from Giotto's scheme in adding niches designed to include statuary above these relief cycles. Though the precise nature of Andrea's contribution is still a matter of scholarly debate, one work generally attributed to him is the marble relief *Sculpture*, which, like the style of the bronze reliefs, is characterized by plastic form, harmonious composition, and attention to detail.

Around 1341, Andrea returned to Pisa, where he maintained a workshop even after 1347, the year he was appointed *capomaestro* at the cathedral of Orvieto. By 1349, however, Andrea had been replaced, and it is frequently assumed either that he died of the plague in 1348 or 1349 or, less probably, that he moved to Florence. The family tradition was carried on by Andrea's sons Nino (fl. 1334–1360s) and Tommaso (fl. 1363–1372), especially Nino, who succeeded his rather at Orvieto. Andrea's sons were less interested in the classicizing aspects of his work, and both of them evolved a mainly Gothic formal vocabulary. In the early *Quattrocento* the suave, lyrical style of their sculpture was still a force to reckon with, as the early work of Jacopo della Quercia demonstrates.

See also **Giotto di Bondone**

Further Reading

Burresi, Mariagiulia, ed. *Andrea, Nino, e Tommaso scultori pisani.* Milan: Electa, 1983.

Castelnuovo, Enrico. "Andrea Pisano scultore in legno." In *Sacre passioni: Scultura lignea a Pisa dal XII al XV secolo,* ed. Mariagiulia Burresi. Milan: Morta, 2000, pp. 152–163.

Clark, Kenneth, and David Finn. *The Florentine Baptistery Doors.* Kampala: Uganda Publishing and Advertising Services, 1980.

Garzelli, Annarosa. "Andrea Pisano a Firenze e una 'Madonna con il cardellino.'" *Antichità Viva,* 36(5–6), 1997, pp. 49–62.

Kreytenberg, Gert. "Andrea Pisano's Earliest Works in Marble." *Burlington Magazine,* 122, 1980, pp. 3–8.

——. *Andrea Pisano und die toskanische Skulptur des 14. Jahrhunderts.* Munich: Bruckmann, 1984.

——. "Eine unbekannte Verkündigungsmadonna als 'Maria gravida' von Andrea Pisano." In *Opere e giorni: Studi su mille anni di arte europea dedicati a Max Seidel,* ed. Klaus Bergdolt and Giorgio Bonsanti. Venice: Marsilio, 2001, pp. 147–154.

Moskowitz, Anita Fiderer. *The Sculpture of Andrea and Nino Pisano.* Cambridge: Cambridge University Press, 1986.

——. *Italian Gothic Sculpture, c. 1250–c. 1400.* Cambridge: Cambridge University Press, 2001.

Paolucci, Antonio. *Le porte del Battistero di Firenze alle origini del Rinascimento.* Modena: Panini, 1996.

Pope-Hennessy, John. *Italian Gothic Sculpture,* 4th ed. London: Phaidon, 1996

FLAVIO BOGGI

PISANO, GIOVANNI (d. by 1319) Giovanni Pisano was the son of Nicola Pisano. Nicola executed the pulpits in the baptistery of Pisa and the cathedral of Siena, and Giovanni is first documented as an assistant to his father in the contract of 1265 for the pulpit in Siena; Giovanni received periodic payments until October 1268, when the pulpit was completed (Bacci 1926; Carli 1943; Milanesi 1854). Nothing certain is known of Giovanni's activities between 1268 and 1278, when his name appears together with Nicola's on the Fontana Maggiore in Perugia. From c. 1285 to c. 1297, Giovanni was at work in Siena, where he is mentioned as *capomaestro* of the project for the cathedral facade in 1290. His name is recorded in Siena in 1314, but in 1319 he is referred to as having died. There is considerable uncertainty regarding the attribution of his early work or supposed early work on the pulpit in Siena, and elsewhere; passages that convey a greater degree of "spiritual tension" have tended to be ascribed to him, whereas those characterized by greater emotional restraint have suggested the hand of Nicola. One image on the Fontana Maggiore is almost certainly by Giovanni: a pair of eagles with enormous claws, powerful breasts, and twisting bodies that seem to anticipate the griffin on the central support of the pulpit in Pistoia.

The facade of the cathedral in Siena was left incomplete on Giovanni's departure c. 1297, and scholars disagree as to whether the present facade reflects his original plan (Kosegarten 1984) or the upper section is a much later design, c. 1370 (Carli 1977; Keller 1937). The program in Siena (unlike the encyclopedic programs of French Gothic cathedrals) is strictly Mariological, and the coherence of its iconography is strong argument for assigning the conception of the entire facade to a single initial project. From early sources we know that a (lost) Madonna and Child stood in the lunette of the central portal flanked by a representative of the commune swearing an oath of allegiance on behalf of Siena, and by a personification of Siena holding up a model of the cathedral. Scenes from the lives of Joachim and Anna and from Mary's childhood adorned the lintel of the central portal; the side lunettes and the gable fields contained mosaics representing further events from Mary's life. On platforms projecting from the towers and between the lunettes of the lower facade were placed prophets and kings of the Old Testament and sibyls and pagan philosophers, i.e., those who in remote times had foreseen the miraculous birth of the savior. Spread out along the upper facade were evangelists and apostles, whose teachings are confirmed by the prophets. Though these were executed in the fourteenth century, they too were probably part of the original plan,

which envisioned the prophets standing like foundations for the New Testament figures above. Around the rose window appeared a seated Madonna and Child flanked by half figures representing the genealogy of Christ; scenes from the life of David, an ancestor of Christ, appeared on one of the tendril columns that originally flanked the portals. The pictorial program of the facade thus revealed the place of Siena within the total redemptive plan of Christian theology. The initial visual impact of the facade comes from an interplay of its chromatic, plastic, and structural effects: the contrasts of color, light, and shadow created by the deep jambs, gables, and gallery; the rich tactile plasticity and rhythmic flow of concave-convex movements across the lower horizontal band of portals and lunettes; and the stepping back of the upper facade behind the gables. The fourteen prophets and sibyls (the originals are in the Museo dell'Opera del Duomo) are dynamic, plastic forms whose gestures and movements embody the excitement of their special enlightenment. The dramatic effect of these figures communicating across real space has no medieval or antique precedent. However, the facade abounds in classicizing motifs such as bead and reel patterns, dentils, masks, acanthus foliage, and all'antica "peopled columns" originally flanking the main portal (Seidel 1968–1969, 1975; Venturi 1927). The traceried bifore and trifore and aspects of the figure style are influenced by French precedents, whereas the alternation of dark and light marble revetment belongs to the Tuscan Romanesque tradition. The facade, then, shows a creative synthesis of antique traditions, local traditions, and northern Gothic influences—the last of these seen also in the undermining of solid surface in favor of perforated mass.

Perhaps as a result of professional difficulties, Giovanni left Siena c. 1297, when the facade was still incomplete (Ayrton 1969). Around this time, or possibly earlier, he executed a number of sculptures for the exterior of the baptistery in Pisa. The remaining fragments (installed in the Museo dell'Opera del Duomo in Pisa) are badly weathered, but these swelling, twisting figures burst with inner energy.

Around 1297, Giovanni received his first commission for a pulpit, from the parish of Sant'Andrea in Pistoia. Pistoia was unusually rich in Romanesque monumental sculptured pulpits, and the proposal for Sant'Andrea insisted that it must not be inferior to one made for San Giovanni Fuorcivitas by Guglielmo, a student of Nicola Pisano; this suggests that there was a strong sense of rivalry among churches. Giovanni's pulpit is signed and dated 1301 and has an inscription that boasts of a "mastery greater than any seen before" (Pope-Hennessy 1972). This richly carved and elegant structure—its parapet poised on Gothic trefoil arches above slender columns with alternating animal and figural supports—reveals Giovanni's debt to Nicola's two earlier pulpits, but it also reveals that Giovanni was completely independent in terms of technique, composition, and expressiveness. Like Nicola's pulpit in the baptistery in Pisa, Giovanni's pulpit in Pistoia is hexagonal and has great structural clarity. But here Giovanni adopts an invention from his father's pulpit in Siena: the narrative reliefs are flanked by figures. All the forms—capitals, figures, narratives—are more energetic than the corresponding elements in Nicola's pulpits. In particular, the lion, griffin, and eagle of the central support are dynamic opposing forces, revolving around the column as hub. Traces of polychromy on the figures as well as remains of the glazed colored background *tesserae* give a hint of the original chromatic effect. The most stunning aspect of this pulpit, however, is the heightened emotional content of the narratives. In the Annunciation, for instance, the awesome message simultaneously thrusts the Virgin away from Gabriel and magnetically draws the figures together. Expressiveness combines

with naturalism to bring the sacred figures down to earth: the Christ child in the Nativity is neither the miniature adult of medieval tradition nor the Herculean child rendered by Nicola but is arguably the first realistic newborn infant in the history of art (Moskowitz 2001). Giovanni's compositional and expressive powers are nowhere more evident than in the Massacre of the Innocents. At first the composition appears chaotic, but closer examination reveals that the violent movements, deep pockets of shadow, and flashing highlights cohere as a series of zigzag vertical and horizontal rhythms generated by the forward motion and gesture of King Herod. In a cinematic sequence, every moment of response is portrayed: to the left of Herod, three women plead before the brutal slaughter; immediately below and at the lower left, several mothers clutch their infants in terror, shielding the babies with their own bodies; at the base, three grieving mothers bend over their dead children. Finally, bringing the eye upward toward Herod again, mother and murderer—like an angel and devil fighting for a soul in the Last Judgment—battle over the body of a screaming infant who has already received the death blow.

A quieter, more intimate side of Giovanni's artistic personality is revealed in a series of depictions of the Madonna and child executed throughout his career. In Giovanni's hands, the image is transformed from austerity and rigidity to an expression of intimacy, as can be seen in a half-length Madonna from a tympanum of the *duomo* in Pisa of the mid-1270s (Keller 1942, 13). In several later Madonnas, the child leans toward his mother, resting his arm on her shoulder. Finally, in the Prato Madonna, universally attributed to Giovanni (c. 1312), the relationship intensifies, as Mary, smiling, bends her head down to direct her gaze at her son. In contrast to the regular, planar features of Giovanni's figure on the tympanum in Pisa, the Prato Madonna is characterized by refined features and delicate transitions in the soft planes and contours.

Giovanni's mastery extended to wood and ivory. He executed a beautiful ivory Madonna and child (Ragghianti 1954; Seidel 1972, 1991) and a series of wood and ivory crucifixes—none documented or dated—which are so compellingly close to his images on the pulpits that the attributions seem valid (Seidei 1971). These, too, mark a turning point in the history of the theme in Italy: the relative quietude of Nicola's representations is now often replaced by an aching pathos reminiscent of some transalpine examples.

In 1302, Giovanni was commissioned to execute a pulpit for the grand Tuscan Romanesque cathedral of Pisa. Because of its location within the vast space of the *duomo*—beneath the cupola, near the south transept—it had to be much larger than the pulpit in Pistoia. Like Nicola's pulpit in Siena, it is octagonal rather than hexagonal. Since each parapet of the bridge leading from stairway to balustrade contains a narrative, there are nine relief fields (an unprecedented number), with the first and last narratives (those on the bridge) on flat panels and the rest on curved slabs. This expanded sequence includes scenes from the life of John the Baptist: the first relief shows the Annunciation to Mary, Mary and Elizabeth in the Visitation, and the Nativity of John the Baptist. Parallels and intersections between the life of Christ and that of John, his precursor, were emphasized in the popular apocryphal literature of this period; and here they are made eloquently clear because the two Nativity scenes are at an angle to each other and thus can be seen simultaneously.

An inscription on the pulpit alludes, in a surprisingly self-conscious way, to difficulties: "The more I have achieved the more hostile injuries have I experienced" (Pope-Hennessy 1972). Further along, there is a reference to the "envy" of others and the "sorrow" of the sculptor who lacks adequate "recognition." Vasari was quite critical of this pulpit, and later in the sixteenth century, when an excuse presented itself, the monument was dismantled (Bacci 1926; Moore et al. 1993). After various proposals for reconstruction in the late nineteenth century, the present version was executed by Peleo Bacci in 1926. Responses continue to be mixed. Documents record the names of dozens of individuals engaged on this pulpit, and certainly the quality of the carving is not as uniform as that on the pulpit in Pistoia. Nevertheless, there are passages of unsurpassed emotional power and inventiveness, such as a saint dragging a resurrected soul toward Christ; moreover, many of the reliefs reveal a continuing engagement with issues of spatial illusionism and naturalism in the treatment of figures and landscape.

Both artist and patron must have felt the challenge posed by the three earlier pulpits and must have sought to surpass them in size, iconographic and sculptural complexity, and decorative richness. The pulpit in Pisa is, then, a recapitulation, synthesis, and amplification not only of the three others but also of the major innovations in almost all the earlier monuments by Giovanni and his father. In addition to the animals and figures supporting the columns—a feature of the earlier pulpits—here there are unusually complex figural supports: in the center the three theological virtues, supported by personifications of the eight liberal arts; *Ecclesia* supported by the cardinal virtues; statue columns of Saint Michael and Hercules (or Samson); and finally a statue column of Christ supported by the evangelists. Not only do the curved narrative panels boldly flout visual expectations; below the parapet, where in earlier works we would see round-headed or pointed trefoil arcades, we now find, supporting the spandrel reliefs, exuberant classical volutes that seem to anticipate the Baroque and are impossible to enclose within the regular geometric contours of architectural norms. Here, as in the convex reliefs above, Giovanni must have relished his radical departure from the expected. In its sheer inventiveness of form, and in the range of emotions and the effectiveness of gestures in the narratives, the pulpit in Pisa represents a tremendous intellectual and artistic achievement.

The last major work by Giovanni is the tomb of Margaret of Luxembourg, wife of Emperor Henry VII. After her death in 1310, a cult grew up around her remains; and reports of miracles led to her beatification in 1313, when the tomb was probably commissioned (Seidel 1987). Much of the original complex is lost, but a major element is extant: an exceptionally fine carving of the empress being raised heavenward by two angels. There is scholarly debate as to whether the group represents the *elevatio animae*, the soul elevated to heaven, fervently desired in the prayers for the dead; or the bodily resurrection, which should occur only at the last judgment but might be granted earlier to a saint. The visual evidence suggests a bodily resurrection, since Margaret is sufficiently weighty to require the physical exertion of the two angels. Also disputed is whether the tomb was a wall monument or, like many later saints' shrines, freestanding (Pope-Hennessy 1987; Seidel 1987).

See also **Pisano, Nicola**

Further Reading

Ayrton, Michael. *Giovanni Pisano: Sculptor.* London: Thames and Hudson, 1969.

Bacci, Peleo. *La ricostruzione del pergamo di Giovanni Pisano nel Duomo di Pisa.* Milan and Rome: Bestetti e Tumminelli, 1926.

Beani, Gaetano. *La pieve di Sant' Andrea.* Pistoia, 1907, p. 28

Carli, Enzo. *Il pulpito di Siena.* Bergamo: Istituto Italiano d'Arti Grafiche, 1943, pp. 4lff.

——. *Giovanni Pisano.* Pisa: Pacini, 1977.

Jászai, Géza. *Die Pisaner Domkanzel: Neuer Versuch zur Wiederherstellung ihres ursprünglichen Zustandes.* Munich, 1968.

——. "Giovanni Pisano." In *Enciclopedia dell'arte medievale,* Vol. 6. Rome: Istituto della Enciclopedia Italiana, 1995, pp. 740–754.

Keller, Harald. "Die Bauplastik des Sienese Doms." *Kunstgesch. Jahrbuch der Biblioth. Hertziana,* 1, 1937.

——. *Giovanni Pisano, mit 152 Bildern.* Vienna: A. Schroll, 1942, p. 66.

Kosegarten, Antje. "Die Skulpturen der Pisani am Baptisterium von Pisa." *Jahrbuch der Berliner Museen,* 10, 1969, pp. 36–100.

Kosegarten, Antje Middeldorf. *Sienesische Bildhauer am Duomo Vecchio.* Munich, 1984.

Milanesi, Gaetano. *Documenti per la storia dell'arte senese,* Vol. 1, *Secoli XIII e XIV.* Siena: O. Porri, 1854.

Moore, Henry, Gert Kreytenberg, and Crispino Valenziano. *L'ambone del duomo di Pisa,* Milan: Franco Maria Ricci, 1993.

Moskowitz, Anita Fiderer. *Italian Gothic Sculpture c. 1250–c. 1400* Cambridge: Cambridge University Press, 2001.

Pope-Hennessy, John. *Italian Gothic Sculpture.* London: Phaidon, 1972.

——. "Giovanni Pisano's Tomb of Empress Margaret: A Critical Reconstruction." *Apollo,* September 1987, p. 223.

Ragghianti, Carlo Lodovico. "La Madonna eburnea di Giovanni Pisano." *Critica d'Arte,* n.s., 1, 1954, pp. 385–396.

Scultura dipinta—Maestri di legname e pittori a Siena, 1250–1450: Siena, Pinacoteca Nazionale, 16 luglio—31 dicembre 1987. Firenze: Centre Di, 1987.

Seidel, Max. "Die Rankensäulen der sieneser Domfassade." *Jahrbuch der Berliner Museen,* 11, 1968–1969, pp. 80–160. .

——. *La scultura lignea di Giovanni Pisano.* Florence: Edam, 1971.

——. "Die Elfenbeinmadonna im Domschatz zu Pisa: Studien zur Herkunft und Umbildung Französicher Formen im Werk Giovanni Pisanos in der Epoche der Pistoieser Kanzel." *Mitteilungen des Kunsthistorischen Institutes in Florenz,* 16, 1972, pp. 1–50.

——. "Studien zur Antikenrezeptionrezep tion Nicola Pisanos." *Mitteilungen des Kunsthistorischen Institutes in Florenz,* 19, 1975, pp. 303–392.

——, ed. *Giovanni Pisano a Genova.* Genoa: SAGEP, 1987.

——. "Un 'Crocifisso' di Giovanni Pisano a Massa Marittima." *Prospettiva*, 62, 1991, pp. 67–77.

Venturi, Adolfo. *Giovanni Pisano: Sein Leben und sein Werk.* Florence: Pantheon, 1927.

ANITA F. MOSKOWITZ

PISANO, NICOLA (c. 1220–1278 or 1284)

Nicola Pisano is generally assumed to have come from southern Italy and thus from the cultural milieu of Emperor Frederick II von Hohenstaufen. Nicola may have arrived in Tuscany as early as c. 1245; a series of carvings in the upper reaches of the cathedral of Siena have been plausibly attributed to him (Bagnoli 1981).

In 1260, Nicola signed and dated the pulpit in the baptistery of Pisa. This pulpit has an unprecedented form; it is a hexagonal freestanding structure whose shape was eminently suited to the centralized plan of the baptistery and echoed Guido da Como's octagonal font occupying the center of the interior space. Its parapet and platform are sustained by seven columns; the central column is surrounded by crouching figures and animals, and the six outer columns alternately rest on lions and on the ground. The columns support trilobed archivolts flanked by representations of the virtues and John the Baptist. Above these rises a balustrade with historiated relief fields separated by triple colonettes. When the pulpit was in its original state, the creamy marble reliefs framed by reddish colonettes and moldings, the speckled and patterned supporting columns, the relief backgrounds filled with colored glazed tesserae (some of which remain), and the polychromy accenting some parts of the figures produced a richly chromatic effect.

The reliefs embellish five of the six sides (the sixth is the entrance to the platform) with scenes from the life of Christ. In a continuous narrative, the first panel shows the *Annunciation, Nativity, Bathing of the Christ Child*, and *Annunciation to the Shepherds*. This is followed by panels illustrating the *Adoration of the Magi, Presentation in the Temple, Crucifixion*, and *Last Judgment*. The figures are powerfully plastic and expressive and reveal the sculptor's study of ancient art and northern Gothic art, enabling him to combine the serene majesty of the former with the deeply felt human experience of the latter. Nicola was not content to present symbolic narratives of transcendental events; his goal was, rather, to tell a human story in a credible and empathic manner. The work is enriched by naturalistic details; the figures convey a sense of bulk and weight, and gestures and movements are rendered with convincing naturalism. This new mode of sculpture was the visual counterpart of the widely diffused apocryphal literature, in which the sparse accounts of the Gospels were enriched with domestic incidents, making the sacred figures human.

In 1265, Nicola signed a contract for a second pulpit, in this case for the cathedral of Siena. Several assistants, including Arnolfo di Cambio and Nicola's son Giovanni, are named in the contract. This pulpit, completed in 1268 and placed within the enormous space of the *duomo*, is octagonal and is larger and more complex than the one in the baptistery in Pisa. Here, the narrative program began at the stairway bridge leading to the pulpit casket, with a figure of Gabriel (now in Berlin) corresponding to Mary of the *Annunciation* seen at the left edge of the first relief (Seidel 1970). As at Pisa, there are three tiers—supporting columns, arcade, and parapet. The central support includes figures representing, for the first time, the liberal arts. The narratives now include the emotionally wrenching *Massacre of the Innocents* and a *Last Judgment* that spreads over two fields, with a full-length figure of Christ the judge between the reliefs. Furthermore, instead of column clusters (as at Pisa), there are corner figures framing the reliefs, resulting in a continuous visual and narrative flow. The classicizing forms of the earlier pulpit give way to more elegantly proportioned figures with softer draperies and refined features—an ideal influenced by French Gothic art. In the narratives, the figures are smaller and more densely packed, and the compositions are organized to suggest movement into depth. Furthermore, Nicola has greatly enlarged his emotional range. The crucified Christ in Siena, for instance, conveys a pathos lacking in the earlier relief: hanging with arms stretched in two great diagonals, shoulders dislocated, abdomen sunken by the weight of the upper torso, and head bent into the chest, the figure conveys human pain and tragedy, intensifying the meaning of the crucifixion.

In 1267, Nicola completed the Arca di San Domenico (tomb of Saint Dominic) in the church of San Domenico in Bologna. The form and structure of the *arca* became the prototype for an entire class of tombs through the fifteenth century (Moskowitz 1994). Many changes have been made to this tomb, but originally it consisted of a freestanding sarcophagus resting atop a series of supporting statue columns representing friars, archangels, and virtues. The sarcophagus, the only part of the original monument that is still in San Domenico, is embellished on all sides with an extensive cycle of biographical reliefs rather than the traditional biblical or symbolic themes. The relief backgrounds show patterns of red and gold *verre églomisé* (much of it restored). The narrative fields are separated by full-length figures projecting in high relief, including the Madonna and child on one long side, the Redeemer on the other long side, and the four church fathers—Augustine, Ambrose, Jerome, and Gregory—at the corners of the sarcophagus. The corner figures, both on and supporting the sarcophagus, project out diagonally, encouraging the observer to move around the ensemble.

The bold and original design of the *arca* has sources as disparate as pulpits, bishops' thrones, holy water fonts, and ancient sarcophagi and was conceived as addressing both laypeople and the Dominican hierarchy. When the tomb was in its original location between the presbytery and south aisle, Dominic's most public and most spectacular miracles were on the side facing the lay congregation, thus serving to promote the cult; and the scenes of the founding and expansion of the Dominican order, which were of greater interest to the clergy, were on the side facing the choir area.

The last major work securely associated with Nicola's name is the Fontana Maggiore ("great fountain") in Perugia, completed in 1278. This is a remarkable secular and civic monument, as original in form and conception among fountains as Nicola's pulpits and the *arca* are, respectively, among pulpits and tombs. The Fontana Maggiore is polygonal and embellished with sculptures; it stands in Perugia's main civic and religious square, and it began not as an artistic project but rather as an engineering and hydraulic problem: it was intended to bring an adequate water supply to Perugia, a town poor in freshwater springs (Nicco Fasola 1951). Precedents for some elements of the fountain's formal structure are found in two- and three-basin liturgical furnishings, such as baptismal and cloister fonts; and also in illustrations of the *fans vitae*, copies of the Holy Tomb, pulpits, and altar *ciboria* (Hoffmann-Curtis 1968; Schulze 1994). However, there is no close prototype for the scale, the complexity of design, or the richness of the program of this indispensably functional urban monument. The sculpture on the basins is uniquely expansive, including scenes from Genesis, prophets, saints, "labors of the months," the liberal arts, various fables, allegorical figures, and even contemporary civic personages. A ring of steps serves as a foundation; on this rests a twenty-five-sided basin with low reliefs separated by colonettes. Above this rises a smaller basin of twelve plain concave sides with figures at the angles and at the center of each face. From here a thick bronze column emerges supporting a third, still smaller basin, also of bronze, which in turn contains three graceful bronze female caryatids. The facets of the superimposed lower basins do not line up, resulting in a syncopated rhythm that impels the viewer to move around the structure. Simultaneously, the vertical elements, together with the diminishing sizes of the basins and the increasing plasticity of the sculpture, draw the eye upward. The effect is of a spiral movement that culminates in, and is resolved by, the caryatid group. The fountain was designed to be seen not only from the ground but also from the balcony of the communal palace (altered at a later date), which was used for announcements to the *piazza* below and as an entrance to the audience hall within for government officials and citizens. Even today, the view from above has its own special effect, as the play of descending water contrasts with the ascending concentric superimposed basins.

Nicola's sculpture provided the source and impetus for the development of his two major assistants. His son Giovanni took up the emotional current of Nicola's style, transforming it into a very personal and highly charged idiom. Arnolfo di Cambio's temperament led him instead toward a starkly monumental and classicizing mode. Nicola's art profoundly influenced not only his immediate successors but also the painting of Giotto and, indeed, the entire naturalistic and classicizing tradition of the art of the following centuries.

See also **Arnolfo di Cambio; Pisano, Giovanni**

Further Reading

Bagnoli, Alessandro. "Novità su Nicola Pisano scultore nel Duomo di Siena." *Prospettiva*, 27, October 1981, pp. 27–46.

Caleca, Antonino. *La dotta mano: Il battistero di Pisa*. Bergamo: Bolis, 1991.

Carli, Enzo. *Il duomo di Siena*. Genoa: SAGEP, 1979.

Cristiani Testi, Maria Laura. *Nicola Pisano: Architetto scultore*. Pisa: Pacini, 1987.

Gnudi, Cesare. *Nicola, Arnolfo, Lapo: L'arca di San Domenico in Bologna*. Florence: Edizioni U, 1948.

Hoffmann-Curtis, Kathrin. *Das Programm der Fontana Maggiore in Perugia*. Düsseldorf: Rheinland-Verlag, 1968.

Kosegarten, Antje Middeldorf. "Die Skulpturen der Pisani am Baptisterium von Pisa." *Jahrbuch der Berliner Museen*, 10, 1968, pp. 14–100.

Moskowitz, Anita Fiderer. *Nicola Pisano's Arca di San Domenico and Its Legacy*. University Park: Pennsylvania State University Press, 1994.

——. *Italian Gothic Sculpture c. 1250–c. 1400*. Cambridge: Cambridge University Press, 2001.

Nicco Fasola, Giusta. *Nicola Pisano: Orientamenti sulla formazione del gusto italiano*. Rome: Fratelli Palombi, 1941.

——. *La fontana di Perugia*. Rome: Libreria dello Stato, 1951.

Schulze, Ulrich. *Brunnen im Mittelalter: Politische Ikonographie der Kommunen in Italien*. Frankfurt am Main: Lang, 1994.

Seidel, Max. "Die Verkündigungsgruppe der Siena Domkanzel." *Münchener Jahrbuch der Bildenden Kunst*, 21, 1970, pp. 18–72.

ANITA F. MOSKOWITZ

PLEYDENWURFF, HANS (ca. 1425–1472) This panel and glass painter was active in Franconia from circa 1450 until about 1472. He established the first significant painting workshop in Nuremberg, which produced works inspired by Netherlandish art. Michel Wolgemut was his pupil and assistant.

Pleydenwurff was born circa 1425 in Bamberg. Nothing is known of his initial training, but he probably went to the Netherlands in the early 1450s. He worked in Bamberg then in Nuremberg, where he became a citizen in 1457. At his death there in 1472, Pleydenwurff was listed as a glass painter. That year, Michel

Wolgemut married his widow, Barbara, and inherited the workshop.

Pleydenwurff's only documented work is the Breslau Altarpiece, of which only fragments survive. Installed in the church of St. Elizabeth in Breslau on June 30, 1462, this large double-winged retable with a carved shrine featured scenes from Christ's Infancy and Passion, and Saints Jerome and Vincent of Teate. The upper part of the Presentation survives (Warsaw, Nationalmuseum). An undamaged wing with the Descent from the Cross (Nuremberg, Germanisches Nationalmuseum) is based on Roger van der Weyden's Deposition Altarpiece of circa 1444 (Madrid, Prado).

Other works have been attributed to Pleydenwurff on the basis of style. Earliest is the half-length Löwenstein Diptych of about 1456. Based on a type popularized by Roger van der Weyden in the Netherlands, it consists of a Man of Sorrows (Basel, Kunstmuseum) and a portrait of the Bamberg canon and subdeacon, Count Georg von Löwenstein (Nuremberg, Germanisches Nationalmuseum). Also ascribed to Pleydenwurff are a large Crucifixion (Munich, Alte Pinakothek), circa 1470, an altarpiece wing with St. Lawrence (Raleigh, North Carolina Museum of Art), after 1462, and wings with Infancy and Passion scenes from the Hof Altarpiece (Munich, Alte Pinakothek), dated 1465. This last was a workshop production, executed by assistants, including Michel Wolgemut.

See also Wolgemut, Michael

Further Reading

Kahsnitz, Rainer. "Stained Glass in Nuremberg." Gothic and Renaissance Art in Nuremberg 1300–1550. New York: Metropolitan Museum of Art, 1986, pp. 87–92.

Löcher, Kurt. "Panel Painting in Nuremberg: 1350–1550." In Gothic and Renaissance Art in Nuremberg 1300–1550. New York: Metropolitan Museum of Art, 1986, pp. 81–86.

Stange, Alfred Deutsche Malerei der Gotik. 10 vols. Berlin: Deutscher Kunstverlag, 1934–1960, vol. 9, pp. 41–44.

Strieder, Peter. Tafelmalerei in Nürnberg 1350–1550. Königstein im Taunus: Karl Robert Langewiesche Nachfolger, 1993, pp. 52–59.

Suckale, Robert. "Hans Pleydenwurff in Bamberg." Berichte des historischen Vereins Bamberg 120 (1984): 423–438.

SUSANNE REECE

POLO, MARCO (1254–1324)   What we know of Marco Polo is based largely on his Divisament dou monde, later known as Libra delle meraviglie del mondo, or simply as Il Milione (after the name Emilione, which Marco Polo and his relatives used to distinguish themselves from the many other Polos in Venice). Tradition has it that Marco dictated this work to Rustichello da Pisa while the two were held in a Genoese prison. Rustichello, a writer of Arthurian romances, transcribed Marco's account into Old French (the preeminent vernacular of the romance genre), and embellished it with narrative and stylistic features typical of a medieval romance. Since people in the Middle Ages regarded Il Milione as a book of marvels, it took a long time before cartographers and explorers (including Christopher Columbus) became aware of its importance as a work of geography.

Marco Polo's work is more than a medieval romance or a book of marvels; it was probably meant to be a straightforward account of two journeys to China: the first by his father Niccolò Polo and his uncle Matteo Polo, and the second by all three Polos. There are numerous discrepancies among the manuscripts and early editions of Il Milione which probably do not reflect Marco's original account or Rustichello's lost rendition of it. There is, however, sufficient information in the most important manuscripts to enable scholars to reconstruct the Polos' two expeditions to China.

In 1260, the two Venetian brothers departed from Constantinople, where they had done business for six years, and arrived in Bukhara (in the Uzbek republic). They were forced to stay there for three years because local wars had cut off the roads leading back to the west. During that time they accepted an invitation to join an envoy from Hulaku Khan to Kublai Khan (grandson of the Mongul conqueror Genghis Khan); and in 1266 they arrived at Kublai Khan's summer palace in Shangtu (near Tolun on the Shan-tien Ho, or Luan River, about 150 miles—240 kilometers—north of Beijing). The brothers stayed at Shangtu for several months before returning to Italy with a message for Pope Clement IV from Kublai Khan.

Not long after their return to Venice in 1269, the brothers decided to bring Marco with them on their second expedition to China. They left Venice in 1271, accompanied by two Dominican monks who were supposed to travel with them to Shangtu but who soon withdrew from the expedition. When the Polos arrived in Acre (Akko) on the Syrian coast, they received letters from the newly elected Pope Gregory X for Kublai Khan. From Acre they went to Ayas (Cilicia) on the southeastern coast of Turkey and presumably took the caravan route to the Turkish cities of Kayseri, Sivas, Erzincan, and Erzurum before arriving at Lake Van. From there the Polos passed through eastern Armenia, where Marco describes Mount Ararat (the traditional site of Noah's landing after the flood), and then south to the Persian cities of Tabriz, Yazd, and Kerman before reaching the ancient Persian port of Hormuz (Bandar Abbas). When they realized that it was unsafe to go to China by ship, the Polos retraced their steps back to Kerman and went north to Mashhad, in northeastern Iran. It is at this point in the narrative that Marco recounts the tale of the "Old Man of the Mountain," one of the best-known episodes in *Il Milione*. From there the Polos went to Balkh (in northern Afghanistan),

where, according to Marco, Alexander the Great married the daughter of Darius, and then to the castle of Taican (present Talikan), known for its nearby salt mountains. They spent a year in the province of Badakhshan while Marco recovered from an illness.

On Marco's recovery, the Polos presumably followed the Oxus (Amu-Dar'ya) and Vakhsh rivers, crossed the Pamirs (known to Marco as the "roof of the world"), and reached the old silk route. The Polos followed the silk route through eastern Turkestan to the Chinese cities of Kashgar (K'a-shih), Yarkand (Soch'e), Khotan (Hotien), Keriya (Yütien), and Cherchen (Ch'iehmo) before arriving in the ancient city of Lop (either Charkhliq or Milan), where they made preparations to cross the desert and the salt-encrusted bed of dry Lop Nor. After thirty days of travel through the desert, they arrived at Sha-Chou (Tun Huang), the first Chinese city under the khan's rule. From there they went to Kan Chou (Zhangye or Chang-yeh) in Kansu province, where they spent a year waiting, presumably, for the khan to send them an escort. They resumed their journey by going south to Lanchou and then north along the Yellow River (and perhaps along the Great Wall) in the direction of Beijing, and arrived at Shangtu in 1275.

Marco spent the next seventeen years serving Kublai Khan on several diplomatic missions to the southern regions of the khan's vast empire, including Yünnan province, Burma (as far as the Irrawaddy River), Cochin China (Vietnam), and even parts of Tibet. Although Marco was impressed by most of these places, his greatest praise and most detailed descriptions are reserved for Hangchou in Chechiang province, the largest and most important city in China at this time. As scholars have pointed out, it was probably Marco's ability to describe in detail the people, customs, and geography of all these places (most of which the khan himself had never seen) that enabled him to remain in the emperor's good graces for seventeen years. Marco, in fact, claims that Kublai Khan rewarded him for his services by making him "governor" of the city of Yangchou, 50 miles (80 kilometers) northeast of Nanking (Nanching). Scholars, however, find it hard to believe that a foreigner could have held such an important position: it is more likely that Marco held a minor post, such as that of inspector.

In 1292, the Polos found an opportunity to return to Venice by joining an envoy escorting the princess Cocacin to her groom, Arghun Khan of Persia, the grandnephew of Kublai Khan. The envoy departed from the port of Zaiton (Chuanchou or Chinchiang in Fuchien province on the Formosa Strait) and sailed along the coasts of China and Vietnam to Sumatra, Ceylon, and the Malabar Coast of India before reaching Hormuz almost two years later. In Hormuz, the Polos learned of Arghun's death and delivered Cocacin to Arghun's brother Kaikhatu. They spent the next nine months in Tabriz before going to Trebizond (the Turkish town of Trabzon on the Black Sea). From there they sailed to Constantinople and Negroponte (a Venetian colony on the Greek island of Euboea) before finally arriving in Venice in 1295. Not long after his return to Venice, Marco was taken prisoner by the Genoese while sailing a galley (possibly in 1296). He remained in prison until 1299, during which time he dictated to Rustichello his adventures in the far east.

The Polos' two journeys to China were the farthest any European had traveled to the Orient since the time of Justinian. In 1246, Giovanni di Piano Carpini, who was a Franciscan emissary of Pope Innocent IV and the author of a history on the Mongols (*Historia mongolorum*), went as far as Karakorum (the ancient Mongolian capital, about 250 miles—400 kilometers—west of Ulaan Baatar). In 1253, William of Rubruck, also a Franciscan friar, went to Karakorum as an envoy of King Louis IX of France. Although both friars left written accounts of their trips to Mongolia, neither account captured the imagination of so many people for so many centuries as Marco's *Il Milione*.

Further Reading

Editions

Benedetto, Luigi Foscolo. *Il libro di Messer Marco Polo cittadino di Venezia detto Milione si raccontano le Meraviglie del mondo*. Milan and Rome: Trèves, Treccani, Tumminelli, 1932.

Marco Polo. *Il libro di Marco Polo detto Milione nella versione trecentesca dell'Ottimo*, ed. Daniele Ponchiroli with an introduction by Sergio Solmi. Turin: Einaudi, 1974.

——. *Il Milione*, ed. Luigi Foscolo Benedetto. Florence: Leo Olschki, 1928.

——. *Il Milione*, ed. Ranieri Allulli. Classici Mondadori. Milan and Verona: Mondadori, 1954.

——. *Milione*, ed. Lucia Battaglia Ricci. Firenze: Sansoni, 2001.

——. *Milione: Le divisament dou monde; il Milione nelle redazioni toscana e franco italiana*, ed. Gabriella Ronchi, intro. Cesare Segre. Milan: Mondadori, 1982.

——. *Il Milione: Introduzione, edizione del testo toscano ("Ottimo")*, ed. Ruggero M. Ruggieri. Biblioteca dell'Archivum Romanicum, Series 1(200). Florence: Olschki, 1986.

——. *Il "Milione" veneto: Ms. CM 211 della Biblioteca Civica di Padova*, ed. Alvaro Barbieri and Alvise Andreose. Venice: Marsilio, 1999.

——. *Milione: Versione toscana del trecento*, ed. Valeria Bertolucci Pizzorusso. Milan: Adelphi, 1975. (With index and glossary by Giorgio R. Cardona.)

Marco Polo: Milione; Giovanni da Pian del Carpine: Viaggi a' Tartari. Novara: Istituto Geografico De Agostini, 1982. (Includes an Italian translation of *Historia mongolorum*.)

English Translations

Bellonci, Maria. *The Travels of Marco Polo*, trans. Teresa Waugh. New York: Facts on File, 1984.

The Book of Ser Marco Polo, the Venetian, Concerning the Kingdoms and Marvels of the East, trans. and ed. Henry Yule. New York:

Scribner, 1929. (3rd ed., "revised throughout in the light of recent discoveries," but not based on Benedetto's critical edition.)

Marco Polo. *The Description of the World*, trans. A. C. Pelliot and P. Pelliot. London: Routledge, 1938.

——. *The Travels of Marco Polo*, trans. Ronald Latham. Harmondsworth, Middlesex: Penguin Books, 1958.

Critical Studies

Barozzi, Pietro. *Appunti per la lettura del Milione*. Genoa: Fratelli Bozzi, 1971.

Bellonci, Maria. *Marco Polo*. Milan: Rizzoli, 1989.

Benedetto, Luigi Foscolo. *La tradizione manoscritta del Milione di Marco Polo*. Turin: Bottega d'Erasmo, 1982.

Brunello, Franco. *Marco Polo e le merci dell'Oriente*. Vicenza: Neri Pozza, 1986.

Capusso, Maria Grazia. *La lingua del Divisament dou monde di Marco Polo*. Pisa: Pacini, 1980.

Hart, Henry Hersh. *Marco Polo: Venetian Adventurer*. Norman: University of Oklahoma Press, 1967.

Komroff, Manuel. *Contemporaries of Marco Polo: Consisting of the Travel Records to the Eastern Parts of the World of William of Rubruck*. New York: Boni and Liveright, 1928.

Marco Polo, Venezia, e l'oriente, ed. Alvise Zorzi. Milan: Electa, 1982.

Olschki, Leonardo. *L'Asia di Marco Polo: Introduzione alla lettura e allo studio del Milione*. Florence: Civelli, 1957.

——. *Marco Polo's Asia: An Introduction to His "Description of the World" Called Il Milione*, trans. John A Scott. Los Angeles and Berkeley: University of California Press, 1960.

Pelliot, Paul. *Notes on Marco Polo*, 2 vols. Paris: Imprimerie Nationale, 1959.

Ross, E. Denison. *Marco Polo and His Book*. Annual Italian Lectures of the British Academy: 1934. Oxford: Oxford University Press, 1934.

Segre, Cesare, Gabriella Ronchi, and Marisa Miianesi. *Avventure del Milione*. Parma: Zara, 1986.

Watanabe, Hiroshi. *Marco Polo Bibliography: 1477–1983*. Tokyo: Toyo Bunko, 1986.

Zorzi, Alvise. *Vita di Marco Polo Veneziano*. Milan: Rusconi, 1982.

STEVEN GROSSVOGEL

POTTER, DIRC (ca. 1368/1370–April 30, 1428)

Dutch poet and diplomat. After he finished high school (the "Latin School,") Potter entered the service of the count of Holland. Having started as a treasury clerk, he was, after 1400, promoted to clerk of the court of justice, bailiff of The Hague, and secretary of the count. As a diplomat he went on a number of journeys to Rome (1411–1412). In his spare time he wrote works of literature: two discourses in prose (after March 1415), *Blome der doechden* (*Flowers of Virtue*), which goes back to the Italian *Fiore di virtù*, and *Mellibeus*, translated from a French translation of Albertanus of Brescia's *Liber consolationis*; but his principal work is *Der minnen loep* (*The Course of Love*, 1411–1412), a treatise in verse about love, larded with stories largely taken from the Bible and from Ovid, in particular from the *Heroides*. The work consists of four books (over eleven thousand lines). Potter distinguishes "foolish," "good," "illicit," and "licit" love; one book is devoted to each of them. Potter derived the classification in Books I, III, and IV from medieval commentaries on *Heroides*, which discern in the *Heroides amor stultus*, *illicitus*, and *licitus*. The "good" love of Book II does not originate from the *Heroides* commentaries, but (at least from Potter's point of view) it forms a whole with "licit" love, which is the highest degree of "good" love. It turns out that Potter knew the complete "medieval Ovid": Ovid's works, the commentaries on these works, and the *accessus*, i.e., the medieval introductions to them. Within the tradition of the "pagan" *artes amandi* (treatises on the art of love), Potter created a Christianized *ars amatoria*. As such he is highly original: *Der minnen loep* is unique in the European context.

Further Reading

Leendertz, Pieter, ed. *Der minnen loep*, 2 vols. Leiden: du Mortier, 1845–1847.

Overmaat, Bernard G. L. "Mellibeus. Arnhem." Ph.d. diss., University of Nijmegen, 1950.

Schoutens, Stephanus. *Dat bouck der bloe-men.* Hoogstraten: Van Hoof-Roelans, 1904 [*Blome der doechden*].

van Buuren, A. M. J. *Der minnen loep van Dirc Potter: studie over een Middelnederlandse ars amandi.* Utrecht: HES, 1979.

——. "Dire Potter, a Medieval Ovid," in Erik Kooper, ed. *Medieval Dutch Literature in Its European Context.* Cambridge: Cambridge University Press, 1994, pp. 151–167.

van Oostrom, Frits P. *Court and Culture: Dutch Literature, 1350–1450.* Berkeley: University of California Press, 1992.

ALFONS M. J. VAN BUUREN

POWER, LEONEL (ca. 1375/85–1445) Composer and music theorist, one of the most prolific and influential in the first half of the 15th century. The first reference to Leonel occurs in 1418 in the records of the household chapel of Thomas duke of Clarence, where he was probably employed as a specialist musician rather than as a cleric. Since his name is given second in the accounts, he may have been one of its most senior members, recruited perhaps as early as 1411–13. After Clarence's death in 1421 Leonel's movements become uncertain, though he may have worked in one of the other English ducal chapels. In 1423 he became a member of the confraternity of the priory at Christ Church, Canterbury, but there is no evidence that this involved any professional duties. That he spent his last years in Canterbury is confirmed by a legal document of 1438 and by records suggesting that from 1439 until his death he acted as master of the Lady Chapel choir of the cathedral.

Most of Leonel's substantial surviving output (over 40 pieces, not counting those with conflicting attributions) is either for the Ordinary of the mass or for Marian services; secular music and isorhythmic motets are lacking. This narrow range of genres is, however, counterbalanced by an unusually wide variety of styles, much wider than that shown by his younger contemporary Dunstable, and his music accurately reflects the important technical changes that occurred during his long career.

Leonel's earliest surviving music comes mainly from the Old Hall Manuscript and bears the hallmark of a skilled and inventive composer fully conversant with the techniques available at the beginning of the 15th century; clearly he was proficient at all levels of elaboration, from austere discant through florid melodic writing to ingenious use of isorhythm. He seems, however, to have taken a particular delight in rhythmic intricacies expressed through notational tricks that are esoteric even by the standards of Old Hall. Some of Leonel's music seems to be contrived around numerical relationships; in this respect he is typical of composers of his time, though his usage is notably less involved than that of Dunstable.

About this time he and others began to group mass movements in pairs, an idea that eventually led to the establishment of the cyclic mass. Only one such cycle survives with an undisputed attribution to Leonel (built on the plainsong *Alma redemptoris mater*), but two more carry conflicting ascriptions. In this and later music he inclined toward the melodically, rhythmically, and harmonically smoother style cultivated from the 1430s onward; and what appear to be his last Marian antiphons are as forward-looking as anything of the period. Most of these more modern-sounding works are preserved only in continental sources, and doubtless there is further music by Leonel among the many anonymous pieces in the earlier Trent Codices and other mid-century continental manuscripts.

Leonel's short treatise in the vernacular "for hem that wilbe syngers or makers or techers" provides a lucid explanation of improvised counterpoint, especially as it involves boys' voices.

See also **Dunstable, John**

Further Reading

Primary Sources

Hamm, Charles, ed. Leonel Power: Complete Works. Corpus Mensurabilis Musicae 50. Rome: American Institute of Musicology, 1969

Hughes, Andrew, and Margaret Bent, eds. The Old Hall Manuscript. 3 vols. in 4. Corpus Mensurabilis Musicae 46, Rome: American Institute of Musicology, 1969–73

Meech, Sanford B. "Three Musical Treatises in English from a Fifteenth-Century Manuscript." Speculum 10 (1935): 235–69.

Secondary Sources

Bent, Margaret. "Power, Leonel." NGD 15:174–79

Bowers, Roger D. "Some Observations on the Life and Career of Lionel Power," Proceedings of the Royal Musical Association 102 (1975–76): 103–27.

GARETH CURTIS

PROSDOCIMUS DE BELDEMANDIS

(d. 1428) Prosdocimus de Beldemandis (Prosdocimo de' Beldomandi), was the author of treatises on arithmetic, geometry, astronomy, and music. After studying in Bologna, he took a doctorate in arts at Padua on 15 May 1409 and received a license in medicine there on 15 April 1411. He was a professor of arts and medicine at Padua from 1422, at the latest, until his death.

Prosdocimus wrote on all four of the quadrivial arts; the following treatises have survived. On arithmetic: Canon in quo docetur modus componendi et operandi tabulam quandam (Padua, 1409 or 1419) and Algorismus de integris sive pratica arismetrice de integris (Padua, 1410). On geometry: De parallelogramo. On astronomy: Brevis tractatulus de electionibus secundum situm lune in suis 28 mansionibus (Montagnana, 1413); Scriptum super tractatu de spera Johannis de Sacrobosco (Padua, 1418); Canones de motibus corporum supercelestium (Padua, 1424); Tabule mediorum motuum, equationum,

stationum et latitudinum planetarum, elevationis signorum, diversitatis aspectus lune, mediarum coniunctionum et oppositionum lunarium, feriarum, latitudinum climatum, longitudinum et latitudinum civitatum; Stelle fixe verificate tempore Alphonsi; Canon ad inveniendum tempus introitus solis in quodcumque 12 signorum in zodiaco; Canon ad inveniendum introitum lune in quodlibet signorum in zodiaco; Compositio astrolabii; and Astrolabium. On music: Expositiones tractatus pratice cantus mensurabilis Johannis de Muris (Padua, possibly 1404); Tractatus pratice cantus mensurabilis (1408); Brevis summula proportionum quantum ad musicam pertinet (1409); Contrapunctus (Montagnana, 1412); Tractatus pratice cantus mensurabilis ad modum Ytalicorum (Montagnana, 1412); Tractatus plane musice (Montagnana, 1412); Parvus tractatulus de modo monacordum dividendi (Padua, 1413); and Tractatus musice speculative (1425).

Prosdocimus based his Algorismus de integris on a similarly titled work of the thirteenth-century polymath Johannes de Sacrobosco; his Scriptum super tractatu de spera Johannis de Sacrobosco is based on the same author's textbook of Ptolemaic astronomy, one of the most widely disseminated medieval astronomical works.

Prosdocimus's musical treatises represent an attempt to survey the entire discipline; no earlier music theorist had attempted such a comprehensive project through separate treatises on the sub-disciplines, and Prosdocimus's musical writings are of great importance because of their scope and clarity. In Parvus tractatulus de modo monacordum dividendi, he described a scale that preserved the standard medieval "Pythagorean" tuning (i.e., with pure perfect fifths, slightly wider than those of present-day equal temperament) but with seventeen notes to the octave (seven naturals, five flats, and five sharps not quite in tune with the flats); this expanded scale may have been an important step toward the tempered tunings of the later fifteenth century. In *Contrapunctus*, he confirmed that medieval scribes did not write all the accidentals they necessarily expected to be performed, and he gave rules that clarify where accidentals are appropriate, even if unwritten. He surveyed the theory of rhythmic mensuration in three treatises, *Expositiones tractatus pratice cantus mensurabilis Johannis de Muris* (a commentary on the *Libellus cantus mensurabilis*, the most widely disseminated medieval treatise on mensuration, which laid the foundation for French fourteenth-century rhythmic notation); *Tractatus pratice cantus mensurabilis*, his own account of fourteenth-century French mensuration; and *Tractatus pratice cantus mensurabilis ad modum Ytalicorum*, an exposition of contemporaneous Italian mensuration (this is the most comprehensive treatment of Italian mensuration in its mature stage). *Tractatus musice speculative* is an attack on the division of the tone into fifths described a century earlier by Marchetto da Padova, based on what Prosdocimus saw as the earlier theorist's abandonment of "Pythagorean" tuning and his faulty logic.

The manuscript Florence, Biblioteca Medicea-Laurenziana, Ashburnham 206, written by Prosdocimus in 1409, is an anthology of the curriculum of the Paduan college of arts and medicine at the time. It includes the *Algorismus de integris* of Johannes de Sacrobosco, the *Algorismus de integris* of Johannes de Lineriis, the *Canones supra tabulas Alphonsi* and the *Scriptum super Alkabicium* of Johannes de Saxonia, the *De septem planetis* of Messahala, the *Tractatus quadrantis novi* and the *Canones de almanach perpetuum* of Profatius Judaeus, and the *De prognosticatione mortis et vite secundum motum lune* of Pseudo-Hippocrates, among shorter works on arithmetic, astronomy, and astrology and several compilations of medical prescriptions.

Further Reading

Editions and Translations

Algorismus de integris magistri Prosdocimi Debeldamandis Patavi simul cum Algorismo de de [sic] *minutiis seu fractionibus magistri Ioannis de Lineriis.* Venice, 1540.

Algorismus Prosdocimi de Beldamandis una cum minuciis Johannes de Lineriis. Padua, 1483.

Coussemaker, Edmond de, ed. *Scriptorum de musica medii aevi nova series*, Vol. 3. Paris: Durand, 1869. (Reprint, Hildesheim: Olms, 1963. Includes *Tractatus de contrapuncto*, pp. 193–199; *Tractatus practice de musica mensurabili*, pp. 200–228; *Tractatus practice de musica mensurabili ad modum Italicorum*, pp. 228–248; *Libellus monocordi*, pp. 248–258; *Brevis summula proportionum*, pp. 258–261.)

Gallo, F. Alberto, ed. *Prosdocimi de Beldemandis "Expositiones tractatus practice cantus mensurabilis magistri Johannis de Muris."* Prosdocimi de Beldemandis Opera, 1. Bologna: Antiquae Musicae Italicae Studiosi, 1966.

Herlinger, Jan, ed. *Prosdocimo de' Beldomandi: Contrapunctus.* Greek and Latin Music Theory 1. Lincoln: University of Nebraska Press, 1984.

——, ed. *Prosdocimo de' Beldomandi: Brevis summula proportionum quantum ad musicam pertinet* and *Parvus tractatulus de modo monacordum dividendi.* Greek and Latin Music Theory 4. Lincoln: University of Nebraska Press, 1987.

——, ed. *Prosdocimo de' Beldomandi: Tractatus plane musice* and *Tractatus musice speculative.* (Forthcoming.)

Huff, Jay A., trans. *Prosdocimus de Beldemandis: A Treatise on the Practice of Mensural Music in the Italian Manner.* Musicological Studies and Documents, 29. American Institute of Musicology, 1972.

Spherae tractatus Ioannis de Sacro Busto Anglici..., Prosdocimi de beldomando patavini super tractatu sphaerico commentaria.... Venice, 1531.

Critical Studies

Baralli, D. Raffaello, and Luigi Torri. "Il *Trattato* di Prosdocimo de' Beldomandi contro il *Lucidario* di Marchetto da Padova per la prima volta trascritto e illustrato."

Rivista Musicale Italiana, 20, 1913, pp. 707–762. (Includes *Tractatus musice speculative*, pp. 731–762.)

Berger, Karol. *Musica Ficta: Theories of Accidental Inflections in Vocal Polyphony from Marchetto da Padova to Gioseffo Zarlino*. Cambridge: Cambridge University Press, 1987.

Favaro, Antonio. "Intorno alia vita ed alle opere di Prosdocimo de Beldomandi matematico padovano del secolo XV." *Bullettino di Bibliografia e di Storia delle Scienze Matematiche e Fisiche*, 12, 1979, pp. 1–74, 115–251. (Includes *Canon in quo docetur modus componendi et operandi tabulam quondam*, pp. 143–145; and *De parallelogrammo*, p. 170.)

——. "Appendice agli studi intorno alla vita ed alle opere di Prosdocimo de Beldomandi matematico padovano del secolo XV." *Bullettino di Bibliografia e di Storia delle Scienze Matematiche e Fisiche*, 18, 1985, pp. 405–423.

Gallo, F. Alberto. "La tradizione dei trattati musicali di Prosdocimo de Beldemandis." *Quadrivium*, 6, 1964, pp. 57–84.

Herlinger, Jan. "What Trecento Music Theory Tells Us." In *Explorations in Music, the Arts, and Ideas: Essays in Honor of Leonard B. Meyer*, ed. Eugene Narmour and Ruth A. Solie. Festschrift Series, 7. Stuyvesant, N.Y.: Pendragon, 1988, pp. 177–197.

Lindley, Mark. "Pythagorean Intonation and the Rise of the Triad." *Royal Musical Association Research Chronicle*, 16, 1980, pp. 4–61.

Sartori, Claudio. *La notazione italiana del Trecento in una redazione inedita del "Tractatus practice cantus mensurabilis ad modum ytalicorum" di Prosdocimo de Beldemandis*. Florence: Olschki, 1938. (Includes *Tractatus pratice cantus mensurabilis ad modum Ytalicorum*, pp. 35–71.)

JAN HERLINGER

PTOLEMY OF LUCCA (c. 1236–1327)

Ptolemy Fiadoni of Lucca (Tolomeo, Tholomeo, Ptolomeo, Bartolomeo) was a member of a family that belonged to the Lucchese commercial elite, though not the aristocracy. He entered the Dominican convent of San Romano at Lucca at an unknown date, but obviously before he accompanied Thomas Aquinas on a journey from Rome to Naples in 1272. He remained in Rome with Aquinas until 1274, probably helping him set up a *studium* of theology in the Neapolitan convent of San Domenico. Ptolemy included a long account of Aquinas's life and works in his *Historia ecclesiastica nova*. Ptolemy may also have visited or lived in Rome during the time of Pope Nicholas III (r. 1278–1280), since his *Historia ecclesiastica* contains interesting descriptions of Nicholas's building projects. *Libellus de iurisdictione imperii et auctoritate summi pontificis* (usually called *Determinatio compendiosa*), written at about this period, seems to breathe the spirit of Nicholas's pontificate. In 1283–1285 Ptolemy visited Provence. In 1285 he was made prior of San Romano in Lucca. In 1288 he was named preacher-general of his order and attended its general chapter in Lucca; he was a *diffinitor* at the general chapters of 1300 at Marseilles and of 1302 at Cologne. During the years 1287–1307 there are frequent documentary references to his presence in the Lucchese convent, often as prior; he was also (from 1300 to 1302) prior of Santa Maria Novella in Florence. During this period he made other trips outside Lucca; for example, Ptolemy witnessed the election of Celestine V at Perugia and his crowning at Aquila and was in Naples during his pontificate in 1294. Ptolemy was in Avignon by 1309 and spent most of the next two decades there, serving at least two cardinals. He was named bishop of Torcello in 1318. Because of a quarrel with the patriarch of Grado, Ptolemy's episcopate was stormy, and he even suffered excommunication and imprisonment. Pope John XXII restored Ptolemy to his see in 1323, probably while the pope was in Avignon attending the festivities for Aquinas's canonization. Ptolemy died in Torcello.

Though he wrote one "scientific" work, *De operibus sex dierum*, published under the title *Exaemeron*, Ptolemy's achievements as a historian and political thinker far outweighed those in philosophy or theology. Besides his *Historia ecclesiastica nova*, which is based not only on Martin of Troppau and other chroniclers but also on numerous canonistic texts, Ptolemy wrote *Gesta Tuscorum*, a volume of annals extending from 1061 to 1303 in which Tuscany and particularly Lucca figured prominently. Ptolemy refers also to a third historical work, *Historia tripartita*, of which no manuscript is known. His desire to exalt the temporal jurisdiction of the papacy found expression in his *Libellus de Iurisdictione imperii et auctoritate summi pontificis*, published as *Determinatio compendiosa de iurisdictione imperii*; and *Tractatus de iurisdictione ecclesie super regnum Apulie et Sicilie*. Krammer, who edited *Determinatio compendiosa* (1909), also edited *De origine ac translatione et statu romani imperii* as a work probably by Ptolemy, but its authorship is uncertain. In about 1302 Ptolemy wrote his continuation of Aquinas's *De regno*; this composite work has usually been referred to as *De regimine principum* and attributed solely to Aquinas. In Ptolemy's continuation, another dimension of his political thought came to the fore: his republicanism. He arranged governments under two main headings, political and despotic, classifying aristocracies and popular governments as political and all forms of absolute rule, including kingship, as despotic. Ptolemy depended heavily on Aristotle's *Politics*, but Artistotle had drawn a sharp distinction between despotic and royal government—a distinction of which Ptolemy shows himself to be well aware in his *De operibus*. Ptolemy's preference for political government was revealed in his claim that this was the regime best suited for inhabitants of Eden, northern Italy, and Rome. In *De operibus* he said that in the state of innocence government would have been, as it was today among the angels, not despotic but political, a

prelacy based on service, not a dominion involving subjection—subjection having come about only as a result of the fall of man. In *De regimine principum* he said that this was also true of northern Italy and Rome, whose inhabitants took pride in their own rationality, though it was not true of the majority of other postlapsarian men, who usually profited more from royal rule. Ptolemy tried to reconcile this view with the frequency of despotism in contemporary Italy by saying that northern Italians could be subjected only by coercion. As for the Roman empire, not it but the church was the legitimate heir of the Roman republic. The virtues of the heroes of the Roman republic, to which Ptolemy also alluded in *Determinatio compendiosa*, recalled, in fact, the pristine state of human nature before the fall of man. Ptolemy's attempt to justify and harmonize republican and hierocratic theories makes him one of the most original political thinkers of the Middle Ages.

See also **Aquinas, Thomas**

Further Reading

Editions

De operibus sex dierum, ed. P. T. Masetti (as *Exaemeron*). Siena, 1880.

De regimine principum, ed. Joseph Mathis, 2nd ed. Turin: Marietti, 1948.

De regno sive de regimine principum. In Thomas Aquinas, *Opuscula omnia*, Vol. 1, *Opuscula philosophica*, ed. Johannes Perrier. Paris: P. Lethielleux, 1949, pp. 220–426.

Gesta Tuscorum, ed. Bernhard Schmeidler (as *Die Annalen des Tholomeus von Lucca*). Monumenta Germaniae Historica, Scriptores Rerum Germanicarum, New Series 8. Berlin: Weidmann, 1930.

Historia ecclesiastica nova, ed. L. A. Muratori. Rerum Italicarum Scriptores, 11. Milan, 1727, pp. 740–1203.

Libellus de iurisdictione imperii et auctoritate summi pontificis, ed. Mario Krammer (as *Determinatio compendiosa de iurisdictione imperii*). Monumenta Germaniae Historica, Fontes Iuris Germanici Antiqui. Hannover and Leipzig: Hahn, 1909.

Tractatus de iurisdictione ecclesiae super regnum Apuliae et Siciliae, ed. Etienne Baluze and Domenico Mansi. In *Miscellanea*, Vol. 1, *Monumenta historica tum sacra tum profane*. Lucca: Riccomini, 1761, pp. 468–473.

Translation

Ptolemy of Lucca. *On the Government of Rulers: De regimine principum—Ptolemy of Lucca with portions attributed to Thomas Aquinas*, trans. James M. Blythe. Philadelphia: University of Pennsylvania Press, 1997.

Critical Studies

Blythe, James M. *Ideal Government and the Mixed Constitution in the Middle Ages*. Princeton, N.J.: Princeton University Press, 1992.

Davis, Charles. "Ptolemy of Lucca and the Roman Republic." *Proceedings of the American Philosophical Society*, 118, 1974, pp. 30–50. (Reprinted in Charles Davis. *Dante's Italy and Other Essays*. Philadelphia: University of Pennsylvania Press, 1984, pp. 254–289.) .

———. "Roman Patriotism and Republican Propaganda: Ptolemy of Lucca and Pope Nicholas III." *Speculum*, 50, 1975, pp. 411–33. (Reprinted in Charles Davis. *Dante's Italy and Other Essays*. Philadelphia: University of Pennsylvania Press, 1984, pp. 224–253.)

Dondaine, Antoine. "Les 'Opuscula fratris Thomae' chez Ptolemée de Lucques." *Archivum Fratrum Praedicatorum*, 31, 1961, pp. 142–203.

Grabmann, Martin. "La scuola tomistica italiana nel sec. XIII e principio del XIV sec." *Rivista di Filosofia Neoscolastica*, 5, 1923, pp. 120–127.

Laurenti, Maria Cristina. "Tommaso e Tolomeo da Lucca 'commentatori' di Aristotele." *Sandalion*, 8–9, 1985–1986, pp. 343–371.

Panella, Emilio. "Priori di Santa Maria Novella di Firenze 1221–1325." *Memorie Domenicane*, 17, 1986, pp. 256–266.

———. "Livio in Tolomeo da Lucca." *Studi Petrarcheschi*, 6, 1989, pp. 43–52.

———. "Rilettura del *De operibus sex dierum* di Tolomeo dei Fiadoni da Lucca." *Archivum Fratrum Praedicatorum*, 63, 1993, pp. 51–111.

Rubenstein, Nicolai. "Marsilius of Padua and Italian Political Thought of His Time." In *Europe in the Late Middle Ages*, ed. J. L. Hale, J. R. L. Highfield, and B. Smalley. London: Faber and Faber, 1965, pp. 44–75.

Schmeidler, Bernhard. "Studien zu Tholomeus von Lucca, 1, Die *Annalen* oder *Gesta Tuscorum* des Tholomeus." *Neues Archiv*, 33, 1908a, pp. 287–308. .

———. "Studien zu Tholomeus von Lucca, 2, *Gesta Lucanorum* des Tholomeus." *Neues Archiv*, 33, 1908b, pp. 308–343.

———. "Studien zu Tholomeus von Lucca, 3, Zur Wiederherstellung der *Gesta Florentinorum* des Tholomeus." *Neues Archiv*, 34, 1909, pp. 725–756.

Schmugge, Ludwig. "Zur Überlieferung der Historia Ecclesiastica nova des Tholomeus von Lucca." *Deutsches Archiv für Erforschung des Mittelalters*, 32, 1976, pp. 495–545.

———. "Kanonistik und Geschichtsschreibung." *Zeitschrift der Savigny-Stiftung für Rechtsgeschichte, Kanonistische Abteilung*, 99, 1982, pp. 219–276.

———. "Fiadoni, Bartholomeo." In *Dizionario biografico degli Italiani*, Vol. 47. Rome: Istituto della Enciclopedia Italiana, 1997, pp. 317–320.

Taurisano, Innocenzo M. *I domenicani in Lucca*. Lucca: Baroni, 1914, pp. 59–76.

Witt, Thomas. "König Rudolf von Habsburg und Papst Nikolaus III. 'Erbreichsplan' und 'Vierstaatenprojekt' insbesondere bei Tholomeus von Lucca, Humbert of Romans, und Bernard Gui." Dissertation, Göttingen, 1957.

CHARLES T. DAVIS

PUCELLE, JEAN (d. 1334) An artist documented as producing the seal of the confraternity of Saint-Jacques-aux-Pèlerins in Paris between 1319 and 1324 and whose name appears in marginal notes along with two other illuminators in the *Belleville Breviary* (B.N. lat. 10483–84), dated 1323–26. His name is also mentioned with two other illuminators in the Bible written by Robert de Billyng (B.N. lat. 11935), and inventory entries of the collection of John, duke of Berry, have suggested that between 1325 and 1328 he made the book known as the *Heures de Jeanne d'Évreux* (New York, The Cloisters) with miniatures and marginalia in *grisaille*. The styles of the miniatures in these manuscripts, however, are all different, and their authorship is the subject of ongoing controversy. At best, one can speak of a "Pucelle style" that manifests a new sense of three-dimensionality in modeled figures and architectural space in manuscripts produced for the royal court in the second quarter of the 14th century.

See also **John, Duke of Berry**

Further Reading

The *Hours of Jeanne d'Évreux Queen of France*, intro. James J. Rorimer. 2nd ed. New York: Metropolitan Museum of Art, 1965.

Blum, Rudolf. "Jean Pucelle et la miniature Parisienne du XIVe siècle." *Scriptorium* 3 (1949): 211–17.

Deuchler, Florens. "Jean Pucelle—Facts and Fictions." *Metropolitan Museum of Art Bulletin* 29 (1971): 253–56.

Morand, Kathleen. Jean Pucelle. Oxford: Clarendon, 1962. [With bibliography.]

ROBERT G. CALKINS

Q

QASMŪNA BINT ISMĀ 'ĪL Qasmūna was the first known Jewish woman writer on the Iberian Peninsula. She is believed to have been the daughter of the famous eleventh-century poet, Samuel Ha-Nagid (Ibn Narīllah), the vizier of the king of Granada and the leader of the Jewish community. He apparently had four children, three sons and one daughter, Qasmūna, whom he instructed in the art of poetry. He reportedly often began a strophe and called on Qasmūna to finish it, a form of recreation common among medieval Arabic peoples. Indeed the first of the three extant poems by Qasmūna is a reply to a short poem by her father concerning someone who harms his benefactor. Qasmūna's clever response compares that person with the moon, which receives its light from the sun and yet sometimes eclipses it. Tradition has it that, upon hearing this, her father said she was a greater poet than he was.

However, Samuel Ha-Nagid wrote his poems in Hebrew, while Qasmūna wrote hers in Arabic. As a Jewish woman, she had no access to Hebrew poetry and certainly no audience for it, even if she had written it. On the other hand, as a member of the court in Granada, she did have access to Arabic poetry, as well as an audience of like-minded women poets. Indeed, although Jewish, she is considered one of the foremost Arabic women poets of Al-Andalus.

Critics have pointed out some Biblical resonances in Qasmūna's poems. They also have underscored the fact that her poems seem to alude to the importance of marriage for women, a very Jewish concept. In effect, her two other poems are laments about her loneliness. The first is about a garden which is going to waste without a gardener. Youth is passing by and the only thing that remains is something the poet does not dare name. In the second poem, she compares herself with a deer in a garden. Critics have commented that her father seems to have been too busy to select a son-in-law. However, one wonders if this is what Qasmūna was complaining about. Obviously, she felt alienated, but her alienation might have been of a more profound nature. Being the daughter of a powerful Jewish official in an Arab court must not have been easy. Being a talented woman with no outlet for her talent must have been even more difficult. Qasmūna could be talking about her spiritual isolation and the waste of her talent. The deer is a restless animal meant to be free, not confined in a garden, however pleasant. What Qasmūna does not dare name could be her frustration.

Further Reading

Garulo, T., *Diwan de las poetisas de al-Andalus*. Madrid, 1986.
Sobh, M., *Poetisas arábigo-andaluzas*. Granada, n.d.

CRISTINA GONZÁLEZ

R

RABANUS MAURUS (Hrabanus, Rhabanus, also known as Magnentius; ca. 780–856). Born in Mainz of a noble family, Rabanus (which means "raven" in Old High German) received the best education available in his day. A favorite pupil of Alcuin, he was called "Maurus" after a disciple of St. Benedict. Rabanus moved in the highest circles of power of the Carolingian world. He became abbot of Fulda in 822 and solicited the patronage of Lothair I to make this one of the outstanding monastic foundations of the age. Rabanus supported Louis the Pious in the political turmoil of the 830s and 840s, and Lothair I on Louis's death. The victory of Louis the German in 840 forced him into exile for about a year; upon his return to German lands, he retired to the abbey of Petersburg until named archbishop of Mainz in 847.

Rabanus was a prolific author and the teacher of some of the most outstanding of the Carolingian scholars, among them Walafrid Strabo. Many of his works have a pedagogical intent. *De institutione clericorum* (before 819) covers ecclesiastical grades, liturgy, liturgical vestments, catechetical instruction, and the Liberal Arts. *De rerum naturis* (after 840; also known as *De universo*) is an encyclopedic work in the style of Isidore of Seville but with an allegorical level of interpretation. His extensive corpus of poetry includes a number of *carmina figurata*, in which the words of poems are arranged in designs to illustrate them. However, it is for his biblical interpretation that Rabanus was most famous in the Middle Ages and early-modern period, even though this material has not been widely studied by modern scholars.

Rabanus wrote commentaries on most books of the Bible: all of the historical books of the Old Testament, many of the books of wisdom literature (significantly, not the Song of Songs), the Major Prophets, Maccabees, the Gospel of Matthew, the Acts of the Apostles, and the Pauline epistles. These are composites of patristic sources, but the extracts from the various patristic works are carefully arranged so as to present allegorical interpretations, mostly having to do with Christ and the church, in a coherent and easily accessible form. These interpretations were widely read before the modern period; they survive in many manuscripts and in printed versions through the 16th century. For his role as a Christian educator, Rabanus earned the title *praeceptor Germaniae*.

See also **Alcuin; Isidore of Seville, Saint; Lothair I, Louis the Pious**

Further Reading

Rabanus Maurus. *Omnia opera. PL* 107–12.

———. *Liber de laudibus sanctae crucis.* In *Vollständige Faksimile-Ausgabe im Original-format des Codex Vindobonensis 652 der Österreichischen Nationalbibliothek,* commentary by Kurt Holter. 2 vols. Graz: Akademische Druck- und Verlagsanstalt, 1972–73.

———. *The Life of Saint Mary Magdalene and of Her Sister Saint Martha: A Twelfth-Century Biography,* trans. David Mycoff. Kalamazoo: Cistercian, 1989.

———. *Martyrologium,* ed. John McCulloh, and *Liber de computo,* ed. Wesley M. Stevens. CCCM 44. Turnhout: Brepols, 1979.

———. *Poems. MGH Poetae* 2.154–258.

Kottje, Raymund, and Harald Zimmermann. *Hrabanus Maurus: Lehrer, Abt und Bischof.* Mainz: Akademie der Wissenschaften und der Literatur, 1982.

Laistner, Max Ludwig Wolfram. *Thought and Letters in Western Europe, A.D. 500 to 900.* London: Methuen, 1957.

Müller, Hans-Georg. *Hrabanus Maurus: De laudibus sancta crucis. Studien zur Überlieferung und Geistesgeschichte mit dem Faksimile-Textabdruck aus Codex Reg. Lat 124 der vatikanischen Bibliothek.* Ratingen: Henn, 1973.

Szoverffy, Josef. *Weltliche Dichtungen des lateinsichen Mittelalters: Ein Handbuch.* Berlin: Schmidt, 1970, Vol. 1.

Turnau, Dietrich W. *Rabanus Maurus, der Praeceptor Germaniae.* Munich: Lindauer, 1900.

E. ANN MATTER

RADEWIJNS, FLORENS (ca. 1350–1400)

Exponent of the Modern Devotion, founder of the Brethren of the Common Life, founder of the monastery of Windesheim. Radewijns was born circa 1350 at Leerdam or Gorinchem and died at Deventer in 1400. He studied at Prague (master of arts) and became a canon in Utrecht. After a sermon of Geert Grote, he converted and accepted the lower position of vicar at Deventer, where Grote lived. For this vicariat he had to be ordained priest. He became the first leader of a congregation of Brethren of the Common Life. These Brethren gave guidance to a convict of schoolboys.

Radewijns compilated two little treatises, which are important because they influenced the treatises of his housemate Gerard Zerbolt of Zutphen. These widely spread treatises gave the Modern Devotion its spiritual fundament. We also have some fragments of Radewijns's letters. He also wrote a (lost?) *propositum,* a set of personal intentions.

In Radewijns's spirituality, humility is a central theme. The idea of externals pulling along the inner man leads to a severe asceticism, as did the idea that a humble inner self has to reflect itself in humble and austere exteriors. By fasting and waking Radewijns had broken his weak nature and almost lost his sense of taste and his appetite. This severe asceticism is colored by the spirituality of the Desert Fathers, which also seems to have influenced his fear of the demon. In his young days Thomas à Kempis lived together with Radewijns. In his biography of Radewijns, Thomas portrays him as a man who incites both love and fear with his straightforwardness.

See also **Thomas à Kempis**

Further Reading

Goossens, Leonardus A. M., ed. *De meditatie in de eerste tijd van de Moderne Devotie.* Haarlem: Gottmer, 1952, pp. 213–254 [*Tractatulus devotus*].

Épiney-Burgard, Georgette. "Florent Radewijns," in *Die deutsche Literatur des Mittelalters: Verfasserlexikon,* ed. Kurt Ruh et al. Berlin: de Gruyter, 2d ed. vol. 7, coll. 968–972.

———. "La Vie et les écrits de Florent Radewijns en langue vernaculaire." *Ons Geestelijk Erf* 63 (1989): 370–384.

Pohl, Michael J., ed. *Thomae Hemerken a Kempis Opera Omnia.* Freiburg: Herder, 1902–1922, vol. 7, pp. 116–210 [with bibliography].

Post, Regnerus R. *The Modern Devotion.* Leyden: Brill, 1968, pp. 317–325.

van Woerkum, M. "Florentius Radewijns. Schets van zijn leven, geschriften, persoonlijkheid en ideeën." *Ons Geestelijk Erf* 24 (1950): 337–346.

——. "Het Libellus 'Omnes, inquit, artes': een rapiarium van Florentius Radewijns." *Ons Geestelijk Erf* 25 (1951): 113–158, 225–268.

——. "Florent Radewijns," in *Dictionnaire de Spiritualité,* ed. Marcel Viller, vol. 5. Paris: Beauchesne, 1964, pp. 427–434.

THOM MERTENS

RAINALD OF DASSEL (ca. 1120–1167)

From 1156 until his death in 1167, Rainald of Dassel was Frederick Barbarossa's most loyal and powerful adviser. Born to a family of Lower Saxon lesser nobility circa 1120, Rainald was educated first at the Hildesheim cathedral school, then in France in the 1140s. He returned to Hildesheim by 1146. Rainald cultivated an interest in arts and letters and would become the chief patron of the "Archpoet" circa 1060.

In 1156, Barbarossa chose Rainald as imperial chancellor. Rainald straightway committed himself to the Hohenstaufen agenda of rejecting papal claims to primacy and establishing German imperial hegemony over northern Italy. Rainald's leadership led to innovations in the chancery almost immediately, including the use of the phrase *sacrum imperium* (Holy Empire) and its variants.

Rainald played a consistently dramatic role in international relations after his elevation to the chancellorship. In 1157, papal legatees met Barbarossa's court in Besançon to protest the imprisonment of Archbishop Eskil of Lund. The Latin text of Pope Adrian IV's letter suggested that the imperial crown numbered among many possible *beneficia* that could be given by the pope. Rainald's translation of the document deliberately rendered *beneficium* as "fief" (*lehen*) rather than "good work" or "favor," Adrian's intended meaning. The subsequent uproar led to a propaganda victory for Rainald and a clear formulation of the imperial position: empire derived from election by the princes and the grace of God, not papal coronation, which was simply a ceremonial act incumbent upon the pope.

Elected archbishop of Cologne at Barbarossa's instigation in 1159, Rainald did not actually take major orders until 1165. Rainald's uncompromising attitude toward the Roman curia led Barbarossa to reject conciliatory papal offers; the result was formal schism with the election of the antipope Victor IV in 1159. In 1162, Rainald oversaw the brutal destruction of Milan, upon whose unconditional surrender he had insisted. Within a few months, however, he had to preside over the failed synod of Saint Jean de Losne, convoked to resolve the papal crisis, but ending in a diplomatic victory for Pope Alexander III, who stubbornly refused to appear and be judged. In April 1164, in Lucca, Rainald orchestrated the election of another antipope, Paschal III. In July 1164, Rainald brought the relics of the Three Kings from Milan to Cologne, where they became the object of a major cult. Late in 1165, Rainald presided over the canonization of Charlemagne in Aachen, the most dramatic step taken in the programmatic sacralization of Barbarossa's imperial rule.

Rainald's uncompromising policy toward the papacy meant that only open conflict could decide the schism. In July 1167, the imperial army won a major victory at Tusculum. Rome was taken, and Alexander III fled in disguise. Triumph was short-lived, however: an epidemic, probably malaria, decimated the German host, killing Rainald and several other princes. Barbarossa returned to Germany with what was left of his army. The political approach of the rest of his reign was markedly more flexible than it had been during the era of Rainald of Dassel.

See also **Frederick I Barbarossa**

Further Reading

Engels, Odilo. *Die Staufer*, 4th ed. Stuttgart: Kohlhammer, 1989.

Ficker, Julius. *Reinald von Dassel: Reichskanzler und Erzbischof von Köln*

1156–1167. Cologne, 1850; rpt. Aalen: Scientia, 1966.

Grebe, Werner. "Studien zur geistigen Welt Rainalds von Dassel." *Annalen des Historischen Vereins für den Niederrhein* 171 (1969): 5–44.

Munz, Peter. *Frederick Barbarossa: A Study in Medieval Politics.* London: Eyre and Spottiswoode, 1969.

JONATHAN ROTONDO-MCCORD

RAMÓN BERENGUER IV, COUNT OF BARCELONA (c. 1114–1162)

On the death of his father in 1131, the young Ramón Berenguer IV became the count of Barcelona at the age of seventeen. The first major event of his reign was the union of the Catalan principalities with the neighboring Kingdom of Aragón. In 1134 Alfonso I the Batallador died childless, and this raised the problem of who was to succeed him. His will, leaving his goods to the military orders, could not be applied; and this, together with the marriage of Ramiro, the brother of Alfonso I, made Alfonso VII of Castile give up all hope of succeeding to the throne. In August 1137 Petronella, born of Ramiro's recent marriage, was immediately promised to Ramón Berenguer, who became prince of Aragon; the marriage took place in 1150. In 1140 the holy see and the military orders gave up their rights over Aragón. It was by diplomatic means that Ramón Berenguer IV ended his disagreement with the king of Castile, whom he met in 1137 and 1140; at these meetings, he swore allegiance to the city of Zaragoza, and prepared a joint expedition against Navarre. Thanks to the diplomatic activities of Oleguer, archbishop of Tarragona, and the seneschal Guillem Ramón de Montcada, the count of Barcelona symbolized the union of the counties inherited from his father with the kingdom of Alfonso I. The Catalano-Aragónese confederation depended on a reciprocal respect for the institutions belonging to each territory.

Ramón Berenguer IV concentrated henceforward on the struggle against Islam. With Alfonso VII he participated in the expeditions to Murcia (1144) and Almerí'a (1147). He later directed campaigns intended to extend his principalities. In 1148 he took Tortosa where the help of Guillem Ramón de Montcada, of the Genoese fleet, and of contingents from Languedoc was decisive for the success of this expedition, recognized by Pope Eugene III as a true crusade. Franchises accorded to the city attracted new inhabitants, while an arrangement with the qādī and the fuqahā' ensured the respect of the Muslim population. On 24 October 1149, the cities of Fraga and Lleida also fell before the troops of Ramón Berenguer IV and Ermengol VII of Urgell. Between 1152 and 1153 Miravet was conquered, and the surviving pockets of Islamic resistance destroyed. Ibn Mardānish, king of Valencia, then swore allegiance to the count of Barcelona, to whom he payed a large tribute. The Ebro River was reached; Ramón Berenguer IV considerably extended the territory of New Catalonia beyond Tarragona. The same thing happened in Aragón, where he annexed Huesca (1154) and Alcáñiz (1157).

His political activities were continued beyond the Pyrenees; the families of Béziers-Carcassonne, of Narbonne and of Montpellier paid homage to him. In 1154 he became the tutor of Gaston V of Béarn; he fought successfully at Toulouse, to which he laid siege with Henri Plantagenet II in 1156. But most of his activities took place in Provence. In 1144, his brother Berenguer Ramón, count of Provence was killed in his wars against the count of Toulouse and the family of Baux, as well as Genoa and Pisa. His son, Ramón Berenguer of Provence, was still a minor and was powerless against so many enemies. In February 1147 Ramón Berenguer IV came to his aid; the leading nobles swore that they would be faithful to him. He wiped out Ramon of Baux, and brought him back in captivity to Catalonia. Three more wars were necessary to put an end to the seditious revolt of Ramon's wife, Stephania of Baux, their children, and their associates. During the summer of 1155 he took their castle at Trinquetaille; at the beginning of 1162, he laid siege to the fortress of Baux and conquered it. He then ensured that Frederick Barbarossa recognized Catalan dominion in Provence, ordering the marriage of his niece Riquilda and his nephew Ramón Berenguer of Provence. It was during the journey to Turin, where he was to meet the emperor, that Ramon Berenguer IV met his death in Borgo San Dalmazzo, on 6 August 1162.

The work of Ramón Berenguer IV was fundamental on institutional and administrative levels. During his youth, in order to oppose the revolt of the Catalan aristocracy, he convened the Assemblies of Peace and Truce. He organized the management of his domain in such a way as to increase his financial resources, which he needed for his expansionary policy. An inspection carried out by Bertran of Castellet in Old Catalonia in 1151 furnished him with a precise inventory of the revenues of his domains; these were administered by bailiffs (*batlles*) or by creditors who accepted them as payment. His vicars (*vicaris*) mainly brought him the fines imposed by tribunals, the tolls levied, and the *parias* (tributes) of the Muslim chiefs. Justice was henceforth carried out by specialists in law, who applied the *Usatges de Barcelona*, a Roman legal code that he had just promulgated. The *Usatges* established the monopoly of the count as regards certain royal rights; castles, mint, and organization of the peace were under his control. The ecclesiastical map was redrawn; the bishoprics of Tortosa and of Lérida (Lleida) were reestablished instead of Roda-Barbastro. In 1154, the metropolitan province of Tarragona, including all the Catalan and Aragónese bishoprics, was also reestablished. Cistercian monks from Grandselve and from Fontfroide

founded Santes Creus and Poblet in New Catalonia; the Templars and Hospitalers, who had received indemnities for their renunciation of Alfonso I's will, were also given domains on the frontier. The count welcomed to his court the first Catalan troubadours, Berenguer of Palol and Guerau of Cabrera. In 1162 he was praised in the first version of the *Gesta comitum barchinonensium*, drawn up at Ripoll. In 1157, on the death of Alfonso VII of Castilla-León, Ramón Berenguer IV had become the most important of the Iberian kings, and the arbiter of their struggles; he had a preponderant role in Occitania. His reign laid the basis for the great Mediterranean expansion of the Catalano-Aragónese confederation.

Further Reading

Aurell, M. "L'expansion catalane en Provence au XIIe siècle." In *La formació i expansió del feudalisme català*. Ed. J. Portella. Girona, 1985. 175–197.

Bisson, T. N. *Fiscal Accounts of Catalonia under the Early Count-Kings (1151–1213)*. Berkeley, 1984.

———. *The Medieval Crown of Aragón: A Short History*. Oxford, 1986.

Schramm, P. E., J. F. Cabestany, and E. Bagué. *Els primers comtesreis; Ramon Berenguer IV. Alfons el Cast, Pere el Catòlic*. Barcelona, 1963.

Soldevila, F. *Història de Catalunya*. 2nd ed. Barcelona, 1963.

MARTÍ AUKELL I CARDONA

RAOUL DE HOUDENC (fl. 1210–20) Radulfus de Hosdenc, *miles,* of Hodenc-en-Bray (Beauvaisis), was the author of an Arthurian romance of 5,938 octosyllabic lines, *Meraugis de Portlesguez,* and three short didactic poems, the *Songe d'enfer,* the *Roman des eles,* and a *Dit.* A second Arthurian romance, the *Vengeance Raguidel* (6,182 lines), whose author names himself as "Raols" is probably also by Raoul de Houdenc. Raoul is one of the most talented of the Chrétien epigones, and *Meraugis de Portlesguez,* concerned with the rivalry of two friends for the love of the fair Lidoine, is one of the best examples of the genre. Both *Meraugis* and the *Vengeance Raguidel,* which is concerned with the avenging of a murdered knight called Raguidel, can best be seen as the work of an author coming to grips with the specter of Chrétien de Troyes. All kinds of humor abound in the two romances, as well as in the short didactic pieces. The *Songe d'enfer* is a vision of Hell notable for a particularly gruesome banquet and some allegorical heraldry; the *Roman des eles* is a guide to *courtoisie.* Raoul was acknowledged, along with Chrétien, to be one of the greatest French poets by Huon de Méry in the *Tournoiement Antécrist* (ca. 1230).

See also **Chrétien de Troyes**

Further Reading

Raoul de Houdenc. "Li dis Raoul Hosdaing," ed. Charles H. Livingston. *Romanic Review* 13 (1922): 292–304.
——. *The* Songe d'enfer *of Raoul de Houdenc,* ed. Madelyn Timmel Mihm. Tübingen: Niemeyer, 1984.
——. *"Le roman des eles": The Anonymous "Ordene de Chevalerie,"* ed. Keith Busby. Amsterdam: Benjamins, 1983.
——. *Sämtliche Werke,* ed. Mathias Friedwagner. 2 vols. Halle: Niemeyer, 1897–1909, Vol. 1: *Meraugis de Portlesguez;* Vol. 2: *La vengeance Raguidel.*
Schmolke-Hasselmann, Beate. *Der arthurische Versroman von Chrestien bis Froissart.* Tübingen: Niemeyer, 1980, pp. 106–15, 117–29.

KEITH BUSBY

RAOUL GLABER (ca. 985–ca. 1046) Born in Burgundy, perhaps out of wedlock, Raoul entered the monastery of Saint-Germain of Auxerre when he was about twelve. By nature restive and averse to discipline, he wandered from monastery to monastery, where, thanks to his literary talents, he was welcomed. From ca. 1015 to 1031, he was the traveling companion of William of Volpiano, abbot of Saint-Bénigne of Dijon and one of the foremost monastic reformers of the day. At William's command, he began a history of the prodigies and wonders surrounding the advent of the year 1000, which he kept with him and added to for the rest of his life. After William's death, Raoul spent time at Cluny (ca. 1031–35), then briefly at Béze, finally returning to Auxerre.

In addition to his Latin *Five Books of Histories,* Glaber wrote a hagiographical *vita* of William and some epigraphy that, due to the jealousy of the monks, was destroyed. He seems to have had difficult relations with a number of people, including his mentor, William, and some of his independence of mind shows up in his writing. His history, dedicated in a later recension to Odilo of Cluny, began with the year 900 and presented the history of the German emperors and French kings, which, as it reached Raoul's own time (Books 3–4), included events from all over the known world and, in his old age (Book 5), included a brief autobiography and anecdotes about anonymous people. Several accounts of the same global material also appear in the independently composed but contemporary history of Adémar de Chabannes.

Often criticized for inaccuracy, gossip, disorganization, and prodigy mongering by modern political historians, Raoul has proven a rich source for social history and mentalities; his theology of history, though crude, prefigures such 12th-century historians as Hugh of Saint-Victor, Otto of Freising, and Joachim of Fiore. Raoul is best known for his apocalyptic interpretation of the two millennial dates 1000 (Incarnation) and 1033 (Passion), which he linked to mass manifestations of religious fervor—heresy, church building, pilgrimage (especially to Jerusalem), and the Peace of God movement. He has accordingly suffered from polemical treatment at the hands of modern historians opposed to the romantic notion of the "terrors of the year 1000."

See also Hugh of Saint-Victor; Joachim of Fiore; Otto of Freising

Further Reading

Raoul Glaber. Les cinq livres de ses histoires (900–1044), ed. Maurice Prou. Paris: Picard, 1886.
——. Rodulfus Glaber opera, ed. John France, Neithard Bulst, and Paul Reynolds. Oxford: Clarendon, 1989.
——. Rodolfo il Glabro: Cronche dell'anno mille (storie), ed. Guglielmo Cavallo and Giovanni Orlandi. Milan, 1989.
France, J. "Rodulfus Glaber and the Cluniacs." Journal of Ecclesiastical History 39 (1988): 497–507.
Iogna-Prat, D., and R. Ortigues. "Raoul Glaber et l'historiographie clunisienne." Studi medievali 3rd ser. 26 (1985): 437–72.
                                    RICHARD LANDES

"RASHI" (SOLOMON B. ISAAC) (c. 1040- 1105)

Solomon b. Isaac, known by the acronym "Rashi" Rabbi Shelomoh [b.] Yiṣḥaq), was born ca. 1040 in Troyes (in the county of Champagne in France) and died in 1105- He was wrongly referred to as "Solomon ha-Yarḥiy" (i.e., from Lunel) by the Dominican polemicist Ramón Martí and by the Christian Hebraists Sebastian Münster and Johannes Buxtorf, and (less incorrectly) "ha-Rav ha-Ṣarfatiy" and "Shelomoh ha-Ṣarfatiy" by Asher b. Saul and by Abraham b. Moses b. Maimon (son of Maimonides), Abraham b. David of Posquières referred to him simply as "ha-Ṣarfatiy." He was the first to compose a detailed and complete commentary, almost line by line, on the Talmud (except for parts not finished before he died). He is also famous for his commentary on the Torah and on several other books of the Bible, although in fact these commentaries have been overpraised. In addition, he wrote some responsa, or legal decisions,

which are of importance also as a reflection of historical conditions. The first known printed Hebrew book was the commentary of "Rashi" on the Torah, but contrary to what virtually every scholar who has written on "Rashi" says, this was not the Reggio (Italy) edition (1475), but Rome, ca. 1470–72 (printed by Ovadyah b. Moses and the brothers Menasseh and Benjamin). This was followed by the Reggio edition, and almost immediately by an edition in Spain (1476), both without the biblical text; the first edition of the text and commentary was in 1482 (additions to the commentary, found in the Spanish Guadalajara and Ixar [Híjar] editions, were reproduced in Kiryat sefer 61 [1986–7]: 533–35). "Rashi"'s commentaries were unknown to Maimonides, and generally in Spain until relatively late; however, in Germany he was highly regarded. Meir b. Barukh of Rothenburg wrote of him "from his waters [commentaries] we drink every day" (responsa, Cremona ed., No. 137). An old saying has it that "all the commentaries of France may be thrown in the trash except those of Parshandata and ben Porata" Parshandata, of course, is "Rashi" (for the saying, see Azulai, Shem ha-gedoliym, s.v. "Rashi," and other sources). As for ben Porata (Joseph), this has been thought to refer to Joseph Ṭov 'Elem of France (contemporary of Rashi, a rabbi in Limoges; however, he is not known to have written any commentaries), but S. D. Luzzatto (Beit ha-oṣar [1881], p. 100) was surely correct in his opinion that it refers rather to Joseph Qara, a student of "Rashi" and possibly the editor of his commentary on the Torah, who wrote commentaries on most of the Bible.

"Rashi" studied at Mayence (Mainz) in Germany, where the yeshivah was headed by Jacob b. Yaqar and Isaac b. Judah, pupils of Rabbēnu Gershom (Gershom b. judah). Another teacher of "Rashi" was Isaac ha-Levy, about whom little is known. Gershom's students had collected his oral comments on the Talmud as they studied with him, and this written collection was known as " *Quntres Magenza*" (or Collection of Mayence), and was used by Natan of Rome in his famous talmudic dictionary *'Arukh*. Later in Italy it was attributed to Gershom himself, and it was printed in the famous Vilna Talmud edition (and see A. Epstein's introduction to *Ma'aseh ha-geonim*, ed. J. Freimann [Berlin, 1909], p. xiii; and see there pp. xxi–ii for citations from "*Rashi*" in that work). "*Rashi*" returned to Troyes where he served as rabbi and head of an important yeshivah, which essentially replaced those of Mayence and worms (where he may also have studied), which were destroyed in the attack on Jews during the First Crusade (see Crusades) in 1096.

"*Rashi*" had only daughters (two or three), one of whom married Meir b. Samuel. All of their children were scholars, the most famous being Samuel ("*Rashbam*") and Jacob ("*Rabbēnu Tam*"). Another daughter, Miriam, married Judah b. Natan, whose commentary on the last pages of the talmudic tractate *Makkot* is in the printed editions (the legend that one of Rashi's daughters wrote the commentary on *Nedarim* may perhaps be a confusion with Judah's commentary on that tractate). The commentary on chapter 10 of *Sanhedrin* ascribed to Rashi is also apparently by Judah (see J. N. Epstein's article on Judah's commentaries in *Tarbiz* 4 [1932], and Saul Lieberman, *Sheqi'in* [*Shki'in* as cataloged by libraries; 1939, rpt. 1970], pp. 92–96; and Ch. Merh aviah, "Rashi's commentary to '*Heleq*'" [Heb.], *Tarbiz* 33 [1964]: 259–86).

While "*Rashi*" is best known to the non-Jewish world for his biblical commentary, in fact his commentary on the Talmud is far more important and has earned him his place as one of the foremost scholars in Jewish history. In addition to these works, he also wrote many responsa, a *siddur*—not actually a prayer book but rather a running compendium of laws and customs relating to blessings,

prayers, holidays, etc. in the manner of similar works by the Geonim Sa'adyah and Amram—and other legal rulings and customs, recorded actually by his students in *Sēfer ha-orah* and *Pardēs*. (It has been argued that *Sēfer ha-orah* was probably written in Provence, but this is unlikely since several statements indicate a French origin; it contains statements also found in the *Siddur*, but sometimes corrupted; Abraham Epstein earlier observed that it is first cited by fourteenth-century Spanish authorities, which is not true, and may even have been written in Spain, but this is even more unlikely. On *Pardēs*, see A. Ehrenreich's introduction to his edition, and V. Aptowitzer, "Zu "*Raschi*"s Pardes," *Zeitschrift für hebraischen Bibliografie* 20 [1917]: 14–16. Much of this work, and the *Sēfer ha-orah*, was taken from the *Ma'aseh geoniym*, written shortly after the time of "*Rashi*." Another important source was the collection *Ma'aseh ha-Makhiyriy*, by the sons of Makhiyr, brothet of Gershom b. Judah, which recorded the customs of the sages of their time and was probably edited by Menaḥem b. Makhiyr (see Leopold Zunz, *Literaturgeschichte der synagogalen Poesie* [Berlin, 1865], pp. 158, 161; Raphael Straus, *Regensburg and Augsburg* [1939], p. 51). On the other hand, it is not possible that the editor Menaḥem whose name appears in *Pardēs*—see f. 13b and No. 166, also possibly No. 150—was that Menaḥem b. Makhiyr, since he mentions "*Rashi*" specifically.

There is no doubt that "*Rashi*"'s talmudic commentary, in addition to making sometimes obscure statements clear (or clearer, at least), helped establish a more accurate text. The text had become corrupted and interpolated over the centuries, and "*Rashi*" utilized *Rabbēnu Gershom*'s autograph corrected copy, and also other manuscripts. Because of the great amount of contact between Italy and France, "*Rashi*" also knew of Italian Jewish scholarship, and cites

Italian commentaries on the Talmud (still unpublished) as *peirush*, or *quntres*, *Romiy*. Contrary to what has sometimes been claimed, he did not know of Natan of Rome's *'Arukh*, although his students later did. Nevertheless, he was in frequent contact with Natan and he addressed inquiries to him, according to Isaac b. Moses of Vienna (thirteenth century, author of *Or zarua'*) and others. Although "*Rashi*" did not, of course, know Arabic and relied on the often erroneous views of Menaḥem b. Saruq and, less frequently, Dunash Ibn Labraṭ, especially in his biblical commentaries, his own grammatical explanations are sometimes valuable (see, e.g., his lengthy discussion of the possible meanings of the conjunction *kiy*, in *Teshuvot*, ed. Elfenbein, No. 251).

The authentic commentary of "*Rashi*" is only on the following tractates: *Berakhot, Shabbat, 'Eruvin, Pesah.im* (chs. 1–9), *Yoma, Sukkah, Beiṣah, Rosh ha-Shannah, Megillah, Ḥagigah, Yevamot, Ketuvot, Soṭah, Giṭṭin, Qidduskin, B.Q., B.M., B.B.* (to fol. 29a), *Sanhedrin* (chs. 1–9), *Makkot* (to fol. 19a), *Shevu'ot, 'A.Z., Zevaḥ.im, Menaḥot, Ḥullin, Bekhorot, 'Arakin, Temurah,* and *Niddah.* The commentary on *Ta'anit* is doubtful, while that on *Zevaḥim* is in fact only partly by him (variant readings are also recorded in the *Diqduqei sofrim*). On *Menaḥot* one should see the commentary attributed to Ibn Adret, and also the new text of "*Rashi*"'s commentary in the Vilna edition. "*Rashi*" is said to have written a commentary also on *Nedarim,* but it is lost (see above on the legend that his daughter wrote that commentary). In the printed text of *B.B.* 29a is written "here Rashi died," but in other manuscripts it is "to here Rashi commented": not that he died but that he did not complete the commentary beyond that point. However, it does appear that he died while writing the commentary on *Makkot* (f. 19b). The printed commentary on *Mo'ed qaṭan* is not by "*Rashi*" but by Gershom b. Judah; however, the actual commentary of Rashi

on that tractate has been published (ed. E. Kupfer, Jerusalem, 1961). A commentary on *Mashkin* attributed to "*Rashi*" was published in 1939 (rpt. 1969).

"*Rashi*"'s talmudic commentaries, unlike those on the Bible, had an almost immediate and lasting impact on Spanish Jewish scholarship as well as that of France and Germany. While talmudic scholarship in Spain soon far outstripped that of the northern European countries, such outstanding scholars as nah. manides, Ibn Adret, Asher b. Yeḥiel and others frequently cited his interpretations, even if sometimes disagreeing.

Bible Commentaries

He clearly intended to write a commentary on all of the books of the Bible, but did not complete it (Berliner stated that the printed commentary ends with Job 40.27; he later published the completion of Job from manuscript, see Bibliography). The commentary on Chronicles (*Divrey ha-yomiyrn*) is not by him but by a German (?) scholar who lived for a time in Narbonne in the twelfth century (Gross, *Gallia judaica*, p. 416, No. 16). It was particularly the commentary on the Torah which earned his fame among ordinary Jews throughout the ages. It became indispensable, especially for the vast majority who did not have a sufficient knowledge of Hebrew to understand all of the text even of the Torah, much less the more complex biblical books. Eventually the study of the weekly *parashah* (portion read in the synagogue service) included the requirement of the study also of "*Rashi*"'s commentary. Unfortunately, his other commentaries were, and are, neglected, just as the study of the other biblical books was neglected. There are critical editions of several of the commentaries (see bibliography), but only that on the Torah has been translated into English (reliable translation).

"*Rashi*" repeatedly emphasized his intention to give the "plain" meaning *(peshuṭo)* of the text, and yet he did not always adhere to that. Already Ibn 'Ezra criticized him for this, noting that there was much allegory or *derash* in his *peshaṭ* (books have been written discussing these topics, although they have overlooked Ibn 'Ezra's criticism).

"*Rashi*"'s commentaries show evidence of good relations with Christians and a generally favorable attitude toward them. So also in his own legal rulings, which detail, for example, common ownership of ovens for baking among Jews and Christians *(Sēfer ha-orah* II, 41); Jews employed Christian laborers (ibid., p. 53); had their horses shoed by Christian blacksmiths and their clothes washed and repaired by Christians (p. 54). Jews borrowed food for their animals from Christian neighbors (p. 56). However, at times there are also polemical statements, although some of these, such as references to "heretics," do not necessarily refer to Christians (on polemics in his biblical commentaries see Shereshevsky, p. 120 ff., and in more detail, in Hebrew, Judah Rosenthal in *Sēfer Rashi*, pp. 45–59, rpt. in his *Meḥqarim vemeqorot* (1967) I, 101–16; however, Rosenthal was inclined to find anti-Christian polemics where none was intended). There are no statements at all about Christians or Christianity in his commentary on the Torah. On Gen. 1.1, he did *not* say, as some have misinterpreted, that *Christians* accuse Jews of having stolen the Land of Israel from the Canaanites; rather "if the *Gentiles* should say." Similarly, he wrote that every Jew has land, since all jews have a "portion" of the Land of Israel, and although the "Gentiles" have conquered it they have no possessive right in it *(Sēfer ha-orah*, pt. II, p. 229, No. 155; Buber correctly noted there that this is because of the law that land can never be stolen; there is a misprint there: *aizeh* should read *ainah*). "Gentiles" in both these statements may mean Muslims, Christians, or any other group.

Customs and Other Things

"*Rashi*" prohibited looking in mirrors of metal or copper on the Sabbath, unless they were attached to a wall, but a glass mirror was permitted *(Pardēs*, p. 42). The reason probably is because one might be tempted to polish a metal mirror in order to see better, but not one made of glass, which is generally clean. He was asked about a Jew who rents an apartment in a building from a Gentile and on the Sabbath he needs to go outside to bring water from the well, and whether this is permitted since there is no *'ēruv* (legal "enclosure" to permit carrying). Rashi replied that it is allowed, based on a legal fiction that assumes he "acquires" the use of the well and courtyard with his rent money, so that in effect it is his private property (ibid., p. 46). Side locks *(pē'ot)* were probably not worn in his time (later medieval manuscript illuminations are ambiguous, some with and some without), for in his commentary to Lev. 19.27 he refers to "one who makes his temples exactly like the back of his ears and forehead" (i.e., hairless). He was firmly opposed to the custom of giving gifts on Purim to Gentile slaves, or to Gentiles in general; for instance, many poor Jews because of embarrassment sent their children with Gentile nurses to the homes of wealthy Jews to receive gifts, and those Jews gave gifts also to the Gentiles. "*Rashi*" complained that the rabbinical requirement of giving on Purim was intended only for Jewish poor *(Siddur*, p. 168, No. 346, and cf. *Pardēs*, No. 205).

"*Rashi*" described the highly unusual practice of Christians in Germany in washing clothes: two rectangular pits were dug and rain water was collected. In the first pit, the water was mixed with excrement (probably urine) of dogs and allowed to ferment to serve as a detergent in which community laundry was soaked, and then rinsed in the second pit. Clothes were first perfumed to remove the odor and then pressed between boards (commentary on *B.B.* 17a; cf. also *Ketuvot* 77a). Some scholars have claimed to have found references to the "investiture controversy" (debate between kings and popes over the authority to appoint bishops) in his commentaries, but in fact there are no such references.

He was completely opposed to "secular" learning. In his commentary to Lev.18.4 he wrote: "Do not depart [from study of the Torah], and do not say 'I have learned the wisdom of Israel, now I shall go and learn the wisdom of the nations.'"

There are some interesting observations concerning the dispersion of the Jews; e.g., on Lev. 36.31, he refers to the "caravans of Jews who *used to* sanctify themselves and go" to the site of the destroyed Temple (since the Christians who at the time occupied Jerusalem did not allow the Jews to go there), or v. 33 ("I will scatter you among the nations"): "this is a harsh measure, since when people of a town are exiled to another place they see each other and are consoled, but the Israelites were scattered as with a winnowing fork, as a man who scatters barley with a sieve and not one [grain] adheres to another" (cf. also on v. 38: "when you are scattered among the nations you will be lost from one another"). On v. 35 he gives an interesting lengthy chronological analogy of the "seventy years" of the Babylonian exile corresponding to the "seventy years" of the sabbatical and jubilee years which were not observed in Israel (see the important notes in the English translation).

"Rashi" also was the source for many proverbial statements which became commonplace in later generations. One of the most important of these was "an Israelite even though he transgresses remains an Israelite," which was used by rabbinical authorities to allow repentant Jews who had been forcibly converted during the attacks of 1096 to return to the Jewish fold. Others are: "with Laban I dwelt and [but] the 613 commandments I kept" (where there is a play on words: *gartiy*, "I dwelt," and *tiryag*, 613), applied to one who remains faithful among bad companions; "prepared for prayer or for war," ready for any circumstance;

"mercy of truth" (*ḥesed shel emet*), attending to the preparation of a dead person for burial. He also related various stories in his talmudic commentaries, derived or adapted from talmudic and geonic sources (see on this the important article of Lewis Landau, "The stories of "*Rashi*" printed in the Babylonian Talmud" (Heb.) in *Eshel Be'er Sheva'*3 [1986]: 101–17).

"*Rashi*" and his grandson "*Rabbēnu Tam*" disagreed over the arrangement of the sections of biblical passages in *tefillin*. To this day some very strict Jews put on two pairs of *tefillin*.

Language

Since the nineteenth century, scholars have been interested in the French glosses (explanations of words or concepts in French, written of course in Hebrew characters) in "*Rashi*"'s commentaries. There are at least ten thousand such words in his commentaries. Elaborate theories of a "Judeo-French" dialect were even developed on the basis of these see also Shereshevsky, p. 14, notes 20–22). Important French glosses appear in other works, most notably the *Siddur*, where the editor has provided a detailed explanation and transcription into Romance. Some of these are of importance not only linguistically, but for customs of the time (note, for example, the use of *salse*, or *sauce*, a mixture of wine and salt in which cooked meat was dipped; *Siddur*, p. 58, No. 118).

A topic that needs further scholarly investigation is the so-called Rashi script. The cumbersome nature of square Hebrew letters, with strokes of varying widths, makes writing extremely burdensome. At an early period a method of nearly "cursive" script was employed, first among Jews in Muslim lands and then in Spain generally (so-called Sefardic script), and in France and Germany the style which has come to be known as "Rashi script," for no apparent reason other than it was modified and used in the first printed edition of his commentary on the Torah.

See also **Asher b. Yehiel; Ibn Adret, Solomon; Ibn Ezra, Moses; Maimonides**

Further Reading

Works by "Rashi"

Pentateuch with Targum Onkelos, Haphtaroth and Rashi's Commentary, tr. M. Rosenbaum and A. M. Silberman (New York, s.a.), 2 vols.; rpt. New York [1965?], 5 vols.

Solomon b. Isaac. Pardēs ha-gadol (Jerusalem, s.a.; photo rpt. of 1870 ed.).

——. Parshan-data, ed. Isaac Maarsen (Amsterdam, Jerusalem, 1930–35; photo rpt. Jerusalem, 1972), critical ed. of commentaries: vol. 1: "minor" prophets, vol. 2: Isaiah, vol. 3: Psalms; with English introductions.

——. Peirushey Rashi 'al ha-Torah, ed. Charles Chavel (Jerusalem, 1982), based on Berliner's editions, with same manuscripts, and "corrections."

——. Rashi 'al ha-Torah, critical ed. Abraham Berliner (Berlin, 1866); second, revised edition (Frankfurt, 1905), based on many more manuscripts.

——. Rashi's Commentary on Ezekiel 40–48, edited on the basis of eleven manuscripts by Abraham J. Levy (Philadelphia, 1931).

——. Sēfer ha-orah (Lemberg, 1905; photo rpt., 1966), ed. S. Buber.

——. Siddur Rashi (Berlin, 1911), ed. S. Buber.

——. Teshuvot Rashi ed. I. Elfenbein (New York, 1943; photo rpt. Benei Berak, 1980).

——. [Teshuvot Rashi. German] Rechtsentscheide Raschis aus Troyes: 1040–1105) Quellen über die sozialen und wirtschaftlichen Beziehungen zwischen Juden und Christen, tr. Hans-Georg von Mutius (Frankfurt; New York, 1986–87), 2 vols.

(responsa of Rashi also in Teshuvot hokhmey Sarfat ve-Lotir, ed. Joel Mueller [Vienna, 1881], Nos. 11–13, 15,16,18 (?), 21–32, 33(?), 34(?), 40–42, 73–84).

——. completion of commentary on Job; ed. A. Berliner in Meliṣ 14: 397 ff., 389 ff., rpt. in Harkavy, Abraham. Me'assef nidah iym (Jerusalem, 1970), pp. 53–56, 69–75;

cf. also I. Maarsen in M.G.W.J. 83 (1939): 442–56.

——. Secundum Salomonem: a thirteenth century Latin commentary on the Song of Solomon [according to "Rashi"], ed. Sarah Kamin, Avrom Saltman (Benei Berak, 1989).

Secondary Literature

Berliner, Abraham. Ketaviym nivhariym (Jerusalem, 1945–49), Vol. 2.

Blumenfeld, Samuel. Master of Troyes. A study of Rashi the educator (New York, 1946); actually only p. 75 ff. is on "Rashi," including excerpts from commentaries.

Hailperin, H. Rashi and the Christian Scholars (Pittsburgh, 1963).

Rashi Anniversary Volume (New York, 1941); collected studies.

Rashi, torato ve-iyshato (New York, 1948); collected studies.

Sed-Rajna, G., ed. Rashi 1040–1990: Hommage a Ephraim E. Urbach (Paris, 1993); I have not been able to see this in time for this article.

Sēfer Rashi (Jerusalem, 1956/57); collected studies.

Shereshevsky, Esra. Rashi the Man and His World (New York, 1982); see critical review by Roth in Hebrew Studies 24 (1983): 221–23 with additional bibliography.

NORMAN ROTH

REINMAR DER ALTE (fl. late 12th c.–early 13th c.) Reinmar der Alte (the old) or, as he is often called by scholars, Reinmar von Hagenau, is the most prolific minnesinger of the twelfth century. He flourished (in the last fifteen or so years of the twelfth and the first years of the thirteenth) at the Babenberg court in Vienna, and probably also traveled widely, as did most courtiers and court retainers. He left no documentary record; we know him only as he presents himself and as other poets refer to him. He lacks the range of Walther von der Vogelweide; the only didactic lyrics he wrote were a few reflections on love, there is no Leich transmitted for him, and the only political songs ascribed to him are a widow's lament and two crusading songs. Yet the view of

him as a singer of only one style of minnesong (courtly love song)—the lament
of the hapless suitor—though influenced
by his own stylization of his persona, is
largely an artifact of scholarship during
the past two centuries. Especially toward
the end of the nineteenth and the first half
of the twentieth century, scholars created
an ever narrower image of Reinmar by
claiming that songs and strophes ascribed
to him were spurious, until the number
of "pseudo-Reinmar" strophes exceeded
those accepted as genuine. If we accept
that he sang (and, in large part, created)
most of the songs and strophes ascribed
to him, it becomes clear that his oeuvre
was rich and varied in addition to being
extensive.

Even the narrow Reinmar canon is
more nuanced than scholars were initially willing to perceive. For one thing,
Reinmar utilizes the woman's voice
more often and in more different ways
than any minnesinger save Neidhart,
whose peasant women and girls reflect
the pastourelle (bucolic) rather than the
Wechsel (exchange) that was Reinmar's
inspiration. One thing becomes clear
in the multifaceted roles the woman's
voices depict: Reinmar's women cannot be equated with his persona's lady.
The lady as the suitor describes her is
recalcitrant, haughty, distant; the noble
woman's voices show someone who, if
she spurns her suitor, does so unwillingly,
constrained by fear of social sanctions.
Often, she demonstrates a desire for her
lover far more impassioned (and physical) than that expressed by "Reinmar" in
his stereotypical role. Indeed, she exposes
his maunderings as misguided at best, lu-
dicrous at worst. Of course, the woman's
voice is Reinmar's projection just as much
as the man's voice, but he surely intends
the incongruity between the stances portrayed to be noted and relished. Just as
Don Quixote is Cervantes's knight of the
woeful countenance, Reinmar's suitor is
doleful. Both are (tragi-) comic fictions.
In many of the songs in the man's voice,
the lady is marginalized, referred to sparingly and obliquely, and the primary subjects of the song are an examination of the
suitor's feelings, the singer's singing, and
the audience's reaction to songs or singer.
The syntax is typically complex; abstractions and legalisms (casuistries) abound.
Imagery is rare; it may be that where
Reinmar tried to introduce imagery (in
part, perhaps, by appropriating strophes
from other singers), his audience rejected
it. Several songs containing a strophe with
some striking image omit this strophe in
most versions and others are transmitted
only once. For many minnesingers songs
are transmitted in multiple versions; for
no singer is this transmission tendency
more common than for Reinmar. Not
only was he prolific, he was apparently
also intent on extending and varying his
repertoire by changing the order and
number of strophes and even, on occasion, the basic tenor of songs. Changes
in wording, form, and most strikingly
voice enable him to make new songs of
old ones. Some of the variants we have
are due to later singers (such as Niune)
appropriating songs or scribes adding
strophes from other versions or deleting
ones they consider inappropriate or corrupt. And some of the textual variants are
due to faulty copying, flawed memory, or
scribal "improvements." Nevertheless,
though most scholars dispute or disre-
gard it, the texts make it abundantly clear
that an authorial intention is behind most
of the variance we find in Reinmar's (and
other minnesingers') songs.

Many minnesingers thematize singing about singing; but Reinmar, with his
unusually introspective and reflective
persona, does so more than most. While
focusing on the theme and engaging that
segment of the listeners most concerned
with singing, other singers, directly, he re-
acts to and may even borrow and adapt
strophes from them. Such an interchange
of allusions and even strophes gave rise
to the notion that he feuded with Walther
von der Vogelweide, with the latter

objecting to Reinmar's ideology of love. Actually, their views on love are quite similar (and similarly diverse, depending on which genre they echo); nevertheless, both singers vie over which of the two is the superior artist. The *Wartburgkrieg*, a fictional account of a contest between singers at the Wartburg in Thuringia, probably reflects their competition (at considerable remove; Reinmar der Alte may have been conflated with Reinmar von Zweter). The coupling of the two singers in the Würzburg Song Codex may be another reflex of their strife. Gottfried von Straßburg pairs both "nightingales" as masters of minnesong. Walther, in his eulogies to Reinmar, praises his art but declares an antipathy toward his person; perhaps the latter is intended to lend veracity to the former, but it is also possible the two simply did not like each other very much. Reinmar arguably caused one of the most egregious instances of multiple ascription by copying a collection of Heinrich von Rugge's songs, or acquiring such a collection, to serve as models. A series of songs by Rugge, to which he may have added songs and strophes of his own, subsequently was copied into codex C twice, once under Rugge's name and once under Reinmar's. The affinities between the two singers are not restricted, however, to one block of songs, so the parallel transmission cannot be explained away as a mere scribal blunder, as scholars have tended to assume. Allusions to or strophes shared with Hartmann von Aue and Heinrich von Morungen probably also reflect Reinmar's willingness to appropriate; he in turn serves as a major model for such singers as Walther von Metze and Rubin.

See also **Hartmann von Aue; Heinrich von Merungen; Neidhart**

Further Reading

Heinen, Hubert, ed. *Mutabilität im Minnesang: mehrfach überlieferte Lieder des 12. und frühen 13. Jahrhunderts.* Göppingen: Kümmerle, 1989.

Jackson, William E. *Reinmar's Women: A Study of the Woman's Song ("Frauenlied" and "Frauenstrophe") of Reinmar der Alte.* Amsterdam: John Benjamin, 1981.

Obermaier, Sabine. *Von Nachtigallen und Handwerkern: 'Dichtung tiber Dichtung' in Minnesang und Sangspruchdichtung.* Tübingen: Niemeyer, 1995.

Schweikle, Günther. *Minnesang in neuer Sicht.* Stuttgart: Metzler, 1994.

Stange, Manfred. *Reinmars Lyrik: Forschungskritik und Überlegungen zu einem neuen Verstädnis Reinmars des Alten.* Amsterdam: Rodopi, 1977.

Tervooren, Helmut. *Reinmar Studien: Ein Kommentar zu den "unechten" Liedern Reinmars des Alten.* Stuttgart: Hirzel, 1991.

Willms, Eva. *Liebesleid und Sängeslust: Untersuchungen zur deutschen Liebeslyrik des späten 12. und frühen 13. Jahrhunderts.* Munich: Artemis, 1992.

Ziegler, Vickie L. *The Leitword in* Minnesang: *Stylistic Analysis and Textual Criticism.* University Park: Penn State University Press, 1975.

HUBERT HEINEN

REINMAR VON ZWETTER (ca. 1200–ca. 1250)

We know this prolific singer of *Sangspruchdichtung* (political and religious thought) only from his songs. They suggest he was born in the Rhineland, grew up in Austria, and was employed as a courtly singer by King Wenzel I of Bohemia in the 1230s. Other internal evidence indicates he sang at the court of the archbishop of Mainz in the 1240s. Reinmar's last datable piece stems from the years 1246 to 1248. He left some 230 single twelve-line, one-stanza songs, all sung to the same tune (called *Frauenehrenton* in manuscript "D") and a *Leich* (lay) without melody. There is also a handful of songs, probably spurious, in other stanzaic forms with which his name is associated. Only a few of his one-stanza songs can be thematically linked together. Most of Reinmar's work is contained in two sources, 219 stanzas in manuscript "C," the famous Manesse Song Manuscript (Heidelberg, no. Cod. Pal. Germ. 848), and 193 stanzas in manuscript "D" (Heidelberg, no. Cod. Pal. Germ. 350). Other stanzas are scattered over some twenty additional manuscripts. The illustration in "C" depicts him as a blind singer dictating his songs, though there is no evidence in the body of his work that he was sight-impaired.

The *Frauenehrenton*, Reinmar's only known melody, is a utilitarian d-based construction, a solid structure for the delivery of all his content-laden stanzas. It is possible that it is not an original composition, since one of Reinmar's confreres in courtly singing accuses him of being a tune thief (*doenediep*).

Reinmar's singing encompasses many of the popular subgenres of *Spruchdichtung*, e.g., political songs, religious songs, cautionary songs, songs of praise, songs about the nature of love, and songs extolling knightly virtue. In this he is a disciple of Walther von der Vogelweide, though his poetry lacks the nuance and lyricism of Walther. Many of his songs have an elegiac quality, lamenting the passing of the heyday of love, honor, and courtly values. In these Reinmar provides a canon for knightly behavior in the first half of the thirteenth century.

His rhetorical style is direct and convincing, underscoring his belief in the old-fashioned values of knighthood (especially *Minne*—courtly love—and honor) and reflecting a natural piety in which he pleads for righteousness, though never in a self-righteous way. His stanzas, especially the political ones, also afford glimpses of his life as a courtly singer. Like Walther before him, Reinmar had to generate political propaganda to suit the occasion. Illustrative are two songs composed in the 1230s, the first issuing a dire warning to those conspiring against Emperor Fredrick II (Roethe: No. 137), the second (composed after a change of patrons) urging willful resistance to the same monarch (Roethe: No. 149).

Pursuing the tradition of Walther's political and religious songs, Reinmar is the link to later singers of *Spruchdichtung* in the second half of the thirteenth century such as Bruder Werner, Meister Alexander, Meister Stolle, der Marner, and Frauenlob. That such a rich assortment of stanzas was collected in more than twenty manuscripts attests to his popularity. For three hundred years he was venerated by the Meistersinger, who counted him among the twelve old masters.

See also **Frauenlob; Frederick II; Walther von der Vogelweide**

Further Reading

Bonjour, Edgar. *Reimar von Zweter als politischer Dichter.* Bern: Haupt, 1922.

Gerhardt, Christoph. "Reinmars von Zweters Idealer Mann." *Beiträge zur Geschichte der deutschen Sprache und Literatur* (Tübingen) 109 (1987): 51–84, 222–251.

Roethe, Gustav. *Die Gedichte Reinmars von Zweter.* Leipzig: Hirzel, 1887.

Schubert, Martin J. "Die Form von Reinmars Leich." *Amsterdamer Beiträge zur älteren Germanistik* 41 (1995): 85–142.

Schupp, Volker. "Reinmar von Zweter, Dichter Kaisers Friedrichs II." *Wirkendes Wort* 19 (1969): 231–244.

PETER FRENZEL

REMIGIO DEI GIROLAMI (d. 1319)

The Dominican Remigio dei Girolami was a well-known teacher and preacher in Florence. He was a member of a family prominent in the wool guild and in municipal civic life. For many years, he was lector of theology in the great Dominican convent of Santa Maria Novella. In addition to his fame as a preacher, he also gained renown as a welcomer of visiting kings, cardinals, and other dignitaries; as an exhorter of civic officials to promote the common good; and as an orator at funerals and commemorative occasions for local and foreign notables. There were few types of public ceremony in Florence or in his order in which he was not at least occasionally a conspicuous participant. Although some of his closest relatives were exiled after the triumph of the Black Guelf faction in 1302, Remigio's own popularity with those in power seems to have continued. In 1313, answering a query from Sienese officials about his political soundness, the Florentine government called him "a leading father to our corporation (*universitati*)."

Remigio also wrote treatises on a rich variety of theological, philosophical, and political subjects, but these seem to have aroused little interest until the second half of the twentieth century, when a number of them were edited. Early in the century, G. Salvadori published some extracts from Remigio's public sermons and advanced the thesis that he must have been Dante's teacher at the time when Dante tells us he was frequenting the "schools of the religious." The theory remains unproved, but it has been widely accepted and is not improbable, for during this period Remigio was the principal lector of one of the two leading schools of the religious in Florence.

Whether he taught Dante or not, Remigio's teaching was important in the Florence of his own day, and it was most emphasized by the chronicle or necrology of his own convent. The entry about Remigio says that at the time of his death he had been a Dominican for fifty-one years and ten months, of which more than forty years had been spent as lector of Santa Maria Novella. Remigio was licensed in arts in Paris, entered the Dominican Order in the "first flower of his youth," and made such rapid progress, according to the necrology, that he became lector at Florence while still a deacon and before being ordained as a priest. He must have become a Dominican in Paris c. 1267–1268, since, as Panella (1982) has shown, he heard Saint Thomas Aquinas during Aquinas's last period of teaching there, from 1269 to 1272. Remigio served in many important positions in his order,

and he was already preacher-general by 1281. He returned to Paris c. 1298 at the express wish of his convent to continue his theological studies and qualify for the *magisterium*. He had returned to Florence in August 1301 but soon went to Rome in the hope of receiving the *magisterium* from Pope Boniface VIII, but this ambition was frustrated by Boniface's sudden death. Remigio finally received the *magisterium* from a fellow Dominican, Pope Benedict XI, probably in 1304 at Perugia; we know that he preached and disputed there, and apparently he did not return to Florence again until 1306 or 1307. This seems to have been his last long absence from the city and the lectorate of Santa Maria Novella, though the necrology says that he gave up teaching and preaching a few years before his death (probably by 1316, when there was a new lector of theology at the convent) and devoted himself to composing and compiling religious books. This activity seems to have consisted in large part in the collecting and editing of his own works.

Remigio's works are contained in four early fourteenth-century double-columned folio volumes and a later collection of Lenten sermons in the *Conventi soppressi* manuscript collection of the National Library of Florence, plus two copies of a commentary on the Song of Songs in the Laurentian Library, also in Florence. The four *Conventi soppressi* volumes are C.4.940, Remigio's treatises; D.1.937, sermons *de sanctis et festis*; G.3.465, questions; and G.4.936, sermons *de tempore*, and those for special occasions. The last includes a section of prologues that Remigio preached at the beginning of his courses. Most are on books of Peter Lombard's *Sentences* or the Bible; but two deal with Aristotle, and one of these is devoted specifically to Aristotle's *Ethics*. Together they comprise some 2,700 folio sides. The four folio volumes, except for the first seventy-four leaves of C.4.940, are all written in the same highly abbreviated hand, with additions, annotations, and corrections by a second hand, evidently that of Remigio himself. Although a few copies of particular sermons have been found in manuscripts of non-Florentine provenance, Remigio's fame was mainly local, and knowledge of his writings was confined almost entirely to his own convent. But his writings must have been important there, for they furnished a rich repository of materials for preaching and for instruction in an important, if somewhat provincial, Dominican school. The purpose of the compilation of these volumes is confirmed by an elaborate web of cross-references, both in the text and in the margins, that connect works in the same volume and in different volumes. Many of the sermons, for example, are merely outlines but often contain references to allegorical and anecdotal material in other sermons and in treatises. As for the treatises (contained in Biblioteca Nazionale, Florence, MS Conventi Soppressi C.4.940), they do not cite the sermons, but they often cite and thereby reinforce each other.

Originality is not the most striking characteristic of Remigio's works. On the other hand, his concern with contemporary events and problems and his intense Florentine patriotism are often apparent. Although Remigio copied quantities of material from Aquinas in his treatise *De peccato usure*, its editor describes Remigio's analysis of the sin of usury as somewhat more flexible than Aquinas's. In a long digression in another treatise, *Contra falsos ecclesie professores*, Remigio tried valiantly, if with only partial success, to find a middle ground between those who exalted and those who decried the claim of the papacy to universal temporal authority. Perhaps the most interesting aspect of Remigio's thought was his effort to fuse the Augustinian concept of peace with the Aristotelian concept of the common good and apply them to the problem of faction in his own city, identifying them with the good of the commune. Several of his treatises and a number of his sermons

are devoted to this theme. He also—like his fellow Dominican Ptolemy of Lucca—tried to inspire his fellow citizens through examples of civic virtue furnished by the heroes of the Roman republic, whose willingness to sacrifice themselves for their *patria* he (again like Ptolemy) did not hesitate to identify with the Christian virtue of *caritas*. Not to be a citizen, he affirmed with Aristotle, was not to be a man; and for Remigio, citizenship required the realization that the good of the part was subordinated to and included in the good of the whole. Of course, the common good of Christendom took precedence over the common good of Florence, and its head should be obeyed whenever possible; but if a command of the pope contravened the peace and well-being of the commune, even that command should be disregarded.

See also **Aquinas, Thomas; Dante Alighieri; Ptolemy of Lucca**

Further Reading

Treatises by Remigio

Contra falsos ecclesie professores (fols. 154v–196v), ed. Filippo Tamburini. Rome, 1981.

De bono comuni (fols. 97r–106r), ed. M. C. De Matteis. In *La "teologia politica comunale" de Remigio de' Girolami*. Bologna, 1977 (text: 1–51).

De bono comuni (fols. 97r–106r), ed. Emilio Panella. In "Dal bene comune al bene del comune: I trattati politici di Remigio dei Girolami nella Firenze dei Bianchi-Neri." *Memorie Domenicane*, 16, 1985, 1–198. (Text, pp. 123–168.)

De bono pacis (fols. 106v–109r), ed. Charles T. Davis. In "Remigio de' Girolami and Dante: A Comparison of Their Conceptions of Peace." *Studi Danteschi*, 36, 1959, pp. 105–136. (Text, pp. 123–136. See also editions by M. C. De Matteis, in *La teologia . . .*, text, pp. 53–71; and Emilio Panella, in "Dal bene comune...," text, pp. 169–183.)

De contrarietate peccati (fols. 124v–130v).

De iustitia (fols. 206r–207r), ed. Ovidio Capitani. In "L'incompiuto 'Tractatus de iustitia' di fra Remigio de' Girolami." *Bullettino dell'Istituto Storico Italiano per il Medio Evo*, 72, 1960, pp. 91–134. (Text, pp. 125–128.)

De misericordia (fols. 197r–206r), ed. A. Samaritani, in "La misericordia in Remigio de' Girolami e in Dante nel passaggio tra la teologia patristico-monastica e la scolastica." *Analecta Pomposiana*, 2, 1966, pp. 169–207. (Text, pp. 181–207.)

De mixtione elementorum inmixto (fols. 11v–17r).

De modis rerum (fols. 17v–70v). (Earlier version with Remigio's corrections in MS Conventi Soppressi E.7.938.)

De mutabilitate et inmutabilitate (fols. 131r–135v).

De peccato usure (fols. 109r–124v), ed. Ovidio Capitani. In "Il 'De peccato usure' di Remigio de' Girolami." *Studi Medievali*, 6(2), 1965, pp. 537–662. (Text, pp. 611–660.)

Determinatio de uno esse in Christo (fols. 7r–11v), ed. Martin Grabmann. In *Miscellania Tomista*. Estudis Franciscans, 24. Barcelona, October–December 1924, pp. 257–277.

Determinatio utrum sit licitum vendere mercationes ad terminum (fols. 130v–131r), ed. O. Capitani. In "La 'venditio ad terminum' nella valutazione morale di S. Tommaso d'Aquino e di Remigio de' Girolami." *Bullettino dell'Istituto Storico Italiano per il Medio Evo*, 70, 1958, pp. 299–363. (Text, pp. 343–345.)

De via paradisi (fols. 207r–352v).

Divisio scientie (fols. 1r–7r), ed. Emilio Panella. In "Un'introduzione alla filosofia in uno 'studium' dei Frati Predicatori del XIII secolo. 'Divisio scientie' di Remigio dei Girolami." *Memorie Domenicane*, n.s., 12, 1981, pp. 27–126. (Text, pp. 81–119.)

Questio de subiecto theologie (fols. 91r–95v), ed. Emilio Panella. In *Il "De subiecto theologie" (1297—1299) di Remigio dei Girolami*. Rome, 1982. (Text, pp. 4–71.)

Quodlibetum primum (fols. 71r–81v) and *Ouodlibetum secundum* (fols. 81v–90v), ed. Emilio Panella. In "I quodlibeti di Remigio." *Memorie Domenicane*, 14, 1983, pp. 1–149. (Text, pp. 66–146.)

Speculum (fols. 135v–l54v).

Questions by Remigio

Extractio ordinata per alphabetum de questionibus tractatis. Biblioteca Nazionale, Florence, MS Conventi Soppressi G 3.465. (See *Questio de duratione monitionum capitulorum Generalium et Provincialium*, ed. Emilio Panella. In "Dibattito sulla durata legale delle 'Admonitiones,'" pp. 85–101; text, pp. 97–101. See also table of contents at the end of the manuscript, ed. J. D. Caviglioli and R. Imbach. In "Brève notice sur *Extractio ordinata per alphabetum* de Remi," *Archivum Fratrum Praedicatorum*, 49, 1979, pp. 105–131; text, pp. 115–131.)

Remigio's Postille

Postille super Cantica Canticorum. Biblioteca Laurenziana, Florence, MSS Conventi Soppressi 362 (fols. 88r–123r; 516, fols. 221r–266v). (The latter MS contains also *Distinctiones* for the letter A, fols. 266v–268v, ed. Emilio Panella. In "Per lo studio di fra' Remigio dei Girolami." *Memorie Domenicane*, n.s., 10, 1979, pp. 271–283.)

Sermons by Remigio

Sermones de diversis materiis. Biblioteca Nazionale, Florence, MS Conventi Soppressi G.4.936, fols. 247r–404v. (See scraps from these sermons, as well as *Versus* and *Rithmi* placed by Remigio at the end of the codex, ed. G. Salvadori and V. Federici. "I Sermoni d'occasione, le sequenze e i ritmi di Remigio Girolami fiorentino." In *Scritti vari di filologia a Ernesto Monaci*, 455–508. Rome: Forzani, 1901. See also the sermons *De pace*, ed. Emilio Panella. In "Dal bene comune . . . ," pp. 187–198. This section of MS Conv. Soppr. G.4.936 also contains prologues to courses on books of the Bible, *Sentences*, and Aristotle's *Ethics*, fols. 276v–345r. See Emilio Panella, ed. *Prologus in fine sententiarum*. In *Il "De subiecto theologie*," pp. 73–75. See also Emilio Panella, ed. *Prologus super librum Ethicorum*. In "' Un'introduzione alla filosofia*," pp. 122–124.)

Sermones de quadragesima. Biblioteca Nazionale, Florence, MS Conventi Soppressi G.7.939.

Sermones de sanctis et de festis. Biblioteca Nazionale, Florence, MS Conventi Soppressi D.1.937.

Sermones de tempore. Biblioteca Nazionale, Florence, MS Conventi Soppressi G.4.936, fols. 1r–246v.

Studies

Davis, Charles T. "An Early Florentine Political Theorist: Fra Remigio de' Girolami." *Proceedings of the American Philosophical Society,* 104, 1960, pp. 662–676. (Reprinted in *Dante's Italy and Other Essays.* Philadelphia: University of Pennsylvania Press, 1984, pp. 198–223.)

Egenter, R. "Gemeinnutz vor Eigennutz: Die soziale Leitidee im *Tractatus de bono communi* des Fr. Remigius von Flotenz." *Scholastik,* 9, 1934, pp. 79–92.

Grabmann, Martin. "Die Wege von Thomas von Aquin zu Dante." *Deutsches Dante Jahrbuch,* 9, 1925, pp. 1–35.

Maccarrone, Michele. " 'Potestas directa' e 'potestas indirecta' nei teologi del XII e XIII secolo." *Miscellanea historiae pontificiae,* 18, 1954, pp. 27–47.

Minio-Paluello, Lorenzo. "Remigio Girolami's *De bono communi.*" *Italian Studies,* 2, 1956, pp. 56–71.

Orlandi, Srefano. *Necrologio di S. Maria Novella,* 2 vols. Florence: Olschki, 1955, Vol. 1, pp. 35–36, 276–307.

Panella, Emilio. "Per lo studio di fra Remigio dei Girolami († 1319)." *Memorie Domenicane,* n.s., 10, 1979.

——. "Il repertorio dello Schneyer e i sermonari di Remigio dei Girolami." *Memorie Domenicane,* n.s., 11, 1980, pp. 632–650.

——. "Remigiana: note biografiche e filologiche." *Memorie Domenicane,* n.s., 13, 1982, pp. 366–421.

——. "Nuova Cronologia Remigiana." *Archivum Fratrum Praedicatorum,* 60, 1990, pp. 145–311.

Pugh Rupp, T. "Ordo caritatis: The Political Thought of Remigio dei Girolami." Dissertation, Cornell University, 1988. (Ann Arbor Microfilms.)

"Remigio Dei Girolami." *Dictionnaire de spiritualité,* 13, 1987, pp. 343–347.

Schneyer, Johannes Baptist. *Repertorium der lateinischen Sermones des Mittelalters für die Zeit von 1150–1350,* Vol. 5. Münster: Aschendorff, 1974, pp. 65–134.

CHARLES T. DAVIS

RENÉ D'ANJOU (1409–1480) Son of Louis II, duke of Anjou, and Yolande of Aragon, the "Good King René" is known for his accomplishments in several areas. This second son of the politically ambitious Yolande was, for strategic reasons, adopted by the duke of Bar. He was married in 1420 to Isabelle of Lorraine. He became duke of Bar in 1430 and duke of Lorraine in 1431, but his claim to the latter title cost him five years in prison. At the death of his elder brother Louis in 1434, René inherited the duchy of Anjou and the family claim to the kingdom of Naples. Although he lost the latter throne to Alfonso of Aragon in 1442, René's prestige and influence nonetheless continued to grow at the court of his brother-in-law, Charles VII, and in France generally. After the death of Isabelle in 1453, he married Jeanne de Laval. René, whose titles derived from the circumstances of aristocratic inheritance, was one of the last obstacles to the unification of France by Louis XI. Deprived of Bar and Anjou by Louis, René retreated in his later years to Provence.

Despite his political reversals, René d'Anjou was known as a good strategist in battle and an expert in warfare. He wrote a treatise on tournaments, the *Traictié de la forme et devis d'un tornoy* (1445–50), and organized several celebrated tournaments on Charles VII's behalf. He was a generous patron of the arts and himself a painter and writer. He composed two richly illuminated allegorical works in verse and prose: the *Mortifiement de vaine plaisance* (1455) and the *Livre du cuer d'amours espris* (1457).

See also **Charles VII**

Further Reading

René d'Anjou. *Le livre du cuer d'amours espris,* ed. Susan Wharton. Paris: Union Générale des Éditions, 1980.

——. *King René's Book of Love (Le cueur d'amours espris,* intro. and commentary F. Unterkircher, trans. Sophie Wilkins.

New York: Braziller, 1975. [Reproduces sixteen illuminations attributed to René.]

Des Garets, Marie Louyse. *Un artisan de la Renaissance française du XVe siècle, le roi René, 1409–1480.* Paris: Éditions de la Table Ronde, 1946.

Lyna, Frédéric. *Le mortifiement de vaine plaisance de René d'Anjou: étude du texte et des manuscrits à peintures.* Brussels: Weckesser, 1926.

JANICE C. ZINSER

RICHARD DE FOURNIVAL (1201–before 1260)

Poet, canon, and chancellor at Amiens cathedral and canon of Rouen, Richard de Fournival produced a rich and varied corpus, composing songs in the trouvère style, the prose *Bestiaire d'amours* and its fragmentary verse redaction, and the Latin *Biblionomia*, the catalogue of his remarkable library. Three other prose treatises, the *Commens d'amours,* the *Consaus d'amours,* and the *Poissance d'amours,* are of questionable attribution.

It is for the *Bestiaire d'amours* that Richard is chiefly known. In this adaptation of the bestiary format, birds and animals represent aspects of the love experience. The text, immediately popular, has been transmitted in numerous manuscripts, richly illuminated. It inspired several literary responses, all anonymous. The earliest is the *Response au bestiaire,* in which the lady to whom the *Bestiaire d'amours* was addressed supposedly replies, turning each of the bestiary examples into an illustration of her need to take care to protect herself against male sexual advances. A verse adaptation, different from the fragmentary verse redaction apparently by Richard himself, also survives; although the author gives his name, he does so in an anagram of such complexity that it remains unsolved. In two 14th-century manuscripts, the *Bestiaire d'amours* is given a narrative continuation, in which the lover captures the lady and receives from her a red rose. In another 14th-century manuscript, the

Bestiaire and its *Response* are embedded in a sequence of prose texts that form a dialogue between lover and lady; although none is a bestiary, all refer to the *Bestiaire,* which clearly inspired the sequence.

We know from the *Biblionomia* that Richard owned some unusual books, including the only known complete copy of the poems of Tibullus. At his death, his library passed to Gérard d'Abbeville and then to the Sorbonne.

Further Reading

Fournival, Richard de. *Le bestiaire d'amour rimé,* ed. Arvid Thordstein. Lund: Ohlssons, 1941.[The anonymous verse adaptation of the *Bestiaire d'amours.*]

——. *Li bestiaires d'amours di maistre Richart de Fornival e Li response du bestiaire,* ed. Cesare Segre. Milan: Riccardi, 1957.

——. *Biblionomia,* ed. Léopold Delisle. *Cabinet des Manuscrits* 2 (1874): 520–35.

——. *Richard de Fournival. l'oeuvre lyrique de Richard de Fournival,* ed. Yvan G. Lepage. Ottawa: University of Ottawa Press, 1984.

SYLVIA HUOT

RICHARD I (1157–1199; r. 1189–99)

Son of Henry II and Eleanor of Aquitaine. Richard the Lionheart was already duke of Aquitaine in right of his mother and heir-apparent to the English throne upon the death of his elder brother, Henry "the Young King," in 1183. His nickname, "the Lionheart" (Fr. "Coeur de Lion"), can be traced back to Gerald of Wales (d. ca. 1223), who compared the king to a lion, and can already be found circulating in a 13th-century romance of Richard's life.

Just as his late brother would have been a disastrous king, Richard could have been a great one had he spent his reign in England rather than on crusade and in the Angevin lands across the Channel. Although a man of knightly prowess, a writer of courtly poetry, patron of culture, cunning politician, and diplomat, Richard exhibited qualities regarded today as repulsive. Even by contemporary standards he could be less than humane, vengeful and beastly; however, he was the ideal martial king and a masterful leader of men. A recent study (by Gillingham) has refuted the view that Richard was homosexual. His reign is most conveniently examined by looking at his role in Angevin politics on the Continent, at his conduct of the Third Crusade, and at the governance of England during his nine-and-a-half-year absence.

Filial piety was not a characteristic of Richard's personality. Henry II sought to maintain the territorial integrity of his lands in France, fighting a doomed struggle against Louis VII (1137–80) and Philip II (1180–1223), a struggle that, under Richard's youngest brother, John, would result in the loss of all English holdings north of the Loire. Richard, desiring effective control of his inheritance, revolted against his father in 1173–74 and again in 1188–89, both times in alliance with the king of France. The warfare was not only patricidal, but fratricidal as well—as John and his brother Geoffrey of Brittany fought against both Henry II and Richard.

Although the conflict was not resolved before the death of Henry, after his return from crusade the fighting decisively favored the Lionheart. The promising course of the wars ended with Richard's death, while fighting a contumacious vassal in Aquitaine: an engagement waged over political issues, not over treasure trove (as some romantic versions of the story have it). Perhaps the greatest tragedy of Richard's early death was not the coming frustration of English ambitions on the Continent but the opportunity denied him to demonstrate his potential greatness as king of England.

Richard was best known in his own day as a crusader, as he is in literature, owing to the once great popularity of Walter Scott's *The Talisman*. For European affairs the most important development of the Crusade was the Treaty of Messina, sealed in 1191. Philip II (Philip Augustus) of France granted territorial boons to Richard, but by this agreement Richard recognized Philip's suzerainty over the Angevin lands on the Continent. Shortly after the two kings arrived in the Holy Land, Philip, a reluctant crusader, fell conveniently ill and returned home, motivated largely by his hope of taking advantage of Richard's absence so as to meddle in the English lordships in France. Richard conducted himself brilliantly as soldier and general and entered into Scott's legend as a revered and worthy opponent and respected friend of Saladin.

After helping to settle the political problems of the Latin kingdom of Jerusalem Richard left for England in October 1192. However, nature and politics interrupted the journey; a victim of shipwreck, he then fell into the hands of the duke of Austria, who delivered him to Henry, the Holy Roman Emperor. Henry, with the active support of Philip of France, kept the Lionheart in captivity until April 1194, when he was released after paying a king's ransom.

Richard had made careful plans for the governance of England during his absence; his kingdom, of course, had been accustomed to an absent king ever since the Norman conquest, owing to the royal policy of ruling personally over their French lands as over their English ones. Richard had a smoothly functioning machinery of government, guided such by able and experienced administrators as William Longchamp, Hubert Walter, and Geoffrey Fitz Peter. Every source of revenue was efficiently exploited, though at Richard's death the treasury was empty—unremitting warfare being the most expensive activity in which a government engages.

Despite the continuing plots of Prince John the country remained loyal to its king and his ministers. In Richard's absence there was less initiation of new institutions than refinement in administration; the great inquest of 1194 checked up on the enforcement of royal judicial, feudal, and financial rights. The role of what would become known as the gentry expanded in the administration of justice; while the end was not foreseen by Richard's ministers, the ultimate result of this enlargement of nonnobles' participation in government gave those of less than noble birth a sense that the government was theirs as well as the king's.

Until recent decades historians have tended to deprecate Richard, as they have Henry V. And yet the popular opinion of his own day is worth something. Wars were not viewed from a modern perspective, nor were their aims to be construed in terms of the goals of modern war. Richard was highly regarded by his contemporaries; perhaps they knew better than we what it meant to be a chivalric hero.

See also **Eleanor of Aquitaine; John; Philip II Augustus; Richard II**

Further Reading

Appleby, John. *England without Richard, 1189–1199.* Ithaca: Cornell University Press, 1965.

Bridge, Antony. *Richard the Lionheart.* London: Grafton, 1989

Gillingham, John. *Richard the Lionheart.* 2d ed. London: Weidenfeld & Nicolson, 1989 [the "select bibliography" and the chapter notes provide a full bibliography].

Gillingham, John. *Richard Coeur de Lion*: *Kingship, Chivalry and War in the Twelfth Century.* London: Hambledon, 1994.

Landon, Lionel. *The Itinerary of King Richard I.* Pipe Roll Society 51. London: Pipe Roll Society, 1935.

Nelson, Janet L., ed. *Richard Coeur de Lion in History and Myth.* London: King's College London, 1992.

Painter, Sidney. "The Third Crusade: Richard Lionhearted and Philip Augustus." In *A History of the Crusades,* gen. ed. Kenneth M. Setton. 2d ed. Vol. 2: *The Later Crusades, 1189–1311,* ed. Robert Lee Wolff and Harry W. Hazard. Madison: University of Wisconsin Press, 1969, pp. 45–86.

JAMES W. ALEXANDER

RICHARD II (1367–1399; r. 1377–99) Born at Bordeaux on 6 January 1367, the second son of Edward the Black Prince, Prince of Wales (d. 1376). After Richard succeeded his grandfather Edward III in 1377, government in his minority was conducted jointly by his three uncles (especially the eldest, John of Gaunt), the earls, and leading officials of his grandfather and father.

Richard displayed courage and leadership during the Peasant Rebellion of 1381 and in the next few years was encouraged by bosom companions and some officials to assert his will over patronage and policies. His prestige was enhanced by his childless marriage in 1382 to Anne of Bohemia (d. 1394), daughter of the late Emperor Charles IV, and by his first major expedition to Scotland (1385). But parliaments were concerned about royal finances, and there was growing disquiet, expressed by some magnates, over failures to check the French in war and over royal indulgence of court intrigues against Gaunt. In 1386 Richard, freed from Gaunt's shadow by the latters expedition to Castile, alienated public opinion by the evasion of financial restraints and the failure to prevent the buildup of an invasion threat from a French armada in Flanders.

In the autumn parliament of 1386 the Commons, abetted by the king's uncle Thomas of Woodstock, duke of Gloucester, and Thomas Arundel, bishop of Ely, secured the dismissal from the chancellorship and the impeachment of a royal favorite, Michael de la Pole, earl of Suffolk. A commission was appointed with wide powers to monitor administration for a year. Determined to evade its control, Richard toured the realm in 1387, seeking support. He prompted the judges to define recent political initiatives as treasonable encroachments on royal prerogative; he aroused suspicions of a sellout to the French by seeking a conference with King Charles VI. In November Gloucester and the earls of Arundel and

Warwick rose in arms and launched an Appeal of Treason against five of the king's supporters. Richard conceded that the appeal would be heard in parliament.

The "Appellants" were joined by Gaunt's son Henry Bolingbroke and by Thomas Mowbray, earl of Nottingham. Richard's close friend Robert de Vere, duke of Ireland, raised an army at his instigation, only to be defeated by the Appellants at Radcot Bridge (in Oxfordshire). In parliament in 1388 the appellees were found guilty; the two in custody, the Londoner Nicholas Brembre and Chief Justice Robert Tresilian, were executed. The Commons impeached other judges and four household officers; the latter (notably Sir Simon Burley, who had tutored the king) were executed.

The Appellants soon lost common purpose and support. The schemes of Gloucester and Arundel for an invasion of France failed, and in August, at Otterburn in Northumberland, the English suffered the worst defeat by the Scots since Bannockburn (1314). In May 1389 Richard declared himself of age and took control of government; in the early 1390s his moderate exercise of authority was underpinned by the returned Gaunt, principal negotiator in attempts to make a final peace with the French.

Richard boosted his authority by suspending the liberties of London (1391–92) and leading an expedition to Ireland (1394–95); London citizens and Irish chieftains alike submitted to his mercy. Continuous truces with the French since 1389 culminated in 1396 in a truce for 28 years; Richard married Charles VT's daughter Isabella.

But the moves in the 1390s toward an Anglo-French rapprochement provoked widespread disquiet; the earl of Arundel was a leading critic, and from 1395 Gloucester emerged as one. In July 1397 Richard arrested Gloucester, Arundel, and Warwick; young nobles made an Appeal of Treason against them for their acts in 1386–88, and they were found guilty in the September parliament. It was announced then that Gloucester had died in custody; Arundel was executed, Warwick sentenced to life imprisonment. The condemnations of 1388 were reversed, and Richard rewarded his noble partisans, such as his half-brother John Holland, earl of Huntingdon, with exalted peerage titles and the forfeited estates of the traitors.

In 1397 Richard had a more solid base of noble support than in 1387 and could call on the many knights and esquires he had retained in recent years, as well as his bodyguard of Cheshire archers. But the general alarm caused by his policies was augmented by the exclusion from the general pardon of January 1398, of those who had ridden against him. Supporters of the Appellants in 1387–88 now had to seek the royal mercy and pay fines. Richard's daring restructuring of magnate power was threatened when, in this session, Bolingbroke accused Thomas Mowbray, his fellow Appellant of 1387–88 and 1397, of treason. In September Richard intervened when the parties were about to settle their quarrel by judicial duel and sentenced Mowbray to exile for life and Bolingbroke for ten years. On the death of Bolingbroke's father, Gaunt, in February 1399 Richard made his banishment perpetual and confiscated the Lancastrian inheritance.

In June, soon after Richard had gone on expedition to Ireland to salvage his 1395 setdement, Bolingbroke sailed widi a small company from France and landed in Yorkshire. He was soon joined by Lancastrian retainers and northern lords, including the earls of Northumberland and Westmorland, disgruntled by Richard's interference in their sphere of influence. Bolingbroke advanced through the Midlands to seize Bristol; Richard's uncle and regent, Edmund duke of York, along with other supporters, was unable to rally effective opposition. From Bristol Bolingbroke moved up through the Welsh marches to capture Chester, the main bastion of Ricardian sentiment.

In Ireland Richard failed to appreciate the urgent need to rally support in person in north Wales and Cheshire; he landed too late in south Wales, moving north to Conway after his forces had disintegrated. The mediating earl of Northumberland betrayed Richard into Bolingbroke's hands; he was conveyed as a prisoner from Flint to the Tower of London. There he was apparently forced to abdicate, and in September a version of this agreement was submitted to the parliament summoned in his name. His requests for a public hearing were refused; the estates accepted the charges made against him in parliament as ground for deposition and acknowledged Bolingbroke's claim to the throne.

The deposed Richard was moved to other prisons, eventually to Pontefract in Yorkshire, where he died (or was killed) after the rising in January 1400 by some of his former favorites—Huntingdon, Huntingdon's nephew Thomas Holland, earl of Kent, John Montague, earl of Salisbury, and Thomas, Lord Despenser. It was easily suppressed. In February Richard's body was brought from his prison for public view in London and buried obscurely in the Dominican friary at Langley, Hertfordshire. In 1416 Henry V moved it to the splendid tomb Richard had prepared for himself in Westminster Abbey.

Richard was 6 feet tall, well built, handsome, and light-haired. Willful, devious, vindictive, sharp-tempered but not bloodthirsty, he was capable of showing affection and inspiring loyalty. He wanted his majesty to awe his subjects but could exert the common touch. He shared the conventional tastes of the higher nobility: hunting, the tournament (mainly as a spectator), courtly poetry. Not notably pious, in maturity he shared with Charles VI an enthusiasm for peace among Christians, an end to the Great Schism of the papacy, and a crusade against the Turks.

His real passion was to stabilize the personal authority of kingship, raising respect for its holy nature by trying to procure the canonization of Edward II and adopting the supposed heraldic arms of Edward the Confessor. His regal ideals and some of the ways in which he tried to project them can be seen in his portrait in Westminster Abbey, in the Wilton Diptych (National Gallery, London), and in his rebuilding of Westminster Hall. Denunciations of his rule are to be found in the poem *Richard the Redeless* and in John Gower's *Tripartite Chronicle*.

See also **Edward III; Gower, John; Henry IV**

Further Reading

Primary Sources

Creton, Jean. *A Metrical History of the Deposition of Richard II*. Ed. J. Webb. *Archaeologia* 20 (1824): 295–423.

Given-Wilson, Chris, ed. and trans. *Chronicles of the Revolution, 1397–1400: The Reign of Richard II*. Manchester: Manchester University Press, 1993.

Hector, L.C., and Barbara F. Harvey, eds. and trans. *The Westminster Chronicle, 1381–1394*. Oxford: Clarendon, 1982.

de Mézières, Philippe de. *Letter to Richard II*. Trans. G.W. Coopland. Liverpool: Liverpool University Press, 1975.

Secondary Sources

Aston, Margaret. *Thomas Arundel: A Study of Church Life in the Reign of Richard II*. Oxford: Clarendon, 1967.

Barron, Caroline M. "The Tyranny of Richard II." *BIHR* 41 (1968): 1–18.

Clarke, Maude V. *Fourteenth Century Studies*. Oxford: Clarendon, 1937.

Du Boulay, F.R.H., and Caroline M. Barron, eds. *The Reign of Richard II: Essays in Honour of May McKisack*. London: University of London, Athlone, 1971.

Gillespie, James L. "Richard II's Archers of the Crown." *Journal of British Studies* 18 (1979): 14–29.

Given-Wilson, Chris. *The Royal Household and the King's Affinity: Service, Politics and Finance in England, 1360–1413*. New Haven: Yale University Press, 1986.

Goodman, Anthony. *The Loyal Conspiracy: The Lords Appellant under Richard II*. London: Routledge & Kegan Paul, 1971.

Harvey, John H. "The Wilton Diptych—A Reexamination," *Archaeologia* 98 (1961): 1–28.

Mathew, Gervase. *The Court of Richard II.* London: Murray, 1968.

Palmer, J.J.N. *England, France and Christendom, 1377–99.* London: Routledge & Kegan Paul, 1972.

Saul, Nigel. *Richard II.* New Haven and London: Yale University Press, 1997.

Scattergood, V. J., and J.W. Sherborne, eds. *English Court Culture in the Later Middle Ages.* London: Duckworth, 1983.

Tuck, Anthony. *Richard II and the English Nobility.* London: Arnold, 1973.

ANTHONY E. GOODMAN

RICHARD III (1452–1485; r. 1483–85) No medieval English king has generated more controversy and emotion, not least as a result of Shakespeare's portrayal of him as the personification of evil. Shakespeare, moreover, clearly reflected images already well formed in early Tudor times. Polydore Vergil, for instance, considered Richard a man who "thought of nothing but tyranny and cruelty"; Sir Thomas More derided him as an ambitious and ruthless monstrosity "who spared no man's death whose life withstood his purpose." Even the king's contemporaries were frequently critical. Dominic Mancini, writing within a few months of his seizure of the throne in June 1483, remarked forcefully on his "ambition and lust for power," and the well-informed Crowland chronicler was scathing on the tyrannical northern-dominated regime that, he believed, Richard established in the south.

Yet the last Yorkist king has always had his admirers as well as critics. Thomas Langton, bishop of St. David's, declared in August 1483 that "he contents the people wherever he goes better than ever did any prince," and the York Civic Records reported "great heaviness" in the city when news arrived of his fete ("piteously slain and murdered") on Bosworth Field in 1485. Modern historians, too, have brought in notably contrasting verdicts, ranging from Charles Ross's conclusion that no one familiar with "the careers of King Louis XI of France, in Richard's own time, or Henry VIII of England...would wish to cast any special slur on Richard, still less to select him as the exemplar of a tyrant" to Desmond Seward's hostile biography of this "peculiarly grim young English precursor of Machiavelli's Prince."

The youngest son of Richard of York, Richard duke of Gloucester proved notably loyal to his brother Edward IV during the crisis of 1469–71 and in the 1470s showed himself as reliable and trustworthy as any of the king's servants (and was rewarded accordingly). His rule of the north during these years was singularly successful; he built a powerful affinity there. Mancini admitted mat he "acquired the favour of the people." No one will ever know for certain whether he set his sights on the throne as soon as he heard of Edward IV's sudden death on 9 April 1483, or if, at first, he merely intended to obtain control of his nephew Edward V so as to prevent the Wydevilles—the family of young Edward's mother—from securing power. What is clear is that the series of preemptive strikes by which he outmaneuvered the queen's family, seized Edward V, eliminated William, Lord Hastings, and rendered the Yorkist establishment impotent, enabled him to become king in his own right before the end of June 1483. The probable murder of his nephews in the Tower of London was the inevitable culmination of this ruthless pursuit of power.

Richard III may have been convinced that he was indeed serving the interest of the nation; such, through the ages, has been the politician's justification for arbitrary action. The critical turning point in his fortunes probably was the rebellion of the duke of Buckingham (hitherto his closest and most spectacularly rewarded supporter) in October 1483. Edward IV's men, who for the most part had accepted

Richard's protectorate and even acquiesced in his usurpation, now deserted him in droves in the south and west. Even more ominously the exiled Henry Tudor, earl of Richmond, emerged at the same time as a potentially serious rival. The king responded vigorously to these threats; the rebellion was put down. In its aftermath, however, given the extent of southern defection and the numbers who now fled the country, he was forced more and more into dependence on his own affinity. This meant, in particular, men from the north. Their advancement in the royal household and appointments to office, not only in southern and western counties but in the Midlands, is amply documented.

Since he reigned for so short a time, it is difficult either to judge Richard's potential and qualities as a ruler or to draw meaningful conclusions about his government. The 15th-century antiquary John Rous, later one of his harshest critics, recorded that he ruled his subjects "full commendably, punishing offenders of his laws, especially extortioners and oppressors of his commons," and won the "love of all his subjects rich and poor." His only parliament—perhaps with his personal encouragement—passed measures dearly benefiting the people; and his establishment of the Council of the North in July 1484 was both popular and enduring.

Though he did make considerable efforts to widen the basis of his support, with the threat of Henry Tudor looming ever larger, his reliance on his own affinity, largely from the north, remained paramount. When he at last faced his rival on the battlefield of Bosworth on 22 August 1485, he was backed largely by the same men who had brought him to power; many, though by no means all, probably fought for him with vigor. However, his own death (in the midst of the action and, according to the Crowland continuator, striving to the end "like a spirited and most courageous prince") made the accession of Henry VII inevitable.

Further Reading

Primary Sources

Armstrong, C.A.J., ed. and trans. *Dominic Macnini: The Usurpation of Richard III.* 2d ed. Oxford: Clarendon, 1969

Pronay, Nicholas, and John Cox, eds. *The Crowland Chronicle Continuations, 1459–1486.* London: Sutton, for the Richard III and Yorkist History Trust, 1986.

Secondary Sources

Dockray, Keith. *Richard III: A Reader in History.* Gloucester: Sutton, 1988 [commentary plus a selection of documents]

Hicks, Michael. *Richard III: The Man behind the Myth.* London: Collins & Brown, 1991

Horrox, Rosemary. *Richard III: A Study of Service.* Cambridge: Cambridge University Press, 1989 [scholarly treatment of politics and government]

Markham, Clements R. *Richard III: His Life and Character, Reviewed in the Light of Recent Research.* London: Smith, Elder, 1906 [very sympathetic]

Pollard, A.J. *Richard III and the Princes in the Tower.* Stroud: Sutton, 1991

Ross, Charles. *Richard III.* London: Eyre Methuen, 1981 [major modern scholarly treatment]

Seward, Desmond. *Richard III: England's Black Legend.* London: Country Life, 1983 [the case against].

KEITH R. DOCKRAY

RICHARD OF SAINT-VICTOR (d. 1173)   A major writer on mysticism in the second half of the 12th century, Richard joined the regular canons of the abbey of Saint-Victor at Paris sometime near the middle of the century (certainly by the early 1150s but perhaps before the death of Hugh of Saint-Victor in 1141). He may have been born in Scotland. He served as subprior and was elected prior in 1161. His writings on the contemplative life were widely known and influenced Bonaventure's treatise *Itinerarium mentis in Deum.*

Richard followed the tradition of Victorine spirituality established by Hugh, but he concentrated more on the stages of development in the mystical life and on what today would be called the psychological aspects of that development. Two of his major mystical writings are symbolic interpretations of biblical persons, objects, and narratives. *De duodecim patriarchiis* (also called *Benjamin minor*) interprets the births and lives of the twelve sons and one daughter of Jacob, recorded in Genesis, as representing the stages of ascetic practice, mental discipline, and spiritual guidance that lead to contemplative ecstasy. *De arca mystica* (also called *Benjamin major*) presents the Ark of the Covenant and the two cherubim that stood on either side of it, described in Exodus, as symbolic of the six kinds or levels of contemplation. Books 4 and 5 of *De arca* give a subtle and influential analysis of types of visionary and ecstatic experience. Richard's *De IV gradibus violentae caritatis* analyzes the stages of the love of God and the transformation of the self by love in the mystical quest. Richard also wrote a commentary on the Book of Revelation, a treatise on the Trinity, mystical comments on various Psalms, a handbook for the Liberal Arts and the study of history (*Liber exceptionum*; digested primarily from works by Hugh of Saint-Victor), a collection of allegorical sermons, and treatises on biblical and mystical topics.

See also **Bonaventure, Saint; Hugh of Saint-Victor**

Further Reading

Richard of Saint-Victor. *Opera omnia*. PL 196.
——. *De Trinitate*, ed. Jean Ribaillier. Paris: Vrin, 1958.
——. *Liber exceptionum*, ed. Jean Châtillon. Paris: Vrin, 1958.
——. *Selected Writings on Contemplation*, trans. Claire Kirchberger. London: Faber, 1957.
——. *The Twelve Patriarchs, The Mystical Ark, and Book Three on the Trinity*, trans. Grover A. Zinn. New York: Paulist, 1979.
——. *Les quatre degrés de la violente charité*, ed. Gervais Dumeige. Paris: Vrin, 1955.
Dumeige, Gervais. *Richard de Saint-Victor et l'idée chrétienne de l'amour*. Paris: Presses Universitaires de France, 1952.
Zinn, Grover A. "Personification Allegory and Visions of Light in Richard of St. Victor's Teaching on Contemplation." *University of Toronto Quarterly* 46 (1977): 190–214.
GROVER A. ZINN

RIEMENSCHNEIDER, TILLMANN (ca. 1460–1531)   Tillmann Riemenschneider is, perhaps, the best known of all German sculptors active during the years around 1500. His father, also Tillmann, was the mint master in Osterrode in Lower Saxony, but by 1483 the younger Riemenschneider was a journeyman carver in southern Germany. Documents place him in the guild of St. Luke in Würzburg, where he was a master by 1485. His workshop was large and successful, with twelve apprentices registered between 1501 and 1517.

Riemenschneider's two sons were also sculptors. From 1505 Riemenschneider served on the Würzburg Council, and he was burgomaster (mayor) in 1520–1521. In 1525 he was fined for refusing to support the bishop against a peasant revolt.

Riemenschneider's sculpture reveals familiarity with German and Netherlandish styles from a broad area. None of his travel is documented, however, and at least some of these regional styles could have been assimilated through the study of exported sculptures. In addition to his carefully worked surfaces, Riemenschneider is known for his excellence in wood, especially linden wood, as well as stone, primarily alabaster and sandstone. His training as a stone carver is usually attributed to his North German origins.

Riemenschneider was an innovative wood carver, experimenting with unpainted surfaces in such early works as the Münnerstadt altarpiece of 1490–1492, the artist's first dated work. This winged altarpiece, dedicated to Mary Magdalene, is currently divided between the Münnerstadt parish church and

Tilmann Riemenschneider. The alter of the Holy Blood, St. Jacob's Church, Rothenburg ob der Tauber, Germay.
© Erich Lessing/Art Resource, New York.

the museums in Munich (Bayersiches Nationalmuseum) and Berlin (Staatliche Museen Preussicher Kulturbesitz). Recent conservation has removed later gilding and polychromy (painting) to reveal Riemenschneider's extraordinarily careful attention to surface detail and nuance, akin to sculptures on a smaller scale, such as ivory carving. The success of Riemenschneider's unpolychromed sculpture is seen in such works as the great altarpiece of the Holy Blood (ca. 1499–1505) still in situ in the Jakobskirche in Rothenburg, and the lindenwood sculpture of Saints Christopher, Eustace, and Erasmus (1494), a fragment of a relief originally representing fourteen helper saints, now in the Metropolitan Museum of Art in New York City (The Cloisters). All these works reveal Riemenschneider's

ability to carve refined drapery and flesh as well to reveal the underlying bone structure. Shortly after the completion of the Rothenburg altarpiece, Riemenschneider created the Creglingen altarpiece (Herrgottskirche, ca. 1505–1510) representing the Assumption of the Virgin in a more elaborate and complex style than the earlier works.

Riemenschneider's works in stone include the sandstone figures carved for the Marienkapelle in Würzburg, including the figures of Adam and Eve (1492–1493), and the nine apostle figures of 1500–1506 (all these now in the Mainfränkisches Museum, Würzburg). Among his most extraordinary achievements, however, are the few surviving works in alabaster such as the Angel and the Virgin Annunciate in Amsterdam of about 1480–1485 (Rijksmuseum), and the St. Jerome with the Lion in Cleveland (Museum of Art), which probably dates before circa 1495. Like some of the linden wood sculptures, these works are sparingly decorated with polychrome and gilt highlights, but they rely on the fineness of the carved surface for their impact.

In addition to altarpieces and architectural sculptures in wood and stone produced for churches in and around Franconia, Riemenschneider's career can be traced through several tomb monuments that attest to his prestige. As early as about 1488 Riemenschneider carved the monument of Eberhard von Grumbach (d. 1487) now in the parish church at Rimpar, depicting the knight in full Gothic armor in relief. The same format is repeated in the tomb monument of Konrad von Schaumberg (d. 1499) in the Marienkapelle in Würzburg. This work, however, of about 1502 is more mature in style, more portrait than effigy. Much grander in scale is the sandstone and marble monument of Archbishop Rudolf von Scherenberg (d. 1495) in the cathedral of Würzburg. Most impressive is the limestone and sandstone tomb of Emperor Heinrich II and Empress

Kunigunde (1499–1513) in the cathedral of Bamberg. Below the relief of the imperial couple are a series of six relief panels illustrating scenes from their lives. Finally, around 1520 Riemenschneider carved the sandstone and marble monument of Archbishop Lorenz von Bibra in Würzburg Cathedral.

Further Reading

Bier, Justus. *Tilmann Riemenschneider.* 4 vols. Würzburg: Verlagsdruckerei, 1925–1978.
——. *Tilman Riemenschneider: Frühe Werke.* Regensburg: Pustet, 1981.
——. *Tilmann Riemenschneider: His Life and Work.* Lexington: University Press of Kentucky, 1982.

PETER BARNET

ROBERT DE BORON (fl. 1180s–1190s) The few facts known about the most important early Grail poet after Chrétien de Troyes are inferred from the epilogue of Robert's *Joseph d'Arimathie,* also called the *Roman de l'estoire dou Graal,* where he names himself and the nobleman in whose company he was writing, Gautier de Montbéliard. Montbéliard is in northern Franche-Comté; Boron is a small village about 12 miles to the northeast. Robert's verse bears traces of his eastern dialect. Gautier left on crusade in 1201, to remain in Palestine until his death in 1212; Robert must have finished the *Joseph* at or before the turn of the century. Robert's incorporation of material from Chrétien's *Conte du Graal* indicates that he wrote after the early 1180s. Other evidence suggests that the *Joseph* might be dated after 1191: Joseph foretells that the Grail will be taken to the "vales of Avaron [Avalon]"— that is, Glastonbury in Somerset; association of the Grail and of Arthurian matter with the abbey was not widespread before 1190–91, when the discovery there of a grave marked as Arthur's was announced.

Joseph d'Arimathie is a verse romance (3,500 octosyllables) that recounts the history of the Grail from the Last Supper and the Descent from the Cross, when Joseph used it to collect Christ's blood, through the imprisonment of Joseph, whom Christ visits and comforts with the holy vessel, until the moment when Joseph's brother-in-law, Bron (or Hebron), the Rich Fisher, is poised to take the Grail from a place of exile outside Palestine to Great Britain. As the *Joseph* draws to a close, the narrator announces that he will relate stories of adventures that Joseph has foretold, including that of the Rich Fisher, if he has time and strength and if he can find them written down in Latin; meanwhile, he will continue with the matter he has at hand.

Robert thus seems to project a complex work consisting of the *Joseph/Estoire,* the narrative to which he will pass immediately, and the fulfillment of Joseph's prophecies. The only manuscript to transmit Robert's verse *Joseph* (B.N. fr. 20047) in fact continues with the fragment of a *Merlin* romance (504 octosyllables), apparently the beginning of the second part; no more of Robert's original work survives.

However, a prose adaptation of the *Joseph,* by an anonymous author referred to as the Pseudo-Robert de Boron, was executed within a few years, and this is linked to a *Merlin* in prose, conjoining the history of the Grail and the history of Britain, that is found complete in a large number of manuscripts (forty-six) and fragments. Two manuscripts also contain a third prose romance, which portrays the Rich Fisher: the Didot *Perceval* (so called because one of the manuscripts was in the Firmin Didot collection). Unlike the first two romances, the Didot *Perceval* is never ascribed to Robert de Boron, nor is there any proof that a verse original of this text existed, yet it is clear that the Didot *Perceval* logically concludes the trilogy. It resembles one of the works projected at the end of the *Joseph/Estoire* and recounts the fulfillment of God's prophecy in the *Joseph* that the Rich Fisher will not die until he is visited by his son's son; it is also closely linked to the prose *Merlin*: finally succeeding at the Grail castle with Merlin's help, Perceval replaces his uncle as Rich Fisher; the hero's triumph coincides with the downfall of the Arthurian kingdom, the founding of which the *Merlin* had recounted.

In the *Joseph/Estoire* and what must have been the original verse *Merlin,* Robert de Boron in effect rewrites the *Conte du Graal* of Chrétien de Troyes. He expands the religious content of the original to provide the Grail's "sacred history," identifying it for the first time with the cup of the Last Supper. In addition, he extends Chrétien's references to pre-Arthurian Britain, which echo Wace's *Brut*, to provide the Grail's "secular history."

Robert's most important contribution is the generative power that infuses his verse. Not only are the prose adaptations of the *Joseph/Estoire* and *Merlin* among the earliest examples of literary prose in French, they also stand at the head of a long tradition that promoted the "translation" of imaginative and historical works written in "unreliable" verse into the "more stable" and "more authoritative" medium of prose. The better-known, more highly respected, Pseudo-Robert de Boron who was thus created, the one to whose authorship the more widely transmitted prose works are attributed, became in the early 13th century an even stronger literary force. He inspired the "completion" of Chrétien de Troyes's unfinished *Conte du Graal* in the anonymous Didot *Perceval*, and he is ultimately responsible for the germination of the Vulgate Cycle.

See also **Chrétien de Troyes**

Further Reading

Robert de Boron. *Merlin, roman du XIIIe siècle,* ed. Alexandre Micha. Geneva: Droz, 1979.

——. *Le roman de l'estoire dou Graal,* ed. William A. Nitze. Paris: Champion, 1927.

——. *Le roman du Graal,* ed. Bernard Cerquiglini. Paris: Union Générale d'Éditions, 1981.

Roach, William, ed. *The Didot Perceval According to the Manuscripts of Paris and Modena.* Philadelphia: University of Pennsylvania Press, 1941.

Cerquiglini, Bernard. *La parole médiévale.* Paris: Minuit, 1981.

O'Gorman, Richard F. "The Prose Version of Robert de Boron's *Joseph d'Arimathie.*" *Romance Philology* 23 (1969–70): 449–61.

——. "La tradition manuscrite du *Joseph d'Arimathie* en prose de Robert de Boron." *Revue d'histoire des textes* 1 (1971): 145–81.

Pickens, Rupert T. "Histoire et commentaire chez Chrétien de Troyes et Robert de Boron: Robert de Boron et le livre de Philippe de Flandre." In *The Legacy of Chrétien de Troyes*, ed. Norris J. Lacy, Douglas Kelly, and Keith Busby. 2 vols. Amsterdam: Rodopi, 1988, Vol. 2, pp. 17–39.

——. "'Mais de ço ne parole pas Crestiens de Troies ¼': A Re-examination of the Didot *Perceval.*" *Romania* 105 (1984): 492–510.

RUPERT T. PICKENS

ROBERT GUISCARD (c. 1015–1085) When Robert Guiscard (Robert de Hauteville) rode into southern Italy in 1047, Norman mercenaries had been playing Lombards against Byzantines there for at least thirty years. Robert's half brothers, older sons of Tancred of Hauteville, had already claimed lands around Aversa, where the eldest, William, had earned the name "Iron-Arm" and had become the first Norman Italian count. William did not welcome Robert's arrival. Eventually another brother, Drogo, gave Robert a miserable outpost in Calabria, which he could control only by ousting the Byzantines. Yet this offered him a base from which to launch ambitious conquests, achieved with prodigious energy. Robert used terror and bloodshed, but his signature strategy was the ruse, as when he allegedly feigned death and penetrated a monastic stronghold inside a coffin, lying on a bed of swords. So wily was this trickster that the name Guiscard ("the clever") was used in the eleventh-century histories featuring his exploits.

Robert also proved his mettle on the battlefield. In 1053, a formidable coalition of Germans from the Holy Roman Empire and their Italian allies, led by Pope Leo IX, engaged the Normans at Civitate, hoping to dislodge them from Italy. Robert distinguished himself in this Norman victory, and soon he was challenging his brother Humphrey for hegemony among the Normans of Italy. Before Humphrey died in 1057, he commended his son Abelard to Robert's care, but Robert promptly claimed his nephew's lands. The boy would grow up to foment insurrections against his uncle but eventually sought asylum in Byzantium after yet another unsuccessful resistance in 1080. Such rebellions punctuated Robert's reign, even as he expanded his domination, seizing Capua from the Lombards and finally—in 1071, after a three-year siege—taking Bari, the last Byzantine foothold in Italy.

Along Robert's path to power, two events of 1059 enhanced his prestige and legitimized his authority. First, having repudiated his wife (the mother of his son, Bohemond), Robert compelled Prince Gisulf II of Salerno to surrender his sister Sichelgaita in marriage. Now linked to a venerable Lombard princely family, Robert also allied himself with the papacy, which sought the support of the Normans in the investiture conflict against the Holy Roman emperor and the imperial antipope. Thus at the synod of Melfi, Robert—who had been thrice excommunicated—acquired a papal blessing and the title of duke of Apulia and Calabria and Sicily.

Before this, Robert had not even visited Muslim Sicily. Yet he now engineered a reconquest increasingly dominated by his younger brother, Roger. Messina fell in 1061, followed by Palermo in 1072. But rebellions in Italy forced Robert to return there, effectively leaving Sicily to Roger. Robert, meanwhile, trained his eye on Byzantium, made enticingly vulnerable by dynastic struggles and the advance of the Seljuk Turks. Emperor Michael VII, desperate for aid from the Normans, had even betrothed his son to Robert's daughter. After Michael was dethroned in a coup in 1078, Robert invoked kinship as a pretext for invading Byzantium. Yet once again Italy drew him back from the campaign, this time to rescue Pope Gregory VII from the Holy Roman emperor Henry IV, who had seized Rome and deposed Gregory. In a mission notorious for its violence and for the alleged burning of Rome, Robert retrieved the pope and took him to Salerno, where he died in May 1085. Robert resumed his Byzantine offensive, taking Corfu while his younger son Roger accompanied Norman forces to the mainland. But Robert died suddenly, on 17 July 1085, when an epidemic of typhoid fever swept through his army. Roger's army promptly deserted, while Sichelgaita took Robert's body to Venosa for burial next to his older brothers in the church of the Holy Trinity. In the twelfth century, his grave attracted a suitable epitaph, which began: "Here lies the terror of the world, Guiscard."

See also **Bohemond of Taranto; Gregory VII, Pope; Leo IX, Pope**

Further Reading

Editions

Amatus. *Storia de' Normanni di Amato di Montecassino*, ed. Vincenzo de Bartholomaeis. Fonti per la Storia d'Italia, Scrittori. Secolo, 11(76). Rome: Tipografia del Senato, 1935.

Geoffrey Malaterra. *De rebus gestis Rogerii Calabriae et Sicliae comitis et Roberti Guiscardi ducis fratris eius*, ed. Ernesto Pontieri. In *Rerum Italicarum Scriptores*, 2nd ed., Vol. 5(1). Bologna: Nicola Zanichelli, 1925–1928.

William of Apulia. *La geste de Robert Guiscard*, ed. Marguerite Mathieu. Palermo: Istituto Siciliano di Studi Bizantini e Neoellenici, 1961.

Critical Studies

Chalandon, Ferdinand. *Histoire de la domina-
tion normande en Italie et en Sicile*, 2 vols.
Paris: A. Picard et Fils, 1907. (Reprint,
New York: B. Franklin, 1960.)

Douglas, David C. *The Norman Achievement,
1050–1100*. Berkeley and Los Angeles:
University of California Press, 1969.

Loud, G. A. *The Age of Robert Guiscard:
Southern Italy and the Norman Conquest*.
Essex: Pearson Education, 2000.

Norwich, John Julius. *The Other Conquest*.
New York: Harper and Row, 1967.
(Published in England as *The Normans in
the South, 1016–1130*.)

Taviani-Carozzi, Huguette. *La terreur du
monde: Robert Guiscard et la conquête
normande en Italie—Mythe et histoire*.
Paris: Fayard, 1996.

Wolf, Kenneth Baxter. *Making History: The
Normans and Their Historians in Eleventh-
Century Italy*. Philadelphia: University of
Pennsylvania Press, 1995.

EMILY ALBU

ROBERT OF ANJOU (1278–1343; r.
1309–1343) Robert of Anjou, king
of Naples ("the Wise") was the third
son of Charles II of Anjou. Robert was
held hostage by the Aragonese from
1285 to 1295. He was created duke of
Calabria and vicar of the Regno for his
father in 1297, and he became prince
of Salerno in 1304. Robert succeeded as
king of Sicily and count of Piedmont,
Provence, and Forcalquier in 1309, despite the claims of his eldest brother's
son, Carobert. Robert's two wives were
Violante of Aragon, sister of James
II; and Sancia of Aragon, daughter of
James II. Robert was survived by two
daughters, Joanna and Maria; the former succeeded him, becoming Queen
Joanna I of Naples.

Robert became king as Emperor Henry
VII was preparing an expedition to Italy
to be crowned. The Guelf party, which opposed Henry's plans, looked to Robert for
leadership, but initially he supported Pope
Clement V, who hoped to form a partnership with Henry to bring peace to Italy.

Clement, recognizing Robert's support,
made him rector of the Romagna (excluding Bologna) in 1310 and supported
a marriage alliance between Robert's heir
and Henry's daughter. This alliance was
never achieved, and relations worsened
when Robert refused to do homage to
Henry in person for Piedmont, Provence,
and Forcalquier. Robert did not prevent
Henry from reaching Rome and being
crowned; but as the Guelfs' opposition to
Henry grew, an army sent by Robert has-
tened the emperor's withdrawal. Robert
became captain of the Guelf league in
February 1313 and soon afterward accepted the lordship of numerous communes. In
April 1313 he became lord of Florence for
five years. Henry responded by condemning Robert, but Henry died in 1313 while
marching on Florence, where an army sent
by Robert was preparing to oppose him.

Meanwhile Frederick of Sicily, supporting Henry in this quarrel (which he had
helped to precipitate), invaded Calabria,
thereby breaking the peace of Caltabellotta.
Robert repulsed him and thereafter made
several unsuccessful attempts (in 1314,
1316, 1325–1326, 1335, and 1339–1342)
to recover Sicily; these attempts further
impoverished his already troubled realm,
and despite his sincere efforts to impose
good justice and administration, Robert
perpetuated corruption and disorder. The
degree of Robert's failure to impose his
ideal of good government is disputed, but
that he failed is not in question.

Robert continued throughout his reign
to be involved in politics farther north. In
1317, the Florentines renewed his lordship
for four years. In 1325, he sanctioned an
offer to make his son Charles of Calabria
lord of Florence. Both Charles and Robert
opposed the expedition by Emperor Lewis
of Bavaria, not least because an alliance
between Lewis and Frederick of Sicily
posed a threat to the Regno.

Robert was religious to the point of
bigotry and was detested by the northern
Ghibellines, but in his own kingdom he
was the most popular of the Angevin

kings—a reputation for which his public works, especially in Naples, and his patronage of the arts and literature may have been partly responsible. Among those whom he patronized were Petrarch and Boccaccio. Simone Martini's picture of Robert worshiping his brother Louis is reputedly the first painted portrait in European art.

See also Boccaccio, Giovanni; Clement V, Pope; Henry VII of Luxembourg; Petrarca, Francesco

Further Reading

Editions

Dominicus de Gravina. *Chronicon de rebus in Apulia gestis, 1333—1350*, ed. Albano Sorbelli. Rerum Italicarum Scriptores, 12(3). Città di Castello: Lapi, 1903.

Mussato, Albertino. *Historia Augusta: Liber IV, Henrici VII; Liber V, De Gestis Italicorum post Henricum Septimum Caesarem*. Rerum Italicarum Scriptores, 10. Città di Castello: Lapi.

Villani, Giovanni, and Matteo Villani. *Croniche*, 13 vols., ed. Ignazio Moutier. Florence: Magheri, 1823–1826.

Critical Studies

Baddeley, St. Clair. *Robert the Wise and His Heirs: 1278–1352*. London, 1897.

Bowsky, W. M. *Henry VII in Italy: The Conflict of Empire and City State, 1310–1313*. Lincoln: University of Nebraska Press, 1960.

Caggese, Romolo. *Roberto d'Angio e i suoi tempi*, 2 vols. Florence: Bemporad, 1922–1930.

Housley, N. "Angevin Naples and the Defence of the Latin East: Robert the Wise and the Naval League of 1334." *Byzantion*, 51, 1981, pp. 548–556.

Léonard, Emile. *Les Angevins de Naples*. Paris: Presses Universitaires de France, 1954.

Monti, Gennaro Maria. *Da Carlo primo a Roberto di Angio*. Trani, 1936.

CAROLA M. SMALL

ROBERT OF MOLESME (ca. 1027–1111)

The founder of the monasteries of both Molesme and Cîteaux, Robert had spent much of his life trying to find or to establish a house where he thought the Benedictine *Rule* was being practiced with sufficient rigor. He spent time in the abbey of Moutier-la-Celle, in the diocese of Troyes; was briefly abbot of Saint-Michel of Langres, then prior of Saint-Ayoul of Provins; and for a period lived as a hermit. In 1075, deciding to try an entirely new Benedictine house, he and a small group of monks founded Molesme, of which he became first abbot (r. 1075–1111). In 1098, believing that even this house was not sufficiently rigorous, he left with a few brothers to found the New Monastery of Cîteaux. Although the monks at Molesme, feeling destitute, had the pope order Robert back to their house in the following year, Cîteaux flourished even without him and became in the 12th century the head of a large and influential order. Molesme, meanwhile, although overshadowed by Cîteaux, also acquired numerous gifts of property, including many priories and cells.

Further Reading

Bouton, Jean de la Croix, and Jean Baptiste Van Damme, eds. *Les plus anciens textes de Cîteaux*. Achel: Commentarii Cistercienses, 1974.

Laurent, Jacques, ed. *Cartulaires de l'abbaye de Molesme*. 2 vols. Paris: Picard, 1907–11.

Lackner, Bede K. *The Eleventh-Century Background of Cîteaux*. Washington, D.C.: Cistercian, 1972.

Spahr, Kolumban. *Das Leben des hl. Robert von Molesme: Eine Quelle zur Vorgeschichte von Cîteaux*. Freiburg: Paulusdruckerei, 1944.

CONSTANCE B. BOUCHARD

ROGER I (1031–1101, r. 1085–1101)

Roger I, count of Sicily, was the brother of Robert Guiscard and was largely responsible for the Norman conquest of Sicily. Roger had been campaigning there since at least 1061, when Messina had fallen, and he took the last

Muslim stronghold, Noto, in 1091. He is said to have had only a handful of soldiers (just 130 knights at the battle of Cerami in 1063), but he became the most powerful figure in the south after his brother's death in 1085. Most scholars agree that Roger I laid the foundations for the later cohesion and wealth of the kingdom of Sicily.

Roger's comital activities can be partially reconstructed from evidence in surviving charters, most of which is published. At a meeting at Mazara in 1093, Roger and his followers divided up the conquered Muslims among their new lords using long lists known as *jara'ida*. One such list in favor of the cathedral at Catania in 1095 is extant in its original form, containing 345 names including fifty-three widows. A grant of peasants made to Guiscard's son, Duke Roger, was confirmed by his uncle to the cathedral of Palermo in the same year. Another element of Roger's documented activity was granting the monks of Saint Philip at Fragalà judicial rights over their peasants, a technique of local government that would be taken up and repeated by Roger II. Roger I's activities were not confined to the island of Sicily: his foundation of the monastery of the Holy Trinity at Mileto in Calabria in 1080–1081, including endowing the house with property and churches in Calabria and Sicily, is recorded in a surviving copy of the original charter. Some judicial rights also appear to have been granted to the abbot in 1093, and Roget confirmed further privileges in a surviving but undated charter. Indeed, Mileto remained his chief residence throughout his life. In 1093, he also clarified a grant and presided over a court case in the Calabrian town of Stilo, and he is recorded as the patron of Greek monks there in 1094 and 1097.

Roger had a mostly cordial relationship with Pope Urban II, and the two cooperated, though sometimes uneasily, regarding the reorganization of the church in Sicily, with the see of Troina transferred to Messina, and Syracuse and Catania given bishops. In an unusual concession, Roger was given responsibility for many of the duties that a papal legate would have undertaken on the island, after he had objected to Urban's appointment of the bishop of Messina to that dignity.

Roger married three times. His first wife, in 1061, was Judith (d. 1080), daughter of William d'Evreux, who is said to have commanded the defense of Troina. His second wife was Eremburga, daughter of William de Mortain. His third wife was Adelasia (d. 1118), daughter of the marquis Manfred of Savona; his and Adelasia's sons were Simon (d. 1105) and Roger II. In addition, Roger I had two illegitimate sons: Jordan, who predeceased his father in 1089; and Geoffrey, who suffered from leprosy. Roger died in 1101, and after a period of minority during which Adelasia governed, Simon and Roger II succeeded him as counts of Sicily.

See also **Robert Giscard; Roger II**

Further Reading

Gaufredus Malaterra. *De Rebus Gestis Rogerii Calabriae et Siciliae Comitis et Roberti Guiscardi ducis fratris eius*, ed. E. Pontieri. Rerum Italicarum Scriptores, 1. Bologna, 1928.

Loud, G. A. "Byzantine Italy and the Normans." In *Byzantium and the West, c. 850–c. 1200: Proceedings of the XVIII Spring Symposium of Byzantine Studies, Oxford, 30 March–1st April 1984*, ed. J. D. Howard-Johnston. Amsterdam: Adolf M. Hakkert, 1988. (Reprinted, with other important essays, in G. A. Loud. *Conquerors and Churchmen in Norman Italy*. Aldershot and Brookfield, Vt.: Variorum, 1999.)

Matthew, Donald. *The Norman Kingdom of Sicily*. Cambridge: Cambridge University Press, 1992.

Ménager, L.-R. *Hommes et institutions de l'Italie normande*. London; Variorum, 1981.

Takayama, Hiroshi. *The Administration of the Norman Kingdom of Sicily*. Leiden: Brill, 1993.

PATRICIA SKINNER

ROGER II (1095–1154)   Roger II created the twelfth-century kingdom of southern Italy and Sicily, known as the Regno. He was the son of Count Roger I of Sicily and his third wife, Adelaide (Adelasia) of Savona, later queen of Jerusalem. Roger I died in 1101, and Roger II succeeded his elder brother, Simon, in 1105. Once he reached his majority, Roger II pursued a clear objective—to accumulate mainland territories in southern Italy. He conquered Calabria in 1122; he succeeded his childless cousin William to the duchy of Apulia in 1127 and was formally recognized as duke of Apulia on 23 August 1128; he acquired the principality of Capua in 1129. Finally, in Palermo, on Christmas day 1130, Roger was crowned king of Sicily, Calabria, and Apulia. The title was conferred, however, by the antipope Anacletus II, following a papal schism. On 25 July 1139, Pope Innocent II made Roger's title official, crowning him king of Sicily, duke of Apulia, and prince of Capua.

According to one chronicler, the celebrations and ceremony for Roger's coronation in Palermo in 1130 were so spectacular that "it was as if the whole city were being crowned." Many scholars have considered Roger's reign equally extraordinary. He ruled over all of Italy south of the Garigliano River, down through Sicily. Although he did not inherit a unified kingdom, accustomed to monarchical rule, he created something resembling one. Roger's rule is impossible to describe easily, for it did not conform to contemporary models of medieval kingship. He bound together the disparate ethnic groups who populated the region. Their coexistence was a practical necessity. He constructed a central government in Palermo that borrowed from the economic, administrative, and legal traditions of his Arab, Norman, Greek, and Italian-Lombard subjects. Roger was the leading feudal lord among feudal lords. He laid the groundwork for *Catalogus baronum*, the list of financial and military obligations owed to the crown by many of his barons. Arab-inspired offices were created to manage finances. A French-inspired chancery, overseen by a chamberlain, issued official court documents in Greek, Arabic, and Latin. A permanent Greek-style bureaucracy or civil service, based in Palermo, helped to manage the vast kingdom. Finally, the king himself, no doubt drawing inspiration from the Byzantium of Justinian, presented himself as a divinely appointed ruler. (Like Justinian, Roger may also have been a lawgiver. A law code, erroneously called the *Assises of Ariano*, has been attributed to him, but more recent scholarship disputes this.)

However one chooses to characterize the kingship of Roger II, he was undeniably successful. Periodic opposition to his rule—in particular, vassal rebellions led by his brother-in-law Rainulf—never lasted long. His foreign policy revealed ambitions, perhaps to expand his kingdom but more likely to safeguard it against external attack. He added much of North Africa to his kingdom while holding off threats from the Greeks, the northern Italians, and the German empire. He maintained a considerable war chest to support his army and navy. Roger's accomplishments did not go unnoticed: a contemporary observed that Roger "did more asleep than others did awake."

Roger II's personality and lineage should not be ignored in assessing his reign. He was described as the fairly stereotypical "Viking" warrior: tall, loud, regal, ruthless, and skilled from childhood on. Roger's upbringing was anything but standard: he was probably raised in the royal court at Mileto in Calabria, where he was schooled in Greek and Arabic. When he was king, his court at Palermo was famous for its eclectic group of western and eastern intellectuals. This tradition continued in Sicily long after Roger's death.

When Roger died, at age fifty-eight, he was survived by his third wife, Beatrice of Rethel, and their new daughter, Constance.

Constance would eventually marry the son of Frederick I Barbarossa, Henry VI, thereby uniting the Norman and Hohenstaufen lines. In 1151, before his death, Roger had ensured the succession by naming and crowning as his heir his fourth son (his oldest surviving son), William I. William's mother was Roger's first wife, Elvira, daughter of Alfonso VI of Castille. A modern historian summed up Roger's reign by noting, "From his father he had inherited a county; to his son he bequeathed a kingdom." This kingdom would endure, largely intact, under the guidance of his son and grandson, William I and William II. They inherited the tradition of a strong, centralized monarchical rule established by their illustrious forebear.

Older scholarship proclaimed that Roger II had created the "first modern state." More recent work has suggested that the kingdom was not so unified as had previously been thought, and that Roger's apparent acceptance of the different cultures over which he ruled was motivated more by political expediency than by laudable tolerance. Roger's reign was an "absolute" monarchy that recognized the weaknesses of this unique kingdom and harnessed its strengths: a large geographic territory, surrounded by ambitious and watchful neighbors, and populated by people of vastly different religious, cultural, and administrative backgrounds. Roger II encouraged tolerance in this multiethnic state when it was politically necessary; overall, he expected strict obedience to his rule.

Roger's last wish, to be buried in the cathedral of Cefalù, which he had founded in 1131 outside Palermo, was not granted; he rests in the cathedral at Palermo. Nevertheless, the fusion of eastern and western architectural and artistic elements at Cefalù reflects the character of Roger's reign: innovative and intimidating political authority set against a glittering backdrop of cultural assimilation and coexistence.

See also **Roger I**

Further Reading

Editions

Alexander of Telese. *Alexandri Telesini Abbatis Ystoria Rogerii Regis Sicilie Calabrie atque Apulie*, ed. Ludovica De Nava. Istituto Storico Italiano per il Medio Evo, Fonti per la Stroria d'Italia, 112. Rome: Nella Sede dell'Istituto, 1991.

Brühl, Carlrichard. *Rogerii II: Regis diplomata Latina*. Codex Diplomaticus Regni Siciliae, Series 1, Diplomata Regum et Principum e Gente Normannorum, 2(1). Cologne: Böhlau, 1987.

Catalogus Baronum, ed. Evelyn Jamison. Rome: Istituto Storico Italiano per il Medio Evo, 1972.

The Liber Augustalis or Constitutions of Melfi Promulgated by the Emperor Frederick II for the Kingdom of Sicily in 1231, trans. James Powell. Syracuse, N.Y.: Syracuse University Press, 1971.

Critical Studies

Abulafia, David. *The Two Italics: Economic Relations between the Norman Kingdom of Sicily and the Northern Communes*. Cambridge; Cambridge University Press, 1977.

——. *Italy, Sicily, and the Mediterranean, 1100–1400*. London: Variorum Reprints, 1987.

——. *The Western Mediterranean Kingdoms 1200–1500: The Struggle for Dominion*. London: Longman, 1997.

Amari, Michele. *Storia dei musulmani di sicilia*, 2nd ed., ed. G. Levi della Vida and C. A. Nallino, 3 vols. Catania, 1930–1939.

Capitani, Ovidio. "Specific Motivations and Continuing Themes in the Norman Chronicles of Southern Italy in the Eleventh and Twelfth Centuries." In *The Normans in Sicily and Southern Italy: The Lincei Lectures 1974*. Oxford; Oxford University Press, 1977, pp. 1–46.

Caspar, Erich. *Roger II (1101–1154) und die Gründung der normannisch-sicilischen Monarchie*. Innsbruck: Wagner, 1904. (See also Italian version: *Ruggero II (1101–1145) e la fondazione della monarchia normanna di Sicilia*, intro. Ortensio Zecchino. Rome, 1999.)

Chalandon, Ferdinand. *Histoire de la domination normande en Italie et en Sicile*, 2 vols. Paris: Librarie A. Picard et fils, 1907. (Reprint, 1991.)

——. "The Conquest of South Italy and Sicily by the Normans" and "The Norman Kingdom of Sicily." *Cambridge Medieval History*, 5, 1926, pp. 167–207.

Cuozzo, Errico. *Catalogus Baronum commentario*. Istituto Storico Italiano per il Medio Evo, 101. Rome: Nella Sede dell'Istituto, 1984.

——. "*Quei maledetti normanni*": *Cavalieri e organizzazione militare nel mezzogiorno normanno*. Naples: Guida, 1989.

Drell, Joanna. "Family Structure in the Principality of Salerno under Norman Rule." *Anglo-Norman Studies*, 18, 1996, pp. 79–103.

——. "Cultural Syncretism and Ethnic Identity: The Norman 'Conquest' of Southern Italy and Sicily." *Journal of Medieval History* 25(3), 1999, pp. 187–202.

Falkenhausen, V. von. "I gruppi etnici nel regno di Ruggero II e la loro partecipazione al potere." In *Società, potere, e popolo nell'età di Ruggero II: Atti delle terze Giornate normanno-sveve—Bari, 23–25 maggio 1977*. Bari: Dedalo Libri, 1979, pp. 133–156.

Jamison, Evelyn. "The Norman Administration of Apulia and Capua, More Especially under Roger II and William I." *Papers of the British School at Rome*, 6, 1913, pp. 211–481. (See also 2nd ed., ed. D. R. Clementi and T. Kolzer, 1987; published as a separate monograph.)

——. "The Sicilian Norman Kingdom in the Mind of Anglo-Norman Contemporaries." *Proceedings of the British Academy*, 24, 1938, pp. 237–285.

Kehr, Karl Andreas. *Die Urkunden der normannisch-sizilischen Könige*. Innsbruck, 1902. (Reprint, 1962.)

Loud, G. A. *Church and Society in the Norman Principality of Capua 1058–1197*. Oxford: Clarendon, 1985.

——. *Conquerors and Churchmen in Norman Italy*. Aldershot: Ashgate, 1999.

——. *The Age of Robert Guiscard: Southern Italy and the Norman Conquest*. Essex: Pearson Education, 2000.

Marongiu, Antonio. "A Model State in the Middle Ages: The Norman-Hohenstaufen Kingdom of Sicily." *Comparative Studies in Society and History*, 4, 1963–1964, pp. 307–321.

——. *Byzantine, Norman, Swabian, and Later Institutions in Southern Italy*. London: Variorum Reprints, 1972.

Martin, Jean-Marie. "Città e Campagna: Economia e Società (sec.VII–XIII)." In *Storia del Mezzogiorno*, Vol. 3, *Alto Medioevo*. Rome: Edizioni del Sole, 1990, pp. 259–381.

——. *La pouille du VIe au XIIe siècle*. Rome: École Française de Rome, 1993.

Matthew, Donald. *The Norman Kingdom of Sicily*. Cambridge: Cambridge University Press, 1992.

Ménager, L. R. *Hommes et institutions de l'Italie Normande*. London: Variorum Reprints, 1981.

Norwich, John Julius. *The Other Conquest*. New York: Harper and Row, 1967. (Also published as *The Normans in the South 1016–1130*. London: Longmans, 1967 and 1981.)

——. *The Kingdom in the Sun, 1130–1194*. London: Longman, 1970.

Takayama, Hiroshi. *The Administration of the Norman Kingdom of Sicily*. Leiden: Brill, 1993.

Wolf, Kenneth Baxter. *Making History: The Normans and Their Historians in Eleventh-Century Italy*. Philadelphia: University of Pennsylvania Press, 1995.

JOANNA H. DRELL

ROLLE, RICHARD, OF HAMPOLE (d. 1349)

Hermit and mystical writer. Little is known of Rolle's life, although some facts can be gleaned from the readings of the liturgical office prepared for the possibility of his canonization, and some conjectures can be made based on his writings. According to the office he came from Thornton, near Pickering, in the diocese of York, and was sent to Oxford with the support of Thomas Neville, archdeacon of Durham. He left the university at nineteen, however, and returned home, where he retired to the forest to live as a hermit. Shortly thereafter he was taken in by John de Dalton, a local squire, and given an eremitic lodging within Dalton's household. This proved inadequate, and he removed to some other place—apparendy against Dalton's will. Rolle seems also at this rime to have been tempted to take a lover (possibly a real person was involved, or perhaps only a diabolical apparition) but resisted the temptation by invoking the precious blood of Jesus.

Rolle's writings contain a number of passages referring to criticism, particularly for irregularity in changing his place of hermitage. However, no record survives indicating either his formal enclosure as a hermit or formal proceedings against him. Records of his education and possible ordination are similarly lacking. We do not know when he took up residence at Hampole, Yorkshire, nor in what relation he stood to the Cistercian convent there, in whose cemetery (later church) he was buried.

Although we have only the vaguest knowledge of his worldly life, Rolle has left us some clear indications of the progress of his spiritual development. In the *Incendium amoris* he describes the reception of the gifts of "heat, sweetness, and song" that are characteristic of his spirituality. The first gift he received was that of actual physical heat warming his breast. At first, he says, he thought that what he felt was some form of temptation; but he came to recognize it as corresponding to a second gift, of sweetness in prayers. Finally, while at prayer in chapel one day, he heard "as it were a ringing of singers of psalms, or rather, of songs." Time and again Rolle writes of this threefold gift of heat, sweetness, and song (*calor, dulcon, canor*).

Works

Rolle's works can be divided into three classes: scriptural commentaries, original mystical treatises, and lyrical and poetic compositions.

The most important scriptural commentaries are the Latin and English commentaries on the Psalter; Rolle also composed Latin commentaries on the first few verses of the Song of Songs, the first six chapters of the book of Revelation, and the Lamentations of Jeremiah. Five other treatises (including, particularly, the *Judica me Deus*) also derive their name and form from their commentary on particular scriptural verses. Another four commentaries are based on biblical texts used in the liturgy or on ecclesiastical texts. All of these lesser commentaries are in Latin. Although the commentaries are based for the most pan on earlier works in the same genre (the Psalter commentaries, for example, derive largely from the "literal" explication in Peter Lombard's *Commentarium*), they also develop a number of themes characteristic of Rolle's interests and teaching, such as devotion to the name of Jesus, and the experience of heat, sweetness, and song. These works probably derive from the period of Rolle's spiritual maturity.

The most important works in Rolle's canon are his three great Latin treatises and his four Latin and English epistolary tracts. The first treatise, *De amore Dei contra amatores mundi*, compares the eternal joys of the lover of God with the passing pleasures of this world. In each of its seven chapters Rolle describes a different aspect of worldly love and shows how the lovers of this world, though they seem happier, will be betrayed in the end into eternal sorrow. The second major treatise, the *Incendium amoris*, deals more specifically than any of Rolle's other writings with his experience of spiritual heat, sweetness, and song and is more autobiographical as well. Although focused on these themes, the *Incendium* also treats discursively a number of theological topics—yet it always returns to Rolle's own spiritual experience and to the idea that God's contemplative gifts to those who love him alone far outweigh the worldly satisfaction of merely intellectual pursuits. The *Incendium* was translated into ME, along with the *Emendatio vitae*, by the Carmelite Richard Misyn. The third of Rolle's Latin treatises, the *Melos amoris*, is in some ways the most difficult of his works to describe: highly alliterative in style and allusive in form, it appears to represent and attempt to reproduce in writing the transformation of contemplative prayer into heavenly song that he describes as the culmination of his spiritual experience. The probable aim of the *Melos* is not so much persuasion as mystagogy—the re-creation in the reader's mind of the author's spiritual experience, which by grace the reader may also attain. The style of the *Melos* has led many to regard it as an immature work; but Arnould, its editor, has pointed out that it more probably manifests the latest stage of his spirituality.

Rolle's most important epistolary tract, and by far his most popular work, is the *Emendatio vitae*. This letter and the parallel English *Form of Living* are addressed in some manuscripts to two of Rolle's disciples—William (Stopes?) in the former case, Margaret Kirkby in the latter—and are probably the last things he wrote. Of particular importance in both is the treatment of the "three stages of love": insuperable, inseparable, and singular. The treatises also exhort Rolle's audience to an immediate rejection of the world's blandishments and conversion to God in the eremitic life. The *Form of Living* was translated into Latin, and the *Emendatio vitae* into English by Richard Misyn and no fewer than six other, independent translators. The themes of the stages of the love of God and the necessity of total conversion to him also occur in Rolle's two other English epistolary tracts, the *Commandment* and the *Ego dormio*. Rolle included a number of lyrics in the *Ego dormio* and the *Form of Living*; a further collection of eight to ten lyrics is attributed to him in two manuscripts. He also wrote the *Canticum amoris*, a Latin hymn of praise to the Virgin Mary.

Rolle's reputation, like that of many influential medieval writers, was so great that many works not written by him came to be associated with his name. Hope Emily Allen's *Writings Ascribed to Richard Rolle* has proven decisive in establishing his canon, although her conclusions regarding chronology and biographical references must still be viewed with some skepticism.

Teaching and Influence

The most distinctive feature of Richard Rolle's spirituality is the experience of the graces of heat, sweetness, and song that follows upon the total conversion from the world to God. He is not always consistent in the hierarchical and chronological ordering of these graces, however; nor despite important similarities, is their description entirely consistent with that of the diree degrees of love—insuperable, inseparable, and singular—found in the later epistles. These three degrees apparendy derive From Richard of St. Victor's *Quattuor gradus violentae charitatis*, minus the fourth (insatiable) degree.

For Rolle the rejection of the false pleasures of this world and a complete conversion to God are the *sine qua non* of the contemplative life, which he believes is most fully lived in the eremitic life. He considered the religious vocation to be comparatively worldly and grouped members of religious orders together with other lovers of this world.

The experience of heavenly song, with that of sensible heat and sweetness in prayer, is particularly characteristic of Rolle's spirituality and that of his followers. Certain sections of *The Cloud of Unknowing* and of Walter Hilton's *Scale of Perfection* and *Of Angels' Song* caution against using words like "heat," "sweetness," or "song" too literally in describing spiritual experience, a feet that suggests that this form of affective mysticism was popular in the later 14th century. These negative comments, together with more positive presentations of this kind of affective mysticism by Thomas Basset, Richard Methley, and John Norton, can be taken as evidence for an informal "school" of Richard Rolle.

Rolle achieved his greatest degree of popular influence with the spread of the devotion (particularly in lyric poetry) to the Passion of Christ and to the Holy Name of Jesus. According to Knowlton the cult of the Holy Name does not seem to have been prominent in England, despite imitations of the "Dulcis Jesu Memoria" and devotional pieces in the tradition of Anselm of Canterbury's *Meditations*, until after the time of Rolle. A number of late-14th- and 15th-century ME lyrics reflect not merely these devotional themes but also the phrasing of Rolle's devotional poems and descriptions of his own spiritual experiences. Rolle was not merely the first of the 14th-century English mystics; he also had the greatest influence on popular piety before the Reformation.

See also **Hilton, Walter**

Further Reading

Primary Sources

Allen, Hope Emily, ed. *English Writing of Richard Rolle Hermit of Hampole.* Oxford: Clarendon, 1931.

Allen, Rosamund S., trans. *The English Writings.* New York: Paulist Press, 1988.

Arnould, E.J.F., ed. *The Melos Amoris of Richard Rolle of Hampole.* Oxford: Blackwell, 1957.

Deanesly, Margaret, ed. *The Incendium amoris of Richard Rolle of Hampole.* Manchester, Manchester University Press, 1915

del Mastro, ML., trans. *The Fire of Love and the Mending of Life.* New York: Doubleday, 1981.

Harvey, Ralph, ed. *The Fire of Love and the Mending of Life, or The Rule of Living of Richard Rolle.* EETS o.s. 106. Oxford: Kegan Paul, Trench, Trübner, 1896.

Ogilvie-Thomson, Sarah J., ed. *Richard Rolle: Prose and Verse.* EETS o.s. 293. Oxford: Oxford University Press, 1988.

Theiner, Paul F., ed. *The Contra amatores mundi of Richard Rolle of Hampole.* Berkeley: University of California Press, 1968.

Secondary Sources

Manual 9:3051–68, 3411–25.

Alford, John A. "Richard Rolle and Related Works." In *Middle English Prose: A Critical Guide to Major Authors and Genres,* ed. A.S.G. Edwards. New Brunswick: Rutgers University Press, 1984, pp. 35–60.

Allen, Hope Emily. *Writings Ascribed to Richard Rolle, Hermit of Hampole, and Materials for His Biography.* New York: Heath, 1927.

Clark, J.P.H. "Richard Rolle: ATheological Re-Assessment." *DownR* 101 (1983): 108-39.

Clark, J.P.H. "Richard Rolle as a Biblical Commentator." *DownR* 104 (1986): 165–213.

Knowlton, Mary Arthur. *The Influence of Richard Rolle and of Julian of Norwich on the Middle English Lyrics.* The Hague: Mouton, 1973.

Watson, Nicholas. "Richard Rolle as Elitist and as Popularist: The Case *Judica me.*" In *De Cella in Seculum: Religious and Secular Life and Devotion in Late Medieval England,* ed. Michael G. Sargent. Cambridge: Brewer, 1989, pp. 123–43.

Watson, Nicholas. *Richard Rolle and the Invention of Authority.* Cambridge: Cambridge University Press, 1991.

MICHAEL G. SARGENT

ROMUALD OF RAVENNA, SAINT (c. 952–1027) Saint Romuald of Ravenna was a monastic reformer and the founder of the Camaldolese order and is considered one of the founders of the Italian eremitical movement of the eleventh century.

Romuald was born into the ducal Onesti family at Ravenna. When he was twenty, his father killed a kinsman in a duel, and Romuald entered the Benedictine monastery of Sant'Apollinare in Classe to perform a forty-day penance for this act. The monastery had a profound effect on him. At the end of the penance he decided to stay, took monastic vows, and entered enthusiastically into a rigorous observance of the Benedictine rule. However, reading the lives of the desert fathers led Romuald to criticize what he considered laxity at Sant'Apollinare, and he soon left the monastery to live as an anchorite in the marshes surrounding Ravenna. About 975, Romuald became the disciple of the hermit Marino and followed him to the vicinity of Venice.

Through Marino, Romuald was drawn into the circle of Venice's doge,

Pietro Orseolo, who was then undergoing a religious conversion. When Orseolo abdicated to join the monastery at Cuxa in the Pyrenees, Romuald and Marino went with him. Romuald remained at Cuxa for ten years, studying the works in its library in order to refine his understanding of the monastic ideal. Although the final shape of his reform was the product of many years of experimentation, the basic notions seem to have been formulated at Cuxa. Romuald's foundations would be among the first expressions of an eleventh-century monastic reform movement that sought to revive the primitive rigor of early Egyptian eremitism.

Romuald returned to Italy on the death of Orseolo in 988. He spent the next ten years based in Pereum, a hermitage in Ravenna's marshes, while he wandered the Apennines seeking followers, founding monasteries, and experimenting with monastic organization. Like a number of other reformers of his time, Romuald was determined to develop a greater spirit of contemplation in monastic houses; accordingly, he established hermitages and cenobitic communities together. But unlike other reformers, Romuald did not believe that a cenobitic life was a necessary prerequisite for an eremitic life. At his foundations, promising candidates were immediately introduced to the life of the hermit. Moreover, he did not subordinate the hermitage to the abbot of the monastery but rather put the cenobites under the moral authority of an experienced hermit. The monastery and hermitage were supposed to complement each other in drawing all monks toward the eremitical ideal of fasting, silence, and solitude.

In 998 Emperor Otto III appointed Romuald abbot of Sant'Apollinare in Classe, but the monks' resistance to his austerity led to his resignation within a year. He then moved to the environs of Rome, near the imperial court, and soon attracted the patronage of several of the emperor's courtiers. When civil unrest at Rome drove the court to Ravenna in 1001, Romuald followed, again settling in Pereum. Romuald now had significant support from the empire. Followers flocked to him. Many, including the imperial chaplain Bruno of Querfurt, went as missionaries to convert the Slavs, inspired by Romuald's insistence that preaching and conversion were the ultimate role of the monk and hermit.

After the death of Otto III in 1002, Romuald left Pereum to wander again in the Apennines. Sometime between 1010 and 1020, he founded a small monastery and hermitage at Camaldoli near Arezzo. This influential institution, famous for its rigor, proved to be his most lasting contribution to eremitical reform. Romuald died at Val di Castro in 1027. By then, his other foundations were already looking to Camaldoli for leadership, and other monastic reformers were drawing inspiration from it.

Romuald had not intended to establish an order separate from the Benedictines. However, after his death the thirty-odd monasteries he had founded drew together around Camaldoli, in part to protect the peculiar customs Romuald had established for them. By the late eleventh century, the Gregorian popes were treating them as an order. The most famous Camaldolese monk, Petet Damian, drew many of his reforming ideals from Romuald. Peter wrote a very influential biography of Romuald in 1042.

See also **Damian, Peter; Otto III**

Further Reading

Edition
Tabacco, Giovanni, ed. *Petri Damiani Vita beati Romualdi.* Fonti per la Storia d'Italia, 94. Rome: Istituto Storico Italiano per il Medio Evo, 1957.

Critical Studies
Belisle, Peter Damian. "Primitive Romauldian/Camaldolese Spirituality." *Cistercian Studies Quarterly,* 31, 1996, pp. 413–429.

Kurze, Wilhelm. "Campus Malduli: Die Frühgeschichte Camaldolis." *Quellen und Forschungen aus Italienischen Archiven und Bibliotheken*, 44, 1964, pp. 1–34.

Leclercq, Jean. "Saint Romuald et le monachisme missionaire." *Revue Bénédictine*, 77, 1962, pp. 307–322.

Phipps, Colin. "Romuald—Model Hermit: Eremitical Theory in Saint Peter Damian's *Vita Beati Romualdi*, Chapters 16–27." *Studies in Church History*, 22, 1985, pp. 65–77.

Schmidtmann, Christian. "Romuald von Camoldi: Modell einer eremitischen Existenz in 10./11. Jahrhundert." *Studia Monastica*, 39, 1997, pp. 329–338.

Tabacco, Giovanni. *Romualdo di Ravenna*. Turin: Bottega d'Erasmo, 1968.

THOMAS TURLEY

RUDOLF VON EMS (ca. 1190–ca. 1255) The presumably Swiss author from Hohenems wrote five surviving quasi-historical epics in verse for important men close to the Staufer court (at first, during the reign of King Heinrich VII) and eventually for King Konrad IV himself, whom he might have accompanied on a campaign to Italy, where the king (and maybe the poet) died in 1254.

The works (based on French and Latin sources) in approximate chronological order are *Der gute Gerhard* (*Good Gerard*), commissioned by Rudolf von Steinach (ministerial of the bishop of Constance) circa 1220; *Barlaam und Josaphat*, after a literary model of abbot Wido von Cappel (near Zürich); *Alexander*, without a known commissioner; *Willehalm von Orlens*, commissioned by Konrad von Winterstetten at the Staufer court in Swabia, before 1243; the French source was provided by Johannes von Ravensburg's *Weltchronik*, dedicated to King Konrad IV Another theory is that Rudolf did not go to Italy and continued the *Weltchronik* beyond "Salomo," after which he added still two later excursus to *Alexander*. If Rudolf had also produced earlier courtly works, which he claimed in *Barlaam und Josaphat*, that is unproven. But an *Eustachius*-Legend, mentioned in *Alexander*, is lost.

Der gute Gerhard, after an unknown source, demonstrates courtly humanity toward a heathen (two manuscripts are extant). *Barlaam und Josaphat* describes the Indian Legend of Buddha after a Latin source of 1220–1223. (Extant in 47 manuscripts; the only illustrated manuscript, of 1469, was done by Diebold Lauber, with 138 drawings.) Alongside the *Laubacher Barlaam* of the Freisinger Bishop Otto II, Rudolf's is the second German version. In *Eustachius*, a high Roman general under Trajan converted to Christianity. *Willehalm von Orlens* is neither an *aventiure*, or courtly chivalric romance (Wolfram), nor a chanson de geste (heroic ballad, like Guillaume), but rather basically a courtly *Fürstenspiegel*, or guide for nobility. An ideal government, Staufer knighthood, exists also in France and England. (Of the twenty-nine extant manuscripts, seven are illustrated, mostly by Diebold Lauber.) A shorter narrative in rhymed couplets, *Wilhalm von Orlens*, was created in the fifteenth century, extant in four manuscripts and one print of Anton Sorg (Augsburg, 1491). Hans Sachs based his drama of 1559 on this print. In 1522, an anonymous Swabian writer reworked Rudolf's epic as stropbic form in the Herzog-Ernst-Tone, a thirteen-line pattern. The story is also recounted in pictures, on a tapestry in Frankfurt of the first quarter of the fifteenth century, in fifteen scenes. The couple Wilhelm and Amelie is also found as a fresco at Runkelstein castle near Bozen. In *Alexander*, Rudolf wanted to portray history, not a heroic or courtly romance. Ten volumes were planned, which were stopped in the middle of the sixth book, however (death of Darius and victory over his followers). The two main sources were the *Historia de preliis* and Curtius Rufus. Fairy-tale portions were left out. (Of the three extant manuscripts, the Munich State Library manuscript was illustrated by Diebold Lauber.) The *Weltchronik* ends, after thirty-six thousand verses, in the middle of the Jewish history of the kings. (Over one hundred manuscripts are extant, as well as reworkings and rhymed bibles.)

Further Reading

Green, Dennis. "On the Primary Reception of the Works of Rudolf von Ems." *Zeitschrift für deutsches Altertum* 115 (1986): 151–180.

Haug, Walter. "Wolframs 'Willehalm'—Prolog im Lichte seiner Bearbeitung durch Rudolf von Ems," in *Kritische Bewährung: Beiträge zur deutschen Philologie: Festschrift für Werner Schröder zum 60. Geburtstag*, ed. Ernst-Joachim Schmidt. Berlin: E. Schmidt, 1974, pp. 298–327.

Walliczek, Wolfgang. "Rudolf von Ems," in *Die deutsche Literatur des Mittelalters. Verfasserlexikon*, ed. Kurt Ruh et al. Berlin: de Gruyter, 1991, vol. 8, coll. 322–345.

Wenzel, Horst. "Höfische Geschichte." *Europäische Hochschulschriften* 1, 284 (1980): 71–87.

Wunderlich, Werner. *Der 'ritterliche' Kaufmann: literatursoziologische Studien zu Rudolf von Ems' "Der guote Gerhart."* Scriptor. Hochschulschriften. Literaturwissenschaft 7. Kronberg im Taunus: Scriptor, 1975.

Zaenker, Karl A. "The Manuscript Relationship of Rudolf von Ems' *Barlaam und Josaphat*." Ph.D. diss., University of British Columbia, 1974.

SIBYLLE JEFFERIES

RUSTICO FILIPPI (c. 1230–c. 1280 or 1285)

The Florentine poet Rustico Filippi (Rustico di Filippo) is credited with initiating the comic style in the medieval Italian lyric. Rustico wrote fifty-seven sonnets transmitted by the Vaticano manuscript Latino 3793, and a *tenzone* with Bondie Dietaiuti found in three other codices. Half of his sonnets were written in the serious style of courtly love; the other half provide one of the earliest examples of the comic, or jocose, style in Italian literature. Brunetto Latini, who considered Rustico one of his closest friends and an accomplished poet, dedicated the *Favolello* to him. Rustico was also the acknowledged teacher of Jacopo da Lèona and is the protagonist of a comic sonnet by Jacopo. Rustico was an ardent Ghibelline.

Rustico's comic sonnets fall into two categories: personal invective, and caricature directed against Florentines of all ages and social conditions. Among the figures he caricatured are warriors who inspire laughter rather than awe, a miser, a cuckolded husband, a man who is the paradigm of laziness, people with offensive body odors, libertines on the prowl, and prostitutes. Rustico displays a great talent for euphemism and uses a plethora of creative metaphors, similes, paraphrases, and hyperbole to describe his characters, the sexual act, and certain parts of the human anatomy. Several of the comic sonnets are linked. For example, there is a three-sonnet group that begins with *Poi che guerito son de le mascelle*, recounting the implausible proposals made by a matchmaker to a poor father with two daughters; and there is a two-sonnet group beginning with *Su, donna Gemma, co la farinata*, which ponders the suspicious reasons behind the sudden loss of weight of a young girl named Mita. The best-known of Rustico's comic sonnets, *Quando Dïo messer Messerin fece*, describes Albizzo de' Caponsacchi as a unique combination of bird, beast, and man—a miracle of God's creation.

In the sonnet describing "*messer Messerin*," and in other sonnets, Rustico frequently compares the targets of his caricatures to animals, at a time when such comparisons were in vogue in the serious courtly love lyric. Whereas in his comic poetry Rustico mocked the overuse of animal comparisons, he avoided them altogether in his twenty-eight sonnets and the *tenzone* in the traditional courtly style. In these compositions, he experimented with various rhetorical devices in order to achieve more drama and more narrative flexibility. Among his innovations, he broke the unity of address, extended personification from the conventional god of love to other items involved in the *psychomachia* of courtly love (the heart, the eyes), and abandoned the extended simile. One sonnet that illustrates all these elements is *Amor fa nel mio cor fermo soggiorno*. The integration of dramatic techniques into the lyric, and the cultivation of a kinetic rather than a descriptive style, reached a culmination in the poetry of the *dolce stil nuovo*. Thus Rustico was an innovator in introducing comic poetry to Italian literature and, to a lesser extent, in the development of the love lyric.

See also **Brunetto Latini**

Further Reading

Editions

Contini, Gianfranco. *Poeti del Duecento*, Vol. 2. Milan and Naples: Ricciardi, 1960, pp. 353–364.

Federici, Vincenzo. *Le rime di Rustico di Filippo, rimatore fiorentino del sec. XIII*. Bergamo: Istituto Italiano d'Arti Grafiche, 1899.

Figurelli, Fernando. *La poesia comico-giocosa dei primi due secoli*. Naples: Pironti, 1960, pp. 74–112.

Marti, Mario. *Poeti giocosi del tempo di Dante*. Milan: Rizzoli, 1956, pp. 29–91.

Massèra, Aldo Francesco. *Sonetti burleschi e realistici dei primi due secoli*. Bari: Laterza, 1920. (See also rev. ed, ed. Luigi Russo, 1940, Vol. 1, pp. 1–30.)

Rustico Filippi. *Sonetti*, ed. Pier Vincenzo Mengaldo. Turin: Einaudi, 1971.

Vitale, Maurizio. *Rimatori comico-realistici*. Turin: UTET, 1956, pp. 99–197. (Reprint, 1976.)

Translations

Dante and His Circle, with the Italian Poets Preceding Him (1100–1200–1300), trans. Dante Gabriel Rossetti. London: Ellis and Elvey, 1892, pp. 360–362.

Poems from Italy, ed. William Jay Smith and Dana Gioìa. Saint Paul, Minn.: New Rivers, 1985, pp. 32–33.

Tusiani, Joseph. *The Age of Dante: An Anthology of Early Italian Poetry Translated into English Verse and with an Introduction*. New York: Baroque, 1974, pp. 56–57.

Critical Studies

Baldelli, Ignazio. "Dante e i poeti fiorentini del Duecento." In *Lectura Dantis Scaligera*. Florence: Le Monnier, 1968.

Buzzetti Gallarati, Silvia. "Sull'organizzazione del discorso comico nella produzione giocosa di Rustico Filippi." *Medioevo Romanzo*, 9(2), 1984, pp. 189–213.

Casini, Tommaso. "Un poeta umorista del secolo decimoterzo (Rustico di Filippo)." In *Scritti danteschi*. Città di Casrello: Lapi, 1913, pp. 225–255.

Folena, Gianfranco. "Cultura poetica dei primi fiorentini." *Giornale Storico della Letteratura Italiana*, 147, 1970, pp. 1–42.

Kleinhenz, Christopher. *The Early Italian Sonnet: The First Century (1220–1321)*. Collezione di Studi e Testi, 2. Lecce: Milella, 1986.

Levin, Joan H. *Rustico di Filippo and the Florentine Lyric Tradition*. American University Studies, 2(16). New York: Peter Lang, 1986.

Marti, Mario. "La coscienza stilistica di Rustico di Filippo e la sua poesia." In *Cultura e stile net poeti giocosi del tempo di Dante*. Pisa: Nistri-Lischi, 1953.

Petrocchi, Giorgio. "I poeti realisti." In *Storia della letteratura italiana*, Vol. 1, *Le origini e il Duecento*, ed. Emilio Cecchi and Natalino Sapegno. Milan: Garzanti, 1965, pp. 575–607. (Reprint, 1979.)

Quaglio, Antonio Enzo. "La poesia realistica." In *La letteratura italiana: storia e testi*, Vol. 1(2), *Il Duecento: Dalle origini a Dante*. Bari: Laterza, 1970, pp. 183–253.

Russo, Vittorio. " 'Verba obscena' e comico: Rustico Filippi." *Filologia e Critica*, 5, 1980, pp. 169–182.

Savona, Eugenio. "Rustico di Filippo e la poesia comico-realistica." In *Cultura e ideologia nell'età comunale: Ricerche sulla letteratura italiana dell'età comunale*. Ii Portico, 57. Ravenna: Longo, 1975, pp. 57–70.

Suitner, Franco. *La poesia satirica e giocosa nell'età dei comuni*. Padua: Antenore, 1983.

JOAN H. LEVIN

RUTEBEUF (fl. 1248–85) The Parisian Rutebeuf composed works in a greater variety of genres than any other medieval poet. Known from a dozen manuscripts, his fifty-five extant pieces illustrate the range of medieval urban poetry. Rutebeuf composed in every vernacular genre except those especially cultivated in the provincial courts of 13th-century France: chivalric epics, romances, and songs of courtly love. At a time when manuscript compilations grouped lyric, dramatic, and narrative pieces separately, Rutebeuf, like his contemporary Adam de la Halle, imposed such a vivid and coherent poetic identity on all his compositions that they were gathered as a corpus in three contemporary compilations. Unlike the vagabond Goliards or jongleurs who traveled from castle to court, Rutebeuf remained in Paris, where he wrote to please many patrons—the royal family, the university, the higher clergy, the papal legate—and to amuse a public in city streets and taverns. While the aristocratic provincial courts were attuned to the refined art of the chanson and the idealizing fantasies of Arthurian romance, Rutebeuf's heterogeneous urban public relished topical works that spoke to issues of the day, such as the Crusades and the proliferation of mendicant orders in Paris. Rutebeuf's political verse follows historical events closely and presupposes familiarity with Parisian topography, personalities, and issues. The notable variety of genres and the historical content that characterize Rutebeuf's poetry are inseparable from Paris, the city that was its essential and nurturing environment, and from the colorful figure of the poet himself.

Although no document preserves any record of Rutebeuf's life, his poems reveal much about his background, training, and relations with patrons. He may have come from the region of Champagne; his earliest polemical poem, the *Dit des Cordeliers* (1249), favors the rights of Franciscan monks in Troyes. Throughout his career, Rutebeuf composed eulogies of nobles from Champagne, although mostly in connection with his role as a Parisian propagandist of papal crusade policy, as in his *complaintes* for Count Eudes de Nevers (1266) and Count Thibaut V of Champagne (1279). Rutebeuf's *Vie de sainte Elysabel* (ca. 1271) was commissioned for Isabelle, daughter of King Louis IX and wife of Thibaut V. Rutebeuf's most prominent benefactors were members of the royal family, such as Alphonse of Poitiers, brother of Louis IX, whom he addresses in his request poem *Complainte Rutebeuf* and in his crusade piece *Dit de Pouille* (ca. 1265) and whom he eulogizes in 1271. The poet also appeals repeatedly to King Philip III the Bold to replace generous benefactors lost on the Crusades. Like the eulogies and commissioned devotional works, Rutebeuf's political poems and appeals for largesse mark his status as a skilled professional poet and his relations with patrons in the highest ecclesiastical and aristocratic circle.

Rutebeuf composed a number of comic pieces like those described in minstrel repertoires. His *Dit de l'herberie* is one of several examples of a dramatic monologue by a quack who amuses an audience with rapid enumerations of coins, exotic places, stones, and herbal remedies. All of Rutebeuf's fabliaux are known in other medieval versions: the story of the Franciscan who enrolls a girl in his monastic order (*Frère Denise*); the tale of the wife who pretends that her midnight rendezvous with the priest is a devotional exercise (*Dame qui fist trois tours autour du moutier*); the account of the bishop who gave Christian burial to a donkey who left him twenty pounds (*Testament de l'âne*). The theme of the obscene *Pet au vilain* is reused in André de la Vigne's farce, the *Meunier de qui le diable emporte l'âme en enfer* (1496).

Rutebeuf also had sufficient clerical training to read Latin and know the student's life. His *Dit de l'université* is a sympathetic account of a peasant boy come to study in Paris who soon squanders his hard-earned funds on pretty city girls. Though not a vulgarizer of philosophical and scientific concepts like his contemporary Jean de Meun, he draws on Latin sources for his saints' lives, miracles, polemical poems, and requests for largesse. In the *Dit d'Aristote,* he translates a passage from the epic *Alexandreis* by Walter of Châtillon; in *Sainte Elysabel,* he abridges a Latin *vita;* in his miracle of the *Sacristain et la femme au chevalier,* he expands an exemplum from the early 13th-century *Sermones vulgares* of the preacher Jacques de Vitry. Rutebeuf's lives of exemplary penitents combine French and Latin sources in the narrative *Sainte Marie l'Egyptienne* and the *Miracle de Théophile,* which dramatizes versions by Gautier de Coinci and Fulbert of Chartres. He even translates and glosses lines from Ovid's *Metamorphoses* in his allegorical *Voie de paradis.*

Rutebeuf's clerical training not only led him to rich literary sources, it also determined his subjects and his style. Rutebeuf's moral poems contribute to the ecclesiastical effort, inspired by the Fourth Lateran Council (1215), to instruct laypeople in religious doctrine: his *Voie de paradis* is an allegorical catechism of confession; three works, the *Etat, Vie,* and *Plaies du monde,* adapt the conventional estates satire of Latin preachers and moralists for a lay public. In contrast with the self-reflective mode of contemporary courtly lyric and moral verse, Rutebeuf's poetry often seeks to turn its hearers toward the outer world of history painted in dramatic moral colors.

Commissioned by supporters of the crusade policies of Louis IX and the pope, Rutebeuf's eleven crusade poems incorporate estates satire and rhetorical techniques of moral persuasion from the didactic tradition to rouse public opinion in favor of increasingly unpopular crusades against Charles of Anjou's Christian rival for the Sicilian throne (1265) and against the Muslims in Tunis (1270). As a professional pamphleteer,

Rutebeuf does not express personal opinions in his poems. He advocates the differing views of the two causes he served in order to sway public opinion and encourage partisans to action; he is an ardent supporter of papal policies in his crusade verse, a fiery Gallican in his defense of university autonomy.

In his fourteen poems supporting the secular university masters against their Franciscan and Dominican rivals and the pope, Rutebeuf again recasts the motifs of didactic poetry to new, polemical ends. Dream allegories, battles of vices and virtues, animal satires, complaints attributed to the church personified—all the resources of the Latin and French satirical tradition are brought to bear on partisan concerns. Knowledge of historical circumstances is essential to the understanding of Rutebeuf's topical poems: the proliferation of mendicant orders in Paris (*Ordres de Paris, Chanson des ordres, Des béguines*); the struggle between mendicants and secular clergy for parish privileges and university chairs (*Discorde de l'université et des Jacobins, Des règles, Dit de sainte Église, Bataille des vices et des vertus, Des Jacobins*); the writings of William of Saint-Amour, banished leader of the university masters (*Dit* and *Complainte de Guillaume*). Out of this factional literature rises a new allegorical figure, Hypocrisy, which comes to overshadow earlier concern with pride and avarice and dominate moral literature of the late 13th and 14th centuries. Personified in Rutebeuf's *Du Pharisien* and *Dit d'Hypocrisie,* hypocrisy is central to Jean de Meun's character False Seeming in the *Roman de la Rose* as well as in late animal satires, such as *Renart le contrefait* and the *Livres de Fauvel.*

Polemical, pious, or entertaining in topic and nonlyric in form, Rutebeuf's poems have a style and shape that owe little to prevailing courtly modes. His characteristic form is the first-person nonmusical *dit,* a rambling, open form, most often cast in octosyllabic couplets or tercets, that accommodates all the topical themes of contemporary history that found little place in courtly song, romance, or epic. In spite of their rhetorical embroidery and rich rhymes, Rutebeuf's poems give an overall impression of artless simplicity and directness. His verses are engaging and amusing: enlivened with frequent irony, animated with proverbs, touched with realistic details. Lively, colloquial direct discourse and dialogue characterize both Rutebeuf's poems and the tableaux of his *Miracle de Théophile*. Often shaped as *complaintes,* Rutebeuf's *dits* pass easily from one subject to another via apostrophes and exclamations that are united more by appeal to emotion than by rigorous logic.

The figure of the poet himself, however, is the element that unifies Rutebeuf's works. Identified by a signature pun as *Rustebeuf qui rudement cevre* ("Rutebeuf who works crudely"), the persona of the poet is protagonist in many of his moral, political, and comic pieces: "Rutebeuf" is the pilgrim in the allegorical *Voie de paradis*; he is the character who goes to Rome in a dream vision to hear news of the election of Pope Urban IV (*Dit d'Hypocrisie*, 1261). It is in his own name that Rutebeuf accuses church prelates of caring less for the Crusades than for "good wine, good meat, and that the pepper be strong" (*Complainte d'Outremer*, ll. 94–95). It is he who witnesses the chaste speech of Alphonse of Poitiers in his eulogy and who is called to judge the comic debate between Charlot and the barber.

Characterization of his poetic persona is most vividly developed in Rutebeuf's best-known works, his ten poems of personal misfortune. His poetic "I" is based on the conventional character type of the poor fool that figures in medieval request verse by Goliards and minstrels and later in the poetry of Eustache Deschamps and François Villon. Picturesquely personal rather than autobiographical in content, his poems of misfortune dramatize an exaggerated, grotesque self, deserted by friends, grimacing with cold and want, and martyred by marriage and a weakness for gambling. In the plaintive or ironic tones of the *Dit d'Aristote*, the *Paix de Rutebeuf*, and *De Brichemer*, the poet reminds his patrons of the virtue of largesse and prompt payment. The *Repentance Rutebeuf* gives a solemn, subjective resonance to the conventional poetry of remorse found in his saints' lives and miracles. Furthermore, in his *Griesche d'hiver, Griesche d'été* and *Dit des ribauds de Grève*, Rutebeuf shows the reader a social world excluded from courtly song, romance, and epic, that of a homeless urban proletariat, stung by white snowflakes in winter and by black flies in summer.

Appreciatively collected by contemporaries, Rutebeuf's poetry was forgotten after his time. But in his works we discover a poetic voice that dramatizes and particularizes the subjective lyric while it speaks with satirical wit and ethical fervor about concerns of the urban world of medieval France.

See also **Adam de la Halle; Deschamps, Eustache; Fulbert of Chartres**

Further Reading

Rutebeuf. *Œuvres complètes de Rutebeuf,* ed. Edmond Faral and Julia Bastin. 2 vols. Paris: Picard, 1959.

——. *Œuvres complètes,* ed. and trans. Michel Zink. 2 vols. Paris: Bordas, 1989–90.

Cerquiglini, Jacqueline. "'Le clerc et le louche': Sociology of an Esthetic." *Poetics Today* 5 (1984): 479–91.

Huot, Sylvia. *From Song to Book: The Poetics of Writing in Old French Lyric and Lyrical Narrative Poetry.* Ithaca: Cornell University Press, 1987, pp. 213–19.

Regalado, Nancy Freeman. *Poetic Patterns in Rutebeuf: A Study in Noncourtly Poetic Modes of the Thirteenth Century.* New Haven: Yale University Press, 1970.

Rousse, Michel. "Le mariage Rutebeuf et la fête des fous." *Moyen âge* 88 (1982): 435–49.

Zink, Michel. "Time and Representation of the Self in Thirteenth-Century French Poetry." *Poetics Today* 5 (1984): 611–27.

———. "*La subjectivité littéraire autour du siècle de saint Louis.* Paris: Presses Universitaires de France, 1985, pp. 47–74.

NANCY F. REGALADO

S

SACCHETTI, FRANCO (c. 1330–1400) Franco Sacchetti was born to a noble Florentine Guelf family, perhaps in Ragusa, where his father did business. Sacchetti spent many years as a merchant. By 1352, he was also composing traditional love poems. In 1354, he married Felice di Nicolò Strozzi. In honor of the Strozzi women, he composed, probably shortly before his marriage, *The Battle of Women*, consisting of 272 mediocre octaves describing the victory of young, beautiful, virtuous ladies over old, ugly, vice-ridden hags. In the early 1360s, during the war between Florence and Pisa, Sacchetti began to be involved in the city's politics and as an administrator of Florentine territories. In 1376 he was sent as ambassador to Bologna; in 1383, when he married for the second time, he was a member of the *otto di balia*; in 1384 he became a prior for the San Giovanni area; during the wars with the Visconti in 1388–1392, he served as counselor to the Florentine government; and throughout the late 1380s and the 1390s he was governor over a series of Florentine territories outside the city.

The 1370s brought a series of sorrows, both personal and public. Sacchetti was in Florence during the plague of 1374. That year and the next saw the deaths of Petrarch and Boccaccio, whom he lamented in sonnets expressing his admiration and sense of loss. Two years later, his first wife died, mourned affectionately in his verse. Meanwhile Florence was threatened by the expansionism of the Milanese and by papal agents who sought to restrict Florentine trade routes across papal territories. To fend off the latter, Sacchetti became involved in the "war of the eight saints" (1375), but hard times and high wartime taxes contributed to the revolt of the *ciompi* (1378). Some of Sacchetti's poems express his views on current political events. "The world is full of false prophets," begins one; another starts, "Wherever virtue is lacking, there all worldly power must soon fail and come to a painful end"; and one ends, "Tell the pope, where he is awaited, that all the limbs fare ill when the head is obstinate in evil."

At the same time, Sacchetti was composing song lyrics, combining a popular immediacy of content with a technical interest in various forms for music. One *cactia* describes how girls, gathering flowers and mushrooms in the woods, are scattered by a thunderstorm while the poet, watching them entranced, gets soaked by the rain. "Blessed be the summertime," begins another song. In 1389, during a moment when tension had relaxed, he took part in the garden conversations and entertainments described in *Il paradiso degli Alberti*. He married for a third time in 1396.

During his later years, Sacchetti began to write in prose. His unfinished *Commentary on the New Testament*, perhaps written in 1381, seeks to apply the evangelists' words to problems and issues of daily life. The use of contemporary moral examples in his biblical commentary led to his writing the *Trecentonovelle* (*Three Hundred Stories*, 1385–1397), accounts of recent events or jokes, unframed but surrounded by personal and moral reflections. The work includes serious issues, despite the frequent stories about pranks and witticisms. Although Sacchetti refers to himself in the preface as "unschooled," his life experiences had made him sensitive to the importance of peace and to the prevalence of injustice. A number of *novelle* comment on how degenerate nobles live by plunder taken from the less fortunate and get away with crimes while the poor, persecuted for minor offenses, have no recourse against the rich and powerful. On the other hand, Sacchetti opposed the presumption of ignorant folk, and several tales present Giotto or Dante wittily putting down ambitious fools. With a clear eye for details of food, dress, and behavior, and with a conversational style, Sacchetti delightfully captured aspects of contemporary life: the difficulty of enforcing dress codes, a chase after a runaway pig, a quarrel between husband and wife, the embarrassment of a youth who trips and falls while eyeing girls, a wet soldier's refuge from his own bare hovel in the warm and well-stocked kitchen of a neighboring ecclesiast. This period also saw the composition of some moral and political *canzoni*, with pleas for peace and moderation. Sacchetti himself collected his poetry over the years into one volume, of which the autograph is preserved in the Laurentian Library in Florence. He compiled his collection of tales in the 1380s and 1390s. Of the 300 stories, 223 survived, a few with gaps or in fragments. Besides these writings, we have sixteen of his letters and a notebook, never intended for publication.

Sachetti died at San Miniato, where he was governor. His tales went unappreciated by the humanists of the following century, but two sixteenth-century manuscripts survived. The first printed edition of a selection of tales appeared in 1724.

See also **Boccaccio, Giovanni**

Further Reading

Editions and Translation

La Battaglia delle belle donne, le Lettere, le Sposizioni di Vangeli, ed. Alberto Chiari. Bari: Laterza, 1938.

Il libro delle rime, ed. Alberto Chiari. Bari: Laterza, 1936.

Opere, ed. Aldo Borlenghi. Milan: Rizzoli, 1957. (*Trecentonovelle, Sposizioni di Vangeli, Libro delle rime, Lettere.*)

Tales from Sacchetti, trans. Mary Steegman. London: Dent, 1908. (Eighty-three prudishly selected tales.)

Trecentonovelle, ed. Vincenzo Pernicone. Florence: Sansoni, 1946.

Il Trecentonovelle, ed. Antonio Lanza. Florence: Sansoni, 1984.

Critical Studies

Barbi, Michele. "Per una nuova edizione delle *Novelle* del Sacchetti." *Studi di Filologia Italiana*, 1, 1927, pp. 87–131.

Caretti, Lanfranco. *Saggio sul Sacchetti*. Bari: Laterza, 1951.

Croce, Benedetto. *Poesia popolare e poesia d'arte*. Bari: Laterza, 1933, pp. 94–105.

Curato, Baldo. *Lettura del Sacchetti*. Cremona: Gianni Mangiarotti, 1966.

Francia, Letterio di. *Franco Sacchetti, novelliere*. Pisa: Tipografia Successori Fratelli Nistri, 1902.

——. *Novellistica*. Milan: Vallardi, 1924, pp. 260–300.

Li Gotti, Ettore. *Franco Sacchetti, uomo "discolo e grosso."* Florence: Sansoni, 1940.

Li Gotti, Ettore, and Nino Pirrotta. *Il Sacchetti e la tecnica musicale del Trecento italiano*. Florence: Sansoni, 1935.

Pernicone, Vincenzo. *Fra. rime e novelle del Sacchetti*. Florence: Sansoni, 1942.

Wilkins, Ernest Hatch. *A History of Italian Literature*, rev. ed., ed. Thomas G. Bergin. Cambridge, Mass.: Harvard University Press, 1974, 117–119.

JANET LEVARIE SMARR

SÆMUNDR SIGFÚSSON INN FRÓÐI
("the learned"; 1056–1133) To his contemporaries, Sæmundr was known as a preeminent churchman and a man of great learning. To modern scholarship, he is known primarily as a founding father of historical writing in Iceland, and of the great dynasty of the Oddaverjar ("men of Oddi"). At various points in the intervening centuries, folklore accused him of sorcery, while scholarly speculation credited him with the *Eddas* and with sagas ranging from *Njáls saga* to *Jómsvíkinga saga*.

"Sæmundr (prestr) inn fróði" is mentioned several times in the *biskupa sögur* (especially *Hungrvaka*, *Kristni saga*, and the sagas of Jón Qmundarson), *Íslendingabók*, annals, genealogies, and in other historical writings. But there is no coherent medieval account of his life, and virtually nothing by him survives in writing, so that much remains unknown.

Sæmundr, the son of a priest, was born into a distinguished family that had lived at Oddi, South Iceland, since about 900. He studied for some years in "Frakkland." The *Oddaverja annáll* for 1077 specifies Paris, but this may be no more than a surmise, as is the suggestion by modern scholars that Sæmundr attended the cathedral school of Notre Dame in Paris. An entertaining account of his return to Iceland in Gunnlaugr Leifesson's *Jóns saga helga* (early 13th century) tells how Jón and Sæmundr outwitted the master astrologer who held Sæmundr in his power. This legend seems to contain the germ of later folktales in which Sæmundr, learned in the black art, uses his cleverness to foil the Devil.

After his return to Iceland in or after 1076, Sæmundr was ordained priest and became a "pillar of the church," building a new church at Oddi dedicated to St. Nicholas, increasing its endowments and clergy, and preaching and dispensing wise counsel in the neighborhood. He probably also had a school there, for he is said in *Sturlu saga* (ch. 1) to have fostered Oddi Þorgilsson, who, like Sæmundr himself, became *fróðr*, "learned (especially in native lore)." Of still greater national importance was Sæmundr's part, with the bishops, in establishing tithe laws (1096) and other ecclesiastical laws.

Little else is known of Sæmundr's life or activities as priest and secular chieftain, because the records are slight and the times relatively uneventful. However, it is known that he and his two brothers married the three daughters of Kolbeinn Flosason. With his wife, Guðrún, he had three sons and a daughter, and their descendants, who came to be known as the Oddaverjar, in many senses built on the foundations laid by Sæmundr at Oddi. Their power and wealth, augmented especially by the tithes and other revenues paid to family-owned churches, overtook those of other chieftainly families during the time of Sæmundr's distinguished grandson Jón Loptsson (1124–1197), and were maintained throughout the following decades without the viciousness found elsewhere. The intellectual tradition of Oddi also flourished. Sæmundr's son, the priest Eyjólfr, had a school there attended by the future St. Þorlákr; Jón Loptsson fostered and educated Snorri Sturluson there. Jón's son, the bishop Páll, compiled a miracle book of St. Þorlákr, and is himself the subject of one of the *biskupa sögur*. The poem *Nóregs konunga tal* was composed around 1190 to celebrate Jón Loptsson's descent through his mother from the Norwegian kings; other works, notably *Orkneyinga saga* and *Skjǫldunga saga*, may have links with Oddi.

Sæmundr is frequently named as an authority by medieval Icelandic historians, and these references provide the main clues about his learning and its transmission. That he composed a work, now lost, on the rulers of Norway from Haraldr hárfagri ("fair-hair") in the late 9th century down to Magnús góði ("the good," d. 1046/7) is suggested by *Nóregs konunga tal* (st. 40), which acknowledges Sæmundr inn fróði as its model for the lives (*ævi*) of these eleven rulers. The scraps of information attributed to Sæmundr elsewhere, however, especially concern the late 10th century: the length of Hákon jarl's reign (in Oddr Snorrason's *Óláfs saga Tryggvasonar*); the number of ships in the Jómsviking fleet at Hjörungavágr (Liavåg) (in AM 510 4to, a late MS of *Jómsvikinga saga*); details of Óláfr Tryggvason's christianization of Norway (in a fifty-word quotation from Sæmundr in Oddr Snorrason's saga); and the date of his death (in Ari Þorgilsson's *Íslendingabók*). Sæmundr is also named in certain versions of the Icelandic annals as authority for the icebound Scandinavian winter of 1047. It seems from all this evidence, and from the example of the near-contemporary *Íslendingabók*, that Sæmundr's legacy to later historiography must have been a chronological scheme, with brief narratives on each ruler, in a sober style but with Christian bias.

Sæmundr's presumed history was probably written rather than oral, especially since the long quotation from Sæmundr in Oddr Snorrason's saga (which survives only in Icelandic versions of a Latin original) is followed by "Svá hefir Sæmundr ritað um Óláf konung í sinni bók" ("Thus has Sæmundr written about King Óláfr in his book"). Storm (1873: 15) and Meissner (1902: 35ff.) nevertheless disputed that there was a written work by Sæmundr. The language seems to have been Latin, for Snorri Sturluson, in his prologue to *Óláfs saga helga* and *Heimskringla*, refers to Ari Þorgilsson as the first writer of history in Norse, although Sæmundr, an older contemporary whom Ari consulted over the writing of *Íslendingabók*, probably completed his history first. The nature of Sæmundr's writing and its influence on other histories of Norway, such as *Fagrskinna*, *Ágrip*, *Historia Norwegiae*, and even on *Knýtlinga saga*, have been much discussed by scholars such as Bjarni Aðalbjarnarson, Siegfried Beyschlag, Svend Ellehøj, and Bjarni Guðnason (see the summary in Andersson 1985).

Sæmundr is also acknowledged as an authority for certain facts about Iceland, including its discovery by the Viking Naddoddr (*Landnámabók*, *Sturlubók* text), but whether such matters were included in the history of Norwegian kings, whether there was a separate work on Iceland, and whether some of Sæmundr's more fragmentary pieces of learning were at first only transmitted orally cannot now be established. The "oral" theory is supported by the report in *Kristni saga*, that "in that year [1118–1119], there was such great loss of life, that the priest Sæmundr the learned said [*sagði*] at the *þing* that no fewer must have died of sickness than had come to the *þing*." It is also possible that Sæmundr simply became a model of learning, to whom miscellaneous facts could be attached. This tendency could apply to such patently clerical facts as the details about the creation of the sun and the moon (in AM 624 4to) or the body of Adam (in AM 764 4to).

The title *Sæmundar Edda* appeared on editions of the *Codex Regius* poems of the *Poetic Edda* until well into this century, and this attribution goes back to 16th- and 17th-century theories that credited Sæmundr first with the *Prose Edda* (now attributed to Snorri) and then with the *Codex Regius* poems. The connection may not be completely unfounded, for it is possible, as Halldór Hermannsson (1932) argued, that Snorri found the poetic materials for his *Edda* at Oddi, and that Sæmundr had a hand in collecting them.

See also **Snorri Sturluson**

Further Reading

Literature

Storm, Gustav. *Snorre SturlassMns Historieskrivning.* Copenhagen: Luno, 1873.

Meissner, Rudolf. *Die Strengleikar: Ein Beitrag zur Geschichte der almordischen Prosalitteratur.* Halle: Niemeyer, 1902.

Halldór Hermannsson. *Sæmund Sigfússon and the Oddaverjar.* Islandica, 22. Ithaca: Cornell University Library, 1932.

Buckhurst, Helen T. McM. "Sæmundr inn fróði in Icelandic Folklore." *Saga-Book of the Viking Society* 11 (1928–36), 84–92.

Einar Ól. Sveinsson. *Sagnaritun Oddaverja. Nokkrar athuganir.* Studia Islandica, 1. Reykjavik: Ísafold, 1937 [English summary, pp. 47–51].

Turville-Petre, G. *Origins of Icelandic Literature.* Oxford: Oxford University Press, 1953 rpt. 1975 [esp. pp. 81–7].

Andersson, Theodore M. "Kings' Sagas (*Konungasögur*)." In *Old Norse–Icelandic Literature: A Critical Guide.* Ed. Carol J. Clover and John Lindow. Islandica, 45. Ithaca and London: Cornell University Press, 1985 [esp. pp. 197–211].

DIANA EDWARDS WHALEY

SALADIN (SALĀH AL-DĪN YŪKSUF B. AYYŪB) (a.h. 564–589 / 1138–1193 c.e.) Sultan of Egypt and Syria, Saladin led military ventures that won back for Islam much of the territory in the Holy Land occupied by Western crusaders. Saladin was born at Tekrit into a Kurdish family in service to 'Imād-al-Dīn Zangī of Mosul; Saladin served 'Imād-al-Dīn's son, Nūr al-Dīn Emir of Syria. At this time, political and moral authority was divided between, the Fātimid caliphate of Cairo and the Abbasid caliphate of Baghdad; regions and cities were held by independent warlords, and wide divisions separated the general population from the military men who wielded power. The crusader states, with their small populations, represented an additional irritating complication, a potential if not an actual threat.

After serving for ten years in Nūr al-Dīn's court at Damascus, Saladin accompanied his uncle Shīrkūh to Egypt on an expedition, during which Shīrkūh seized effective power in Cairo in 1169; Shīrkūh died almost immediately, and Saladin succeeded him in command. He played a dual role as Fātimid vizier and as Nūr al-Dīn's subordinate until the caliph's death in 1171 and Nūr al-Dīn's in 1174. Saladin proclaimed himself sultan of Egypt, with authority over Mesopotamia, and initiated the Ayyūbid dynasty. Part of the rest of his career was spent in a power struggle with the Zangids, in the course of which he successfully established his power in Syria, where he took Damascus and later Aleppo with the aid of his brother Tūrānshāh. He failed, however, to subdue the city of Mosul completely, or to win unqualified approval from the Abbasid caliphs.

Saladin represented himself as the champion of Islam against the crusaders, a role whose potentialities had been developed by Nūr al-Dīn, and his intermittent campaigns against the crusader states culminated in the battle of Hattin (near Tiberias) in 1187, in which he destroyed the field army of the Latin Kingdom of Jerusalem; he went on to capture Jerusalem and take most of the crusader strongholds. Tyre, however, provided the crusaders with a base, and Saladin's victories prompted the calling of the Third Crusade in 1189, during which the western armies were able only to capture Acre. Although the engagements between

Cristofano dell' Altissimo (c. 1525–1605). Portrait of Saladin, Sultan of Egypt. © SEF/ Art Resource, New York.

Christian and Muslim forces were to a degree politically indecisive, they greatly influenced cultural life in the West owing to the famous encounter between England's King Richard the Lionheart (r. 1189–1199) and Saladin. The sultan's ensuing reputation for generosity and chivalry earned him a place of honor in medieval romance, and even Dante located his soul in Limbo. The crusaders were not strong enough to recapture Jerusalem but neither could Saladin clear them from the coast. This stalemate led to a truce in 1192, the Peace of Ramleh [Ramla], shortly after which Saladin died.

During the late 1100s, trade was an important source of revenue, which Saladin needed for his military campaigns. The armament industry and the slave trade flourished, and anecdotal evidence indicates that trade routes remained open even while wars were being fought nearby, and that huge profits could be made from military supplies (although risks of loss were also high). During the Third Crusade (1189–1192) there was considerable interference with Mediterranean shipping, but Saladin enjoyed the benefits of an open trade route between Egypt and India (via the Red Sea, thanks to the extension of his control over Yemen).

Saladin unquestionably changed the pattern of Middle Eastern history, not so much because he established his own dynasty (the Ayyūbids were short-lived) but, immediately, because he gave the coup-de-grâce to the ailing Fāṭimid dynasty. He also made Europe aware that retaining crusader states would involve enormous effort and expense. As a corollary to this, he demonstrated the increasing importance of an efficient, if expensive, professional army, which later contributed to the refinement of the Mamluk system; this, arguably, led to a profound change in the economic and social resources of Egypt and Syria.

See also **Dante Alighieri; Richard I**

Further Reading

Ehrenkreutz, Andrew S. *Saladin*. Albany: State U of New York P, 1972.
Gibb, H.A.R. *The Life of Saladin: From the Works of Imad ad-Din and Baha ad-Din*. Oxford: Clarendon, 1973.
Lyons, Malcolm Cameron, and D.E.P. Jackson. *Saladin: The Politics of the Holy War*. Cambridge and New York: Cambridge UP, 1997.

MALCOLM C. LYONS

SALIMBENE DE ADAM (1221–C. 1289) What we know of Fra Salimbene de Adam of Parma is based entirely on the *Chronicle*, his only extant work. In it Salimbene tells us that he was born to Guido de Adam and Inmelda de Cassio, members of two well-established families in Parma. He was christened Balian of Sidon but was simply called Ognibene by his family. In 1238 he entered the Franciscan order and was given the name Salimbene by the last friar Saint Francis had admitted to the order. During his novitiate, Salimbene met Bernard of Quintavalle, the first friar Saint Francis had admitted to the order; and Elias of Cortona, the order's first minister general.

After completing his novitiate at Fano, Salimbene went to a convent in Lucca where he studied music and first saw the Holy Roman emperor Frederick II. From there he moved to Siena, where he continued his study of music and came into contact with the theories of Joachim of Fiore through the work of Hugo of Digne. From 1243 to 1247 Salimbene was in Pisa, where his education in Joachism continued under Rudolf of Saxony. Salimbene's acquaintance with some of the most distinguished people of his rime continued during his trips to France in 1247–1248. At Provins he met the Joachist Gerard of Borgo San Donnino. At Villefranche and at Sens he met Giovanni di Piano Carpini, the Franciscan provincial general of Germany and Spain, who had been an emissary for

Pope Innocent IV at the court of the khan Guyuk at Karakoram in Mongolia. At Hyères Salimbene heard the lectures of Hugo of Digne, and at Auxerre he met Saint Louis of France. In 1248 he was ordained a priest at Genoa; later he was sent to Ferrara, where he remained for seven years. He probably spent the years 1279–1285 in Reggio Emilia and its province, where, in 1283, he began working on the *Chronicle*. In 1287 he moved to Montefalcone, where he died shortly after 1288.

Despite his close contact with several of the leading thinkers of his time, and despite the opportunities to study at several of the most important universities of his day (he spent a week studying at the University in Paris but left without the permission of his superiors), Salimbene's intellectual background is regarded by scholars as superficial. His knowledge of the Bible was thorough, as is shown by his extensive use of biblical quotations throughout the *Chronicle*; but as scholars have indicated, these quotations are used to support statements which often have little if anything to do with the Bible. Scholars concur that even when Salimbene discusses issues about which he was knowledgeable (such as the prophesies of Joachim of Fiore and the relative merits and shortcomings of Elias of Cortona), he is often subjective and biased.

Salimbene's numerous acquaintances and travels provided him with plenty of material for his *Chronicle*. Besides narrating famous and less-known events in Italy and France, the *Chronicle* also narrates personal moments in Salimbene's life and that of his family. The *Chronicle* is regarded by scholars as historically accurate for the most part, but its importance is not purely historical. As Baird (1986) has shown, it is the earliest account of the spread of Joachism within the Franciscan order, as well as an important document of Franciscan life in the thirteenth century and the extent to which the Franciscan order had deviated from Saint Francis's original rule. Salimbene does not hesitate

to reveal his own worldly interests while narrating the worldliness of his age. His narrative, however, also includes *exempla* of spiritual piety; as seen in his characterizations of Saint Louis of France, John of Parma (minister general of the Franciscan order), and even himself (Salimbene's visions of the holy family are narrated in great detail). In fact his extensive use of *exempla* gives the *Chronicle* a narrative style that anticipates Boccaccio's *Decameron*. The *exempla* are an integral part of the *Chronicle* and are used not only to illustrate a moral but also to produce comic effects. Moreover, these *exempla* are rich in detail making the characterizations both vivid and realistic (Auerbach 1957).

In addition to vivid portraits of well-known and lesser-known people of his time, Salimbene himself often appears in the *Chronicle*, giving the work an autobiographical dimension. He comes across as having a great interest in worldly matters, and (as Baird notes) he often expresses contempt for qualities he himself is guilty of, indicating a contradictory or ambiguous personality. Nevertheless, Salimbene's candid and uninhibited nature suggests that he is true to himself throughout the *Chronicle*, even when his evaluation of others (e.g., Elias of Cortona) is not as truthful.

The *Chronicle* has come down to us in a single manuscript: (Vatican Latin 7260) of which the first 277 folios are missing. The manuscript, written by Salimbene himself, narrates events from 1168 to 1287. The years 1168–1212 are based on Sicardo of Cremona's *Chronicle*; and the historic events occurring from 1212 to 1283 (the year Salimbene began writing the work) seem to have much in common with two chronicles attributed to Albert Milioli: *Liber de temporibus* and *Cronica imperatorm*. Not until the twentieth century did Salimbene's *Chronicle* receive the scholarly and critical attention it deserves.

See also **Frederick II; Giovanni di Piano Carpini; Joachim of Fiore**

Further Reading

Editions and Translation

The Chronicle of Salimbene de Adam, trans. Joseph L. Baird, Giuseppe Baglívi, and John Robert Kane. Medieval and Renaissance Texts and Studies, 40. Binghamton, N.Y.: Medieval and Renaissance Texts and Studies, 1986. (With bibliography.)

Cronica Fratris Salimbene de Adam, 2 vols., ed. Ferdinando Bernini Scrittori d'Italia, 187–188. Bari: Laterza, 1942.

Salimbene de Adam. Cronica, 2 vols., ed. Giuseppe Scalia. Scrittorl d'Italia, 232–233. Bari: Laterza, 1966.

Critical Studies

Auerbach, Erich. Mimesis. New York: Doubleday, 1957, pp. 187–188.

Auzzas, Ginetta. "Salimbene da Parma." In Dizionario critico della letteratura italiana, 3 vols. Turin: UTET, 1973, Vol. 3, pp. 293–294.

Carile, Antonio. Salimbene e la sua opera storiografica: Delle lezioni tenute alla. Facoltà di Magistero dell'Università di Bologna nell'anno accademico 1970–1971. Bologna: Pàtron, 1971.

Coulton, George Gordon. From Saint Francis to Dante. New York: Russell and Russell, 1968.

Crocco, Antonio. Federico II nella Cronica di Salimbene. Naples: Empireo, 1970.

D'Alatri, Mariano, and Jacques Paul. Salimbene da Parma: Testimone e cronista. Rome: Istituto Storico dei Cappuccini, 1992.

Sainati, Augusto. Studi di letteratura latina medievale e umanistica: Raccolti in occasione del suo ottantacinquesimo compleanno. Padua: Antenore, 1972.

Violante, Cinzio. La cortesia chiericale e borghese nel Duecento. Florence: Olschki, 1995.

STEVEN GROSSVOGEL

SALUTATI, COLUCCIO (1331–1406)

Coluccio Salutati was born at Stignano, on the frontier between Ghibelline Lucca and Guelf Florence, and was carried into exile when the Ghibellines seized power in the area shortly after his birth. He was raised and educated at Bologna, where he studied under Pietro da Moglio, a member of the third generation of Italian humanists. Salutati was trained as notary and in 1350–1351, after his father's death, he returned to Stignano with his family and began practicing his profession. Between 1351 and 1367 Salutati earned his living as a notary, but by 1356 he was already playing a major political role in the rural commune of Buggiano, of which Stignano formed one of four villages. He married a local woman, Caterina di Tomeo di Balducci, in 1366. In 1367 he moved to Todi to become its chancellor; in 1368 he moved to Rome, where he worked in the papal chancery under Francesco Bruni. After being unable to find suitable employment with the papacy, Salutati became chancellor of Lucca with Bruni's help in 1370. Almost immediately, however, he became embroiled in a factional dispute, and in 1371 he lost his position and reluctantly returned to Stignano. He had lost his first wife while he was still in Lucca; sometime between 1372 and 1374, widowed with a small boy, he married Piera, the daughter of Simone Riccomi. He and Piera had at least eight children.

Salutati was called to Florence in 1374 to assume the newly created secretaryship of the tratte, the office supervising elections to Florentine offices; in 1375 he became chancellor. As the official responsible for conducting the Florentine government's correspondence with the provinces and with foreign powers, he almost immediately established his reputation as the greatest author of official letters in western Europe. He was able to demonstrate his virtuosity immediately, because 1375 marked the beginning of a three-year war between Florence and the papacy, a war whose major battles were propaganda campaigns designed to retain and attract allies. Perhaps his greatest epistolary triumphs came in 1390–1406, when he assumed responsibility for representing to western European powers the issues involved in Florence's bitter struggle with the Visconti of Milan. Florence's archenemy, Gian Galeazzo Visconti, is said to have stated that "a letter of Salutati's was worth a troop of horses." Having been chancellor for thirty-one years, during which time he navigated the troubled waters of Florentine political life with unerring tact, Salutati died in 1406.

Salutati was influenced, after 1367, by Petrarch's concern with integrating Christianity and pagan letters, but he never achieved the mature Petrarch's confidence in their harmoniousness. Salutati, who is less classicizing in style than Petrarch and more obviously intrigued by scholastic philosophy and theology, betrays, the weak welds in Christian humanism. Although he was a family man and a devout Florentine patriot, his *De seculo et religione* (1381), praising the superiority of the monastic life, represented a genuine ascetic element in his thought. His last private letters unambiguously affirm his allegiance to Christian truth over and against pagan culture. Nonetheless, up to the last year of his life his devotion to ancient literature remained strong. Under his influence, Florence brought the great Greek scholar Manuel Chrysoloras from Constantinople in 1397 to teach Greek at the university. Whereas a previous attempt in 1360–1362, with Leonzio Pilato, had failed to arouse the interest of the city's young people, the arrival of Chrysoloras marked the rebirth of Greek studies in western Europe.

Salutati made Florence the capital of this major movement in European cultural and intellectual life through his prestige as chancellor; the fame of his public letters; his eagerness to relate classical studies to moral and religious problems of his day; his effort to encompass within a continuous tradition the ancient Latin authors, the church fathers, and the medieval rhetoricians; and his successful introduction of Hellenic studies into the Latin west. That Florence was the center of humanistic studies down to the mid-fifteenth century testifies enduring intellectual legacy.

See also **Petrarca, Francesco**

Further Reading

Epistolario di Coluccio Salutati, ed. Francesco Novati. Fonti per la Storia d'Italia, 15–18. Rome. 1891–1916.

Ullman, Berthold L. *The Humanisum of Coluccio Salutati*. Medioevo e Umanesimo, 4 Padua: Antenore, 1983.

Witt, Ronald G. *Hercules at the Crossroads: The Life, Works, and Thought of Coluccio Salutati*. Durham, N.C.: Duke University Press, 1983.

RONALD G. WITT

SANCHO III, KING OF NAVARRE (r. 1000–1035) The reign of Sancho III Garcés, known as "el Mayor" (1000–1035) was a pivotal one, not only for Navarre but for all of Christian Spain. Possessed with prodigious political talents, he brought his small kingdom of Navarre to its apogee in the Middle Ages. Because the decline of Muslim influence in the region left him relatively free to focus his attentions elsewhere, he made no serious efforts to continue the Reconquest. Instead, he set about unifying all the Christian states except Castile under his rule. His cultural and political influences were French, and by his outlook and his actions he helped draw Spain out of its isolation and incorporate it into the rest of Western Christendom.

His inheritance was small—little more than a string of tiny counties in the foothills of the Pyrenees—but by skillful manipulation of marriage alliances, Sancho was able to widen his domains by acquiring adjacent territories. An important factor in his success was the marriage of his sister Urraca to King Alfonso V of León. Through Urraca, Sancho III continued to be a real power in that kingdom even after Alfonso's death. While Urraca served as regent for her son, Vermudo, Sancho gained control of Aragón and the old Marches counties of Sobrarbe and Ribagorza to the east of Aragón.

From his base in León, Sancho extended his influence to Castillian affairs through his brother-in-law García Sanchez, the count of Castile. When García Sanchez was murdered in 1029, Sancho took possession of Castile in his sister's name and designated his own son, Fernando, as heir. The Navarrese dynasty was firmly established in Castile in 1032 when Fernando married his first cousin Sancha, sister of Vermudo III, whose dowry brought to Navarre the disputed lands between the Cea and Pisguerga rivers.

Not all of Sancho's attempts to bring the Pyrenean states under Navarrese hegemony were so fruitful. By holding out the prospect of a military alliance against the Muslims in the central Ebro basin, he forced the count of Barcelona, Ramón Berenguer I (1018–1035), to become his vassal, although neither party would benefit much from this coalition. He tried to press his rights to succession in the duchy of Gascony, but his attempt to link the two Basque-speaking regions under one banner ultimately failed.

His political strength remained in Spain, however, and the high point of his career took place in 1034 when he occupied of the city of León, unseating his nephew Vermudo. Finally, possessing a political authority that encompassed Navarre, León, Aragón, and Castile, he styled himself Emperor of Hispania ("rex Dei gratia Hispaniarum") and coined money in affirmation of his new imperial dignity, thereby laying claim to a peninsular supremacy that had previously been attributed to the king of León.

His imperial career was short-lived, however. He died suddenly the next year, and Vermudo III regained León, ruling it until 1037. Although he governed a unified kingdom, Sancho's adherence to the patrimonial concept of kingship, as was the custom in France, which declared royal domains heritable and divisible among his heirs, made any permanent union of these states impossible. In his will Sancho stipulated that his several realms be divided among his sons, all of whom eventually bore the title of king: Navarre was granted to García III Sánchez (1035–1054); Castile, to Fernando I (1035–1065); and Aragon, to Ramiro I (1035–1063). As a result, the new frontier kingdoms of Castile and Aragón attained the status of kingdoms, and ultimately would overshadow Navarre and León.

His permanent influence on medieval Spanish culture extended far beyond territorial expansion and royal inheritances, however. During his reign, feudal concepts of law and landholding current in France penetrated into the peninsula. Under his aegis, Romanesque artistic styles, especially in architecture, became well established in Spain. He encouraged the pilgrimage to Santiago de Compostela, a principle vehicle for transmission of French ideas. For the convenience of the pilgrims, he modified and improved the difficult route through Álava and the Cantabrian Mountains. And during his reign Cluniac reform was introduced into the monasteries of Oña, Lerie, and San Juan de la Peña.

See also **Alfonso V, King of Aragón, The Magnanimous; Ramón Berenguer IV, Count of Barcelona**

Further Reading

Lacarra, J. M. *Historia del reino de Navarra en la Edad Media*. Pamplona, 1975.
O'Callaghan, J. F. *A History of Medieval Spain*. Ithaca, N.Y., 1975.
Pérez de Urbel, J. *Sancho el Mayor de Navarra*. Madrid, 1950.

THERESA EARENFIGHT

SANCHO IV, KING OF CASTILE

(1258–1295) Sancho IV, the second son of Alfonso X and Queen Violante, was born on 12 May 1258 in Valladolid. His sobriquet, "el Bravo," referred to his strength of will and determination. After the sudden death of his older brother Fernando de la Cerda in 1275, Sancho, rejecting the claims of his nephew,

Alfonso de la Cerda, and demanded recognition as heir to the throne. Although Alfonso X acknowledged him, continual pressure from France and the papacy led the king to propose giving a portion of his dominions to his grandsons, Alfonso and Fernando, known collectively as the Infantes de la Cerda. Breaking with his father, Sancho, with the consent of the estates of the realm assembled at Valladolid in 1282, assumed royal authority, though he did not take the crown. A desultory civil war followed until the death of Alfonso X on 4 April 1284. Unreconciled and disinherited by his father, Sancho IV, nevertheless, was acclaimed as king and crowned at Toledo.

His situation was exceedingly precarious. Not only did Alfonso de la Cerda, supported by France, dispute his claim to the throne, but the pope had excommunicated Sancho and placed an interdict on his kingdom. The pope also denied the legitimacy of his marriage to his cousin, María de Molina; thus, their children would be considered illegitimate and lack any claim to inherit the throne. By challenging his father and by making many promises that he was unable to carry out, Sancho IV also weakened the authority of the crown.

Throughout his reign he was engaged in an intense struggle to gain control of the straits of Gibraltar in order to prevent any Moroccan invasion in the future. Immediately after his accession he had to provide for the defense of the southern frontier against a new challenge by Abū Yūsuf, the Merinid emir, Alfonso X's last ally. Landing at Tarifa in April 1285, he besieged Jerez while his troops devastated a broad zone from Medina Sidonia to Carmona, Écija, and Seville. While Sancho IV sent his Genoese admiral, Benedetto Zaccaria, to protect the mouth of the Guadalquivir, a Castilian fleet of about one hundred ships waited in the straits to relieve Jerez or to disrupt the emir's communications with Morocco. When Sancho IV marched southward from

Seville to Jerez, Abk Yksuf decided not to test his fortunes in battle, and retreated to the safety of Algeciras in August. Two months later Sancho IV made peace with the emir.

Meanwhile, after the failure of the French crusade against Aragón, Sancho IV, because of continuing concern over the claims of Alfonso de la Cerda, was under pressure to enter an alliance with either kingdom. On the one hand, Philippe IV of France was Alfonso's cousin while Alfonso III of Aragón had custody of the two Infantes de la Cerda. Lope Díaz de Haro, lord of Vizcaya, who had much to do with securing Sancho IV's recognition as heir to the Castilian throne, preferred the alliance with Aragón as a guarantee that Alfonso de la Cerda would not be free to press his claims. Lope was the most influential person in the realm because the king had given him control over the royal household and finances as well as custody of all royal strongholds. Other members of the royal council eventually convinced Sancho IV that he had entrusted Lope with far too much authority. Thus the king turned against him in 1288 and caused his death in a violent scene.

Now free to decide for himself, Sancho IV broke with Aragón and allied with France. He expected that the continual threat of French intervention on behalf of the Infantes de la Cerda and papal opposition to the legitimation of his marriage and his children would be eliminated. He also promised to give the Infantes joint rule over Murcia and Ciudad Real as an independent realm, provided they renounced all claims to Castile. At that, Alfonso III of Aragón liberated the Infantes and proclaimed Alfonso de la Cerda as king of Castile. Inconclusive border warfare followed until 1291, when the new king of Aragón, Jaime II, concerned about his capacity to retain the kingdom of Sicily against papal opposition, decided to make peace. Jaime II left the Infantes de la Cerda to fend for themselves and agreed with Sancho IV on zones of future exploitation and conquest in North Africa.

The conclusion of this treaty came at an opportune moment because the Merinids were preparing to resume hostilities as soon as the truce with Castile ran out. Although Benedetto Zaccaria, again in Castilian service, defeated the Moroccan fleet in August 1291, Abū Ya'qūb, the Merinid emir, invaded Spain soon after. In the spring of 1292, Sancho IV, aided by Muḥammad II of Granada (who feared the Merinids), besieged Tarifa, a port often used by Moroccan forces entering Spain. Sancho IV entered the town in triumph on 13 October 1292. The king of Granada, who had expected that Tarifa would be restored to him, now broke with Castile and joined the Moroccans in a new siege of Tarifa in 1294. Nevertheless, Alfonso Pérez de Guzmán, known thereafter as "el bueno," successfully defended Tarifa until a Castilian and Catalan fleet compelled the enemy to withdraw. The capture and subsequent defense of Tarifa was the first stage in closing the gates of the peninsula to future Moroccan invasions.

Not long after Sancho IV died on 25 April 1295, his wife María de Molina, whom he married at Toledo in July 1282, became regent for their son, Fernando IV. Sancho wrote a book of counsel titled *Castigos e documentos* for Fernando.

See also **Alfonso X, El Sabio, King of Castile and León; Molina, María de; Philip IV the Fair**

Further Reading

Gaibrois de Ballesteros, M. *Historia del reinado de Sancho IV.* 3 vols. Madrid, 1922.

JOSEPH F. O'CALLAGHAN

SAXO GRAMMATICUS (13th century) Toward the end of the 12th century, the Danish historian Sven Aggesen wrote that his old associate Saxo was composing a full-length history of the Danish kings of the previous century. Four MS fragments of this work (one, from Angers, probably autograph), a compendium of around 1345, and an edition printed at Paris in 1514 from a lost MS provide the surviving evidence for Saxo's achievement. It was printed under the title of *Danorum Regum Heroumque Historiæ* ("The History of the Kings and Heroes of the Danes"), but is usually known by the earlier description *Gesta Danorum* (alias *De Gestis Danorum*).

Saksi was not an uncommon name in medieval Denmark, and the historian cannot be identified for sure with any who bore it. *Grammaticus* "the learned" and *Longus* "the tall" are posthumous by-names. From his own words, we learn that he came from a warrior family, and that he joined the household of King Valdemar I's foremost adviser, Absalon, bishop of Roskilde (1158–1192) and archbishop of Lund (1178–1201), who encouraged him to write history. His partiality for Zealand suggests that he came from that island. He may have been educated abroad, and his familiarity with church business argues that he became a clerk of some sort, but probably not a monk. He was also familiar with war and seamanship. In Absalon's will, "my cleric Saxo" was forgiven a small debt, and required to send two borrowed books to the Cistercians of Sorø. Saxo completed his work under the patronage of Archbishop Anders (1201–1223), probably after 1216, and dedicated it to Anders and King Valdemar II.

During Saxo's lifetime, Denmark achieved dominance over the Baltic lands; Danes also came into closer contact with the intellectual life of the southern countries their ancestors had raided. Saxo aimed to provide them with a national history in Latin comparable to those of other European peoples. The only foreign historians he mentions are Bede, Dudo of St.-Quentin, and Paulus Diaconus; he was less influenced by them in his concept of the nation than by Vergil's *Aeneid*, and by the historical abridgments of the Roman authors Valerius Maximus and Justin. His view of morals and mythology owed much to Horace, Ovid, and Cicero; and the tone of his work coincides with the humanistic scholarship of the 12th century as expounded in the schools of northern France (e.g., by William of Conches and John of Salisbury), as well as with the contemporary epics of Galterus de Castellione (*Alexandreis*) and Geoffrey of Monmouth (*Historia regum Britanniae*).

Other Danish authors (e.g., the Roskilde Chronicler, the Lejre Chronicler, Sven Aggesen) had made pioneer attempts to record the Danish past in Latin, but Saxo found them inadequate. He had no use for the annalists of Lund, nor for conventional chronology, and the northern genealogists failed to provide him with enough kings. He claimed to be restoring lost native traditions and interpreting runic memorials, but these claims seem unfounded. He took most of his legendary and heroic material from wandering Icelanders and their MSS, relocating stories from their international repertoire within Denmark. He claimed that Archbishop Absalon's own words were his main source for modern history, but he must have used other written sources now lost. His debt to biblical ideas and language was small.

The work published in 1514 begins with a preface including a geographical description of the northern world, and is divided into sixteen books of unequal length. Books 1–4 deal with the Danes before the birth of Christ, 5–8 with the period down to the establishment of the Church in Denmark. Books 9–12 cover events from the Conversion to the promotion of Lund as a metropolitan see, and 13–16 run from 1104 to 1187.

The first eight books differ from the rest in the greater fluency of the prose and the inclusion of verse in a variety of meters. The basic subdivisions are the reigns of over seventy kings. Saxo begins with the election of the eponymous Dan as the first ruler, and the dethronement of the first two kings, Humblus and Lotherus, by unjust and justified violence. Then Skioldus and Hadingus appear as types of the heroism, luck, and virtue essential for effective kingship even in a pagan world. These kings, and Frotho I in Book 2, are names derived from Old Norse poetry and invested with attributes and episodes. With Kings Ro (Book 2) and Høtherus (Book 3), he made versions of the legends now found in the *Snorra Edda* and *Skjǫldunga saga's* epitome. Amlethus, the prototype of Hamlet, whose career appears in Books 3 and 4, was imported from an undiscovered source, and served as a type of cunning hero dogged by the unkindness of fate and human corruption, a pattern for both kings and tyrannicides. The rest of Book IV tells of the patriotic duelist Uffo, already celebrated by Sven Aggesen as vindicator of the Danish frontier, and known in Anglo-Saxon sources (e.g., *Widsith, Beowulf*, and the Mercian genealogy). The heathen gods, introduced in Book 1 as malign but fallible illusionists, enslave men's minds and lust for their daughters (Baldr and Nanna, Óðinn and Rinda, Book 3).

King Frotho III, an imaginary Danish Caesar contemporary with Christ, takes up Book 5. Helped by his witty companion Erik the Eloquent, he builds an empire over the northern world and civilizes it by enforcing two law codes. His story is enlivened by romance, adventure, and horror, but illustrates the power of words over weapons. In Book 6, this power is taken to excess, when the Danes elect the rustic poet Hiarno to rule them. This same power becomes beneficial and invigorating in the case of the degenerate Ingellus (see Ingjaldr of *Skjǫldunga saga*) and his dauntless and poetic champion Starcatherus, whose satire shamed the king into doing his duty and destroying his enemies. Stories of love, magic, and murder occupy the reign of Halfdanus in Book 7, which ends with the revival of the Danish empire under Haraldus Hyldetan, who is taught the secret of military success by Óðinn. The great fight of Bråvalla, in which Óðinn betrays Haraldus to his enemies, begins Book 8; and later on, Starkatherus contrives his own death after a poetic outburst on the duty of vengeance. Jarmericus (Ermanaric the Goth) then appears, as the victim of another treacherous counselor, and in the reign of Snio, famine drives the Lombards to emigrate from Denmark. In two voyages to the underworld, Danish adventurers witness the malign and morbid condition of the old gods and giants. The mighty King Gøtricus is prevented from overthrowing Charlemagne by assassination and Saxo's "Old Testament" ends with Viking heroism betrayed by the heathen gods, powerless against fate.

In Book 9, the supreme Viking Regnerus (Ragnarr loðbrók ["hairybreeches"]) achieves empire over the whole North, including the British Isles, only to die in Ella's snake pit as a punishment for persecuting the new faith accepted by his less successful rival Haraldus. His avenging sons fail to preserve his empire, and efforts to hold England by a succession of alternately Christian and pagan kings culminate with Gormo's marrying the English heiress Thyra. The English throne falls to their sons by inheritance, but Gormo dies of grief at the death of the elder. More tribulations afflict his successors Haraldus and Sveno in Book 10 (echoes here of Adam of Bremen and the *Roskilde Chronicle*), until both king and people accept the true faith, and Sveno's son Kanutus wins a Christian empire over the whole northern world, including England. He leaves a vigorous Church and a military law code to posterity, and after his son's death the Danes show their probity by accepting the Norwegian Magnús as king in observance of a sworn pact.

In these two books, written sources are distorted and augmented by Nordic legend: tales of Ragnarr, Ívarr, Gorm, the Jómsvikingar, and Palnatoki. From 11 onward, more Latin sources were available, and in 11 to 13 the reigns of Sven II and his five sons (1047–1134) are presented with an eye to earlier accounts, modified or rejected at will. Each ruler serves as an example of good or bad kingship according to his effectiveness against the Slavs and the unruly nobility and people of Denmark. Kings purge their own guilt by spectacular penances, and the people incur death and destruction for the slaying of King Knud (Cnut) the Saint (1086) and Knud (Cnut) Lavard (1131). Book 14 (four times as long as any other) covers the period of civil wars, conspiracy, and dissension among king, bishops, and nobles from 1134 to 1178, when Valdemar I and Absalon succeeded in conquering the Rugian Slavs and restoring unity to the kingdom. Book 15 covers Absalon's first years as archbishop of Lund (1178–1182) and the rebellion of the Scanians against his authority. Book 16 relates how his political mission was fulfilled in the early years against Knud (Cnut) VI (1182–1187) by the declaration of Danish independence against the Emperor Frederick Barbarossa, and by the subjugation of the Pomeranian Slavs.

In the last three books, a copious narrative is enlivened by reported speech and digressions on Norwegian, German, and Slavic affairs. The main source may have been Absalon's own words, but Saxo and the compiler of *Knýtlinga saga* (ca. 1260) perhaps used an earlier written source now lost. Books 9–16 are usually supposed to have been written first, before 1201; and the earlier books in the time of Valdemar II. Much of the text must relate to contemporary issues and personalities, but it is difficult to find Saxo advocating any official policy. His patrons were the most powerful men in the kingdom, but he was an idiosyncratic critic of the times, hoping to inspire his fellow countrymen to political unity and civic virtue by the example of former days, as well as to impress learned foreigners. Simplified and excerpted versions of his work were current in Denmark in the later Middle Ages, but it was only after 1514 and the appearance of Anders Sørensen Vedel's Danish translation in 1575 that his view of the Nordic past was widely received both at home and abroad.

See also Cnut; Sunesen, Anders; Sven Haraldsson (Forkbeard)

Further Reading

Editions

Pedersen, Christian, ed. *Danorum Regum Heroumque Historiæ*. Paris.

Badius, 1514 [based on complete MS Books 10–16 reproduced in E. Christiansen's trans.; the whole edition was reprinted with minor alterations at Basel in 1534 and Frankfurt in 1576].

Stephanius, Stephanus J., ed. *Saxonis Grammatici Historiæ Danicæ Libri XVI*. Søro: Crusius, 1645 [usually bound with the following work].

Stephanius, Stephanus J. *Notæ Uberiores in historian Danicam Saxonis*. Sorø: Cntsius, 1645. Reproduced (ed. H. D. Schepelem) by Museum Tusculanum, Copenhagen, 1978. [There were further editions by C. A. Klotz (Leipzig, 1771), P. E. Müller (Copenhagen, 1839, with Prolegomena and Notæ Uberiores by J. M. Velschow, 1858), and A. Holder (Strassburg, 1886).]

Olrik, Jørgen, and H. Ræder, eds. *Saxonis Gesta Danorum*. Vol. 1. Copenhagen: Levin & Munksgaard, 1931. Vol 2. *Indicem Verborum Continens*, by Franz Blatt. Copenhagen: Levin & Munksgaard, 1957. For the 14th-century abridgment, of which four MSS survive, see: Langebek, J., ed. *Thomæ Gheysmeri Compendium Historiæ Danicæ*. In SRD, vol. 2, pp. 286–400. Copenhagen: Godiche, 1773.

Gertz, M. Cl., ed. *Scriptores Minores Historiæ Danicæ*. 2 vols. Copenhagen: Gad, 1917–18. Vol. 1 rpt. by Selskabet for Udgivelse af Kilder til Dansk Historie, Copenhagen, 1970. The four Saxo MS fragments appear in facsimile in vol. 5 of Corpus Codicum Danicorum Medii Aevi. Ed. Johannes Brøndum-Nielsen. Copenhagen: Munksgaard, 1962.

Translation

Elton, Oliver, trans. *The First Nine Books of the Danish History of Saxo Grammaticus*. Folklore Society Publications, 33. London: Nutt, 1893; rpt. 2 vols. New York: Norrœna Society, 1905.

Ellis Davidson, Hilda, ed., and Peter Fisher, trans. *Saxo Grammaticus. The History of the Danes. Books I–IX*. 2 vols. Cambridge: Brewer Totowa: Rowman and Littlefield, 1979–80.

Fisher, Peter. "On Translating Saxo into English." In Friis-Jensen, Karsten, ed. *Saxo Grammaticus: A Medieval Author Between Norse and Latin Culture*. Copenhagen: Museum Tusculanum, 1981, pp. 53–64.

Christiansen, Eric, trans. *Saxo Grammaticus: Danorum Regum Heroumque Historia. Books X–XVI: The Text of the First Edition with Translation and Commentary*. 3 vols. British Archaeological Reports, International Series, vols. 84 and 118 (in two parts). Oxford: B.A.R., 1980–81

Bibliographies

A survey of the most important work done to 1930 was given by Jørgen Olrik in the Latin and Danish Prolegomena to his edition. See further: Skovgaard-Petersen, Inge. "Saxo." *KLNM15* (1970), 49–50, and "Saxo" in *Dansk Biografisk Lexicon* 12 (1982), 641–3.

Laugesen, Anker Teilgaard. *Introduktion til Saxo*. Copenhagen: Gyldendal, 1972, pp. 86–7 [meager].

Literature

Two collections of articles contain much recent work: Boserup, Ivan, ed. *Saxostudier. Saxo-kollokvierne ved Københavns universitet*. Copenhagen: Museum Tusculanum, 1975. Friis-Jensen, Karsten, ed. *Saxo Grammaticus: A Medieval Author Between Norse and Latin Culture* [see above]. These are referred to below as *Saxostudier* and *Saxo-Culture*.

(a) Myth and Legend

Turville-Petre, E. O. G. *Myth and Religion of the North: The Religion of Ancient Scandinavia*. New York: Holt, Rinehart and Winston; rpt. Westpori: Greenwood, 1975, pp. 27–34.

Ellis Davidson, H. R. *Gods and- Myths of Northern Europe*. Harmondsworth: Penguin, 1964.

Dumézil, Georges. *La Saga de Hadingus.* Paris: Presses Universitaires, 1953 [trans. by D. Coltman as *From Myth to Fiction: The Saga of Hadingus* (Chicago: University of Chicago Press, 1973) and reviewed by E. O. G. Turville-Petre in *Saga-Book of the Viking Society* 14 (1953–55), 131–4].

Andersson, Theodore M. "*Niflunga saga* in Light of German and Danish Materials." *Mediaeval Scandinavia* 7 (1974), 22–30.

Dollerup, Cay. *Denmark, Hamlet and Shakespeare.* 2 vols. Salzburg Studies in English Literature, Elizabethan and Renaissance Studies, 47. Salzburg: Institut fúr englische Sprache und Literatur, Universität Salzburg, 1975.

Lukman, Niels. "Ragnar loðbrók, Sigfrid, and the Saints of Flanders." *Mediaeval Scandinavia* 9 (1976), 7–50.

Smyth, Alfred P. *Scandinavian Kings in the British Isles 850–880.* Oxford: Oxford University Press, 1977 [on Ragnarr and his sons].

Strand, Birgit. *Kvinnor och Män i Gesta Danorum.* Kvinnohistoriskt arkiv, 18. Gothenburg: [n.p.], 1980 [English summaryl

Bjarni Guðnason. "The Icelandic Sources of Saxo Grammmaticus." In *Saxo-Culture,* pp. 79–93.

Martinez-Pizarro, Joaquin. "An *Eiriks þáttr málspaka?* Some Conjectures on the Source of Saxo's Ericus Disertus." In *Saxo-Culture,* pp. 105–19.

Skovgaard-Pedersen, Inge. "The Way to Byzantium: A Study in the First Three Books of Saxo's History of Denmark" In *Saxo-Culture,* pp. 121–33.

Strand, Birgit. "Women in Gesta Danorum." In *Saxo-Culture,* pp. 135–67.

(b) History and Ideology

Skovgaard-Petersen, Inge. "Saxo, Historian of the Patria." *Mediaeval Scandinavia* 2 (1969), 54–77.

Damsholt, Nanna. "Kongeopfattelse og kongeideologi hos Saxo." In *Saxostudier,* pp. 148–55.

Riis, Thomas. "Bruddet mellem Valdemar den Store og Eskil 1161. Søborg, diplomerne og Saxo." In *Saxostudier,* pp. 156–66.

Skyum-Nielsen, Niets. "Saxo som kilde til et par centrale institutioner i samtiden." In *Saxostudier,* pp. 175–92.

Weibull, Curt. "Vem var Saxo?" *Historisk tidsskrift* (Denmark) 78 (1978) 87–96.

Riis, Thomas. *Les institutions politiques centrales du Danemark 1100–1332.* Odense University Studies in History and Social Sciences, 46. Odense: Odense University Press, 1977, pp. 14–31, 86–150.

Johannesson, Kurt. *Saxo Grammaticus. Komposition och världsbildi Gesta Danorum.* Stockholm: Almqvist & Wiksell, 1978 [in Swedish, but for an English summary see his "Order in Gesta Danorum and Order in the Creation," in *Saxo-Culture,* pp. 95–104].

Malmros, Rikke. "Blodgildet i Roskilde historiografisk belyst." *Scandia* 45 (1979), 46–66 [English summary].

Weibull, Curt. "Saxos berättelser om de danske vendertågen 1158–1185." *Historisk tidsskrift* (Denmark) 83 (1983), 35–70.

Sawyer, Birgit. "Saxo-Valdemar-Absalon." *Scandia* 51 (1985), 33–60 [English summary].

Sawyer, Birgit. "Valdemar, Absalon and Saxo: Historiography and Politics in Medieval Denmark." *Revue Belge de philologie et d'histoire* 63 (1985), 685–705

Skovgaard-Pedersen, Inge. *Da Tidernes Herre var nær. Studier i Saxos historiesyn.* Copenhagen: Den danske historiske Forening, 1987.

(c) Latinity, Verse, and Manuscripts:

Blatt, Franz [Indledning and Præfatio to the Index (vol. 2) of Olrik and Ræder's 1931 edition]

Saxostudier, pp. 1–114, contains thirteen articles in Danish on the language, construction, and analogues of Saxo's work

Friis-Jensen, Karsten. *Saxo og Vergil.* Copenhagen: Museum Tusculanum, 1975 [French summary].

Boserup, Ivan. "The Angers Fragment and the Archetype of Gesta Danorum." *Saxo-Culture,* pp. 9–26.

Friis-Jensen, Karsten. "The Lay of Ingellus and Its Classical Models." *Saxo-Culture,* pp. 65–78.

Friis-Jensen, Karsten. *Saxo Grammaticus as Latin Poet: Studies in the Verse Passages of the Gesta Danorum.* Analecta Romana; Instituti Danici, Supplementum 14. Rome: Bretschneider, 1987.

Friis-Jensen, Karsten. "Was Saxo a Canon of Lund?" *Cahiers de l'institut du moyen-ge grec et latin* 59 (1989), 331–57.

ERIC CHRISTIANSEN

SCHONGAUER, MARTIN (ca. 1450–1491) Known today primarily as an engraver, this artist, active in Colmar and the Upper Rhine area from circa 1470 until about 1491, was nicknamed Hübsch Martin (Fair Martin) by his contemporaries in praise of his abilities as a painter. He is important as an assimilator of Netherlandish art. His work was influential in Germany, and he attracted many followers, including Albrecht Dürer.

Martin Schongauer was probably born circa 1450 in Colmar, a town south of Strasbourg. Although some have proposed a birth date of about 1430, this view has not found widespread acceptance. His father, Caspar, was a goldsmith, and Martin probably first trained in his shop. His rather apparently wanted his son to become a cleric, for Schongauer's name appears in the 1465 matriculation records of the University of Leipzig. After only one semester, however, he returned to Colmar and began training as a painter. Caspar Isenmann, active in Colmar circa 1435–1472, is often cited as his teacher, but no evidence, documentary or stylistic, supports this assumption. As a journeyman, Schongauer likely traveled to Cologne, then to the Netherlands. His experience of works by the major Netherlandish masters—Roger van der Weyden, Robert Campin, Dieric Bouts, and Hugo van der Goes—is evident in his overall style and in his appropriation of Netherlandish compositions, motifs, and figure types. After his travels, Schongauer settled in Colmar, where he purchased a house in 1469 and again in 1477. He remained there until 1489, when he became a citizen of nearby Breisach. He died there in 1491.

None of Martin Schongauer's paintings are signed. The only dated work attributed to him is the Madonna of the Rose Arbor (Colmar, church of St. Martin), dated 1473 on the reverse. The figure types and detailed, naturalistic rendering of plants and birds are inspired by Netherlandish art. This work's date has been used to establish Schongauer's chronology.

Scholars agree that the earliest preserved works by Schongauer are two wings from the altarpiece commissioned by Jean d'Orlier, preceptor of the Antonite monastery of Isenheim, about 1470 (Colmar, Musée d'Unterlinden). They feature an Annunciation on the exterior, and on the interior, an Adoration and Jean d'Orlier presented by St. Anthony. Schongauer painted several small devotional paintings in the 1480s: two Holy Families (Munich, Alte Pinakothek; Vienna, Kunsthistorisches Museum), an Adoration of the Shepherds (Berlin, Gemäldegalerie), and two versions of the Virgin and Child at a Window (private collections). His last painting, a Last Judgment fresco in Breisach Minster, is based on Roger van der Weyden's Last Judgment Altarpiece of about 1445 (Beaune, Musée de l'Hôtel Dieu).

One-hundred sixteen monogrammed engravings survive, which include both religious and secular subjects. Schongauer's great contributions to the medium were his innovative use of stipling (dots), hatching (fine lines), and crosshatching to create tonal effects like those in paintings, and his adoption of complex compositions derived from paintings. The works are divided into two periods. The early engravings date to the early 1470s. Compositions, as in Christ Carrying the Cross, tend to be intricate and crowded with figures, and the system of modeling inconsistent. Mature works, from the late 1470s until his death, contain smaller groups, or single figures, and the modeling is more controlled and logical, as in the Wise and Foolish Virgins.

A number of drawings attributed to Schongauer also survive. The recent attribution of a watercolor Study of Peonies (private collection) provides insight into Schongauer's working methods (Koreny 1991: 591–596). It was probably executed as a preparatory study from nature for the 1473 Madonna of the Rose Arbor.

Further Reading

Baum, Julius. *Martin Schongauer*. Vienna: A. Schroll, 1948.

Le beau Martin: Gravures et dessins de Martin Schongauer vers 1450–1491. Colmar: Musée d'Unterlinden, 1991.

Châtelet, Albert. "Martin Schongauer et les primitifs flamands." *Cahiers alsaciens d'archéologie, d'art et d'histoire* 22 (1979): 117–142.

Dvorak, Max. "Schongauer und die niederländische Malerei," in *Kunstgeschichte als Geitstesgeschichte: Studien zur abendländischen Kunstentwicklung*. Munich: Piper, 1924, pp. 151–189.

Koreny, Fritz. "A Coloured Flower Study by Martin Schongauer and the Development of the Depiction of Nature from van der Weyden to Dürer," *Burlington Magazine* 133 (1991): 588–597.

Rosenberg, Jakob. *Martin Schongauer Handzeichnungen*. Munich: Piper, 1923.

Shestack, Alan. *The Complete Engravings of Martin Schongauer*. New York: Dover, 1969.

SUSANNE REECE

SERCAMBI, GIOVANNI (1348–27 May 1424) Giovanni Sercambi was born in Lucca, where his father ran a book and paper store; he thus grew up with a good library at hand. He was educated by private tutors for a government career, and he prospered by supporting the rise to power of the Guinigi family. After 1400, however, feeling neglected by the Guinigi, he withdrew from politics and began to write. Sercambi's works include A *Chronicle of the Affairs of Lucca* (from 1164–1424, including events in which he had participated); the *Monito*, a compendium of advice on finance and administration based on his own experiences in public service; and, in his final years, the *Novelle*, a collection of 155 tales.

The book of advice, dedicated to the Guinigi, advocates practical measures for maintaining control: taking a census of the citizens, forbidding them to possess arms, and ensuring that the legislative council is filled with one's own friends and relatives. The novelle, which draw in part on Sercambi's history of Lucca, are similarly hard-boiled; the collection is filled with tales of deceit, fraud, theft, clerical misbehavior, and the self-serving manipulations of lovers, parents, children, dealers, and clients. A few of the tales are about Sercambi himself, e.g., how he escaped an attack by highway robbers.

The tales are framed by an account of a plague in 1374, during which a group of men and women travel around Italy to avoid the disease. As on some of the actual penitential pilgrimages occasioned by recurring plagues, the travelers agree to pool their money, hear mass every morning, and refrain from sexual activity during the journey. Boccaccio's influence is clear in the setting (the plague), in the inclusion of occasional poems, and in more than twenty of the tales; but instead of having various members of the group narrate in turn, Sercambi's travelers appoint one storyteller to keep them entertained. This character often tells stories appropriate to the places they are visiting: stories of theft near Naples, of Roman history at Rome, of Venetian customs at Venice. Many of the stories are drawn from contemporary or recent events, as well as from Roman myth and history, popular fabliaux, and other medieval collections of tales, such as the *Disciplina clericalis* and the *Decameron*. The titles of the stories suggest the moral categories of preachers' *exempla*: "On Great Prudence," "On Supreme Avarice," "On Supreme Justice," "On Vain Lust," and so forth.

Sercambi's style is rough, and his tales were rarely mentioned before the late 1700s, when one of the two fifteenth-century manuscripts was found. However, since its first printing in Venice in 1816, the *Novelle* has been reprinted many times.

See also **Boccaccio, Giovanni**

Further Reading

Editions and Translation

Le croniche, ed. Salvatore Bongi. Rome: Fonti per la Storia d'Italia Pubblicate dall'Istituto Storico Italiano, 1892.

Italian Renaissance Tales, trans. Janet Smarr. Rochester, N.Y.: Solaris, 1983, pp. 49–68.

Novelle, ed. Giovanni Sinicropi. Scrittori d'Italia, 250–251. Bari: Laterza, 1972.

Novelle, ed. Luciano Rossi, 3 vols. Rome: Salerno, 1974.

Critical Studies

Alexanders, James W. "A Preparatory Study for an Edition of the *Novelle* of Giovanni Sercambi." Dissertation, University of Virginia, 1940.

Di Francia, Letterio. *Novellistica*, Vol. 1. Milan: Vallardi, 1924, pp. 223–260.

Di Scipio, Giuseppe Carlo. "Giovanni Sercambi's *Novelle*: Sources and Popular Traditions." *Merveilles et Contes*, 2, 1988, pp. 25–36.

The Italian Novella: A Book of Essays, ed. Gloria Allaire. New York: Routledge, 2003.

Marietti, Marina. "Imitation et transposition du *Décaméron* chez Sercambi et Sermini: Réécriture et contexte culturelle." In *Réécritures*, Vols. 1–2, *Commentaires, parodies, variations dans la littérature italienne de la Renaissance*. Paris: Université de la Sorbonne Nouvelle, 1984, Vol. 2, 9–68.

Nicholson, Peter. "The Two Versions of Sercambi's *Novelle*." *Italica*, 53, 1976, pp. 210–213.

Petrocchi, Giorgio. "Il novelliere medievale del Sercambi." *Convivium*, 17, 1949.

Plaisance, Michel. "Les rapports ville campagne dans les nouvelles de Sacchetti, Sercambi, et Sermini." In *Culture et société en Italie du Moyen Age à la Renaissance*. Paris: Université de la Sorbonne Nouvelle, 1985, pp. 61–73.

Pratt, Robert A. "Chaucer's Shipman's Tale and Sercambi." *Modern Language Notes*, 55, 1940, pp. 142–145.

Salgarolo, David. "The Jews and Conversion in the Medieval and Renaissance Italian Novella." *NEMLA Italian Studies*, 11–12, 1987–1988, pp. 27–40.

Salwa, Piotr. "*Il novelliere sercambiano* e il suo contesto lucchese." *Kwartalnik Neofilologiczny*, 33(2), 1986, pp. 207–225.

———. *Narrazione, persuasione, ideologia: Una lettura del "Novelliere" di Giovanni Sercambi, lucchese*. Lucca: Maria Paccini Fazzi Editore, 1991.

Swennen Ruthenberg, Myriam. "The Revenge of the Text: The Real-Ideal Relationship between Giovanni Sercambi's *Croniche* and *Novelliere*." Dissertation, New York University, 1994.

Vivarelli, Ann W. "Giovanni Sercambi's *Novelle* and the Legacy of Boccaccio." *Modern Language Notes*, 90, 1975, pp. 109–127.

JANET LEVARIE SMARR

SEUSE, HEINRICH (1295/1297–1366)

This Dominican priest served as a confessor, preacher, and teacher to religious men and women in the German south. His poetic works in the mystical tradition served to inspire those in his care.

Born into a patrician family in or near Constance, Seuse did not seek out ministerial service but followed in the footsteps of his religiously oriented mother, whose name he chose to use. At thirteen he entered the monastery at Constance. Following a general course of study there, he may have studied briefly in Strasbourg before attending the *studium generate* (early form of university education) in Cologne around 1324 or 1325, where he studied with Meister Eckhart. Seuse probably remained in Cologne until the master's death in 1327, when he returned to Constance and was appointed lector at the monastery. At the age of forty, around 1335, Seuse was told by God to abandon the ascetic practices he had followed for twenty-two years. This turning point in his personal life also marked a change in his professional career: Seuse became an itinerant preacher and spiritual adviser, concentrating his activities in Switzerland, the Alsace, and along the Upper Rhine. Because he supported the pope in a power struggle with Ludwig of Bavaria, Seuse was forced to leave Constance in 1338 or 1339; some eight years later he probably returned. Around 1348 he was transferred to the Dominican monastery in Ulm, where he remained until his death more than fifteen years later. He was canonized in 1831.

In his last years, Seuse undertook the editing of his works for publication, his *Ansgabe letzter Hand;* the works he chose make up the *Exemplar.* Included are his life *(Vita),* which chronicles in third-person narrative the life of the *Diener der ewigen Weisheit* (Servant of Eternal Wisdom), Seuse himself. The authorship of the *Vita* is disputed; the Töß sister Elsbeth Stagel, one of Seuse's spiritual charges, probably played a role in the editing, if not the writing of the work. Following are Seuse's earliest works, the *Büchlein der ewigen Weisheit (Little Book of Eternal Wisdom)* and the *Büchlein der Wahrheit (Little Book of Truth),* two of the most popular devotional tracts in the late medieval mystical tradition. Both are written as dialogues between the Servant and the personification of eternal wisdom and truth, respectively. The *Exemplar* concludes with the *Briefbüchlein (Little Book of Letters),* an edited version of Seuse's correspondence with the Dominican sisters in his charge, primarily those at the convent of Töß. The *Little Book of Love (Minnebüchlein),* whose authenticity is doubtful, and a larger collection of letters, the *Großes Briefbuch* (Great Book of Letters), also survive. Both sets of letters by Seuse are more characteristic of the homiletic rather than the epistolary genre. Indeed, few of his homiletic works are extant, although he was charged with the responsibility of preaching; only two German sermons are accepted as authentic works of the Dominican friar, but neither is included in the *Exemplar.* The *Horologium sapientiae (Clock of Wisdom)* is the only extant work of the Dominican in Latin; it is an expanded version of the *Büchlein der ewigen Weisheit.*

The religious content of Seuse's work, which draws on the Bernhardian tradition, stands in marked contrast to the speculative mystical theology of his teacher Eckhart.

Because of his poetic style and the preeminence of love imagery in his writings, Seuse often is characterized as the *Minnesänger* among the medieval German mystics.

See also **Meister Eckhart**

Further Reading

Bihlmeyer, Karl, ed. *Heinrich Seuse. Deutsche Schrifien.* 1907; rpt. Frankfurt am Main: Minerva, 1961.

Boesch, Bruno. "Zur Minneauffassung Seuses." *Festschrift Josef Quint anläßlich seines 65. Geburtstages übefreicht,* ed. Hugo Moser, Rudolf Schutzeichel, and Karl Stackmann. Bonn: Semmel, 1964, pp. 57–68.

Clark, James M. *The Great German Mystics: Eckhart, Tauler and Suso.* Oxford: Blackwell, 1949.

Colledge, Edmund, and J. C. Marler. 'Mystical' Pictures in the Suso 'Exemplar' *Ms Strasbourg 2929." Archivum Fratrurn Praedicatorum* 54 (1984): 293–354.

Filthaut, Ephrem M., ed. *Heinrich Seuse. Studien zum 600. Todestag, 1366–1966.* Cologne: Albertus Magnus, 1966.

Haas, Alois M., and Kurt Ruh. "Seuse, Heinrich OP," in *Die deutsche Literatur des Mittelalters: Verfasserlexikon,* 2d ed., ed. Kurt Ruh et al. Berlin: de Gruyter, 1992, vol. 8, cols. 1127–1129.

Hamburger, Jeffrey E. "The Use of Images in the Pastoral Care of Nuns: The Case of Heinrich Suso and the Dominicans" *Art Bulletin* 71 (1989): 20–46.

Künzle, Pius. *Heinrich Seuses Horologium sapientiae.* Spicilegium Friburgense 23. Freiburg im Breisgau: Universitätsverlag, 1977.

Stoudt, Debra L. "The Structure and Style of the Letters of Seuses *Großes Briefbuch." Neuphilologische Mitteilungen* 90 (1989): 359–367.

Tobin, Frank. "Coming to Terms with Meister Eckhart: Suso's Buch der Wahrheit." *Semper idem et novus. Festschrift for Frank Banta,* ed. Francis G. Gentry. Göppingen: Kümmerle, 1988, 321–344.

Tobin, Frank. *Henry Suso: The Exemplar, with Two German Sermons.* Mahwah, N.J.: Paulist, 1989.

Walz, Angelus. "Bibliographiae susonianae conatus." *Angelicum* 46 (1969): 430–491.

DEBRA L. STOUDT

SHEM TOV OF CARRIÓN (ca. 1290–
1360) Shem Tov Yiẕhaq ben Arduti'el,
Castilian rabbi and poet whose *Proverbios
morales*, addressed to Pedro I and quoted
in the Marqués de Santillana's *Prohemio e
carta*, synthesizes Semitic poetics with the
Spanish idiom in a permutation of a literary
formula: the getting of wisdom. Its relative
success has eclipsed Shem Tov's Hebrew
compositions *Ma'aseh ha-rav*, a *maqáma*
featuring a debate between pen and scis-
sors; *Vam qohelet*, a *baqashah* consisting of
two thousand words beginning with the letter *mem*; and, finally, *Ha-vidui ha-gadol*, a
prayer of confession for Yom Kippur. This
oeuvre provides a useful frame of reference for gauging the ethical, rhetorical, and
philosophical dimensions of the *Proverbios
morales*. Shem Tov also translated Yisra'el
ha-Yisra'eli's liturgical treatise *Miẕvot ze-
maniyot* from Arabic into Hebrew; the authorship of other titles sometimes attributed to him is dubious. Excluding inferences
from his work, the scant known biographical information is obtained from a *díwán*
(book of poetry) written by Shmu'el ben
Yosef ben Sason, and places him in Carrión
de los Condes in 1338.

Drawing on the language of parem-
ology, medieval philosophy, the Bible,
Talmud, and Arabic wisdom anthologies, *Proverbios morales* examines the
ostensible dilemma posed to the individual by the unpredictability of human
existence and endorses adherence to the
Aristotelian mean in ethical matters, recognition of circumstances in social conduct, and ultimate faith in the Creator.
Here, all things exist in complementary
opposition—night and day, loss and gain,
and so on; therefore wealth is ephemeral,
happiness is momentary, and power mere
vanity. For the individual, successful negotiation of such a world requires the
perspicacious appraisal of circumstance
since an action once advantageous may
now be disadvantageous, as Shem Tov
shows in a paradox on speech and silence. For the monarch, God's representative, duty requires that he vouchsafe

truth, justice, and peace, the foundations
of political order.

The poem's language is consistent in
its general phonetic, morphological, and
syntactic features with medieval Castilian.
Its distinctive traits include homoioteleu-
ton rhyme, complex hyperbaton, phra-
seological parallelism, the prevalence of
parataxis over hypotaxis, and the accumulation of grammatical functions in
pleonastic pronouns.

The suggestion that the poem may be
a vestige of a rabbinical *mester de clerecía*
(clerical poetry) could ultimately establish its otherwise uncertain generic identity. The 725 alexandrine stanzas reveal a
sustained tone of self-assurance in Shem
Tov's poetic voice, equally adept at evoking poignancy, melancholy, or whimsy.
The antonymic parallelism of his compositional technique, derived from Arabic
and Hebrew poetics, sometimes interpreted as indicative of moral relativism,
serves to enunciate extremes that define a
center of equilibrium.

Each of the six extant manuscripts
preserves multiple variants and stanza sequences, several suggest the complex social
profile a single work may possess. One is
redacted in Hebrew *aljamía* (Cambridge),
another includes an anonymous prose
prologue (Madrid), and a third records
219 stanzas written from memory and entered into evidence during proceedings for
the crime of heresy (Cuenca). The first example implies genesis of the poem's main
body for purposes of Jewish education.
The latter pair allude to its essentially oral
performance character; the commentator
advocates memorizing the work, "que
todo omne la deuiera decorar. Ca esta fue
la entençio del sabio rraby que las fizo,"
["that each person should memorize.
That was the intention of the wise rabbi
who made it"] and the defendant charged
with heresy swears he recorded "quantas
a la memoria me han venido" ["as many
as have come to memory"].

That the *Proverbios morales* were
presented to Pedro I for his edification

seems apparent, but the assertion that it was written specifically for a Christian audience warrants appraisal. That hypothesis relies upon the poem's redaction in Castilian, an opening apostrophe and closing reference to Pedro I, and a *captatio benevolentiae* summarizing the Jewish poet's situation when addressing a Christian audience of superior social rank. The delivery of medieval Jewish sermons in a vernacular places a correlation between language choice and intended audience here in doubt. The use of the V(*os*) form of address, required for addressing a social superior, is limited to the poem's introductory and concluding passages, the main body prefers the *T(ú)* form suitable for an equal or inferior in status. It may be inferred therefore that Shem Tov composed the *Proverbios morales* for a destinatory of equal or inferior status—that is, the Jewish community, and redacted occassional material in order to accommodate the poem for presentation before a different audience.

A subtle poetic composition, *Proverbios morales* succeeds in incorporating the complexity of human existence into a persuasive discourse on ethics and philosophy that addresses the dynamic of the individual in society.

See also **Pedro I the Cruel, King of Castile**

Further Reading

Alarcos Llorach, E. "La lengua de los *Proverbios morales* de don Sem Tob," *Revisía de Filología Española* 35 (1951), 249–309.

Perry, T. A. *The "Moral Proverbs" of Santob de Carrion: Jewish Wisdom in Christian Spain*, Princeton, N.J., 1987.

Zemke, J. *Critical Approaches to the "Proverbios Morales" of Shem Tov de Carrión*. Newark, Del., 1997.

JOHN ZEMKE

SHUSHTARĪ, AL-, ABŪ AL-HASAN (b. 1212)

The medieval Hispano-Arabic mystical poet Abū al-Ḥasan al-Shushtarī,

who was born and who lived most of his life in Muslim Spain, introduced the colloquial *zajal* to the field of Ṣūfi (Islamic mystical) poetry. The *zajal* is the well-known strophic poem that uses the colloquial as its medium—in this case, the Andalusian medieval dialect—and particularly originated in Muslim Spain during the Middle Ages. As a "popular" art form that had not been used before or thought appropriate for sublime Ṣūfi expression, the Hispano-Arabic zajal that existed at the time was especially perfected by another Andalusian poet, Ibn Quzmān, who mainly wrote satirical and courtly love zajals. There is today enough evidence that this type of zajal was performed, sometimes by means of choral singing. In the East, Ṣūfi poets like Ibn al-Farīd of Egypt (d. 577) had been using the classical form of the Arabic *qaṣīda*, with its traditional framework of monorhyme and monorhythm and with classical Arabic language to express thoughts. In Spain, however, strophic poetry—namely the *muwashshaḥa* and the zajal—evolved in Andalusian Arabic verse, demonstrating the influence of Romance popular literre. In other words, the *muwashshaḥa* and the zajal in their inception in Arabic literature became uniquely associated with al-Andalus. But it was Al-Shushtarī who first chose the zajal for Ṣūfi purposes.

Therefore, most important about Al-Shushtarī in this context is that his strophic poetry forms a link between two areas of interest in the literature of Muslim Spain: the formal and esoteric, on the one hand (represented by the mystical philosophy of Ibn ʿArabī and Ibn Sabʿīn, two Ṣūfi whom Al-Shushtarī followed), and the "popular" aspect of the Hispano-Arabic literary world (represented by the informal zajal and its master, Ibn Quzmān) on the other. Through the unity of these two strands, Al-Shushtarī sought to interpret and make accessible mystical ideas and to propound an understand-ing of Ṣūfism virtually synonymous with a vibrant, aesthetic perceptiveness. He therefore represents an important melding of the esoteric spirituality of Ṣūfism and a kind of emerging lay spirituality.

This yoking of a theological and an aesthetic perspective significantly illuminates the act and art of interpretation, which is the main area of concern in Al-Shushtarī's poetry. Ṣūfi scriptural (i.e., Qur'ānic) exegesis plays a fundamental role in this literary self-awareness that permeates the poetry. Consistent textual references such as "understanding" and "grasping allusions," "words," "terms," "symbols," or "signs" underline the concept of critical interpretation. Like all Ṣūfis, Al-Shushtarī did not deal with texts—scripture or otherwise—superficially. He constantly asked his audience to "untie symbols" and to "grasp ultimate meanings," urging them to think, to analyze, and to put parts of a poem together in the service of the whole, as if inviting them to join his Ṣūfi path by interpreting his songs. Hence, this literary self-consciousness ultimately reflects a mystical self-consciousness as well, while the Ṣūfi principle of Qur'ānic exegesis shaped the way Ṣūfi poets, such as Al-Shushtarī, composed poetry and the way they expected it to be interpreted.

Al-Shushtarī utilized the means provided by this mystical tradition for symbolic expression, but his innovation in the use of the zajal for such marks his contribution in the field. He could not merely depend on the techniques provided by traditional rhetoric to achieve a combination of artistry and mysticism. In al-Shushtarī, the concept of "interpretation" in itself becomes the main concern, and the poetry comes to express the interrelation between critical perceptiveness of text and mystical views. It is this integration that Al-Shushtarī's strophic poetry fully realizes.

This relationship between the lyrical and the mystical manifests itself in three main features that act as systems of reference and regulation that afford the audience effective ways of responding spiritually as well as aesthetically to

the lyrics. These reference systems are regarded from the standpoint of their mystico-aesthetic correspondence to convey Al-Shushtarī's mystical and aesthetical philosophy simultaneously.

The first aspect is the idea of the multiple levels of meaning existing within the poems—that is, the symbolism. This feature directly translates into two areas of interest: the network of Ṣūfi doctrines and symbolic terminology as well as the literary self-conscious mode characterized by direct textual references. The major reference is that of *ramz* (symbol), hence underlying the symbolic composition of the poems and suggesting the application of symbolic interpretation in order to discern the text's binary dimension. In other words, Al-Shushtarī does not merely use symbols but calls attention to this use and to symbolic critical reading.

The second major area that also displays literary self-consciousness is structure—specifically ring composition and its relation to the theme of the "reflexive." The ring structure embodies a circular principle of interpretation, which is most appropriate to the Ṣūfi mode of perception and to the tradition of composing ophic poetry. Ṣūfi exegesis, called *ta'wī*, is the internal interpretation of the Qur'ān and seeks the inner level or primary meaning through returning the outward, literal plane of scripture to its original, hidden spiritual essence—hence a circular, reflexive movement. And in strophic poetry, the nature thereof allows the poet to utilize his strophes as movable structural units, which is more feasible than dealing with single lines in the more restrictive form of a classical qasida. Al-Shushtarī could also use the interplay beeen the different parts of the zajal or *muwashshaḥa* (such as the *matla*, the *qufl*, and the *kharja*) to solidify the ring composition. Moreover, the phenomena of borrowing and of composing a poem based on an already established kharja (the last line in the song)—that is, starting from the end—or based on an established prosodic pattern (contrafaction) are all typical compositional techniques that enhance the circular effect. Thus, Al-Shushtarī was very conscious of specific structural patterns and their significance to the art of critical interpretation.

The third manifestation of that general literary concern lies in the element of performance itself, which is naturally realized with the pioneering use of the zajal. Because this is a poem composed to be sung or performed in public (sometimes in a choral manner), it affords the audience or recipients interaction with the art presented. The active participation involved here is what distinguishes Al-Shushtarī's mystical work, adding a new dimension to Ṣūfi poetry in general, and invigorating the whole mystical experience. Ṣūfi poetry here is thus no longer intellectually exclusive or highly theoretical and unreached, but a living part of the mystical existence. Al-Shushtarī even included within the lyrics themselves, and among his other created personalities, the persona of the *zajjal* (the zajal's composer) or singer—that is, the persona of the poet/artist.

The two other personae are the ascetic, pious *faqir* (epithet for Ṣūfi) and its symbolic counterpart, a wanton drunk. The first persona, the wandering, "ecstatic" Ṣūfi, seems to embody the character of Al-Shushtarī himself, a Ṣūfi faqir who wandered in various lands and took his zajal singing in the streets and marketplaces. At times, however, Al-Shushtarī adopts the Quzmāni wanton persona; as he says in his "Zajal 99," he literally puts on his defiant and unorthodox hat (exchanging his turban for a monk's hood). Of course, this device of putting on literary masks serves an important artistic purpose: the personalities ultimately join to form an underlying unity between literature and Ṣūfism.

As has been shown, the use of symbols and circular structure are ways of enhancing the concept of Ṣūfi exegesis and establishing the necessity of critical interpretation. In the same manner, drawing attention to performance and to various personae or voices

further proves how Al-Shushtarī was aware that he presented a new art—not merely a Ṣūfi philosophical treatise or didactic poetry—and that he was interested in the intricate artistry of composition.

In the final analysis, the novel aesthetic position of Al-Shushtarī is that critical interpretation, from the Ṣūfi perspective, is a "circular" process in which an "essential," spiritual truth becomes a poem: then by means of interaction with an interpreting audience (through public performance) the poem is returned to its origins. The correspondence between the theological dimension and the aesthetic dimension has one purpose: to illuminate the nature of the process of interpretation when linked to religious hermeneutics. Al-Shushtarī's poetry illustrates his characteristic blend of appealing and melodic simplicity, on the one hand, and sophisticated and even enigmatic complexity on the other. He was able to make "perfect form" (i.e., (zajals and *muwashshahas*) in art indistinguishable from mystical pursuit.

See also Ibn Quzmn

Further Reading

Corbin, H. *Creative Imagination in the Sufism of Ibn ʿArabī*. Trans. R. Manheim. Princeton, N.J., 1969.

Monroe, J. *Hispano-Ambic Poetry*. Berkeley, 1974.

"Prolegomena to the Study of Ibn Quzmān: The Poet as Jongleur." In *The Hispanic Ballad Today: History, Comparativism, Critical Bibliography*. Ed. S. G. Armistead, A. Sanchez-Romeralo, and D. Catalán. Madrid, 1979. 77–129.

Shushtarī, al-, A. al-Ḥasan. *Dīwān*. Ed. A. S. al-Nashshar. Cairo, 1960.

Stern, S. M. *Hispano-Arabic Strophic Poetry*. Ed. L. P. Harvey. Oxford, 1974.

OMAIMA ABOU-BAKR

SIGER OF BRABANT (ca. 1240– November 10 1284) This scholastic philosopher, an important representative of thirteenth-century heterodox

Aristotelianism, played a prominent role in the debate on the proper place of philosophy with respect to theology and Christian faith.

The details of Siger's biography are largely unknown. He was born around 1240 or shortly thereafter in Brabant and started his academic career circa 1255–1260 in Paris, where he received an M.A. in 1260–1265. On November 10, 1284, he died in Orvieto, killed by his secretary.

His oeuvre includes commentaries on Aristotle's *Physics, Metaphysics,* and *On the Soul,* and a number of separate questions dealing with logic, philosophy of nature, metaphysics, and ethics. Most of his writings resulted from his teaching as a master of arts at Paris. His published work probably dates from around 1270 and thereafter.

In his early writings, Siger professes the ideal of the pure philosopher searching for truth unaided by Christian revelation and trying to reveal the exact teachings of Aristotle, the philosopher par excellence. This attitude was seen as a serious threat to theology by a number of theologians, whose reaction was reflected in the famous Parisian Articles of 1270 and 1277, issued by Bishop Stephen Tempier. In his later work, however, Siger is less radical and steers a middle course between philosophy and Christian faith.

Of central importance was Siger's theory of the human intellect. In line with the teachings of Averröes, Siger holds that humans receive intellectual knowledge from a single, pure intellectual substance, which is the last of the hierarchy of intellectual substances and which consists of an active and a potential part. Only this pure intellectual substance is immortal; final personal responsibility therefore has no place. The theory evoked a sharp and detailed criticism of Thomas Aquinas. Toward the end of his career, Siger no longer defended it, mainly because of the attack of Thomas Aquinas, which seems to have convinced him that he was wrong.

See also **Aquinas, Thomas**

Further Reading

Philosophes Médiévaux 3 (1954): 12–14; (1972–1974): 24–25; (1981–1983) [editions of most of Siger's works].

Gauthier, R. A. "Notes sur Siger de Brabant." *Revue des sciences philosophiques et théologiques* 67 (1983): 201–232; 68 (1984): 3–49.

Hissette, Roland. *Enquête sur les 219 articles condamnés à Paris le 7 mars 1277.* Louvain: Publications Universitaires de Louvain, 1977.

Van Steenberghen, Fernand. *Maître Siger de Brabant.* Louvain: Publications Universitaires de Louvain, 1977.

———. "Publications récentes sur Siger de Brabant," in *Historia Philosophia Medii Aevi;* ed. Burkhard Mojsisch and Olaf Plua, vol. 2. Amsterdam: Grumer, 1991, pp. 1003–1011 [bibliography].

MAARTEN J. F. M. HOENEN

SIGHVATR ÞÓRÐARSON With more than 160 stanzas and half-stanzas, Sighvatr's *oeuvre* is the most fully attested of all the skalds. Even so, the original context of many stanzas is uncertain and only one poem, *Bersǫglisvísur* ("Plain-speaking Verses"), approaches complete preservation. Although no saga centering on Sighvatr exists, his distinguished career is documented by numerous episodes, some anecdotal and perhaps dubiously reliable, in the various versions of *Óláfs saga helga.* An Icelander born near the turn of the 11th century, Sighvatr belonged to a skaldic kindred, being the son of Þórðr Sigvaldaskáld and the uncle of Óttarr svarti ("the black"). His childhood was spent independently of his father, who seems to have been attached to the Jómsvíkingar, and in a non-Snorri anecdote his legendary fluency in poetic improvisation is attributed to his having caught and eaten a miraculous fish. Following a successful petition to St. Óláfr to accept him as a court poet, his adult career began with his *Víkingarvísur*

("Verses on the Viking Expedition"; the title is editorial). Here, Sighvatr used information from eyewitnesses (including his father?) to enumerate Óláfr's battles in the Baltic, England, France, and Spain. *Nesjavísur* ("Nesjar Verses"), by contrast, is based on Sighvatr's own participation in Óláfr's victorious sea-battle against Earl Sveinn Hákonarson (1016). Sighvatr also became personally involved in peace missions. His embassy (*ca.* 1017) to Earl Rognvaldr of Västergötland is described in *Austrfararvísur* ("Verses on a Journey to the East"). This collection of verses gives vivid, humorous, almost chatty impressions of a difficult route, inhospitable heathen people, and a favorable diplomatic outcome, although its exact documentary significance remains controversial. Subsequently, with the high rank of *stallari* ("marshall"), Sighvatr went to England to gather intelligence about Knud (Cnut) the Great's designs in Norway. He described this mission in a sparsely preserved sequence entitled *Vestrfararvísur* ("Verses on a Journey to the West"; 1025–1026). Sighvatr's close relationship with Óláfr, richly documented in the *lausavísur* and other compositions, brought him landed property and also benefited other Icelanders, including his nephew Óttarr. Tradition has it that he was instrumental in the naming of Óláfr's son Magnús, and in return the king sponsored Sighvatr's daughter at baptism. A pilgrimage to Rome (1029–1030) precluded his participation in the king's final battle at Stiklastaðir. His sorrow is expressed in some very eloquent and touching memorial *lausavísur*. His *erfidrápa* ("memorial lay"), perhaps composed some years later, appears to have focused on Óláfr's battles, sainthood, and miracles. Spurning an invitation from Sveinn, the temporary regent of Norway, Sighvatr attached himself to Óláfr's widow, Ástriðr, in exile in Sweden, and composed verses eulogizing her political efforts on behalf of Magnús, her stepson. Returning to Norway with Magnús

(1035), he forestalled civil war with the poem entitled *Bersǫglisvísur*, which, by mingling candid admonition with sweet persuasion, brought the new king to recognize the grievances of Sveinn's erstwhile supporters. He also mediated between Ástriðr and Álfhildr, the mother of Magnús. Despite his declaration to Knud that he could serve only one lord at a time, Sighvatr was capable of political independence. Most notably, he composed a *drápa* and an affectionate memorial *flokkr* in honor of Erlingr Skjálgsson, Óláfr's brother-in-law and long-time foe (d. 1028). Some MSS connect his name with a poorly attested *Tryggvaflokkr* for Tryggvi Óláfsson (son of Óláfr Tryggvason, and an unsuccessful contender against Earl Sveinn); poems praising Earl Ívarr and the Swedish king Qnundr Jakob are also reported. His *Knútsdrápa* ("Lay in Honor of Knud") was composed after Knud's death (1035), perhaps on the occasion of Magnús's reconciliation with Hardacnut (1038). Its coverage included Knud's English campaign, the battle of Helgeå, and the king's pilgrimage to Rome. It is distinctive formally for its *klofastef* ("broken refrain") and very restrictive *tøglag* versification. Sighvatr's death probably occurred around 1043. His verse distinguishes itself by sincerity, loyalty, humor, and general strength of personality. Such is the air of spontaneity that his poems appear to be retrospective assemblages of occasional or anecdotal verses. Colloquial and proverbial touches sit side by side with foreign words, which, combined with the breadth of geographical references, give his verse a somewhat cosmopolitan feel. Mythological kennings occur seldom, except in *Erlingsflokkr*, perhaps because they were out of keeping with the newly Christian ethos. Also scarce are obscure, neologistic compound nouns and kennings, of the sort so often found in other skalds' work. The general effect is simplicity, commonly offset by a difficult word order or an intricate plaiting of several short sentences within the one *helmingr*. With Sighvatr, then, skaldic discourse seems to be both in touch with its traditions and also opening itself to international contacts, in conformity with the expansion of Norwegian and Danish hegemony during his lifetime.

See also Cnut

Further Reading

Editions

Finnur Jónsson, ed. *Den norsk-islandske skjaldedigtning*. Vols. 1A-2A (tekst efter håndskrifterne) and 1B-2B (rettettekst). Copenhagen and Christiania [Oslo]: Gyldendal, 1912–15; rpt. Copenhagen: Rosenkilde & Bagger, 1967 (A) and 1973 (B).

Kock, Ernst A., ed. *Den norsk-isländska skjaldedikwingen*. 2 vols. Lund: Gleerup, 1946–50 [contains some improvements on Finnur Jónsson's edition].

Jón Skaptason. "Material for an Edition and Translation of the Poems of Sigvat Þórðarson, *skáld*." Diss. State University of New York at Stony Brook, 1983.

Translations

Hollander, Lee M. *The Skalds: A Selection of Their Poems with Introduction and Notes*. Princeton: Princeton University Press, 1945; 2nd ed. Ann Arbor: Michigan University Press, 1968 [brief biography, together with translations of selected stanzas, with emphasis on *Austrfararvísur*, *Vestrfararvísur*, and *Bersglisvísur*].

Campbell, Alistair. *Skaldic Verse and Anglo-Saxon History*. London: Lewis, 1971 [translation of Sighvatr's verses on English topics and discussion of their historical value].

Turville-Petre, E. O. G. *Scaldic Poetry*. Oxford: Clarendon, 1976 [brief biography, with small selection of stanzas and translations].

Whitelock, Dorothy, ed. *English Historical Documents c. 500–1042*. 2nd ed. London and New York: Eyre Methuen Oxford University Press, 1979 [English translation of Sighvatr's verses on English topics].

Fell, Christine. "*Víkingarvísur*." In *Specvlvm Norroenvm: Norse Studies in Memory of Gabriel Turville-Petre*. Ed. Ursula Dronke *et al*. Odense: Odense University Press, 1981, pp. 106–22 [text, translation, and discussion of *Víkingarvísur*].

Literature

Finnur Jónsson. *Den oldnorske og oldislandske Litteraturs Historie*. 3 vols. 2nd ed. Copenhagen: Gad, 1920–24 [account of Sighvatr's career and poems].

Vestlund, Alfred. "Om strofernas ursprungliga ordning i Sigvat Tordarsons *Bersǫglisvísur*." *Arkiv för nordisk filologi* 46 (1929), 281–93 [analysis and rearrangement of stanza order in *Bersǫglisvísur*].

Moberg, Ove. *Olav Haraldsson, Knut den Store och Sverige*. Lund: Gleerup, 1941 [historical account of Sighvatr's verses].

Campbell, Alistair. *Encomium Emmae reginae*. Camden Society Third Series, 72. London: Royal Historical Society, 1949 [historical value of Sighvatr's verses on English topics].

Holtsmark, Anne. "Uppreistarsaga." *Maal og minne* (1958), 93–7 [the theme of betrayal in *Erfidrápa*].

Hallberg, Peter. *Den fornisländska poesien*. Verdandis skriftserie, 20. Stockholm: Bonnier, 1962 [selections, chiefly from *Ausufararvísur*].

Vries, Jan de. *Altnordische Literaturgeschichte*. 2 vols. Grundriss der germanischen Philologie, 15–6. Berlin: de Gruyter, 1941–42 rpt. 1964–67, vol. 1 [general account of Sighvatr's career and compositions].

Bǫðvar Guðmundsson. "Rǫðin á Bersöglisvísum." *Mfmir* 9.1 (1970), 5–8 [reply to Vestlund, urging conservative approach to the prose sources].

Höskuldur Þrainsson. "Hendingar í dróttkvæðum hætti hjá Sighvati Þórðarsyni." *Mímir* 9.1 (1970), 9–29 [Sighvatr's practice with *hendingar*].

Frank, Roberta. *Old Norse Court Poetry: The Dróttkvætt Stanza*. Islandica, 42. Ithaca and London: Cornell University Press, 1978 [detailed analyses of selected stanzas from *Austrfararvísur*, the memorial *lausavísur*, and the *Erfidrápa*].

Fidjestøl, Bjarne. *Det norrøne fyrstediket*. Øvre Ervik: Alvheim & Eide, 1982 [discussion of stanza allocation and sequence in the known praise poems].

RUSSELL POOLE

SIMON DE MONTFORT, EARL OF LEICESTER (ca. 1208–1265) A younger son of the Simon de Montfort who led

the crusade against the Albigensian heretics in southern France, he first came to England in 1230 to pursue a ramily claim to the earldom of Leicester. Simon quickly won King Henry III's favor, secured the family inheritance, and married the king's sister in 1238. He thus aroused the resentment of established baronial families, who saw him as a self-seeking interloper. But his political career followed a path different from that of Henry's other favorites.

Simon was a proud, ambitious, and self-confident man who developed strong ecclesiastical friendships. Although he was at the center of affairs in the 1240s and 1250s, he came to despise Henry's military incapacity and to condemn his conduct of government. In 1258 he joined other magnates in imposing baronial government upon the king in the Provisions of Oxford. When Henry plotted to regain his power, Simon emerged as the chief advocate of the Provisions and Henry's implacable enemy. He rejected the arbitration of Louis IX of France and, though outnumbered, defeated Henry at the Battle of Lewes, 14 May 1264.

Simon now virtually ruled England, with the king as his prisoner, but he could not legitimize his authority. Faced with, the hostility of the pope and most of the barons, he tried to strengthen his position by including representatives of the towns and counties in the parliament of January 1265, the first time they had been convened together, Simon's position weakened as some of his supporters deserted him, complaining of his arrogance and use of power to enrich his family; he was defeated and killed at the Battle of Evesham, 4 August 1265.

For some years he was popularly venerated as a saint who had died for the liberties of the realm. It was, in reality, the kings need for taxation that ensured the development of the medieval parliament, not Simon's novel expedient of convening all the interested parties, simultaneously, in 1265.

Further Reading

Bemont, Charles. *Simon de Montfort, Earl of Leicester, 1208-1265.* New ed. Trans. Ernest F. Jacob. Oxford: Clarendon, 1930.

Carpenter, DA. "Simon de Montfort: The First Leader of a Political Movement in English History." *History76* (1991): 3–23.

Knowles, C.H. *Simon de Montfort, 1265–1965.* London: Historical Association, 1965 [covers Simon's changing reputation].

Labarge, Margaret Wade. *Simon de Montfort.* London: Eyre & Spottiswoode, 1962.

Maddicott, J.R. *Simon de Montfort.* .Cambridge: Cambridge University Press, 1994 [the best account of his life].

C.H. KNOWLES

SLUTER, CLAUS (ca. 1345–1405/06)

Artist who also achieved prominence as one of Philip the Bold of Burgundy's *valets de chambre*, a position he acquired after the death of his master, Jehan de Marville, Sluter was born in Haarlem in Holland; after working in Brussels from 1379 to 1385, he became an assistant to Marville, then *valet de chambre* to Philip, in Dijon. The Chartreuse de Champmol in Dijon, a project begun by Marville and his workshop, features one of Sluter's and the workshop's finest accomplishments, the *Well of Moses* (ca. 1395–1406). Sluter also finished the tomb of Philip the Bold, now in the Musée des Beaux-Arts in Dijon, which had been begun by his predecessor. His primary achievement in his art was to free sculpture from its purely structural function, enabling the figures to dominate the architectural setting. Sluter infused his work with energy and an emotive quality unsurpassed by his contemporaries.

See also **Philip the Bold**

Further Reading

Morand, Kathleen. *Claus Sluter: Artist at the Court of Burgundy.* Austin: University of Texas Press, 1991.

Snyder, James. *Northern Renaissance Art.* New York: Abrams, 1985.

MICHELLE I. LAPINE

SNORRI STURLUSON (1178/9–1241)

Snorri Sturluson was outstanding as a man of letters, and as a man of the world. More is known about him than about most authors of his time. He figures prominently in the major events of his day as recorded by his nephew Sturla Þórðarson in his *Íslendinga saga*, the chief item in the *Sturlunga saga* collection. We also gain glimpses of Snorri from other sagas of the *Sturlunga* collection, from Sturla Þórðarson's *Hákonar saga Hákonarsonar*, and from sagas of contemporary Icelandic bishops, especially Guðmundr Arason, as well as from annals, genealogies, letters, and verses by Snorri and his contemporaries.

Snorri's intelligence and driving ambition made him exceptional, but, at the same time, his life reflects his age and its contradictions, not least that between political turbulence and intellectual achievement.

Snorri is named in a near-contemporary source among the eight most powerful laymen in Iceland while still in his twenties. In 1215–1218 and 1222–1231/5, he held the almost presidential position of lawspeaker (*lǫgsǫgumaðr*) to the *Alþingi*, and he became the richest man in the land.

Snorri owed his worldly success to a combination of luck and shrewd management. He was born into the clan of the Sturlungar, who took their name from his father, the chieftain Sturla Þórðarson of Hvammr (d. 1183), and gave their name to one of the most tempestuous ages in Iceland's history, the "Age of the Sturlungs." Snorri's relations with his brothers Þórðr and Sighvatr and nephew Sturla Sighvatsson varied throughout their lives, but at their worst were tragically destructive. In 1227–1228, for instance, Snorri and Þórðr ousted Sturla Sighvatsson from the family chieftainship (*goðorð*) in Dalir. In 1236, Sturla attacked Snorri's farm at Reykjaholt and had his son Órækja mutilated.

Although born into the Sturlungar, Snorri was brought up among the Oddaverjar, being fostered at Oddi, a prime center of learning, by the great chieftain Jón Loptsson (d. 1197). Partly through the agency of his foster-kinsman Sæmmdr Jónsson, Snorri married Herdis, daughter of Bersi inn auðgi ("the wealthy") in 1199. He inherited Bersi's estate at Borg two years later. In 1206, Snorri moved to Reykjaholt, his main home for the rest of his life, and took over the *goðorð* there, later extending his influence (often by a shared or temporarily entrusted *goðorð*) still farther throughout the west of the country and into the northern and southern quarters. Herdis remained in Borg until her death in 1233, but before that, in 1224, Snorri had found another partner, Hallveig Ormsdóttir, a member of the Oddaverjar and the richest woman in Iceland.

Snorri also allied himself with other chieftainly families through his daughters' marriages: Hallbera's to Árni Magnússon óreiða ("the unready") of the Ámundaætt and then to Kolbeínn ungi ("the young") of the Ásbirningar; Ingibjg's to Gizurr Þorvaldsson of the Haukdœlir; and Þórdís's to Þorvaldr Vatnsfirðingr. But Þorvaldr was burned to death at the instigation of Sturla Sighvatsson in 1228, and the other three marriages turned sour, and with them the alliances, which proved to be the death of Snorri, because Gizurr and Kolbeinn were leaders of the expedition that killed him.

Snorri's dealings with his fellow Icelanders, as lawspeaker, chieftain, and neighbor, and the personality that emerges from them, are far too intricate even to outline here. In essence, Snorri shunned violence and cherished an ideal of peace, which, however, could not prevail against the violence of the times or his own greed for power and ostentatious wealth. He figures variously as a reconciler, an equivocator, or a coward. His practical sense and legal expertise were often put to the service of his friends, but often used in deviously self-promoting ways; and where legal means failed, he did not flinch from inciting others to violence.

Snorri began early to court the favor of Scandinavian rulers by sending youthful praise poems to the Norwegian kings Sverrir Sigurðarson and Ingi Bárðarson, and the earl Hákon galinn ("the mad"). Hákon sent lavish gifts in return and an invitation to Norway, but died before Snorri was able to take up this offer. Snorri did, however, make the journey to see Hákon's widow, Kristin, now remarried in Gautland, during his Scandinavian visit of 1218–1220. The main focus of the visit was the Norwegian court, and Snorri spent the two winters with Earl Skúli, regent to the young King Hákon Hákonarson, becoming a royal retainer and receiving titles from them culminating in lendr maðr ("baron," literally "landed-man") as well as magnificent gifts. The glory and generosity of these rulers were celebrated in Snorri's grand metrical sampler Háttatal, and Snorri is credited with two panegyrics for Skúli alone, from which only a refrain survives. Snorri also cut a political deal in Norway, making a promise (which he kept little or not at all) to persuade the Icelanders to accept Norwegian rule, while Skúli in return gave up his intention to punish a fracas between the Oddaverjar and Norwegian traders by invading Iceland.

Snorri again sailed to Norway in 1237, thus escaping from the tightening web of hostility between Icelandic clans and within his own, and there he learned of the deaths of Sighvatr Sturluson and la ighvatsson in the battle of Ǫrlygsstaðir (1238). Snorri stayed with Earl Skúli and his son Pétr, thus taking the wrong side in what became a fatal rift between Skúli and King Hákon. It was later rumored in Iceland that Skúli had secretly granted Snorri the title of "jarl," but certainly Snorri gave Hákon grounds enough for anger and a charge of treason by leaving Norway in defiance of his ban. The king's anger joined that of Gizurr Þorvaldsson, Snorri's alienated and ambitious son-in-law. Acting in delayed response to a letter from the king that had been brought to him by Árni óreiða, another former son-in-law, Gizurr, led the force of seventy men that attacked Reykjaholt on September 22, 1241. Kolbeinn ungi and one of Hallveig Ormsdóttir's sons were also in the company. A party of five warriors discovered Snorri hiding in the cellar and, despite his injunction "do not strike" (eigi skal hǫggva), killed him there.

To posterity, Snorri's role as a man of letters, a preserver of poetic, mythological, and historical traditions, a composer of technically ingenious verse, and a writer of at times superb prose far exceeds his importance as magnate and statesman. Yet Sturla Þórðarson only rarely refers to this side of his life, calling him a good skáld, and reporting spiteful comments about Snorri's poetic attempts to ingratiate himself with the Norwegian monarchy and about his tendency to compose verses rather than act. He also tells how Snorri's nephew Sturla Sighvatsson spent a winter at Reykjaholt in 1230–31, and had copies of Snorri's sǫgubǽskr made. What saga books these were is not clear, but Snorri probably wrote his Prose Edda, his separate Óláfs saga helga, and most of Heimskringla in the relatively peaceful decade 1220–1230. That he also composed Egils saga has been argued often and persuasively, if not conclusively.

See also **Sturla Þórðarson**

Further Reading

Literature

Sigurður Nordal. Snorri Sturluson. Reykjavik: Porláksson, 1920; rpt. Reykjavik: Helgafell, 1973

Paasche, Fredrik. Snorre Sturlason og Sturlungeme. Oslo: Aschehoug, 1922; 2nd ed. 1948

Einar Ól. Sveinsson. The Age of the Sturlungs: Icelandic Civilization in the Thirteenth Century. Trans, Jóhann S. Hannesson. Islandica, 36. Ithaca: Cornell University Press, 1953; rpt. New York: Kraus, 1966

Simon, John. "Snorri Sturluson: His Life and Times." Parergon 15 (1976), 3–15

Ciklamini, Marlene. *Snorri Sturluson.* Twayne's
World Authors Series, 493. Boston: Twayne,
1978.

DIANA EDWARDS WHALEY

SPINELLO ARETINO (c. 1350–1410)

The painter Spinello Aretino (Spinello
di Luca Spinelli) was born into a family of goldsmiths. Spinello was active
in the principal towns of Tuscany, and
his art, like that of his contemporaries
Agnolo Gaddi and Antonio Veneziano,
is characterized by profound insight into
Giottesque concerns with light, space, and
form. To this should be added his highly
expressive treatment of line and, in certain works, an interest in richly wrought
surface textures and luminous color. His
skills in narrative composition and design
were cleverly applied in the many important monumental fresco commissions that
punctuate his career.

1370s–1385: Arezzo and Lucca

It would appear that Spinello spent
his formative years in Arezzo, and it is
likely that he trained under the local
painter Andrea di Nerio, whose influence can be detected in the austere and
powerfully modeled forms of Spinello's
fresco *Virgin and Child with Saints
and a Donor* (1377; Arezzo, Museo
Diocesano). By the early 1380s, Spinello
had moved to Lucca, where the measured style of his earlier Aretine phase
had evolved to take greater account of
the decorative qualities of line and color;
these developments suggest that he was
responding to the sumptuous aspects of
contemporary Lucchese artistic culture,
especially the art of Angelo Puccinelli.
In 1384, it is documented that Spinello
had recently executed an altarpiece for
the Olivetan order in Lucca; today, its
principal components are generally identified as a central *Virgin and Child with
Angels* (Fogg Collection, Cambridge,
Massachusetts), two flanking panels of
Saint Pontianus and *Saint Benedict* (both
in the Hermitage, Saint Petersburg),
and three predella scenes (Galleria
Nazionale, Parma). The pre-della scenes
were designed with a remarkable degree
of spirited narrative detail, and some
of the motifs indicate that Spinello was
familiar with the monumental fresco cycles of the Camposanto in nearby Pisa.
Spinello's sojourn in Lucca culminated in
another commission from the Olivetan
order: a grand polyptych for the high,
altar of Santa Maria Nuova in Rome. Its
central panel (now missing) was signed
and dated 1385.

1386–1398: Arezzo, Florence, and Pisa

Spinello is documented in Arezzo in
1386. He was in Florence the following
year, by which point he had joined the
Arte dei Medici e degli Speziali and had
received payment for two designs of statues intended for the cathedral facade. In
this same period, he was commissioned
by the Alberti family to work on two
great fresco cycles: scenes from the *Life
of Saint Benedict* (c. 1387–1388) for the
sacristy of the Olivetan foundation of San
Miniato al Monte, and episodes from the
Life of Saint Catherine of Alexandria (c.
1390) for the private chapel of the Alberti,
the Oratorio di Santa Caterina in Antella
(outside Florence). Spinello's powers of
narrative composition, which were already evident in the predella scenes of the
Lucchese altarpieces, are fully developed
in both fresco cycles, in which the facial
expressions and individual gestures of the
robustly modeled figures have been intelligently selected. In these years, Spinello's
use of rhythmic line intensified, as can
be seen in his next project, frescoes depicting scenes from the *Lives of Saints
Ephysius and Potitus* (1390–1391) in
the Camposanto of Pisa. Here, Spinello
emphasizes the calligraphic forms of the
undulating drapery and also exhibits an
interest in antique models, for his great
battle scenes rely on reliefs from Roman

sarcophagi for their effects. Following this commission in Pisa, Spinello returned to Florence, where he probably completed the cycle in Antella, as well as executing frescoes of episodes in the *Life of Saint John the Baptist* (now destroyed) in the Manetti Chapel in Santa Maria del Carmine. Spinello is again documented in Arezzo in 1395–1397.

1399–1411: Florence, Siena, and Arezzo

Between 1399 and 1401, Spinello was once again working in Florence, where he collaborated with Niccolò di Pietro Gerini and Lorenzo di Niccolò on the high altarpiece of Santa Felicita (1401; Accademia, Florence). Spinello's austerely designed saints from the right wing are in marked contrast to his dancing angels in the central panel, whose furious movements and fully activated drapery forms are remarkable for their expressive force. In the following years Spinello was mostly occupied with commissions in Arezzo, but by late 1404 he was in Siena to paint frescoes for the Sant'Ansano Chapel (now destroyed) in the cathedral. His years in Siena culminated in a commission, on which his son Parri Spinelli assisted him, to decorate the Sala di Balia in the Palazzo Pubblico with frescoed scenes from the *Life of Pope Alexander III* (1407–1408); these are remarkable for their engaging anecdotal elements and expressively characterized human figures.

Spinello occupies an important position in the development of Tuscan painting. His interest in the principles of Giotto's art and his competence in monumental mural painting were to influence Masaccio and others; at the same time, his lavish effects of color and pattern, decorative use of line, and freshness of narrative anticipated the late Gothic style of Lorenzo Monaco and Lorenzo Ghiberti.

See also **Giotto di Bondone**

Further Reading

Bellosi, Luciano. "Da Spinello Aretino a Lorenzo Monaco." *Paragone*, 187, 1965, pp. 18–43.

Boggi, Flavio. "Painting in Lucca from the Libertà to the Signoria of Paolo Guinigi: Observations, Proposals, and New Documents." *Arte Cristiana*, 87, March-April 1999, pp. 105–116.

Boskovits, Miklos. *Pittura fiorentina alila vigilia del rinascimento, 1370–1400*. Florence: Edam, 1975, pp. 141–147, 430–432.

Calderoni Masetti, Anna Rosa. *Spinello Aretino giovane*. Florence: Centro Di, 1973.

Fehm, Sherwood A. "Notes on Spinello's So-Called Monte Oliveto Altarpiece." *Mitteilungen des Kunsthistorischen Institutes in Florenz*, 17, 1973, pp. 257–272.

Fremantle, Richard. *Florentine Gothic Painters: From Giotto to Masaccio—A Guide to Painting in and Near Florence*. London: Secker and Warburg, 1975, pp. 343–354.

Weppelmann, Stefan. "Andrea di Nerio o Spinello Aretino?" *Nuovi Studi*, 4, 1999, pp. 5–16.

———. "Sulla pittura del trecento aretino tra le botteghe di Andrea di Nerio e Spinello Aretino." *Proporzioni*, 1, 2000, pp. 28–36.

FLAVIO BOGGI

STAINREUTER, LEOPOLD (ca. 1340–ca. 1400)

An Austrian by birth, the cleric Leopold Stainreuter studied at the Universities of Paris and Vienna, becoming court chaplain to Duke Albrecht III of Austria (d. 1395). Stainreuter was a prominent translator of Latin theological tracts, having rendered the *Rationale divinorum officiorum* of Guilelmus Durandus (d. 1296) for the ducal court. Apparently at the behest of the duke's steward, Hans von Liechtenstein, Stainreuter translated Latin books on pilgrimage (called *Pilgerbüchlein*). Stainreuter, as translator and popular theologian, joins the so-called *Wiener Schule* (Viennese School), formed from authors with close ties both to the Habsburg court and the University of Vienna: Heinrich von Langenstein, Nikolaus von Dinkelsbühl, Thomas Peuntner, Nikolaus Kempf, and Nikolaus von Astau. (Johannes von Gelnhausen, Rudolf Wintuawer, Friedrich der Karmeliter, and Ulrich von Pottenstein are also associated, however tangentially, with the Viennese School.)

Central concerns of the authors named were religious instruction and edification, to which ends they translated Latin writings into the vernacular. Believing that literature should offer practical instruction for daily living and should promote the conversion of souls, they aimed their catechetical literature at a broad audience, embracing clerics, the laity, common people, and the nobility. Augustinianism was the theological direction of the school, Stainreuter having been active in the monastery of the Augustinian Hermits in Vienna.

Stainreuter also found his voice as historian, translating and composing dynastic history. For his 1385 translation of the *Historia tripartita*, the three-part church history by Cassiodorus, he wrote, as a type of introduction, a panegyric poem to Duke Albrecht III, labeled an "Epistel in daz lob des furstleihen herren herczog Albrechten czw Österreich" (Epistle of praise of his princely duke Albrecht of Austria). In the work Stainreuter identifies himself both as *chapplan, prueder Lewpoltz* (Brother Leopold, chaplain) and *lesmaister* (lector). Noteworthy is his employment of genealogy, a topic carried to fullness in his *Österreichische Chronik von den 95 Herrschaften* (begun in the late 1380s), an influential compendium of Austrian history borrowing the frame of world history, and commissioned by Duke Albrecht III. The *Chronik*, sometimes called the *Chronica patrie*, is a detailed, annalist prose history—based in part on the religious chronicle *Flores temporum* focusing on Austria from its earliest times through the rule of Duke Albrecht. (The concluding events are the death of the duke in 1395 and the pilgrimage of

Duke Albrecht IV in 1398.) Stainreuter's *Chronik* is nourished by its vivid historical awareness, as indicated by its opening references to Seneca as helmsman, of the value of memory *(gedechtnüs)*, and of history writing itself. There follows a fabulous pseudo-history, insistent in its efforts to legitimate Habsburg rule, placing Austria in a historical context that is both inventive and tendentious. As valuable as any of the Austrian historical events reported by Stainreuter is his allusion to a very early German Bible. He reports (in paragraph 388) that Queen Agnes of Hungary (d. 1364), *het ain bibel, die waz ze deütsche gemachet* (possessed a Bible written in the German tongue).

By the 1980s scholarship on Leopold Stainreuter seemed stable and serene. For all the vague remarks in the critical literature of the type that works were "ascribed" to him, a consensus had emerged that he was a translator and historian of note. Now that consensus has been shattered. Paul Uiblein recently shook Stainreuter research to its foundations, claiming Stainreuter was in fact the beneficiary of a kind of mistaken identity. Uiblein identifies our author, instead, as a certain Leopold of Vienna (Leupoldus de Wienna), a cleric of similar background who studied theology in Paris and taught the same in the theological faculty of the University of Vienna, established in 1384. At some point before this, Leopold had become court chaplain of Duke Albrecht III of Austria. Among his ducal duties was the preparation of translations; for these, as well as for his teaching at the university, he was recognized in 1385. In that year Duke Albrecht interceded on Leopold's behalf with Pope Urban VI, so that the chaplain might receive a benefice. That Leopold of Vienna already enjoyed the favor of the pope is shown by the bestowal of the title "papal honorary chaplain" in 1385.

Suffice it here to say that scholarship on Leopold Stainreuter is in flux; it is not yet certain when, or how, researchers might sort through the claims and counterclaims, and make a cogent case for the achievements of either "Leopold." Until that time, the literary patronage of the Habsburg dukes, primarily Albrecht III, will be more opaque than once believed. What is clear is that in late-fourteenth-century Austria a court historiography arose animated by nobles and confected of genealogy, historical fact, and fable.

Further Reading

Boot, Christine, ed. *Cassiodorus' Historia Ecclesiastica Tripartita in Leopold Stainreuter's German Translation MS ger. fol.1109.* 2 vols. Amsterdam: Rodopi, 1977.

Uiblein, Paul. "Leopold von Wien (Leupoldus de Wienna)," in *Die deutsche Literatur des Mittelalters. Verfasserlexikon,* 2d ed., ed. Kurt Ruh et al. Berlin: de Gruyter, 1985, vol. 5, cols. 716–723.

WILLIAM C. McDONALD

STEPHEN II, POPE (d. 757, r. 752–757)   Pope Stephen II is sometimes identified as Stephen III—his predecessor, the original Stephen II, having died in 752 before being consecrated. Stephen became pope at a time of flux that gravely threatened the papacy. Since the late seventh century, the control of the Byzantine empire over its Italian possessions had steadily deteriorated. This decline allowed a succession of popes to assume de facto control over the duchy of Rome and to formulate an increasingly persuasive ideology justifying the right of the successors of Saint Peter to guide the orthodox in Italy, i.e., the true Romans who spurned the heretical iconoclastic policy of the emperors. However, another Italian power, the Lombard kingdom, was eager to exploit the decline of Byzantium. The Lombards became increasingly aggressive, and in 751 the Lombard king, Aistulf (r. 749–756), seized the exarchate, an important Byzantine territory around Ravenna, and threatened to occupy the duchy of Rome.

Stephen's central concern throughout his pontificate was to provide security for what was coming to be called the Republic of Saint Peter. After diplomacy failed to avert the Lombard threat and after approaches to Constantinople made clear that his theoretical overlord was incapable of protecting Rome, Stephen turned to Pepin III, king of the Franks. Pepin was perhaps grateful to the papacy, which had approved his seizure of the Frankish crown in 751, and indicated that he was willing to support Stephen's cause. Stephen thereupon journeyed to Francia in 753–754. After lengthy negotiations, the two parties entered a treaty of friendship, and Pepin agreed to protect the papacy and to restore to it extensive territories described in a written document. For his part, Stephen solidified the claim of the Carolingians to the throne by reanointing Pepin and his sons and by forbidding anyone to replace the Carolingians as kings. He also bestowed on Pepin and his sons the vague title *patricius Romanorum*, which implied that the Frankish rulers were responsible for protecting the Romans.

These negotiations resulted in a successful Frankish expedition to Italy in 755, which exacted from Aistulf a promise to restore extensive territories. However, once Pepin left Italy, Aistulf refused to respect his promise and again threatened Rome. Stephen's appeals led to a second Frankish expedition in 756 and another defeat for Aistulf. Pepin's agents now took possession of formerly Byzantine cities and territories in the exarchate and the Pentapolis and granted them to the pope, in a document known as the Donation of Pepin. Although these territories did not encompass all that Pepin had promised in 754, they and the duchy of Rome constituted the core of what was in effect an independent papal state. Stephen II followed up this success by playing a significant role in the election of Desiderius (757–774) to succeed Aistulf under terms favorable to the papacy.

When Stephen II died, there remained many uncertainties about the exact boundaries of the papal state, the future course of action of the new Lombard king, and the relationship between the papacy and the Frankish monarchy. However, Stephen's successes in expanding the republic of Saint Peter and in gaining a protector for it marked a turning point not only in papal and Italian history but also in the history of the west and its relationship with the east.

See also **Pepin III the Short**

Further Reading

Editions

Codex Carolinus, ed. Wilhelm Gundlach. Monumenta Germaniae Historica, Epistolae Merowingici et Karolini aevi, 1. Berlin: Weidmann, 1892, pp. 487–505.

Le liber pontificalis, 3 vols., ed. Louis Duchesne, 2nd ed. Bibliothèque des Écoles Françaises d'Athènes et de Rome. Paris: E. de Boccard, 1955–1957, Vol. 1, pp. 440–462.

Critical Studies

Miller, David Harry. "The Roman Revolution of the Eighth Century: A Study of the Ideological Background of the Papal Separation from Byzantium and Alliance with the Franks." *Mediaeval Studies*, 36, 1974, pp. 79–133.

Noble, Thomas F. X. *The Republic of Saint Peter. The Birth of the Papal State, 680–725.* The Middle Ages. Philadelphia: University of Pennsylvania Press, 1984, pp. 61–107.

RICHARD E. SULLIVAN

STEPHEN LANGTON (ca. 1155–1228) Stephen Langton and his brother Simon were two of the most influential figures of their age. Stephen was born in Langton-by-Wragby, near Lincoln. His early education was probably at the Lincoln cathedral school, but ca. 1170 he moved to Paris and studied and then taught, for about twenty years, around the Petit Pont, probably at the school of

Peter the Chanter. Like the Chanter and Peter Comestor, Stephen was interested in practical moral questions and in biblical studies. He was at his best when discussing, in a common-sense way, the problems of everyday life. He sided most definitely with the active rather than the contemplative life.

Stephen's fame came not from his theology but from his preaching and biblical commentaries. He was known as *Linguatonans*—thundering tongue. About 500 of his sermons survive. He is credited with the division of the Bible into more or less its present chapters; he was well known for his corrections to the text; and he commented on most of the Bible according to both the literal and spiritual senses. His commentaries circulated in a number of forms, some with only one sense, some with both. He also wrote commentaries on Peter Comestor's *Historia scholastica*.

While in Paris, he was a close friend of Lothar of Segni, who as Pope Innocent III made him a cardinal in 1206. In December 1206, Stephen was elected archbishop of Canterbury; but owing to disputes over his election between King John Lackland and the Canterbury chapter (backed by Innocent III), he was not allowed to take his seat until 1213. Until then, he lived in exile at the abbey of Pontigny.

Stephen was closely involved with Magna Carta and may have been its author. He worked hard to maintain the role of mediator during the events that led to 1215 and saw the charter not as innovation but as restatements of the rights and duties of kingship. Innocent read Langton's mediation with the barons as an indirect challenge to himself and suspended him as archbishop for two years. The dispute was eventually settled by the deaths of John and Innocent, and Stephen returned to England in 1218.

He attended the Fourth Lateran Council in 1215 and was very much in sympathy with its reforming principles. Back in England, he avidly pursued church reform, holding the first provincial council to legislate in England in 1222 in Oxford. He himself was active in administration of his see. He presided over the translation of the relics of Thomas Becket at Canterbury in 1220. He played a major role in the coronation of the boy-king Henry III (1220) and became his adviser. He died in Sussex in 1228.

See also Innocent III, Pope; John; Peter Comestor; Peter the Chanter

Further Reading

Stephen Langton. *Commentary on the Book of Chronicles,* ed. Avrom Saltman. Ramat-Gan:Bar-Ilan University Press, 1978.

——. *Der Sentenzenkommentar des Kardinals Stephan Langton,* ed. Artur Michael Landgraf. Münster: Aschendorff, 1952.

——. *Selected Sermons of Stephen Langton,* ed. Phyllis Barzillay Roberts. Toronto: Pontifical Institute of Mediaeval Studies, 1980.

Baldwin, John W. *Masters, Princes, and Merchants: The Social Views of Peter the Chanter and His Circle,* 2 vols. Princeton: Princeton University Press, 1970, Vol. 1, pp. 25–31.

Longère, Jean. *Œuvres oratoires de maîtres parisiens au XIIe siècle: étude historique et doctrinale.* Paris: Études Augustiniennes, 1975.

Powicke, Frederick Maurice. *Stephen Langton: Being the Ford Lectures Delivered in the University of Oxford in Hilary Term 1927.* Oxford: Clarendon, 1928.

Roberts, Phyllis Barzillay. "Master Stephen Langton Preaches to the People and Clergy: Sermon Texts from Twelfth-Century Paris." *Traditio* 36 (1980): 237–68.

——. *Stephanus de Lingua-Tonante: Studies in the Sermons of Stephen Langton.* Toronto: Pontifical Institute of Mediaeval Studies, 1968.

LESLEY J. SMITH

STOSS, VEIT (ca. 1445/1450–1533) The famed sculptor was born in Horb am Neckar and died in Nuremberg

on September 20, 1533. Virtually no documentation exists about Stoss's training and earlier years. His earliest secure sculptures show his familiarity with the heightened realism of the art of Nikolaus Gerhaert and Martin Schongauer, suggesting a stay on the Upper Rhine, perhaps in Strasbourg. Rogier van der Weyden's paintings, likely through other artistic intermediaries, also influenced the young sculptor. Although scholars have suggested the Stoss collaborated on altarpieces in Rothenburg (1466) and Nördlingen, nothing is known about his very earliest production. He certainly was an established sculptor when, in 1477, he moved to Kraków from Nuremberg, where he had married before 1476. Between 1477 and 1489 he created the Mary Altarpiece for St. Mary's in Kraków. Measuring 13.95 × 10.68 meters, this is probably the period's largest winged retable. Several of the apostles in the Death and Coronation of the Virgin in the corpus are about 2.8 meters tall. Here and in the relief scenes of the inner and outer wings, Stoss provides his figures with little space. Most are located within a shallow stage with a sharply tilted ground plane. Stoss's virtuosity in cutting highly animated draperies with deep, crisp folds is best observed in the richly polychromed (multicolored) and gilt corpus statues. For a project of this magnitude, the artist employed several assistants likely including a few of his seven sons. The Mary Altarpiece, the red marble Tomb of King Casimir IV Jagiello (1492) in Wawel Cathedral in Kraków, and his cast bronze Tomb Plate of Callimachus (Filippo Buonaccorsi, d. 1496) in the city's Dominican Church, among other works, exerted a tremendous influence on other artists active in Poland and eastern Prussia.

In 1496 Stoss moved back to Nuremberg. Three years later he completed stone statues of the Man of Sorrows and Mater Dolorosa plus three reliefs of the Last Supper, Christ on the Mount of Olives, and the Arrest of Christ that patrician Paulus Volckamer set in the eastern choir wall of St. Sebaldus church. The emotional appeal of the figures, notably Christ and Mary, who look beseechingly at the viewers passing in the ambulatory, coupled with a growing clarity of form define Stoss's more developed style. His career, however, was temporarily sidetracked. Having lost 1,265 guilders speculating on copper, Stoss forged a promissory note in 1503. After being convicted, he was branded on both cheeks and banned from leaving the city. In 1504 Stoss fled and worked briefly in Münnerstadt, where he polychromed Tillmann Riemenschneider's Mary Magdalene Altarpiece (1490–1492) and painted four scenes of the Martyrdom of St. Kilian on the wings. These are Stoss's only documented paintings; he also created ten engravings during this decade. Stoss returned to Nuremberg and through the intercession of Emperor Maximilian resumed his career. For the choir of St. Sebaldus, he made the limewood St. Andrew (1505–1507), in which the clear and stable pose of the apostle contrasts with the marvelous billowing drapery.

Stoss carved both small-scale and large statues throughout the 1510s and 1520s for local patrons and churches. His greatest feat was the Angelic Salutation (1517–1518), an over-life-size Annunciation suspended from the choir vault in St. Lorenz church. Supported by an angel holding *sanctus* bells, Gabriel and Mary float before the high altar. They are enframed by a giant rosary complete with roses, beads, small figured roundels, a group of joyous angels, and, at the apex, God. The ensemble included a great crown above, now lost, and Jakob Pülmann's candelabrum. Commissioned by Anton II Tucher, Nuremberg's highest official, the Angelic Salutation was covered for much of the liturgical year. With the advent of the Reformation in Nuremberg, the whole group was sheathed permanently from 1529 until circa 1806. The Reformation also affected Stoss's

final great commission, the Mary Altar (1520–1523) ordered by the artist's son, Andreas Stoss, who was the prior of the local Carmelite convent. Stoss's preparatory drawing is today in the University Museum in Kraków. The sculptor had yet to be paid when the convent was dissolved in 1525.

After a long legal battle, the altarpiece was transferred by Stoss's heirs to Bamberg in 1543 and is now in the cathedral. Like several of Stoss's later carvings, the Mary Altar was stained but never polychromed. Stoss continued working at least until 1532. His impact on regional sculpture, at least before 1525, was considerable.

See also **Maximilian; Riemenschneider, Tillmann; Schongauer, Martin**

Further Reading

Baxandall, Michael. *The Limewood Sculptors of Renaissance Germany.* New Haven, Conn.: Yale University Press, 1980.

Kahsnitz, Rainer. "Veit Stoss in Nürnberg. Eine Nachlese zum Katalog und zur Ausstellung." *Anzeiger des Germanischen Nationalmuseum* (1984): 39–70.

——, ed. *Veit Stoss in Nürnberg: Werke des Meisters und seiner Schule in Nürnberg und Umgebung.* Munich: Deutscher Kunstverlag, 1983.

——, ed. *Veit Stoss: Die Vorträge des Nürnberger Symposions.* Munich: Deutscher Kunstverlag, 1985.

Lutze, Eberhard. *Veit Stoss,* 4th ed. Munich: Deutscher Kunstverlag, 1968.

Oellermann, Eike. "Die monochromen Holzbildwerke des Veit Stoss." *Maltechnik* 82 (1976): 173–182.

Sello, Gottfried. *Veit Stoss.* Munich: Hirmer, 1988.

Skubiszewski, Piotr. *Veit Stoss und Polen.* Nuremberg: Germanisches Nationalmuseum, 1983.

Soding, Ulrich. "Veit Stoss am Oberrhein: Zur Kunstgeschichtlichen Stellung der 'Isenheimer Muttergottes' im Louvre." *Jahrbuch der Staatlichen Kunstsammlungen in Baden-Württemberg* 29 (1992): 50–76.

JEFFREY CHIPPS SMITH

STRICKER, DER

STRICKER, DER (ca. 1190–ca. 1250) This itinerant poet, known only by his pseudonym, was probably born toward the end of the twelfth century in the Middle German region. A major portion of his life was spent in Austria, where he died about 1250, if the last poems for which reliable dates exist are taken as *terminus post quern.* Clearly not a member of the nobility, he seems to have worked for various audiences and patrons, although none is known to us by name. His oeuvre, consisting of nearly 170 works and spanning a wide variety of genres, attests not only to his versatility and originality but also to his considerable knowledge of theological and legal issues. He is familiar with the works of Hartmann von Aue and Wolfram von Eschenbach. The paucity of information regarding the poet extends to the chronology of his works. While it is generally assumed that his two longer works, *Daniel von dem Blühenden Tal* and *Karl der Große,* are products of his youth, it remains impossible to establish a sequence for *Pfaffe Amis,* various stories of medium length, and his vast output of short narratives consisting of fables, prayers, didactic poems, and a corpus of *Mären* (stories or tales) that constitute his actual claim to fame. *Daniel von dem Blühenden Tal,* consisting of 8,478 verses and transmitted in four extant manuscripts, is a highly original treatment of the Arthurian romance genre. Denounced by earlier scholarship, which viewed Stricker's *novum* of an unproblematic hero and an active, functioning society as a serious misunderstanding of the genre, it is recognized today as the coherent and skillful text that introduced the notion of *ratio* as a means to avoid the pitfalls of human life. The popularity of Stricker's *Karl* is attested to by twenty-four manuscripts and twenty-three fragments. Whether it was written in the wake of the Charlemagne revival or occasioned by the moving of his remains to Aachen in 1215 or by the transport of Charlemagne reliquaries to Zurich in 1233 still must be determined. Although Stricker's primary source was the *Chanson de Roland,* modern scholarship has been reluctant to label the 12,206 verse narrative simply a reworking of his source. Yet, attempts to explain it in its historical context as a political piece aimed at renewing interest in crusading efforts or as confirmation of the Hohenstaufen emperors as legitimate heirs to Charlemagne are inconclusive as well. A comprehensive interpretation remains a desideratum.

Stricker's shorter narratives are transmitted in fifty-three manuscripts and range from 10 to circa 2,500 verses. Counted among the latter are *Die Frauenehre,* Stricker's praise of women, and *Pfaffe Amis,* a cyclical narrative arranged in twelve episodes that castigates the folly of man. The thematic emphasis on *prudentia* and self-knowledge, either as underlying message or overtly stated, extends to many of the shorter works, which range from purely religious to profane, from entertaining to moralizing. Viewed as a whole, the shorter narratives present a canon of values appropriate to men and women and to all social classes.

See also **Charlemagne; Hartmann von Aue; Wolfram von Eschenbach**

Further Reading

Bartsch, Karl. *Karl der Große von dem Stricker.* Quedlin-burg: Basse, 1857; rpt. Berlin: de Gruyter, 1965.

Ehrismann, Otfrid. *Der Stricker: Erzählungen, Fabeln, Reden. Mittelhochdeutsch/ Neuhochdeutsch* Stuttgart: Re-clam, 1992.

Fischer, Hanns. "Strickerstudien: Ein Beitrag zur Liter-aturgeschichte des 13. Jahrhunderts." Ph.d. diss., Lud-wig Maximilian-Universität, Munich, 1953.

——. *Studien zur deutschen Märendichtung.* Tübingen: Niemeyer, 1968, 2d ed. 1983.

——. *Der Stricker: Verserzählungen I.* Tübingen: Niemeyer, 1960, 4th ed. Johannes Janota, ed. 1979.

——. *Der Stricker. Verserzählungen II* Tübingen: Niemeyer, 1967, 4th, ed. Johannes Janota, 1983.

Geith, Karl-Ernst. *Carolus Magnus: Studien zur Darstellung Karls des Großen in der deutschen Literatur des 12. und 13. Jahrhunderts,* Bibliotheca Germanica 19. Bern: Francke, 1977.

Henderson, Ingeborg, *Strickers Daniel von dem Blühenden Tal: Werkstruktur und Interpretation.* Amsterdam: Benjamins, 1976.

Henne, Hermann. *Der Pfaffe Amis.* Göppingen: Kümmerle, 1991.

Hofmann, Klaus. *Strickers Frauenehre: Überlieferung, Textkritik, Edition, literaturgeschichtliche Einordnung.* Marburg: Elwert, 1976.

Mettke, Heinz. *Fabeln und Mären von dem Stricker.* Halle: Niemeyer, 1959.

Moelleken, Wolfgang W. *Die Kleindichtung des Strickers,* 5 vols. Göppingen: Kümmerle, 1973–1978.

Räkel, Hans-Herbert. "Die Frauenehre von dem Stricker," in *Österreichische Literatur zur Zeit der Babenberger,* ed. Alfred Ebenbauer. Vienna: Halosar, 1977.

Resler, Michael. *Der Stricker: Daniel von dem Blühenden Tal.* Tübingen: Niemeyer, 1983.

———. *Der Stricker: 'Daniel of the Blossoming Valley' (Daniel von dem Blühenden Tal).* New York: Garland, 1990.

Schwab, Ute. *Die bisher unveröffentlichten geistlichen Bispelreden des Strickers.* Göttingen: Vandenhoeck and Ruprecht, 1959.

———. *Der Stricker, Tierbispel.* Tübingen: Niemeyer, 1960, 3d ed. 1983.

Thamert. Mark Lee. "The Medieval Novelistic 'Märe': Telling and Teaching in Works of the Stricker." Ph.d. diss., Princeton University, 1986.

Wailes, Stephen L. *Studien zur Kleindichtung des Stricker.* Berlin: Schmidt, 1981.

Ziegeler, Hans-Joachim. *Erzählen im Spätmittelalter.* Munich: Artemis, 1985.

INGEBORG HENDERSON

STURLA ÞÓRÐDARSON (July 29, 1214–July 30, 1284)

Sturla Þórðdarson attained eminence as a historian, poet, and legal expert. His literary fame is based on his histories: *Íslendinga saga* ("History of the Icelanders"), which covers in detail the period from 1183 to 1242, and *Hákonar saga Hákonarsonar,* a chronicle of the reign of the Norwegian king Hákon Hákonarson (1217–1263). He also composed a version of *Landnámabók* ("Book of Settlements") known as *Sturlubók.* Although much of his skaldic poetry has been lost, the surviving verses are generally considered conventional rather than exceptional in inspiration and in expression. In the last two decades of his life, he was an acknowledged authority on his native law. Following Iceland's integration into Norway (1264), the Norwegian king Magnús Hákonarson (1263–1280) appointed him a member of the commission charged with revising provincial law.

Sturla was born the illegitimate son of a major chieftain, Þórðr Sturluson, in the northwest of Iceland. Although his illegitimacy was a distinct social disadvantage, his upbringing was privileged. In his infancy, he was raised by his grandmother Guðný, a woman of remarkable intellect and energy. His father trained him early in the duties of a chieftain, which included participation in legal affairs and in armed ventures. At age thirteen, he was delegated to empower his uncle Snorri to administer his father's chieftaincy al the *Alþingi.* In his late teens, he guarded Bishop Guðmundr and his retinue of paupers during his visitation of western Iceland. Subsequently, Sturla joined his brothers in protecting their father's territory from the depredations of Snorri's son Órækja. These missions involved him in open or barely concealed enmities that would test his organizational skills and would develop his abilities as a chieftain.

In 1235, Sturla joined his uncle Snorri, the great writer and historian. A closeness developed between the two. Although Sturla would ascribe demeaning foibles to Snorri in *Íslendinga saga,* the fact remains that Snorri assigned to Sturla the administrative powers that made Sturla, at age twenty-six, one of the foremost chieftains of western Iceland (1240). Sturla acknowledged his debt by naming his oldest son after his uncle and by joining Óraekja in seeking blood revenge for the slaying of Snorri (1241).

In the internecine struggles of the thirties and forties, the power of Sturla's clan, the Sturlungar, had been truncated. Increasingly, the Norwegian king manipulated the internal jockeying for power. Sturla was embroiled in these fights, both because two of the main contestants, Þórðr Kakali and Þorgils Skarði, were his cousin and nephew respectively, and because he felt compelled to protect his own territorial interests. His fortunes fluctuated as he participated, sometimes reluctantly, sometimes actively, in bitter feuds. Tragedy also touched his life. In 1253, Sturla had allied himself with Gizurr Þorvaldsson, the chieftain who had ordered Snorri's death. To strengthen the alliance, Sturla had affianced his daughter to Gizurr's son Hallr. At the end of the wedding celebration, Gizurr's manor, Flugumýrr, was put to the torch. The bride barely escaped in the attack that was futilely launched in revenge for the slaying of both Snorri and of Snorri's nephew, Sturla Sighvatsson. Moreover, Þorgils Skarði, for a brief time the major chieftain in northern Iceland and Sturla's close associate, was slain in 1258.

A period of uncertainty, dashed hopes, ill-fated alliances, and ventures ended in Sturla's exile to Norway in 1263. His stay at the court was prolonged. It was also an intellectually busy and fruitful time. Appointed court historian, he composed the official history of Magnús's father, King Hákon Hákonarson, a work based on eyewitness reports and on records in the royal chancery. Sturla was also busy with the revision of the provincial laws, including Icelandic law. He returned to Iceland with the first codification of the amended law, the so-called *Jámsiða* ("iron side"), in 1272. He then assumed the highest judiciary post. In 1277, his jurisdiction as lawman was restricted to northern and western Iceland. Concomitantly, he was summoned to Norway on charges

that he was less active in discharging his duties than the newly appointed lawman for eastern and southern Iceland. Still, he was honored by the king, who appointed him a member of the court with the rank of knight (*skutilsveinn*). Again he assumed the post of royal biographer by writing the history of Magnus's reign, of which only one page survives. He resigned his post as lawman when he felt unable to cope with the question of jurisdiction over church property that pitted landowners against the bishop. He died in 1284, respected by his contemporaries for his scholarliness and integrity.

His literary work was extensive. He probably wrote, as a prologue to *Landnámabók*, an account of Iceland's christianization, *Kristni saga*, and also a lost version of *Grettis saga*. A 14th-century clerical author credits Sturla with a fantastic story about the troll-woman Selkolla. Less certain is the conjecture that he was responsible for the oldest versions of Icelandic annals and for a list of lawspeakers that has survived only in a MS of the 17th century.

See also **Hákon Hákonarson; Magnús Hákonarson; Snorri Sturluson**

Further Reading

The primary sources for Sturla's life are his own *Íslendinga saga*, other sagas in the collection known as *Sturlunga saga*, and *Árna saga biskups*.

Literature

Ker, William Paton. *Sturla the Historian.* The Romanes Lecture, 1906. Oxford: Oxford University Press, 1906; rpt. in *Collected Essays of W. P. Ker.* Ed. Charles Whibley. London: Macmillan, 1925.

Einar Ól. Sveinsson. *The Age of the Sturlungs: Icelandic Civilization in the Thirteenth Century.* Trans. Jóhann S. Hannesson. Islandica, 36. Ithaca: Cornell University Press, 1953; rpt. New York: Kraus, 1966.

Magerøy, Hallvard. "Sturla Tordsson." In *Norsk biografisk leksikon* 15. Oslo: Aschehoug, 1966, pp. 188–201 [contains bibliography].

Jón Jóhannesson. *A History of the Old Icelandic Commonwealth: Íslendinga saga.* Trans. Haraldur Bessason. University of Manitoba Icelandic Studies, 2. Winnipeg: University of Manitoba Press, 1974.

Ciklamini, Marlene. "Biographical Reflections in *Íslendinga saga*: A Mirror of Personal Values." *Scandinavian Studies* 55 (1983), 205–21.

Guðrún Ása Grímsdóttir and Jónas Kristjánsson, eds. *Sturlustefna. Ráðstefna haldin á sjö alda ártíð Sturlu Þórðarsonar sagnaritara 1984.* Reykjavik: Stofnun Árna Magnússonar, 1988.

MARLENE CIKLAMINI

SUCHENWIRT, PETER (fl. 14th c.)

Neither the birth date nor death date is known for this most famous German herald of the fourteenth century. The name Suchenwirt is apparently a professional one derived from *such den wirt* (get the innkeeper); he calls himself *chnappe von den wappen* (page of the weapons, poem 30, ll. 169–189). His name appears in twelve documents from 1377 to 1407, all dealing with his house in Vienna. His name also appears in a eulogy by Hugo von Montfort (1357–1423), who was with him on Duke Albrecht III's Prussian crusade of 1377. Suchenwirt's language, perspective, and sympathies suggest that he was an Austrian. The best source of information about his life is found in his poetry.

There are fifty two poems by Peter Suchenwirt extant in at least thirty three manuscripts. The main manuscript containing Suchenwirt's works, called "A," is in the National Library in Vienna (no. a3045, 503 pages from beginning of fifteenth century). The poems range in length from 57 lines to 1,540 lines. They include a number of different genres: four death laments; eighteen elegies (*Ehrenreden*); eleven historical and political occasional poems; fifteen moral allegories and spiritual didactic poems; four comic poems. The general term *Ebrenrede* was coined by Alois Primisser, Suchenwirt's first editor, and was applied to Suchenwirt's poems honoring famous Austrian nobles. These were poems that followed a strict formula: a formal expression of humility; general praise of the hero; description of hero's specific deeds; repetition of general praise; prayer for intercession of his soul (if the hero was already deceased); description of his coat of arms, both shield and helmet; name of the hero; a short closing prayer.

The subject matter of his political comments is especially enlightening. He discusses the ramifications of a division of property, the political consequences of a tax on wine, and the interrelationships among the classes; these are not generally the subject matter for chronicles or historical songs.

Suchenwirt (and a certain Gelre in the Low Lands) are unique in writing *Ehrenreden*. Their poetry places them within a long and illustrious tradition whose origins are in the death lament, the political-historical song, and in the so-called "tournament and siege poetry."

The heroes of the *Ehrenreden* follow similar life patterns with crusades against the heathens in Prussia, pilgrimages to the Holy Land, expeditions into Italy, and in the so-called numerous local campaigns in their homelands.

Further Reading

Achnitz, Wolfgang. "Peter Suchenwirts Reimtraktat 'Die zehn Gebote' im Kontext deutschspracher Dekaloggedichte des Mittelalters. Mit Textedition und einem Abdruck der Dekalog-Auslegung des Johannes Künlin." *Beiträge zur Geschichte der deutschen Sprache und Literatur* 120 (1998): 53–102.

Blosen, Hans. "Überlegungen zur Textuberlieferung und Textgestaltung bei einem Gedicht von Peter Suchenwirt," in *Probleme altgermanistischer Editionen,* ed. Hugo Kuhn, Karl Stackmann, and Dieter Wuttke. "Wiesbaden: Steiner, 1968.

Brinker-von der Heyde, Claudia. "Suchenwirt, Peter," in *Die deutsche Literatur des Mittelalters. Verfasserlexikon,* 2d ed., ed.

Kurt Run et al. vol. 9. Berlin: de Gruyter, 1995, cols. 481–488.

Busse, Kaarl Heinrich von. "Peter Suchenwirt's Sagen über Livlane." *Mittheilungen aus dem gebiete der Geschichte Liv-, Esthh- und Kurland's,* ed. Gesellschaft für Geschichte und Altertumskund der russischen Ostsee-Provinzen. 3. Riga: Nicolai Kymmel, 1845, pp. 5–21.

Docen, Bernard Joseph. "Die Schlacht bei Sempach. 1386. Von Peter Suchenwirt." *Sammlungfür altdeutsche Literatur und Kunst* 1, no. 1 (1812): 152–160.

Friess, Godfried Edmund. "Fünf unedierte Ehrenreden Peter Suchenwirts." *Wiener Sitzungsberichte der Akademie der Wissenschaften, Phil.-hist. Klasse* 88 (1877): 99–126.

Primisser, Alois, ed. *Peter Suchenwirt's Werke aus dem vierzehnten Jahrhunderte. Ein Beytrag zur Zeit- und Sittengeschichte.* Vienna: J.B. Wallishausser, 1827; rpt. Vienna: H. Geyer, 1961.

Van D'Elden, Stephanie Cain. *Peter Suchenwirt and Heraldic Poetry.* Vienna: Halosar, 1976.

STEPHANIE CAIN VAN D'ELDEN

SUGER (1081–1151) Abbot of Saint-Denis from 1122 to 1151, Suger is one of the most interesting representatives of French monastic culture in the 12th century, combining an extraordinary devotion to his monastery with an understanding of the weaknesses and potential strengths of the kings of France. He was an ardent administrator and builder, and, if he is best remembered for his desire to adorn his church, he also reformed the liturgy and improved the life of the community, earning the praise of Bernard, abbot of Clairvaux.

Suger also stands out from most of his contemporaries because of the much clearer picture we have of his personality and achievements. He himself wrote a Latin vita of Louis VI, in which he gives a vivid picture of the king's attempts to subdue the turbulent aristocracy in the Paris region, his own role in this process, and the king's special devotion to St. Denis.

He also wrote two works concerning his administration of the monastery's lands and the building and consecration of the new church. A small number of his charters and letters survive, and his image and his words are preserved in several places in the church of his abbey.

Suger was born of a modest knightly family probably not too far from Saint-Denis and was given as an oblate to the abbey. During his early years, he seems to have realized how the abbey had lost prestige, power, and wealth since the time of Charlemagne and Charles the Bald; how the reciprocal devotion of saint and king had been a strength to both; and how the church's small size and decayed furnishings no longer served the needs of the monks or the crowds of pilgrims coming there. Throughout his long life and particularly during his abbacy, it was his purpose to remedy these three lacks.

Suger tells us how as a youth he used to look at the abbey's muniments and how he was aware not only of its lost domains, but also how through mismanagement it was receiving much less revenue than it should. The first portion of his book on the administration of the abbey, *De rebus in administratione sua gestis,* described how he carefully and painstakingly tried to recover what was owed to the abbey and to increase its revenues. For example, increases came from getting more revenues from the town of Saint-Denis or acquiring a wealthy priory like Argenteuil, but they also came from clearing forests, planting new crops and vines, settling new inhabitants on the land, enforcing ancient rights against the encroachments of local lords, building houses, granges, and courts, establishing new churches, and converting cash rents into payments in kind.

Suger also learned from the monastery's history that it had been a frequent beneficiary of royal munificence. Lands, money, and precious objects had been given to Saint-Denis by kings of France from Dagobert on. He knew, too, that it was in times of peace and harmony that Saint-Denis had prospered most. An opportunity to recreate that special harmony between king and abbot arose from the fact that Louis VI, once a pupil at the abbey, had a particular devotion to the martyrs and confidence in Suger. Although Suger was to become regent while Louis VII was on crusade, and it was then that he acted as a royal "minister" of the king, it was really during the reign of Louis VI (d. 1137) that troublesome enemies of both king and abbey, like the lords of Le Puiset, were brought to heel. The ancient relationship between *regnum* and *monasterium* was not only enhanced but refashioned when Louis VI returned the crown of his father, Philip I, to Saint-Denis; took the royal standard from the abbey's altar as he left for war in 1124, declaring that if he were not king he would do homage to the abbey; granted the fair of the Lendit what amounted to an immunity from royal justice; and declared that the kings of France should be buried at Saint-Denis.

The more rigorous administration of the monastic lands and the creation of symbols that emphasized Saint-Denis's special importance for the French were antecedent to Suger's intention to tear down the old church and replace it with a larger one with more splendid hangings, stained glass, altars, crosses, and other objects. Though this must have long been planned for, Suger tells in his *De consecratione ecclesie sancti Dionisii* that once construction started the work proceeded quickly, the western narthex and towers being consecrated in 1140, and the translation of the saints to their new reliquaries and the construction of the eastern end with the new ambulatory and stained-glass windows completed in 1144. If stylistically the chevet anticipates many features of the Gothic churches of the Île-de-France, the church also incorporates many of Suger's major concerns: the preservation of the past, a harmonious adaptation of the old to the new, an emphasis on the liturgy, and most of all the exaltation of the saints.

Suger was inventive and eclectic. He reshaped and adorned objects that had been in the church; if he was not given the precious stones he needed, he bought them. So, too, he found the sources for his conception of the church in writings as diverse as saints' lives, liturgical texts, biblical commentaries, chronicles, and the writings of Pseudo-Dionysius the Areopagite, as well as in buildings he had seen.

Suger was a small man and an assertive one, and on behalf of his church he considered any means legitimate. In his last years, as regent, he had had to spend much of his time away from Saint-Denis, and money that had been intended for the rebuilding of the nave he used for the king's needs. He died at Saint-Denis in 1151.

Further Reading

Suger. *Vie de Louis VI le Gros* (*Vita Ludovici VI*), ed. and trans. Henri Waquet. Paris: Les Belles Lettres, 1929.

———. *Abbot Suger on the Abbey Church of Saint-Denis and Its Art Treasures*, ed. and trans. Erwin Panofsky. 2nd ed. Princeton: Princeton University Press, 1979. [*Liber de rebus in administratione sua gestis*, chs. xxiv–xxxiv; *Libellus de consecratione Sancti Dionysii; Ordinatio.*]

Bur, Michel. *Suger, abbé de Saint-Denis, régent de France.* Paris: Perrin, 1991.

Cartellieri, Otto. *Abt Suger von Saint-Denis, 1081–1151.* Berlin: Ebering, 1898.

Gerson, Paula L., ed. *Abbot Suger and Saint-Denis: A Symposium.* New York: Metropolitan Museum of Art, 1986.

THOMAS G. WALDMAN

SUNESEN, ANDERS (ca. 1160–1228)

Anders Sunesen was archbishop of Lund from 1201/2 to 1223/4. His father, Sune Ebbesen, was a cousin of Archbishop Absalon and one of the wealthiest men in Denmark. In the 1180s, Anders studied abroad. He probably received his main training in Paris (arts and theology), but also visited Italy (for law studies in Bologna?), and England (for an unknown purpose). After becoming a master of arts perhaps by 1186, and of theology some years later, he spent some time teaching, probably theology in Paris, before becoming chancellor to King Knud VI (r. 1182–1202). His first-known job as chancellor was on an embassy in 1195 that tried to reconcile Philippe Auguste of France with his Danish queen, Ingeborg. In 1201/2, Anders succeeded Absalon as archbishop of Lund and left the chancellery to his brother Peter, bishop of Roskilde, Denmark. In 1204, Anders was named papal legate to Denmark and Sweden. During the years 1206–1222, he cooperated with King Valdemar II (r. 1202–1241) in the subjugation and christianization of pagan populations in the Baltic area, in particular Estonia. Though initially reluctant, he seems in the end to have obeyed a papal summons to attend the Fourth Lateran Council in Rome in 1215. In 1222, he petitioned the pope to be relieved of his duties as archbishop due to "an incurable bodily infirmity." His successor, Peder Saksesen, was consecrated in 1224. Anders died in 1228, leaving various possessions to Lund chapter, including a collection of books.

As archbishop, Anders was an able administrator and politician on good terms with both pope and king. A later legend, modeled on the story of Moses in Exodus 17, credits him with prayer that secured Danish victory in the decisive battle against the Estonians at Lyndanis on June 15, 1219. This legend is often combined with another, according to which the Danish flag, *Dannebrog*, was sent from heaven during the battle.

Anders produced no literary works in Danish, as far as is known. Apart from administrative documents, the following Latin works have been attributed to Anders: (1) *Hexaemeron*, a theological poem in 8,040 hexameters, extant. (2) *De vii ecclesiae sacramentis*, also in hex-ameters, now lost. (3) Two sequences, "Missus Gabriel de celis" and "Stella solem preter morem"; "Missus," however, seems to predate Anders, and his authorship of "Stella" is also doubtful. (4) A Latin version of the Law of Scania, extant; the attribution rests on slender evidence, but is generally accepted.

The *Hexaemeron* is preserved in one medieval MS (Copenhagen, Royal Library, E don. var. 155 4to) from the second half of the 13th century, originally in the cathedral library at Roskilde. Anders probably composed the work in Paris in the early 1190s. It consists of twelve books and combines a commentary on Genesis 1–3 (Books 1–4) with an exposition of the main points of systematic theology, excluding the sacraments (5–12 plus a digression on divine names in 2–3). Main sources include, for the commentary on Genesis, Peter Comesior's *Historia scholastica* and Richard of St. Victor's *Allegorie*, and for the remaining part of the work, Stephen Langton's *Summa* and *Quaestiones*. As a whole, the *Hexaemeron* takes the reader from the Creation (1) to the Day of Judgment (12). A second proemium in Book 10 marks off two main parts: creation and fall (1–9), recreation in Christ (10–12). Anders shows great skill as a poet of hexameters. In his handling of the Latin language and of verse technique, he dissociates himself from the classicizing school represented by Saxo. The poem seems to have had a very limited diffusion, probably because so much learning is packed into it that it makes for very difficult reading.

See also **Peter Comestor; Philip II Augustus; Richard of Saint-Victor**

Further Reading

Editions
Leges Provinciales Terrae Scaniae ante annos 400 Latinæ redditae per Andream Suonis F. Ed. Amoldus Hvitfeldius. Copenhagen, 1590.

Andreae Sunonis filii archiepiscopi Lundensis Hexameron libri duodecim. Ed. M. Cl. Genz. Copenhagen: Gyldendal, 1892 [includes edition of the sequences].

Skånske lov. Anders Sunesøns parafrase. Aakjær, S. and E. Kroman, eds. In *Danmarks gamle Landskabslovemed Kirkelovene* 1.2. Ed. Johs. Brøandum-Nielsen and Poul Johs. Jørgensen. Danish Society of Language and Literature. Copenhagen: Gyldendal, 1933.

Andreae Sunonis Filii Hexaemeron Post M. Cl. Gertz. Ed. Sten Ebbesen and L. B. Mortensen. Corpus Philosophorum Danicorum Medii Aevi, 11.1–2. Danish Society of Language and Literature. Copenhagen: Gad, 1985–88 [contains English introduction in part 1 and extensive bibliography in part 2].

Literature

Kabell, Aage. "Ueber die dem dänischen Erzbischof Anders Sunesen zugeschriebenen Sequenzen." *Archivum latinitatis medii aevi* 28 (1958), 19–30.

Christensen, A. E. "Sunesen, Anders." *Dansk Biografisk Leksikon* 14. Copenhagen: Gyldendal, 1983, pp. 208–11.

Mortensen, Lars Boje. "The Sources of Andrew Sunesen's Hexaemeron." Université de Copenhague, *Cahiers de l'Institut du moyen âge grec et latin* 50 (1985), 113–216.

Ebbesen, Sten, ed. *Anders Sunesen, stormand—teolog—administrator—digter.* Copenhagen: Gad, 1985 [contains fifteen studies on Sunesen, with English summaries and extensive bibliography].

Ebbesen, S. "Corpus Philosophorum Danicorum Medii Aevi, Archbishop Andrew (+1228), and Twelfth-Century Techniques of Argumentation." In *The Editing of Theological and Philosophical Texts from the Middle Ages.* Ed. Monika Asztalos. Acta Universitatis Stockholmiensis, Studia Latina Stockholmiensia, 30. Stockholm: Almqvist & Wikselt, 1986, pp. 267–80.

STEN EBBESEN

SVEN HARALDSSON (Forkbeard) (r. 987–1014)

Sven Haraldsson was king of Denmark 987–1014. Sven seized power through a revolt against his father, Harald Gormsson (Bluetooth), who fled to the Wends and died of his wounds on November 1, 987. That Sven was captured and ransomed from the Wends following this revolt is highly dubious. According to Adam of Bremen, Sven's revolt was a pagan reaction, but its motives were more likely political; there is no other indication that Sven was a pagan. In Sven's time, Viking raids against England were resumed, and in 994 he led a raid together with Óláfr Tryggvason. He probably also took part in the raid in 991 and the battle of Maldon, but apparently not in the great raids of 997–1002 and 1009–1012. In 1003–1004, however, he conducted a raid, possibly to avenge the death of his sister Gunnhild and her husband, Pallig, in Æthelred's massacre of the Danes on November 13, 1002. In 1013, he led a raid that, in a strikingly short time, achieved the conquest of England, when Æthelred gave up resistance and left the country at Christmas, his subjects having acknowledged Sven as king. Sven's English reign was brief, however; he died on February 3, 1014, in Gainsborough and was buried first in England, then in Roskilde.

Sven also reasserted his father's claim to Norway, which had been seized, possibly with the help of Æthelred, by Óláfr Tryggvason around 995. Sven supported the sons of Earl Hákon, and, having married the widow of the Swedish king Erik Bjarnarson and thereby gaining influence in Sweden, he also supported his young stepson Olav (Skötkonung) Eriksson. Together with these allies, he won a decisive victory over Óláfr Tryggvason in the battle of Svlðr (Svold) and thereby restored traditional Danish overlordship over Norway.

The sources for Sven's reign are contradictory. While Thietmar and Adam of Bremen depict him as a cruel and evil ruler who was punished by the Lord with captivity, exile, and foreign conquest, and whose position was very insecure, according to the *Encomium Emmae*, he "was practically the most fortunate of all the kings of his time." Both views are obviously biased, but Sven's career to a large extent bears out the encomiast's view. To be able repeatedly to leave Denmark on prolonged campaigns, he must have enjoyed a secure position at home, suggested also by the fact that the fortifications built late in his father's reign were allowed to decay. He had remarkable political and military success in Scandinavia as well as in England.

Sven was the first Danish king to strike coins with his name on them. Only one type is known, imitating an Anglo-Saxon coin and struck by an English moneyer who apparently also worked for Óláfr Tryggvason and for Olav Eriksson. The coins of the three kings are so different, however, that they are more likely to be independent imitations than struck by the same moneyer. At the same time, imitations of English coins, but without the Danish king's name on them, began to be produced in large numbers in Lund, which developed into a town early in Sven's reign.

See also **Adam of Bremen; Óláfr Tryggvason**

Further Reading

Editions

Campbell, Alistair, ed. and trans. *Encomium Emmae Reginae*. Camden Society Third Series, 72. London: Royal Historical Society, 1949.

Thietmar von Merseburg, *Chronik*. Ed. Werner Trillmich. Ausgewähite Quellen zur deutschen Geschlchte des Mittelalters, 9. Berlin: Rütten & Loening, 1957.

Adam Bremensis. *Gesta Hammaburgensis Ecclesiae Pontificum*. In *Quellen des 9. und 11. Jahrhunderts zur Geschichte der hamburgischen Kirche und des Reiches*. Ed. Werner Trillmich and Rudolf Buchner. Ausgewähite Quellen zur deutschen Geschichte des Mittelalters, 11. Berlin: Rütten & Loening, 1978.

Translations

Adam of Bremen. *History of the Archbishops of Hamburg-Bremen*. Trans. Francis J. Tschan. Records of Civilization: Sources and Studies. New York: Columbia University Press, 1959.

Literature

Skovgaard-Petersen, Inge. "Sven Tveskseg i den ældste danske historiografi. En Saxostudie." In *Middelalderstudier tilegnede Aksel E. Christensen på tresårsdagen II. september 1966*. Ed. Tage E. Christensen et al. Copenhagen: Munksgaard, 1966, pp. 1–38.

Stenton, F.M. *Anglo-Saxon England*. 3rd ed. Oxford History of England, 2. Oxford: Clarendon, 1971.

Demidoff, Lene. "The Death of Sven Forkbeard—in Reality and Later Tradition." *Mediaeval Scandinavia* 11 (1978–79), 30–47.

Sobel, Leopold. "Ruler and Society in Early Medieval Western Pomerania." *Antemurale* 25 (1981), 19–142.

Andersson, Theodore M. "The Viking Policy of Ethelred the Unready." *Scandinavian Studies* 59 (1987), 284–95.

Brown, Phyllis R. "The Viking Policy of Ethelred: A Response." *Scandinavian Studies* 59 (1987), 296–8.

Sawyer, Peter. *Da Danmark blev Danmark*. Gyldendal og Politikens Danmarkshistorie, 3. Copenhagen: Gyldendal; Politiken, 1988.

Sawyer, Peter. "Swein Forkbeard and the Historians." In *Church and Chronicle in the Middle Ages*. Ed. Ian Wood and G.A. Loud. London: Hambledon, 1991, pp. 27–40.

NIELS LUND

SVERRIR SIGURÐARSON (r. 1177–1202)

SVERRIR SIGURÐARSON (r. 1177–1202) King of Norway 1177–1202, Sverrir Sigurðarson was a native of the Faroe Islands, where his paternal uncle held the bishopric of Kirkebø (Kirkubæur). Here, Sverrir grew up and received his education. At the age of twenty-four, he was consecrated a priest, and his Norwegian mother revealed to him that his true father was the then long-dead King Sigurðr munnr ("mouth") Haraldsson. This revelation caused Sverrir to go to Norway in 1176, quit the clergy, and fight his way to the throne in fierce opposition to the powerful Archbishop Eysteinn, who had supported Magnús Erlingsson and crowned him king in 1164. Sverrir was proclaimed king in 1177 in Trondheim, and a few years later he had succeeded in gaining control of the larger part of the country. After the battle at Fimreiti in 1184, where King Magnús fell together with the majority of the Norwegian aristocracy, Sverrir became the sole ruler of Norway, although having constantly to fight an array of pretenders to the kingdom.

Our knowledge about Sverrir comes primarily from his saga, *Sverris saga*, which presents us with a fascinating personality, seemingly embodying great contrasts. He describes himself as being fierce as the lion and mild as the lamb, both symbols found on his royal seal. His biography does indeed exhibit his wit and down-to-earth philosophy, but also the new Christian ethics of mildness and forgiveness toward one's enemies. Sverrir's complex background and subtle mind are reflected in his irony and humor, displaying great self-confidence. Sverrir was a brilliant military leader on sea as well as on land. His ingenious tactics in warfare were so untraditional that he has been called a coward despite being victorious; his guerilla attacks were often of a kind that most Norse noblemen avoided. Sverrir had a profound knowledge of the Bible. His national-church policy brought him into lasting conflict with the Norwegian bishops; eventually, the archbishop left the country. Sverrir was excommunicated by him and later by the pope.

Sverrir's struggle with the Church is set forth in a document he himself commissioned. From his *Oratio contra clerum Norvegiae* ("Speech Against the Norwegian Clergy"), as well as the contemporary *Sverris saga*, we learn about his political ideology, drawn partly from Old Testament values. At the same time that he carried out his controversies with the international Church, Sverrir introduced those theocratic traits into his dynastic policy that are so extraordinary for the 13th-century Norwegian monarchy. During his reign, Sverrir strengthened the centralization of the king's administra-

tion, and the finances of the Crown were improved by a new system of taxation.

After the Reformation, Sverrir was celebrated as the king who had the courage to speak against the authority of Rome. In the 19th-century Norwegian struggle for national independence, Sverrir became a symbolic figure for the national identity. Present-day interest in the development of the state as an institution has made Sverrir and his royal descendants much valued as the creators of a strong and highly centralized state as early as the 13th century.

Further Reading

Literature

Cederschiöld, Gustaf. *Konung Sverre*. Lund: Gleerup, 1901.

Paasche, Frederik *Kong Sverre*. Oslo: Aschehoug, 1920.

Koht, Halvdan. *Kong Sverre*. Oslo: Aschehoug, 1952.

Gathome-Hardy, Geoffrey M. *A Royal Impostor: King Sverre of Norway*. Oslo: Aschehoug London: Oxford University Press, 1956.

Holm-Olsen, Ludvig. "Kong Sverre i sökelyset." *Nordisk tidskrift* 34 (1958), 167–81.

Helle, Knut. *Norge blir en stat, 1130–1319*. Handbok i Norges historie, 3. 2nd ed. Bergen, Oslo, and Tromsø: Universitetsforlaget, 1974.

Gunnes, Erik. *Kongens ære: Kongemagt og kirke i "En tale mot biskopene."* Oslo: Gyldendal, 1971.

Lunden, Kåre. *Norge under Sverreætten 1177–1319*. Oslo: Cappelen, 1976.

Ólafia Einarsdóttir. "Sverrir—præst og konge." In *Middelalder, Methode og Medier. Festskrift til N. Skyum-Niehen*. Ed. Karsten Fledelius et al. Copenhagen: Museum Tusculanum, 1981, pp. 67–93; rpt. in *Norske Historikere i Utvalg VI*. Oslo: Universitetsforlaget, 1983, pp. 126–41, 336–8.

       ÓLAFÍA EINARSDÓTTIR

SYRLIN, JÖRG THE ELDER (1420/1430–1491) AND JÖRG THE YOUNGER (1455–1523) Father and son were highly successful joiners and masons. Based in Ulm (Baden-Württemberg), they supplied furniture, altars, fountains, and other carvings for towns throughout Swabia and southern Germany. Yet were they also sculptors? The answer to this question ultimately determines the level of their fame. Recent scholarship suggests that most carvings attributed to the pair are by other Ulm sculptors with whom they collaborated. The careers of the Syrlins are relatively well documented. Jörg the Elder signed and dated (1458) an oak lectern with sculpted evangelist symbols now in the Ulmer Museum. More important, his signatures appear on the sedilia (chancel seats, 1468) and elaborate choir stalls (1469–1474) in the Minister cathedral in Ulm. This is the finest extant late Gothic cycle in Germany. It includes ninety nine exquisite oak busts and reliefs of philosophers and sibyls, each distinguished by fine facial characterizations and varied natural poses. Traditionally, scholars ascribed the sculpture and the carpentry to Jörg the Elder, though already in 1910 Georg Dehio challenged this view by arguing that Jörg's signatures and monograms pertain only to his production as a joiner. The sculpture of these and other carvings ascribed to Jörg are quite varied in their styles rather than the work of a single hand. In later-fifteenth-century Ulm, it was common for a single master to receive a commission for a complex altarpiece. This artist then engaged a collaborative team of sculptors, joiners, and painters. Between 1474 and 1481, Jörg and his colleagues created the Münster's monumental high altar. Although the altar was destroyed on July 20, 1531, during the Protestants' iconoclastic cleansing of the church, Jörg the Elder's intricate presentation drawing (81 × 231 cm; Stuttgart, Württembergisches Landesmuseum) displays his talents as a designer, notably his adept mastery of architectural ornament. The sculptor of the altar is unknown, though Michel Erhart of Ulm has been suggested.

Jörg the Younger trained with and assisted his rather before assuming con-

trol of the workshop in early 1482. Under his direction the atelier's production seems to have expanded, though again his role as sculptor is doubtful. Inscriptions and other documentation link him with projects at the Benedictine abbeys of Ochsenhausen, Zweifalten, and Blaubeuren. For Zwiefalten Jörg prepared choir stalls, a sacrament house, and seven altars between 1509 and the dedication of the choir in 1517. He was aided by Christoph Langeisen, an Ulm sculptor. Langeisen was likely just one of several participating sculptors. Little survived the rebuilding of the church in the mid-eighteenth century. Passion reliefs from one of these altars, today in the Württembergisches Landesmuseum in Stuttgart, are attributed to Nikolaus Weckmann (active 1481–1526), another Ulm sculptor to whom the majority of carvings once ascribed to Jörg the Younger are now credited. It appears that the son too was primarily a joiner and contractor. In 1493 his workshop created the elaborate choir stalls at Blaubeuren, which while loosely patterned on those in the Ulm Münster include far fewer sculpted busts.

Jörg the Younger, like his father, excelled as a designer. In 1482 one of the Syrlins completed and signed the Fish Trough fountain opposite the city hall in Ulm. The pair probably collaborated on the project; some scholars believe the showy twisting of the spire relates to other architectural drawings, such as the plan for a new western tower for the Münster, ascribed to the son. The three sandstone sculptures of knights, now in the Ulmer Museum, are by yet another hand.

See also **Erhart, Michel**

Further Reading

Baum, Julius. *Die Ulmer Plastik der Spätgotik.* Stuttgart: J. Hoffmann, 1911.
Dehio, Georg. "Über einige Künstlerinschriften des   deutschen   15.   Jahrhunderts."

Repertorium für Kunstwissenschaft 33 (1910): 18–24.

Deutsch, Wolfgang. "Der ehemalige Hochaltar und das Chorgestühl, zur Syrlin- und zur Bildhauerfrage," in *600 Jahre Ulmer Münster: Festschrift,* ed. Hans Eugen Specker and Reinhard Wortmann. Forschungen zur Geschichte der Stadt Ulm 19. Ulm: Stadtarchiv, 1977, pp. 242–322.

——. "Syrlin der Jüngere oder Niklaus Weckmann?" In *Meisterwerke Massenhaft: Die Bildhauerwerkstatt des Niklaus Weckmann und die Malerei in Ulm um 1500.* Stuttgart: Württembergisches Landesmuseum, 1993, pp. 7–17.

Koepf, Hans. *Die gotischen Planrisse der Ulmer Sammlungen.* Foschungen zur Geschichte der Stadt Ulm, 18. Ulm: Stadtarchiv, 1977, nos. 8, 30, 31, 49.

Schneckenburger-Broschek, Anja. "Ein Niederländer als schwäbisches Genie: Neues zum Ulmer Chorgestühl." *Zeitschrift des deutschen Vereins für Kunstwissenschaft* 40 (1986): 40–68.

Seifert, Hans. *Das Chorgestühl im Ulmer Münster.* Königstein im Taunus: K.R. Langewiesche Nachfolger, 1958.

Vöge, Wilhelm. *Jörg Syrlin der Ältere und seine Bildwerke, 2 vols. Berlin: Deutsche Verein für Kunstwissenschaft,* 1950.

JEFFREY CHIPPS SMITH

T

TANNHÄUSER, DER (fl. mid–13th c.) The lyrical works of Tannhäuser, a thirteenth-century traveling singer and composer, are preserved in the famous Zurich Manesse family and Jena manuscripts of courtly love poetry known as *Minnesang.* The name is toponymic, but as several villages are called Tannhausen, the poet's place of origin cannot be determined. We know only that he was for a time at court in Vienna under the patronage of Duke Frederick II. The first song *(Leich)* can be dated to 1245, the sixth to 1264–1266. The language is South German.

The range and quality of the surviving poetry reveal Tannhäuser as a fine poet of great versatility. All three major categories of Middle High German verse are represented: *Minnesang, Leich,* and *Sangspruch.* The six *Minnelieder,* preserved in the Manesse manuscript, can be grouped as two summer songs, two winter songs—all relatively conventional—and two *Minne* (courtly love) parodies in which the poet's optimism is obviously misplaced in the face of the impossibility of his lady's absurdly exaggerated demands.

The *Leiche,* likewise in the Manesse manuscript, are probably Tannhäuser's best-known pieces. There are seven, five of them *Tanzleiche,* the earliest such dance songs in German literature. The first is a panegyric on Duke Frederick, and princes and patronage return later in *Leich* 6. *Minne* is a theme in several, and 2 and 3 both contain love stories. The shortest, 7, is a riddle. Recurring motifs are nature, May, and dancing, lending the *Leiche* a consistently jovial tone. The poet delights in references to contemporary narrative literature. A passion for geographical locations is no doubt intended to underscore the vast experience of the traveling singer, though some feel that in *Leich* no. 5 this reaches the level of parody.

There are sixteen *Sangsprüche* in three cycles in the Manesse manuscript and—though authenticity is open to question—a further cycle of four in the Jena manuscript. The principle theme of the Manesse *Sangsprüche* is the experience (and the poverty) of the traveling singer, patronage, and the death of the patron. The Jena cycle is more pious, including prayers of atonement. Other lyrical works attributed to Tannhäuser in Jena, Kolmar, and Wiltener manuscripts are at best of dubious authorship.

Tannhäuser was held in particular esteem in ensuing centuries, his love poetry being celebrated by the *Meistersänger,* who named a melody *(Tannhäuserton)* after him and cast him as the thirteenth member at the gathering of the "12 old masters." By contrast, a pious rejection of sexuality underlies the late medieval

Tannhäuser legend, in which the poet endangers his soul by his service to Venus but turns to Mary in the end. In the poems *Tannhäuser und Venus* and *Tannhäuser und Frau Welt*, the Minnesinger takes his leave of the goddess despite her allure. The fifteenth-century *Tannhäuser-Ballads* develops this, with Tannhäuser then traveling to Rome to seek absolution. The pope (Urban IV) tells him he can no more be saved than the papal staff can produce life. When the dry stick begins to bud, the pope sends for Tannhäuser, but too late; the poet has returned to Venus and the pope is damned. The most familiar modern version of the legend is Wagner's opera, in which it is merged with the story of the *Wartburgkrieg*.

Further Reading

Thomas, J.W., trans. *Tannhäuser: Poet and Legend*. Chapel Hill: University of North Carolina Press, 1974.

GRAEME DUNPHY

THEODORA (c. 500–548) Theodora became empress of Byzantium in 527. She had been born in poverty and had spent her youth as a notoriously virtuosic courtesan in Constantinople. But she reformed, and her cleverness and strong personality attracted the young Justinian, who made her his wife and, on his ascent to the throne as Justinian I, his consort.

Although Theodora differed with Justinian on theology and, as a strong adherent of Monophysitism, sometimes worked against his policies, she was his invaluable ally and counselor. Her advice helped him rescue his throne during the Nika riots (532), and her death from cancer in 548 was a grievous blow to him personally and politically.

Theodora had risen from the dregs of society and never felt totally secure on her throne; she intrigued constantly to ward off any challenge she saw to her husband or to her own standing with him. Thus, it is said, Theodora became jealous of the Ostrogothic queen of Italy, Amalasuntha, who was famous for cleverness and beauty, and—anxious lest this woman come to the capital and attract Justinian—conspired to have her murdered as a part of the dynastic tangles of the Ostrogothic court. Theodora's support of the Monophysites was played on by the Roman legate Vigilius, who promised her his aid in return for her influence in having him made pope (537). However, Vigilius found it impossible to keep his promise, and Theodora became his implacable foe. At her urging, Justinian had Vigilius abducted and brought to Constantinople to be coerced into supporting religious policies that Theodora had helped frame. Vigilius's degradation was Theodora's last triumph before her death.

Several portrait busts surviving from this period have been identified as Theodora, notably one that is now in the Castello Sforzesco in Milan. Even more striking is her austere portrayal, together with her retinue, in a famous mosaic panel in the church of San Vitale in Ravenna. Fired by the sensational account given of her by the historian Procopius, artists and writers of modern times have continued to be fascinated by her image: she has been the fanciful subject of an opera by Donizetti, a play by Sardou, numerous novels, and at least one (Italian) movie.

See also **Justinian I**

Further Reading

Bridge, Antony. *Theodora: Portrait in a Byzantine Landscape*. London: Casseil, 1978.

Browning, Robert. *Justinian and Theodora*, rev. ed. London: Thames and Hudson, 1987.

Diehl, Charles. *Theodora: Empress of Byzantium*, trans. Samuel R. Rosenbaum. New York: Ungar, 1972. (Originally published 1904.)

Procopius of Caesarea. *History of the Wars* and *Secret History*. Loeb Classical Library

Series. London and Cambridge, Mass.: Heinemann/Harvard University Press, 1914–1935. (With reprints; translations.)

JOHN W. BARKER

THEODULF OF ORLÉANS (ca. 760–821)

A Goth born in Spain, Theodulf was forced to flee his homeland, coming to the court of Charlemagne in 780. By 798 he was named bishop of Orléans by Charlemagne. In 801 Pope Leo III honored him with the title of archbishop. Theodulf enjoyed high visibility and favor in the courts of Charlemagne and his successor, Louis the Pious. His luck changed, however, in 817, when he was accused of conspiring against the emperor, whereupon he was removed from his bishopric and imprisoned. He died, thus disgraced, in 821.

Although Theodulf is best known today as one of the preeminent poets of the Carolingian renaissance, he was probably more valued among his contemporaries for his theological and pastoral works. Around 800 he composed his first *Capitula*, a manual for parish priests, in an attempt to institute a reform within his diocese, and a second somewhere between 800 and 813. Forty-one copies survive throughout Europe and England, written between the 9th and 12th centuries, attesting to the popularity of the work. At Charlemagne's request he wrote the *Libri Carolini* under the pretense that it was actually the emperor's work. He also wrote *De ordine baptismi* and supervised a revision of the Bible at his scriptorium.

Theodulf's *Capitula* was widely used during the Anglo-Saxon monastic reform and survives in four English manuscripts. In Latin and English it became a standard work for the clergy and a source for Anglo-Saxon prose. Vercelli Homily III and Assmann Homilies XI and XII draw from the *Capitula*; Ælfric seems to have used it in his pastoral letters; and Wulfstan used it in composing his homilies. The *De ordine baptismi* was also known to the Anglo-Saxons. The text, surviving in BL Royal 8.C.iii, was used by Wulfstan in Homily VIII.

See also **Charlemagne; Wulfstan of York**

Further Reading

Primary Sources

Napier, Arthur S., ed. *The Old English Version of the Enlarged Rule of Chrodegang...*; *An Old English Version of the Capitula of Theodulf...* EETS o.s. 150. London: Kegan Paul, Trench, Trübner, 1916.

Theodulf. *Opera Omnia.* PL 105.

Secondary Sources

Gatch, Milton McC. *Preaching and Theology in Anglo-Saxon England: Ælfric and Wulfstan.* Toronto: University of Toronto Press, 1977.

Godman, Peter. *Poets and Emperors: Frankish Politics and Carolingian Poetry.* Oxford: Clarendon, 1987.

McKitterick, Rosamond, ed. *Carolingian Culture: Emulation and Innovation.* Cambridge: Cambridge University Press, 1994.

HELENE SCHECK

THIBAUT DE CHAMPAGNE (1201–1253)

The most illustrious of the trouvères and one of the most prolific, Thibaut IV, count of Champagne and king of Navarre, grandson of the great patroness of poets Marie de Champagne, was also an important political figure. After several years' education at the royal court of Philip II Augustus, young Thibaut began his life as a ruler under the regency of his mother, Blanche of Navarre. He later took part in the war of the newly crowned Louis VIII against the English, appearing at the siege of La Rochelle in 1224, and continued to serve the king, his overlord, thereafter. In 1226, however, he withdrew his support during the royal siege of Avignon and returned home in secret. Upon the king's death a few months later, Thibaut was accused of having poisoned him, but nothing came of this apparently groundless charge. The following year, he allied himself with other feudal powers in an attempt to dethrone Blanche of Castile, widow of Louis VIII and regent for their son Louis IX, but the queen succeeded in detaching him from the rebellious group and making him her defender. Attacked by his erstwhile allies, Thibaut was saved by the royal army.

Thibaut's relations with the crown, however, were unsteady, particularly after 1234, when he succeeded his uncle Sancho the Strong as king of Navarre, and it was not until 1236 that a final peace was achieved, based on the vassal's submission. Three years later, he left for the Holy Land as head of the crusade of 1239; the undertaking was marked from the start by discord among the Christian leaders and by Muslim military superiority, the result of which was Thibaut's decision in 1240 to withdraw from his charge and return to France. There, armed struggles engaged his attention through the following years, and in 1248 he made a penitent's pilgrimage to Rome. He died in Pamplona. He had been betrothed twice, married three times, divorced once, widowed once, and had fathered several children. The rumor has persisted since his day that the great love of his life was none other than Blanche of Castile, but apart from offering a tempting key to his political shifts, it seems to have no merit.

As a trouvère, Thibaut was immediately successful, seen as equaled only by his great predecessor Gace Brulé. Dante was to consider him one of the "illustrious" poets in the vernacular, and the medieval songbooks that group their contents by composer place his works before all others. The over sixty pieces ascribed to him with reasonable certainty, almost all preserved with music, show a majority of courtly chansons, none anticonventional in theme or form but most marked by an unusual development of imagery, especially allegorical, use of refrains, or self-confident lightness of tone. The other works, revealing a style similarly charac-

teristic of Thibaut, are *jeux-partis* (among the earliest known), debates, devotional songs (including one in the form of a *lai*), crusade songs, *pastourelles*, and a *serventois*.

See also **Blanche of Castile; Louis IX; Philip II Augustus**

Further Reading

Brahney, Kathleen J., ed. and trans. *The Lyrics of Thibaut de Champagne.* New York: Garland, 1988.

van der Werf, Hendrik, ed. *Trouvères-Melodien II.* Kassel: Bärenreiter, 1979, pp. 3–311.

Wallensköld, Axel,ed. *Les chansons de Thibaut de Champagne, roi de Navarre.* Paris: Champion, 1925.

Bellenger, Yvonne, and Danielle Quéruel,eds. *Thibaut de Champagne, prince et poète au XIIIe siècle.* Lyon: La Manufacture, 1987.

SAMUEL N. ROSENBERG

THIETMAR OF MERSEBURG (975–1008/1018)

Born into the comital house of Walbeck in eastern Saxony, Thietmar received his primary education at the royal convent of Quedlinburg. In 987, his father transferred him from Quedlinburg to the monastery of Berge, outside of Magdeburg. Thietmar remained at Berge for three years, continuing his education, apparently with the expectation that he would eventually join the community. When a place could not be obtained for him there, he was moved to the cathedral at Magdeburg (November 1, 990). Thietmar studied at the cathedral's school, then among the empire's preeminent centers of learning, and was formally admitted to the chapter circa 1000, during the reign of Archbishop Giselher. Professional advancement came to him during the reign of Giselher's successor, Archbishop Tagino. The archbishop elevated him to the priesthood in 1004 at a ceremony attended by Emperor Henry II, and thereafter he seems to have joined the archbishop's entourage.

It was due to Tagino's favor, moreover, that Thietmar was chosen by Henry II to succeed the recently deceased bishop of the see of Merseburg (1008). As Bishop of Merseburg, Thietmar inherited a host of problems deriving from that diocese's troubled history. Emperor Otto I had founded the bishopric in 968, in conjunction with his elevation of Magedeburg to the status of archbishopric. For a variety of reasons, it was suppressed in 981, its property being divided among neighboring dioceses and its cathedral transformed into a proprietary monastery of the archbishops of Magdeburg. Although the diocese was restored by Henry II in 1004, its boundaries and property rights remained a matter of dispute. Thietmar seems to have occupied most of his career in attempts to regain diocesan lands ceded to neighboring dioceses during the period of Merseburg's suppression (i.e., 981–1004). Similar issues led to a long running property dispute with the Saxon ducal house of the Billunger.

Thietmar's chief gift to posterity is his history, the *Chronicon*, which he composed between 1012 and his death in 1018. The work is divided into eight books and survives in two manuscripts at Brussels and Dresden, the latter now available only in the form of a facsimile. The Dresden manuscript is particularly valuable as it was produced under Thietmar's direction and includes corrections and additions made in his own hand. In compiling the *Chronicon*, Thietmar drew heavily at times on the work of other historians, but much of his material is based on his own observations and experiences, especially in the later books. Indeed, for events in the reign of Emperor Henry II, he is often our unique informant. It is generally assumed that Thietmar's original intention was to focus on the history of his diocese. If so, his theme must have rapidly expanded to include the history and deeds of the Ottonian kings, their lineage, and other topics as well. Thietmar was nothing if not opinionated and ex-

pressed views on subjects ranging from politics to the (in his opinion) shocking character of contemporary women's fashions. He subjected monastic reform and its advocates to a withering critique and offered negative characterizations of Lotharingians, Bavarians, Italians, and others lacking the good fortune to have been born Saxon. With his detailed commentary on the career of Duke Boleslav Chrobry, Thietmar is one of the most important witnesses for the emergence of the medieval Polish state, and his detailed descriptions of Slavic social customs and religion are some of the earliest on record. Thietmar's testimony is especially valuable for the history of Ottonian policy in the east, German relations with the western Slavs, and the family histories of the east Saxon aristocracy.

See also **Otto I**

Further Reading

Chronicon (*Die Chronik des Bischofs Thietmar von Merseburg und ihre Korveier Überarbeitung*). ed. Robert Holtzmann. Monumenta Germaniae Historica, Scriptores rerum Germanicarum, nova series 9. Berlin: Weidmann, 1935.

Leyser, Karl. *The Ascent of Latin Europe.* Oxford: Clarendon Press, 1986.

Lippelt, Heinrich. *Thietmar von Merseburg. Riechsbischof und Chronist.* Mitteldeutsche Forschungen 72. Cologne: Böhlau, 1973.

Warner, David A. "Thietmar of Merseburg on Rituals of Kingship." *Viator* 26 (1995): 53–76.

——. *Ottonian Germany.* Manchester: Manchester University Press, 1999.

DAVID A. WARNER

THOMAS À KEMPIS (1379/1380–1471)

An author of spiritual writings, Thomas (Hemerken) à Kempis (also Hamerkein, Malleolus) was born some time between September 29, 1379, and July 24, 1380, at Kempen near Cologne. At the age of thirteen he left for Deventer to attend classes at the chapter's school of the Lebuinus Church. In 1399 he applied for admission to a monastery of the Canons Regular at Zwolle called St. Agnietenberg. This monastery, a daughter-house of Windesheim, was pervaded by the spirit of the *Devotio moderna* (Modern Devotion) movement. After taking the habit in 1406 and after his solemn profession in 1407, Thomas was ordained a priest in 1413 or 1414. He evolved into a prolific transcriber and author of several spiritual writings. From 1425 till 1430 (and in a second term starting in 1433), he performed the task of subprior and combined it with the assignment of a novice master. In this last quality he developed as a musician, preacher, and history teacher. For the job of procurator Thomas turned out to be less suited; he held that office for only one year in 1443. He died on either May 1 or July 24, 1471.

Thomas à Kempis is credited with thirty-one treatises, as well as three cycles of *sermones* (sermons), some *cantica* (catechetic songs), and *epistolae* (letters). Depending on the goal he had in mind or the audience he wanted to reach, he used different genres. He proved to be a pious historian in, e.g., his *Chronicon Montis sanctae Agnetis*. One can discover his qualities as a musician and writer of letters in his *Cantica* and *Epistolae*. His output consists in large part of practical-ascetic works, such as his *Libellus de disciplina claustralium*, *Vita boni monachi*, *Manuale parvulorum*, and *Doctrina iuvenum*.

His famous *De Imitatione Christi* is included in this category as well. This work deserves a wider treatment here, as it is one of the most influential spiritual texts of the late Middle Ages and can be considered the most widely read book in Christianity, with the exception of the Bible. In the centuries-old fight about the authorship of this fifteenth-century treatise, forty serious candidates have been taken into account. Among them Augustin, Bernard, Jan van Ruusbroec, Geert Grote, Joannes Gersen, abbot of Vercelli, Jean Gerson,

and, finally, Thomas à Kempis, were the most prominent. On the basis of the excellent linguistic and codicological (manuscript) investigations of L.J.M. Delaissé, it is now generally accepted among scholars that Thomas à Kempis has to be regarded as the author of the four *libelli* (books) that form *De Imitatione Christi*. The first four treatises of Thomas à Kempis's autograph of 1441 (Brussels, Koninklijke Bibliotheek, manuscript no. 5855–5861) form, in this order, books I, II, IV, and III of *De Imitatione Christi*. They have the following incipits (first lines):

1. *Qui sequitur me, non ambulat in tenebris*
2. *Regnum Dei intra vos est dicit Dominus*
3. *De sacramento. Venite ad me omnes qui laboratis*
4. *Audiam quid loquator in me Dominus Deus*

In other manuscripts and incunabula, treatises I, II, and IV often appear as a unity. If one considers the contents of these works and the titles given by Thomas in his autograph of 1441, this unity is not purely a coincidence. A codex belonging to a monastery of Canons Regular at Nijmegen, now in the Royal Library in Brussels (manuscript no. 22084), makes clear that the four *libelli* of *De Imitatione Christi* already circulated in 1427, fifteen years before Thomas completed his final redaction in the autograph mentioned above.

In treatise I, *Admonitiones ad spiritualem vitam utiles*, Thomas formulates, for beginners in spiritual life, some points of advice concerning a life in silence, prayer, and study. In treatise II, *Admonitiones ad interna trahentes*, Thomas merely describes the mental state that the young religious has to develop to consider prayer as a privileged place where one is able to meet Christ personally instead of a mechanical duty. Treatise III, *De interna consolatione*, is Thomas's personal testimony of his intimate relationship with

Christ in daily life of the monastic community. Thomas points out that the life of a person who is looking for God is not without obstacles. He wrote this book, furthermore, to provide consolation. Finally, treatise IV of the *De Imitatio Christi* contains reflections on the Holy Eucharist that are characteristic of the time in which the *Imitatio* was composed but not strictly coordinated with the contents of the first three books. It is especially in these books that Thomas develops the concept of a "journey" for the faithful. Here he first describes the inner disposition from which one can be open to Christ and follow Him in the most appropriate and fruitful way. From studies made after those of Delaissé mentioned above, the conclusion can be drawn that Thomas made the stylistic improvements in the *Imitatio* not because of his love for the beauty of the (Latin) language, the *latinitas*, but for catechetical reasons.

Other treatises, like the *Orationes et meditationes de vita Christi*, have a more theological character. In his *Hortulus rosarum* and *Soliloquium animae*, Thomas shows his gifts as a spiritual writer. All but one of his works were composed in Latin; he wrote a small treatise in Middle Dutch: *Van goeden woerden to horen ende die to spreken*. Finally, he compiled his *sermones* in three coherent cycles.

One can easily conclude that the quantity of scholarly contributions on the sources, style, and theology in Thomas à Kempis's *opera omnia* (complete works) stands in no proportion to the enormous amount of literature devoted to his authorship of the *Imitatio*. The study of his theology is in an early stage; up until now, no attempt has been made at a synthesis. Recent investigation has shown that Thomas's originality lies in his view that the ascetic structuring of life is explained by the mystical longing that Thomas wants to develop in each person. In his theological anthropology, mystical aspirations are exclusively nourished and purified by a realization of the self in an ascetic way of life. Furthermore, his spirituality is strongly Christ-centered.

Further Reading

Ampe, Albert, and Bernhard Spaapen. "Imitatio Christi. I. Le livre et l'auteur.—II. Doctrine," in *Dictionnaire de spiritualité*, ed. Marcel Viller. Paris: Beauchense, 1932ff, vol. 7, cols. 2338–2355.

Delaissé, L. J. M. *Le Manuscrit autographe de Thomas à Kempis et "L'Imitation." Examen archéologique et édition diplomatique du Bruxellensis 5855–5861.* 2 vols. Paris: Erasme, 1956.

Ingram, John K., ed. *The Earliest English Translation of the First Three Books of De imitatione Christi* ... London: K. Paul, Trench, Trubner, 1893.

Pohl, Michael Joseph, ed. *Thomae a Kempis canonici regularis ordinis S. Augustini Opera Omnia*, 7 vols. Freibourg im Breisgau: Herder, 1902–1922.

Puyol, Pierre-Édouard. *L'auteur du livre De Imitatione Christi. Première section: la contestation.* Paris: Retaux, 1899.

van Dijk, Rudolf, Th.M. "Thomas Hemerken à Kempis," in *Dictionnaire de spiritualité*, ed. Marcel Viller. Paris: Beauchense, 1932ff., vol. 15, cols. 817–826.

van Geest, Paul. "Thomas Hemerken a Kempis," in *Die deutsche Literatur des Mittelalters: Verfasserlexikon*, ed. Kurt Ruh et al., vol. 9. Berlin: de Gruyter, 1978, cols. 862–882.

——. "Introduction," in *Thomas a Kempis: La vallée des Lis*. Bégrolles-en-Mauges: Abbaye de Bellefontaine, 1992, pp. 11–48.

——. "De sermones van Thomas a Kempis; een terreinverkenning." *Trajecta* 2 (1993): 305–326.

——. *Thomas a Kempis (1379/80–1471): een studie van zijn mens- en godsbeeld: analyse en tekstuitgave van de Hortulus Rosarum en de Vallis Liliorum.* Kampen: Kok, 1996.

Weiler, Anton G. "Recent Historiography on the Modern Devotion: Some Debated Questions." *Archief voor de geschiedenis van de katholieke kerk in Nederland* 26 (1984): 161–184.

"The works of Thomas à Kempis," trans. Michael Joseph Pohl. 6 vols. Ph.d. diss., University of London, 1905–1908.

PAUL J. J. VAN GEEST

THOMAS D'ANGLETERRE (fl. 2nd half of the 12th c.) Eight fragments totaling 3,146 octosyllabic lines, distributed among five manuscripts, are all that remain of Thomas's *Tristan*, composed ca. 1175 for the nobility of Norman England. The author may have been a clerk at the court of Henry II Plantagenêt in London. The fragments of Thomas's *Tristan* preserve essentially the last part of the story, from Tristan's exile in Brittany to the lovers' deaths. Line 3,134 of the epilogue, the adaptations by Brother Robert (Old Norse) and Gottfried von Strassburg (Middle High German), and the Oxford *Folie*, however, all indicate that Thomas had composed a complete version, one that followed the biographical structure and general movement of the original legend, though Thomas made numerous modifications to it.

Placing Arthur in the mythic past and situating the story in an England ruled over by King Marc, Thomas's reworking is dominated by rationality; the poet tones down the fantastic elements and shows a certain logic in the ordering of events and in the behavior and motivation of the characters. It is possible to suppose that Thomas would have described the *amur fine e veraie* experienced by the protagonists when Tristan first came to Ireland (see 1. 2,491), with the love potion only confirming that love. In keeping with the milieu for which he wrote, Thomas eliminated or reworked overly "realistic" episodes (harp and lyre, Iseut and the lepers, life in the forest of Morois), bringing the story into line with the new courtly ideals. A master hunter, Tristan (like his "pupil" Iseut) is also a musician and poet as well as an artist capable of creating the marvelous statues of the Hall of Images.

The principal contribution of Thomas, as scholar and moralist, is in his minute analysis of love and the other mysteries of human nature. Characters reveal themselves through monologues, debates, and lyric laments; and their self-examination is analyzed through the narrator's long interventions. The action is motivated less by exterior agents than by *inner* adventure, the wanderings of the protagonists' consciences, which, alone seems to interest Thomas. The paradox in Thomas's version is thus the narration, within the story of a love seen as absolute and perfect, of an analysis of love that shows Tristan's desire for change (*novelerie*) and his fundamental dissatisfaction. This analysis is coupled with reflections on jealousy and on Tristan's obsession with taking the place of the Other (Iseut or Marc) and feeling himself the pleasure experienced (or not) by the Other. Iseut's role is to express, in actions and lyric laments, her passion, tenderness, and pity for her lover's plight. Thomas uses the technique of "gainsaying": the quarrel between Iseut and Brangain allows the queen to reveal the positive side of *fin'amor*, which had been depicted by Brangain as folly and lechery. Characters like Cariado, Iseut of the White Hands, Tristan the Dwarf, and, undoubtedly, the faithful Kaherdin in the lost episodes, are there to fill out this "mirror" of the multiple faces of love.

The language available to Thomas was not yet as subtle and supple as his analyses. Words like *desir, voleir, poeir*, even *raisun*, whose meanings seem still too imprecise or overcharged, are significant less in themselves than through the systems of oppositions into which they fit. Repetitions bordering on redundancy, anaphora, antitheses, and rhetorical questions occur almost too frequently. Thomas, however, is capable of realistic depiction, as in the description of London, the doctors who treat Tristan, or the storm. The death scene is characterized by a rhythm wedded to the circularity of desire that conveys, in the echoing of certain rhyme pairs (*confort/mort, amur/dulur, anguissus/desirus*), the very essence of love.

Thomas makes good the ambitious program articulated in the epilogue: to complete a narrative (*l'escrit*) in which all lovers, whatever their manner of loving, can find pleasure, recall their own passion through the exemplary destiny of Tristan and Iseut, and perhaps escape—for that seems to be the moralist's ultimate goal—the torments and deceits of passion.

See also Béroul; Gottfried von Straßburg; Henry II

Further Reading

Thomas d'Angleterre. Le roman de Tristan par Thomas, ed. Joseph Bédier. 2 vols. Paris: SATF, 1902–05.
——. Les fragments du roman de Tristan, poème du XIIe siècle, ed. Bartina H. Wind. Geneva: Droz, 1960.
——. Thomas of Britain: Tristran, ed. and trans. Stewart Gregory. New York: Garland, 1991.
Baumgartner, Emmanuèle. Tristan et Iseut: de la légende aux récits en vers. Paris: Presses Universitaires de France, 1987.
Fourrier, Anthime. Le courant réaliste dans le roman courtois en France au moyen âge. Paris: 1960, pp. 19–109.
Hunt, Tony. "The Significance of Thomas' Tristan." Reading Medieval Studies 7 (1981): 41–61.

EMMANUÈLE BAUMGARTNER

THOMAS OF CELANO (c. 1190–1260)

Thomas of Celano was a Franciscan hagiographer, the author of the first two lives of Francis of Assisi. Little is known about Thomas's early life, except that he was apparently from a noble family and received a good education. He joined the Franciscan order in the first years of its existence, probably in 1215, and volunteered for the first Franciscan mission to Germany in 1221. He seems to have shown administrative talent, for the next year he was made custos of a substantial part of the central European province, and in 1223 he was appointed vicar for the entire province while its minister was in Italy. In 1224, Thomas returned to Italy. He may have been present when Francis died in 1226.

Thomas's reputation as a preacher and stylist and his status as a relatively early follower of Francis seem to be the reasons Pope Gregory IX commissioned him in July 1228 to write an official life of the saint. While preparing the work, Thomas amassed a huge collection of anecdotes from friars and laymen that became a source for several later lives of Francis. By February 1229, he had finished what would come to be called Vita prima. Written in cursus, or rhythmical prose, the Vita prima is a skillful attempt to convey the interior life of Francis as early Franciscans knew it. But in many ways it is also a conventional stereotyped hagiography. It emphasizes Francis's spiritual journey and ideals but omits some of the quirkiest and most compelling episodes of the saint's life. In 1230, Thomas edited the Vita prima into a liturgical epitome, the Legenda ad usum chori.

Although the Vita prima was greeted with enormous enthusiasm when it first appeared, by the early 1240s many friars were voicing dissatisfaction with it, apparently because so many favorite stories about Francis had been left out. In 1244, the Franciscan general chapter invited all friars who had known Francis ro submit their reminiscences so that a new, more complete vita could be composed. Thomas was once again called on to be the author. From materials he had not used in his first life and from recently submitted anecdotes, Thomas crafted the Memoriale in desiderio animae de gestis et verbis sanctissimi patris nostri Francisci, usually called the Vita secunda. Like the first life, it tells the story of Francis's conversion; but in its second part the anecdotes are arranged as a kind of prolonged character study of the subject. The Vita secunda—unlike the Vita prima—confronts matters of controversy within the order, especially a growing dispute over the relaxation of the rule. Thomas clearly depicts Francis as favoring a strict adherence to the rule and lamenting the corruption of his order by those who sought to relax it.

If "laxists" found the general message of the *Vita secunda* distasteful, many throughout the order complained that it gave insufficient attention to Francis's miracles, a subject that had been carefully elaborated in the *Vita prima*. To remedy this, Thomas composed a *Tractatus de miraculis* in 1255–1256 that detailed almost 200 of Francis's miracles. Thomas may also be the author of the *Legenda sanctae Clarae*, a life of Francis's friend Saint Clare written in the mid-1250s.

Thomas died in 1260 at Tagliacozzo. His works survived, despite a directive of the Franciscan chapter general of 1266 ordering that they and all other lives of Francis be destroyed to facilitate acceptance of Bonaventure's *Legenda maior* as the only official version of Francis's life.

See also **Bonaventure, Saint; Francis of Assisi, Saint**

Further Reading

Edition

Thomas of Celano. *Saint Francis of Assisi: First and Second Life of Saint Francis, with Selections from the Treatise on the Miracles of the Blessed Francis*, trans. Placid Hermann. Chicago, Ill.: Franciscan Herald, 1963.

Critical Studies

Bontempi, Pietro. *Tommaso da Celano, storico e innografo*. Rome: Scuola Salesiana del Libro, 1952.

De Beer, Francis. *La conversion de Saint François selon Thomas de Celano*. Paris: Éditions Franciscaines, 1963.

Facchinetti, Vittorino. *Tommaso da Celano: Il primo biografo di San Francesco*. Quaracchi: Collegio di San Bonaventura, 1918.

Miccoli, Giovanni. "La 'conversione' di San Francesco secondo Tommaso da Celano." *Studi Medievali* Series 3(5), 1964, pp. 775–792.

Moorman, John R. H. *Sources for the Life of Francis of Assisi*. Manchester: Manchester University Press, 1940. (Reprint, Farnborough: Gregg, 1966.)

Spirito, Silvana. *Il francescanesimo di fra Tommaso da Celano*. Assisi: Edizioni Porziuncola, 1963.

THOMAS TURLEY

THOMASÎN VON ZERCLAERE (fl. early 12th c.)

Born into an ancient noble family in Cividale in Friulia, northern Italy, around 1185, Thomasîn was a member of the monastic cathedral of Aquileia and so later came into close contact with Wolfger von Erla, the German patriarch of Aquileia known for his patronage of such famous German poets as Walther von der Vogelweide. We might assume that Wolfger commissioned Thomasîn to compose his famous book of courtly etiquette, *Der Welsche Gast* (*The Italian Visitor*), consisting of about 14,800 verses. Thomasîn dated his Middle High German poem by telling us that he wrote it twenty-eight years after the loss of Jerusalem to the Arabs in 1187, that is, in 1215. The intention with his treatise was to improve the desolate state of the German nobility. It is the first German *Hofzucht* (courtly primer) ever written, and this by a nonnative speaker; it addresses young noblemen and women, teaching them the norms of courtly behavior. Thomasîn also added a general lesson about courtly love that he based on his *Buch von der Höfischeit* (*Book of Courtliness*), which he had previously composed in the Provençal language. In his book the poet emphasizes the value of constancy (*staete*), moderation (*mâze*), law (*reht*), and generosity (*milte*). Thomasîn drew from many different sources but mentions only the *Moralia* by Pope Gregory the Great (d. 604), a highly popular Latin moral treatise. Nevertheless, the text demonstrates Thomasîn's extensive knowledge of theological and secular literature of his time. The poet was clearly opposed to Walther von der Vogelweide's polemics against the pope, warned of the threatening spread of hereticism, and appealed to the

German knighthood to embark on a new crusade. For him, knighthood must be subservient to the church and must pursue primarily religious and moral ideals. However, Thomasîn did not hesitate to recommend courtly literature as reading material for young noble people because some of the best-known protagonists in Middle High German literature would provide them with models of ideal behavior. The *Welsche Gast* proved to be an enormously popular didactic treatise and has come down to us in some two dozen manuscripts (thirteen complete, eleven as fragments), of which almost all are illustrated.

See also **Gregory VII, Pope; Walther von der Vogelweide**

Further Reading

Huber, Christoph. "Höfischer Roman als Integumentum? Das Votum Thomasîns von Zerclaere." *Zeitschrift für deutsches Altertum* 115 (1986): 79–100.

Neumann, Friedrich. "Einführung," in *Der Welsche Gast des Thomasîn von Zerclaere. Cod. Pal. Germ. 389 der Universitätsbibliothek Heidelberg.* Wiesbaden: Reichert, 1974, Kommentarband, pp. 1–65.

Röcke, Werner. *Feudale Anarchie und Landesherrschaft*: *Wirkungsmöglichkeiten didaktischer Literatur. Thomasîns von Zerclaere "Der Welsche Gast."* Bern: Lang, 1978.

Ruff, E. J. F. *"Der Welsche Gast" des Thomasîn von Zerclaere: Untersuchung zu Gehalt und Bedeutung einer mhd. Morallehre.* Erlangen: Palm und Enke, 1982.

Thomasîn von Zerclaria. *Der Welsche Gast*, ed., Heinrich Rückert. Quedlinburg: Basse, 1852; rpt. ed. Friedrich Neumann. Berlin: de Gruyter, 1965.

ALBRECHT CLASSEN

TORQUEMADA, TOMÁS DE (1420–1498)

Born in the town from which he drew his surname, in the province of Palencia, in 1420. He was nephew to the no less famous Cardinal Juan de Torquemada, author of the *Tractatus contra Midianitas*, written in defense of the Jewish *conversos* (Christian converts) from whom he, and correspondingly Tomás, were said to have been descended. As a young man, Tomás entered the Order of St. Dominic in the priory of San Pablo in Valladolid, and resided as a friar in the convent at Piedrahita. He was later appointed prior of the convent of Santa Cruz in Segovia, a title he retained throughout his career; and at about the same time was chosen to be a confessor of Queen Isabel and King Fernando: it is in this role that he appears in the only painting that is believed to depict him faithfully, Berruguete's *Virgin of the Catholic Kings*, in the Prado.

On 11 February 1482 he was appointed by papal bull as one of seven new inquisitors to continue the work of the recently founded Inquisition (the first two inquisitors had been appointed in 1480). In 1483 a new central council, the Consejo de la Suprema y General Inquisición, was set up by the king and queen to govern the inquisition, and Torquemada was chosen to head it as inquisitor general. On 17 October 1483 another papal bull, which conceded control of the inquisitions of the Iberian Peninsula to the crown, also appointed Torquemada as joint inquisitor general of the three realms of Aragón, Catalonia, and Valencia. In this role, he was empowered to intervene in any part of the peninsula in a way that not even the crown was always able to. Torquemada subsequently played a key role in forcing through the introduction of the new inquisition in the realms of the Crown of Aragón, which still retained their old inquisitors from the medieval inquisition. In May 1484 Torquemada appointed new inquisitors for the eastern kingdoms, but faced enormous opposition, fundamentally because the new appointees were all Castilians and their tribunal was not subject to the laws of the kingdoms; in Aragón one of the appointees, Pedro Arbués, was murdered in 1485. To find a way out of the impasse, in February 1486 pope Innocent VII sacked all the existing papal inquisitors in the Crown of Aragón, and secured the simultaneous withdrawal of the Castilian nominees. This left the way open for Torquemada to start again with new appointees.

The important contribution made by Torquemada to the new inquisition is confirmed by the fact that he wrote its first rule book, the *Instrucciones*, first drawn up in November 1484 and then later amplified in versions of 1485,1488, and 1498. Together with additions made in 1500, these early rules were known as the *Instrucciones Antiguas*, and laid down all the procedures of the tribunal in its early period. Torquemada must not, however, be viewed as all-powerful. As inquisitor general he was no more than chairman of the Suprema and could be overruled by it; moreover, his commission, which came from the pope, could be revoked at any time. In 1491 and again in 1494, while Torquemada was still functioning, additional and temporary (until 1504) inquisitor generals were appointed to aid the work of the inquisition, proof that he did not hold unquestioned power.

No documentary proof whatsoever exists for attributing to Torquemada the evidently anti-Semitic philosophy of the early inquisition, or responsibility for the bloody excesses of the tribunal; but neither is there any reason to question the traditional view that sees him as the driving spirit behind its early years. It is unquestionable that he was a major force behind the expulsion of the Jews in 1492: King Fernando stated expressly, in a letter that he sent to several nobles, that "the Holy Office of the Inquisition has provided that the Jews be expelled from all our realms." A story of uncertain origin states that when the Jews tried to buy their way out of the expulsion, Torquemada burst into the presence of the king and queen and threw thirty pieces of silver on the table, demanding to know for what price Christ was to be sold again.

A strong supporter of religious reform, Torquemada in 1482 founded the beautiful monastery of Santo Tomás in Avila, where he died on 16 September 1498.

Further Reading

Kamen, H. *Historia de la Inquisitión en España y América*. Madrid, 1984. Lea, H. C. *A History of the Inquisition of Spain*. 4 vols.

HENRY KAMEN

TORRE, ALFONSO DE LA (fl. mid-15th c.)

Theologian and writer in the vernacular active in the mid-fifteenth century, remembered nowadays as the author of the *Visión deleytable*, a philosophical dialogue and survey of the seven liberal arts, natural theology, and ethics. The work is in large part a cento of older texts, mostly unidentified and at times heavily amplified and supplemented by the author, and bound together by an allegorical dialogue. The *Visión* enjoyed a certain currency in its own century and in the two following. By the end of the seventeenth century it had undergone eleven printings, had been translated into Catalan and Italian and, unbelievably, back into Spanish.

What is most notable, indeed astonishing, about Torre's dialogue and the thought it expresses is the fundamentally Averroist and rationalist direction of its argument, especially of its theology. The main index to this tendency is, of course, the author's choice of sources, in some instances unremarkable, in others quite otherwise. Thus the passages on the liberal arts depend largely on Isidore of Seville and Al-Ghazāli. The pages on cosmology, on the influence of the spheres on the sublunary world, are from a source Torre calls simply "Hermes," but which is in fact the *Latin Asclepius*, very well known and influential in Western Christendom. But the matter on natural theology comes not from a Christian source, but from

Maimonides's *Guide for the Perplexed*. This notable text brings to the *Vision* unaltered the Maimonidean teaching about the nature of God, eminently his existence, unity and incorporeity, but also his power, omniscience, and Providence. One should add that the passages in the *Guide* that express views at odds with what we could call common Christian theology—on providence, for example, or on the nature of evil—are preserved in the *Visión* without embarrassment. There is also in Torre's text, as we should note in fairness, a series of chapters that speak plain Christian language. But the author makes absolutely no effort to reconcile the sense of these pages with the rest of his argument, and one might indeed reasonably guess that this passage is a sop, a concession to the Christian reader, who elsewhere in the work is induced to accept views that at best are on the outer limits of orthodoxy.

The rationalist strain is sustained in the *Visión* in passages entirely separate from those directly and extensively dependent on the *Guide*. In a pair of lines early in the work Torre alludes hastily to Maimonides's theory of prophecy, roughly the view that God speaks to his prophets "mediante la lunbre yntelectual" (by means of intellectual enlightenment). In a second short passage he refers clearly to Maimonides's notion that the Bible speaks one language to the wise and learned and another to the vulgar, or in Leo Strauss's words, that Scripture "is an esoteric text, and that its esoteric teaching is akin to that of Aristotle." More important, perhaps, the *Visión's* chapters on ethics make few significant allusions to Christianity, or indeed, even to the idea of rewards and punishments in the other world.

Torre at one point says that the will of God can be understood in two senses, as what he wills directly and as what he wills virtually as he foresees the consequences of his first decision. Significantly, this theme is not Maimonidean; it savors

of Christian scholasticism, and is possibly of Scotist or nominalist tendency. In other words, Torre's rationalism is not an accident. When he presents unmodified Maimonidean teachings that are at variance with those of Christian theology, the choice of doctrine is not innocent; it is certainly not made in ignorance. Torre was, as we have seen, a legitimate theologian, a *bachiller en teología*, and the knowledge of Christian divinity revealed in details of the course of the *Visión* is fully professional. His choice of themes, therefore, must have been fully deliberate. What, then, are we to think of this strange book and its author? Was Torre a crypto-Jew? Perhaps; the case is interesting. One should note that the mixture in the *Visión* of Jewish authorities and Christian is in no way alien to later medieval Jewish Averroism; the conversion of Shlomo Halevy/Pablo de Santa María was due in great part to his early familiarity with Aquinas. Torre's final plea to the Infante don Carlos not to show his book to a third person is itself revealing. Maimonides himself lays it down firmly that high doctrine should not be revealed to the vulgar.

See also Averroës, Abu 'L-Walīd Muhammad B. Ahmad B. Rushd; Isidore of Seville, Saint; Maimonides

Further Reading

Strauss, L. *How Fārābī Read Plato's Laws*. Damascus, 1957.

Torre, A. de la. *Visión deleytable*. 2 vols. Salamanca, 1991.

CHARLES FRAKER

TOSCANELLI, PAOLO DAL POZZO

(1397–May 1482) Noted Florentine physician, mathematician, astronomer, and leading cosmographer of his day. Born into a family of rich Florentine merchants and bankers, Toscanelli studied medicine (he is sometimes referred to as Paul the Physician) at the University of Padua, the principal seat of scientific learning in Italy. Here he acquired a sound theoretical education, which he combined with a Florentine appreciation of pragmatism and practical experience. He was a scientist with a businessman's eye for calculations. Toscanelli numbered among his close friends and acquaintances important humanists like Nicholas of Cusa, Filippo Brunelleschi, Angelo Poliziano, Cristoforo Landino, and Leon Battista Alberti; he also knew Marsilio Ficino and Giovanni Pico, although he disagreed with them on the subject of astrology.

If little has survived of Toscanelli's own writings, we know from the tributes of his contemporaries that he was held in great regard. Toscanelli was interested in a wide variety of subjects, including optics and agriculture. One surviving manuscript shows that his observations on comets were remarkably accurate for his day. Highly empirical, he founded his geographical theories more on contemporary travel accounts and his own research than on classical sources such as Ptolemy. He is reported to have interviewed travelers and visitors recently returned from Asia and Africa: he knew Marco Polo's *Divisament du monde* (c. 1298) and Niccolò dei Conti's account of Asia based on his travels (1435–1439), written by his contemporary, Poggio Bracciolini.

Early biographers of Toscanelli credit him with having theorized about the possibility of reaching the Indies via the Atlantic, and of making his idea known to King Alfonso V of Portugal (r. 1438–1481) and Christopher Columbus (1451–1506). In 1474, Toscanelli is said to have written a letter defending the notion that one could sail west from Europe and reach the spice regions of "Cathay" to Portuguese canon Fernão Martins de Reriz, a familiar at court and later cardinal. The information was meant for the king. Toscanelli and Martins had been friends of Nicholas of Cusa for many years; both had been present at his death in 1464. A world map supposed to have

accompanied the letter and now also lost, greatly underestimated the true expanse of the Atlantic, showing "Cipangu" (Japan) lying 3,000 nautical miles (some 3,450 miles or 5,555 kilometers) west of the Canaries and at about the same latitude. Having learned of this letter and map, Columbus wrote to Toscanelli from Lisbon some years later (c. 1480) requesting a copy of the map. A transcription of Toscanelli's response survives in a book (*Historia Rerum Ubique Gestarum* by Aeneas Silvius [Pope Pius II]) that Columbus once owned. The veracity of this correspondence has been disputed, and even if authentic, Toscanelli's miscalculation of the earth's circumference probably only confirmed Columbus's own ideas rather than implanted them as has been claimed.

The text of the letter encourages Columbus to undertake such a westward voyage for several reasons: commercial (the East was rich in precious commodities); practical (a voyage across the Atlantic, as Toscanelli misconstrued it, would be quicker than the route around Africa); and pious (Christian Europe would be able to resurrect its mission to Asia, which had been abandoned in the fourteenth century, and mount a crusade to reconquer the Holy Land).

Years after his death, Toscanelli's fame as a scientist had not waned; in 1493, Ercole d'Este, duke of Ferrara, sent to Toscanelli's heir in Florence seeking to obtain his manuscripts and maps.

See also **Columbus, Christopher; Polo, Marco; Nicholas of Cusa**

Further Reading

La Carta perduta: Paolo dal P.T. e la cartografia delle grandi scoperte. Florence: Alinari, 1992.

Flint, Valerie I.J. *The Imaginative Landscape of Christopher Columbus.* Princeton, NJ: Princeton UP, 1992.

Garin, Eugenio. "Ritratto di Paolo dal Pozzo Toscanelli." *Belfagor* 3 [anno 12] (1957):

241–257; rpt. in *Ritratti di umanisti.* Florence, 1967, pp. 41–66.

Morison, Samuel Eliot. *Journals and Other Documents on the Life and Voyages of Christopher Columbus.* New York: Columbia UP, 1963.

Phillips, J.R.S. *The Medieval Expansion of Europe.* Oxford and New York: Oxford UP, 1988.

Revelli, Paolo. *Cristoforo Colombo e la scuola cartografica genovese.* Genoa: Consiglio Nazionale delle Ricerche, 1937.

GLORIA ALLAIRE

TRAINI, FRANCESCO (fl. 1321–1345)

The painter and illuminator Francesco Traini (Francesco di Traino) is generally considered the most important Pisan artist of the second quarter of the *Trecento*, when Pisa was under the rule of Francesco Novello della Gherardesca. Traini's career is still a focus of debate among scholars, but all would agree that he was one of the most original painters in fourteenth-century Italy. Traini's only surviving signed work is an altarpiece depicting Saint Dominic between eight scenes from his life (1344–1345; Pisa, Museo Nazionale di San Matteo). Since the nineteenth century, this altarpiece has been a valuable point of reference in attempts to identify a larger body of Traini's work.

Documented Life and Career: 1321–1345

Nothing is known about Traini's formative years; but to judge from his securely identifiable work, he was indebted to Sienese artistic traditions, especially the art of Simone Martini and Lippo Memmi, who were both active in Pisa in the early fourteenth century. This debt is evident in Traini's expressive treatment of line, his use of richly wrought surface textures, and his interest in spirited narrative detail. In addition, the Giottesque traditions of Florentine painting in general and the San Torpè Master in particular have been identified as possible sources for the more forcefully expressive elements in Traini's recognized oeuvre. Traini must already have been established as an independent painter with a certain reputation c. 1321, for in July and August 1322 it is recorded that he was paid for having decorated two important rooms in the Palazzo degli Anziani in Pisa. His success during the following decade is indicated by the fact that in December 1337 he committed himself to taking on an apprentice (by the name of Giovanni) for a period of three years. Traini is next recorded in December 1340 and February 1341, when he was involved in a commission to paint a banner for the confraternity of the Laudi of the cathedral in Pisa. In 1344 and 1345, Traini received payment for the signed Saint Dominic Altarpiece, which adorned an altar in the powerful Dominican church of Santa Caterina

Francesco Traini. *The Triumph of St. Thomas Aquinas.*
© Scala/Art Resource, New York.

in Pisa. Albizzo delle Statere, a wealthy Pisan citizen who was active in public life, had allocated funds for its execution in his will of 1336; the status of this commission suggests that Traini's art was held in high regard by his contemporaries. Traini is not thought to have survived the Black Death in 1348.

Panel Paintings, Frescoes, and Illuminations: 1320s–1340s

The Saint Dominic Altarpiece is considered one of the greatest achievements of Pisan *Trecento* panel painting. It shows a monumental standing figure of the saint, whose solid form is crisply delineated and defined by robust modeling. At each side of the saint are four episodes from his life, contained within quatrefoils; these are characterized by a remarkably fresh sense of narrative. For example, in one scene—*Saint Dominic Saving Pilgrims from a Shipwreck*—the painter was careful to evoke a variety of responses ranging from a desperate struggle for life by those in the water to the gratitude of the drenched figures who have been saved. Profound insights into psychological nuances and individual characteristics are evident throughout the altarpiece and are a hallmark of Traini's style generally, as can be seen in the *Saint Anne with Virgin and Child* (1330s; Princeton University Art Museum) and the *Archangel Michael* (c. 1330s; Lucca, Museo Nazionale di Villa Guinigi). The *Saint Anne with Virgin and Child* has a highly innovative design: an immobile and matronly Anne with a wizened face is juxtaposed with a suave, youthful Virgin who tenderly supports a lithe and nimble infant. The *Archangel Michael* depicts a heroic figure whose activated pose and spirited drapery convey a powerful sense of energy.

There are still differences of opinion regarding the exact nature of Traini's activity as a fresco painter in the Camposanto of Pisa. Since 1974, when Bellosi attribut-

ed the *Triumph of Death* and stylistically similar frescoes to Bonamico Buffalmacco, some scholars have held that Traini's contribution was limited to the bold designs of the Crucifixion (1330s). Traini's career as an illuminator is less contentious, but it too is a subject of divergent critical opinions, which concern the role of collaborators or intervention by a shop. The quality of Traini's illuminations is perhaps best seen in Lucano Spinola of Genoa's copy of Dante's *Inferno* (c. 1330; Chantilly, Musée Condé), which manifests a remarkable sensitivity to glance, gesture, and the fall of drapery.

The legacy of the marked expressive power of Traini's art can be discerned in the work of a number of important younger painters active in northwestern Tuscany. These painters include Francesco Neri of Volterra and Angelo Puccinelli of Lucca, both of whom used Traini's robust chiaroscuro, powerful volumes, and eccentric characterization of figures.

See also **Martini, Simone**

Further Reading

Balberini, Chiara. "Problemi di Miniatura del Trecento a Pisa: Gli Antifonari di San Francesco." *Critica d'Arte*, 63(7), 2000, pp. 44–60.

Bellosi, Luciano. *Buffalmacco e il Trionfo della Morte*. Turin: Einaudi, 1974.

——. "Sur Francesco Traini." *Revue de l'Art*, 92, 1991, pp. 9–19.

Carli, Enzo. *Pittura pisana del Trecento*, Vol. 1. Milan: A. Martello, 1959.

——. *La pittura a Pisa dalle origini alla "Bella Maniera"* Pisa: Pacini Editore, 1994.

Dalli Regoli, Gigetta. *Miniatura pisana del Trecento*. Venice: N. Pozza, 1963.

Meiss, Millard. *Francesco Traini*, ed. Hayden B. J. Maginnis. Washington, D.C.: Decatur House, 1983.

Polzer, Joseph. "Observations on Known Paintings and a New Altarpiece by Francesco Traini." *Pantheon*, 29, 1971, pp. 379–389.

Testi Cristiani, Maria. "Francesco Traini, i 'Chompagni' di Simone Martini a Pisa e la Madonna 'Linsky' con Bambino, Santi, e Storiette del Metropolitan Museum." *Critica d'Arte*, 64(9), 2001, pp. 21–45.

FLAVIO BOGGI

TREVISA, JOHN (early 1340s?–1402) Translator of informational works. Born probably in Cornwall, Trevisa entered Exeter College, Oxford, in 1362 and remained there until 1365. In 1369 he entered Queen's College and subsequently became a fellow. He was ordained priest in 1370. Trevisa was expelled from Queen's in 1378 for alleged misuse of college property but appears to have returned there for lengthy periods in 1383–86 and 1394–96. It was possibly after his expulsion from Queen's that he became vicar of Berkeley in Gloucestershire and chaplain to Thomas, Lord Berkeley. He was also a nonresident canon of Westbury-on-Trym, near Bristol.

Trevisa's major undertakings were his translations of several lengthy Latin works. The first that can be securely dated is his translation of Ranulf Higden's *Polychronicon*, a universal history, which he completed in 1387. His translation of the *De proprietatibus rerum*, the medieval encyclopedia of Bartholomaeus Anglicus, was finished in 1398. He produced this translation, as well as one of Giles of Rome's *De regimine principum*, a treatise on kingship, under the patronage of Thomas, Lord Berkeley. Trevisa also translated several shorter works: the apocryphal *Gospel of Nicodemus*, Richard FitzRalph's antimendicant sermon *Defensio curatorum*, and William Ockham's *Dialogus inter militem et clericum*. His only original works seem to be two brief essays on translation that preface some manuscripts of his *Polychronicon* translation: the "Dialogue between a Lord and a Clerk on Translation" and the "Epistle... Unto Lord Thomas of Barkley upon the Translation of *Polychronicon*...."

Trevisa's achievement as a translator has several important aspects. Most

obviously, he made accessible to an English audience such widely popular Latin informational works as the *Polychronicon* and *De proprietatibus rerum*. The influence of these translations was considerable. Both appear to have circulated widely (given their massive sizes) in manuscript and were printed by Caxton and de Worde, respectively, in the late 15th century. The *Polychronicon* was reprinted in the 16th century, while the *De proprietatibus* achieved an extended influence through Thomas East's revised edition in 1582 of *Batman vppon Bartholome*, a commentary on the work by Stephen Batman. In the latter form it was still being read and used in the late 17th century.

Trevisa also had a valuable role as neologizer. His translations expanded the lexical range of English, particularly in his use of new scientific and technical terminology. His fluent and generally accurate renderings of Latin prose demonstrated the possibilities of English prose as an instructional medium, thereby extending his influence into form as well as content.

Trevisa has also been credited with a role in the translation of the Wycliffite Bible. He was certainly at Oxford at the same time as Wyclif and Nicholas Hereford. However, his involvement in the Wycliffite translation remains uncertain, although there is at least some circumstantial evidence for it. His authorship has also been urged for a translation of Vegetius's *De re militari* into ME, but this seems unlikely.

See also **Caxton, William; Ockham, William of; Wyclif, John**

Further Reading

Primary Sources

Babington, Churchill, and J.R. Lumby, eds. *Polychronicon Ranulphi Higden*, 9 vols. Rolls Series. London: Longmans, 1865–86.

Perry, Aaron J., ed. *Dialogus inter Militem et Clericum; Richard FitzRalph's Sermon: "Defensio Curatorum"; and Methodius:*

"*Þe Bygynnyng of þe World and þe Ende of Worldes*". EETS o.s. 167. London: Humphrey Milford, 1925.

Seymour, M.C., gen. ed. *On the Properties of Things: John Trevisa's Translation of Bartholomaeus Anglicus De proprietatibus rerum*. 3 vols. Oxford: Clarendon, 1975–88.

Waldron, Ronald A., ed. "Trevisa's Original Prefaces on Translation: A Critical Edition." In *Medieval English Studies Presented to George Kane*, ed. Edward Donald Kennedy et al. Woodbridge: Brewer, 1988, pp. 285–99.

Secondary Sources

New *CBEL* 1:467–68, 806.

Manual 8:2656–61, 2866–77.

Edwards, A.S.G. "John Trevisa." In *Middle English Prose: A Critical Guide to Major Authors and Genres*, ed. A.S.G. Edwards. New Brunswick: Rutgers University Press, 1984, pp. 133–46.

Fowler, David C. *John Trevisa*. Aldershot: Variorum, 1993.

A.S.G. EDWARDS

TROTULA OF SALERNO Trotula is the name given to a number of medical treatises on the diseases of women, most of which seem to have come from the medical university of Salerno. Whethier a twelfth-century Trotula of Salerno actually existed, whether Trotula was a woman, and what and for whom Trotula wrote have been a subject of scholarly debate for many years. Benton (1985) suggested that a female physician named Trota wrote a *Practica* (*Practice of Medicine*) containing obstetrical and gynecological material while teaching at Salerno. Unlike many other universities in the Latin west, Salerno was formed by a community of medical practitioners who were not necessarily clerics; this anomaly would probably account for the remarkable presence of a woman teacher. The *Practica*, in Latin, was not copied after c. 1200; it was supplanted by other Latin works on gynecology and cosmetics taken from various male writers. The name Trotula (probably a diminutive of Trota) was attached to these later writings, which were in turn translated into a number of European vernaculars. Benton held that the genuine writings of Trota were more practical in character than those of her fellow Salernitan physicians, but this conclusion is difficult to support.

Further Reading

Benton, John F. "Trotula, Women's Problems, and the Professionalization of Medicine in the Middle Ages." *Bulletin of the History of Medicine*, 59, 1985, pp. 30–53.

Green, Monica H. "Women's Medical Practice and Health Care in Medieval Europe." *Signs*, 14, 1989, pp. 434–473. (Reprinted in *Sisters and Workers in the Middle Ages*, ed. Judith Bennett, et al. Chicago, Ill.: University of Chicago Press, 1989, pp. 39–78.)

The Trotula: A Medieval Compendium of Women's Medicine, ed. and trans. Monica H. Green. Philadelphia: University of Pennsylvania Press, 2001.

FAYE MARIE GETZ

U

UBERTINO DA CASALE (1259–c. 1329) The Franciscan reformer Ubertino da Casale was the author of the *Arbor vite crucifixe Jesu*—sometimes translated as *The Tree of the Crucified Life of Jesus*. This work had a strong effect on later Franciscan rigorists and on some prelates and monarchs; figures who were influenced by it include Dante, Giovanni dalle Celle, Saint Catherine of Siena, Saint Bernardino, John Brugman, and King Martin I of Aragon.

Most of our information about Ubertino until the time when he composed the *Arbor vite* in 1305 comes from its first prologue, but its chronology is not always clear. Ubertino was a native of Casale Monferrato in the diocese of Vercelli and in the Franciscan province of Genoa. He was received into the Franciscan order (Friars Minor) at age fourteen. Scholars disagree about the next period of his life. Some think that he remained in his province for a considerable time, until c. 1284 or 1285; but others—on the basis of his own testimony that he studied for nine years *et Parisius fui*—believe that after his novitiate he went to Paris and remained there until c. 1284. In any event he spent the years 1285 to 1289 (dates on which all the scholars agree) at Santa Croce in Florence. There, he was probably a subordinate lector in its *studium*, since he says that he was occupying the office of lector when he heard, at Pentecost, of John of Parma's death, which occurred in March 1289 (*Arbor vite*, 5.3).

It seems likely that Ubertino's studies in Paris had preceded this period in Florence rather than that, as some scholars hold, he went to Paris only after 1289. Ubertino associates Paris with a time when he was lax and ambitious. He tells us that his coming to Tuscany was accompanied by a conversion to a more ascetic life. Half of his four-year stay in Florence coincided with the lectorate there of the reformer who was to have the greatest influence on him, Petrus Johannis Olivi. Ubertino would have been exposed to Olivi's doctrine of *usus pauperi*, or "poor use," as essential to the Franciscan way of life—that is, the austere use of necessities and the avoidance of economic security and all superfluity. He must also have heard Olivi prophesy the persecution of the "spiritual" church by the "carnal" church. Ubertino's first meetings with Olivi—and with Margaret of Cortona, Cecilia of Florence, and John of Parma (who was in retirement at Greccio)—must have taken place just before or during 1285–1289. His crucial encounter with Angela of Foligno may also have been at this time. (There is conflicting evidence in the manuscripts on the date of this meeting: some say "in the twenty-fifth year of my religion.") According to Ubertino, these were the meetings that brought about his real conversion, after "almost fourteen years of external observance." It is difficult to believe that he then relapsed into what he calls laxity and ambition.

Ubertino learned a great deal from Olivi at Santa Croce; but unlike Olivi, he had no vocation to be a professional theologian, or to continue as a lector. Instead, Ubertino abandoned teaching to become a wandering preacher, traveling through Tuscany, Umbria, and the Marches, and denouncing both the heresy of the Brethren of the Free Spirit and the corruption of the official church. It is clear from the *Arbor vite* that he considered the resignation of Pope Celestine V and the subsequent election of Pope Boniface VIII illegitimate—a point on which he differed from Olivi. In the *Arbor vite* he identified Boniface, as well as Boniface's successor Pope Benedict XI, with the mystical Antichrist. How far Ubertino went in expressing these radical views in his public sermons is uncertain, but some hint of his opinions must have reached Benedict XI, because the pope summoned and arrested him. Ubertino was freed only because of the entreaties of a delegation of Perugian citizens; he was then sent by his Franciscan superiors to La Verna for an extended period of meditation. He used that time to write the *Arbor vite*, although he can hardly have composed the whole artful and almost interminable work, as he avows, in three months and seven days in 1305, without premeditation and with the aid of just a few books. Perhaps he was referring only to the nucleus of this vast work—a conjecture that might explain how Angelo Clareno could have described it as a "small" book. In any case, the more extreme opinions in the work were evidently not known to Ubertino's enemies among the Friars Minor for a long time, for they attacked only his defense of Olivi and were unable to keep Ubertino from exerting considerable influence in high ecclesiastical circles.

Ubertino also became the confidant and servant of a prominent cardinal, Napoleone Orsini, who looked kindly on the Spiritual faction of the Franciscans. Ubertino was appointed Orsini's chaplain in 1306 (though their connection seems to have begun earlier) and as late as 1324 was still doing important diplomatic work for him, helping conduct negotiations between Pisa and Aragon. In 1307, Ubertino was in Tuscany trying to further efforts on behalf of the Florentine exiles and was also undertaking juridical activity against the heretics of the Free Spirit. At about this time, he was also becoming increasingly involved in defending the interests of the Spiritual Franciscans; he served as procurator for various Spiritual groups, carrying their cases as far as Avignon.

Orsini's protection, and perhaps that of Cardinal James Colonna as well, must have been vital to Ubertino during the many years when he was able to frustrate the designs of the Franciscan leaders against him. He also seems to have elicited some sympathy from the popes to whom these leaders complained about him—Clement V and John XXII. At the time of the Council of Vienne (1310–1312), Ubertino wrote polemical treatises defending Olivi, advocating the doctrine of "poor use" for the Franciscan order, and pleading that at the very least the Spirituals should be allowed to follow the will of Francis and be free from persecution by the order. These writings were reflected to some extent in the bulls of Clement V, although in the end Clement refused to grant the Spirituals exemption from their superiors. The Spirituals fared worse under John XXII, but after their downfall Ubertino was not turned over to the authorities of the order. Instead, he secured from John a bull (20 October 1317) permitting him to enter the Benedictine house of Gembloux in the diocese of Liège, though there is no record that he ever set foot there. Ubertino was still in Avignon in 1322, when John asked him and a number of cardinals, bishops, Franciscans, Dominicans, and other clerics for their opinion on whether, as the Franciscans asserted, Christ and his apostles had owned nothing either individually or in common. The pope eventually issued a bull condemning the Franciscans' claim that only their order, which professed corporate as well as individual poverty, fully imitated the life of Christ and his apostles; in this bull, John came very close to quoting some of Ubertino's earlier arguments against the practices of the Franciscan community.

But Ubertino's longtime defense of Olivi finally made it possible for the Franciscan community to bring him down. In 1325, in a bull directed to the Franciscans, John described Ubertino as a fugitive—Ubertino having fled from Avignon in fear of imminent condemnation—and ordered his arrest. Ubertino may have escaped to the court of Lewis of Bavaria, and he may have helped in the writing of some of Lewis's attacks on John XXII; this hypothesis rests mainly on Albertino Mussato's testimony that Ubertino and Marsilius of Padua accompanied Ludwig to Rome in 1328. There is contemporary testimony that Ubertino preached on behalf of Ludwig's Franciscan antipope Peter Corbara.

The date and manner of Ubertino's death are unknown, though a later tradition of the Fraticelli (a Spiritual Franciscan group) held that it was violent.

Ubertino was an interesting combination of ascetic, polemicist, and diplomat. He was a gifted rhetorician and, particularly in his polemical works, a brilliant satirist. He poured into the *Arbor vite* his often moving meditations on Christ's life and the similarities between Christ and Saint Francis. This work, obviously constructed in large part from Ubertino's earlier sermons and treatises, also contains a multitude of long and short extracts from various authorities: the church fathers; Bernard, Bonaventure, Olivi, and other Franciscan writers; and Thomas

Aquinas. There are surely also many sources that have not yet been identified. The fifth book of the *Arbor vite*, containing Ubertino's views on ecclesiastical history, is mainly based, as Manselli (1965, 1977) has shown, on Olivi's *Postilla in Apocalypsim*. Ubertino's polemical treatises are vivid, supple, and remarkably readable, despite the technicality of their arguments. In these works, the historical dimension disappears, and "poor use" is emphasized much more than corporate expropriation. In 1322, the pope commanded Ubertino to enlarge his oral opinion on whether Christ and the apostles had possessed nothing, either individually or in common. Ubertino did so in the unpublished treatise *De altissima paupertate* (*Treatise on the Highest Poverty*), largely copied—although with significant omissions, additions, and modifications—from Olivi's question 8, *De altissima paupertate*, in the series of questions called *De perfectione evangelica*. Ubertino's summary of that treatise, *Reducendo igitur ad brevitatem*, was included in a famous collection of opinions on the question, in manuscript Vatican Latinus 3740, and attracted a marginal note in the pope's own hand. This summary drew a number of its arguments from Olivi's question 9, dealing with whether *usus pauper* was included in the Franciscan vow of evangelical poverty. Cardinal Orsini's opinion contained in the same collection follows a line of argument similar to Ubertino's and may actually have been written by Ubertino.

Ubertino's doctrines regarding poverty are the most interesting aspect of his thought. They seem to have undergone considerable development over his lifetime. In the *Arbor vite*, Ubertino accepted the official Franciscan view, shared by all factions, that as followers of evangelical perfection, if not as prelates transferring goods to the poor, they absolutely embraced corporate as well as individual poverty. To this he added Olivi's view that "poor use" was necessary to the observance of the highest poverty, and that the persecution of those who followed "poor use" was a sign of the appearance of the Antichrist and the coming of the "last age."

In Ubertino's polemical treatises, this historical dimension of his thought disappears entirely, and he is much more concerned with poor use than with corporate expropriation. In his final treatise, written when he was nominally a Benedictine, Ubertino was unwilling to accept the traditional view that the holding of collective property by monastic corporations according to human law was no breach of evangelical perfection. He did, however, clearly affirm, against the Franciscans, that possession according to natural (though not civil) law was inseparable from the use of consumable things. The Franciscans' theory, on the other hand, maintained that Franciscans had only the use of such things, whose ownership always rested with the donors or was held by the pope. Ubertino now evidently regarded this theory as a pitiful pretense. He also thought that it was ultimately inimical to Olivi's doctrine of "poor use," a doctrine to which—despite his careful editing and revision of Olivi's question concerning the highest poverty—he always remained faithful.

See also **Boniface VIII, Pope; Catherine of Siena, Saint; Celestine V, Pope; Dante Alighieri**

Further Reading

Editions

Arbor vitae crucifixae Jesu. Venice: Andrea de Bonettis de Papia, 1485. (Reprint, ed. Charles T. Davis. Turin: Bottega d'Erasmo, 1961.)

Declaratio fratris Ubertini de Casali et sociorum eius contra falsitates datas per fratrem Raymundum procuratorem et Bonagratiam da Bergamo, ed. F. Ehrle. *Archiv für Literatur und Kirchengeschichte des Mittelalters,* 3, 1887, pp. 160–195.

Decretalis etiam, ed. F. Ehrle. *Archiv für Literatur und Kirchengeschichte des Mittelalters,* 3, 1887, pp. 130–135.

Reducendo igitur ad brevitatem, ed. Charles T. Davis. In "Ubertino da Casale and His Conception of *Altissima Paupertas.* " *Studi Medievali,* Series 3(22.1), 1981, pp. 41–56.

Rotulus iste, ed. F. Ehrle. *Archiv für Literatur und Kirchengeschichte des Mittelalters,* 3, 1887, pp. 89–130.

Sanctitas vestra, ed. F. Ehrle. *Archiv für Literatur und Kirchengeschichte des Mittelalters,* 3, 1887, pp. 48–89.

Sanctitati apostolice, ed. F. Ehrle. *Archiv für Literatur und Kirchengeschichte des Mittelalters,* 2, 1886, pp. 374–416.

Super tribus scelribus Damasci, ed. A. Heysse. *Archivum Franciscanum Historicum,* 10, 1917, pp. 103–174.

Tractatus Ubertini de altissima paupertate Christi et apostolorum eius et virorum apostolicorum. Codex Vienna Staatsbibliothek, 809, fols. 128r–159v.

Critical Studies

Bihl, Michael. "Review of Biographies of Ubertino, by Huck, Knoth, and Callaey." *Archivum Franciscanum Historicum,* 4, 1911, pp. 594–599.

Blondeel, E. "L'influence d'Ubertin de Casale sur les écrits de S. Bernardin de Sienne" and "Encore l'influence d'Ubertin de Casale sur les écrits de S. Bernardin de Sienne." *Collectanea Franciscana,* 6, 1936, pp. 5–44, 57–76.

Callaey, Frédégand. *L'idéalisme franciscain spirituel au XIV siècle: Étude sur Ubertin de Casale.* Louvain, 1911.

——. "L'influence et la diffusion de l'*Arbor vitae* de Ubertini de Casale." *Revue d'Historie Ecclésiatique,* 17, 1921, pp. 533–546.

——. "L'infiltration des id–es franciscaines spirituales chez les frères mineurs capucins au XVI siècle." In *Miscellanea Francesco Ehrle,* Vol. 1. Rome: Biblioteca Apostolica Vaticana, 1924.

Colasanti, G. "I Santi Cuori di Gesùe di Maria nell'*Arbor vitae* (1305) di Ubertino da Casale, O. Min." *Miscellanea Francescana,* 59, 1959, pp. 30–69.

Damiata, Marino. *Pietà e storia nell' "Arbor vitae" di Ubertino da Casale.* Florence: Edizioni Studi Francescani, 1988, pp. 195–215.

——. "Ubertino da Casaie: Ultimo atto." *Studi Francescani,* 86, 1989, pp. 279–303.

Daniel, Randolph. "Spirituality and Poverty: Angelo da Clareno and Ubertino da Casale." *Medievalia et Humanistica,* n.s., 4, 1973, pp. 89–98.

Davis, Charles T. "Ubertino da Casaie and His Conception of *Altissima Paupertas.*" *Studi Medievali*, Series 3(22.1), 1981, pp. 1–41.

Douie, Decima L. *The Nature and the Effect of the Heresy of the Fraticelli.* Manchester: University Press, 1932, pp. 120–152. (Reprint, 1978.)

Ehrle, F. "Die Spiritualen, ihr Verhältniss zum Franzis Kanerorden und zu den Fraticelen." *Archiv für Literatur und Kirchengeschichte des Mittelalters*, 1, 1885, pp. 509–569; 2, 1886, pp. 106–164; 3, 1887, pp. 553–623; 4, 1888, pp. 1–190.

——. Zur Vorgeschichte des Konzils von Vienne." *Archiv für Literatur und Kirchengeschichte des Mittelalters*, 2, 1886, pp. 353–416; 3, 1887, pp. 1–195.

Godefroy, P. "Ubertin de Casale." *Dictionnaire de théologie catholique*, 15, 1950, pp. 2021–2034.

Guyot, B. G. "*L'Arbor vitae crucifixae Iesu* d'Ubertin de Casale et ses emprunts aux *De articulis fidei* de S. Thomas d'Aquin." In *Studies Honoring Ignatius Charles Brady, Friar Minor*, ed. Romano Stephen Almagno and Conrad L. Harkins. Saint Bonaventure, N.Y.: Franciscan Institute, 1976, pp. 293–307.

Hofer, J. "Das Gutachten Ubertins von Casale über die Armut Christi." *Franziskanische Studien*, 11, 1924, pp. 210–215.

Huck, Johann Chrysostomus. *Ubertin von Casale und dessen Ideenkreis: Ein Beitrag zum Zeitalter Dantes.* Freiburg im Breisgau: Herder, 1903.

Ini, A. M. "Nuovi documenti sugli Spirituali di Toscana." *Archivum Franciscanum Historicum*, 66, 1973, pp. 305–377.

Knoth, E. *Ubertin von Casale: Ein Beitrag zur Geschichte der Franziskaner an der Wende des 13. und 14. Jahrhunderts.* Marburg, 1903.

Manselli, Raoul. "Pietro di Giovanni Olivi ed Ubertino da Casale (a proposito della *Lectura super Apocalipsim* e dell'*Arbor vitae crucifixae Iesu).*" *Studi Medievali*, Series 3(6), 1965, pp. 95–122

——. "L'anticristo mistico: Pietro di Giovanni Olivi, Ubertino da Casale, e i papi del loro tempo." *Collectanea Franciscana*, 47,1977, pp. 5–25.

Martini, A. "Ubertino da Casale alla Verna e la Verna nell'Arbor Vitae." *La Verna*, 11, 1913, pp. 273–344.

Oliger, Livarius. "De relatione inter Observantium querimonias Constantienses (1415) et Ubertini Casalensis quoddam scriptum." *Archivum Franciscanum Historicum*, 9, 1916, pp. 3–41.

Potestà, G. L. "Un secolo di studi sull' *Arbor vitae*: Chiesa ed escatologia in Ubertino da Casale." *Colléctanea Franciscana*, 47,1977, pp. 217–267.

——. *Storia ed escatologia in Ubertino da Casale.* Milan: Vita e Pensiero, 1980.

Zugaj, M. "Assumptio B. M. Virginis in *Arbor Vitae Crucifixae Jesu* (a. 1305) Fr. Ubertino de Casali, O. Min." *Miscellanea Francescana*, 46, 1946, pp. 124–156.

CHARLES T. DAVIS

UGUCCIONE DA PISA (c. 1125 or 1130–30 April 1210)

Under the entry *Pis* in *Derivationes*, Uguccione states that he was born in Pisa—without, however, indicating the year, which has had to be estimated by his biographers. The date of his election as bishop of Ferrara is likewise uncertain. He completed his studies at Bologna, where in all probability he wrote his grammatical treatises. Later, he began to lecture on Gratian's *Decretum*, perhaps at the monastery of Saint Nabore and Saint Felice, where Gratian had taught. One of Uguccione's students was Lothar, a count of the Segni, who later became Pope Innocent III. Uguccione headed the diocese of Ferrara until his death. During his years as bishop he was given important assignments by popes Celestine III and Innocent III, his former pupil, mostly for the purpose of resolving a crisis at Nonantola, which was governed by an *abate* insufficient to the task. The archbishop of Ravenna, Guglielmo Curiano, also entrusted Uguccione with settling disputes between the inhabitants of Ravenna and those of nearby Rimini. The outline of these biographical events agrees with the traditional view according to which Uguccione da Pisa, bishop of Ferrara, was, as both lecturer on grammar and canonist, the author of all of the works mentioned below. Muller (1991, 1994) has challenged this view, arguing that the grammarian and the canonist should not be identified as the same person.

It will be useful to point out links among Uguccione's works, based on internal cross-references. The *De dubio accentu* and *Rosarium* are cited in *Derivationes* and explicitly referred to by name in the *Agiographia*, which is itself referred to by name in the *Summa decretorum*. These references constitute the writer's claim to authorship and the basis for all further critical discussion of his works.

De dubio accentu: This brief treatise provides the correct pronunciation of a number of compound words or words in which the penultimate syllable is followed by a mute plus a liquid. In a set of appendixes, Uguccione deals with more specialized issues relating, again, to pronunciation, and also to spelling. Giovanni Balbi's *Catholicon* often draws on this text, while occasionally deferring to Bene da Firenze's teachings.

Rosarium: This treatise on grammar, cited twice in the *Derivationes*, is preserved in a single manuscript dating from 1382, Erfurt Ampl. Q. 69 (252), ff, 1–63. It provides a summary of *ars grammatica*, based on the eight parts of speech. A list of conjugated verb forms, arranged alphabetically (*amo, amas*, etc. to *zelo, zelas*), appears on leaves 24ra–54rb.

Derivationes: Preserved in more than 200 extant manuscripts, this lexicon comprises the entire patrimony of *the* Latin language, classified by the principles of word derivation. It constitutes a fundamental stage in the development of medieval Latin lexicography because it organizes a large amount of linguistic data into derivational groupings and because it integrates into this scheme erudition passed down from antiquity, to be preserved and passed on to future generations. The work remains unpublished.

Agiographia: This short text also uses the word derivation format, which, in its most noteworthy section, presents a list of saints' names, arranged according to the liturgical calendar; these are then glossed with reference to traditional hagiographical aspects relating to holy deeds leading to canonization. The work serves as a bridge between Uguccione's two major texts; it is cited in the *Summa decretorum*, and it makes, in turn, an explicit reference to the *Derivationes*.

Summa decretorum: Uguccione worked on this text from 1178 to at least 1188. However, some questions arise as to whether the commentary regarding cases 23–26 is authentic or the work of one of Uguccione's continuators. Relatively recently, this text has been subjected to renewed scrutiny by historians of canon law, in an attempt to understand Uguccione's views on the thorny issue of the relationship between the two supreme authorities on earth—the papacy and the empire. According to some, Uguccione's thinking on this subject may have inspired Dante's *Monarchia*; indeed, Dante explicitly cites the *Derivationes* in his *Convivio* (4.6.5). The *Summa decretorum* also deals with a number of questions pertaining to the theology of the sacraments. For the manuscript tradition of this *Summa*, still unpublished, readers should consult Leonardi (1956–1957).

Expositio de symbolo apostolorum: This text is attributed to Uguccione in Trombelli (1775) and codex 2633 in the University Library of Bologna but is not cited by him in any of his other works. It offers a commentary on the twelve articles of the *credo*, thereby constituting itself a catechism on the fundamental beliefs of the Christian faith. This brief exposition may be the fruit of Uguccione's pastoral activity, undertaken during the last twenty years of his life as bishop of Ferrara.

See also **Gratian, Innocent III, Pope**

Further Reading

Editions

De dubio accentu—Agiographia—Expositio de symbolo apostolorum, ed. Giuseppe

Cremascoli. Spoleto: Centro Italiano di Studi sull'Alto Medioevo, 1978.

Derivationes. Florence: Accademia della Crusca, 2000.

Il"De dubio accentu" di Uguccione da Pisa, ed. Giuseppe Cremascoli. Bologna, 1969.

Expositio Domini Huguccionis Ferrariensis Episcopi de Symbolo Apostolorum, ed. Joannes Chrysostomus Trombelli. In *Bedae et Claudii Taurinensis itemque aliorum veterum Patrum opuscula*, Bologna, 1755, pp. 207–223.

L *"Expositio de symbolo apostolorum " di Uguccione da Pisa*, ed. Giuseppe Cremascoli. *Studi Medievali*, 14, 1973, pp. 364–442.

Häring, Nicholas M. "Zwei Kommentare von Huguccio, Bischof von Ferrara." *Studia Gratiana*, 19, 1976, pp. 355–416.

Critical Studies

Austin, H. D. "Glimpses of Uguiccione's Personality." *Philological Quarterly*, 26, 1947, pp. 367–377.

———. "Uguiccione Miscellany." *Italica*, 27, 1950, pp. 12–17.

Cremascoli, Giuseppe. "Saggio bibliografico." *Aevum*, 42, 1968, pp. 123–168.

Leonardi, Corrado. "La vira e l'opera di Uguccione da Pisa decretista." *Studia Gratiana*, 4, 1956–1957, pp. 37–120.

Marigo, Aristide. *I codici manoscritti delle "Derivationes" di Uguccione Pisano*. Rome: Istituto di Smdi Romani, 1936.

Müller, Wolfgang P. "Huguccio of Pisa: Canonist, Bishop, and Grammarian?" *Viator*, 22, 1991, pp. 121–152.

———. *Huguccio: The Life, Works, and Thought of a Twelfth Century Jurist*. Washington, D.C.: Catholic University of America Press, 1994.

Riessner, Claus. *Die "Magnae Derivationes" des Uguccione da Pisa und ihre Bedeutung für die romanische Philologie*. Rome: Edizioni di Storia e Letteratura, 1965.

GIUSEPPE CREMASCOLI
TRANSLATED BY RICHARD LANSING

ÚLFR UGGASON (fl. ca. 1000)

Úlfr Uggason was an Icelandic skald who flourished around the year 1000. He married Járngerðr, daughter of Þórarinn Grimkelsson and Jórunn Einarsdóttir from Stafaholt (*Landnárnabók* S76, H64). His wife's family were descendants of Hrappr, son of Bjrn buna Veðrar-Grímsson, one of the most prominent early settlers in Iceland. His father's family is unknown.

Úlfr is represented in three sagas. *Njáls saga* portrays him as a cautious man. In ch. 60, he makes a brief appearance as the loser in an inheritance claim he contests with Ásgrímr Elliða-Grimsson. In ch. 102, he refuses to commit himself openly to physical violence in the cause of the antimissionary party in the events surrounding the conversion of Iceland to Christianity. Both here and in *Kristni saga* (ch. 9), a single verse of Úlfr's is preserved in which he responds to a poetic incitement to push the foreign evangelist Þangbrandr over a cliff. Likening himself to a wily fish, he asserts that it is not his style to swallow the fly (*esat mínligt... flugu at gína*)!

However, Úlfr is best known for his composition of a skaldic picture poem, *Húsdrápa* ("House-lay"), which commemorates a splendid new hall that Óláfr pái ("peacock") had built at Hjarðarholt. The *drápa* celebrates both the builder of the hall and the mythological stories depicted on its carved panels, *Laxdæla saga* (ch. 29) describes the hall and the occasion upon which Úlfr delivered his poem, the marriage feast of Óláfr's daughter Þuriðr. Excellent stories (*ágætligar sgur*) were carved on the wainscoting and on the hall ceiling, and these splendid carvings surpassed the wall hangings. *Laxdæla saga* does not preserve the poem, but comments only that *Húsdrápa* was well crafted (*vel ort*) and that Úlfr received a good reward for it from Óláfr. These events are usually dated, according to the saga's chronology, to about 985.

Fortunately for posterity, Snorri Sturluson preserved fifty-six lines of *Húsdrápa* in his *Edda*, mostly as half-stanzas illustrating points of skaldic diction in *Skáldskaparmál*. Out of these verses, editors have conventionally reconstructed a *drápa* of twelve stanzas or half-stanzas, which probably had the refrain *hlaut innan svá minnum* ("within have appeared these motifs").

There are three known mythological subjects Úlfr treated in *Húsdrápa*, and there may have been more. Snorri states that Úlfr composed a long passage in the poem on the story of Baldr, of which we now have five half-stanzas (7–11 in Finnur Jónsson 1912–15). They deal with the procession of supernatural beings and their mounts riding to Baldr's funeral. In *Gylfaginning*, chs. 33–35 (Finnur Jónsson 1931: 63–8, Faulkes 1987: 48–51), Snorri gives a prose account of the funeral and other events that led up to and followed Baldr's death, for which *Húsdrápa* was probably one of his main sources.

Two other known subjects of *Húsdrápa* were Þórr's fight with the World Serpent, Miðgarðsormr, a popular choice with Viking Age skalds and sculptors (sts. 3–6), and the otherwise unrepresented myth of how the gods Heimdallr and Loki, said by Snorri to have taken the form of seals, wrestled for a "beautiful sea-kidney" (probably the necklace Brísíngamen) at a place called Singasteinn. Only one stanza (2) of this section survives, although from Snorri's summary it seems likely to have been longer in the complete *drápa*.

It may be surmised that Úlfr's pictorial praise poem in honor of Óláfr pái was, in a late 10th-century Icelandic context, something of a hearkening back to the courtly, aristocratic style of skalds like Bragi Boddason and Þjóðólfr of Hvin, who lived about a century earlier than Úlfr. Judging by *Laxdœla saga*'s account of Óláfr, his splendid style of living, and Irish royal connections, he would have been flattered by an implicit comparison with Norwegian princelings and their skaldic encomiasts.

See also **Bragi Boddason; Snorri Sturluson**

Further Reading

Editions

Kahl, B. *Kristni saga. Þáttr Þorvalds ens víðforla. Þáttr Ísleifs biskups Gizurarsonar. Hungrvaka*. Altnordische Saga-Bibliothek, 11. Halle: Niemeyer, 1905 [see pp. 1–57].

Finnur Jónsson, ed. *Den norske-islandske skjaldedigtning*. Vols. 1A-2A (tekst efter håndskrifterne) and 1B-2B (rettet tekst). Copenhagen and Christiania [Oslo]: Gyldendal, 1912–15; rpt. Copenhagen: Rosenkilde & Bagger, 1967 (A) and 1973 (B), vol. 1A. pp. 136–9; vol. 1B, pp. 128–30.

Finnur Jónsson, ed. *Edda Snorra Sturlusonar*. Copenhagen: Gyldendal, 1931 [lines from *Húsdrápa* pp. 89, 90, 94, 96–100, 147, 152, 165, 168].

Einar Ól. Sveinsson, ed. *Laxdæla saga*, Oslenzk fomrit, 5. Reykjavik: Hið íslenzka fornritafélag, 1934.

Einar Ól. Sveinsson, ed. *Brennu-Njáls saga*. Íslenzk fornrit, 12. Reykjavik: Hið íslenzka fomritafélag, 1954.

Jakob Benediktsson, ed. *Íslendingabók. Landnámabók*. Íslenzk fornrit, 1. Reykjavik: Hið íslenzka fornritafélag, 1968.

Turville-Petre, E. O. G. *Scaldic Poetry*. Oxford: Clarendon, 1976, pp. 67–70 [Baldr's funeral strophes from *Húsdrápa*].

Frank, Roberta. *Old Norse Court Poetry: The Dróttkvætt Stanza*. Islandica, 42. Ithaca and London: Cornell University Press, 1978 [texts and discussion of *Húsdrápa* pp. 104–5, 110–2, 170].

Translations

Gudbrand Vigfusson and F. York Powell, eds. and trans. "Christne saga." In *Origines Islandicae: A Collection of the More Important Sagas and Other Native Writings Relating to the Settlement and Early History of Iceland*. 2 vols. Oxford: Clarendon, 1905 rpt. Millwood: Kraus, 1976, vol. 1, pp. 370–406.

Hollander, Lee M. *The Skalds: A Selection of Their Poems, with Introductions and Notes*. New York: American-Scandinavian Foundation, 1945; 2nd ed. Ann Arbor: University of Michigan Press, 1968, pp. 49–54.

Magnús Magnússon and Hermann Pálsson, trans. *Njal's saga*. Harmondsworth: Penguin, 1960 [esp. pp. 144 and 220–1].

Magnús Magnússon and Hermann Pálsson, trans. *Laxdæla saga.* Harmondsworth: Penguin, 1960 [esp. pp. 111–3].

Faulkes, Anthony, trans. *Snorri Sturluson. Edda.* Everyman Classics. London and Melbourne: Dent, 1987 [lines from *Húsdrápa,* pp. 67–8, 71, 74–7, 116, 121, 132–3, 135].

Bibliographies
Hollander, Lee M. *A Bibliography of Skaldic Studies.* Copenhagen: Munksgaard, 1958.

Bekker-Nielsen, Hans. *Old Norse-Icelandic Studies: A Select Bibliography.* Toronto Medieval Bibliographies, 1. Toronto: University of Toronto Press, 1967.

Literature
Lie, Hallvard. "Billedbeskrivende dikt." *KLNM* 1 (1956), 542–5.

Lie, Hallvard. *"Natur"* og *"unatur"* iskaldekunsten. Avhandlinger utg. av Det norske Videnskaps-Akademi i Oslo. II. Hist.-filos. kl. No. 1. Oslo: Aschehoug, 1957; rpt. in his *Om sagakunst og skaldskap. Utvalgte avhandlinger.* Øvre Ervik: Alvheim & Eide, 1982, pp. 201–315.

Lie, Hallvard. "Húsdrápa," *KLNM* 7 (1962), 122–4.

Turville-Petre, E.O.G. *Myth and Religion of the North: The Religion of Ancient Scandinavia.* New York: Holt, Rinehart and Winston, 1964; rpt. Westport: Greenwood, 1975.

Strömbäck, Dag. *The Conversion of Iceland: A Survey.* Trans. and annotated by Peter Foote. Text Series, 6. London: Viking Society for Northern Research, 1975.

Schier, K. "Balder." In *Reallexikon der germanischen Altertumskvnde* 2. Gen. ed. Johannes Hoops. Berlin and New York; de Gruyter, 1976, pp. 2–7.

Schier, Kurt. "Die Húsdrápa von Úlfr Uggason und die bildliche Überlieferung altnordischer Mythen." In *Minjar og menntir: Afmælisrit helgað Kristjáni Eldjárn, 6 desember 1976.* Ed. Guðni Kolbeinsson *et al.* Reykjavik: Menningarsjóður, 1976, pp. 425–43.

Schier, Kurt. "Húsdrápa, 2. Heimdall, Loki und die Meerniere." In *Festgabe für Otto HMfler zum 75. Gebunstag.* Ed. Helmut Birkhan. Philologica Germanica, 3. Vienna: Braumüller, 1976, pp. 577–88.

Clover, Carol J. "Skaldic Sensibility." *Arkiv för nordisk filologi* 93 (1978), 63–81.

Clunies Ross, Margaret. "Style and Authorial Presence in Skaldic Mythological Poetry." *Saga-Book of the Viking Society* 20 (1981), 276–304.

Kuhn, Hans. *Das Dróttkvætt.* Heidelberg: Winter, 1983 [esp. pp. 295–6].

Meulengracht Sørensen, Preben. "Thor's Fishing Expedition." In *Words and Objects: Towards a Dialogue Between Archaeology and History of Religion.* Ed. Gro Steinsland. Institute for Comparative Research in Human Culture, Oslo. Ser. B: Skrifter, 71. Oslo: Norwegian University Press, 1986, pp. 257–78.

MARGARET CLUNIES ROSS

ULRICH VON ETZENBACH (fl. 2d half of the 13th c.)
A German author who contributed to the emerging German culture at the Bohemian court in Prague of the House of the Přemysl. He began writing his *Alexander* romance around 1270 under the patronage of King Ottokar, and completed it in 1286 under King Wenzel II, Ottokar's son. The legendary romance *Wilhelm von Wenden* was written around 1290, whereas the date of Ulrich's *Herzog Ernst* version D (attribution uncertain) cannot be confirmed.

We do not know much about Ulrich apart from what he mentions about himself in his works. He was born in Northern Bohemia (*Alexander,* vv. 27627f.) and acquired a solid education, though he probably did not become a cleric. His knowledge of Latin was very good, and so his familiarity with "classical" Middle High German literature, to which he refers often.

The *Alexander,* which has been preserved in six manuscripts and several fragments, deals with the famous history of the Macedonian ruler Alexander the Great and follows his conquest of the Persian Empire and all the lands extending to the river Indus. The text is based primarily on the Latin epic poem *Alexandreis* (thirteenth century), composed in hexametric verse by Walther of Châtillon, but then also on the *Nativitas et victoriae Alexandri Magni* regis (*Birth and Victories of Alexander the Great King*, ca. 950–970) by the Archpriest Leo (which again was based on the tenth-century *Historia preliis*).

For both Walther and Ulrich, Alexander's victories laid the foundation for the third of four secular empires that would, according to biblical traditions, come and go before Christ's return and the Day of Judgment. For religious reasons Alexander's activities are cleansed from any negative elements as in the older tradition; even murderous slaughter and killing of enemy troops are exculpated. Moreover, the important aspects of Alexander's curiosity leading to his exploration of the world (dive into the sea in a glass bubble; flight in the air with the help of griffins) are eliminated as well, because he is seen as God's instrument and made to an ideal ruler in the tradition of the *Fürstenspiegel* (didactic texts for princes). In many respects, Alexander is modeled after Ottokar II, whom Ulrich wanted to idealize through his work.

In *Wilhelm von Wenden*, preserved only in one manuscript, now in Dessau, King Wenzel II and his wife, Guta of Habsburg, are immortalized in the figure of Prince Wilhelm of Parrit and his wife, Bene (the Good One). Wilhelm secretly departs from his dukedom to make a pilgrimage to Jerusalem and to convert to a Christian. Bene accompanies him but is left behind in a foreign country after she delivers twins, whom Wilhelm sells to Christian merchants to be free of this burden on his pilgrimage. Because of Bene's virtuous lifestyle she is later elected (!) the ruler of that country, and when by chance the family eventually reunites again after many years, they all convert to Christianity and thus missionize the entire country. Both the role of the strong woman and the tolerant attitude toward non-Christian religions are remarkable. Ulrich used as his model either *Guillaume d'Angleterre* by Chrétien de Troyes, or the *Eustachius* legend in the *Legenda aurea* (*Golden Legendary*).

Herzog Ernst D finally, extant in one manuscript (Gotha, called "d"), follows the tradition of goliardic narratives (*Spielmannsepen*) in which the young Bavarian duke has to leave Germany because of political and military conflicts with his father-in-law, the irrational and impetuous emperor, and explores the world of the Orient. Both this text and the *Alexander* were later translated into Czech.

See also **Walter of Châtillon**

Further Reading

Behr, Hans-Joachim. *Literatur als Machtlegitimation*. Munich: Fink, 1989.

Classen, Albrecht: "Ulrichs von Etzenbach *Wilhelm von Wenden—ein Frauenroman?*" *Literaturwissenschaftliches Jahrbuch* 30 (1989): 27–43.

Kohlmayer, Rainer: *Ulrichs von Etzenbach "Wilhelm von Wenden."* Meisenheim: Hain, 1974.

Rosenfeld, Hans-Friedrich, ed. *Ulrich von Etzenbach. "Wilhelm von Wenden."* Berlin: Akademie-Verlag, 1957.

——, ed. *Herzog Ernst D*. Tübingen: Niemeyer, 1991.

Toischer, Wendelin, ed. *Ulrich von Etzenbach*: "*Alexander.*" Prague: Verein für Geschichte der Deutschen in Böhmen, 1888.

ALBRECHT CLASSEN

ULRICH VON LIECHTENSTEIN (ca. 1200–1275) Ulrich von Liechtenstein's action-filled life as a political *ministeriale* in Austria in the middle two fourths of the twelfth century is well documented in contemporary records. As a literary parallel to his life, Ulrich created with his *Frauendienst* (*Service of Ladies*), compiled around 1255, though doubtless utilizing songs composed earlier, a fictional verse romance in which his persona, the minnesinger Ulrich, woos a recalcitrant lady with songs, adventures, including a cross-country tournament for which he dresses himself as Venus, and misadventures. In one of these he disables a finger while fighting to gain his lady's approval. When he learns that she doubts he was really injured, he chops the finger off and sends it to her in a jeweled casket, accompanied by a verse booklet proclaiming his love. His misadventures, which often echo literary motifs, are recounted with rollicking humor. His attempted tryst with the lady in her chambers, in the course of which he is hoisted up to and let down (literally: let fall) from her window in a basket and is so distraught at being rejected that he tries to drown himself, forms a high point of his hapless service. Angered by her consistent rejection of him, he turns to the service of a new lady, undertaking yet another marathon tournament, this time as King Arthur. In the midst of all his feverish service of a lady, he explicitly takes some time off to enjoy the company of his wife. Whereas songs more or less punctuate the narrative in the first half of the work (though their motifs often seem to have inspired its plot), they dominate the second half. Here, the framework often becomes little more than a poetological commentary on the songs, though as in many *razos*, or reasons (i.e., prose commentaries), of the troubadours—a possible inspiration for this part of the work—the commentary consists largely of paraphrase, and praise of the songs' excellence. Ulrich's fifty-seven songs and one *Leich* (poem), though accomplished, pale somewhat against the originality of their frame. His models were Walther von der Vogelweide (whom he quotes without attribution), Wolfram von Eschenbach (whose dawn songs he parodies), and Gottfried von Straßburg. He also doubtless learned from singers such as Gottfried von Neifen (whose use of the motif of the lady's rose-red mouth he exaggerates to comic effect) and probably influenced others in turn, such as Steinmar. A set of strophes he shares with Heinrich von Veldeke and Niune (Kraus, no. 58 XII) probably bears the former's name through scribal misascription and was adapted into two shorter songs by the latter.

In addition to the *Frauendienst*, he wrote the *Frauenbuch*, a didactic treatise in debate form in which a lady and a knight discuss who is responsible for the sad state of the world. In the end the lady is declared free of blame. Though it lacks the innovative sparkle (and the occasional narrative tedium) of the former work, its earnestness and apparent sincerity remind us that despite the ubiquity of humor and playfulness in Ulrich's larger work, he seems to have taken the exhortations to be constant, loyal, pure, and kind (good)that permeate both works to heart. Despite all the weaknesses and absurdities that he clearly recognizes in contemporary life and (especially) letters, he valorizes courtly ideals and seeks to promote *hôher muot* (courtly good cheer).

See also **Heinrich von Veldeke; Walther von der Vogelweide**

Further Reading

Bechstein, Reinhold, ed. *Ulrich's von Lichtenstein Frauendienst.* 2 vols. Leipzig: Brockhaus, 1888.

Kraus, Carl von, ed. *Deutsche Liederdichter des 13. Jahrhunderts.* 2 vols.; 2d ed. Gisela Kornrumpf. Tübingen: Niemeyer, 1978.

Lachmann, Karl, ed. *Ulrich von Lichtenstein.* Berlin: Sander, 1841; rpt. Hildesheim: Olms, 1974.

Thomas, J. W., trans. *Ulrich von Liechtenstein's Service of Ladies.* Chapel Hill: University of North Carolina Press, 1969.

HUBERT HEINEN

ULRICH VON TÜRHEIM (fl. ca. 1230–1245) After Gottfried von Straßburg had left his *Tristan* as a torso around 1210, two authors picked up the fragment and provided their own conclusions—Heinrich von Freiberg (ca. 1280–1290) and Ulrich von Türheim. The latter composed his *continuatio* (continuation) roughly between 1230 and 1235, adding a total of 3,730 verses. Uirich's conclusion of the *Tristan* was commissioned by the imperial cup-bearer (*Reichsschenk*), the Augsburg nobleman Konrad von Winterstetten (d. 1243). Sometime after that Ulrich wrote the continuation of Wolfram von Eschenbach's *Willehalm*, the so-called *Rennewart*, comprising more than 36,000 verses, completed before 1250. Among his earliest literary enterprises, however, we find Ulrich's short narrative *Clîges*, which is extant only in a fragment from circa 1230 and based on Chrétien de Troyes's *Cligès*.

An Ulrich von Türheim appears in the documents of the bishop and the cathedral chapter of Augsburg between 1236 and 1244. We assume that he was identical with our poet.

For his *Tristan* continuation, Ulrich relied heavily on the *Tristan* version by Eilhart von Oberg, *Tristrant*. Here, Tristan marries Isolde Whitehand, without sleeping with his newlywed. Her brother Kaedin learns about this scandalous situation and challenges Tristan, who then tells him of Isolde the Fair. Together they travel to England and meet Isolde secretly. Tristan spends one night with her alone, whereas Kaedin is duped by a chambermaid. Later Tristan is falsely accused of having failed in his service for the queen, and the latter orders him to be beaten and chased away when he shows up at court in the guise of a leper. The lovers overcome the conflict and misunderstanding, however, and Tristan can spend some time at court hidden behind his mask, until he is discovered and then returns to Arundel with Kaedin. Now Tristan fully accepts his wife and sleeps with her. When he later helps Kaedin in a secret love affair, Kaedin is killed and Tristan badly wounded. He requests help from Isolde the Fair, and asks that in case of her arrival the ship should set a white sail. When Isolde the Fair approaches the coast, jealous Isolde Whitehand deceives her husband and tells him that the sail is black. Despairing, Tristan dies, and when his true love has finally arrived at the bed, she drops dead next to him. King Marke has both buried together; a rosebush and a grapevine planted on their grave later intertwine, symbolizing the everlasting love of Tristan and Isolde the Fair.

Ulrich's *Rennewart* focuses on the history of the eponymous hero, who is, after the victory over the Saracens (described by Wolfram von Eschenbach in his *Willehalm*), baptized and married to King Loys' daughter Alise. Rennewart assumes the kingdom of Portebaliart and continues with his battles against the heathens. Alise dies at the birth of her child Malefer, who is soon after kidnapped by merchants and brought to Terramer, who wants to raise him as an opponent to Christianity, though to no avail. Rennewart, deeply grieved, joins a monastery where he lives for twenty more years. Two times he enters the battlefield again, however, and there he meets his son and entrusts him with the rulership of Portebaliart. Malefer later conquers the Oriental empire of his grandfather Terramer and marries the queen of the Amazons, Penteselie, who delivers a child with the name Johann who will continue with the religious struggle against the heathens. When Terramer's son Matribuleiz attacks France anew, Willehalm returns from his hermitage, a move that immediately convinces the Saracens, reminded of their previous defeat, to return home. Willehalm erects a monastery near Muntbasilière where he will eventually meet his death.

This *continuatio* was, along with Wolfram's epic, highly popular and is extant in thirteen manuscripts and twenty-nine fragments. Ulrich relied in part on the French tradition of the *chansons de gestes* (heroic songs), which are focused on Guillaume d'Orange. The Augsburg citizen Otto der Bogner supplied Ulrich, as he indicates in his *Rennewart*, with the manuscripts of the French texts (vv. 10270–10282). Ulrich probably composed his works for the royal court of the Hohenstaufen family.

See also **Eilhart von Oberg; Gottfried von Straßburg; Wolfram von Eschenbach**

Further Reading

Grubmüller, Klaus. "Probleme einer Fortsetzung." *Zeitschrift für deutsches Altertum* 114 (1985): 338–348.

McDonald, William C. *The Tristan Story in German Literature of the Late Middle Ages and Early Renaissance.* Lewiston, Maine: Edwin Mellen Press, 1990.

Spiewok, Wolfgang, ed. *Das Tristan-Epos Gottfrieds von Straßburg. Mit der Fortsetzung des Ulrich von Türheim.* Berlin: Akademie-Verlag, 1989.

Ulrich von Türheim. *Rennewart,* ed. A. Hübner. Berlin: Weidmann, 1938; 2d ed., 1964.

——. *Tristan,* ed. Th. Kerth. Tübingen: Niemeyer, 1979.

Westphal-Schmidt, Christa. *Studien zum Rennewart Ulrichs von Türheim.* Frankfurt am Main: Haage und Herchen, 1979.

ALBRECHT CLASSEN

URBAN II, POPE (c. 1035–1099, r. 1088–1099) Pope Urban II (Odo of Lagery, Eudes de Châtillon) was a church reformer and founder of the crusading movement. Urban was a native of France and was descended from a noble family of Châtillon–sur–Marne, near Soissons; Odo was his baptismal name. During his early school days at Reims, he came under the influence of Saint Bruno, the founder of the Carthusian order, who remained a potent influence in shaping his goals and values even after he had become pope. Odo's early career followed a pattern common among young clerics of noble lineage. After becoming archdeacon of Reims by 1160, he abandoned his career among the secular clergy and entered the monastery of Cluny. There, too, he advanced rapidly. By c. 1070 he was prior of Cluny; then Pope Gregory VII recruited him into the papal service in 1079–1080 and soon named him cardinal-bishop of Ostia.

Odo served Gregory diligently, at times at considerable peril to himself, notably when he was a papal legate in Germany during some of the darkest days of the pope's struggle against King Henry IV. When Gregory died at Salerno on 25 May 1085, Odo seemed a likely successor, but the choice fell instead on Abbot Desiderius of Monte Cassino, who reigned briefly as Pope Victor III. Shortly before his death (in 1087), Victor recommended that Odo be elected to succeed him. On 12 March 1088, the cardinals who had assembled at Terracina complied with Victor's suggestion, and Odo was crowned as Pope Urban II the same day.

The papacy was at this point in dire straits. Since Rome and the patrimony of Saint Peter were in the hands of Henry IV's supporters, papal revenues were greatly reduced, an antipope (Clement III) had the backing of the emperor, and the church reform movement seemed to be faltering. The great achievement of Urban's pontificate was to redress and, in large measure, to reverse this situation.

Urban was in many ways far more successful in implementing the papal reform program than Gregory VII had ever been. He achieved this in part by an unremitting round of meetings with bishops, the clergy, and powerful laymen, in which he preached, argued, bargained, and cajoled to induce his hearers to accept the main planks of the reformers' platform—to refrain from simoniacal appointments to church offices, to restore church property to clerical control, and to commit the clergy at every level to celibacy. At the same time, Urban sought, with considerable success, to reduce the political tension resulting from the confrontations that had marked the pontificate of Gregory VII. In place of confrontation, Urban offered negotiation; instead of demands, he advanced proposals; and he preferred to outmaneuver his opponents rather than challenge them directly.

Urban saw clearly that his reform program could succeed in the long run only if it was securely anchored in the church's legal structure. Accordingly, he devoted a great deal of time and effort to persuading church councils to adopt the principal

Council of Clermont. Arrival
of Pope Urban II in France.
Miniature from the Roman de
Godefroi de Bouillon. 1337.
Ms. fr. 22495, fol. 15.
© Bridgeman-Giraudon/Art
Resource, New York.

tenets of his program as church law. He
also lavished time and attention on his
role as supreme judge in the ecclesiastical
court system, and his decisions became
an integral part of the canonical jurispru-
dence of later generations.

Urban is best-known, however, as the
pope who proclaimed the First Crusade. At
the council of Clermont on 27 November
1095, Urban called on the knights, nobles, and bishops of Christendom to join
in an expedition to push back Turkish
armies that had occupied Asia Minor
and to help the Byzantine emperor restore Christian control over the Levant.
He further promised that participants in
this expedition would receive spiritual rewards, as well as a share in the conquests
that they achieved. The council adopted
his proposals, which quickly aroused a
broad and enthusiastic response—probably broader and more enthusiastic, indeed, than Urban had anticipated. The
pope devoted a great deal of time and effort over the following months to spelling
out the implications of his proposal and
refining arrangements for its organization
and implementation.

By the fall of 1096, crusaders from
France, Germany, and England were
on the way to their rendezvous at
Constantinople. In Italy, Urban's proposal
aroused interest at first mainly among the
restless Norman conquerors of the south,
who saw it as an opportunity to secure a

foothold in Byzantine territories; and the
merchants of a few maritime cities in the
north, especially Genoa and Pisa, who
perceived that the venture, if successful,
might open up profitable commercial opportunities in the Middle East.

After the initial bands of crusaders had
departed, Urban once more directed his
attention to the implementation of church
reform and endeavored to resolve the issues that had put the papacy at odds with
the principal monarchs north of the Alps.
Although he achieved some successes, his
program was still incomplete when he fell
ill in the summer of 1099. At the beginning of July, the crusading armies that he
had dispatched to the east had taken the
city of Jerusalem. News of this momen-
tous victory had not yet reached Rome
when Urban died on 19 July 1099.

See also **Gregory VII, Pope; Henry IV,
Emperor**

Further Reading

Editions

The Councils of Urban II, Part 1, *Decreta
    Claromontensia*, ed. Robert Somervilie.
    Amsterdam: Hakkert, 1972.
Jaffé, Philipp. *Regesta pontificum Romanorum*,
    2nd ed., 2 vols.
Leipzig, 1885–1888, Vol. 1, pp. 657–701.
    (Reprint, Graz: Akademische Druck- U.
    Verlagsanstalt, 1956. Includes some of
    Urban's letters.)

Patrologia Latina, 151, cols. 283–558. (Texts of most of Urban's surviving letters.)

Critical Studies

Becker, Alfons. *Papst Urban II (1088–1099)*, 2 vols. Schriften der Monumenta Germanise Historica, 19. Stuttgart: A. Hiersemann, 1964–1988. Furhmann, Horst. *Papst Urban II. und der Standder Regularkanoniker.* Munich: Beck, 1984.

Gossman, Francis J. *Pope Urban II and Canon Law.* Washington, D.C.: Catholic University of America Press, 1960.

Kuttner, Stephan, "Brief Notes: Urban II and Gratian." *Traditio*, 24, 1968, pp. 504–505.

——. "Urban II and the Doctrine of Interpretation: A Turning Point?" *Studia Gratiana*, 15, 1972, pp. 53–86.

Somerville, Robert. "The Council of Clermont and the First Crusade." *Studia Gratiana*, 20, 1976, pp. 323–337.

——. "Mercy and Justice in the Early Months of Urban II's Pontificate." In *Chiesa diritto e ordinamento della "Societas Christiana" net secoli XI e XII: Atti della nona Settimana internazionale di studio, Mendola, 28 agosto–2 settembre 1983*. Milan: Vita e Pensiero, 1986, pp. 138–158.

JAMES A. BRUNDAGE

V

VALERA, DIEGO DE (1412–c. 1488)
According to Valera himself, he was
born in 1412 and lived to a ripe old age,
probably dying late in 1488. His father,
Alonso Chirino de Guadalajara, was the
chief royal physician to Juan II of Castile
and author of at least two medical treatises, one of which was printed in Seville
in 1506. In 1427 Valera joined the royal
court at the age of fifteen and served as
one of the *donceles* of Juan II, and then
Prince Enrique (the future Enrique IV).
He was present at the Christian victory
of LaHigueruela just outside the Naṣrid
capital of Granada in 1431, and was made
a knight at the conquest of Huelma.

In 1437 Valera began a series of travels and adventures throughout western
Europe, being included by Fernando del
Pulgar in his *Claros varones de Castilla*
among a select list of famous knights er-
rant "que con ánimo de cavalleros fueron
por los reinos estraños a fazer armas con
qualquier cavallero que quisiese fazerlas
con ellos, e por ellas ganaron honrra para
sí e fama de valientes e esforçados cavalleros para los fijosdalgos de Castilla." He
was present at sieges, which Charles VII
of France directed against the English,
traveled to Prague, helped Albert V in
his campaigns against the Hussites, and
was rewarded by being made a member
of several chivalrous orders. Returning to
Castile, it was not long before Valera was

on his travels again with the king's backing and accompanied by a royal herald,
this time visiting Denmark, England, and
Burgundy, taking part in a famous tournament near Dijon, and returning subsequently on yet another mission to the
court of Charles VII of France.

Valera took part on the royal side at
the battle of Olmedo in 1445, but he
was soon to fall out of favor due to his
habit of preferring unsolicited advice
in letters addressed to Juan II and then,
subsequently, to Enrique IV. As a result
he passed into the service of the count of
Plasencia, Pedro de Estúñiga, for several
years. By his own detailed account in his
final chapter of the *Crónica abreviada*,
Valera played an important role in the
downfall of Álvaro de Luna, who was beheaded in Valladolid in 1453.

Apart from short periods of judicial office in Palencia and Segovia as
well as some service in the noble house
of Medinaceli, Valera spent most of his
later life in Puerto de Santa María, from
where he continued to write letters of political and military advice, in particular to
Fernando the Catholic.

Valera was a prolific author whose
main interests were devoted to chronicles
and short treatises of a chivalrous, political, or moral nature. Carriazo established
a chronological list of his works as follows: *Arbol de las Batallas*, a translation

of the famous French treatise on the laws of arms by Honoré Bonet, done for Álvaro de Luna (prior to 1441); *Espejo de Verdadero Nobleza*, a treatise on the origins and nature of nobility, dedicated to Juan II (ca. 1441); *Defensa de virtuosos mugeres*, dedicated to Queen María of Castile (prior to 1443); *Exhortatión a la paz*, addressed to Juan II (ca. 1448): *Tratado de las armas*, for Afonso V of Portugal (ca. 1458–1467); *Providencia contra Fortuna*, dedicated to the marquis of Villena (ca. 1465); *Ceremonial de Príncipes*, also dedicated to the marquis of Villena (ca. 1462–1467); *Breviloquio de virtudes*, for Rodrigo Pimentel, count of Benavente; *Origen de Roma y Troya*, for Juan Hurtado de Mendoza; *Origen de la casa de Guzmán*; *Doctrinal de príncipes*, dedicated to Fernando the Catholic (ca. 1475–1476), perhaps one of Valera's more original works; *Preheminencias y cargos de los oficiales de armas*, for Fernando the Catholic; *Geneología de los Reyes de Francia*, dedicated to Juan Terrin; *Crónica abreviada de Espana* (1479–1481); *Memorial de diversas hazanas*; and *Crónica de los Reyes Católicos*.

In addition Carriazo listed another two works, a lost work on the Estúñiga family, and another of dubious attribution, also lost, on *Ilustres varones de España*. In between all these works, the extraordinarily productive Valera also managed to write a considerable number of short poems of a moralistic or courtly love nature.

Further Reading

Pulgar, F. del. *Claros varones de Castilla.* Ed. R. B. Tate. Oxford, 1971.

Valera, M. D. de. *Crónica de los Reyes Católicos.* Ed. J. de Mata Carriazo. Madrid, 1927.

——. *Memorial de diversas hazañas.* Ed. J. de Mata Carriazo. Madrid, 1941. This edition includes the *Crónica abbreviada* as well.

ANGUS MACKAY

VAN DER WEYDEN, ROGIER

VAN DER WEYDEN, ROGIER (1399/1400–1464) Flemish painter, a student of Robert Campin, known in his day as second only to Jan van Eyck, Rogier van der Weyden was born in Tournai in French-speaking Hainaut, but the economic life of the area depended heavily on Flanders rather than France. In the 1430s, rather than seek employment at the Burgundian court, he moved to Brussels as the head of a large workshop. As a guild member, he catered heavily to Germanic circles of patronage, which did not, however, prevent his appreciation of the achievements of the court painter van Eyck. The influence of his predecessor can be detected in early works such as the *Annunciation* of ca. 1435, now in the Louvre, from his attention to detail in the patterning of the floor and fabrics to the symbolic objects filling the panel with meaning. Simultaneously, van der Weyden began to move beyond van Eyck's stylistic accomplishments to create a style of his own, as exemplified by his *Lamentation* (ca. 1435–38) in the Prado. In a shallow, undefined space, van der Weyden focuses the viewer's attention upon the monumental figures actively demonstrating their grief. He rejects the disguised symbolism so favored by van Eyck in order to explore more fully the emotive capabilities of composition. Van der Weyden, although not employed directly by the Burgundian court, did produce some works for its most prominent members. An example is his *Altarpiece of the Seven Sacraments* (ca. 1453–55) in the Musée Royal des Beaux-Arts of Antwerp, executed for Jean Chevrot, bishop of Tournai, in which he expanded the Gothic cathedral interior as depicted in van Eyck's earlier *Madonna in the Church*. He and van Eyck shared a client in the person of Nicolas Rolin, chancellor of Flanders. Van der Weyden also painted a nativity altarpiece (1452–55), now in Berlin, for Pieter Bladelin, who was the chief tax collector in Flanders for Philip the Good.

See also **Campin, Robert; Van Eyck, Jan**

Further Reading

Davies, Martin. *Rogier van der Weyden*. London: Phaidon, 1972.
Panofsky, Erwin. *Early Netherlandish Painting*. New York: Harper and Row, 1971.
Snyder, James. *Northern Renaissance Art*. New York: Abrams, 1985.

MICHELLE I. LAPINE

VAN EYCK, JAN (ca. 1380–1441) As one of the most famous painters of his day, van Eyck had the special privilege of being a *valet* to Philip the Good, duke of Burgundy. His role as court painter extended into the realm of diplomacy, as van Eyck was one of Philip's emissaries to Spain between 1424 and 1430. Van Eyck began his career in the Burgundian court after the death of his former patron, John of Bavaria. Although he served Philip directly, his production of panel painting for him went unrecorded. However, accounts of patronage do exist for members of Philip's circle. Van Eyck's reputation as a great master emerged from his superrealistic and sensual treatment of the panel, his rich and precise handling of clothing and jewels. Van Eyck fully exploited oil paint as his medium, evidenced by his exquisite details and nearly invisible brushwork. As was practiced by the majority of northern painters, van Eyck infused the objects in his world with secondary, allegorical, and christological meanings. The most obvious expression of his disguised symbolism can be found in his treatment of the Virgin and Child, a subject van Eyck repeatedly explored. His *Madonna in the Church* (ca. 1437–38), now hanging in the Gemaldegalerie-Staatliche Museen in Berlin, represents a beautifully executed example of his style and iconographic approach: the large size of the Virgin in comparison with her surroundings emphasizes her status. The *Ghent Altarpiece* (1432), which has sparked many a debate concerning attribution and assemblage, was done in collaboration with his brother Hubert and represents the only painting known by van Eyck prior to 1433.

Van Eyck produced his most renowned work for the members of the Burgundian court or people closely linked to it, particularly the two-thirds of his paintings that contain portraits. The *Arnolfini Wedding Portrait*, which rivals the altarpiece in reputation, was painted for Giovanni Arnolfini in 1434. Arnolfini settled in Flanders with his half-French wife after Philip the Good appointed him to a position at court. Baudouin de Lannoy, lord of Molembaix, commissioned a work in honor of his membership in the order of the Golden Fleece, founded by Philip in 1430. The inclusion of the order's collar in his portrait of 1435 advertises his newly acquired status. Van Eyck served Philip and the court of Burgundy for a sixteen-year stint that ended with his death in 1441. It was during his tenure as artist of the court that van Eyck developed the detailed, naturalistic style that had such a great impact on all who followed him.

See also **Van der Weyden, Rogier**

Further Reading

Dhanens, Elisabeth. *Hubert and Jan van Eyck*. New York: Alpine, 1970.
Henbison, Craig. *Jan van Eyck: The Play of Realism*. London: Reaktion, 1991.
Panofsky, Erwin. *Early Netherlandish Painting*. New York: Harper and Row, 1971.
Snyder, James. *Northern Renaissance Art*. New York: Abrams, 1985.

MICHELLE I. LAPINE

VENEZIANO, PAOLO (died c. 1362) The earliest undisputed date for Paolo Veneziano is 1333, when he signed and dated a triptych, the *Dormition of the Virgin*, formerly at San Lorenzo in Vicenza and now in the civic museum there. An art collector in Venice mentions him in a memorandum of 1335. His *Madonna and Child Enthroned* in the Crespi collection in Milan is signed and dated August 1340. A signed deposition by Paolo of March 1341 is in the Venetian archives, where there was once a document of September 1342 commissioning a throne for use in a state festival from a painter named Paolo. This Paolo, who appears to be the same artist, enjoyed official status at the time. In April 1345, Paolo and his sons Luca and Giovanni signed and dated a panel used to protect the enamel and gold Pala d'Oro on the high altar of the basilica of San Marco. The cover, which is still in place, depicts episodes from the legend of Saint Mark, with half-figure saints and the *Man of Sorrows* above. A Venetian archival document of January 1346 records payment to Paolo fot an altarpiece for the chapel of Saint Nicholas in the ducal palace; two scenes from the life of Nicholas in the Soprintendenza at Florence may have once belonged to it. An *Enthroned Madonna and Child* at Carpineta in the Romagna bears Paolo's signature and the date 1347. A document of April 1352 in the archives at Dubrovnik relates to an altarpiece by him which is now lost. In 1358, Paolo and his son Giovanni signed and dated the *Coronation of the Virgin* now in the Frick Collection. Paolo died sometime between then and September 1362, when a Venetian archival document mentions him as deceased.

A large body of undocumented work is attributed to Paolo and his workshop, which is known to have included his sons Luca, Giovanni, and probably Marco, and at least one other artist. This body of work may be divided into two groups. One group falls within Paolo's documented career and is widely accepted, although with differences of opinion concerning chronology and autograph share; the other group is placed before that and is controversial. Important works among the former group are as follows: the votive tomb lunette of Doge Francesco Dandolo in Santa Maria dei Frari in Venice, painted around the time of the doge's death in October 1339; the *Enthroned Madonna and Child* with angels and donors in the Accademia in Venice, probably c. 1340; the polyptych from Santa Chiara in the same museum,

depicting the *Coronation of the Virgin* and scenes from the lives of Christ, Saint Francis, and Saint Clare, probably from the early 1340s; a dismembered polyptych in San Giacomo Maggiore, Bologna, possibly c. May 1344, when the church was consecrated; a crucifix in the church of Saint Dominic at Dubrovnik, probably the òne mentioned in a document of March 1348; dated polyptychs of 1349 at Chioggia, 1354 in the Louvre, and April 1355 formerly at Piran in Istria; and another late polyptych, dismembered, at San Severino in the Marches.

The other group of works, which is a subject of debate, should be attributed to Paolo's early period. It includes the panel masking the sarcophagus of the Blessed Leo Bembo, dated 1321, once in San Sebastiano, Venice, and now at Vodnjan in Istria; the dated *Coronation of the Virgin* of 1324 in the National Gallery in Washington; five panels from the early life of the Virgin and her parents at Pesaro; an altarpiece with half-length Madonna and child and four scenes from their lives in San Pantalon, Venice; sixteen panels from the legend of Saint Ursula in the Volterra collection in Florence; and a polyptych with an image and narrative of Saint Lucy, originally in her church at Jurandor and today in the bishop's chancellery at Krk in Dalmatia. The undated works were apparently done during the 1320s, in the order listed. The painted donor figures in a wood relief of 1310 at Murano have also been ascribed to Paolo, but they seem too early to have been painted by him and may show the hand of his master. It also has been suggested that Paolo and his workshop illuminated manuscripts and designed or executed mosaics and embroideries.

Although a long Venetian mosaic tradition survived into the fourteenth century, relatively little work on panel or in the other pictorial media was produced in the period immediately before Paolo. The traditional view is that Paolo was the founder and first great master of Venetian *Trecento* painting, and this view would have to be upheld unless the works assigned to him before his documented activity are rejected. Some of these works, particularly the panels at Pesaro, show the direct influence of Giotto's frescoes in nearby Padua; others, such as the *Coronation of the Virgin* in Washington, show the intrusion of Gothic style and iconography into the local Byzantine tradition. These same ingredients—the Byzantine, the Gothic, and the Giottesque—are the fundamental elements in Paolo's later works, in which the Gothic becomes more pronounced. The Byzantine and Gothic are so harmoniously blended as to suggest their ultimate common source in the distant classical past; the same might be said of the Giottesque. The influence of the Saint Cecilia Master and the school of Rimini may also be detected. The published literature assumes that, despite the obvious similarities, Paolo attained his style independendy of direct Sienese influence. Such examples as his Accademia *Madonna*, which is close to Duccio's in the Pinacoteca at Siena; and his figures of Saint Catherine in the Sanseverino polyptych and in a panel at Chicago, which resemble Simone Martini's fresco of that saint at Assisi, suggest otherwise. The bold patterns and glowing colors give Paolo's paintings an opulence unequaled even by the Sienese.

Paolo Veneziano had a profound influence on Venetian pictorial art, particularly panel painting, until the end of the fourteenth century. The style that he instituted was continued by Lorenzo Veneziano (whose dated works range from 1357 to 1372) and others into the fifteenth century and the international Gothic style. Paolo had relatively little influence on the mainland, which, with the exception of Istria and Dalmatia, responded to more progressive artistic stimuli.

Further Reading

Lucco, Mauro, ed. *La pittura nel Veneto: Il Trecento*. Milan: Electa, 1992.

Muraro, Michelangelo. *Paolo da Venezia*. University Park and London: Pennsylvania State University Press, 1970.

Pallucchini, Rodolfo. *La pittura veneziana del Trecento*. Venice and Rome: Istituto per la Collaborazione Culturale, 1964.

Il Trecento adriatico: Paolo Veneziano e la pittura tra oriente e occidente, ed. Francesca Flores d'Arcais and Giovanni Gentili. Milan: Silvana, 2002.

BRADLEY J. DELANEY

VILANOVA, ARNAU DE

VILANOVA, ARNAU DE Arnau de Vilanova is a figure of unusual interest for his role in medieval intellectual history. Though he called himself "Catalanus" and grew up in Valencia, it seems likely that he came there with his parents from a village outside Daroca (in Aragón) during the Christian resettlement of the city after its reconquest in 1237/8. We can infer his medical training at the *studium* of Montpellier in the 1260s, but it is only with the 1280s that we can begin to reconstruct his biography in detail. During that decade he was in Barcelona in medical attendance on the kings of Aragón-Catalonia, first Pedro III el Gran and then Alfonso III. It was in this same period that his translation of Galen's *De rigore* from Arabic into Latin was finished (Barcelona, 1282); Arnau had presumably learned Arabic growing up in Aragón or Valencia. His other medical translations—of Avicenna's *De viribus cordis* and of Abulcasis's *De medicinis simplicibus*—though undated, may also have been completed in these years.

During the 1290s Arnau was apparently back at Montpellier, this time as a regent master, though occasionally he can also be found advising the new king, Jaime II, on his family's health. This was a period of gr°eat intellectual fruitfulness. Arnau composed a number of scientific works in these years, in which he developed aspects of medical theory. Simultaneously, his personal theological views were maturing along Joachimite lines; like the spiritual Franciscans with whom he was also beginning to establish close ties, he viewed the contemporary church, its institutions and orders, as corrupt, and he took that corruption to manifest the coming end of a historical age. When Jaime II sent him to Paris and to King Philip le Bel in 1300 to negotiate the status of the disputed Vail d'Aran, Arnau took the opportunity to defend these views as set out in his *De adventu antichristi* before the theologians of the Sorbonne: as a result, he was imprisoned as a heretic and released only at the intervention of the French monarch.

Seeking vindication, Arnau went now to Pope Boniface VIII, treating the pope successfully for the ailment of a stone and winning his agreement that Arnau's views, while rash, were not heterodox. With this assurance, Arnau renewed his attack on his adversaries, the scholastic theologians—Dominicans, in particular—whom he accused more harshly than ever of faithlessness, of having abandoned the study of the Bible for secular sciences. The installation of a friend as Pope Clement V in 1305 gave Arnau still more support and allowed him the calm to return to intellectual reflection and composition, in both his fields of activity. His most careful work on clinical medicinae, the *Regimen sanitatis* prepared for Jaime II, was written at this time, as was his *Speculum medicinae*, an ambitious attempt to draw current medical theory together synthetically. Yet simultaneously (1306) he was composing his *Expositio super antichristi*, doctrinally the most complex of his theological writings. He looked now to Clement as the authority destined to lead the reform of the church and society that would enable them to confront the Antichrist, and he believed that he had won over Jaime II and his brother Frederigo III of Sicily (Trinacria) to his program. But in 1309 Arnau went too far in his claims about Jaime, who thereupon broke completely with his former advisor and friend. Frederic, however, continued faithful, implementing Arnauldian spiritual principles in his kingdom even after Arnau's death in 1311.

On balance, Arnau enjoyed more success as a physician than as a theologian and reformer. A council at Tarragona condemned a dozen of his theological works in 1316, and most of the several Beguine communities inspired by his ideal of a lay spirituality dwindled away where they were not suppresssed outright. The taint of heterodoxy may have contributed to the later ascription to Arnau of many alchemical works, none with any verisimilitude. His genuine medical writings are numerous, however, and enjoyed great popularity down to the sixteenth century—particularly his *Regimen sanitatis* for Jaime II and the *Medicationis parabole* dedicated to Philip le Bel in 1300. Arnau's more abstract scientific writings are often original attempts to develop some particular aspect of medical theory and to imbed it within a broader naturophilosophical framework, and—like his *Aphorismi de gradi-bus*—they show considerable breadth of knowledge and imagination. Often harshly critical of his academic colleagues, he was particularly severe on their overdependence upon Avicenna's *Canon*, which had been the dominant authority behind the thirteenth-century schools. (To be sure, his own works are heavily marked by Avicennan problems and conclusions.) In 1309 he was one of three advisors who helped Clement V draw up a new curriculum for the medical faculty at Montpellier, one that made the works of Galen rather than Avicenna the core of medical instruction at that school. Attempts have been made to see his theological and medical positions as unified, but in many respects he seems to have been able to keep his two lives/passions compartmentalized.

See also **Avicenna; Clement V, Pope; Jaime II**

Further Reading

Arnaldi de Villanova Opera Medica Omnia. vols. 2, 3, 4, 6.1, 15, 16, 18, 19 published to date. Barcelona, 1975–.

Crisciani, C. "Exemplum Christi e Sapere. Sull'epistemologia di Arnaldo da Villanova," *Archives Internationales d'Histoire des Sciences* 28 (1978), 245–92.

García Ballester, L. "Arnau de Vilanova (c. 1240–1311) y la reforma de los estudios medicos en Montpellier (1309)," *Dynamis* 2 (1982), 97–158.

Perarnau, J. *L'"Alia Informatio Beguinorum" d'Arnau de Vilanova.* Barcelona, 1978.

Santí, F. *Arnau de Vilanova: L'obra espiritual.* Valencia, 1987.

MICHAEL MCVAUGH

VILLANI, GIOVANNI (c. 1280–1348) The Florentine chronicler Giovanni Villani was a merchant and politician as well as a writer. He was the author of the *Nuova cronica* (*New Chronicle*), a history of Florence set in a much wider context, beginning with the tower of Babel and extending to 1348, the year when he died of the plague. In this work, he combined municipal patriotism and a cosmopolitan outlook with a passion for statistics and detail. Despite its length, it was (like Dante's *Comedy*) a great popular success, circulated in many fourteenth- and fifteenth-century manuscripts. However, although there were a number of subsequent printings, it was given a critical edition only quite recently (Porta 1990–1991).

Giovanni Villani was born into a mercantile family of some standing in Florence. Giovanni's father served a term as a prior—a member of the main governing board of the city—in 1300; and Giovanni and his three brothers were able to secure positions with two of the leading Florentine banking and commercial houses. Giovanni himself became a successful and rich businessman, though he must have lost most of his fortune in the great financial crash of the 1340s. He was

also successful socially and politically. He married, as his second wife, a woman from the aristocratic Pazzi family; and he held a place in the ruling Florentine oligarchy, serving in various communal offices, including three terms as prior. His business career not only gave him intimate knowledge of the power struggles in his own city but also put him in touch with the wider world. He was able to travel extensively and receive reports from all over western Europe at a time when Florence was one of its richest and most populous cities. In this golden age, Florence enjoyed—as Giovanni observed in a meticulous statistical description of its trade and resources c. 1338—an income greater than that of many kingdoms. At this time, its banking and mercantile companies controlled and manipulated a disproportionately large concentration of capital and trade. Of these companies, the most powerful were the Bardi and the Peruzzi. As early as 1300, Giovanni was a shareholder with the Peruzzi firm, and c. 1302 he went to Bruges in its service; he was connected with it for a number of years, as were several of his relatives. Then, probably by 1312, but certainly by 1322, he transferred his activities to a new but rapidly growing firm, the Buonaccorsi, in which he and his brother Matteo became prominent—in fact, Giovanni was its codirector by 1324. Certainly by the late 1320s its operations were varied and widespread, including not only banking but also trading in many commodities, and extending over a vast area: southern and northern Italy, southern and northern France, Brabant, Flanders, England, and various parts of the Mediterranean. Although Giovanni mentions other places from time to time, it is these regions of which he seems to have had real knowledge. At least for those chapters of his chronicle that cover the period 1300–1348, we may suppose that conversations, oral reports, and merchants' letters are at least as important a source as chronicles and official documents.

Giovanni's access to both official and private documents must have made possible his unusually rich and accurate statistics about such things as armies, tax revenues, cloth production, wine consumption, coinage parities, and the number of castles in private and in communal hands. No doubt his collection of such quantitative information was greatly facilitated by the various offices and appointments entrusted to him by his city and his guild. Apart from his three priorates, these were mostly financial. As a municipal official, for example, he supervised the commune's money and the building of a stretch of the third circle of walls. As an official of the Calimala guild, he served on the *mercanzia* council of eight and oversaw the making of Andrea Pisano's bronze doors for the Baptistery. He also went on some diplomatic missions: he was sent to Cardinal Bertrand de Pouget in Bologna in 1329 and a little later to negotiate (unsuccessfully) for the surrender of Lucca. Most of his office-holding was in 1320–1330. After that, he may have been under a cloud, having been tried for barratry in 1331 for his part in building the walls, even though he was cleared of the charge. The fact that Charles of Calabria, then lord of the city, entrusted to the Buonaccorsi company the collection of the taxes from three of the six districts of Florence to pay for the building of those very walls may not have helped Villani's reputation. But real disaster came later, in 1346, after the collapse of the great Florentine commercial companies. Then Giovanni was imprisoned for alleged misconduct as the representative of the Buonaccorsi in negotiations with the communal government about their bankruptcy liabilities. Giovanni does not mention this personal disgrace, but he does express remorse for his share of responsibility in the losses of the small investors in the great companies. We do not know how long his imprisonment lasted. He died in 1348, some two years after it began, and was buried in Florence in the church of the Santissima Annunziata. His brother Matteo and his nephew Filippo continued his chronicle.

For the most part, the opinions Giovanni Villani expresses in his chronicle are remarkably balanced and moderate. His patriotism as a Florentine, for example, was real but not exaggerated. He knew that Florence was sometimes unjust to its neighbors, and though he praised its resilience and resourcefulness in times of crisis, he often deplored its lack of talent for war. He disliked *signori* and signorial government, but he could not always conceal his admiration for a despot as brilliant as Castruccio Castracani, despite the defeats Castruccio inflicted on Florence. Giovanni favored republican government and connected it with political liberty. But he bitterly condemned factional strife and considered the rule of a benevolent *signore* like King Robert of Naples sometimes necessary to restrain it. Villani was also critical of republican regimes representing one class, whether that class was aristocratic, mercantile, or (especially) artisan.

Giovanni was not only a moderate patriot and republican but also a moderate, though very loyal, Guelf. The rival Ghibelline party had been driven out of Florence in the late 1260s, before Giovanni was born, at the same time that the rule of the Ghibellines' Hohenstaufen patrons in southern Italy had given way to the rule of Charles of Anjou, called in by the pope to govern the kingdom of the Two Sicilies. The Ghibellines remained strong in the north and in some parts of Tuscany, but Guelf Florence, Angevin Naples, and the papacy, despite occasionally violent quarrels, were linked by strong economic and political bonds. For Giovanni, these bonds seem to have been ideological as well, reinforced by sincere religious feeling. He regarded Charles of Anjou as a new Charlemagne, summoned to Italy to rescue the Roman church from the Hohenstaufen Lombards. Giovanni devoted perhaps his most sustained literary effort to a long and eloquent account of Charles's Italian campaigns. He also portrayed Florence as usually an ally of the church, from the struggle between Pope Gregory VII and the Emperor Henry IV in the late eleventh century down to his own time. The intervals during the later period when the pope and Florence were at odds worried Giovanni, as did the taxation of the Florentine clergy without their consent by his own commune. At the same time, he did not hesitate to criticize individual popes and Angevin rulers for avarice and immorality, and his fellow Guelfs for factionalism. He thought that the expulsion of the White Guelfs in 1302 was disgraceful, but he was glad that their assault on the city in 1304 did not succeed. He was also glad that Henry VII failed to capture Florence in 1312, but he said that the emperor's original intention had been to deal justly with Guelfs as well as Ghibellines. Such urbane judiciousness was appropriate to a rich businessman who numbered kings and princes among his acquaintances and had wide experience of the world.

In the prologue to the *Nuova cronica*, Giovanni says that his pride in the noble origins of his city and his desire to delight and instruct his fellow citizens had impelled him to write its history. In Book 9, Chapter 36, he relates that he began to write in 1300, after returning to Florence from Rome, where he had participated in the great papal jubilee. Seeing the ancient Roman ruins, reading the ancient histories, and reflecting on the decline of Rome had inspired him to tell the story of the rise of Florence, an offspring of Rome. Whether or not Giovanni began his chronicle immediately after his return to Florence, it is evident that he wrote primarily for Florentines and that one of his main purposes was to celebrate their successes without omitting their blunders and failures. The history of no other European city except Rome had hitherto been told at such length. Giovanni also conveys a sharp awareness of developments in the physical shape and monuments of Florence—for example, its central octagonal church, the Baptistery, which he says travelers assured him was the most beautiful in the world; its other churches and public buildings, whose siting and arrangement he compared, following an old Florentine historical tradition, with those of similarly named Roman monuments; the dimensions of its walls, towers, and bridges; and even the emblems on the banners of its militia and the decoration on its war cart, or *carroccio*. He is also aware that Florence is not just a city but a European power, and his ability to see Florence as part of a greater world is one of his main merits as a historian. Giovanni also likes to include a good story or a vivid detail, from wherever it comes. He touches on such topics as astral portents, monstrous births, costumes, public feasts, civil and religious rituals, relics, epidemics, earthquakes, inscriptions, apparitions, the lions behind the communal palace in Florence, coins, Gog and Magog, Muhammad, what might have happened, famous men (like Aquinas, Dante, and Giotto, of whom he writes pocket biographies), sea battles, sermons, governments, and expedients for increasing public revenue. Given such variety, it is no wonder that many critics have accused Giovanni Villani of being episodic and lacking a unifying theme or point of view. Porta believes that Giovanni did revise the chronicle extensively but that his main purpose was probably to introduce new information at many points—a process made easier because the chronicle is for the most part organized not thematically but year by year.

Giovanni certainly wants to instruct as well as entertain and inform his readers. He says that he wants to show future Florentines which actions of their predecessors they should imitate and which they should avoid. The guidance he offers is more moral than intellectual. It is true that much shrewd commentary on business, politics, and war is scattered through his book, but he has no single large lesson to teach. His analysis of the secondary causes of a particular Florentine victory or defeat can be thorough and penetrating, as, for example, in his explanations of the failure of Florence to acquire Lucca after the death of Castruccio Castracani. Very often, however, he is content—as a devout and right-thinking Florentine Guelf—to attribute such disasters to the wrath of the deity at the wickedness of the Florentines: their pride, avarice, and envy. Giovanni knows the Old Testament well, and his God, like Yahweh, is swift to punish. Sometimes, particularly in the later books of his chronicle, he seeks scientific, or at any rate astrological, explanations; but he consistently denies that the influence of the stars negates free will or men's responsibility for their actions, and he expresses again and again his conviction that the stars are immediately and totally subject to God's commands. He does try to account rationally for one great problem in thirteenth-century and early fourteenth-century Florence: factionalism. He does so by a literal application of Dante's metaphor about the opposition between the two peoples who, according to Florentine legend, shared in populating the city, the allegedly "noble and virtuous" Romans and the allegedly "rough and fierce" Fiesolans. For Dante, "Romans" were all those willing to submit to the emperor's laws; "Fiesolans" were those "barbarians" who resisted it. For Giovanni Villani, the two names designate two peoples who actually participated in populating Florence and whose imperfect mixing produced chronic strife. He finds the story of this mixing in the *Chronica de origine civitatis* (written before 1231) and its Italian translations. (It is very unlikely that he was able to find the origin, as some scholars have maintained, in the so-called Malispinian chronicle, which was almost certainly written after his own and was largely copied from a compendium of his work.) In the *Chronica de origine civitatis*, the

Roman origins of Florence were exalted and Julius Caesar himself was included among the founders of the city; but though the Fiesolans were represented as fierce enemies of the Romans, they were not depicted as barbarians. This Giovanni could have found in no surviving work before Dante's *Inferno*, circulated c. 1314. Probably Giovanni was also paraphrasing Dante's words in *Paradiso* (15.109–111), as Aquilecchia (1965) has suggested, when he referred in Book 9, Chapter 36, to the rise of Florence and the decline of Rome.

Up to this point in his chronicle, Giovanni is mainly concerned with describing the steady ascent, despite occasional disasters, of Florence, the child of Rome. Afterward, misfortunes multiply and the direction of Florence's development is not so clear. But Giovanni retains much of his optimism until the 1340s, the imposition and overthrow of Walter de Brienne's regime, and the subsequent financial crash. Neither communal nor personal calamities slowed the chronicler's busy pen. It continued right up to his death to provide an invaluable picture of the attitudes of the fourteenth-century oligarchy of Florence toward its past and present, and, especially for the period from c. 1320 to 1348, a narrative source for medieval Florentine history of inexhaustible richness and variety.

See also **Dante Alighieri; Malispini, Ricordano**

Further Reading

Editions

Villani, Giovanni. *Cronica*, 8 vols., ed. Ignazio Moutier. Florence: Magheri 1823. (Reprinted in Florence: Coen, 1844; Milan: Borroni e Scotti, 1848.)

——. *Selections from the First Nine Books of the "Croniche Florentine" of Giovanni Villani*, trans. Rose E. Selfe, ed. Philip H.Wicksteed. Westminster: A. Constable, 1896.

——. *Cronisti del Trecento*, ed. Roberto Palmarocchi. Milan: Rizzoli, 1935, pp. 153–466.

——. *Nuova cronica*, 3 vols., ed. Giuseppe Porta. Parma: Fondazione Pietro Bembo; U. Guanda, 1990–1991.

Critical Studies

Aquilecchia, Giovanni. "Dante and the Florentine Chroniclers." *Bulletin of the John Rylands Library*, 48(1), 1965, pp. 30–55.

Arias, G. "Nuovi documenti su Giovanni Villani." *Giornale Storico della Letteratura Italiana*, 34, 1899, pp. 383–387.

Bec, Christian. "Sur l'historiographie marchande à Florence au XIVe siècle." In *La chronique et l'histoire au moyen-âge: Colloque des 24 et 25 mai 1982*, ed. D. Poiron. Paris, 1984, pp. 45–72.

Becker, Marvin B. *Florence in Transition*, Vol. l, *The Decline of the Commune*. Baltimore, Md.: Johns Hopkins University Press, 1967.

Bruni, Francesco. "Identità culturale e mito delle origini: Firenze nella *Cronica* di Giovanni Villani." In *Storia delle civiltà letteraria Italiana*, Vol.1, *Dalle origini al Trecento*, ed. G. Barberi Squarotti. Turin: 1990, part 2, pp. 716–728.

Castellani, A. "Sulla tradizione delk *Nuova cronica* di Giovanni Villani." *Medioevo e Rinascimento*, 2, 1988, pp. 53–118.

——. "Pera Baducci lla tradizione della *Nuova Cronica* di Giovanni Villani." *Studi di Filologia Italiana*, 48, 1990, pp. 5–13.

Cipolla, C. M. *The Monetary Policy of Fourteenth-Century Florence*. Berkeley: University of California Press, 1982.

Davis, Charles T. "Dante, Villani, and Ricordano Malispini." In *Dante and the Idea of Rome*. Oxford: Clarendon, 1957, pp. 244–262.

——. "The Malispini Question." *Studi Medievali*, Series 3(10.3), 1970, pp. 215–254. (Reprinted in *Dante's Italy and Other Essays*. Philadelphia: University of Pennsylvania Press, 1984, pp. 94–136.)

——. "Il buon tempo antico." In *Florentine Studies: Politics and Society in Renaissance Florence*, ed. N. Rubinstein. London, 1968, pp. 45–69. (Reprinted in *Dante's Italy and Other Essays*. Philadelphia: University of Pennsylvania Press, 1984, pp. 71–93.)

——. "Topographical and Historical Propaganda in Early Florentine Chronicles and in Villani." *Medioevo e Rinascimento*, 2, 1988, pp. 35–51.

Della Torre, A. "L'amicizia di Dante e Giovanni Villani." *Giornale Dantesco*, 12, 1904, pp. 33–44.

Del Monte, A. "La storiografia fiorentina dei secoli XII e XIII." *Bullettino dell'Istituto Storico Italiano per il Medio Evo e Archivio Muratoriano*, 62, 1950, pp. 175–282.

De Matteis, M. C. "Ancora su Malispini, Villani, e Dante: Per un riesame dei rapporti tra cultura storica e profezia etica nell'Alighieri." *Bullettino dell'Istituto Storico Italiano per il Medio Evo e Archivio Muratoriano*, 82, 1970, pp. 329–390.

——. "Malispini da Villani o Villani da Malispini? Una ipotesi sui rapporti tra Ricordano Malisini, il 'Compendiatore,' e Giovanni Villani." *Bullettino dell'Istituto Storico Italiano per il Medio Evo e Archivio Muratoriano*, 84, 1973, pp. 145–221.

Fiumi, Enrico. "La demografia fiorentina nelle pagine di Giovanni Villani." *Archivio Storico Italiano*, 108, 1950, pp. 78–158.

——. "Economia e vita privata dei fiorentini nelle rilevazioni statistiche di Giovanni Villani." *Archivio Storico Italiano*, 111, 1953, pp. 207–241.

Frugoni, Arsenio. "G. Villani *Cronica*, XI, 94." *Bullettino dell'Istituto Storico Italiano per il Medio Evo e Archivio Muratoriano*, 77, 1965, pp. 229–255.

Green, Louis. *Chronicle into History: An Essay on the Interpretation of History in Florentine Fourteenth-Century Chronicles*. Cambridge: Cambridge University Press, 1972.

Hartwig, Otto. *Quellen und Forschungen zur ältesten Geschichte der Stadt Florenz*, 2 vols. Marburg: N. G. Elwert'sche Verlagsbuchh., 1875–1880.

Hyde, J. K. "Medieval Descriptions of Cities." *Bulletin of the John Rylands Library*, 48(2), 1966, pp. 308–340.

Imbriani, V. "Sulla rubrica dantesca nel Villani." In *Studi danteschi*. Florence, 1891, pp. 1–175.

Lami, V. "Di un compendio inedito della cronica di Giovanni Villani nelle sue relazioni con la storia fiorentina malispiniana." *Archivio Storico Italiano*, Series 5, 1890, pp. 369–416.

Link-Heer, Ursula. "Italienische Historiographie zwischen Spätmittelalter und fruher Neuzeit." In *Grundriss der romanischen Literaturen des Mittelalters*, Vol. 11(1).

Heidelberg: C. Winter Universitätsverlag, 1987, pp. 1068–1129. (See especially pp. 1078–1088.)

Luiso, F. P. "Le edizioni della *Cronica* di Giovanni Villani." *Bullettino dell'Istituto Storico Italiano per il Medio Evo e Archivio Muratoriano*, 49, 1933, pp. 279–315.

——. "Indagini biografiche su Giovanni Villani." *Bullettino dell'Istituto Storico Italiano per il Medio Evo e Archivio Muratoriano*, 51, 1936, pp. 1–64.

Luzzati, Michele. "Ricerche sulle attivita mercantili e sul fallimento di Giovanni Villani." *Bullettino dell'Istituto Storico Italiano per il Medio Evo e Archivio Muratoriano*, 81, 1969, pp. 173–235.

——. *Giovanni Villani e la compagnia dei Buonaccorsi*. Rome: Istituto della Enciclopedia Italiana, 1971.

Mattucci, Andrea. "Da Giovanni Villani al primo Guicciardini: I mondi separati della *narrazione* e del *discorso*." In *Machiavelli nella storiografia fiorentina: Per la storia di un genere letterario*. Florence: Olschki, 1991, pp. 3–30.

Mehl, Ernst. *Die Weltanschauung des Giovanni Villani: Ein Beitrag zur Geistesgeschiehte Italiens im Zeitalter Dantes*. Leipzig: Tuebner, 1927.

——. "G. Villani und die *Divina Commedia*." *Deutsches Dante-Jahrbuch*, 10, 1928, pp. 173–184.

Meissen T. "Atiia, Totila, e Carlo Magno fra Dante, Villani, Boccaccio, e Malispini: Per la genesi di due leggende erudite." *Archivio Storico Italiano*, 152, 1994, pp. 561–639.

Milanesi, G. "Documenti riguardanti Giovanni Villani e il palazzo degli Alessi in Siena." *Archivio Storico Italiano*, n.s., 4, 1856, pp. 3–12.

Morghen, Raffaello. "Dante, il Villani, e Ricordano Malispini." *Bullettino dell'Istituto Storico Italiano per il Medio Evo e Archivio Muratoriano*, 41, 1921, pp. 171–194.

——. "La storiografia fiorentina del Trecento: Ricordano Malispini, Dino Compagni, e Giovanni Villani." In *Libera cattedra di storia della civiltà fiorentina—Secoli vari:'300,'400, '500*. Florence: Sansoni, 1958, pp. 69–93.

Najemy, J. M. *Corporatism and Consensus in Florentine Electoral Politics, 1280–1400*. Chapel Hill: University of North Carolina Press, 1982.

——. "L'ultima pane tiella Nuova Cronica di Giovanni Villani." *Studi di Filologia Italiana*, 41, 1983, pp. 17–36.

Neri, F. "Dante il primo Villani." *Giornale Dantesco*, 20, 1912, pp. 1–31. Ottokar, Nicola. *Il commune di Firenze alla fine del Dugento*. Florence: Vallecchi, 1926. (See also 2nd ed. Turin: Einaudi, 1962.)

Pezzarossa, Fulvio. "La tradizione fiorentina della memorialistica." In *La "memoria" dei "mercatores": Tendenze ideologiche, ricordanze, artigianato in versi nella Firenze del Quattrocento*, ed. Gian-Mario Anselmi, Fulvio Pezzarossa, and Luisa Avellini. Bologna: Pàtron, 1980, pp. 39–149.

——. "Le geste e' fatti de' Fiorentini: Riflessioni a margine di un'edizione della cronica di Giovanni Villani." *Lettere Italiane*, 45, 1993, pp. 93–115. Porta, Giuseppe. "Censimento dei manoscritti delle cronache di Giovanni, Matteo, e Filippo Villani, 1." *Studi di Filologia Italiana*, 34, 1976a, pp. 61–129.

——. "Testimonianze di volgare campano e francese in G. Villani." *Lingua Nostra*, 37, 1976b, pp. 8–9.

——. "Censimento dei manoscritti delle cronache di Giovanni, Matteo, e Filippo Villani, 2." *Studi di Filologia Italiana*, 37, 1979, pp. 93–117.

——. "Aggiunta al censimento dei manoscritti delle cronache di Giovanni, Matteo, e Filippo Villani," *Studi di Filologia Italiana*, 44, 1986a, pp. 65–67.

——. "Sul testo e la lingua di Giovanni Villani." *Lingua Nostra*, 47, 1986b, pp. 37–40.

——. "La storiografia fiorentina fra il Duecento e il Trecento." *Medioevo e Rinascimento*, 2, 1988, pp. 119–130.

——. "Giovanni Villani storico e scrittore." In *I racconti di Clio: Tecniche narrative della storiografia—Atti del Convegno di Arezzo, 6–8 novembre 1986*, ed. Roberto Bigazzi, et al. Pisa: Nistri-Lischi, 1989, pp. 147–156.

——. "Les rapports entre l'Italie et la France dans la persepective des chroniqueurs florentins du XIVe siècle." In *Die kulturellen Beziehungen zwischen Italien und den anderen Laendern Europas im Mittelalter*, ed. Danielle Buschinger and Wolfgang Spiewok. 1993a, pp. 147–156.

——. "Le varianti redazionali come strumento di verifica dell'autenticità di testi: Villani e Malispini." In *La filologia romanza e i codici: Atti del Convegno di Messina, 19–22 dicembre 1991*, Vol. 2. Messina, 1993b, pp. 481–529.

Ragone, Franca. "Le scritture parlate: Qualche ipotesi sulla redazione delle cronache volgari nel Trecento dopo l'edizione critica della *Nuova Cronica* di Giovanni Villani." *Archivio Storico Italiano*, 149, 1991, pp. 783–810.

Rubinstein, Nicolai. "The Beginnings of Political Thought in Florence." *Journal of the Warburg and Courtauld Institutes*, 5, 1942, pp. 198–227.

Santini, Pietro. *Quesiti e ricerche di storiografia fiorentina*. Florence: Seeber, 1903.

CHARLES T. DAVIS

VILLARD DE HONNECOURT (Wilars dehonecort; Vilars dehoncort; fl. 1220–30)

Picard artist now known only through a portfolio of thirty-three parchment leaves of drawings in Paris (B.N. fr. 19093). Some leaves have been lost from the portfolio; the maximum number that can be proven to be lost is thirteen, with the possible loss of two additional leaves.

Villard addressed his drawings to an unspecified audience, saying that his "book" contained "sound advice on the techniques of masonry and on the devices of carpentry . . . and the techniques of representation, its features as the discipline of geometry commands and instructs it." The subjects of Villard's drawings are animals, architecture, carpentry, church furnishings, geometry, humans, masonry, mechanical devices, recipes or formulae, and surveying.

Villard traveled extensively, and most of the identifiable monuments that he drew date to the first quarter of the 13th century. He drew, and perhaps visited, the cathedrals of Cambrai, Chartres, Laon, Meaux, Reims, and the abbey of Vaucelles in France; the cathedral of Lausanne in Switzerland; and the abbey of Pilis in Hungary.

There is no documentary evidence that Villard designed or built any church any-

Villard de Honnecourt (c. 1225–c. 1250). Drawing of flying buttresses of Reims Cathedral, 1230–35. © Bridgeman-Giraudon/Art Resource, New York.

where or that he was in fact an architect. It has been proposed that he may have been "a lodge clerk with a flair for drawing" or that his training may have been in metalworking rather than masonry. It may be that Villard was not a professional craftsman but rather an inquisitive layman who had an opportunity to travel widely.

Further Reading

Barnes, Carl F., Jr. "Le 'problème' Villard de Honnecourt." In *Les batisseurs des cathédrales gothiques*, ed. Roland Recht. Strasbourg: Éditions les Musées de la Ville de Strasbourg, 1989, pp. 209–23.

——. *Villard de Honnecourt: The Artist and His Drawings, A Critical Bibliography*. Boston: Hall, 1982.

——, and Lon R. Shelby. "The Codicology of the Portfolio of Villard de Honnecourt

(Paris, Bibliothèque nationale, MS fr. 19093)." *Scriptorium* 40 (1988): 20–48.

Hahnloser, Hans R. *Villard de Honnecourt: Kritische Gesamtausgabe des Bauhuttenbuches ms. fr. 19093 der Pariser Nationalbibliothek.* Vienna: Schroll, 1935; rev. ed. Graz: Akademische Druck- und Verlagsanstalt, 1972. [Best facsimile edition.]

CARL F. BARNES, JR.

VILLEHARDOUIN, GEOFFROI DE (ca. 1150–before 1218)

Author of the *Conquête de Constantinople,* one of the earliest historical works written in French prose, and one of two eyewitness accounts of the Fourth Crusade. Villehardouin was born into a noble Champenois family. He served the count of Champagne, Thibaut III, as marshal after 1185. In this capacity, Villehardouin developed the mediating abilities that would serve him so well. We know of three disputes he mediated, one involving the count himself.

Count Thibaut III of Champagne (d. 1202) was one of the organizers of the Fourth Crusade, so Villehardouin was at the heart of the planning. He was one of the six ambassadors sent to Venice in 1201 to negotiate passage in Venetian ships. In 1203, he was sent to Isaac II, whom the crusaders had restored to the throne of Constantinople, to see that the Latins would be paid as agreed. He carried out negotiations between the emperor Baudouin and Boniface of Montferrat, the new leader of the crusade, when the two fell out. Because of his outstanding services, Villehardouin was made marshal of Romania in 1205. The rest of his life is obscure. He last appears in the records in 1212 and was certainly dead by 1218, when his son arranged a memorial for him.

The *Conquête,* which begins with the preaching of the crusade by Foulques de Neuilly and ends suddenly in 1207, was composed after the events it relates, although Villehardouin probably made notes and certainly used documentary sources. The prose is straightforward and unrhetorical. The story is told in excellent chronological order.

Villehardouin seems to have intended his work as a defense of the crusade against critics who pointed out that the crusaders attacked only the Christian cities of Zara and Constantinople and never got to Jerusalem at all. Villehardouin lays chief blame for these unfortunate facts on those who failed to join the crusade at Venice and help pay for passage, forcing the crusaders to repay Venice by attacking Zara, and those who deserted later, leaving too small a fighting force for a real holy war. He does not, however, hold blameless those who participated or remained; their sins, particularly their greed, caused further disasters and offended God.

Villehardouin's narrative was more widely read than Robert de Clari's, the other eyewitness account of the Fourth Crusade. Six manuscripts of the *Conquête* are extant, and two more were used in early editions before they disappeared. In addition, two manuscripts of an abbreviation exist. Villehardouin's work was also incorporated in the *Chronique de Baudouin d'Avesnes,* a 13th-century compilation that circulated widely.

Further Reading

Villehardouin, Geoffroi de. *La conquête de Constantinople,* ed. Edmond Faral. 2 vols. 2nd ed. Paris: Les Belles Lettres, 1937.

Joinville and Villehardouin. *Chronicles of the Crusades,* trans. Margaret Shaw. Harmondsworth: Penguin, 1963.

Beer, Jeanette M.A. *Villehardouin, Epic Historian.* Geneva: Droz, 1968.

Dufournet, Jean. *Les écrivains de la IVe croisade: Villehardouin et Clan.* 2 vols. Paris: SEDES, 1973.

LEAH SHOPKOW

VILLON, FRANÇOIS (1431–1463)

Of all the lyricists of late-medieval France, Villon is the most celebrated among both scholars and general readers. Students of premodern literature inside and outside the francophone world have encountered him in his original Middle French; and thousands of people who have little or no French have read versions of his poems in the major European languages.

It was not always thus. The circle of contemporaries who knew of Villon's literary abilities was a modest one. He tells us in his *Testament* that an earlier work, the *Lais*, is already in circulation and being referred to by a title not of his choosing. On the other hand, the number of early sources preserving his poems is small; and his readers were in general not found among the rich and powerful. Although some such personages come in for mention in his verses, it is usually in the context of appeals for money, or of distant, uneasy, or downright irreverent allusion; Villon was not a success with well-off patrons of literature. The fame he sought eluded him. He seemingly hoped for a career as a court poet and exerted himself to catch the eye of such highly placed connoisseurs as Charles d'Orléans; but for unknown reasons, he did not achieve more than a small gift of money here and there. Greater success in his lifetime, however, might well have spelled later obscurity; his *poésies de circonstance*, composed, we must assume, to curry favor, competent though they are, are by and large forgettable. Rather than spend much of his career in turning out pleasing official verse, he was driven by circumstance, and perhaps also by a jarring personality, to live by expedients, know misery, reflect on it, and write amateur poetry of a unique stamp.

The body of Villon's works is of moderate dimensions: some 3,300 lines. It comprises independent pieces in fixed form (ballades and rondeaux) and two unified compositions, the *Lais* and the *Testament*. The *Lais*, dated 1456, is a series of burlesque legacies occasioned by being, as Villon asserts, crossed in love, and consequently deciding to quit Paris, perhaps never to return. The *Testament*

(1461) takes up again the legacy pattern but refines it into the articles of a last will and testament, complete with legal clauses and phraseology, the fiction now being that the author is near death and bethinking himself of soul and body as well as of worldly goods. This, Villon's major work, written, in octaves (eight-line strophes of octosyllabic verse), contains fixed-form pieces as well, some of which may antedate or even postdate 1461. The whole amounts to a personal literary anthology as well as the poet's artistic testament and monument. The rest of his *œuvre* is made up of a fulsome *Louange* of Princess Marie d'Orléans, with attached double ballade and much Latin adornment; a *Ballade franco-latine*, even more latinate; a number of difficult poems in the jargon of the medieval French underworld; and some ballades made up of the rhetorical devices dear to the schoolroom and fashionable court. Jumbled in with them are some pieces so intensely felt, so personal, so perfectly marrying form and content, that they belong by right to the greatest world literature. Among these are the *Épître à ses amis*, Villon's De *profundis*; the yes-and-no meditation on fate and individual responsibility best called *Débat de Villon et de son cœur*, and the *Ballade des pendus*, with its unbearable yet inescapable vision of legally executed bodies (including the poet's?) and its reiterated solicitation of prayer for their souls. Villon's last poems appear to fit into the interval between his last imprisonment and appeal, the commutation of his death sentence to a ten-year exile, and his departure in 1463 to an unknown end.

Villon was born into a poor family (*Testament*, ll. 273–75) in 1431, the year marked by the death of Jeanne d'Arc, celebrated in the *Testament* (ll. 351–52) as *... Jehanne la bonne Lorraine/Qu'Engloys brulerent a Rouen* ("Joan, the brave girl from Lorraine/Burned by the English at Rouen"). The Hundred Years' War was dragging on; disease, food-shortages, and protracted spells of cold, wet weather afflicted everyone, the poor especially. It was out of harsh necessity, no doubt, that the future poet's mother entrusted her child to a presumed relative, Guillaume de Villon, the kindly chaplain of the Parisian church of Saint-Benoît-le-Bétourné not far from the Sorbonne, who would be the boy's *plus que père* (*Testament*, 1. 849).

Young François, originally called de Montcorbier or des Loges, took the surname of his adoptive father, and much else besides: security, relative comfort, clerical status, and the opportunity for the best formal education then available. In 1449, he obtained the baccalaureate degree and three years later the License and the degree of Maître ès Arts. This and his connections ought to have smoothed Villon's path into the learned professions; but these were overpopulated in the mid-15th century. To enter the secular or regular clergy was apparently not for him a viable choice; nor, in the absence of an independent income or a patron, was it possible for him to become a professional writer. He turned to living by his wits, in the company of other unemployed *clercs* and even more lowly individuals; and this led him into repeated brushes with the law, mainly for theft but once for manslaughter. As an *écolier*, he was entitled to the church's protection from the full rigor of secular justice; but it looks as if he lost the benefit of clergy, as well as many months of freedom, when he was condemned to prison at Meung-sur-Loire in 1461 by the bishop of Orléans.

It was his long police record, rather than one final and spectacular crime, that drove the exasperated secular authorities in late 1462 to pass a capital sentence; the Parlement, on appeal, commuted this to a ten-year banishment from Paris and its environs. Sadly, it is owing to his activities as part-time criminal that much of the information about Villon has come to us, for the abundant records have been preserved in the Paris archives. They supplement the hints, half-truths, special pleading, and downright lies that bestrew the poet's own writings.

Such a biographical excursus is particularly indicated in Villon's case, for much of his work is highly personal without always being informative or even candid. His feelings take precedence over the exact cause for them, his hatred for his enemies overshadows the ways whereby the latter have earned his resentment, and the possibility that the poet himself might somehow have provoked or deserved rough handling is pushed far into the background. Yet the interweaving of concrete if unreliable allusions to persons and events on the one hand, of passionate response on the other, makes of Villon an autobiographical lyricist to an unusual degree.

His themes, though, are universal ones, colored by his cultural milieu and his own subjectivity. Adversity, suffering, insecurity, the hunger for love, the transitoriness of youth and of all good things, the approach of death, the faith that sees beyond it—these are the timbers of which his work is built. Through the 2,000 lines of the *Testament*, he turns these notions over and over, in a composition structured by association of ideas and shifting moods rather than logical or formal progression. This begins as early as the first stanzas, which move with great rapidity from the testator's age and mental condition to his state of health and thence to his recent hardships and the person responsible for them; and with the name of Bishop Thibaut d'Aussigny, the memory of the preceding summer's incarceration, and probable degradation from clerical status, comes flooding back, making him sacrifice syntax to sarcasm: yes, he will pray for his enemy—with a cursing psalm. For good measure, he adds a prayer for Louis, *le bon roy de France*. On he goes, intermingling complaint, piety, and half-admissions of unsatisfactory behavior. Yet a sinner in his situation is pardonable: *Neccessité fait gens mesprendre/Et faim saillir le loup du boys* ("It's need drives folks to go astray/And hunger, the wolf to leave the woods";

ll. 167–68). He has abundant grounds for lamentation. His youth has flown; he is prematurely old, poor, rejected by his kin, disappointed in love, regretting his old friends (where are they now?), knowing that death will come for him as it has for the lovely ladies and great potentates of the past. These are themes to which he returns, obsessively but not uninterruptedly; for a great number of bequests remain to be formulated and the whole apparatus of the fictitious testament to be worked in.

There is a good deal of humor in all this, of a rough, pun-filled, scabrous character; and the poet takes advantage of the safety afforded by the last-will-and-testament schema to take verbal revenge on the individuals and classes who have earned his disapproval; after all, the document, according to the poetic fiction, will not be read until after his decease. We are led once again to the theme that underlies the *Testament* as a whole. It sometimes is expressed with gentle gravity, as in the *Ballade des dames du temps jadis*; in grimmer moments, the poet's thought turns to scenes com monly beheld in Paris: the piled-up and anonymous bones in the Cemetery of the Innocents, the cadavers of executed criminals dangling from the Montfaucon gibbet, the last agony awaiting each man and woman. In the Europe of the 15th century, the body's death was but a stage in the soul's journey; prayers and allusions to Heaven and Hell throng the octaves and fixed-form pieces. In the intervals of anxiety about death and what is in store for himself and all humankind, Villon repeatedly turns to common experience, particularly its darker side. Happiness is rare and fleeting; sorrow, fear, physical discomfort, and decrepitude—these are the lot of the human race. Why had Villon, why had so many men and women known suffering? Why does a just God permit malevolent Fortune to afflict the innocent? The poet's own stance, at least as early as the independent *Épître à ses amis* (presumably

composed during the 1461 incarceration at Meung-sur-Loire) is that of a blameless victim, and he cries out with the words of the archetypical righteous sufferer, job (11. 1–2): *Ayez pictié, ayez pictié de moy/ A tout le moins, s'i vous plaist, mes amis!* ("Have pity, do have pity upon me,/You at least, if you please, who are my friends"). This explicit kinship with Job is affirmed repeatedly through the *Testament*; it has become the poet's characteristic way of making sense of what has befallen him, of understanding, as well, the human condition.

Villon's themes are by no means original, nor is his use of archetypes in working them out. As an educated man, he was steeped in the Latin classics and in the Bible, those storehouses of human experience and its literary expression; to allude to traditional topoi, stories, and personages was second nature for him, as it was for other writers of the day. His preoccupation with death and decay, his frequent melancholy, his startling coarseness, his mingling of jest and seriousness, are also features common in late-medieval writing, and in the visual arts as well. What sets him apart is the immediacy of his communication with the reader. His verse revivifies the notion of lyric: not poems to be sung, but poems expressive of feeling. Unlike the conventional and impersonal *je* of much contemporary writing, Villon's *je* most frequently is his unique and unruly self, temporarily brought to order by the discipline of his octaves and his fixed-form pieces. Much 15th-century poetry treats of love, again in courtly and stereotyped ways, for the stylized worship of the lady was still very much alive. Villon writes of love, too, but mostly from his own limited experience: it is a snare and a delusion, at best a fleeting joy. By and large, women are sensual and venal (but not to be condemned, for it is *nature femeninne* [*Testament*, 1. 611] that moves them), and in any case their attractiveness soon withers. Indeed, woman's charms, such a staple among mainstream masculine writers of the period, do not feature much here except in the context of bitter reminiscence and of regret for the transitoriness of all things desirable. It would in fact not be easy to find another major poet so indifferent to beauty; but then visual description of any sort does not stand out in Villon's verses. He inclines to naming persons and places, to evoking action and speech and gesture, rather than to painting word pictures. Even his self-description is limited to a few qualifiers: *sec et noir*; *plus maigre que chimere* ("skinny and dark"; "thinner than a wraith"). What he does give us is his reactions to his experience, and a sketch of late-medieval France as he knew it. This is a world of people living by their wits and not hampered by scruples: entertainers, prostitutes, counterfeiters, tavern keepers and tavern haunters, jailers and moat cleaners, peddlers, beggars, dissolute monks—Villon's poetry opens the door upon a teeming world, lacking in grace or nobility but intensely alive. Most vital of all are the poet's own self and experience, given expression that transcends his own time and milieu so as to be at once personal and universal.

Villon's works have been preserved in a number of manuscripts and fragments, and in a printed edition of 1489, These early sources vary in completeness, from the *Lais*, the *Testament*, and numerous independent pieces, down to two or three ballades; they differ also in degree of reliability. The manuscript copies, the incunabulum, and also the many 16th-century printings of his works attest to a moderate readership over the course of about a century. Villon then, like most medieval writers, underwent an eclipse, with one edition at the end of the 1600s and three in the 1700s. The years from 1832 onward have seen an increasing flow of editions, translations, historical notes, and interpretive essays; and the stream shows no sign of drying up. Villon continues to be subject to much critical scrutiny, some

of it closer to creative writing than to explication of the texts, but much of it responsible and serious. We can now read Villon's often difficult and allusive verses with a fair approximation to his own meaning.

See also **Charles d'Orléans**

Further Reading

Villon, François. *Complete Poems*, ed. and trans. Barbara N. Sargent-Baur. Toronto: Toronto University Press, 1994.

——. *Le lais Villon et les poèmes variés*, ed. Jean Rychner and Albert Henry. 2 vols. Geneva: Droz, 1977.

——. *Le Testament Villon*, ed. Jean Rychner and Albert Henry. 2 vols. Geneva: Droz, 1974–85.

——. *François Villon: Œuvres*, trans. André Lanly. 2 vols. Paris: Champion, 1969.

——. *François Villon: ballades en jargon*, trans. André Lanly. Paris: Champion, 1979.

——. *The Poems of François Villon*, trans. Galway Kinnell. New York: New American Library, 1965.

Burger, André. *Lexique complet de la langue de Villon*. 2nd ed. Geneva: Droz, 1974.

Champion, Pierre. *François Villon: sa vie et son temps*. 2nd ed. 2 vols. Paris: Champion, 1934.

Fox, John Howard. *The Poetry of Villon*. London: Nelson, 1962. LeGentil, Pierre. *Villon*. Paris: Hatier, 1967.

Peckham, Robert D. *François Villon: A Bibliography*. New York: Garland, 1990.

Sargent-Baur, Barbara N. *Brothers of Dragons: Job dolens and François Villon*. New York: Garland, 1990.

Siciliano, Italo. *François Villon et les thèmes poétiques du moyen âge*. Paris: Nizet, 1934.

Sturm, Rudolf. *François Villon, bibliographie et matériaux littéraires (1489–1988)*. Munich: Saur, 1990.

Vitz, Evelyn Birge. *The Crossroad of Intentions: A Study of Symbolic Expressions in the Poetry of François Villon*. The Hague: Mouton, 1974.

Ziwès, Armand, and Anne de Bercy. *Le jargon de maître François Villon interprété*. 2nd ed. 2 vols. Paris: Puget, 1960.

BARBARA N. SARGENT-BAUR

VINCENT DE BEAUVAIS (ca. 1190–ca. 1264) The author of a most spectacular encyclopedia of medieval culture and thought, Vincent de Beauvais joined the Dominican house at Paris ca. 1220, shortly after its founding, and probably moved to the new Dominican house in his native region of Beauvais toward the end of the same decade. Vincent served as lecturer to the monks of the nearby Cistercian abbey of Royaumont, founded by King Louis IX in 1228 and through this association, mediated by Abbot Ralph, won the favor of the king and ultimately the support of the royal purse for his scholarly projects.

The first half of the 13th century was a time of intellectual "consolidation," when several scholars, Vincent among them, felt the need to integrate the results of the intellectual explosion of the 12th century with the traditional learning of western civilization. Vincent entitled his work *Speculum maius*, a mirror to the world and its truths, which he compares implicitly with, earlier attempts, perhaps the *Imago mundi* of the 12th century, sometimes attributed to Honorius of Autun. The *Speculum* originally comprised two parts: the *Naturale* and the *Historiale*. The *Naturale* beings with a treatise on theology (the triune God, archetype and creator of the universe; angels; demons; account of Creation and the exitus of all reality from God), proceeds to a consideration of the Fall, Redemption, and the sacraments of the church, and concludes with a summation of natural philosophy, including a description of the physical universe and the nature of human being. The *Historiale* gives an account of history from the Creation story of Genesis to 1244 in his earliest edition, and extended to 1254 in his later version. Its popularity is attested by several translations into the vernacular, including French, Catalan, and Dutch verse. After revising and reorganizing his work, Vincent produced a third volume, the *Doctrinale*, that contained a treatise on knowledge and the arts, including all the fields of science, from grammar and mechanics to politics, law, and medicine: in short, all that is useful to know to live a fruitful and productive life, both public and private. Although Vincent had intended to publish a fourth part, the *Morale*, he never accomplished his goal. The tract entitled *Morale* that began to circulate in the 14th century with the first three parts is in fact an anonymous compilation drawn from the *Summa theologica* of Thomas Aquinas.

In the last years of his life, Vincent composed treaties for the royal court. On the death of the dauphin Louis in January 1260, he wrote his *Epistola consolatoria super morte filii*. Within the next year or so, he published at the request of Queen Marguerite a tract on the education of princes, *De eruditione filiorum nobilium*, for the tutors of Prince Philip. Finishing this work, Vincent returned to his treatise concerning royal government requested by Louis IX. Sometime before Pentecost 1263, he presented the first part, *De morali principis institutione*, to his patron. But as with his *Speculum*, Vincent never finished this work: the second part was only supplied at a later date by a fellow Dominican, William Peraldus.

See also **Aquinas, Thomas; Louis IX**

Further Reading

Vincent de Beauvais. *De eruditione filiorum nobilium*, ed. Arpad Steiner. Cambridge: Mediaeval Academy of America, 1938.

Gabriel, Astrik. *The Educational Ideas of Vincent of Beauvais*. 2nd ed. Notre Dame: University of Notre Dame Press, 1962.

Lusignan, Serge, A. Nadeau, and M. Paulmier-Foucart, eds. *Vincent de Beauvais: Actes du Colloque de Montréal, 1988*. Montreal, 1990.

McCarthy, Joseph M. *Humanistic Emphases in the Educational Thought of Vincent of Beauvais*. Leiden: Brill, 1976.

Paulmier-Foucart, M., and Serge Lusignan. "Vincent de Beauvais et l'histoire du *Speculum majus*." *Journal des Savants* 1990, pp. 97–124.

MARK ZIER

W

WACE (ca. 1100–after 1174) Born on the island of jersey, Wace received his training first at Caen, then at Paris or, less likely, at Chartres; the influence of Hugh of Saint-Victor on his work is evident. Early in the 1130s, *maistre* Wace returned to Caen, where he occupied the position of *clerc lisant* (this term, used by Wace himself, most likely meant "reader of the lessons in the church service"); between 1165 and 1169, King Henry II of England rewarded him for his literary work with the prebend of a canon at Bayeux. He must have sojourned in England, since he knew the English language and gives precise geographical details of that country, especially of the Dorset area. Charters at Bayeux that bear his signature are not helpful in more precisely dating his life, which is known exclusively from personal remarks in his *Roman de Rou*.

Wace began his literary career with a series of hagiographical poems, of which three, signed by him, are preserved. From his stay in England, the center of St. Margaret's cult, he probably brought back a *Vie de sainte Marguerite* (742 lines), the first and stylistically by far the best of thirteen verse adaptations of this legend into French. His *Conception Nostre Dame* (1,810 lines) was designated as propaganda in favor of the establishment of the feast of the Immaculate Conception, as furthered by Abbot Anselm of Bury-Saint-Edmunds (r. 1121–46) against formidable opposition, especially from St. Bernard of Clairvaux. As a Norman, Wace would have had great interest in the life of the Virgin, for the Normans were among the first in France to establish the feast of the Immaculate Conception, which was often called the *fete aux Normands*. In the *Conception Nostre Dame*, Wace introduces the technique of grouping different episodes in one poem, in this case five that lead from the establishment of the feast to the Assumption of the Virgin. The same technique is found in his *Vie de saint Nicolas* (1,563 lines), written probably for a citizen of Caen, Robert, son of Tiout; containing twenty-three independent episodes, without any advancement in time, it testifies to the popularity of the saint in Normandy in the first half of the 12th century. The three poems, all in rhymed octosyllabic lines, can be dated ca. 1135–50.

Wace's reputation as an adapter of Latin works on popular topics might have brought him the commission by Eleanor of Aquitaine, newly wed to Henry II, to "translate" Geoffrey of Monmouth's *Historic reg'um Britanniae* (ca. 1136). Wace could not immediately locate a copy of this text and consequently based most of his adaptation on the *Britannici sermonis liber vetustissimus* (possibly by the archdeacon Walter of Oxford, a close friend of Geoffrey of Monmouth who is mentioned by Geffrei Gaimar), written in the early 1130s with the intent of ingratiating the Celtic part of the population with the new Norman rulers by stressing the Britons' claim to Britain, tracing its history back to the Trojans, in particular to Aeneas, with the help of early Welsh chronicles and Nennius. According to these sources, Brutus (folk etymology of *Brytt* 'Briton'), Aeneas's great-grandson, led the Trojans out of Greek captivity to Britain; the *Liber vetustissimus* then depicted the legendary history of Brutus's descendants on this island through the 8th century, when the Celts had to abandon all hope of reconquering the country from the Anglo-Saxons. It was this text that Geoffrey reedited and brought to renown thanks to the interest of the Norman dynasty in the predecessors of the Anglo-Saxons, renown that also had its repercussions on Wace's *Roman de Brut*, or *Geste des Bretons* (1155), since scribes of later manuscripts constantly altered the text by increasingly modeling it on Geoffrey's work. In the critical edition, the *Roman de Brut* is narrated in 14,866 octosyllabic verses; the manuscript Durham Cathedral C. iv. 1 (Anglo-Norman; 13th c.) inserts 670 decasyllabic verses containing the prophecies of Merlin related by a certain Elias; Lincoln Cathedral 104 (Anglo-Norman; 13th c.) adds 640 Alexandrines of the same prophecies by a certain William; and B.L. Add. 45103 (Anglo-Norman; 13th c.) contains yet another version of the prophecies, also in Alexandrines, and anonymous. B.N. fr. 1450 (Picard; 13th c.) goes even further and inserts between lines 9,798 and 9,799 Chrétien de Troyes's romances *Erec, Perceval, Cligés, Yvain,* and *Lancelot,* in that order.

Wace is remarkably critical of his source, frequently stressing that he is not certain of a fact; conversely, he romanticizes the dry events of history in order to make them palatable to an audience of noble laypersons. In particular, his work contains several episodes that presage the spirit of courtly love, such as King Aganippus's love "from afar" for Cordeïlle, King Leïr's youngest daughter, or Uther Pendragon's love from reputation only for Ygerne; but he also stresses the catastrophic consequences of passion, illustrated, for example, by the episodes of Locrin's and Mordred's adulterous relationships. Though he eliminates the most fantastic elements in his source, such as Merlin's prophecies, he adds many picturesque details, among them a mention of the institution of the Round Table, a detail that to date has not been satisfactorily explained. Wace's work was enormously popular (twenty-six manuscripts have preserved it in complete or fragmented, form), and ca. 1200 the priest Layamon of Raston in Worcestershire adapted it into Middle English, swelling it to nearly 30,000 lines; it is Layamon who reports that Wace had dedicated his work to Eleanor, which is possible though not mentioned in the text.

While in the *Roman de Brut* Wace was highly successful in converting pseudohistory into narrative fiction, he was less so in the *Roman de Rou* (i.e., Rollo), or *Geste des Normands* (11,440 octosyllabic lines; plus a prologue of 315 lines and the first 4,425 lines of the work, in Alexandrines; in addition, there exists the first draft of a prologue in 750 octosyllabic lines). The work was commissioned by Henry II, who wanted a poem similar to the *Brut* with respect to the history of Normandy. Wace especially had recourse to Dudo de Saint-Quentin's unreliable *De moribus et actis primorum Normanniae ducum,* from the first years of the 11th century, Guillaume de Jumièges's *Gesta Normannorum ducum* of 1071, Guillaume de Poitiers's *Gesta Guillelmi* (ca. 1078), and William of Malmesbury's *Gesta regum Anglorum* of the first half of the 12th. Wace began the project in 1160. He was uncomfortable with real history and its sources, excelling only when he narrated legendary material, such as stories about Duke Richard I, the Richard of Normandy in the *Chanson de Roland*, and events during the reigns of kings William II Rufus and Henry I (r. 1100–35), where he was a historian in his own right, drawing from personal information. Occasionally, he also gives firsthand information concerning the reign of the Conqueror, such as details about William's fleet in 1066, having as a small child heard his father comment on it. The commission did not excite Wace: for a while, he even attempted another meter, the Alexandrine (one of the first authors, if not the first, to do so); the work thus advanced so slowly that Henry II grew impatient and commissioned the much younger Benoît de Sainte-Maure, whose *Roman de Troie* (ca. 1165) had superseded the *Brut* as a literary success, with the same task. Wace, bitterly disappointed, interrupted his work after having narrated the Battle of Tinchebrai, in which Henry I defeated his older brother Robert Curthose and annexed Normandy (1106). Since he mentions Henry II's siege of Rouen in 1174, it is assumed that he died soon after that date.

Wace is undoubtedly the most brilliant author of the first period of Norman literature; the modern reader is also struck by his conscientiousness, honesty, and—for the period—highly critical, even scholarly approach to literature.

See also **Benoît de Sainte-Maure; Bernard of Clairvaux; Chrétien de Troyes**

Further Reading

Wace. *Le roman de Brut de Wace*, ed. Ivor Arnold. 2 vols. Paris: SATF, 1938–40.

——. *The Conception Nostre Dame of Wace*, ed. William Ray Ashford. Chicago: University of Chicago Libraries, 1933.

——. *Le roman de Rou de Wace*, ed. Anthony J. Holden. 3 vols. Paris: Picard, 1970–73.

——, ed. *Wace: La vie de sainte Marguerite*, ed. Hans-Erich Keller. Tubingen: Niemeyer, 1990.

——.. *La vie de saint Nicolas par Wace, poème religieux du XIIe siècle*, ed. Einar Ronsjö. Lund: Gleerup, 1942.

Keller, Hans-Erich. *Étude descriptive sur le vocabulaire de Wace*. Berlin: Akademie, 1953.

——. "The Intellectual Journey of Wace." *Fifteenth Century Studies* 17 (1990): 185–207.

Pelan, Margaret. *L'influence du "Brut" de Wace sur les romans français de son temps*. Paris: Droz, 1931.

HANS-ERICH KELLER

WALAFRID STRABO (ca. 808–849)

A Carolingian scholar and poet, Walafrid (Strabo means "the squinter") was born in Swabia and educated at Reichenau and later at Fulda under Rabanus Maurus. He served from 829 to 838 as tutor to Louis the Pious's youngest son, Charles the Bald. After 838, he was the abbot of Reichenau; for political reasons, he was expelled by Louis the German in 840 but reinstated in 842. Walafrid died on August 18, 849, crossing the Loire to visit his former student, Charles the Bald.

To modern readers, Walafrid's most famous works are his poems, including the *Visio Wettini*, a hexameter treatment of visions of Hell, Purgatory, and Paradise written at the age of eighteen and dedicated to his former teacher, Wettin of Reichenau; and *De cultura hortorum* (or *hortulus*), a medicinal description and allegorical interpretation of twenty-three herbs and flowers. Other poems include hagiography and praises of important people (including Louis the Pious and the empress Judith, mother of Charles the Bald). In the Middle Ages, he was also famous for his exegesis, much of it based on the longer works of Rabanus Maurus, including commentaries on the Pentateuch, the Psalms, and the canonical epistles. This exegesis remains in need of further critical study. The *Glossa ordinaria*, published as a work of Walafrid in Migne's *Patrologia Latina*, Vols. 113–14, is now known to have been written in the

12th century and erroneously ascribed to Walafrid in the 15th.

See also **Louis the Pious; Rabanus Maurus**

Further Reading

Walafrid Strabo. *Poems. MGH Poetae* 2.259–473.

Traill, David A., ed. and trans. *Walahfrid Strabo's Visio Wettini: Text, Translation and Commentary.* Bern: Lang, 1974.

Duckett, Eleanor Shipley. *Carolingian Portraits: A Study in the Ninth Century.* Ann Arbor: University of Michigan Press, 1962, pp.121–60.

Godman, Peter. *Poets and Emperors: Frankish Politics and Carolingian Poetry.* Oxford: Clarendon, 1987.

Onnerfors, Alf, Johannes Rathofer, and Fritz Wagner, eds. "Über Walahfrid Strabos Psalter-Kommentar." In *Literatur und Sprache im europaischen Mittelalter: Festschrift für Karl Langosch zum 70. Geburtstag.* Darmstadt: Wissenschaftliche Buchgesellschaft, 1973, pp. 75–121.

E. ANN MATTER

WALLĀDAH BINT AL-MUSTAFKI Wallādah, who lived in Córdoba in the eleventh century, was the daughter of Caliph Muḥammad al-Mustakfi. Her house was a meeting place for writers. She had a tempestuous relationship with the famous poet Ibn Zaydūn, who dedicated many of his poems to her. Wallādah accused him of sleeping both with her slave and his own secretary, a man by the name of 'Ali. In turn, she had affairs with Muhya, a woman poet, and with the vizir. Her relationship with Ibn Zaydūn ended badly. Most of her nine extant poems are about him. Some are delicate love poems, such as: "Expect my visit at dusk, for I find that night is the best time to hide secrets. What I feel for you is such that by its side the sun would not shine, the moon would not rise and the stars would not begin their nocturnal journey." Some are obscene satirical poems: "You are called the hexagonous,

a name that will endure beyond your life: faggot, buggerer, philanderer, fucker, cuckold, thief."

Although Wallādah's lifestyle was unconventional, her poetry was not. In addition to panegyrical poems, a genre she seems not to have cultivated, satirical and love poems were very popular among the poets of al-Andalus. The works of women poets, for the most part, took the form of a dialogue with their male counterparts. In accordance with this fashion, Wallādah's love and satirical poems consist of dialogues with Ibn Zaydūn. However, if she followed established genres, she did so with originality and flair. Wallādah held her own against the best male poets of her time. Indeed, she was considered brilliant.

It is said that Wallādah had the following two verses embroidered on her tunic: "By God, I was made for glory and I proudly follow my own path" and "I offer my cheek to whomever loves me and give a kiss to whomever desires me." She seems to have followed her mottos, because she became a legendary poet and lover who has excited the imagination of readers for centuries.

See also **Ibn Zaydūn**

Further Reading

Garulo, T. *Diwan de las poetisas de al-Andalus.* Madrid, 1986.

Sobh, M. *Poetisas arábigo-andaluzas.* Granada, n.d.

CRISTINA GONZÁLEZ

WALTER OF CHÂTILLON (fl. 1160–1190) One of most celebrated poets of the twelfth century, whose *Alexandreis* reveals the author's interest in the East and in world geography.

Despite Walter of Châtillon's reputation as an extraordinary poet in Latin, we know little about his life. He was born near Lille, then in the county of Flanders. After studying at schools in France (probably at Paris, possibly at Reims or Orléans), he taught at a number of schools in northern France, including one at Châtillon. After studying at Bologna, he joined the court of William, archbishop of Reims, who eventually made Walter a canon, probably of Amiens. In addition to numerous lyrics in Latin on a wide variety of subjects (religious, erotic, and satirical) and a treatise against the Jews, Walter wrote his best-known work, the *Alexandreis* (between 1171 and 1181), which he dedicated to Archbishop William. *The Alexandreis,* a ten-book epic in dactylic hexameters, takes its form, diction, and style from the classical epic tradition. Its primary model is Lucan's *Bellum civile,* its primary historical source, Quintus Curtius Rufus's *Historia Alexandri Magni.*

Although the *Alexandreis,* which covers the life of Alexander the Great, is more restrained than some versions of the story in the Alexander romance tradition, it nevertheless reveals Walter's considerable interest in the East. By contrast to the Alexander romance, the *Alexandreis* follows Curtius's more "realistic" depiction of the East. Alexander does not confront any of the monstrous races or exotic peoples described in the romance. For example, rather than encountering the Brahmans, the legendary inhabitants of India famed for their ascetic life and philosophy, Walter's Alexander meets the Scythians. His Scythians, however, presented as idealized primitives living in accordance with Nature's dictates, have much in common with the Brahmans of the romance.

Walter's Alexander seems to be a paradigm for crusaders—in particular for crusading kings such as Philip Augustus (r. 1180–1223). Critics have argued that he serves, on the one hand, as a positive model of prowess to be imitated and as a negative warning against pursuing the wrong things in the Holy Land: wealth and fame rather than the salvation of his soul.

A catalogue of the lands of Asia in Book 1 and a description of a map carved on the inside of the dome of the tomb of the Persian emperor Darius in Book 7 define the natural limitations of the world. This map is a typical medieval *mappamundi* of the tripartite type: the *orbis terrarum* has a circular form and is oriented to the East, with Asia filling the top half of the circle, Europe and Africa the two quarters on the bottom. The world is ringed by a surrounding Ocean. Like contemporary *mappamundi,* Walter's includes places and peoples of significance from all periods in biblical, ancient, and medieval history. Walter presents as unnatural Alexander's ambition to cross the Ocean, to see the regions of the extreme East, and to conquer the peoples of the Antipodes. When Alexander begins to fulfill this ambition by invading the Ocean, the goddess Nature intervenes and arranges his death. Although Walter's *Alexandreis* was widely known during the Middle Ages—it survives in some 200 manuscripts and was familiar to such prominent vernacular poets as Dante and Chaucer (whose Wife of Bath alludes casually to Darius's tomb in her "Prologue" [ll. 497–499])—the poem has been largely (and undeservedly) forgotten.

See also Chaucer, Geoffrey; Dante Alighieri; Godfrey of Viterbo; Philip II Augustus

Further Reading

Kratz, Dennis. *Mocking Epic: Waltharius, Alexandreis, and the Problem of Christian Heroism.* Madrid: José Porrúa Turanzas, 1980.

Lafferty, Maura K. "Mapping Human Limitations: The Tomb Ecphrases in Walter of Châtillon's *Alexandreis." Journal of Medieval Latin* 4 (1994): 64–81.

Ratkowitsch, Christine. *Descriptio Picturae: Die literarische Funktion der Beschreibung von Kunstwerken in der lateinischen Grossdichtung des 12. Jahrhunderts.* Vienna: Verlag der Österreichischen Akademie der Wissenschaften, 1991.

Walter of Chatillon. *Alexandreis*. Ed. Marvin L. Colker. Padova, Italy: Antenore, 1978.
——. *Alexandreis*. Trans. R. Telfryn Pritchard. Toronto: Pontifical Institute of Medieval Studies, 1986.
——. *Alexandreis*. Trans. David Townsend. Philadelphia: U of Pennsylvania P, 1997.

MAURA K. LAFFERTY

WALTHER VON DER VOGELWEIDE
(ca. 1170–ca. 1230) In service largely at the Hohenstaufen courts, Walther is considered the greatest of the German courtly singers of the High Middle Ages. Some would argue for his poetic primacy among European singers in any language. Internal evidence in his songs suggests he was active between the early 1190s and the late 1220s. His *Minnesang* (love singing), in which he sang the painful joy of unrequited love for a woman of high station *(hôhe minne)*, shows influences of fashionable German courtly singers such as Heinrich von Morungen and Reinmar der Alte. Walther also sang of the so-called *nidere minne* (down-to-earth love), an amorous relationship both physical and mutual that has close parallels in Latin secular love songs. His political, personal, didactic, and religious songs *(Sangspruch)* reflect the vicissitudes of his career as well as the turbulent political events of the *sacrum imperium*, known later as the Holy Roman Empire.

Extant today are over six hundred stanzas in some three dozen manuscripts. Walther's music has been entirely lost save for five melodies, two of them fragmentary and another two from manuscripts written three centuries later. Accordingly, readers must use their imaginations to re-create the conditions of performance and the effect of the melodies and their accompaniments.

Walther's name appears only once in nonliterary documents of his lifetime, a 1203 entry in the travel accounts of Bishop of Passau directing that five shillings be given the singer *(cantor)* for a fur coat. But other thirteenth-century singers and romanciers provide ample encomia, or formal praise, for this towering figure of German lyric singing. Gottfried of Straßburg in his *Tristan* (ll. 4751–4820) calls him the nightingale carrying the banner of *Minnesang*, praising Walther's high (tenor?) voice and his dexterity in the polyphonic style of the day (organum). His artistry is also celebrated by, among others, Reinmar von Zweter, Bruder Werner, and Rudolf von Ems. In the waning Middle Ages he is enthroned by the Meistersinger as one of the Twelve Old Masters. Only one contemporary provides negative criticism: Thomasin von Zerklaere castigates him as a slanderer of Pope Innocent III and a deceiver of men *(Der welsche Gast*, 11. 11091–11268).

The songs classified as *Minnesang*—the sequence can only be surmised—are normally categorized in the following major groups: early songs of elevated love *(hôhe minne)* linked to Reinmar at the Viennese court; later *Minnesang*; songs of down-to-earth love *(nidere minne)*; and late songs. Augmenting the difficulties of dating these songs is the strong possibility of revision in the course of the singer's career or changes developing from the orality of the pieces.

Walther's assumed apprenticeship at the Viennese court, in the 1190s under the tutelage of Reinmar der Alte (Reinmar von Hagenau), produced a number of early songs. Some of these have been linked to a "Reinmar feud" *(Reinmar-Fehde)*, a quasi debate revealing the outlines of a serious polemic with his former mentor on the nature of *minne*. Reinmar is the representative of the traditional (since the 1160s) ideas inherent in the troubadour lyric: his love, unrequited and unconsummated, is for an unapproachable lady of a higher station. Walther, on the other hand, hints at a more mutual love; his lady is valued not for her cold, Turandot-like majesty but for a more immediate and shared joy. The Reinmar debate began in the 1190s and seemed to continue until after Walther's departure from Vienna in 1198. Emblematic of this exchange is Walther's *Ein man verbiutet âne pfliht* (no. L. 111,22ff), a response to Reinmar's *Ich wirbe umb allez daz ein man* (*Minnesangs Frühling*, no. 159,1ff), in which, using the same melody and stanzaic form, he weaves Reinmar's key motifs into his song to produce an ironically critical response to his mentor.

It is difficult to separate what seem to be the more mature songs of the Reinmar debate from Walther's non-Reinmar–related songs of the period circa 1205–1215, a time in which he achieved mastery of language. Here the singer composed his most effective and inventive songs, sharply breaking with the traditional German *Minnesang* (as performed by Heinrich von Morungen, Reinmar, and others), with its prickling tensions and the incessant conjectures about an impossible love. Walther's style now becomes pointed, ironic, playful, and original. Though still dancing around the theme of *hôhe minne*, many of his songs now suggest an equal relationship with a young woman whose station is not of importance and whose designation increasingly becomes the generically female *wîp* (woman) rather than the socially hierarchical *frouwe* (lady). In *Si wunderwol gemachet wîp*, (L. 53,25ff), he sings of the physical attributes of a woman not of the nobility, completing his catalog of adulation with an unprecedented image of the woman, unclothed, stepping cleanly from her bath.

Among the songs of this period are some that appear outside the scope of the *Minne* theme. The so-called *Preislied* (panegyric) *Ir sult sprechen willekomen* (L. 56, 14ff) is possibly a response to the troubadour Peire Vidal (fl. ca. 1187–1205), whose unkind characterizations of German deportment probably rankled at German-speaking courts. Walther's praise of German (*tiutschiu*) woman and, by extension, German culture is unique in medieval song.

During these years Walther also composed songs with bucolic settings about the real and physical love of a young woman who seems tangential to courtly circles (songs of *nidere Minne*, sometimes called *Mädchenlieder*). In "Herzeliebez frouwelîn" (L. 49, 25ff) he is charmed by a woman or girl whose glass ring he values more than the gold ring of a queen. "Nement, frowe, disen cranz" (L. 74, 20ff) projects a dream vision of his beloved, a pretty girl *(wol getânen maget)* portrayed in the scenery of the *Carmina Burana*, that is, under a blossoming tree on a meadow graced by flowers and the singing of the birds.

"Under der linden" (Beneath the Linden Tree, no. L. 39,11ff) is Walther's most celebrated love song. In the tradition of the Latin *pastourelle*, it contains the same predictable imagery as in "Nement, frowe, disen cranz." But Walther brings to this tradition a deceptively simple language expressing the essence of the lovers' joy, deftly combined with a playful and delicate web of motifs to form a song with complex levels of meaning.

Walther's position at court required him also to excel at the art of *Sangspruch*. The term pertains to songs in which love is not the primary matter: political pieces, songs of personal invective, requests for favors from a patron, crusade songs, and songs with a didactic or religious content. Each piece is normally restricted to one stanza, though in some cases several stanzas composed in the same tune (*Ton*, plural *Töne*) can be bound together to form a performance piece. Walther's *Sangspruch* provides a glimpse of the events of his life as well as the fortunes of the empire under the Hohenstaufen rulers and its ongoing struggle with the papacy. These songs were composed largely for patrons at the electoral courts—kings, dukes, counts, and bishops—who expected from the singer both workmanlike compositions and persuasive performances. Occasional songs in the best sense, they were composed about specific events or personalities. In editions of Walther they are usually grouped into cycles of stanzas of identical metrical and musical form *(Ton)*. Some, though not all, of the stanzas of a *Ton* have the same general thematic content. Modern scholarship has given them associative names that apply to some though not all of the stanzas in the *Ton*. In the "Konig-Friedrichston" (King Friedrich Tune, no. 26,3ff), for example, King Friedrich (later the emperor Friedrich II) plays a major role only in a few of the stanzas. Each of these *Töne* contains between three and eighteen stanzas.

Walther's best-known *Ton*, the "Reichston" (Imperial Tune, L. 8,4ff), may well be the earliest. A triad of long stanzas (twenty-four lines each), it begins pensively with the trademark image of Walther sitting on a stone in the pose of the philosopher (*Ich saz ûf eime steine*, I sat upon a stone). In the second song (L. 8,28), Walther moves out of the meditative mode and into the political, calling for the crowning of the true emperor, the Hohenstaufen candidate Philipp of Swabia rather than the papally sanctioned Otto of Brunswick, dynastic leader of the Welf party. With pointed imagery he declares the clergy of Rome corrupt and the times out of joint. In the third song (L. 9,16), assuming the persona of a pious hermit, he indicts the pope as being too young (Innocent III was only thirty-nine), an anomaly symptomatic of the ills besetting the curia at Rome and its imperial policy.

In 1198 Walther left Vienna and attached himself to various Hohenstaufen courts in the middle German regions, continuing both positive and negative associations with Philipp of Swabia (in the five stanzas of the first "Philippston," Philipp Tune, L. 18,29ff). Despite Walther's ardent propaganda for the imperial candidate, he complains of Philipp's parsimony. This theme of a patron's miserly qualities would become a favorite of the later generation of *Sangspruch* singers in the thirteenth century.

The "Wiener Hofton" (Viennese Court Tune, L. 20, 16ff), largely composed after Walther's departure from Vienna in 1198, reveals an ambivalence about the Viennese court, combining a longing to return to this desirable venue with an uneasiness about his relations with the reigning Duke Leopold VI. Walther continues to sing in the causes of Philipp until the would-be emperor's death in 1208, but gradually in the course of the first decade of the thirteenth century, he forms new courtly associations, most prominently with Hermann, Landgrave of Thuringia, and his son-in-law, Dietrich, Margrave of Meißen. These princes are forced to change allegiance after Philipp's death, leaving the imperial candidacy open to his archrival, Otto of Brunswick. Walther reflects the new loyalties in the "Ottenton" (Otto Tune, L. 11, 6ff), in which he welcomes the new kaiser to the Reichstag (imperial diet) in Frankfurt, declaring that his patron, the Margrave of Meißen, is as loyal to the emperor as an angel is to God. Less than a year later the margrave and other princes (like the fallen angels) are in open rebellion, preparing the way for a new-Hohenstaufen pretender, the young Friedrich II, grandson of Barbarossa.

As was the lot of singers employed by the courts, Walther continued the propaganda commissioned by his various patrons. In one of his sharpest and most amusing pieces, "Unmutston" (Disgruntled Tune, L. 34,4), Walther rants against that most ardent enemy of the Hohenstaufen interests, Pope Innocent III, for his collecting of German monies to finance the Albigensian Crusade in 1213, accusing the Roman clergy of feasting on capons and wine while the German laity grows lean from fasting.

There is evidence that Walther was able to gain a modicum of independence as overseer of a fief. In 1220 he composed a song of request to King Friedrich for his own house, playing on his lord's sympathy for a homeless singer whose wearisome life was a procession of one-night stands. ("König-Friedrichston," L. 28,1). Apparently Walther was successful, for in the same *Ton* (L. 28,31) he proclaims triumphantly his thanks to the king, grateful that he need no longer go begging at the courts of base lords for shelter.

Since these songs of praise and political propaganda were produced on demand to suit the shifting political alliances of a turbulent period of imperial history, one might properly ask to what extent Walther's songs reflect his own values. Many are outright propaganda, although of a kind wrought with the highest poetic skills and a deft sense of language. And yet many pieces reveal a personality sharply troubled by the woeful state of the mutable world and impelled by a desire to return to the established, predictable, and more ethical patterns of time past. The "Wiener Hofton" bewails the uncouth behavior of courtly youth (L. 24,3), marking its disparity with the days when one did not spare the rod with ill-mannered children. More personal and sadder echoes of this nostalgia permeate the "Elegie" (Elegy, L. 124,1 ff), generally held to have been composed in Walther's old age. It too complains of the uncourtly behavior of young people, but combines it with what must have been an old man's deeply personal sense of an irretrievable past. And yet, in the last stanza, it is clear that it is a song of outright propaganda, urging knights to undertake a crusade, possibly that of Frederick II in 1227. Walther was still the paid entertainer whose patron called the tune.

The manuscripts also contain a scattering of personal and religious songs of one or more stanzas that cannot properly be called *Sangspruch*. One is the "Palästina-Lied" (Palestine Song, L. 14,38ff), also a recruiting song for a crusade, containing the only complete and proven melody among Walther's songs. Another is the *Leich* (L. 3,1ff). This most virtuosic of all medieval lyric forms—derived from the liturgical sequence—is a large-format song built on a series of versicles and responses that undergo repetition and variation. It may have been specifically composed for groups of singers and instrumentalists, who would have sung and played it antiphonally in unison or possibly with rudimentary polyphony (*organum*). With its many repetitions and variations, it often approached the complexity of a fugue. This is Walther's longest single performance piece, a prayer to the Mother of God (hence called a *Marienleich*), marked by lush praise of the Virgin commingled with references to the Trinity, biblical prefigurations, and elements of Christian theology. Yet even in this, Walther's most pious work, the singer cannot refrain from references to the Roman curia and its "unchristian things" *(unchristliche dinge)*.

The legacy of Walther's *Sangspruch* was a set of models and patterns for a century of professional singers who followed. His love songs, on the other hand, marked in a sense the end of *Minnesang*. The art had soared in the songs of Morungen and Reinmar. Walther moved through the exhausted concept of *hôhe minne* and brought the love song back to earth. But after him no other Minnesinger approached his or his predecessors' mastery of the art.

See also **Frederick II; Heinrich von Morungen; Reinmar der Alte**

Further Reading

Bäuml, Franz, ed. *From Symbol to Mimesis: The Generation of Walther von der Vogelweide.* Göppingen: Kümmerle, 1984.

Bein, Thomas. *Walther von der Vogelweide.* Stuttgart: Reclam, 1997.

Brunner, Horst, et al. *Walther von der Vogelweide: Die gesamte Überlieferung der Texte und Melodien—Abbildungen, Materialien, Melodiestranskription.* Göppingen: Kümmerle, 1977.

——, et al. *Walther von der Vogelweide: Epoche—Werk—Wirkung.* Munich: Beck, 1996.

Cormeau, Christoph, ed. *Walther von der Vogelweide: Leich, Lieder, Sangsprüche.* Berlin: de Gruyter, 1996.

Goldin, Friedrich. "Walther versus Reinmar," in *The Regeneration of Poetic Language in Medieval German Literature: Vernacular Poetics in the Middle Ages*, ed. Lois Ebin. Kalamazoo: Western Michigan University, 1984, pp. 57–92.

Hahn, Gerhard. *Walther von der Vogelweide: Eine Einführung.* Munich: Artemis, 1986.

Halbach, Kurt Herbert. *Walther von der Vogelweide*, 4th ed. Stuttgart: Metzler, 1983.

Jones, George Fenwick. *Walther von der Vogelweide.* New York: Twayne, 1968.

McFarland, Timothy, and Silvia Ranawake, eds. *Walther von der Vogelweide: Twelve Studies.* Oxford: Oxford University Press, 1982.

Mück, Hans-Dieter. *Walther von der Vogelweide: Beiträge zu Leben und Werk.* Stuttgart: Stöffler and Schütz, 1989.

Müller, Jan-Dirk, and Franz Josef Worstbrock, eds. *Walther von der Vogelweide: Hamburger Kolloquium 1988 zum 65. Geburtstag von Karl-Heinz Borck.* Stuttgart: Hirzel, 1989.

Nix, Matthias. *Untersuchungen zur Funktion der politischen Spruchdichtung Walthers von der Vogelweide.* Göppingen: Kümmerle, 1993.

Scheibe, Fred Karl. *Walther von der Vogelweide, Troubadour of the Middle Ages: His Life and His Reputation in the English-Speaking Countries.* New York: Vantage, 1969.

PETER FRENZEL

WENCESLAS (November 26, 1361–August 6, 1419)

Wenceslas IV (Václav, Wenzel, king of the Romans 1378–1400, king of Bohemia until 1419) was the eldest son of Charles IV by his third wife, Anna of Schweidnitz. Wenceslas was born on November 26, 1361, in Nuremberg. He was elected king of the Romans on June 10, 1376, and assumed control of imperial affairs as Staathalter in February of the following year. After Charles's death, he inherited the Bohemian crown. Wenceslas has not enjoyed the good reputation of his father. In particular, he has been generally condemned for his sloth, vacillation, and drunkenness.

Wenceslas was faced immediately with several serious problems. First was the Swabian City League, established July 4, 1376. The growth of the league, aimed directly against the mortgage policies of his rather, led to a major war, lasting until 1389. The second problem was the Great Schism, which broke out in the fall of 1378. Wenceslas supported the pope in Rome, Urban VI. In 1380 he traveled to Paris in an attempt to convince French King Charles V to withdraw support from the Avignon pope, Clement II. When this effort failed, on the advice of Urban VI, Wenceslas allied himself with Richard II of England. The alliance and resulting marriage between the English king and Wenceslas's sister Anna marked a total break with the traditional pro-French Luxembourg policy. Within the empire, a group of southern principalities, led by Leopold III of Austria and Archbishop Pilgrim II of Salzburg, supported Clement VII.

During the first years of his reign, Wenceslas sought to resolve the problems of the cities. The *Landfriede* (peace) of Nuremberg (1383) marks the first attempt to divide the empire into districts or counties *(Kreise)*, anticipating the later reforms of Albrecht II and Maximilian I. After the league's defeat at Döffingen (1388), the *Landfriede* of Eger (1389) provided a modicum of stability for the next several decades. The political autonomy of the cities was recognized, while they were banned from making further leagues.

After 1390, problems in Bohemia consumed most of Wenceslas's energy. He tended to support the towns and lower nobility; this provoked resistance from the great nobles and higher clergy. The archbishop of Prague, Jan z Jenštejna (1379–1396) in particular proved a serious opponent of the crown. The torture and murder of the vicar general of Prague,

John of Pomuk (March 20, 1393) by royal officials provoked a noble Fronde in 1394. Wenceslas's cousin, Margrave Jost of Moravia, joined with the nobles and took the king prisoner (May 8, 1394) with the collusion of Duke Albrecht III of Austria. Jost was named regent, but the intervention of Wenceslas's half-brother John of Görlitz and Ruprecht II of the Palatinate led to the king's release. As Wenceslas now turned on his opponents, a civil war broke out. The deaths of Albrecht III (August 29, 1395) and John of Görlitz (March 1, 1396) brought an end to the fighting. Wenceslas's other half-brother, king Sigismund of Hungary, was able to negotiate a peace settlement among Jost, Wenceslas, and the nobles. In return, Sigismund was recognized as Wenceslas's heir and named imperial vicar.

After the battle of Nikopolis (September 28, 1396), Sigismund turned to securing his Hungarian lands. This left Wenceslas, after a ten-year absence from Germany, faced with an angry crowd of princes at the imperial diets of Nuremberg (1397) and Frankfurt (1398). The four Rhenish electors issued a series of demands. The *Landfriede* and Schism were perennial sticking points. Wenceslas's elevation of Giangalleazzo Visconti to the duchy of Milan (April 11, 1395) also provoked the electors' ire. In June 1400 the Rhenish electors demanded that Wenceslas appear before them to answer to their complaints. Their request coincided with a renewal of hostilities among Wenceslas, Jost, and the nobles. Wenceslas's Bohemian problems did not, in the eyes of the electors, excuse his refusal to appear. On August 20, 1400, the four Rhenish electors declared Wenceslas deposed and elected the count palatine, Ruprecht III, king of the Romans.

Wenceslas refused to recognize his deposition, but he was too occupied with Bohemian affairs to do much about it. The death of Ruprecht of the Palatine in 1401 presented Wenceslas with an op-portunity to regain the German throne. Unfortunately he could not count on support from his family. Indeed, both Sigismund and Jost were able to secure election to the imperial throne. Jost's death—perhaps from poison—in January 1411 cleared the way for an agreement between Sigismund and Wenceslas. The latter agreed to relinquish his German crown in return for half the imperial revenues and recognition of his position in Bohemia.

The last years of Wenceslas's reign in Bohemia saw the beginnings of a religious and political crisis that would later erupt in the Hussite revolution. Since the time of Charles IV, a series of radical preachers, among them Conrad Waldhause, Jan Milíc, and Matthew of Janov, had been attacking the higher clergy. The marriage between Anne of Bohemia and Richard II of England led to the growth of a Wycliffite faction among Czech scholars at the University of Prague. Jerome of Prague, along with his student Jan Hus, appeared as leaders of the Wycliffite Czechs. The ideological struggles were connected with political struggles in the university between the Czech minority and the three German-dominated "nations."

After the Roman pope Boniface IX (1389–1404) supported the Rhenish electors in 1400, Wenceslas turned to support the Czech reformers. He agreed to recognize the Council of Pisa (1408) and at the council of Kutná Hora ordered the German masters of the university to do so as well. The Kutná Hora decrees (January 18, 1409) broke the Germans' control over the university, giving the Czech nation three votes to one for all three of the German nations. A number of German masters left, later forming the core of the University of Leipzig.

The principal architects of the Czech victory were Jerome of Prague, Jan Hus, and Jakoubeck of Stríbro. In the wake of the Kutná Hora decrees, Archbishop Zdynek of Prague (1399–1411) excommunicated a number of royal officials and placed Prague under the interdict. Wenceslas ordered the city's clergy to ignore the decree. Zydnek agreed to submit to the king, but then fled the kingdom, seeking the aid of Emperor Sigismund. The archbishop died in Bratislava in September 1411, and after his departure, the Hussite movement became more radical. A group of reformers began calling for the administration of the cup to the laity *(utraquism)*. In 1412 Hus and Jakoubek publicly declared the Roman pontiff to be antichrist, leading to their excommunication. Along with the new archbishop, Conrad of Vechta, Wenceslas made a furtive attempt to restore Catholicism. Hus turned to the nobility for support, and at a synod in February 1413, Wenceslas again changed his mind, ordering the archbishop's commission to declare that there was no heresy in Bohemia.

In 1414 Emperor Sigismund requested that Hus appear before the Council of Constance to explain his program. Under a guarantee of safe-conduct, Hus went to Constance but soon found himself imprisoned. Over 250 Czech nobles protested this action, but to no avail. On July 6, 1415, Hus was burnt as a heretic in Constance. Reprisals against other Hussites had already begun. The German burghers of Olomouc had burned two lay preachers a week earlier; Jerome of Prague was burnt in May of the following year. Hus's death led fifty-eight Hussite nobles to form a Hussite league in September 1415. A Catholic alliance followed a month later. In 1416 Wenceslas again tried to restore Catholicism in Prague, but resistance from the university faculty and nobility forced a compromise on the question of *utraquism*.

The election of Pope Martin V in 1417 increased pressure on Wenceslas to take a hard line against the heretics. In the spring of 1419, Wenceslas arrested priests in Prague who granted the cup to the laity, and appointed Czech and German Catholics as *Bürgermeister* (mayors) in the Nové Mesto. On July 30, 1419, the radical preacher Jan

Zelivsky led a procession through the city to the New Town Hall demanding the release of imprisoned Utraquist priests. A scuffle broke out, and thirteen of the council members were thrown out the window. The first defenestration of Prague led to the outbreak of a great revolt. Not long after, on August 6, 1419, Wenceslas died. While most works ascribe his death to a stroke, research by a Czech neurologist suggests that the actual cause of death was acute alcohol poisoning.

Wenceslas was married twice, to Johanna of Bavaria (d. 1386) and Sophia of Bavaria (d. 1425). He had no children and all his lands fell to Emperor Sigismund.

See also **Charles IV; Charles V the Wise; Richard II**

Further Reading

Baethgen, Friedrich. *Schisma und Konzilzeit, Reichsreform und Habsburg Aufstieg.* Munich: Deutscher Taschenbuch Verlag, 1973.

Gerlich, Alois. *Habsburg-Luxembourg-Wittelsbach im Kampf um die deutschen Königsthrone: Studien zur Vorgeschichte Königtums Ruprechts von der Pfalz.* Wiesbaden: Steiner, 1960,

Hlaváek, Ivan. *Das Urkunden- und Kanzleiwesen des böhmischen und römischen Königs Wenzel (IV.) 1376–1419: Ein Beitrag zur spätmittelalterlichen Diplomatik.* Stuttgart: Hiersemann, 1970.

Kaminsky, Howard. *A History of the Hussite Revolution.* Berkeley: University of California Press, 1967.

Lindner, Theodor. *Geschichte des deutschen Reiches unter König Wenzel.* Braunschweig: C. A. Schwetschkte und Sohn, 1875/1880.

Speváek, JiYí. *Václav IV. 1361–1419. K predpokladûm hustiské revoluce.* Prague: Svoboda, 1986.

WILLIAM BRADFORD SMITH

WERNER DER GÄRTNER (fl. circa 1250–1280) The creator of one of the most realistic narratives of the Middle

Ages, Werner der Gärtner (the gardener) composed *Helmbrecht*, a short epic of 1,934 lines written in rhyming couplets, between 1250 and 1280, although some dispute this dating. Detailing a drastic picture of contemporary life, Werner depicts the decline of chivalry as well as the moral decay of the peasantry. The work has been variously described as a *Dorfgeschichte* (village tale), *Verspredigt* (rhymed sermon), and exemplum (moral tale). *Helmbrecht* survives in two manuscripts: "A" refers to the famous *Ambras Book of Heroes* (Heldenbuch) from 1504 to 1515, a costly parchment manuscript in Vienna (Nationalbibliothek) copied by Hans Ried; and "B," the "Leombach Manuscript" (1413), a paper manuscript. A third, illustrated manuscript, now lost, was still extant at the start of the nineteenth century. Manuscript "A," regarded as the original version, points to the Austrian-Bavarian region as its place of composition. Little is known of Werner, who is generally thought to have been a cleric, a wandering minstrel, or an occasional poet. He was an educated man whose work was intended for a sophisticated, noble audience.

This moral-didactic tale centers on the generation gap between father and son, between older conservative values and newer progressive aspirations. Werner begins with a description of the elaborate and highly inappropriate cap with which Helmbrecht, the farmer's son, hopes to find acceptance among the knights. The younger Helmbrecht rejects the farmer's life and instead aspires to become a knight, a calling for which he is clearly unsuited. His mother and sister provide him with expensive clothing (a contravention of the sumptuary laws); father Helmbrecht provides him with a costly steed, but only after trying to dissuade his son from leaving the farm (vv. 233–258; 279–298; 329–360). Helmbrecht easily finds acceptance with a band of robber knights and soon becomes the worst in his gang. After a year of plundering, he returns home and tells his father about the depravity and immorality of the knights. The elder Helmbrecht again tries to convince his son to remain on the farm and offers to share all that he has with him (vv. 1098–1114). Helmbrecht scoffs at this offer and returns to his band of robber knights, taking with him his sister Gotelint, who secretly has agreed to marry his friend Lemberslint. The marriage proves ill-fated, for after the wedding breakfast the judge and his hangmen appear and try them on the spot. Helmbrecht's nine companions are summarily hanged. Helmbrecht's life is spared but only after he has been maimed and blinded as punishment for his behavior toward his parents. It is in this pitiful condition that Helmbrecht returns home for the last time. Unlike before, he does not find a compassionate father ready to help him, but rather a disdainful father who turns him out (vv. 1713–1760; 1775–1813). Helmbrecht suffers a miserable existence in the forest until he is finally captured by peasants whom he had wronged and is hung.

The three conversations between father and son mark the tale's progress. The lesson is clear: parents should be strict in educating their children; children should obey their parents (the Fourth Commandment); one should be content with one's station in life *(ordo mundi)*. Whether or not Werner actually witnessed the events he describes, these events accurately reflect the social unrest occasioned by the end of the Hohenstaufen reign in the late thirteenth century. Werner addresses the major social issues of his time by depicting the collapse of the feudal system, the decline of chivalry, and the new self-assertiveness of the peasants; his social criticism is directed at peasants and knights alike.

Further Reading

Banta, Frank G. "The Arch of Action in Meier Helmbrecht." *Journal of English and German Philology* 63 (1964): 696–711.

Helmbrecht, ed. and trans. Helmut Brackert, Winfried Frey, and Dieter Seitz. Frankfurt am Main: Fischer-Taschenbuch Verlag, 1972; rpt. 1990.

Jackson, W. T .H. "The Composition of Meier Helmbrecht." *Modern Language Quarterly* 18 (1957): 44–58.

Kolb, Herbert. "Der 'Meier Helmbrecht' zwischen Epos und Drama." *Zeitschrift für deutsche Philologie* 81 (1962): 1–23.

Meier Helmbrecht von Wernher der Gartenaere, ed. Friedrich Panzer. Halle: Niemeyer, 1902; 10th ed., Hans-Joachim Ziegeler. Tübingen: Niemeyer, 1993.

Seelbach, Ulrich. *Bibliographie zu Wernher der Gartenaere*. Berlin: Schmidt, 1981.

——. *Kommentar zum Helmbrecht von Wernher dem Gartenaere*. Göppingen: Kümmerle, 1987.

Sowinski, Bernhard. *Wernher der Gartenaere: Helmbrecht. Interpretation.* Munich: Oldenbourg, 1971.

Wernher der Gartenaere: Helmbrecht, trans. Linda Parshall, ed. Ulrich Seelbach. New York: Garland, 1987.

LYNN D. THELEN

WILIGELMUS (fl. c. 1099–c. 1120)

Wiligelmus (Guglielmo, Wiligelmo) is often considered the first great Italian sculptor. His reliefs on the facade of Modena cathedral are among the first important sculptural programs of northern Italy, as part of the early development of Romanesque sculpture. His identity as the creator is known from an inscription held by the figures of the prophets Enoch and Elijah: *Inter scultores quanto sis dignis onore—Claret scultura nunc Wiligelme tua* ("How much honor you deserve among sculptors is now shown by your sculpture, Wiligelmo"). Wiligelmus's oeuvre has been identified at Modena and elsewhere through stylistic comparisons with these prophets, carved from the same block as the inscription.

Wiligelmus's principal work is the sculptural assemblage on the west facade of the cathedral of Modena, presumably executed c. 1106–1110, including the inscription plaque; four reliefs from

Genesis; two reliefs of *genii* with overturned torches; numerous capitals and decorative reliefs; and the program of the central portal, containing an elaborate scroll motif and twelve reliefs of prophets. The present placement of some of the reliefs is the result of changes made to the facade in the late twelfth century by the Campionese masters, who added the lateral portals and relocated the first and fourth reliefs from Genesis above them. Some scholars hold that these reliefs were created as part of liturgical furnishings for the interior of the cathedral (Quintavalle 1964–1965), but the evidence suggests that they were originally intended as part of a sculptural program decorating the facade.

The four reliefs from Genesis flanking the central portal serve as a monumental introduction to the cathedral and constitute the first large-scale frieze devoted exclusively to biblical subjects. The general themes are the creation, the fall, and the promise of salvation as revealed in the flood. The frieze concludes with the ark as the ship of salvation—an Old Testament prefiguration of salvation and the mission of the church. *Labors of the Progenitors* and *Cain and Abel Offering to God*, which flank the main portal, present a lesson to the faithful about giving the fruits of one's labors to God (and the church). Textual similarities between the inscriptions and the liturgical drama *Ordo representacionis Ade* suggest that performance and image were intended to work together to educate audiences about the roles of church and faithful in the history of salvation. Wiligelmus's Genesis frieze should thus be seen as an important early example of the development of large-scale didactic Romanesque sculptural programs.

Wiligelmus's figures are conceived as bold, massive, vital forms of great monumentality and plasticity. They convey an impressive sense of weight, as seen in the angels holding God's *mandorla* and Abel's slumping body in *Cain Killing*

Abel. Figures emerge from the relief plane and fully occupy the space that is allotted to them, even bursting into the frame of the plaque (e.g., *Enoch and Elijah*). These forms have large heads, hands, and feet; broad faces with lead–inset eyes; hair articulated by long, wavy parallel strokes; and beards punctuated with drill holes. Solemn, full of *gravitas*, these bodies express the narrative action with clear, bold gestures. Wiligelmus animates his figures with palpable human expressions (especially notable is the anguish on Cain's face as he is killed by Lamech). Most of these sculptures make prominent use of inscriptions, either identifying figures or including more extensive biblical, liturgical, or secular texts; the inscription plaque held by Enoch and Elijah is an example.

Numerous sources and models for Wiligelmus's style have been suggested, including ivory, metalwork, and manuscripts as well as early Romanesque sculpture in Aquitaine and Bari. The most direct and most apparent source of inspiration is Roman sculpture. Local, provincial Roman works clearly provided models for several of the reliefs in Modena. The *genii* with overturned torches and the arrangement of the prophets Enoch and Elijah on the inscription plaque are clearly derived from Roman sarcophagi. Wiligelmus's access to these sources can be explained by *Relation translationis carports sancti Geminiani* (*Account of the Translation of the Body of Saint Geminianus*), which mentions the miraculous discovery of a quarry of building materials, presumably the necropolis or other parts of the Roman city of Mutina (Modena). Wiligelmus adopted not only formal arrangements of figures from these Roman sources but also the sense of solidity and *gravitas* that distinguishes his sculptures. Furthermore, the obvious source of inspiration for the arrangement of the frieze around the central portal is the Roman triumphal arch. This suggests a certain conscious use of antique forms to connote both the venerable antiquity of Modena and the triumph of the church.

In addition to the program at Modena, Wiligelmus appears to have worked at the cathedral in Cremona before the earthquake of 1117. The four large prophets from the jamb of the portal are stylistically analogous to his work at Modena. Fragments of a frieze from the cathedral of Cremona, clearly modeled after Wiligelmus's reliefs in Modena, appear to have been executed by his workshop. Wiligelmus apparendy directed a large workshop that trained numerous sculptors who continued his work at Modena and carried his style elsewhere. The two lateral portals at Modena—Porta della Pescheria (north, by the Master of the Artù) and Porta dei Principi (south, by the Master of San Geminiano)—are products of the school of Wiligelmus. These two portals follow Wiligelmus's basic scheme from the west portal, but with smaller, less massive, though more lively figures. The Porta dei Principi is the earliest example of the northern Italian form of a two-story porch-portal supported by lions or *atlantes* bearing columns. That this form developed in the context of Wiligelmus's workshop further indicates his seminal role in the development of northern Italian Romanesque sculpture.

Additional sculpture by the workshop of Wiligelmus can be found at the Benedictine abbey of Nonantola, the cathedral of Piacenza, the Pieve di Quarantoli, and the Cluniac abbey of San Benedetto Polirole. The most noteworthy pupil of Wiligelmus is Master Nicholaus.

Further Reading

Crichton, George Henderson. *Romanesque Sculpture in Italy.* London: Routledge and Kegan Paul, 1954.

Francovich, Geza de. "Wiligelmo da Modena e gli inizii della scultura romanica in Francia e in Spagna." *Rivista dell'Istituto Nazionale di Archeologia e Storia dett'Arte,* 7, 1940, pp. 225–294.

Frugoni, Chiara. *Wiligelmo: Le sculture del duomo di Modena.* Modena: F. C. Panini, 1996.

Gandolfo, Francesco. "Note per una interpretazione iconologica delle storie del Genesi di Wiligelmo." In *Romanico padano, romanico europeo*, ed. Arturo Carlo Quintavalle. Parma: Artegrafica Silva, 1982, pp. 323–337.

Lanfranco e Wiligelmo: Il duomo di Modena (Quando le cattedrali erano bianche), 3 vols., ed. E, Castelnuovo, V. Fumigalli, A. Peroni, and A. Settis. Modena: Panini, 1984.

Porter, Arthur Kingsley. *Romanesque Sculpture of the Pilgrimage Roads*, 10 vols. Boston: Marshall Jones, 1923. (Reissue, New York, 1966.)

Quintavalle, Arturo Carlo. *La cattedrale di Modena: Problemi di romanico emiliano*, 2 vols. Modena: Editrice Bassi, 1964–1965.

——. *Da Wiligelmo a Nicola*. Parma, 1966.

——, ed. *Wiligelmo e la sua scuola*. Florence: Sadea-Sansoni, 1967.

——. *Romanico padano, civiltà d'occidente*. Florence: Marchi e Bertolli, 1969.

——. "Piacenza Cathedral, Lanfranco, and the School of Wiligelmo." *Art Bulletin*, 55, 1973, pp. 40–57.

——. *Wiligelmo e Matilda: L'officina romanica*. Milan: Electa, 1991. Salvini, Roberto. *Wiligelmo e le origini della scultura romanica*. Milan: Aldo Martello, 1956.

——. *La scultura romanica in Europa*. Milan: Garzanti, 1963.

——. *Il duomo di Modena e il romanico nel modenese*. Modena: Cassa di Risparmio di Modena, 1966.

Wiligelmo e Lanfranco nell'Europa romanica. Atti del Convegno, Modena, 24–27 ottobre 1985. Modena: Panini, 1989.

SCOTT B. MONTGOMERY

WILLEM OF HILDEGAERSBERCH (ca. 1350–1408/1409)

The most important author and performer of *sproken* (short verse narratives) in Middle Dutch literature, Willem was born around 1350 in Hillegersberg, near Rotterdam (county of Holland). He died between June 1408 and April 1409. He was not of noble heritage and seems to have received a rather restricted education. We can probably take seriously the verses in which he states that he is ashamed of his lack of knowledge of Latin. Willem was an itinerant poet, performing at aristocratic courts, in abbeys, and in towns. He maintained a close relationship with the court in The Hague, judging by his frequent appearances in the writings about the counts of Holland. Between 1383 and 1403, Willem is mentioned no fewer than thirty-two times.

Much of Willem's oeuvre survives; 120 *sproken* can be attributed to him. His name is mentioned in forty of them. Two manuscripts contain almost all known *sproken* written by him: The Hague, Koninklijke Bibliotheek (manuscript no. 128 E 6) and Brussels, Koninklijke Bibliotheek (manuscript no. 15.659–661), preserving 117 and 119 *sproken*, respectively. Fragments and *sproken* in other miscellanies prove that Willem of Hildegaersberch was very esteemed in his days.

The *sproke*, a short poetic genre, was performed from the fourteenth century onward by itinerant artists in the Middle Dutch area. It has an average length of 180 to 200 verses, but shorter as well as longer *sproken* are found. The *sproke* can be mainly narrative as well as demonstrative, mostly with no lyrical tenor. It generally implicitly or explicitly moralizes or serves a didactic purpose. Moral truth and Christian or worldly ethics are often stressed. The genre of the *sproke* is very close to the exemplum, the parable, and the sermon. Willem mostly writes rhyming couplets, but he sometimes switches to a strophic form.

Willem's poems treat a large diversity of themes. He speaks about religious subjects, such as Christian virtues or the Easter gospel. On the other hand, he does not hesitate to criticize the clergy. An important part of Willem's oeuvre was meant to be recited at court, and these texts are consequently directly addressed to the lords. Here he is concerned with worldly virtues like honor and justice, especially complaining about their decline. He considers it to be his duty to advise the lords in matters of government and to confront them with the truth. His criticism concerns especially the rogues who surround the lords and deceive them. Willem of Hildegaersberch was conscious that he depended to a very large extent on the favor of the lords. This is why he sometimes felt obliged to soften the truth. In those cases he formulated his criticism in an indirect way. Thus, no one had to feel offended, and the person in question always had the possibility to say the criticism did not apply to him or her. The way to make his criticism indirect is fiction. Willem uses dissociating elements: he wraps his criticism in exempla, allegories, or (animal) fables, for example.

Further Reading

Bisschop, Willem, and Eelco Verwijs, eds. *Gedichten van Willem van Hildegaersberch.* The Hague: Nijhoff, 1870.

Hogenelst, Dini. *Sproken en sprekers. Inleiding op en repertorium van de Middelnederlandse sproke.* 2 vols. Amsterdam: Prometheus, 1997.

Meder, Theo. *Sprookspreker in Holland. Leven en werk van Willem van Hildegaersberch (circa 1400).* Amsterdam: Prometheus, 1991 [German summary].

van Oostrom, Frits P. *Court and Culture: Dutch Literature, 1350–1450.* Berkeley: University of California Press, 1992.

AN FAEMS

WILLIAM DURANDUS (c. 1230 or 1231–1 November 1296) William Durandus (Guillelmus Duranti, Guillaume Durand) is called the Elder to distinguish him from a nephew with the same name. The elder "William Durandus was born in Puimisson, near Béziers in Provence. We know practically nothing about his family or early life before his ordination as subdeacon in the cathedral of Narbonne c. 1254 and his enrollment in the list of canons at the cathedral of Maguelonne at about the same time. Not long after taking clerical orders, William began formal legal studies at the University of Bologna;

he earned a doctorate in canon law there c. 1263. He may have lectured at the university before he became a papal chaplain and "general auditor" under Pope Urban IV (r. 1261–1264). Early in his long and increasingly difficult career in the service of the papal curia, William befriended the best-known canonist in Europe, Cardinal Henricus de Segusia (Henry of Susa), known as Hostiensis.

Under Pope Clement IV (1265–1268), William continued his service as papal chaplain and auditor. He also finished the first edition of his first publication, *Aureum repertorium* (c. 1264–1270), a short index and commentary on Gratian's *Decretum* (c. 1140) and on Pope Gregory IX's *Liber extra* (1234). *Aureum repertorium* was soon followed by William's massive and—during the medieval period—definitive textbook on procedural law, *Speculum Iudiciale* (c. 1271–1276). The enduring fame of this work earned William the nickname Speculator, by which he was commonly known during and after his lifetime.

In the summer of 1274, William attended the Second Council of Lyon and held the official title of *peritus* (theologian) for Pope Gregory X (1271–1276). William later assisted in the post-conciliar editing of the canons of the council, and some twenty years afterward he published the final version of *In sacrosanctum Lugdunese concilium commentarius* (c. 1293–1294), his long commentary on the council's decrees.

By 1279, William was ordained a priest and was made dean of the cathedral of Chartres by Pope Nicholas III (r. 1277–1280). In 1280, Nicholas appointed him *rector et capitaneus generalis* of a portion of the papal states (including a part of Tuscany and the diocese of Rieti). In 1281, the new pope, Martin IV (r. 1281–1285), added to William's official duties rule of the turbulent Romagna. From 1282 to 1286, William coordinated the war efforts of the papacy in the Romagna, leading the pro-papal Guelfs to a precarious interim victory over the Ghibellines.

In 1285, William submitted his resignation from the papal service to Pope Honorius IV (r. 1285–1287). Within a month, William was elected bishop of Mende in his native Provence by the cathedral chapter. He was consecrated bishop by the archbishop of Ravenna in 1286 but (inexplicably) remained in Rome for another five years before taking up residence in Mende in July 1291.

William's prolific literary production during his episcopacy demonstrates his conscientious application of his learning to pastoral care (not to mention his capability as an encyclopedic polymath). The works he published in this period include the following: *Constitutiones synodales* (c. 1292), a collection of statutes and instructions for the reform of the clergy of his diocese; *Ordinarium* (c. 1291–1293), a book regulating the liturgical services of the cathedral of Mende; his commentary on the Second Council of Lyon; *Rationale divinorum officiorum* (c. 1291–1296), a long allegorical commentary on the entire liturgy (including the mass, divine office, and church year); and *Pontificale* (*Bishop's Book, c.* 1293–1295), which provided rubrics and prayers for liturgical services performed only by a bishop. Modern scholarship has revealed that William's *Rationale* and *Pontificale* were two of the most important liturgical texts of the entire medieval period in Europe.

William had been a resident bishop for only four years when he succumbed to the persistent entreaties of his friend Benedict Gaetani, now Pope Boniface VIII (r. 1294–1303), to return to Rome and assume official duties in the papal states. In September 1295, William was appointed rector of the Anconian March and the Romagna, territories that were in a state of near-anarchy since the Ghibelline faction had mobilized itself for war with the Guelfs. William's command of the papacy's war effort failed, however, when he lost the city of Imola to the Ghibellines

and presided over the defeat of a pro-papal Bolognese army in April 1296. By the end of the summer of 1296, William, who was by then in his sixties, seems to have had little if any official responsibility in the papal states. He continued to reside in Rome, where he died.

William Durandus the Elder was buried in the church of Santa Maria Sopra Minerva. A thirty-line epitaph praising his life and works was inscribed there in marble, possibly at the request of his nephew William Durandus the Younger, who succeeded him as bishop of Mende.

There are numerous incunabula and early printed editions of *Aureum repertorium super toto corpore iuris canonici,* but as of the present writing there was no modern edition. *Speculum iudiciale* survives in more than 100 medieval manuscripts; there are numerous incunabula and early printed editions but (again as of this writing) no modern edition. A manuscript (possibly written or corrected by Durandus himself) of *Constitutiones synodales* was published in a diplomatic edition (Berthelé and Valmary 1905). The only known printed edition of *In sacrosanctum Lugdunese concilium commentarius* is that of 1569. The *Pontificale* was published in the magisterial edition of Andrieu (1940). The *Rationale divinorum offciorum* survives in hundreds of medieval Latin manuscripts, as well as numerous medieval vernacular translations; the first modern critical edition is Davril and Thibodeau (1995, 1998). Although a complete modern biography of Durandus has yet to be written, the bibliography of secondary sources is voluminous; selected references are listed below.

Further Reading

Primary Sources

Andrieu, Michel, ed. *Le pontifical romain au Moyen-Âge,* Vol. 3, *Le pontifical de Guillaume Durand.* Studi e Testi, 88. Vatican City: Biblioteca Apostolica Vaticana, 1940.

Aureum repertorium super toto corpore iuris canonici. Venice: Paganinus de Paganinis, 1496–1497.

Berthelé, J., and M. Valmary, eds. "Les instructions et constitutions de Guillaume Durand le Spéculateur," *Académie des Sciences et Lettres de Montpellier: Mémoires de la Section des Lettres*, Series 2(3), 1905, pp. 1–148.

Davril, Anselme, and T. M. Thibodeau, eds. *Guillelmi Duranti Rationale divinorum officiorum I–IV, V–VI.* Corpus Christianorum, Continuatio Medieaevalis, 140 and 140A. Turnhout: Brepols, 1995; 1998.

In sacrosanctum Lugdunese concilium commentarius sub Gregorio X Guilelmi Duranti cognomento Speculatoris commentarius, ed. Simone Maiolo. Fano: Iacobus Moscardus, 1569.

Speculum iudiciale, illustratum, et repurgatum a Giovanni Andrea et Baldo degli Ubaldi. Basel: Froben, 1574. (4 parts in 2 vols.; the best-known and most widely available text. Reprint, Darmstadt: Aalen, 1975.)

Secondary Sources

Baimelle, Marius. *Bibliographie du Gévaudan*, n.s., fasc. 3. Mende: n.p., 1966. (Pamphlet. Good though dated bibliography for the life and works of Durandus and his nephew.)

Boyle, Leonard. "The Date of the Commentary of William Duranti the Elder on the Constitutions of the Second Council of Lyons." *Bulletin of Medieval Canon Law*, n.s., 4, 1974, pp. 39–47.

Douteil, Herbert. *Studien zu Durantis "Rationale divinorum officiorum" als kirchenmusicalischer Quelle.* Kölner Beiträge zur Musikforschung, 52. Regensburg, 1969.

Dykmans, Marc. "Notes autobiographiques de Guillaume Durand le Spéculateur." In *Ius populi Dei: Miscellanea in honorem Raymundi Bidagor.* Rome, 1972, pp. 121–142.

Faletti, Louis. "Guillaume Durand." *Dictionnaire de droit canonique*, 5, 1953, pp. 1014–1075.

Gy, Pierre-Marie, ed. *Guillaume Durand, évêque de Mende (v. 1230–1296): Canoniste, liturgiste, et homme politique— Actes de la Table Ronde du CNRS Mende 24–27 mai 1990.* Paris: Centre National de la Recherche Scientifique, 1992. (Collection of papers; at the time of its publication it represented the most up-to-date research on Durandus.)

Leclerq, Victor. "Guillaume Duranti, évêque de Mende, surnommé le Spéculateur." In *Histoire Littéraire de la France*, Vol. 20. Paris: Librairies Universitaires, 1895, pp. 411–480.

Ménard, Clarence C. "William Durand's *Rationale divinorum officiorum*: Preliminaries to a New Critical Edition." Dissertation, Gregorian University (Rome), 1967. (Groundbreaking work that was the basis for a recently published edition of the *Rationale*.)

Thibodeau, Timothy M. "*Enigmata figurarum*: Biblical Exegesis and Liturgical Exposition in Durand's *Rationale*". *Harvard Theological Review*, 86, 1993, pp. 65–79.

TIMOTHY M. THIBODEAU

WILLIAM I (1027/28–1087; r. 1066–87) First Norman king of England; known as "the Conqueror." Born in 1027 or 1028 at Falaise in Normandy, William was the only, but illegitimate, son of Duke Robert of Normandy. His mother, Herleva, was the daughter of a tanner or, more probably, an undertaker of Falaise. Subsequently Robert married her off to a minor noble from the Seine Valley, Herluin de Conteville, by whom she had two further sons, Odo, later bishop of Bayeux (from 1050), and Robert, subsequently (from ca. 1060) count of Mortain.

William became duke of Normandy at the age of seven, when his father died in July 1035 while returning from a pilgrimage to Jerusalem. That he became duke at all, given his age and illegitimacy, was probably due to the lack of other candidates. Though Robert had taken the precaution to have him formally designated duke before departing for the Holy Land, William's rule in Normandy was to face serious challenges for more than twenty years. Law and order collapsed in the duchy during his minority, ducal power and property were usurped by contending nobles, and several members of his court, including some cousins, were murdered in factional disputes. This disorder culminated in a serious rebellion in western Normandy in 1047, led by Count Guy of Brienne, suppressed only with the help of the French king Henry I, who assisted William in defeating the rebels at the Battle of Val-es-Dunes near Caen.

In the years immediately after this success the domestic situation in Normandy was stable enough for William to start aggressive operations on his southern border, capturing the frontier fortresses of Domfront and Alençon in 1051/52. This in turn brought him into conflict with the overlord of Maine, Count Geoffrey Martel of Anjou, and with his erstwhile ally King Henry, and was also followed by renewed revolt in Normandy by a hitherto loyal supporter, his uncle Count William of Arques. The Duke's position was saved by his own military prowess and activity, and smashing defeats were inflicted on French armies at Mortemer in 1054 and Varaville in 1057. The latter marked the end of the young duke's struggle for survival.

From 1062 onward William's chief concern seems to have been the acquisition of the county of Maine, after the death of the childless Count Herbert II. He was aided in this by the fact that the new king of France, Philip I, was a minor, while Anjou was weakened by a succession struggle between the sons of Geoffrey Martel. By 1065 William had placed a garrison in Le Mans, installed a Norman bishop, secured the fealty of the leading nobles of the county, and had his eldest son, Robert, recognized as count. But his hold over Maine was never fully consolidated and was to remain a problem for the rest of his life.

In 1051 the childless king of England, Edward the Confessor, had designated William, his cousin, as his successor. One source suggests that the duke visited England in 1051. This seems unlikely, given how difficult his position was in Normandy at that time; probably Archbishop Robert of Canterbury (a Norman) had acted as intermediary while on his way to Rome in that summer. Whether Edward persisted in his intention of having William as his heir also seems doubtful; he may have changed his mind several times. William's chance of securing the succession was much enhanced when his potential rival, Harold of Wessex, Edward's brother-in-law, visited Normandy in 1064 or 1065 and was persuaded or forced to swear fealty to the duke and to support his claim. Many details remain obscure; we cannot be certain why Harold went to Normandy, whether Edward sent him or not, or even the date of his visit.

Nor did it have any immediate effect on the English succession. When Edward died on 5 January 1066 Harold succeeded him. The designation of 1051 and Harold's oath had given William a *casus belli*, and he used them to orchestrate a propaganda campaign to secure recruits from all over France and to gain papal support. The invasion was launched, after some delays, at the end of September 1066, and on 14 October the Norman and English armies met a few miles north of Hastings. After a desperate struggle the English were defeated and Harold killed. Within two months the surviving English magnates and the church leaders had surrendered, and William was crowned king of England in Westminster Abbey on Christmas Day 1066.

This merely marked the start of the conquest of England. To begin with William sought to emphasize the continuity of his rule with that of Edward, and to use Englishmen in his government. His first earl of Northumbria, Copsi, was an Englishman, and even Archbishop Stigand of Canterbury, whose appointment had been canonically dubious and who was regarded with disapproval by the papacy, was retained until 1070. But widespread rebellion, in the west and north in 1068, and more seriously in the north and in the fen country of East Anglia in 1069 and 1070¾the latter with Danish support—led to a major change in policy and the widespread replacement of English landowners by Frenchmen. The king was under obvious pressure to satisfy what Orderic Vitalis called "his envious and greedy Norman followers." So serious was the revolt of 1069 that William resorted to the harshest of measures to quell it, devastating much of Yorkshire to prevent further rebellion and thereby condemning many of the inhabitants to death by starvation. Inured as they were to violence, contemporary chroniclers were shocked by the barbarity of his actions.

But this drastic treatment worked. The last bastion of English resistance, the Isle of Ely, surrendered in 1071. Thereafter William's rule in England was not seriously threatened. There was admittedly another rebellion in 1075, led by the Norman earl Roger of Hereford and the Breton earl Ralph of Norfolk, but this was crushed by William's subordinates, under the direction of Archbishop Lanfranc, while the king remained in Normandy. Indeed, in his later years, William was largely an absentee ruler, not visiting the country at all between 1076 and 1080 and spending eleven of his last fifteen years in Normandy. In his absence England was ruled largely by his half-brother Odo of Bayeux (until his disgrace and imprisonment in 1082) and Lanfranc. Queen Matilda played a similarly crucial role in Normandy until her death in 1083.

After 1070 renewed problems on the Norman frontiers helped to keep William in the duchy. The king suffered the only serious military setback of his life at Dol on the Breton border in September 1076. Relations with the king of France, Philip, deteriorated. Maine became restive under Norman rule. And worst of all, the king's son Robert Curthose rebelled, probably in the spring of 1078. There was an indecisive battle at Gerberoi in eastern Normandy in January 1079, in which William was slightly wounded. Although there was a temporary reconciliation early in 1080, relations remained difficult

and Robert went into exile again in 1084. The root of the problem seems to have been Robert's wish to have an independent role in Normandy, of which he had been designated as duke before Hastings, and William's determination to keep his son firmly under supervision.

William's last visit to England came in 1085–86, to organize the defense of the kingdom against a threatened Danish invasion. But the most important result of this visit was the Domesday Book. Its purpose has been much debated. Probably it was a guide to both the resources of the country and the ownership of particular estates, made necessary by the large-scale redistribution of land caused by the Conquest.

The first draft of the Domesday survey was probably nearly completed when William held a court at Salisbury in August 1086, where he exacted a comprehensive oath of loyalty from his magnates and the more important of their undertenants. Eleven months later, when campaigning at Mantes on the Norman border, he was taken seriously ill. He was carried to Rouen, where he died on 9 September 1087. On his deathbed he agreed to Robert's succession as duke of Normandy, his second surviving son, William Rufus, succeeding as king of England. He was buried at the monastery of St. Étienne at Caen, which he himself had founded a quarter of a century earlier.

Much of William's success came from a partnership with a small group of Norman nobles, such men as William Fitz Osbern, Roger de Montgomery, and his own half-brothers. It was not surprising that this group of seven or eight men were the chief beneficiaries of the Conquest. In ecclesiastical matters his chief adviser was Lanfranc, abbot of St. Étienne at Caen in 1063 and archbishop of Canterbury in 1070. Though favoring the moral reform of the clergy, William was always concerned to vindicate his own control of the church and to limit papal interference. He was not above appointing his half-brother

Odo as bishop when the latter was well below the canonical age. After 1066 he was generally content to adopt existing English laws and institutions but to exploit them to the full; contemporaries agreed that his government was harsh and predatory. The Anglo-Saxon Chronicle called him "stern beyond all measure to people who resisted his will."

William was tall, strong, and of harsh voice and imposing appearance, tending to corpulence in later life. He married ca. 1050 Matilda, daughter of Baldwin V of Flanders, by whom he had four sons (one of whom, Richard, died young) and four or perhaps five daughters.

See also **Edward the Confessor; Harold Godwinson; Lanfranc of Bec**

Further Reading

Primary Sources

Chibnall, Marjorie, ed. and trans. *The Ecclesiastical History of Orderic Vitalis.* 6 vols. Oxford: Clarendon, 1969–80.

Foreville, Raymonde, ed. and trans, (into French). *Histoire de Guillaume le Conquérant.* Paris: Les Belles Lettres, 1952 [the chronicle of William of Poitiers].

van Houts, Elisabeth M.C., ed, and trans. *The Gesta Normannorum Ducum of William of Jumièges, Orderic Vitalis and Robert of Torigni.* 2 vols. Oxford: Oxford University Press, 1992–95.

Wilson, David M., ed. *The Bayeux Tapestry: The Complete Tapestry in Colour.* London: Thames & Hudson; New York: Knopf, 1985 [fascinating illustrated account of the campaign of 1066].

Secondary Sources

Barlow, Frank. *Edward the Confessor.* Berkeley: University of California Press, 1970.

Bates, David. *Normandy before 1066.* London: Longman, 1982

Bates, David. *William the Conqueror.* London: Philip, 1989 [excellent bibliography].

Douglas, David C. *William the Conqueror.* London: Eyre & Spottiswoode, 1964.

John, Eric. "Edward the Confessor and the Norman Succession." *EHR*94 (1979): 241–67.

Le Patourel, John. *The Norman Empire.* Oxford: Clarendon, 1976.

Loyn, H.R. *The Norman Conquest.* 3d ed. London.

Hutchinson, 1982 [the best of several general books].

van Houts, Elisabeth M.C. "The Origins of Herleva, Mother of William the Conqueror." *EHR*101 (1986): 399–404.

GRAHAM A. LOUD

WILLIAM OF AUVERGNE (William of Paris; 1180/90–1249)

Born in Aurillac in the Auvergne, William was canon of Notre-Dame in Paris by 1223, regent master at Paris in 1225, and bishop of Paris in 1228. A secular master himself, William was, however, an early champion of the mendicant orders, allowing Roland of Cremona to hold the first Dominican chair in theology (1229). Known for his fairness and good sense, he was confessor to Blanche of Castile and friend and adviser to Louis IX.

William left a vast corpus of works in encyclopedic style, including a series of tracts sometimes called his *Magisterium divinale* (1123–40), which included *De universo. Cur Deus homo, De fide et legibus,* and *De Trinitate.* His *De vitiis et virtutibus* rivaled that of William Peraldus (the two men were often confused) in popularity. One of the first theorists of Purgatory, he was also among the first theological users of Aristotle in Paris, and he sought out texts of Avicenna, Maimonides's *Guide,* Avicebrol, and others in the service of orthodox belief.

See also **Blanche of Castile; Louis IX**

Further Reading

William of Auvergne. *Opera omnia.* 2 vols. Paris: Andraeas Pralard, 1674; repr. Frankfurt am Main: Minerva, 1963.

——. *De Trinitate,* ed. Bruno Switalski. Toronto: Pontifical Institute of Mediaeval Studies, 1976.

——. *The Immortality of the Soul = De immortalitate animae,* trans. Roland J. Teske.

Milwaukee: Marquette University Press, 1991.

——. *The Trinity, or, The First Principle = De Trinitate, seu De primo principio*, trans. Roland j. Teske and Francis C. Wade. Milwaukee: Marquette University Press, 1989.

Bernstein, A.E. "Esoteric Theology: William of Auvergne on the Fires of Hell and Purgatory." *Speculum* 57 (1982): 509–31.

Marrone, Steven P. *William of Auvergne and Robert Grosseteste: New Ideas of Truth in the Early 13th Century*. Princeton: Princeton University Press, 1983.

Quentin, Albrecht. *Naturkenntnisse und Naturanschauungen bei Wilhelm von Auvergne*. Hildesheim: Gerstenberg, 1976.

Rohls, Jan. *Wilhelm von Auvergne und der mittelalterliche Aristotelismus: Gottesbegriff und aristotelische Philosophie zwischen Augustin und Thomas von Aquin*. Munich: Kaiser, 1980.

Valois, Noel. *Guillaume d'Auvergne, évêque de Paris (1228–1249), sa vie et ses ouvrages*. Paris: Picard, 1880.

LESLEY J. SMITH

WILLIAM OF CONCHES (ca. 1085–ca. 1154)

Named by John of Salisbury as one of his teachers, William is most often associated with the so-called School of Chartres, as a student of Bernard of Chartres and a master there, although Richard W. Southern has called into question whether William actually taught at Chartres, as opposed to Paris. John of Salisbury calls William a grammarian, and much of William's extant work is in the form of glosses on authoritative texts widely used in the schools. He glossed Boethius's *De consolatione Philosophiae*, Macrobius's *In somnium Scipionis*, Plato's *Timaeus*, Priscian's *Institutiones grammaticae*, and Juvenal. He may be the author of *Moralium dogma philosophorum*. His gloss on *De consolatione* identified the World Soul with the Holy Spirit, although the gloss on the *Timaeus* presents the World Soul as a concept with many hidden meanings. William's glosses on Macrobius and the *Timaeus* analyze the nature of *fabula*

and *integumentum* as these apply to the "cloaking" of philosophical and theological truth in words and images in literary texts and imaginative narratives. William's interest in physics and cosmology is revealed in his *Philosophia mundi* (entitled *Dragmaticon* in a later revision), a systematic treatment of physical, cosmological, geographical, and meteorological phenomena and questions, summing up scientific knowledge in the era before the translation of Aristotle's scientific works. He sought to discern the true workings of nature and shunned "miraculous" explanations, even for biblical events, when a more straightforward explanation might be found. William made use of translations-adaptations of medical works from the Arabic, such as Constantine the African's *Pantegni*.

See also **John of Salisbury; Macrobius; Martianus Capella**

Further Reading

William of Conches. *Glosae in luvenalem*, ed. Bradford Wilson. Paris: Vrin, 1980.

——. *Glosae super Platonem*, ed. Édouard Jeauneau. Paris: Vrin, 1965.

——. *Philosophia*, ed. Gregor Maurach with Heidemarie Telle. Pretoria: University of South Africa, 1980.

——. *Das Moralium dogma philosophorum des Guillaume de Conches, lateinisch, altfranzösich und mittelnieder-frankisch*, ed. John Holmberg. Uppsala: Almqvist and Wiksell, 1929.

Gregory, Tullio. *Anima mundi: la filosofia de Guglielmo di Conches e la scuola di Chartres*. Florence: Sansoni, 1955.

Häring, Nikolaus M. "Commenatry and Hermeneutics." In *Renaissance and Renewal in the Twelfth Century*, ed. Robert L. Benson and Giles Constable with Carol D. Lanham. Cambridge: Harvard University Press, 1982, pp. 173–200.

Jeauneau, Édouard. "Deux rédactions des gloses de Guillaume de Conches sur Priscien." *Recherches de théologie ancienne et médiévale* 27 (1960): 212–47.

——. "*Lectio philosophorum*": recherches sur l'École de Chartres. Amsterdam: Hakkert, 1973.

Parent, Joseph-Marie. *La doctrine de la création dans l'École de Chartres: études et textes.* Paris: Vrin, 1938.

Southern, Richard W. *Platonism, Scholastic Method, and the School of Chartres.* Reading: University of Reading, 1979.

Wetherbee, Winthrop. *Platonism and Poetry in the Twelfth Century: The Literary Influence of the School of Chartres.* Princeton: Princeton University Press, 1972.

GROVER A. ZINN

WILLIAM OF OCKHAM (ca. 1285–1347)

Philosopher and Franciscan theologian. William studied in London and Oxford. His writings include commentaries on the *Sentences* of Peter Lombard and lectures on Aristotle's logic and physics and reflect the influence of his fellow Franciscan John Duns Scotus (d. 1308).

Ockham was an outstanding dialectician and theologian, but his outspoken views were not without controversy. Although summoned in 1324 to the papal court at Avignon to justify his teaching on transubstantiation, there was no formal condemnation of his doctrines. His study of the papal constitutions on apostolic poverty led to his involvement in the debate over Franciscan poverty and the attack on John XXII (1316–34) as a heretic. Under the protection of Emperor Louis IV of Bavaria, the political opponent of the pope, Ockham wrote several political works, including the *Dialogue*, where he discussed his views on the errors of the papacy and its rights with respect to the Holy Roman Empire.

Ockham's doctrines marked a turning point in the history of philosophy and theology. He held that logic was separate from theology, that they are both true, and that they represent different kinds of truth. Thus theology cannot be proved by logic. This *via moderna* ("modern way") marked the separation between faith and reason and was a hallmark of late-medieval philosophy.

Ockham is usually associated with the rule of "Ockhams razor." Known also as the law of parsimony or economy, the dictum became a foundation stone of scientific method: the simpler a theory or explanation is, the less chance for error.

Ockham died 10 April 1347 in Munich and was buried in the Franciscan church. His nominalist philosophy, which emphasized the fundamental reality of individually existing things, and his political theory on the limitation of papal power, were to be highly influential in Reformation thought.

See also **Duns Scotus, John**

Further Reading

Courtenay, William J. "Nominalism and Late Medieval Thought: A Bibliographical Essay." *Theological Studies* 33 (1972): 716–34

Courtenay, William J. "Late Medieval Nominalism Revisited: 1972–1982." *Journal of the History of Ideas* 44 (1983): 159–64

Leff, Gordon. *William of Ockham: The Metamorphosis of Scholastic Discourse.* Manchester: Manchester University Press, 1975

William of Ockham. *Philosophical Writings: A Selection.* Ed. and trans. Philotheus Bohner. Edinburgh: Nelson, 1957.

PHYLLIS B. ROBERTS

WILLIAM OF SAINT-AMOUR (ca. 1200–1272)

William is now chiefly remembered for his ferocious campaign against the mendicant orders. We know nothing of his life until he became master of arts in Paris (by 1228). By November 1238, he had received the doctorate in canon law and was also canon of Beauvais and rector of Guerville. He went on to study theology in Paris and ca. 1250 was a regent master.

From about this time, William began his attacks on the mendicant way of life, and it was through his influence that the Dominicans were suspended from teaching in 1254 for having in effect broken the closed shop of masters by ignoring the suspension of classes in the previous year and continuing to teach.

William never substantially amended his views on the mendicants, and his subsequent fate depended on who was pope at the time. Innocent IV (r. 1243–54) was sympathetic, and he flourished. Alexander IV (r. 1254–61) was cardinal protector of the Franciscans, and William was deprived of his privileges and expelled from France. Clement IV, although disagreeing, allowed him to return to Saint-Amour, where he died. His most famous polemical work is *De periculis novissimorum temporum* (1256).

Further Reading

Douie, Decima L. *The Conflict Between the Seculars and the Mendicants at the University of Paris in the Thirteenth Century*. London: Blackfriars, 1954.

Dufeil, M.M. *Guillaume de Saint-Amour et la polémique universitaire parisienne, 1250–1259*. Paris: Picard, 1972.

LESLEY J. SMITH

WILLIAM OF SAINT-THIERRY

(1070/90–1148) Born in Liège, William of Saint-Thierry studied at the schools of Reims and perhaps at Laon under Anselm of Laon, where he may have met Peter Abélard. For unknown reasons, he renounced his studies and in 1113 became a monk in the Benedictine monastery of Saint-Nicasius in Reims. In 1118, he became abbot of Saint-Thierry, near Reims. As a close friend and admirer of Bernard of Clairvaux, he wished to change orders and become a Cistercian. However, Bernard dissuaded him until 1135, when William became a monk in the newly founded Cistercian monastery of Signy, where he died in 1148.

On several occasions, William encouraged Bernard's literary activities. Bernard's early work, the *Apologia*, a fierce attack on the traditional Benedictine monastic lifestyle, was written at William's request and dedicated to him. About 1138, William, shocked by the theological audacity of Abélard, persuaded Bernard to oppose him, adding to his request a list of Abélard's errors, published as the *Disputatio adversus Abaelardum*. Bernard's intervention resulted in Abélard's condemnation at the Council of Sens in 1141. William was also instrumental in bringing about Bernard's famous series of sermons on the Song of Songs. When both were ill, they spent some time together in the infirmary of Clairvaux, talking about the *Canticle*. William also intended to write a life of Bernard but completed only the first book, the so-called *Sancti Bernardi vita prima*.

William published many works on devotional and exegetical themes, among which are the *Expositio in epistolam ad Romanos* (in reaction to Abélard's commentary on Paul's Epistle to the Romans), the *Expositio super Cantica canticorum* (a commentary on the Song of Songs), as well as two compilations on the Song of Songs from the works of Ambrose and Gregory the Great and a treatise on the relation between body and soul (*De natura corporis et animae*). Author of *De natura et dignitate amoris* and *De contemplando Deo*, William is also considered to be the author of the famous *Epistola ad fratres de Monte Dei*, about the solitary and contemplative life.

For William, the act of faith is part of and subsumed under mystical knowledge and contemplation. Faith is a pretaste of the vision of the divine. Reason helps faith in the process of understanding itself, raising it to the level of full mystical knowledge characterized by love. William supports his reflections on mystical knowledge with quotations from many sources, mainly patristic, while also frequently referring to profane, classical authors. He, like the "monastic theology" he helped to create, can thus be seen as part of the so-called 12th-century renaissance.

See also **Abélard, Peter; Anselm of Laon; Bernard of Clairvaux**

Further Reading

William of Saint-Thierry. *Opera.* PL 180, 184, 185.

——. *On Contemplating God,* trans. Sister Penelope. Kalamazoo: Cistercian, 1977.

——. *The Nature and Dignity of Love,* trans. Thomas X. Davis. Kalamazoo: Cistercian, 1981.

——. *On Contemplating God; Prayer, Meditations,* trans. Sister Penelope. Kalamazoo: Cistercian, 1971.

——. *On the Nature of the Body and the Soul,* trans. B. Clark. In *Three Treatises on Man: A Cistercian Anthropology,* ed. Bernard McGinn. Kalamazoo: Cistercian, 1977.

——. *Exposé sur le Cantique des cantiques,* ed. jean M. Déchanet, trans. Pierre Dumontier. Paris: Cerf, 1962.

——. *The Mirror of Faith,* trans. Thomas X. Davis. Kalamazoo: Cistercian, 1979.

——. *Lettre aux frères de Mont-Dieu (Lettre d'Or),* ed. and trans. Jean M. Déchanet. Paris: Cerf, 1975

Bell, David N. *The Image and Likeness: The Augustinian Spirituality of William of Saint-Thierry.* Kalamazoo: Cistercian, 1984.

Déchanet, Jean M. *William of Saint-Thierry: The Man and His Work.* Spencer: Cistercian, 1972.

BURCHT PRANGER

WIRNT VON GRAFENBERG (fl. 1204–1210)

Author of the Middle High German Arthurian romance *Wigalois,* written between 1204 and 1210, Wirnt is thought to be a *ministerial* (clerical administrator) from the town of Gräfenberg north of Erlangen.

No documents associate him with any particular court at which *Wigalois* might have been written, but Berthold IV, count of Andechs and duke of Meran, is his most likely patron. References to characters from *Erec* and *Iwein* as well as the first part of *Parzival* attest to the author's familiarity with the works of his famous contemporaries Hartmann von Aue and Wolfram von Eschenbach. Although earlier treatments of the *Wigalois* story, such as Renaud de Beaujeu's *Le Bel Inconnu,* existed outside of Germany, Wirnt insists that his source was a story told by a squire. It has been suggested that the citing of an oral source served as a pretext to set his own emphasis rather than following slavishly the demands of the genre.

The *Wigalois* romance consists of 11,708 verses and is written in rhymed couplets. The story of Gawein's son, it is divided into five distinct parts: the hero's upbringing in his mother's fairy kingdom; his arrival at Arthur's court and his adventures in the Arthurian realm; his adventures in the otherworldly realm of Korntin and ultimate triumph over the prince of darkness, the heathen King Roaz of Glois; the hero's wedding and coronation; and the avenging of the murder of a wedding guest. While earlier scholarship insisted on viewing Wirnt's hero as the unproblematic knight of fortune's wheel, more recent work detects a flawed character in need of God's mercy who submits to the will of God. It is God who provides the supreme guidance through the supernatural obstacles of Korntin and grants victory. Wirnt's novelty is the Arthurian knight as God's champion in the eschatological conflict between heaven and hell. He uses the genre to send a message of apocalyptic urgency to his contemporary society, drawing obvious parallels between that society and Wigalois's antagonist. Both have lost sight of the ultimate good, and thus the story of Wigalois serves as a vehicle to reaffirm God's grace as our only hope for salvation. Wirnt's romance has enjoyed surprising popularity, judging not only by the relatively large number of extant manuscripts but also by its influence on contemporary as well as subsequent German authors writing in the latter thirteenth and fourteenth centuries. Noteworthy later adaptations of the story include a fifteenth-century chapbook, a Yiddish rendition transmitted in manuscripts from the sixteenth century, and a nursery tale dated 1786. Wirnt himself became the hero of Konrad von Würzburg's verse narrative *Der Welt Lohn*, in which he is depicted as a knight who learns to forsake the things of the world and to serve God. The story of Wigalois has also contributed valuable material to the body of Arthurian iconography, ranging from the Wigalois frescoes in Runkelstein castle near Bolzano in South Tyrol and woodcuts illustrating the chapbook version to picture cycles in two of the manuscripts. One of these, the parchment codex no. *Ltk 537* of Leyden, is considered the only significant illuminated Arthurian manuscript of the fourteenth century.

See also **Hartmann von Aue; Konrad von Würzburg; Wolfram von Eschenbach**

Further Reading

Cormeau, Christoph. *'Wigalois' und 'Diu Crone': Zwei Kapitel zur Gattungsgeschichte des nachklassischen Aventiureromans.* Zurich: Artemis, 1977.

Freeland, Beverly M. "*Wigalois A*: A Prototype Edition of Wirnt von Gravenberg's *Wigalois.*" Ph.d. diss., University of California, Los Angeles, 1993.

Henderson, Ingeborg. "Manuscript Illustrations as Generic Determinants in Wirnt von Gravenberg's *Wigalois,*" in *Genres in Medieval German Literature*, ed. Hubert Heinen and Ingeborg Henderson. Göppingen: Kümmerle, 1986.

Kapteyn, J. M. N. *Wigalois, der Ritter mit dem Rade.* Bonn: Klopp, 1926.

Thomas, J. W. *Wigalois, The Knight of Fortune's Wheel.* Lincoln: University of Nebraska Press, 1977.

INGEBORG HENDERSON

WITTENWILER, HEINRICH (ca. 1350– ca. 1450)

Author of the *Ring*, a comic-didactic verse satire of the early fifteenth century, Heinrich Wittenwiler employs chiefly High Alemannic language in the poem, with occasional Bavarianisms. As shown by his knowledge of the local dialect, which he places in the mouths of the peasants in the *Ring*, Wittenwiler probably stemmed from the Toggenburg area of Switzerland. The poem exists in only one manuscript, located in the Meiningen (Thuringia) archives.

Wittenwiler served as *advocatus curiae* at the episcopal court in Constance, where, as a high official of the bishop, he would have moved in circles favorable to the Austrian nobility and inimical to disruptive forces such as the city guilds and the Bund ob dem See (Dutch marine commerce alliance). His use of *Sachliteratur* (technical writing) shows him to have been a man of great learning and wide-ranging interests. He is mentioned in documents from the last two decades of the fourteenth century, although the composition of the *Ring* falls in the first decade of the fifteenth, probably during the episcopate of Albrecht Blarer.

Wittenwiler derived the basic structure of the *Ring* from the short force *Metzen hochzît (Metz's Wedding)*, but expanded it to almost ten thousand lines with extensive allegorical, didactic, and satirical passages. Set in the village of Lappenhausen, the first of three sections deals with Bertschi Triefnas's devotion to Mätzli Rüerenzumph, the antipode of all ideals of courtly beauty. During his wooing, Bertschi accidentally inflicts a head wound on Mätzli, who, while receiving treatment, is impregnated by the doctor Chrippenchra. To cover up his misdeed, the doctor persuades Mätzli to marry Bertschi.

In the second section, a lengthy debate on the pros and cons of marriage, as well as instruction for Bertschi in religion, manners, virtue, hygiene, and home economics, precede the wedding. At the wedding feast, the villagers display every possible form of bad manners and finally abandon themselves to wild dancing. A minor incident at the dance leads, in the third section, to an all-out war between Lappenhausen and

neighboring Nissingen. The conflict esca-
lates until it involves most of southwestern
Germany and figures from the Germanic
epics. Fro Laichdenman, the local astrologer, betrays Lappenhausen to its enemies, and the village burns to the ground.
Bertschi, the only survivor, laments his
failure to follow the wise teachings of his
mentors and moves to the Black Forest to
lead the life of a hermit.

To underscore Wittenwiler's method
of alternating didacticism with bucolic
bawling *(gpauren gschrai)*, the manuscript
differentiates by means of red or green
marginal stripes those passages that can
serve as stylistic models (red) from those
that satirize peasant mores (green). Read
as an allegorical work, the *Ring* strongly
associates peasants with images of a carnal and sinful humanity; read politically,
it expresses the disgust of an urban nobility faced with a series of peasant revolts.

Further Reading

Jones, George Fenwick, trans. *Wittenwiler's
Ring and the Anonymous Scots Poem
Colkelbie Sow.* Chapel Hill: University
of North Carolina Press, 1956; rpt. New
York: AMS, 1969.

Lutz, Eckhart Conrad. *Spiritualis Fornicatio.*
Sigmaringen: Thorbecke, 1990.

Plate, Bernward. *Heinrich Wittenwiler.*
Darmstadt: Wissenschaftliche
Buchgesellschaft, 1977.

Riha, Ortrun. *Die Forschung zu Heinrich
Wittenwilers "Ring" 1851–1988.*
Würzburg: Königshausen and Neumann,
1990.

Wießner, Edmund. *Heinrich Wittenwilers "Ring."*
Leipzig: Redam, 1931; rpt. Darmstadt:
Wissenschaftliche Buchgesellschaft, 1964.

Wittenwiler, Heinrich. *Der Ring,* ed. Rolf
Bräuer, George F. Jones, and Ulrich Müller.
Göppingen: Kümmerle, 1990 [facsimile ed.].
                                      JIM OGIER

WITZ, KONRAD (ca. 1400/1410–
1445/1446) In 1896, Daniel Burckhardt
of the Öffentlichen Kunstsammlung in

Basle published his observations on the
stylistic similarity between the panels of
an incomplete Heilsspiegel Altar (Altar of
Human Salvation) in Basle and the panels
from the St. Peter Altar in Geneva, which
are signed by Konrad Witz and dated
1444. This artist, whose distinctive style
had little influence on later German art,
had been forgotten since his death.

Konrad Witz was probably born in
Rottweil in Württemberg circa 1400–
1410; he is first documented by his entrance into the Basel painters' guild on
June 21, 1434. The Council of Basle
(1431–1437), which brought high church
officials to the city, thus increasing the
possibilities for important artistic commissions, was probably the motivation
for his move. On January 10, 1435, he
became a citizen of Basle, and he married
shortly thereafter. In 1441 and 1442 he
was paid for unknown paintings in the
Kornhaus (granary). One of the wings
of his altarpiece for the high altar of St.
Peter in Geneva is signed and dated 1444.
In 1446 he is recorded as dead, leaving
his widow and five young children.

The Heilsspiegel Altar, dated circa
1435 and partially destroyed and dismembered in the iconoclasm of 1529, was
painted for the choir of the church of St.
Leonhard in Basle. Based on the *Speculum
humanae salvationis (Mirror of Human
Salvation),* which places Old Testament
an other prefigurations next to their fulfillment in the New Testament and Last
Judgment, it is the earliest and largest altar in this tradition in the fifteenth century.
The center and predella (lower alter panel)
are lost, but seven of the eight scenes from
the inner wings survive. Five are in the
Kunstmuseum in Basle and the other two
in the Gemäldegalerie in Berlin and the
Musée des Beaux Arts in Dijon. Since they
show Old Testament or historical scenes
with two figures standing before a gold
background, the missing center must have
shown their fulfillment: an Adoration of
the Magi or a *Christus Salvator* (Christ
as Savior) are most often suggested. The

outside panels seen on the closed altar showed single figures standing in narrow rooms. Five of the original eight survive: four in Basle and one in Dijon.

The St. Peter Altarpiece (Geneva, Musée d'Art et d'Histoire) also lacks its center and predella, probably destroyed by iconoclasts in 1535, when the remaining panels were separated. Today the inner wings show the Adoration of the Magi on the left and the donor presented to the Virgin by St. Peter on the right. The left outside wing represents the Miracle of Fishes and Calling of St. Peter, and the right outside wing the Freeing of St. Peter from Prison. The landscape of the Miracle of Fishes gives an accurate view of the shores of Lake Geneva with the Savoy Alps and Mont Blanc and is considered to be the first topographical landscape portrayed in northern European art. New research considers the connection of this panel to the politics of Savoy. Other undated paintings attributed to Wirz are the Annunciation (Nuremberg, Germanisches Nationalmuseum), the Meeting at the Golden Gate (Basel, Kunstmuseum), and Saints Catherine and Mary Magdalene in a Church (Strasbourg, Musée de l'Oeuvre Notre-Dame).

The physical presence of figures and materials is more important in Witz's paintings than depiction of rich costumes or detailed settings. His tempera technique and strong, simple colors increase the immobility that characterizes his figures, and strong shadows help to define his space. The forms on the outside wings in their narrow rooms resemble those in some miniatures of the Utrecht school circa 1430.

Further Reading

Deuchler, Florens. "Konrad Witz, la Savoie et l'Italie: Nouvelles hypothèses à propos du retable de Genève." *Revue de l'art* 71 (1986): 7–16.

Gantner, Joseph. *Konrad Witz*. Vienna: A. Schroll, 1942.

Rott, Hans. *Quellen und Forschungen zur südwestdeutschen und schweizerischen Kunstgeschichte im XV. und XVI.* *Jahrhundert 3: Der Oberrhein* 2. Stuttgart: Strecker und Schröder, 1936, pp. 20–25.

Schauder, M. "Konrad Witz und die Utrechter Buchmalerei," in *Masters and Miniatures: Proceedings of the Congress on Medieval Manuscript Illumination in the Northern Netherlands (Utrecht, 10–13 December 1989)*, ed. K. van der Horst and Johann-Christian Klamt. Doornspijk: Davaco, 1991, pp. 137–147.

MARTA O. RENGER

WOLFRAM VON ESCHENBACH
(fl. first half of the 13th c.) The greatest German epic poet of the High Middle Ages, Wolfram wrote *Parzival, Willehalm, Titurel*, and nine lyric poems. Internal evidence in his works makes it likely that he composed *Parzival* between 1200 and 1210, worked on *Willehalm* after 1212, and left it unfinished sometime after 1217, possibly as late as the 1220s. Wolfram's few lyric poems, most of them amorous exchanges between two lovers ("dawn songs"), were probably completed early in his career, and the two fragments that make up *Titurel* were composed either during or after his work on *Willehalm*. Wolfram must have lived from about 1170 to the 1220s. He names himself in both *Parzival* and *Willehalm* and characteristically interjects remarks about his personal life and circumstances, so that we seem to have ample biographical information about Wolfram. Yet it is difficult to know how much of it is true or how much is only a pose.

If we take Wolfram at his word, he was a poor man, probably not a ranked administrator (*ministeralis*, ministerial), dependent on wealthy patrons for support. He must have been at the court of Landgrave Hermann of Thuringia, who, he says, provided the French source for *Willehalm*, and he claims to have been a military man with a wife and young daughter. Wolfram was probably born in the Middle Franconian town of Ober-Eschenbach, today renamed Wolframs-Eschenbach. His grave was seen there in the fifteenth century and again in the early seventeenth century, but there is no sign of it today. He was well acquainted with the works of the leading poets of his day: Heinrich von Veldeke, Hartmann von Aue, Gottfried von Straßburg, Walther von der Vogelweide, and Neidhart von Reuental. He surely knew Eilhart von Oberge's *Tristant*, the German *Alexanderlied, Rolandslied, Kaiserchronik, Nibelungenlied,* and other heroic sagas. Yet Wolfram claims not to be able to read or write (see *Parzival* strophe 115, ll. 27–30; Willehalm 2,16–22). Such remarks may well have been made in reaction to poets like Hartmann and Gottfried, who boasted of their learning and their literary abilities.

Wolfram's *Parzival*, an Arthurian romance of over 25,000 lines in rhymed couplets, is based on Chrétien de Troyes's *Perceval* (also called *Le Conte del Graal*). It is not a translation in the modern sense, rather an adaptation, expansion, and completion of Chrétien's work. There are several important differences. Chrétien's romance is unfinished. Although there are several continuations, his work stops after 9,234 lines. Wolfram provides his *Parzival* with a detailed prehistory and brings his story to a logical conclusion, while maintaining the general sequence of events found in his source. The prehistory (the first two books) deals with Parzival's father, Gahmuret, and how he eventually marries Herzeloyde, but is killed in battle. Striken by the news of Gahmuret's tragic death, Herzeloyde gives birth to Parzival and resolves to raise him in the wilderness, far from the knightly world of the court.

Wolfram takes Chrétien to task in an epilogue for not having told the story properly then goes on to say that a certain "Kyot," who told the true tale, might well be angry about that (*Parzival* 827, 1–4). Earlier Wolfram had claimed Kyot as his source on several occasions and had gone into great detail about how Kyot had found the true story of the Grail in a dis-carded Arabic manuscript in Toledo. In the manuscript there was a report about the Grail and the Grail family by a part-Jewish astronomer named Flegetanis, who had read about the Grail in the stars. Kyot, a Provençal Christian, had to learn Arabic to read the manuscript. Then he read in Latin chronicles and finally found the story of the Grail Family, which he eventually located in Anjou. All in all, an elaborate invention, especially since we have no real evidence of such a Kyot.

Another striking difference between Wolfram and his source is the nature of the Grail. In Chrétien it is a dish or bowl, in Wolfram a fantastic stone with the pseudo-Latin name of *lapsit exillis*. The angels, who had remained neutral during Lucifer's rebellion, were banished to the stone. Later, a human family became the guardians of the Grail and lived from the food and drink that the Grail miraculously provided. Anyone who has been in the presence of the Grail will not die for a week thereafter, only a virgin can carry the Grail, and inscriptions appear on the stone to name children who are called to the Grail. They grow up to become knights and ladies and are sent out to occupy thrones that lack rulers. The knights defend the Grail Castle and are forbidden to marry or to have a love relationship with a woman (Wolfram calls them "templars"). Only the Grail King may have a wife, but King Anfortas had been wounded by a poisoned spear while performing chivalric deeds in the service of a lady, and been kept alive by the power of the Grail, yet suffering excruciating pain. Nevertheless, although the Grail cannot be found by any seeker, an inscription on the Grail announced that a stranger would come and Anfortas would be healed if he asked the question without prompting during the first night. The stranger would then become Grail King.

Of course, Parzival is destined to be that stranger. He grows up ignorant of knighthood until he encounters some knights, riding through the forest.

Impressed by their armor, Parzival is intent on becoming a knight himself. His desire for knighthood stems from the paternal side of his genetic makeup, and his mother reluctantly allows him to leave. Still, she dresses him in fool's clothing in the hope that the ridicule he will surely receive will force his return. However, Parzival's handsome appearance impresses people, and he eventually reaches King Artus's court, only to be told that he should get his own armor by attacking Ither, a knight outside the court who is feuding with Artus, if he wants to become a knight.

Parzival kills Ither with his crude javelin, unaware that Ither is a blood relative, strips him of his armor, puts it on, and rides off on Ither's horse. He arrives at the castle of Gurnemanz, who gives him a short course in knightsmanship and admonitions about how to behave as a knight. Traveling on to Pelrapeire, Parzival wins the beautiful Condwiramurs by defeating her besiegers. After some rime, Parzival leaves Condwiramurs to visit his mother, but he arrives instead unwittingly at Munsalvæsche, the Grail Castle. There he is received with great honor, sees the Grail procession and the bloody lance, hears the lamenting of the people, and receives a sword from King Anfortas, who is obviously in great pain. But Parzival, mindful of Gurnemanz's advice not to ask too many questions, remains silent. The next morning the Grail company has disappeared, and Parzival leaves to try to find them. Two days later, he comes to King Artus's court, which has been eager to meet the Red Knight, as he was called by the knights he had defeated, and sent to Artus. His arrival occasions a feast at the Round Table, and Parzival is duly admitted to that select company. At this crowning moment of Parzival's knightly career, the ugly Grail messenger, Cundrie, appears and castigates him verbally for having failed to ask about An-fortas's suffering. Publically humiliated, Parzival leaves, angrily blaming God for his shame and determined to find the Grail and rectify things.

After Parzival's humiliation by Cundrie in front of Artus and his knights, that other paragon of chivalry, Gawan, is challenged to defend his honor. He then takes over center stage of the narrative with his quest for four queens and four hundred maidens held captive at Schastel Marveille. His adventures predominate from Book VII through XIV, except for Book IX, where the story returns to Parzival. Book IX is crucial for Parzival, angry as he is at God but with his thoughts on the Grail and his wife, Condwiramurs. Four and one-half years have passed since Parzival was at the Munsalvæsche and had failed to ask the question. Now, on Good Friday, he is directed to his uncle, the hermit Trevrizent, who tells him about his family and his relationship to the Grail King Anfortas. In addition, Parzival learns all about the Grail, about his motner's death, and the fact that he had killed a relative, Ither, in his effort to become a knight. Hesitatingly, Parzival admits that he was the one who had visited the Grail Castle but had not asked the question. After this confession, Trevrizent gives Parzival a new understanding of the relationship of God and humans, so that he makes his peace with God through penance. Nevertheless, he will still wander in search of the Grail Castle.

Gawan, in the meanwhile, has cleared his family name, rescued the queens from Schastel Marveille, and won the hand of Orgeluse. He has one last task to complete: single combat with Gramoflanz in the presence of his uncle, King Arms, who arrives with all his court. Before that can happen, Gawan fights with Parzival but is spared when they recognize each other. Parzival rights in place of the wounded Gawan against Gramoflanz and defeats him. King Artus then arranges a reconciliation among all the parties involved, and a joyous nuptial celebration ensues. Parzival leaves the festivities alone and encounters his heathen half-brother, Feirefiz, in combat. Just when it appears that Parzival will be defeated, Feirefiz throws aside his sword and magnanimously discloses his identity first. Now Parzival, with his new awareness of God and having been tested to the point of death, is ready to be summoned to the Grail. Cundrie appears, announces that Parzival has been called, and they leave for Munsalvæsche accompanied by Feirefiz. There Parzival asks the question, Anfortas is healed, and a short time thereafter Parzival is reunited with Condwiramurs, who arrives at the castle with their twin sons.

In Wolfram's *Parzival* we see two ideal realms, that of King Artus and that of the Grail. The knights of Artus's Round Table represent the highest secular ideal of chivalry, epitomized in the person of Gawan. The Grail knights on the other hand have a special relationship to God. They are chosen for divine purposes. Parzival belongs to both realms by virtue of his inheritance: from his father, the skill and desire to excel in knightly combat; from his mother, his genealogical relationship to the Grail family and his destiny to succeed Anfortas as King of the Grail Castle. We see in his story first his misguided striving to become an exemplary knight, then his angry confusion when he is humiliated at what should have been his moment of highest honor. Finally, he learns to adjust his sights from the goals of his own ambition and accept the purposes that God has for him. The twofold structure of the work embodied in the figures of Gawan and Parzival shows both knights succeeding in their particular tasks of freeing two groups of people. For one it is a worldly success, for the other, a transcendent, spiritual achievement.

Wolfram's other major work, *Willehalm*, is quite different from *Parzival*. Not only is it unfinished, but it is also not an Arthurian romance. Its source is the Old French *chanson de geste, La Bataille d'Aliscans*, one of the twenty-four poems in the cycle about Guillaume d'Orange and his family. This is heroic poetry that revels in combat and death, Christians against heathens, good against evil. Wolfram himself takes notice of the difference when he states: "Whatever I recounted earlier about fighting [. . .] ended in some way other than in death. *This* fighting will settle for nothing less than death and loss of joy" (*Willehlm* 10, 22–26). Yet for Wolfram, love and courtly attitudes are not lacking. *Willehalm* deals with the conflict between religions and the love that makes the religious conflict tragic. It involves immense slaughter and suffering on both the Christian *and* the heathen sides, and the religious differences and the human experience of the struggle give the work a much greater depth. Although he has transformed the material of his source perhaps to an even greater extent than in *Parzival*, Wolfram still preserves the essential sequence of events of his source as far as his story goes. One final difference: the *chanson* is written in tirades—stanzas of a varying number of ten-syllable lines, with each tirade, or *laisse*, having the same assonance. Wolfram uses the rhymed couplets of the courtly romance.

Willehalm begins in the midst of the first great battle of Aliscans. The heathen emperor Terramer had summoned huge armies and landed not far from Willehalm's fortified city of Oransche. Terramer's purpose is to force the return of his daughter Arabel to her husband, Tybalt, and to the religion of her people. Arabel, now called Gyburg after her baptism, had fallen in love with Willehalm when he was a prisoner in heathendom. She had helped him escape, left Tybalt to flee with Willehalm, and converted to Christianity. Her former husband and her son have come with the Saracen forces.

In the course of the first battle, Willehalm loses all his knights, including young Vivianz, who is the outstanding fighter for the Christians. Willehalm himself is barely able to escape the slaughter by donning the armor of King Arofel, whom he had slain, and riding away through the heathen ranks, almost unnoticed.

He spends the night at Oransche with Gyburg, then leaves early the next morning to seek help from King Louis. Gyburg is left to defend the fortress with her ladies and a handful of survivors.

Having arrived in Laon, Willehalm receives an extremely cold welcome. King Louis and the queen, Willehalm's sister, are most reluctant to do anything for him. Willehalm, in great rage at the insulting treatment and deeply concerned about Gyburg's fate, grabs the queen by her braids and threatens to cut her head off. When Willehalm's rather, mother, and brothers, who are present at court, hear what has happened at Aliscans and Oransche, they immediately pledge help. Eventually, Willehalm's anger is appeased by the intervention of his niece, Alyze; Louis, whose life had also been threatened by Willehalm, is mollified so that he, too, offers to send imperial forces under Willehalm's command to raise the siege at Oransche.

Before setting out for Oransche with the French troops, Willehalm obtains from Louis the services of Rennewart, a huge young heathen who had been working as a kitchen boy, having rejected baptism. Rennewart is eager to fight, believing that his relatives had refused to ransom him after he was abducted by merchants. He asks for a gigantic club, bound with iron bands, as his weapon, but he forgets it repeatedly on the way to Oransche. (In *Aliscans*, Rainouras is a burlesque figure who eventually dominates the fighting in the second battle. Wolfram's Rennewart, however, despite some boorish acts, is portrayed as a young nobleman in undeserved circumstances. He is actually Gyburg's long-lost brother!)

Willehalm hastens back to Oransche with the French troops, only to discover that Terramer's forces had withdrawn to the coast where the air was better without having stormed the fortress successfully. Gyburg and her meager forces had been able to hold them off. One by one, Willehalm's father and his brothers

arrive with their armies, and the stage is set for the second battle. However, before it begins, a meeting of all the leaders takes place, at which all voice their resolve and support for the battle. Gyburg alone adds a temporizing voice. Tearfully she expresses her sorrow that she is the cause for the huge loss of life on both sides and makes a moving plea for the Christians to spare the heathens, if possible.

In the ensuing battle the Christians are victorious, but the loss of life on both sides is immense. Rennewart, who had forcibly "persuaded" the wavering French not to desert, plays a leading role in the victory. Terramer manages to escape to his ships, and the expected confrontation between Rennewart and his father does not take place. Indeed, when the battle is over Rennewart is missing. Willehalm grieves at the apparent loss of Rennewart and about the terrible slaughter that has occurred. In a gesture of respect for the noble heathens, he gives orders to have their fallen kings embalmed and buried according to their own rites. At this point the narrative breaks off.

Most scholars believe that *Willehalm* is a fragment, basing their argument on the fact that too many narrative strands are left untied. Others feel that, for whatever reasons, Wolfram may have been unable to finish it and devised an emergency conclusion (the *Notdach* theory). Still others maintain that *Willehalm* is complete as it stands, that with the tragic quality of the poem Wolfram has put an entirely new meaning into the substance of his source and that for him any continuation of the Rennewart story had become irrelevant. One further, more recent position is that Wolfram intended it to be a fragment. No matter how one looks at the ending, or lack thereof, *Willehalm* is still a powerfully moving work, dealing with problems that have been with us, as Wolfram says: "since Jesus was plunged into the Jordan to be baptized" (*Willehalm* 4, 28f). Wolfram seems to have been deeply affected himself by the tragedy of it all, if one can judge by his numerous self-reflective remarks throughout the poem.

The two fragments usually called *Titurel* from the name of the old Grail King in the first line of the first fragment deal with the two young lovers, Schionatulander and Sigune, from Wolfram's *Parzival*. It is as if Wolfram attempted to flesh out the briefly mentioned story of their tragic love. Written in four long-line strophes that resemble the *Nibelungenlied* strophes to a limited degree, the first fragment deals with the discovery of the mutual love of the two young people, and the second fragment describes an idyll in the woods that is interrupted by the catching of a hunting dog who had been running through the woods trailing a fantastically elaborate leash with a story depicted on it. Sigune wishes to read the story to its end, but the dog escapes as she loosens the leash to read more and carries the leash away. She promises Schionatulander her love as a reward for retrieving the leash. We know from *Parzival* that Schionatulander gets killed in the attempt, and Sigune is left mourning over his dead body when Parzival meets her. A later poet named Albrecht (von Scharfenberg?) took on the task of completing *Titurel*, and he did so with a vengeance. There are over 6,000 strophes in his so-called *Jüngerer Titurel*, compared with Wolfram's 170! Although it is poetically inferior, Albrecht's work was thought for a long time to be Wolfram's because he identifies himself as Wolfram early on in the work, disclosing his own name only at almost the very end.

There are many problems in *Titurel*. These include the manuscript tradition, the precise text of the poem, and the relationship of the two fragments to each other. Even the theme of love is treated strangely, portraying the exuberance and joy of the naive young lovers trying to act so properly as courtly lovers, yet with a background of impending tragedy on the basis of family history. It is a work of changing moods with somberness predominating.

Wolfram's lyric poems generally describe the parting of lovers at dawn and follow a tradition found in Provençal and Old French poetry. For the most part the lady is the dominant figure. She is the one who is awake as dawn is breaking and must wake her lover so that he can leave without being seen. But Wolfram also includes a sympathetic watchman in several instances, and in one poem he is the dominant speaker. The poems generally end with one last embrace and then the tearful parting as the sun rises higher. Wolfram's dawn songs, among the first in German of that genre, are marked by their striking imagery and their sensitive portrayal of the lovers. His few other poems are similar to more traditional *Minnelieder* (courtly love songs) but show his complete mastery of that type.

See also **Eilhart von Oberg; Gottfried von Straßburg; Hartmann von Aue**

Further Reading

Bumke, Joachim. *Die Wolfram von Eschenbach Forschung seit 1945. Bericht und Bibliographie.* Munich: Wilhelm Fink, 1970.

——. *Wolfram von Eschenbach*, 6th ed. Stuttgart: Metzler, 1991; 7th ed., 1997.

Gibbs, Marion E., and Sidney M. Johnson, trans. *Wolfram von Eschenbach: Willehlam.* Harmondsworth: Penguin, 1984.

Gibbs, Marion E., and Sidney M. Johnson. *Wolfram von Eschenbach: "Titurel" and the "Songs."* New York: Garland, 1988 [with English trans.].

——. *Medieval German Literature: A Companion.* New York: Garland, 1997, pp. 174–205.

Green, D. H. *The Art of Recognition in Wolfram's "Parzival."* Cambridge: Cambridge University Press, 1982.

Groos Arthur. *Romancing the Grail.* Ithaca, N.Y.: Cornell University Press, 1995 [on *Parzival*].

Hatto, Arthur T., trans. *Wolfram von Eschenbach: Parzival.* Harmondsworth: Penguin, 1980.

Heinzle, Joachim. *Stellenkommentar zu Wolframs "Titurel."* Tübingen: Niemeyer, 1972.

Heinzle, Joachim, ed. *Wolfram von Eschenbach: Willehlam.* Frankfurt am Main: Verlag Deutscher Klassiker, 1991 [with German trans.].

——, ed. *Willehalm: nach der Handschrift 857 der Stiftsbibliothek St. Gallen.* Tübingen: Niemeyer, 1994.

Kiening, Christian. "Wolfram von Eschenbach: Willehalm," in *Mittelhochdeutsche Romane und Heldenepen,* ed. Horst Brunner. Stuttgart: Reclam, 1993, pp. 212–232.

Kühn, Dieter, trans. *Wolfram von Eschenbach: Parzival.* Frankfurt am Main: Insel, 1986.

Lachmann, Karl, ed. *Wolfram von Eschenbach,* 6th ed. Berlin: de Gruyter, 1926 [reprinted often].

Leitzmann, Albert, ed. *Wolfram von Eschenbach,* 5 vols. Halle (Saale): Niemeyer, 1902–1906 [reprinted often].

Lofmark, Carl. *Rennewart in Wolfram's "Willehalm": A Study of Wolfram von Eschenbach and His Sources.* Cambridge, England: Cambridge University Press, 1972.

Mertens, Volker. "Wolfram von Eschenbach: Titurel," in *Mittelhochdeutsche Romane und Heldenepen,* ed. Horst Brunner. Stuttgart: Reclam, 1993, pp. 196–211.

Mohr, Wolfgang. *Wolfram von Eschenbach. Titurel. Lieder.* Göppingen: Kummerle, 1978, pp. 101–161.

Mustard, Helen M., and Charles E. Passage, trans. *Wolfram von Eschenbach: Parzival.* New York: Vintage Books, 1961.

Nellmann, Eberhard, ed. *Wolfram von Eschenbach: Parzival.* Frankfurt am Main: Verlag Deutscher Klassiker, 1994 [German trans. Dieter Kühn].

Passage, Charles E., trans. *Wolfram von Eschenbach: Willehlam.* New York: Ungar, 1977.

——. trans. *Wolfram von Eschenbach: Titurel.* New York: Ungar, 1984.

Poag, James F. *Wolfram von Eschenbach.* New York: Twayne, 1972 [good general introduction in English].

Pretzel, Ulrich, and Wolfgang Bachofer. *Bibliographie zu Wolfram von Eschenbach,* 2d ed. Berlin: Schmidt, 1968.

Schmidt, Elisabeth. "Wolfram von Eschenbach: Parzival," in *Mittelhochdeutsche Romane und Heldenepen,* ed. Horst Brunner. Stuttgart: Reclam, 1993, pp. 173–195.

Schröder, Werner, ed. *Wolfram von Eschenbach: Willehalm.* Berlin: de Gruyter, 1978 [with German trans. Dieter Kartschoke; rev. 1989].

Walshe, Maurice O'C. *Medieval German Literature.* Cambridge, Mass.: Harvard University Press, 1962, pp. 156–175 [concise treatment].

Wapnewski, Peter. *Die Lyrik Wolframs von Eschenbach: Edition. Kommentar. Interpretation.* Munich: Beck, 1972 [songs, with German trans.].

SIDNEY M. JOHNSON

WOLGEMUT, MICHAEL (1434/1437–1519)

Born in Nuremberg between 1434 and 1437, Michael Wolgemut was the city's foremost painter and printmaker in the late fifteenth century. Wolgemut trained with his father, Valentin, a painter, and worked as a journeyman with Gabriel Mälesskircher in Munich before returning to Nuremberg in 1471. A year later he married Barbara, the widow of the noted painter Hans Pleydenwurff. Whether he had collaborated earlier with Hans is uncertain. Wolgemut developed a large workshop that specialized in the production of large retables, woodcuts, and designs for stained glass windows. The artist's pupils included his stepson, Wilhelm Pleydenwurff, and Albrecht Dürer, who was in the shop from 1486 until 1489.

Wolgemut's first documented painting is the high altar completed in 1479 for the St. Marienkirche in Zwickau. This complex polyptych includes painted wings depicting the Passion of Christ (exterior) and Infancy (middle) that cover the nine life-size standing statues of saints on the inner wings and in the corpus, a painted and carved winged predella (lower altar panel), and a Last Judgment covering the back of the altar. Wolgemut employed a team of now anonymous joiners, painters, and sculptors on this and similar elaborate projects, notably the Peringsdorfer Altar made circa 1486 for the Augustinian Cloister in Nuremberg (today in the Friedenskirche) and the high altar (1506–1508) in the church of St. Johannes and St. Marrinus in Schwabach. In his paintings, including his independent portraits, such as that of Levinus Memminger circa 1485 (Madrid, Museo Thyssen-Bornemisza), Wolgemut displayed his familiarity with Netherlandish art, notably the works of Rogier van der Weyden and Dirk Bouts. His clearly defined figures are located in the extreme foreground before deep landscapes.

Today the artist is best known for his prints. In addition to independent woodcuts, Wolgemut recognized the potential of illustrating books. The artist, his stepson, and his shop supplied 96 woodcuts for Stephan Fridolin's *Schatzbehalter* (1491) and 1,809 woodcuts using 645 different blocks for Hartmann Schedel's *Liber Chronicarum* (*Nuremberg Chronicle*, 1493), both published by Anton Koberger in Nuremberg. The latter with its maps, city views, portraits, and elaborate illustrations was the century's most ambitious publishing project and was marketed across Europe.

Wolgemut's career spanned four decades. His last major picture, the *Epitaph of Anna Gross* (Nuremberg, Germanisches Nationalmuseum), dates around 1509. In 1516 Albrecht Dürer affectionately recorded his mentor's likeness in a portrait (Nuremberg, Germanisches Nationalmuseum). Wolgemut died on November 30, 1519, in Nuremberg.

Further Reading

Bellm, Richard. *Wolgemuts Skizzenbuch im Berliner Kupferstichkabinett*. Studien zur deutschen Kunstgeschichte 322. Baden-Baden: P. H. Heitz, 1959.

Fridolin, Stefan. *Der Schatzbehalter: Ein Andachts- und Erbauungsbuch aus dem Jahre 1491*, ed. Richard Bellm. 2 vols. Wiesbaden: G. Pressler, 1962.

Füssel, Stephan, ed. *500 Jahre Schedelsche Weltchronik*. Pirckheimer Jahrbuch 9. Nuremberg: Carl, 1994.

Rücker, Elizabeth. *Die Schedelsche Weltchronik: Das größte Buchunternehmen der Dürer-Zeit*, 33d rev. ed. Munich: Prestel, 1988.

Scholz, Hartmut. *Entwurf und Ausführung: Werkstattpraxis in der Nürnberger Glasmalerei der Dürerzeit*. Ph.d. diss., University of Stuttgart, 1988. Berlin: Deutscher Verlag für Kunstwissenschaft, 1989.

Stadler, Franz Izra. *Michael Wolgemut und der Nürnberger Holzschnitt im letzten Drittel des XV. Jahrhunderts*. 2 vols. Studien zur deutschen Kunstgeschichte 161. Strasbourg: J. H. E. Heitz, 1913.

Strieder, Peter. *Tafelmalerei in Nürnberg, 1350 bis 1550*. Königstein im Taunus: K. Robert, 1993, pp. 65–85, 200–219.

Wilson, Adrian. *The Making of the Nuremberg Chronicle*. Amsterdam: Nico Israel, 1976.

JEFFREY CHIPPS SMITH

WULFSTAN OF YORK (d. 1023)

Bishop of London 996–1002, bishop of "Worcester 1002–16, and archbishop of York 1002–23, who served two kings (Æthelred II and Cnut) as adviser and author of legislation while addressing the pressing moral and ecclesiastical issues of his time. One of two great stylists in the history of OE prose (with Ælfric), Wulfstan had a distinguished career as a homilist and statesman. Although educated as a Benedictine, he was very much a public figure who began signing himself "Lupus" ("Wolf") early in his career, as he developed a reputation for spoken and written eloquence and for moral reform. The 12th-century *Liber Eliensis* (*Book of Ely*) provides the only medieval information, much of riiat questionable, about his life.

When he assumed the sees of Worcester and York in plurality (holding both simultaneously) upon the death in 1002 of Archbishop Eadulf, Wulfstan had experienced the worst ravages of the Danes and the largely ineffectual responses of Æthelred's army. With its rich library and scriptorium removed from the worst of the fighting Worcester provided him an opportunity to study important patristic and canonical texts and thus to develop as a writer and reformer. Much of his work was also done at York, where he performed the functions of a leader of the church. Extant manuscripts from both centers show Wulfstan's hand in the annotations. In addition several versions of his "commonplace book" survive, containing collections of materials intended for use in his own work. Either at Worcester or York he wrote versified entries for 957 and 975 in the D version of the Anglo-Saxon Chronicle.

Wulfstan's reputation grows from his sermons. These include a series of eschatological works, impassioned calls for repentance in response to signs of the coming of Doomsday. Another series on the elements of Christian faith treats the subjects of baptism, the Creed, the gifts of the Holy Spirit, and the duties of a Christian. In both series he draws on a variety of Latin sources largely from the Carolingian period and shapes his work to specific audiences. Only two of his sermons are proper to the church year, and those address the matter of penance during Lent. Wulfstan's sermons are topical, hortative, and utilitarian messages rather than explications of the Gospels or hagiographic narratives.

The best-known sermon also seems to have been the most popular in its time: *Sermo Lupi ad Anglos* (*The Sermon of Wolf to the English*), so called from the opening words of its rubric. Surviving in five manuscript versions, this work probably was composed in 1014, the year in which Æthelred was exiled. The *Sermo Lupi* is noteworthy for drawing on themes and materials that engaged Wulfstan throughout his career, here brought together and presented urgently when it seemed that God was punishing the English at the hands of the Danes. In particular Wulfstan uses phrases from his eschatological sermons in depicting the present evils that presage the end of the

world. He ends with a typical exhortation to return to the faith of baptism, where there is protection from the fires of hell.

As trusted counselor to Æthelred, and to his Danish successor Cnut, Wulfstan wrote a variety of legislation intended to reassert the laws of earlier Anglo-Saxon kings and bring order to a country that had been unsettled by war and the influx of Scandinavians. Although he put into writing edicts that had been decreed by the ruling witan, or council, Wulfstan echoed there the concerns about present conditions and the urgency for change expressed in his homiletic writings. The laws are of three distinct types: short codes addressing such specific issues as the need to christianize the Danelaw, protect the clergy and the church, and reinforce a hierarchical social order consistent with the past; drafts of legislation for Æthelred and Cnut; and a comprehensive, formal code for Cnut. Through these legal writings Wulfstan used his influence to press for social, moral, religious, and political reforms extending even to the obligations of the king.

Beginning about 1005 a remarkable interchange occurred between Wulfstan and his talented contemporary Abbot Ælfric of Eynsham. Wulfstan requested from Ælfric two pastoral letters in Latin treating duties of the secular clergy. Shortly thereafter he asked Ælfric to translate the letters into OE. Although the versions that survive today bear evidence of Wulfstan's revisions, they are important because they strongly influenced his own prescriptions for the secular clergy, the *Canons of Edgar*, as well as the code he drafted for Æthelred at Enham in 1008. These and other letters by Ælfric formed part of a group of canonistic materials including Frankish capitularies and Wulfstan's translation of Amalarius's *De regula canonicorum*, materials that underlie one of Wulfetan's sermons on baptism, his *Institutes of Polity*, and certain legal codes, in addition to the *Canons of Edgar*.

Because they provide yet another strong example of his reforming philosophy, Wulfstan's own canonistic works command interest. The *Canons of Edgar*, so-called because they hark back to better times during the reign of Edgar, provide instruction on proper conduct and training for the secular clergy and detailed instructions on their duties, including how to conduct the mass. The *Institutes of Polity* form a treatise on the organization of society, an early example of estates literature that attempts to define the duties of each class. His lengthy discussion of the bishop's role provides insight into the career Wulfstan fashioned fot himself. Wulfstan also translated prose portions of the Benedictine office into OE, presumably to help the secular clergy with their devotions.

The effectiveness of Wulfstan's writing owes much to his rhythmic style, distinctive vocabulary, and use of rhetorical figures. He usually wrote with two-stress, alliterating, sometimes rhyming phrases syntactically independent of one another, which he could use to build toward a powerful climax. His stylistic touches include a large stock of intensifying words, repeated phrases, and forceful compounds. Figures of sound as taught by medieval manuals of rhetoric appear prominently in his work. All of these tools Wulfstan used in his attempts to restore England to the order and piety it had enjoyed before the Viking depredations.

See also Ælfric; Cnut

Further Reading

Primary Sources

Bethurum, Dorothy, ed. *The Homilies of Wulfstan*, Oxford: Clarendon, 1957.

Fowler, Roger, ed. *Wulfstan's Canons of Edgar*. EETS o,s. 266. London: Oxford University Press, 1972.

Jost, Karl, ed. *Die "Institutes of Polity, Civil and Ecclesiastical": Ein Werk Erzbisch of Wulfstans von York*. Schweitzer anglistische Arbeiten 47. Bern: Francke, 1959.

Ure, James M., ed. *The Benedictine Office: An Old English Text*. Edinburgh University Publications in Language and Literature 11. Edinburgh: Edinburgh University Press, 1957.

Whitelock, Dorothy, ed. *Sermo Lupi ad Anglos*. 3d ed. New York: Methuen, 1966.

Secondary Sources

Bethurum, Dorothy. "Archbishop Wulfstan's Commonplace Book." *PMLA* 57 (1942): 916–29.

Bethurum, Dorothy. "Wulfstan." In *Continuations and Beginnings: Studies in Old English Literature*, ed. Eric G. Stanley. London: Nelson, 1966, pp. 210–46.

Gatch, Milton McC. *Preaching and Theology in Anglo-Saxon England: Ælfric and Wulfstan*, Toronto: University of Toronto Press, 1977.

Ker, N.R. "The Handwriting of Archbishop Wulfstan." In *England before the Conquest: Studies in Primary Sources Presented to Dorothy Whitelock*, ed. Peter Clemoes and Kathleen Hughes. Cambridge: Cambridge University Press, 1971, pp. 315–31.

Richards, Mary P. "The Manuscript Contexts of the Old English Laws: Tradition and Innovation." In *Studies in Earlier Old English Prose*, ed. Paul E. Szarmach. Albany: SUNY Press, 1986, pp. 171–92.

Stafford, Pauline. "The Laws of Cnut and the History of Anglo-Saxon Royal Promises." *ASE* 10 (1981): 173–90.

Whitelock, Dorothy. "Wulfstan's Authorship of Cnut's Laws." *EHR* 70 (1955): 72–85.

Wormald, Patrick, "Æthelred the Lawmaker." In *Ethelred the Unready*, ed. David Hill. BAR Brit. Ser. 59. Oxford: BAR, 1978, pp. 47–80.

MARY P. RICHARDS

WYCLIF, JOHN (ca. 1330–1384)

WYCLIF, JOHN (ca. 1330–1384) The most distinguished English philosopher and theologian of the later 14th century and a significant influence on the emergence of the heretical Lollard movement. His popular fame as a church reformer, however, is largely unjustified and only dates from the Reformation period.

Wyclif was probably born in Yorkshire. For most of his adult life he was a scholar and teacher at Oxford, and only in his last decade did he make any impression on a wider stage, first as a royal servant and then as the inspiration of heresy. He first appears in the records as a fellow of Merton College in 1356, as master of Balliol College in 1360, and later as warden of Canterbury Hall, an appointment that involved him in a struggle with the regular clergy. He proceeded from Arts to Theology in the late 1360s and became a doctor of theology about 1372–73. He was, it appears, a conventional academic and like most of his contemporaries was supported, as an absentee, by the revenues of various benefices, none of great value. He was granted a canonry at Lincoln in 1371, though the promise of a prebend there with substantial resources was never fulfilled. In 1374 he was granted the Leicestershire benefice of Lutterworth, which was in the gift of the crown.

This undoubtedly was a reward for services as a polemicist and a diplomat. He defended the crown's right to tax the clergy and even its violation of sanctuary in order to arrest crown debtors, and in 1374 he took part in a diplomatic mission to Bruges. By 1378 he was compelled to withdraw from politics, although his lay patrons continued to protect him from the assaults of church authorities who had secured papal condemnation of his views on the subject of civil and divine lordship. In 1381 he was forced to leave Oxford, retiring to Lutterworth, where he died of a stroke at the end of 1384. Although his enemies alleged that he had inspired the Peasant Rebellion of 1381, this view cannot be substantiated and his earlier strong royatism makes it inherently unlikely.

Increasing knowledge of the development of scholastic philosophy has enhanced Wyclif's reputation as a thinker. A man of great learning and incisive mind, he was a vigorous defender of realist metaphysics against the nominalism of William of Ockham. In this he followed the tradition active during his formative years in Oxford, but he went beyond his teachers as an independent thinker.

As a philosopher his views remained acceptable, but when he began teaching theology he clashed with the authorities.

His early theological concern with questions of dominion and grace probably arose more from his activities as a royal servant than from philosophical principles. Concurrently with his royal service, however, he became involved in biblical studies, writing a commentary on the whole Bible, something none of his contemporaries did. His reverence for scripture led to a fundamentalist view of the Bible as eternally present in God and probably influenced his denial of transubstantiation in the eucharist, an opinion in accord with his metaphysical views. There has been recent debate on whether metaphysics or biblicism gave the first impetus to this opinion, the issue that led to his final breach with orthodoxy. Even by the end of his life Wyclif had probably not worked out his precise belief in the nature of the eucharist, but it may have come close to the later Lutheran doctrine of consubstantiation.

His influence survived his death, and his eucharistic views were, in a simplified form, one of the hallmarks of later Lollardy. More important perhaps was the production by his followers, under the influence of his biblicism, of two English versions of the Bible, the staple reading for heretical groups and material for works of orthodox devotion. His philosophical views were taught for a time in Oxford and spread also to Bohemia, where they influenced the thought of religious reformers. Later his theological teachings also reached Bohemia and probably contributed to the more radical wing of Hussite thought. A substantial number of Wycliffite manuscripts have survived in libraries there.

By this time the church authorities were taking steps against his writings. Forty-five articles from his works were condemned at Prague in 1403, 267 articles were condemned after Archbishop Arundel's purge at Oxford in 1409, and the attacks continued at the councils of Rome (1413) and Constance (1415). At the last a command was issued for the exhumation and burning of his body, though this part of the sentence was not carried out until 1428.

See also Ockham, William of

Further Reading

Kenny, Anthony. *Wyclif*. Oxford: Oxford University Press, 1985 [best introduction].

Kenny, Anthony, ed. *Wyclif in His Times*. Oxford: Clarendon, 1986 [valuable essays on many aspects of the man and his influence].

Leff, Gordon. *Heresy in the Later Middle Ages: The Relation of Heterodoxy to Dissent, c. 1250–c. 1450*. Manchester: Manchester University Press, 1967 [a good summary of Wyclif's teachings].

McFarlane, K.B. *John Wycliffe and the Beginnings of English Nonconformity*. London: English Universities Press, 1952 [illuminating and good for biography unfair to Wyclif as a thinker].

Thomson, Williell R. *The Latin Writings of John Wyclyf. An Annotated Catalog*. Toronto: Pontifical Institute, 1983 [the best bibliographical treatment of Wydif's writings].

Workman, Herbert B. *John Wyclif: A Study of the English Medieval Church*. 2 vols. Oxford: Clarendon, 1926 [the fullest life, though the interpretation is colored by Reformation apologetics].

J.A.F. THOMSON

Index